MW01625921

1849

The Philadelphia Mint Strikes Gold

Roman Goddess of Abundance, by Hubert Schutter in 1861. This mural adorned the ceiling of Treasury Secretary Samuel P. Chase's office suite in the Treasury building. Its cornucopia of "yellow boys" is emblematic of the economic boom of the preceding decade driven by California gold.

1849 The Philadelphia Mint Strikes Gold

Michael F. Moran and Jeff Garrett
Foreword by Richard G. Kelly and Nancy Oliver

1849
The Philadelphia Mint Strikes Gold

3101 Clairmont Road • Suite G • Atlanta, GA 30329

ISBN: 0794842453

Printed in China

Correspondence concerning this book may be directed to Whitman Publishing, Attn: 1849, at the address above.

About the coin on the cover: The Smithsonian 1849 double eagle is probably the most iconic and desirable coin in its vast collection. The coin is a direct result of the California Gold Rush, and is a tangible link to one of the most important phases of American history. As is well documented in this book, the flow of bullion from the gold fields of California led to the legislation of March 3, 1849, authorizing the production gold dollars and double eagles.

If you enjoy *1849: The Philadelphia Mint Strikes Gold*, you will also enjoy *History of the United States Mint and Its Coinage*, by David W. Lange; *America's Money, America's Story*, 2nd edition, by Richard Doty; and *Striking Change: The Great Artistic Collaboration of Theodore Roosevelt and Augustus Saint-Gaudens*, by Michael F. Moran.

CONTENTS

FOREWORD

Few numismatic works can match the level of research accomplished by Mike Moran and Jeff Garrett in *1849: The Philadelphia Mint Strikes Gold*. We were genuinely impressed with the depth of the research, and the quality of the writing. Their book is written in the style of numismatic history at its best.

This is a fine account of the debates and prejudices concerning the establishment of mints at New York and San Francisco on both the East Coast and the West. It was interesting to read the indirect sparring between Patterson of Philadelphia and Gwin of California, and the personalities of both in their dealings with others who would influence their professional statures.

Not only should this book be in every numismatist's library, but major libraries should also carry a copy, for it is not just a numismatic work. Its contribution to United States history is evident throughout.

It is a most pleasant and easy read—even for those who may have limited knowledge of numismatics—and a fascinating account of history during that trying period of the California Gold Rush and its effect on the United States. *1849: The Philadelphia Mint Strikes Gold* comes with our highest recommendation.

Lastly, we cannot resist a note here that this new book by Moran and Garrett is quite timely, for we are about to release our book on the complete history of the first San Francisco Mint, once located on Commercial Street in San Francisco. The authors touch on this mint facility; they have put together a very fine piece of work.

Richard G. Kelly and Nancy Oliver
California

Richard Kelly and Nancy Oliver are award-winning historical/numismatic researchers and authors who make their home in Northern California. Partners for 40 years, they have co-authored six books concerning numismatic history. Together they have also been contributors to the monthly American Numismatic Association magazine The Numismatist, *and have a column therein called "Numismatic Chronicles." Rich and Nancy enjoy attempting to solve numismatic mysteries, and they have met with success many times in their efforts.*

PROLOGUE

CALIFORNIA

The young army lieutenant leaned eagerly against the ship's railing to get his first view of the California coastline. As the ship entered Monterey Bay on January 26, 1847, his eyes settled upon a sight of unmatched splendor. Everything on shore looked bright and beautiful. The hills were covered with grass, flowers, and serene live oaks. The low adobe houses with red tiled roofs and whitened walls contrasted starkly with the groves of dark pine trees behind them. It was a scene as far away from war as any could be.

The West Point–trained officer prepared to go ashore, not knowing what to expect. When the Mexican-American War began, Lieutenant William Tecumseh Sherman (fig. 1) had been stuck with recruiting duty in Pittsburgh with no escape in sight. Finagle as he might, he could secure no frontline assignment. Finally orders arrived assigning him to Company F of the Third Artillery, bound for California. With the long journey around the Cape behind him, he disembarked to find the war over in California. Major John C. Frémont and Brigadier General Stephen W. Kearny had easily overcome the Mexican opposition. Now Sherman settled down to garrison duty while his classmates garnered fame and experience in Mexico.

By June 1847, Frémont and Kearny had each taken leave, and Colonel R.B. Mason became the ranking Army commander—in essence the military governor of Califor-

Fig. 1. The young Lieutenant W.T. Sherman, bright-eyed and red-headed, was remembered by fellow cadets at the U.S. Military Academy as one of the brightest and most popular fellows.

nia. He chose Sherman as his adjutant general, bestowing upon the young man a role beyond his years in the military administration of this new territory, which would not be granted statehood until 1850. Sherman took an immediate liking to Mason, describing the colonel as a man of great experience and stern character. While some found Mason harsh and severe, Sherman found him kind and agreeable. Sherman respected him for his good sense, and Mason, in turn, gave Sherman his unlimited confidence.

All was routine, until one spring day in 1848, when two Americans came into the military headquarters at Monterey seeking Governor Mason. They had been sent by Captain John Sutter (an immigrant from Switzerland and formerly a captain in the Swiss artillery) on special business and they insisted upon seeing the governor *in person*. Without standing upon ceremony, Sherman ushered them into Mason's office. A short time later, Mason called the lieutenant into the room. Sherman saw upon the colonel's table a series of papers and about a half ounce of gold. Mason asked Sherman if he had ever seen gold before. Sherman had when he had been in upper Georgia in 1844. However, that gold was much finer than the example lying on Mason's table. It had been kept in phials and transparent quills. This metal glittered in small flakes and appeared to be placer gold, found in streambeds. First, Sherman picked up a piece and put it in his mouth, finding it metallic in taste. Next, he ordered his clerk to find an axe and a hatchet. Getting the tools, Sherman took the largest piece and beat it flat. Beyond a doubt, this glittering material was a metal, and a pure malleable metal at that. Still, neither Mason nor Sherman attached much importance to the fact that the two men had brought in gold. Only in great quantities would this gold be significant.

Sutter had written a letter to Mason stating that, for the general benefit of settlers in the area, he was engaged in erecting a sawmill at Coloma, 40 miles up the American fork of the Sacramento River and above his fort at New Helvetia. He had incurred considerable expense and now sought a "preemption" to the quarter section of land on which the mill was located, embracing the tailrace in which this particular gold had been found.

Mason instructed Sherman to prepare a reply. California was still a Mexican province held by the United States as a conquest. As the war was not yet terminated, no laws of the United States applied to it—including land laws. Additionally, preemption laws could only be applied after a public survey. Mason shared little of Sutter's concern about the legal title to his holdings. There were no settlements within 40 miles, and Sutter was not likely to be disturbed by trespassers.

As the spring and summer of 1848 advanced, reports came fast and furious about gold at Sutter's mill and in the surrounding area. Sherman's description of the situation was vivid.

> Stories reached us of fabulous discoveries, and spread throughout the land. Everybody was talking of "Gold! Gold!!" until it assumed the character of a fever. Some of our soldiers began to desert; citizens were fitting out trains of wagons and pack mules to go to the mines. We heard of men earning fifty, five hundred, and thousands of dollars per day, and for a time it seemed as though somebody would reach solid gold.

Prices began to escalate in Yerba Buena (soon to be renamed San Francisco), particularly for mules, horses, and mining supplies. Sherman could not escape the infection, and he convinced Mason that it was their duty to go and see it with their own eyes in order to report back to the government in Washington.

On June 17, Mason's party, with the enthusiastic Sherman at the lead, set out for Sutter's Fort. They went first to Yerba Buena, finding it almost stripped of male inhabitants. Two or three ships were abandoned in the harbor for lack of a crew. Next they crossed the bay to Sausalito with horses in tow, and worked their way to Petaluma. It being the dry season, they traveled the plain from Sonoma to the Sacramento River. Everywhere along the way, they saw evidence of neglect in the fields, cattle roaming in the wheat, and mills sitting idle.

Following the Sacramento River, they reached Sutter's Fort only to find little sign of habitation, except for the fort itself, its staffers, and an old adobe house originally known as the hospital. The entrance to the fort was a large gate, closed at night, with two ship's cannons for protection. Inside was a large structure with a good shingle roof, used as a storehouse. All around the fort walls were rooms that served as Sutter's living quarters, a blacksmith's shop, and a carpenter's shop. Here within the walls was a beehive of commercial activity. The little party found preparations under way at the fort to celebrate the Fourth of July. The locals were pleased to have the military governor as the honored guest.

Here, Mason and Sherman learned the story of the discovery. Sutter had employed, or was a partner with, a man named James Marshall to build a sawmill at Coloma. Marshall had been part of a battalion of Mormons sent to California during the war. When the soldiers mustered out, the church leadership asked that Marshall and others remain behind to earn some money before returning to Utah, as the settlement at Great Salt Lake was desperate for hard currency.[1] Marshall thus recruited four members from the battalion and some Indians. The sawmill had been erected over a dry channel of the river that was to serve as the tailrace from the mill. However, the tailrace did not carry the water away from the mill fast enough. In early January 1848, Marshall was digging a ditch to help the water escape when he discovered the gold.

Marshall forbade his men from prospecting at the sawmill. It being placer gold, the men eventually moved downstream to a place called Mormon Island, where they discovered one of the richest placers ever. Word then flashed through the Mormon community like wildfire.

Leaving the fort, Mason and his party found about 200 Mormons working their claims on the island, also known as the Mormon Diggings. Some were washing for gold with tin pans, while others were using close-woven Indian baskets. However, most employed what were termed ripple machines or cradles. The gold here came in fine, bright scales. In his memoirs many years later, Sherman recalled the scene vividly.

> In the midst of a broken country, all parched and dried by the hot sun of July, sparsely wooded with live oaks and struggling pines, lay the valley of the American River, with its cold mountain stream coming out of the Snowy mountains to the east. In this valley is a flat, or gravel bed, which in high water is an island, or is overflown [*sic*], but at the time of our visit was simply a level gravel bed of the river. On its edges men were dipping and filling buckets with the finer earth and gravel, which was carried to a machine made like a baby's cradle, open at the foot, and at the head a plate of sheet-iron or zinc, punctured full of holes. On this metallic plate was emptied the earth, and water was then poured on it from buckets while one man shook the cradle with violent rocking by a handle. On the bottom were nailed cleats of wood. With this rude machine four men could earn from forty to one hundred dollars a day, averaging sixteen dollars or a gold ounce, per man per day. While the sun blazed down on the heads of the miners with tropical heat, the water was bitter cold, and all hands were either standing in the water or had their clothes wet all the time; yet there were no complaints of rheumatism or cold.

The hillsides were thickly strewn with canvas tents and crude huts, which Mason euphemistically called "bush arbors." A store had been erected and several shanty boarding houses were in operation.

Colonel Mason correctly observed that the miners were on public land and that the gold was the property of the United States. He then concluded that, while all of the miners were trespassers, the government benefitted by the extraction of the gold. Therefore, he would not interfere. The reasoning might have been convoluted but the miners were not going to leave willingly and he did not have the force to remove them. However, in his report to Washington, Mason would be much more forceful in pointing out that the government was entitled to rents for the gold removed from these lands. Continued delay in this matter would only make its implementation that much more difficult.

The next day, Mason and Sherman continued up the American River, stopping at various mining camps. At Coloma, the sawmill stood unfinished, with the tailrace just as Marshall had left it. There were few miners in the area because of the claims of Sutter and Marshall. In addition, Marshall was guarding the site.

The following day, using Marshall as a guide, they crossed to the north side of the river, to an area of dry diggings. Little pools of water stood in the beds of the streams, and these were used to wash the dirt. Here, the gold came in every conceivable size and shape, with some specimens weighing four or five ounces. Sherman learned that some diggings were extremely rich, but on a whole, the strikes were much more random than at the river. A fellow could strike a pocket and collect several thousand dollars of gold; or he could be shifting about and prospecting here and there while spending all the money he had. At all the sites visited by the officers, countless Indians were employed by the miners to augment their efforts.

Little stores were springing up at every point among the diggings. Here flour, bacon, and the like were sold at exorbitant prices. After the trip, Sherman would invest in such an operation and do quite well financially when he cashed out.

The party spent nearly a week in the gold fields. Yet they did not penetrate the full extent of the gold discovery, confining themselves to the several forks of the American and Yuba rivers. Lack of forage for the horses forced them to work their way back to the Sacramento Valley. Still, they were there long enough to be quite bewildered by the tales of the recent discoveries.

Mason estimated conservatively that some 4,000 men were working in the gold district, of whom more than half were Indians, and that from \$30,000 to \$50,000 worth of gold was mined daily. Governor Mason even went so far as to recommend that a mint should be established somewhere near Yerba Buena. He correctly noted that no capital was needed to mine this gold. A man needed only his labor and a little luck to strike it rich. It seemed as if everyone Mason met in the gold fields had his two, three, or four pounds of gold to show the colonel. Never before had there been anything like this gold strike to generate wealth for the working man.

As the party returned, they gave their official sanction to the veracity of the news emanating from the gold fields, adding new force to the gold fever. Upon their arrival at Monterey, Mason had an immediate problem. News was waiting for them that the war was virtually over. The volunteers were threatening to desert en masse for the gold fields. Even the soldiers who had traveled with Mason and Sherman would ultimately desert. The math was simple. A soldier returning from furlough had just made as much money in one week as he would be paid in the Army for five years. Mason was able to hold the volunteers temporarily in place only by promising them quick and honorable discharges.

After the trip, Sherman suggested that Mason send a special courier to Washington with details of the strike. Sherman drafted the report to which Mason made a few changes before affixing his signature. They had returned with a few samples of the gold given to them along their route. Sherman advised Mason to have additional purchases made in Yerba Buena in order to provide Washington with a large sample of commercial gold. Captain Joseph Libbey Folsom, delegated with this task, returned with an oyster can full of the yellow metal that he had purchased for $10 an ounce, the going rate for unassayed gold at the customs house in Yerba Buena.[2]

Now they had to find someone to courier the report and the gold to the East Coast. That man was Lieutenant Lucien Loeser. He had just been promoted, and by Army practice was entitled to a leave back home. Sherman's oyster can full of gold was on its way.

The arrival of that gold in Washington would change everything in the United States. It would fuel rapid industrialization across the Northern states with a supporting rail system. It would leave few institutions untouched, least of all the United States Mint at Philadelphia.[3] The Mint would be shaken to its very foundation and only just barely survive. However, to understand the events that would unfold at the Mint, the story must begin almost at its establishment, in 1794.[4]

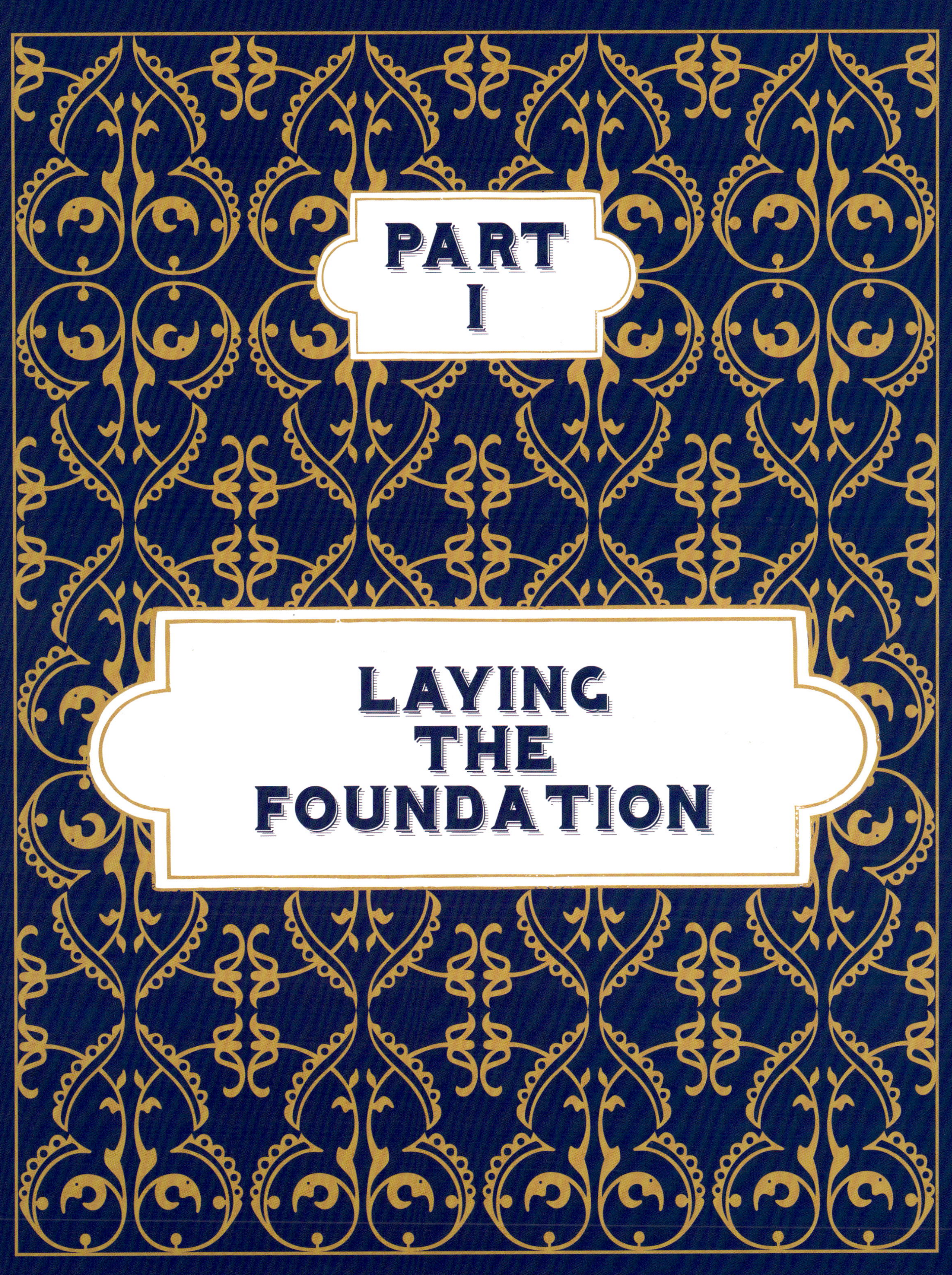

PART I

LAYING THE FOUNDATION

CHAPTER 1

STEPCHILD

Elias Boudinot stepped out of the Pennsylvania State House, where Congress was meeting, onto Chestnut Street. It was December 8, 1794. The House of Representatives had just taken up the annual report from Mint director David Rittenhouse, submitted the previous December. Stale as it was, it was discouraging to hear. Troubles had been encountered in filling the roster of positions called for in the Mint's enabling legislation. Once adequate people had been found, Rittenhouse complained that the bonding requirements of the two most important officers, the coiner and assayer, were too onerous, creating the unintended effect of preventing the coinage of gold and silver. In closing, Rittenhouse pointed out the need for a refiner at the Mint. A considerable portion of the bullion they were receiving was below coin standard, requiring the assayer to take on the added burden of refining.[1] Up to this point, the only remedial action taken by Congress was to reduce the bonding requirements.

From the entrance to the Pennsylvania State House, it was a two and a half block walk through the heart of the nation's financial district to the Bank of the United States (unaffectionately nicknamed the BUS). This institution, the brainchild of Alexander Hamilton, was chartered by Congress and served as the quasi-central bank. All Congressman Boudinot wanted was some copper cents, just a small token to prove the Mint's worth to the populace. It was not to be; a surprised Boudinot was told that there were none to be had. The bank could not get them from

Fig. 2. The first United States Mint. Even in this idealized image, the first mint has an appearance of being cobbled together.

the Mint. This surprised Boudinot; he knew the Mint had been producing copper coinage since 1793.

Elias Boudinot was not a man to be put off, having served previously as president of the Continental Congress and serving now as a congressman from New Jersey. He turned, retraced his steps to the State House, and moved beyond the financial district to Seventh Street. It was like entering another world. This mint (fig. 2) was a mean affair. Originally the site of a distillery, over the years the buildings had been modified and added to.[2] The whole facility gave the impression of a cobbled-together operation. All things considered, it was just as well that it was not located on Chestnut Street with the rest of the financial establishment.

The American government had previously had the best of intentions for the Mint. Prior to the Revolution, the colonies had been prohibited by Great Britain from establishing public mints. It was a bone of contention, as trade with the mother country was constantly draining *specie*, silver and gold coins, from the 13 colonies. After the Revolution, the circulating medium came from America's trading partners and consisted primarily of Spanish dollars and their fractional parts. Over the preceding century, Mexican and South American mines controlled by Spain had fed a torrent of silver to their colonial mints that made the Spanish milled dollar an international monetary unit.

The Constitution gave Congress the power to coin money, to regulate the value of said coin money and the value foreign coins, and to fix the standard of weights. The Coinage Act of April 2, 1792, established the U.S. Mint and set the value of the dollar to be the same as that of the Spanish milled dollar. The dollar was to contain 371.25 grains of pure silver or 416 grains of standard silver—silver diluted by alloy. It also set the value of gold at 15 times an equivalent amount by weight of silver. Thus, by giving legal-tender status to both metals, this act put the United States on a bimetallic standard.

The next day, December 9, an exasperated Boudinot reported his experience at the Mint on the floor of the House. Yes, the Mint had coined copper cents. But quantities had been constrained because the officers of the Mint could not get them distributed. Congress had not appropriated money for the necessary transportation expense. He railed emotionally that the New Jersey Legislature several years back had authorized a private-contract coinage of coppers with more being made in a few months than had ever been made in the Philadelphia Mint. The costs at the U.S. Mint must be such that each cent cost two cents to make. Then he back-peddled saying he could not tell exactly how many cents it cost to make the copper pennies. He was wrong, but the damage was done. Others added to the fray, saying that outside of Philadelphia, the Mint was of absolutely no use. Boudinot now found himself on a committee of inquiry to report on the state of the Mint and measures necessary to improve it.[3]

Not surprisingly, it was Boudinot who reported on behalf of the committee to the House exactly two months later. The report was thorough, giving an intimate view of the Mint and its operations. The cost of the land had been $4,266.66 and the buildings $22,720.45. The works consisted of two rolling mills, one for hot and the other for cold metal, worked by four horses and requiring five men in attendance. A drawing machine, powered by the horse mill and worked by the same men as the rolling mills, equalized the strips from the rolling mills for cutting planchets. Three cutting presses were utilized to create the planchets of both the larger and smaller coins. It was intended that the horse mill work the cutting presses. However, with work lacking, one man operated each cutting press. There were three coining presses, modified to be self-feeding and discharging. A fourth press was under construction with plans to dedicate it to dollars and medals. Furnaces were also in place for annealing and to support assay melting and refining. In addition, the mint maintained two forges. Boudinot noted there would be a substantial cost savings if the facility had access to waterpower or steam power in place of the four horses.

When it came to a review of the operations and recommendations, the tone was tempered, the words measured. The end result was an even-handed, fair treatment of the Mint. The difficulties encountered so far were typical of those in any enterprise in its formative stage. Complicating the situation, no works of such large scale, requiring both force and precision, had been attempted in the United States. Having failed to obtain skilled workmen in Europe to man the mint, Americans had been recruited to learn their skills on the job. Hampering the situation even more, some of the machinery necessary for the mint and the tools for making said machinery, could be brought from the outside, but most had to be made on site.

Yet the morale of the Mint was good, with the men claiming that their output was as good as any of the more experienced mints in Europe. Most of their problems had been overcome and they were confident that future coinage would be substantial.

In spite of this optimism, Boudinot pointed out problems. To keep expenditures at a minimum, the land purchased for the mint was now found to be too small. Great delays had been encountered in processing bullion, some of which was substandard. All bullion deposited at the mints in Europe had to first be brought to standard at the expense of the depositor. This was done outside the Mint in the private sector. Very few people in the United States possessed the needed skills, making it necessary to establish such a department at the Mint. The assayer had performed the job to date but that negated the system of checks and balances instituted at the Mint for security purposes. A melter refiner must be added.

There remained two more issues. The officers of the Mint complained that the standard for silver coins contained too much alloy that would, in their words, cause the coins to "wear black." They wanted fineness increased from its mandated level of 892 to 900.[4] Also the real problem with copper coin distribution was who paid for the cost of shipping the heavy cents and half cents from the mint to the banks along the eastern seaboard.

Boudinot picked up on all the issues. He recommended provision be made for a melter refiner with the cost of the refining born by the depositor. For the sake of efficiency, depositors should bring bullion to the Mint in quantities of no less than 200 ounces of silver or 20 ounces of gold. The standard for silver coins should be altered to nine parts pure silver to one part alloy. The United States should pick up the cost of distributing copper coins. And finally, the Mint should be able to give preference to bullion brought to the Mint at or near standard for purposes of coining.[5] On the closing day of the Third Congress, Boudinot's recommendations were enacted, with the exception of the change in alloy for silver coins, which would stay at the old rate.[6]

• • • •

In June 1795, the seriously ailing David Rittenhouse resigned his position as director of the Mint. Thomas Jefferson had pushed the original appointment of Rittenhouse by George Washington. Rittenhouse, who suffered from poor health throughout his lifetime, had been unable to reject the entreaties of both Washington and Jefferson. He was a noted scientist with mathematical skills and member of the American Philosophical Society. The society, founded in 1743, drew its membership from all the leading scientific circles of the United States and beyond. With its meeting hall situated just off of Chestnut Street, at the State House Yard (now known as Independence Square), the American Philosophical Society was at the seat of American power.

Now there would be a changing of the guard at the Mint. Where would this plum fall? Would it remain within Jefferson's influence or Alexander Hamilton's? The previous April, acting on advance knowledge of Rittenhouse's retirement, Tench Coxe, a Treasury Department high-level functionary, approached Dr. Benjamin Rush, asking him on his doorstep if he would take the director's position. Recalling the meeting in his autobiography,

Rush related that he rejected it on the spot. It would not pay a third of what he was earning from his medical practice.[7] Coxe, who was noted for his devious political dealings, might have been freelancing. However, he had withdrawn his support of Hamilton the preceding year in favor of Jefferson. Consequently, Hamilton, now working in the private sector, openly disliked Coxe. Likewise, Jefferson had withdrawn to Monticello, temporarily forsaking politics.[8] If Coxe was Jefferson's proxy in a quiet tug of war between these two political opposites over the Mint, Hamilton prevailed as his man, Henry William De Saussure, received the appointment.

De Saussure, a prominent lawyer from South Carolina, felt unqualified for the post and promptly showed it by supporting the Mint's practice of using nine parts pure silver to one part alloy, simply ignoring the mandated standard. Rittenhouse had ordered the change in October, 1794, expecting Congress to follow suit in line with Elias Boudinot's committee's recommendation. De Saussure then refused to countermand the practice "under the weighty sanctions of Mr. Rittenhouse's authority." He simply stated that some mistake had prevented Congress from acting on the proposal.

De Saussure also found himself over his head with technical difficulties. The iron used for the rollers in the rolling mills failed with maddening frequency. Replacements were, at times, faulty. Lack of working dies, coupled with their excessive wear, caused suspensions of coining. A better selection of steel and more skill in the hardening of the dies helped. But the greatest difficulty was the substandard bullion brought to the mint for coinage. Meanwhile, no move had been made to fill the melter refiner position. In exasperation, the Mint director resigned on October 14, 1795. In his final report, De Saussure summed up the situation at the Mint succinctly. If the Mint were regularly supplied with bullion of the legal standard, capacity would be adequate to coin in a mix of denominations $3 million annually in gold and silver.[9]

• • • •

Elias Boudinot (fig. 3) was a Hamilton man. Though philosophically the two were in lockstep, there was a personal reason for Boudinot's allegiance. When Hamilton came to the colonies at age 17, he lived with Boudinot in northern New Jersey doing preparatory work at a grammar school before entering King's College.[10]

Like Hamilton, Boudinot had retired from politics, not standing for reelection to Congress in the autumn of 1794. Approached now to take De Saussure's place, he was at first reluctant. He believed he lacked the necessary knowledge of chemistry. Dr. Rush was consulted and preferred another candidate. Regardless, the position was offered once more to Boudinot and he accepted. His nomination was sent to the Senate for confirmation on December 10, 1795.[11] Rush, in support, loaned Boudinot some chemistry books that he believed would get him up to speed.[12]

Fig. 3. Elias Boudinot, after he had retired from the Mint, in an 1817 painting by Thomas Sully. As a former president of the Continental Congress, he brought political prestige to the position of Mint director.

Knowledge of chemistry was the least of Boudinot's problems when he took the reins of the Mint. Among his first acts, he ordered the Mint to comply with the mandated alloy standard. Not only were the Mint's actions against the law, they defrauded the depositors. The Mint's policy had been to pay on each deposit on the basis of nine parts silver to one part alloy. However, if the Mint had paid based upon the legally mandated alloy, the depositor would have received more in face value. When this fact became public knowledge in 1798, depositors petitioned Congress for redress, which added to the Mint's poor standing with certain members of the House.[13]

A year later, Boudinot still did not have a melter refiner and bullion was a headache. He complained in his first annual report over the lack of a bullion fund to either purchase bullion or anticipate payments due to depositors. When bullion came into the mint, each deposit had to be treated individually, requiring melting three and four times to recover all of the silver and gold to minimize wastage. It was a long and inefficient process, pushing the

Mint's cost structure above where Boudinot felt it ought to be. Some of his other problems were more political, such as lacking an appropriation to cover the overall wastage at the end of the operating year.[14]

Boudinot got his melter refiner, Joseph Cloud, who was approved by the Senate on January 2, 1797.[15] He also got a House inquiry into the expenses at the Mint. At the heart of this inquiry was the role foreign coins were playing in the nation's specie supply and the attendant impact on the Mint's operating cost structure.

• • • •

Congress had moved to regulate foreign coinage with the law of February 9, 1793. Effective the following July 1, the law required, after a three-year interval from the start of gold and silver coinage at the Mint and so proclaimed by the President, that no foreign coins except Spanish milled dollars and their fractions be legal tender in the United States. As laws went, this one was both well intentioned and reasonably well-crafted. The three-year period gave the Mint time after commencing production of gold and silver coins to ramp up output to replace their foreign counterparts. It also provided a source for bullion for the Mint, instructing the Treasury Department to forward foreign coins received in satisfaction of federal taxes and fees to the Mint for recoining. It was assumed that the nation's banks would follow this lead. The problem was simply that these coins were still legal tender. No one any distance from the Mint was going to voluntarily take the time and expense for recoining. Furthermore, the law did not compel Treasury to send its foreign coins to the Mint either.

The inquiry now brought to light the fact that no such coinage proclamation had been forthcoming from the president. As a result action on a bullion fund appropriation for the Mint was put on hold. President John Adams then responded to this oversight by issuing the required proclamation, on July 22, 1797, that terminated legal-tender status for foreign silver coins on October 15, 1797 and for foreign gold coins on July 31, 1798. As the termination date for the silver coins rapidly approached, these coins began to lose value based upon their expense for recoinage, striking the rural population, isolated from the banks on the eastern seaboard, the hardest.

With the convening of the second session of the Fifth Congress in December 1797, the bungling of the call on foreign silver coins and the expected similar furor over foreign gold coins was front and center on the congressional agenda. Aggravating matters, the expected flood of foreign silver coins into the Mint for recoining had not materialized.

Debate opened in the House on December 11 and spilled into the following January. It was proposed that the provisions of the Foreign Coin Act of 1793, setting forth the deadline for acceptance of foreign coins in payments to the government, be suspended for two years or until the end of the next session of Congress.[16] With legal-tender status of foreign gold coins set to expire in the coming months, no one really believed that the Mint could strike enough eagles and half eagles to adequately replace these coins. Besides in the backcountry where there were no banks, gold and not paper currency was the primary monetary instrument. What paper money there was, was often traded at a discount due to the remoteness of the issuing bank.

Three alternative solutions now came to the forefront. Congress must either not call in the foreign coins, enlarge the Mint to facilitate the recoining, or have no Mint at all. Some thought the Mint useless. Other, calmer heads recognized that it was not the lack of mechanical force at the Mint, but want of bullion.[17] Philadelphia Congressman Samuel Sitgreaves took the Mint's position that suspending the act would deny the Mint bullion that it badly needed to increase coinage.[18]

On the other hand the Mint also took criticism for delays in processing bullion deposits. No bank at any distance, say New York or Baltimore, would send their bullion to the Mint. They could not afford to tie up their hard currency for as long as six months while incurring the expense of transportation and insurance to boot. Only the Philadelphia banks could afford to have the foreign specie recoined. In addition, the Mint would not take in more bullion from the local banks than it could work in one mass. This practice, in effect, forced the local banks to aggregate deposits while waiting for the Mint to call for them. It did, however, expedite refining at the Mint by alleviating the need to conduct repeated meltings over numerous small deposits to maximize precious metal recovery.

Expanding the Mint was easily dismissed. Why do that when the seat of government would be removed from Philadelphia in two years? Unspoken was the assumption that the Mint would move with it.[19]

John Swanwick, who resided in Philadelphia, did not help matters when he observed that United States gold coins were so scarce in the interior of the country that when one passed in commerce, it was often hoarded as a pocket piece. An Englishman had lately informed Swanwick that, in 1795, he had seen a large quantity of American eagles in a goldsmith's shop in London for the purpose of melting down—"So rapidly," the Englishman said, "do [y]our eagles take their flight."[20]

Into this sometime rough debate, Albert Gallatin (fig. 4), representative from Pennsylvania and future secretary of the Treasury, was a voice of reason. It was clear, he said, that the United States certainly had no excess of circulating specie than was necessary for commerce and that withdrawing any portion of it would be a mistake. Then he asked what had happened to the substantial revenues from the federal customs houses. Why had more of

Fig. 4. Albert Gallatin, in a painting by Gilbert Stuart (circa 1803), would guide the Treasury Department through the administrations of Jefferson and Madison.

it not shown up at the Mint for recoining. He also noted that there was a much easier way of providing the Mint with bullion, without encountering the difficulties of forcing the foreign coins out of circulation. Congress could simply make an appropriation of $100,000 for the purchase of bullion for the Mint.[21]

Later in the debate, Gallatin returned to his main point. The law of 1793 was basically broken into two parts. The first directed that all foreign gold and silver coins that came into the Treasury should be recoined. The second provided that, after a certain period, all foreign coins should be called out of circulation. However, with the first having not been carried into effect, it was highly unreasonable that the second should be undertaken. If foreign coin could not be gotten to the Mint, the law ought to be repealed and an appropriation for bullion purchases made.[22]

Gallatin had raised the issue of the lack of Treasury remittances of foreign coins into the Mint enough times now that a formal response from Treasury was demanded. Secretary Oliver Wolcott, a Yale-trained lawyer, answered that the value of specie from customs collections at ports distant to Philadelphia was often transmitted by paper transactions. No particular portion of the specie contained in the vaults of the BUS was specifically earmarked as belonging to the United States. However, the secretary noted that the BUS had always been willing to cooperate in facilitating the operations of the Mint and would at any time advance the foreign coins in their possession for recoining. Wolcott noted that in 1795 and 1796 there was a scarcity of foreign silver coins available for recoining. French and Spanish gold was available but there was a ready market for these coins and they would have been recoined at a loss anyway. The secretary provided no explanation for this market disparity in gold values. Finally, Wolcott came forth with the statement that the condition and prospects of the Treasury during the years 1795 and 1796, were such as to dissuade the secretary from advances not appearing to be of primary importance. Cutting through the bureaucratic language, the United States was strapped financially and could not afford to tie up its funds for the amount of time it would take the Mint to recoin its foreign money. Wolcott then closed, by stating disingenuously that under existing arrangements, no difficulty would be found in supplying the Mint with any sums for recoinage of which the Mint might be found competent.[23] Gallatin had his answer.

The issue of suspending of the call provision in the Foreign Coin Act of 1793 was really never in doubt. The call provisions clearly worked to the disadvantage of the rural portion of the population. Having just experienced an insurrection over whiskey excise taxes in western Pennsylvania, Congress was in no mood to antagonize these people again. Particularly since one of the sticking points of that tax was that it be paid in hard-to-get specie. On February 1, 1798, President Adams signed into law the suspension of the call on foreign coin.[24] At the same time, Congress did nothing about providing adequate bullion to the Mint for coinage. There was not even any substantial debate on this subject.

On April 30, 1802, Congress would again suspend the call provisions of this act giving foreign specie another three-year lease on life.[25] Like an elixir, Congress would become hooked on this easy solution to the lack of American circulating coins.

••••

Throughout this period, Boudinot had another vexing and more immediate problem on his hands. Gold and silver aside, copper coins were a financial necessity to the young country. They passed in everyday commerce. They were paid out for daily wages. Yet there was no indigenous source for this metal. The Mint must import its needs. At the same time the seigniorage from these copper coins (the difference between the face value of a coin and the costs of its bullion, alloy, and manufacture) created a significant offset to operating expenses thereby benefiting the Philadelphia Mint's bottom line. On the other hand, seigniorage from silver and gold coinage that passed into commerce based upon intrinsic value was nil. Boudinot could handle many of the production issues at the Mint but a shortage of copper coinage, adversely impacting his costs of operations, would be a death knell.

In 1796 Boudinot, at Washington's instigation, had settled on the British as the primary supply of his copper planchets. He approached two potential suppliers in 1797, the Company of Copper Miners and Boulton, Watt & Company, for trial shipments. The Company of Copper Miners product was wholly unacceptable. Yet as 1797 waned, no shipment had yet appeared from Boulton. It finally arrived on December 4. It was worth the wait, as Boudinot found Boulton's planchets exactly as specified. The Mint director then asked Boulton to send twenty tons of copper planchets in the spring, and again in the autumn of 1798.

Time and distance now tripped up Boudinot. Boulton noted that the Mint director had requested 15 tons in June 1797. This was the order they filled that arrived in late spring 1798. With the copper planchets again satisfactory, Boudinot wrote asking if the firm could supply 40 to 50 tons annually. Then, a yellow fever epidemic caused the mint to shutdown that summer. It made no difference, as Boudinot did not hear from Boulton.

It was not until June 1799 that Boudinot received 10 tons of copper planchets from the English firm. In the interim, Boudinot had become worried, writing many letters and submitting repeated orders to Boulton. While the shipments were still short on quantity, Boulton's attitude seemed to improve. Boudinot had also asked the English firm's advice on die hardening to which they had been forthcoming.[26] What Boudinot did not know was that a severe winter in Britain froze the canals in that country, preventing Boulton from shipping at the desired levels sooner.

October 1799 brought another shipment from Boulton.[27] The supply relationship was now established.[28] However, cent shortages prior to this point had cost the Mint dearly in terms of needed political support.

1849

CHAPTER 2

BARE-KNUCKLES BRAWLING

The congressional debate of 1797 over the legal-tender status of foreign coins left unanswered another immediate question. Would the mint, now sorely unpopular in the land, remain in Philadelphia? L'Enfant's plan for the nation's new capital, located along the banks of the Potomac River in Virginia and Maryland, included 17 reservations for public institutions but assigned no uses to any of them. Yet by 1798 the commissioners in charge were assigning functions to them, one of which was a mint square, obviously intended as the new permanent site of the Mint.[1]

With the decision made that all offices of the government were to be moved to the newly created Washington City on December 1, 1800, the question of the Mint's status in Philadelphia became paramount. Elias Boudinot, in his annual report of January 8, 1800, to President John Adams, diplomatically asked for guidance. Remaining in Philadelphia would require legislative authorization. Boudinot argued that the Mint was in great measure supported by the bullion passing through the various Philadelphia banks. Deprived of this source for coinage, he correctly predicted that the mint, located in the financially isolated new capital, would frequently be without silver and gold for coinage while the carrying cost for operations would remain unchanged. Boudinot asked for a prompt decision from Congress. The equipment and structures must be kept in good repair unless the intent was to move

the mint. In that case, only maintenance necessary to maintain immediate activity would be needed.[2]

Faced with making this decision, Congress balked. The Senate Finance Committee recognized that removal of the Mint would "in many respects be inconvenient." However the prospect of keeping the Mint in Philadelphia away from the immediate oversight and direction of the principal officers of the government was questioned.[3] With that conundrum, the Sixth Congress simply authorized the Mint to remain in Philadelphia until March 4, 1801, leaving the issue to be dealt with by the Seventh Congress.[4] Then, in an about face with President-elect Thomas Jefferson and the Democratic Republicans about to take power, the Sixth Congress on its last day in lame duck session, March 3, 1801, extended the mint's stay in Philadelphia for two more years until the beginning of the Eighth Congress.[5] Clearly the Federalists in Philadelphia were worried over the disposition of the Mint under the Democratic Republicans and were hoping for more control in two years.

They had reason to be fearful. In February 1802, the House established yet another committee to review the Mint at Philadelphia. The committee immediately put Boudinot on the spot, requesting that he fully assess Mint operations.

Boudinot's detailed response only added fuel to the fire. The machinery at the mint would definitely last another year, but after that would probably need some maintenance and repairs. In particular, the horses were old and ought to be replaced within the year. However, if the Mint were to be made permanent in Philadelphia, conversion to steam power should be considered. The lots on which the mint was located were too small, cramping operations. The Mint director argued that Philadelphia had expanded westward so that these lots were now in the center of the city. As a result they had appreciated somewhat in value and their sale would facilitate a move to a larger location, more remote from the city center.

Boudinot got to the heart of the matter when he stated that the machinery at the mint was specific to minting coins and had no value beyond scrap if sold. The basic expenses of the Mint were $20,000 annually and $15,000 on a net basis after deducting the seigniorage from the copper coinage. Boudinot had a bid in hand from a group of Philadelphia businessmen to take over the coinage function using the existing mint facilities, charging the government on a percentage basis for silver and gold and on a weight basis for copper coins.[6]

Not surprisingly, this committee reported back to the full House on April 2, 1802, with a bill to abolish the Mint.[7] Sensing the odds were against the Mint surviving in Philadelphia, Boudinot wrote directly to President Jefferson on April 17. It was an appeal for severance compensation for the workmen at the Mint, should Congress act adversely. The men had endured static wages in the face of inflation driven by the trade disruptions caused by the French and British conflict that would become known as the Napoleonic Wars in Europe. They had submitted, without complaint, under the assumption that their employment was permanent. In addition, their skills developed over time at the Mint would be difficult to transfer to the private sector. Boudinot closed by saying that this compensation for past service should not be applied to the officers of the Mint.[8] Boudinot's plea was to no avail; President Jefferson considered the issue of the mint's location to be within the responsibility of the Congress and washed his hands of it.[9]

The ensuing debate in the House was vigorous. Proponents of the measure to abolish stated that Boudinot's response to their inquiry gave sufficient information to act. With the recent peace, albeit possibly temporary, in Europe, foreign silver and gold coins were again flowing into the country. After March 3, 1803, the mint must be moved to Washington. Why incur this expense and move equipment in questionable repair? The secretary of the Treasury could be empowered to contract with the BUS or with individuals for the supply of copper coinage. However, the Bank of the United States was not in the minting business. The government had been spending $20,000 annually for ten years and what had they received for this expenditure? The Mint should be terminated. That was a cheap shot; the Mint had performed reasonably well given the circumstances over that period.

Calmer heads raised concerns. Who would determine the purity of the foreign specie? Bank paper provided a useful alternative to coins, but would that always be the case? What would happen should hostilities in Europe resume and the flow of foreign specie be interrupted again? The opposition argued for a one-year postponement of the decision, until the next session of the Seventh Congress. This motion failed.[10] With the votes in hand, the House, on April 26, 1802, passed the bill to abolish the Mint.[11]

The problem for the faction against the Mint was that only six more working days remained in the first session of the Seventh Congress. While the Democratic Republicans held a majority in the Senate, the Federalists still had substantial numbers in this chamber. There just wasn't time available to move the legislation into and out of the Finance Committee and back to the floor for a vote. And the bill's supporters lacked the votes to force this legislation directly to the floor for an immediate consideration.

With the convening of the second session, on December 6, 1802, supporters of the Mint in the House were prepared. On December 22 John Randolph of Virginia (fig. 5) moved that the House resolve itself into a Committee of the Whole to once again consider abolishing the Mint. Randolph had foolishly assumed the motion to be

Fig. 5. John Randolph, vitriolic opponent of the Mint, in a depiction by John Wesley Jarvis (1811).

perfunctory and left the floor before the question was called. It narrowly failed; the House expressed a desire to wait for the forthcoming Mint annual report for any new information. The fight was on.

Randolph had a reputation for a sharp tongue and made enemies easily. The next day, he was at his sarcastic best. The information at hand from the last session was sufficient enough, he declared. The director himself had reported that the machinery would not last. In the elapsed time since his report, had the machinery renewed itself? The horses were old and worn out. Had they grown any younger? Were the cramped quarters somehow enlarged? The Mint director had recommended a change in location and conversion to steam power. There having been no general election between the sessions, Randolph presumed that no change in sentiment had taken place. Thus, Randolph had made his motion believing his subject perfectly matured.

Randolph was wrong. Supporters of the Mint were organized and ready to make their case. Their arguments were laced with inside information on the Mint. The facility had coined more than $500,000 in the year just ended. Though the Mint was an expense to Treasury, it was not an expense to the nation. The exportation of an equivalent amount of bullion to be coined on contract in Europe and then shipped back would have cost at least 5 percent, more than Mint operating expenses.

Randolph retorted that, notwithstanding all the issues, no member of Congress ever saw a coin. That was an overstatement; they certainly had seen copper coinage. Randolph went on to say he had not seen a gold coin from the Mint in two years. Supporters had an answer for this issue as well. Banks, as part of their capital accounts, were holding gold coins. It was the practice of banks to count the specie in their vaults once a month. The burden of this practice was considerably lessened when the specie was in gold and not silver.

Andrew Gregg, a congressman from Pennsylvania, made a motion to postpone the subject until receipt of the Mint director's report. It easily carried with 47 ayes to 28 nays. Supporters of the Mint now had the upper hand.[12]

Boudinot's report reached the House on January 11, 1803. Every talking point made by supporters was mirrored in the report, making it clear that the Mint's defense had been orchestrated. Boudinot also made the point that if Congress adjourned without taking any action in regard to the Mint, its activity in Philadelphia lacked legislative authorization to continue. Nor could its equipment be moved to Washington without money authorized for the expenses. Without any action, the nation would be without a mint. In addition, the skills and professional knowledge accumulated by the workforce would be lost.

In reaction the House appointed a five-member committee on January 25 to report back a recommendation. Originally the committee was composed of two members from the rural South and two members from New England. The fifth was from Maryland. However, he asked to be excused and Samuel Mitchill (fig. 6), a politician from New York City, was appointed in his place. Educated at the University of Edinburgh and a former professor of chemistry, botany, and natural history at Columbia College, Mitchill was immune to Randolph's rhetoric.[13]

Mitchill came before the full House three days later. The committee had been split and Mitchill had cast the deciding vote. But Mitchill was not going to make a report. Instead, he wished to report by submitting a bill. His maneuver was a masterstroke. Now the debate switched to the merits of his proposed bill, as opposed to an up-or-down vote on the continued existence of the U.S. Mint. The issue was no longer so clear-cut. Mitchill, in support of his move, repeated what was well understood—unless a provision was made by law, the Mint could not continue in Philadelphia and must be moved to Washington. Money would be needed for the move and more money would be needed to cover the expense of breaking up the operation in Philadelphia. Furthermore, any shortage of copper and small silver coins

Fig. 6. Through Representative Samuel L. Mitchill's adroit leadership, the Mint at Philadelphia gained a new lease on life in 1803. Thereafter, its location would be reviewed on a five-year basis for an indefinite period of time.

Fig. 7. Portrait of Dr. Benjamin Rush, treasurer of the Mint, by Thomas Sully (circa 1812–1815).

would only be aggravated during the move. On motion to allow the committee to report the bill, supporters of the Mint won by a solid majority.[14]

Mitchill wasted no time reporting H.R. 24 on February 1, 1803. It extended the operation of the Mint for five years from the expiration of its present term and provided $500 for maintenance to replace horses and repair machinery.[15]

Randolph had lost. Mitchill, by choosing a five-year term, picked off enough of the opposition to reverse the action from the first session in the House. The bill easily carried the Senate. On the last day of second session, the bill came back to the House where it was amended, dropping out the $500 appropriation, in an attempt to starve the Mint of the extra cash needed to improve operating efficiency. The opposition's intent was more clearly revealed in a second motion, seeking to cut the term from five years to one year. This amendment narrowly failed.[16]

The Philadelphia Mint now had a five-year reprieve. It was not the best of situations but the alternative had been extinction. The only losers in this legislative logroll were the four old horses at the mint. Mitchill had risen to the occasion brilliantly. The ultimate irony of someone from New York City saving the Mint at Philadelphia would not be understood for another generation when the two cities would be locked in a fierce struggle for financial supremacy.

• • • •

In this adverse environment, the officers of the Mint became embroiled in a bitter family dispute. Dr. Benjamin Rush (fig. 7) had fallen upon hard times when his Philadelphia medical practice declined precipitously over his unorthodox procedure of bleeding yellow fever patients. Dr. Nicholas Way, the Mint's treasurer and a friend of Rush, had died of the feared disease in the epidemic of 1797. Rush was married to Boudinot's niece. Whether Rush came to Boudinot or Boudinot sought to help Rush is not clear. Everybody knew the treasurer's job was a sinecure with little real work attached to it. Rush now wanted it. He and President John Adams had been close friends since their days serving together in the Continental Congress. Adams was happy to choose Rush over the numerous other applicants.[17] The Senate, with some hesitation, approved the appointment on November 27, 1797.[18]

What should have been a cordial family relationship soured in 1800 over a contested will. Matters quickly deteriorated when the two men refused to speak to each other.[19] Boudinot took it a step further, accusing Rush of neglecting his work and asking him to resign. That only inflamed matters. It was difficult to neglect a job with so minimal requirements, yet defending one's minimal efforts could also be embarrassing. Rush, by his own admission, said that the job took only a few minutes of his day, three or four times a week. Once a quarter, he had to work for a few hours preparing his accounts for inspection. He even had a clerk to sign bullion receipts for him.[20] Instead of resigning, Rush dug in.

The feud broke into the open in 1802. Boudinot had written Secretary of the Treasury Albert Gallatin asking that Gallatin send an auditor from Washington, alleging that Rush had not settled his accounts for more than a year.[21] This accusation ultimately landed in Thomas Jefferson's hands. Rush countered by accusing Boudinot of certain improper practices inconsistent with the integrity expected of Mint officers. Boudinot asked the other officers to testify as to his innocence. Several in response sought unsuccessfully to reconcile the two men.

Next, Rush took the unprecedented step of making his accusations specific in a letter to the officers. Boudinot had, for personal purposes, used the mint's iron, tools and workmen, permitted his tenant farmer to receive commissions on articles purchased for the Mint, and stolen horse dung from the mint's stable. Boudinot, in his defense to the secretary of the treasurer, admitted two very minor repairs to his carriage made by Mint workmen. He did admit to having his watch repeatedly recalibrated by the chief coiner. And yes, his farmer had hauled away the mint's horse dung because a hostler could not be found to remove it without charge; that the same individual had saved the Mint hundreds of dollars by his judicious purchases of mint supplies.[22] Ultimately, the charges against Boudinot were dropped. However, it was clear that a culture of laxness, brought about in part by the long periods of inactivity, was developing at the mint.

Elias Boudinot turned 65 in 1805. He had just completed a house in Burlington, New Jersey. Rush correctly believed that Boudinot was going to resign. He promptly wrote Thomas Jefferson, asking for the appointment. He claimed that he had been induced by all of the other officers at the Mint as well as other considerations to seek the office of director. He made his case, reminding Jefferson of his large sacrifices during the Revolution. Just what these were, he did not say. He admitted to financial setbacks in his practice of medicine, coupled with his large family and the approach of old age, that made this position particularly enticing to him.[23]

Now, would Thomas Jefferson give Benjamin Rush what he had once peremptorily rejected?

1849

CHAPTER 3

THE COMING OF THE PATTERSONS

Thomas Jefferson had specific ideas as to who should succeed Elias Boudinot at the Mint. It was not Benjamin Rush. The position was not a sinecure and Jefferson wanted the best man available. To the president's mind, that meant someone as strong in mathematics as Rittenhouse had been. With Alexander Hamilton killed in a duel in 1804, the president had a clear field from which to make his selection.

It certainly was no surprise that the president turned to the membership of the American Philosophical Society (APS) to fill the position. While Jefferson was the president of the APS, more in title than reality, he fulfilled the position with great pride. He had turned to the Society in 1803, sending Meriwether Lewis to consult with its leading members before he embarked on his great expedition of the vast territory acquired through the Louisiana Purchase. Jefferson specified one man in particular, an old friend, Robert Patterson, to give advice on scientific instruments for the journey.[1] The two had a comfortable, easy relationship. Both men were enthusiasts of ciphers and other codes. As a joke, Patterson, some four years before, had sent Jefferson a letter in cipher that was nothing short of perfection. The problem was, that neither Jefferson, nor anyone else for more than two hundred years, could unscramble what turned out to be, essentially, the preamble from the Declaration of Independence.[2]

Robert Patterson (fig. 8) had immigrated to America in 1768 at the age of 25. Of Scotch-Irish heritage, it was nat-

Fig. 8. Posthumous portrait of Dr. Robert Patterson, executed by Rembrandt Peale in 1830.

ural for him to settle in the Philadelphia area where there were many people of similar background. He took part in the American Revolution, ultimately serving as a brigade major. In 1779 he accepted a position as professor of mathematics and natural philosophy at the University of Pennsylvania. Here, life settled into a pleasant routine until 1805 when Thomas Jefferson called him to the Mint.

Jefferson was as aware as Benjamin Rush that Boudinot was preparing to leave. He wasted no time, tapping Patterson in a short note on April 27, 1805. Perhaps the most important detail of this communication was its postscript.

> I should be sorry to withdraw you from the college; nor do I perceive that this office need do it. Its duties will easily admit your devoting the ordinary college hours to that institution. Indeed it is possible that the Mint may sometime or other be discontinued that I could not advise a permanent living be given up for it.[3]

Jefferson's honest advice to an old friend was given without heed to the precedent that it could be setting of part-time directors. Patterson took the president at his word, continuing his position at the university and serving additionally as vice provost from 1810 to 1813.

Thus the 62-year-old Patterson embarked on a new career. What he found was a reasonably well-run manufacturing operation under chief coiner Henry Voigt and assistant coiner Adam Eckfeldt. Patterson took a liking to Eckfeldt, who had been hired by Rittenhouse to harden the dies. Boudinot had judged the man much more valuable and promoted him to his present position. Now, Eckfeldt had the management of the whole coining department.[4]

Patterson was also satisfied with the melter refiner, Joseph Cloud. Cloud gained admittance to the American Philosophical Society, with Patterson's approval, in 1806 and would serve as a curator of the Society from 1814 to 1822.

The long periods of idleness, for lack of bullion and specie to coin, had to disturb Patterson. To make matters worse, President Jefferson complained to Patterson that dollar coins were being exported as quickly as they were being struck; he called their coinage lost labor. Neither man was forthcoming as to why they were leaving the country but Patterson had a simple solution. He stopped their coinage in 1804.[5] He extended this solution to the eagle gold coin, also under export pressure. After the fact,

James Madison, as secretary of state, provided formal instructions, in accordance with the president's wishes, to terminate dollar coin production on May 1, 1806.[6]

Discontinuing the two coins most prone to export did not address Patterson's immediate and overriding problem of acquiring a steady supply of bullion to efficiently drive the Mint's coining activities. In December 1805, the Bank of the United States came to him with a proposition. To prevent the export of the legal-tender Spanish milled dollars as much as possible, the bank would bring them to the Mint in large quantities for recoining into half dollars and smaller denominations, provided the Mint upheld its part of the bargain in a timely manner.

The Bank of the United States had grown into the nation's first truly national business enterprise, with nine branch offices along the Atlantic seaboard, from Boston to Savannah and near the Gulf coast at New Orleans. It was led by the highly capable Philadelphia banker Thomas Willing.[7] Patterson signed on to this proposal in what was to become an ongoing partnership. As a result, he asked authorization from Jefferson for the hiring of a few additional men and one extra horse for the rolling mill.[8]

The deal was good for Patterson. For a trivial expense, he could increase the coinage of silver and gold, better satisfying the financial interests in the country. What he did not address was the benefit to the Bank of the United States of such an arrangement. If Spanish specie was being exported to satisfy negative trade balances, there was a reason.

When Alexander Hamilton originally fixed the weight and silver content of the American dollar in 1792, he based it upon the assay results of a number of circulated Spanish milled dollars. His intent was to make the value in metal of the American dollar equivalent to that of the Spanish dollar. However, his number was low due to the wear and abrasion these coins had received in commerce. While Hamilton's value of 371.25 grains of pure silver for the American dollar was acceptable for domestic purposes against the worn Spanish dollars, it overvalued the dollar in export markets. A freshly minted Spanish dollar contained about 375 grains of pure silver.[9] Thus, Spanish dollars were the specie of choice to settle foreign debts.

For the Bank of the United States, this same rule basically held true. The bank received the Spanish dollars on a nominal basis equal to the American dollar. The Mint then received these dollars from the Bank of the United States on a bullion basis, repaying the Bank in American dollars based upon the aggregate of silver bullion received. In nearly all cases, the bank could do no worse than break even, and if the culls were eliminated, they stood to gain.

Patterson soon learned that there was another, less-palatable part of the bargain. The Bank of the United States wanted half dollars. Any denomination less would require more time for counting when the books were periodically reconciled. Patterson found he could not force them to take smaller denomination pieces. Production of half dimes stopped, while it was sporadic at best for dimes and quarters. The country would have to rely upon heavily circulated fractional Spanish specie, where the nominal value was well above the intrinsic value. This situation put him at odds with his boss. Jefferson recognized that the lesser denominations were more valuable to the public. These small coins would also be less susceptible to export. Indeed, if Jefferson could have his way, the law would be amended to allow two- and three-cent pieces in silver and "golden dollars" which would all be large enough to handle and a great convenience to the public.[10] Here Jefferson was suggesting substituting gold for silver in the dollar coin. Perhaps Jefferson was letting his bias show, inferring that a silver dollar coin was inconvenient in everyday commerce and that this fact might have played some part in his desire to have its production discontinued.

• • • •

Patterson inherited another issue at the Mint that had nothing to do with inadequate coin production. His 61-year-old engraver, the diminutive Robert Scot, had held his position since 1793, virtually the beginning of the Mint. Scot's profession was bank-note, map, and other flat-plate engraving, and he had limited skill as a diesinker. His designs in the intervening years had been adequate, but were really a hodgepodge of mediocrity. In Patterson's opinion, Scot, while a marvelous and faithful officer, was so infirm as to not be expected to continue in his position for long.[11] Besides, Patterson wanted improvements and questioned Scot's ability to successfully execute new designs.

Whether it was at Patterson's initiative, or Jefferson taking a hand in the situation, a call was put out to the American consul in Leghorn, Italy, Joseph Clay, seeking a replacement for Scot.[12] He, in turn, contracted with Moritz Fürst to proceed to the United States to be employed at the Mint as a diesinker at a salary well above that of the engraver. When Fürst arrived in 1807, he was rejected. John Reich had the inside track, and would be a lot cheaper.[13]

Reich had arrived in Philadelphia from Bavaria sometime before 1801 under an indenture. He had Americanized his given name, Johann Matthaus, to simply John. In some capacity, Reich had had the good fortune to meet Thomas Jefferson and convince him of his talents. Jefferson had in turn recommended him to Boudinot. Otherwise he expected that a man of Reich's skills would surely find work in the publishing business.[14] One of the officers of the Mint, most likely the well-to-do Boudinot, then purchased Reich's indenture. Boudinot was pleased with the samples of his work, but hesitant to employ him without testing him first.[15]

Boudinot had a specific project in mind. Scot had a contract in hand for the execution of several medallions for

Fig. 9. This medal, possibly the first commemorative struck at the mint, celebrates the 25th anniversary of the signing of the Declaration of Independence as well as the inauguration of Thomas Jefferson. It was executed by John Reich on a contract basis. The similarity of the image of Jefferson found on this medal to that used on the Jefferson Indian Peace Medal indicates that Reich worked on both medals.

the Indian nations. This work had to have been the Jefferson Indian peace medal. Boudinot insisted that Scot employ Reich to work under him on the execution of this commission. However the compensation that Scot threw Reich's way barely covered living expenses.[16] His work was excellent which led to chief coiner Henry Voigt pairing with Reich on another project.

There was a move afoot in Philadelphia to commemorate the Declaration of Independence, followed 25 years later by the triumph of republicanism upon Thomas Jefferson's inauguration. Jefferson himself had complained that the only medals authorized by Congress were for military exploits and that the Declaration of Independence certainly merited a medal.[17] Voigt saw this work as a way to keep Reich employed and attached to the Mint. The chief coiner supported Reich while he was sinking the die. The two would share the profits from the public sale of the medal. Voigt thought sales would be quite extensive, considering the workmanship and the subject at hand. Boudinot was agreeable to this scheme which involved the use of the coin presses when they were not employed in the business of the Mint. Even with Boudinot's permission to strike the medal at the Mint, Voigt hesitated.

The chief coiner sent a specimen strike of the commemorative medal (fig. 9) to President Jefferson for his approval. He then asked Jefferson's approval to use the mint's coin presses on this project, as an endorsement of Boudinot's permission.[18] Jefferson's reply was a masterful avoidance of the question. He thought the commemoration of the Declaration of Independence worthy of a medal and Reich's execution certainly of great merit. He had friends to whom he wished to give an example of the medal. Could Voigt send him four more and information on the price and he would see that Reich was paid?[19] Nowhere in the reply did Jefferson grant permission to use the mint's presses on such a purely private venture. Yet where did Jefferson think these four medals, as well as the one in his possession, were coming from?

Thus, a grey area of Mint operations was created. The law governing the Mint and its operation was silent regarding the execution of medals. Scot clearly benefited financially from the execution for the government of the Indian peace medals. Now Reich and Voigt would benefit from this quasi-private venture. Jefferson had given his implied approval. Precedence was born.

Yet there was still no position for Reich. The intense focus of Congress upon the Mint and its expense at that point prevented Boudinot from attempting anything of this sort. Meanwhile, Reich struggled to make it on his own. Concurrently, the rumor reached Jefferson that Scot would not employ him for fear of being supplanted in spite of that fact that Scot was independently wealthy.[20] The president refused to intervene.

As Patterson took the helm at the Mint, he was informed that the Navy Department was to have use of the mint machinery to strike a medal authorized by Congress honoring Commodore Edward Preble for his victory at Tripoli. Again, the work bypassed Scot and went to Reich. The resulting medal struck at the Mint in early 1806 was outstanding, Reich's best work. Subsequently dissatisfied with his remuneration, Reich wrote directly to President Jefferson to complain. He got nowhere. Jefferson rebutted that while he was the American representative in Paris, he had contracted with Pierre Du Vivier and Augustin Duprè for Revolutionary War medals. No man living should be paid more than these fine artists. Jefferson had instructed the secretary of the Navy to pay Reich based upon the president's estimate of the value of Reich's work. Jefferson meant to pay what the work was worth, no more and no less. The president thought the medal (fig. 10) the best he had ever seen, but would regret extremely if his opinion of the work should be diminished by Reich's continuing opinion that the artist had not received justice.[21] Perhaps Jefferson's pique at having his judgment of compensation questioned is what stirred up the job offer at Leghorn to Moritz Fürst.

Patterson had another take on the situation. He was anticipating coin production to exceed $1 million in 1807. Unwilling to rely solely on Scot for the necessary die

Fig. 10. In 1806 John Reich stepped up his game considerably with the execution of the Edward Preble medal, awarded by Congress for Preble's victory in the naval action at Tripoli.

Fig. 11. John Reich's Capped Bust design first appeared in 1807 on the quarter and half dollar. It was later placed on the half dime and dime. In its original form and later modified for close-collar striking, this design lasted until 1838, making it the first design series with any longevity used in the United States.

preparation, he pushed the president to hire Reich as an assistant. By now, the man was readying to return to Europe, despairing of making a living in the United States. Patterson knew the Mint would be stopped cold in its tracks if Scot resigned or died with no replacement. His closing comment to Jefferson tipped his hand. He had another agenda.

> A small salary however would retain [Reich] in the country and secure his services to the Mint and in truth the beauty of our coins would be greatly improved by his masterly hand.

Patterson wanted new coin designs.

Patterson supported his position, saying that Reich's salary would save the government money by avoiding the necessity of going outside to have dies engraved for medals, implying that Scot was not capable. Now this work might be executed by an artist in their service at little or no expense to the government.[22] The issue of compensation for medal work had taken a turn in reverse.

Ignoring the possibility of any hurt feelings from Scot, Patterson put Reich to work immediately on providing new design devices on the American coinage. The changes were applied to the half dollar and half eagle coins in 1807 and to the smaller silver and gold coins as the occasion arose for Patterson to order their striking. On the obverse was a buxom Miss Liberty with mob cap. Reich varied the configuration of the cap from the gold coins to the silver coins. This design was better suited to the larger tondo of the half dollar. Years later, it was recalled that Liberty's adornment was taken from life and intended as a work of good taste from the style of the times. Reich was given a miniature from which he copied his design.[23] However, some were not pleased and called the image a likeness of Reich's fat mistress.[24] For the reverse, Reich determined upon two different heraldic eagles, one for the gold coins and one for the silver coins (fig. 11).

Were these designs an improvement over the existing works? Only somewhat. Reich's competence in medal designs was clear for all to see. However, it is quite another thing to successfully apply those same artistic skills to a general coinage design. United States silver and gold coins were required by the Mint Act of 1792 to have a figure emblematic of Liberty on the obverse and an eagle on the reverse. Thus, artistic license was restricted. Second, relief, used to great effect in medals, had practical limitations for general coinage, arising from the need to achieve an adequate die life during mass production. A second concern involving relief, although less so with a manual screw press, was the need to bring up all the features of the design with one blow of the coin press, a must for cost efficient coinage. Finally, these coins were struck with an open collar creating a minimal rim. Anything above the lowest relief would subject the coin to additional wear, impacting its intrinsic value and impairing its ability to stack for counting purposes.

• • • •

Patterson met his production goal for 1807, but in December of that year politics reared its ugly head. At President Jefferson's urging, Congress passed the Embargo Act, prohibiting American ships from engaging in foreign trade. This was done in response to British and French depredations on American shipping in their struggle for European domination. The much-hated act had the unintended side effect of reducing foreign specie circulating in the United States. Bullion provided to the Mint by the Bank of the United States and other Philadelphia banks declined over the 15 months the act was in effect. In fact, foreign specie declined to such an extent that Congress allowed the exemption making these coins legal tender to lapse in April 1809. Now, only American coins, Spanish dollars, and their fractions were legal tender. If only Patterson had had the bullion available at that point, the elixir of foreign specie might have been extinguished permanently.

One good thing came out of the Tenth Congress. With virtually no fanfare, the Mint's lease on life at Philadelphia was extended another five years to March 4, 1813.[25]

The specter of legal-tender foreign coins returned in December 1810. The 20-year charter of the Bank of the United States would expire in the following year, and its renewal was in doubt. Thomas Willing had retired as its president in 1807. The institution was pressuring state banks, when presenting their bank notes for collection, by demanding specie in payment. Should the Bank of the United States not be rechartered, they must liquidate and pay their stockholders, mostly foreign, in this medium. On the other hand, if legal-tender status were again granted to foreign specie, particularly gold coins, some of the pressure from the Bank of the United States on the state banks would be relieved. There was also recognition in Congress that a great drain on the circulating specie of the United States would occur should action not be taken to augment the supply.[26] The obligation of the Bank of the

United States to shareholders amounted to $7 million, seven years of output from the Mint at peak production with adequate bullion supply.[27]

The exemption effort died in the House. Spanish gold coins had depreciated in intrinsic value by 4 percent since the last extension of legal-tender status in 1806. No one knew how to treat the Spanish doubloons still in circulation in the rural areas and, above all, no one wanted to appropriate money to reimburse current holders for the depreciated value of these coins. Consequently, the move to extend legal-tender status again failed.[28]

• • • •

It happened. President James Madison took no position, effectively undercutting the efforts of his secretary of the Treasury, Albert Gallatin, to extend the Bank of the United States charter. The House tabled the measure. In the Senate, the young senator from Kentucky, Henry Clay, took the floor and effectively killed the extension with his oratory. When the tally in the Senate reached a tie, Vice President George Clinton cast the deciding vote against the Bank of the United States.[29]

It should not have happened. There were people outside of Washington who knew better. One voice of reason rising in support of the Bank of the United States was the Pennsylvania State Legislature, led by one of its members, Nicholas Biddle. Left unchecked by the Bank of the United States, state banks would issue too many paper notes on too little specie reserve. The inflationary effect would be disastrous. Killing the Bank of the United States also stripped the government of its lender of last resort and its primary agent for making payments. It was a voice in the wind. The country would have to experience the resulting calamity before appreciating what had just been said.[30]

Seven million dollars in hard currency left the country, mostly to Great Britain, to make liquidation payments to shareholders. Worse, with war clouds on the horizon, the government was left with no central bank to finance military expenditures. It was an act of financial imbecility. Henry Clay would rue this day in the not too distant future. Meanwhile, the American public, not understanding the implications of the dismantling of the Bank of the United States, would blame the Mint for the lack of specie. All the Mint could do was to request an exemption from Madison's renewed embargo of British goods to import copper from Boulton.[31]

When the bill to continue the Mint in Philadelphia came up for consideration in the House of Representatives at the end of 1812, not surprisingly there were objections. The motion was made to move the Mint to the seat of government in Washington. Two Congressmen from Philadelphia effectively beat back this effort. They argued that the Mint must be located in a great commercial city to gain access to needed bullion. The unsaid great commercial city was Philadelphia, which was still the financial capital of the country. Furthermore, it was doubtful that the officers and laborers at the Mint would make any such move. The motion failed, drawing little support.[32] Philadelphia got five more years and Patterson felt good enough about his situation at the Mint to retire from the University of Pennsylvania in 1814.

A changing of the guard within the Mint officers also occurred at this time. Benjamin Rush died of typhus fever on April 19, 1813.[33] President Madison nominated Rush's son, James, to the position.[34] This appointment was only remarkable in that it established the principle of family succession within the Mint. Attitudes had changed for fierce old Republicans, like Rush and Patterson. Henry Voigt died on February 2, 1814. Patterson wasted no time in advancing Adam Eckfeldt to the position that he had performed for some time. Madison submitted the nomination to the Senate 10 days later.[35]

The Mint weathered the first two years of the War of 1812 with adequate bullion. In fact, there were only minor interruptions following the discontinuance of the Bank of the United States in 1811. However, virtually all coin production in this period went to the banks in the form of half eagles and half dollars. The roof fell in 1814 when the United States nearly ran out of money to fund the war, suspending specie payments. Bullion supply turned on a dime, slowing to a trickle with gold being the first to go. Patterson complained that prices for gold and silver bullion had risen to prohibitive levels as people held on to their hard currency. The state banks, relieved of the burden of maintaining specie reserves against their currency, began to issue paper money without restraint. The major banks even began issuing notes in fractional parts of a dollar, called tickets.[36] These would quickly become derisively known as *shinplasters*.

Without bullion from the banks or copper from England, coinage output in 1815 was virtually nil.[37] With essentially nothing to do, the Mint might as well have closed its doors.

CHAPTER 4

LIKE A SLUMBERING PHOENIX

The year 1816 began just like 1815 ended. There was no central bank and specie payments remained suspended, meaning everybody hoarded their hard money. American monetary policy was in shambles. It could not be worse.

For the Mint, it got worse. The letter from Robert Patterson to President James Madison from January 11, 1816, summed it up.

> I have the mortification to inform you that this morning about 2 o'clock, a fire broke out in the mill house, a wooden building, belonging to the Mint which is consumed together with an adjoining building containing the rolling and drawing machines & also the milling house.
>
> The front part of the building, containing the coining presses, the office, & assayer's department is uninjured.
>
> The manner in which this fire originated is perfectly unaccountable. No fire is ever kept in the part of the building where it was first discovered, nor had any of the workmen been there for some days.
>
> No loss of gold or silver will be sustained of any consequence nor will the copper coinage be in the least impaired.[1]

Patterson, normally a man of few words when it came to official communications, had just laid out the picture without pointing out how truly damaging the fire really was. The Mint director avoided the fact that, without the ability to generate planchets, there would be no gold or silver coinage until repairs were made. For a nation that must return to specie payments to normalize the economy, this fire was a disaster.

Patterson then made a decision with larger implications than just the Mint. He decided to replace the horse mill that powered the rolling and drawing machines with steam power. Philadelphia had completed the Fairmount Water Works in September 1815. Although the distribution system would not be ready on a wide scale, using hollowed out logs, until 1817, the change looked like a good long-term decision. The risk was how the introduction of steam power would impact production over the short- and medium-term.

There was a political motive as well. In December 1816, the issue of the continuing the Mint in Philadelphia would again be in front of Congress. Having the steam enhancements in place with their expected cost savings and increased production,[2] would allow supporters of the Mint to argue that Philadelphia be made permanent.[3] However it was not to be; the Mint received another five-year extension instead.[4]

For secretary of the Treasury and native Philadelphian, Alexander James Dallas (fig. 12), the decision was simple.

Fig. 12. As Treasury secretary, A.J. Dallas had the misfortune to inherit an empty treasury and no central banking system. This was compounded by a fire at the mint, which halted all specie production except copper coins.

If he was ever to get specie payments reinstated, he must have the specie with which to do it. He had no alternative but to return to foreign coins. On March 20, 1816, Dallas wrote to John Calhoun in the House of Representatives. Calhoun was no novice when it came to Mint affairs, having read law in the office of former Mint director Henry William De Saussure. Dallas needed the Foreign Specie Law of 1806 revived. Spanish gold had been circulating in the country on a bullion basis, alleviating the issue of its depreciated value. Following his predecessors, he optimistically asked that the law run for three years in the expectation that production from the Mint would take up the slack in the meantime.[5]

In what amounted to the legislative equivalent of the speed of light, the necessary authorization to make certain foreign gold coins, French crowns, and five-franc pieces legal tender for three years was enacted on April 29.[6]

• • • •

The Democratic Republicans, learning from their error, moved on April 16, 1816, to charter the Second Bank of the United States to correct for the vast expansion of paper currency brought about by the suspension of specie payments. Established state banks had made large profits by extending loans and bank-note issues without regard to specie reserves held in their vaults. In addition, newly chartered state banks could open with only a tiny amount of borrowed specie on hand while indulging in profligate lending of their own notes. Also in August 1816, plans were put in place to resume specie payments on February 20, 1817.

The new bank's charter empowered it to act as the federal government's exclusive agent, holding its deposits, transferring federal funds, and dealing with federal collections and payments. In exchange, the bank received an annual payment of $1.5 million and all federal deposits were non-interest bearing. In addition, the bank and all of its branches were exempt from state taxation. The government would hold 20 percent of the stock, thus becoming a minority owner in the bank, with limited say on its board of directors. It was a good deal for the bank and its shareholders—too good for its own good.

The Madison administration first turned to Thomas Willing to return as head of the reconstituted Bank of the United States. Now over 80 years old, he declined. They then botched the appointment by naming William Jones, an alcoholic political crony and former secretary of the Navy.[7]

The Bank of the United States began operations by returning state bank notes to the issuing banks for redemption in specie. A contraction of circulating paper currency to stem a growing speculative bubble was the intended effect had the Bank of the United States not begun issuing its own paper notes in addition to the state bank notes.

In spite of the Mint having bullion in its vaults to start the year 1817, and Patterson's belief that the "stagnation" in the circulation of specie would ease and the flow of bullion to the Mint would approach normal levels, the Mint's output stalled in both 1817 and 1818.[8] There was no question that the Bank of the United States had the specie in their vaults in 1817 as a result of their redemption activities. Obviously there were production problems with the switch over to steam power at the Mint. Patterson was silent on the issue. The simple fact was Patterson did not authorize payment to the engine fabricator until June 24, 1817.[9]

• • • •

By the end of 1818, the lack of specie in general circulation had reached a critical point. An inquiry was conducted in the Senate on the feasibility of banning exportation of specie from the country.

Simply put, resumption of specie payments had not gone well. Since the conclusion of the Napoleonic Wars, the British had been dumping their manufactured goods, no longer in demand in their peacetime economy, into the American market draining specie to settle trade balances. In addition, Chinese trade was booming. The Chinese valued Spanish dollars above all other hard currency and were willing to pay a premium for them. American merchants participating in the trade were now forced to pay a premium of 8 to 10 percent to get this specie from brokers. Spanish dollars had become a vanishing entity and banks were struggling to maintain enough hard currency to back their paper money.

Yet banning the export of specie was like cutting off one's nose to spite one's face. This foolishness, if it could be enforced, would reduce foreign trade to a cumbersome barter system. Secretary of the Treasury William Crawford (fig. 13) wisely opposed this move and effectively headed it off.[10]

There was another issue factoring into the specie drain the government did not want to acknowledge. $4 million of debt associated with the Louisiana Purchase was due. Held by foreigners, this debt had to be paid in specie. Beginning in 1818, the Bank of the United States, acting as the government's agent, began accumulating this hard currency in order to facilitate the repayment. This action only acerbated the situation and explained why the Mint had a relatively small amount of bullion to coin in 1818.

Hand in glove with the exportation ban was the issue of reauthorizing legal-tender status for foreign gold coins and the French silver coins that would expire in the coming spring. Secretary Crawford opposed extending this act for foreign gold coins but did not see how extending the status of legal tender to foreign silver coins could be avoided. In response, Crawford pushed Patterson to commit to increased production. Patterson, in the interim, had

Fig. 13. William Crawford succeeded A.J. Dallas as Treasury secretary in late 1816. He was the first to attempt to adjust the gold-to-silver ratio in order to restore gold to the circulating specie of the country.

constructed a new foundry and refining furnace that were now nearly complete. The Mint director answered that, with adequate bullion, operating five days per week and making repairs on the sixth, he could strike 35,000 gold coins weekly. Or he could strike 145,000 silver coins based upon a mix of 40 percent half dollars and 60 percent smaller coins. That was basically double or triple in dollar amounts, depending upon the mix of gold, the level achieved before the specie suspension. To accomplish this production, Patterson would need a higher appropriation for wastage and sundry expenses and authority to hire additional workmen. If Crawford wanted even more production, it would be necessary to construct a new building, taking an estimated 12 months.

Crawford also queried the Mint director as to what changes were necessary in U.S. law to secure more gold coinage than in previous years. While Patterson was not one to take the initiative in such matters of government policy, he did not hesitate to answer the question, bringing to light in simple terms a fundamental flaw in the American specie system. The value of gold relative to silver needed to be increased so that the ratio of the one to the other was greater than that in Europe. The legal standard of 15 to 1 needed to be raised to 16 to 1. United States gold was now undervalued, explaining why eagles were taking flight to the melting pots of the London bullion dealers. If the United States were to overvalue gold by, in Patterson's estimate, 10 percent, the gold flow would reverse and the Mint would have no problem securing the necessary bullion. To accomplish this would require the recall and recoinage of existing American gold coins.[11]

When Hamilton formulated key parts of the Mint Act of 1792, the comparative ratio of gold to silver was 15 to 1. Gold, at that point, had recently declined in value relative to silver from its level of 15.6 to 1 in colonial times. During the Napoleonic Wars, gold reversed course, appreciating against silver and now stood at something approximating 15.5 or 16 to 1. Having set the silver content of the American dollar at 371.25 grains of pure silver, Hamilton used the ratio to determine $1 of pure gold to be 24.75 grains. Thus, he arrived at 247.5 grains of pure gold in an American eagle coin.[12] Patterson's recommendation would reduce the gold in an eagle to 232.031 grains.

Crawford now went to work on both the House Committee on Ways and Means and the Committee on Finance in the Senate. William Lowndes, chairman of the Ways and Means Committee, reported to the House on behalf of the special committee appointed to examine and recommend amendments to the laws regulating American and foreign coins. Lowndes got to the central point of the foreign coin issue quickly. The committee did not believe that the United States could dispense with foreign coins anytime soon. Bullion sources available to the Mint were too restricted to hope to change this situation, regardless of Mint capacity.

The committee did recognize that coins issued from the Mint needed to be protected from being melted and exported by enacting laws that would give them an advantage in domestic commerce compared to foreign coins of equal purity and weight. They noted that, in countries like the United States that relied on a mixed circulation of paper and specie, the impact of large imports that must be paid in specie was disproportionately felt. In addition, the banks removed a large portion of the hard currency due to their obligation to pay specie on demand. Removing the obligation to pay specie would eliminate the only check upon the banks in the issuance of their paper currency and credit—an act none were willing to authorize.

The committee acknowledged that gold had been more stable in value over time than silver. The inconvenience of coin shortages would, in great measure, go away if gold were the only legal tender for debts above a moderate amount. The committee seemed on the verge of opting for the gold standard. But then Lowndes drew away, saying that the public considered silver as the standard of value and that the committee would not recommend a limit on the legal tender of silver coins. He did agree that the gold to silver ratio should be returned to its original valuation in the colonies of 15.6 to 1.

Lowndes then broached a subject that Patterson had not. An advantage could be afforded American coinage in domestic commerce over equivalent foreign coins, particularly the Spanish dollar, by assigning a lower value to the foreign coins for commercial purposes or by reducing the weight of the American dollar. Arbitrarily assigning a reduced value to foreign specie was impractical. However, exacting a seigniorage on American coins, in effect reducing silver content, would produce the desired result. Domestic coinage would then be more valuable at home than abroad. However, this action would break the link to intrinsic value.

The committee then fixed upon a set of recommendations. The increase in the gold to silver valuation from 15 to 15.6 amounted to 4 percent. They recommended reducing the silver content of the dollar coin by 4 percent or 14.85 grains for seigniorage. Applying the 15.6 to 1 ratio to the silver content of the dollar before reduction for seigniorage gave a gold content for the eagle of 237.98 grains. No thought was given to the fact these would be awkward numbers for both the assayer and melter refiner to work with at the Mint. The committee recommended an appropriation expanding the capacity of the Mint. Also, they were willing to consider making certain foreign gold and silver coins legal tender for another 18 months.[13]

The actual bill introduced rounded the gold content of the eagle down to 237 grains and restricted Spanish specie and American coins of less value than a half dollar to legal tender in amounts not exceeding $5.[14] However, the bill omitted any appropriation to expand the Mint's capacity. These were solid recommendations that would have gone far in solving the nation's shortage of circulating hard currency. However, they violated two cornerstones of Alexander Hamilton's monetary policy at the founding of the Mint—free coinage and intrinsic value.

The committee's work died on the floor of the House. Instead, Congress extended legal-tender status for foreign coins. However, gold coins would no longer be current after November 1, 1819. French crowns and five-franc pieces that were not in demand for the China trade would continue as legal tender for two more years.[15]

• • • •

Crawford soon had bigger problems than the failure of Congress to act upon his recommendations to retain American coinage in domestic circulation. The post-war years had seen a tremendous expansion of the American economy. However, the withdrawal of the specie to pay the Louisiana Purchase debt coincided with a change in monetary policy at the Bank of the United States from an inflationary expansion of their currency to a deflationary tight money policy in order to reflect their depleted specie reserves and to counteract the excesses of 1817 and 1818. Coupled with a decline in European demand for American agricultural products, the speculative bubble that had been building since the end of the war burst. The United States quickly slipped into a depression known as the Panic of 1819. Once again, the banks in the United States suspended specie payments.

There was more to the shift at the Bank of the United States to a tight money policy in 1819. Under Jones's leadership, the bank had put lavish lending policies in place, particularly in the Western part of the country to fuel the agricultural exports. He had also done away with the bank's initial policy of demanding specie when redeeming state bank notes. In so doing, Jones lost control of state bank lending, adding to the flood of paper currency. When Jones reversed course, he only made a bad situation worse. America's leading financier and one of the Bank of the United States directors, Stephen Girard, quit in disgust.

Matters came to a head when Jones was implicated in a major defalcation at the Baltimore branch of the Bank of the United States. It put the bank on the brink of insolvency. Dividends were suspended and Jones was sacked. The new head, Langdon Cheves, a former speaker of the House of Representatives, was forced into a much tighter money policy of restricting loans than conservative economic management would have dictated to bring the bank back to a solid financial condition.

It was said that Cheves saved the bank but ruined the people. The agricultural segment of the economy was hardest hit. Thomas Jefferson, who had foolishly cosigned notes of friends, was forced to the brink of bankruptcy. Crops withered and businesses collapsed. The bank had alienated a large segment of the population. One such individual was the popular military leader, future president Andrew Jackson, and he would not forget.[16]

Little noted at the time, Nicholas Biddle, the financially adept Pennsylvania legislator, was appointed to the bank's board in 1819.[17]

• • • •

Again, bullion deposits at the Mint slowed to a trickle. Eckfeldt used the down time, four or five months in 1819, to complete improvements to the mint's machinery that had been more or less underway since the fire. Evidently, the conversion to steam power was still not where Eckfeldt wanted it. Once specie payments were resumed and deposits began to flow again, it was clear from production that Mint capacity had been substantially increased due to Eckfeldt's enhancements. In the approximately seven months the Mint was in operation, $1.4 million, in mostly half dollars, was struck.[18] In 1820 the Mint lost another three months to a lack of bullion deposits. However, it still ended the year coining $1.8 million, including substantial quantities of half eagles.[19]

• • • •

As 1820 drew to a close, Secretary William H. Crawford found he was going to have to revisit the issue of specie. Complaints had been made about the loss of legal-tender status for Spanish gold. The Spanish had long since adjusted their gold to silver ratio to 16 to 1. The loss of these doubloons to American commerce put New Orleans, the major Southern port, at a severe disadvantage.[20] On March 3, 1821, the Senate and House enacted an extension of the legal-tender statute for foreign coins, reinstating the gold coins of Britain, France, Portugal, and Spain for two years.[21]

That was the simple part. Crawford also had to reopen the issue of the gold to silver ratio. Undervalued American gold had continued to flow out of the country in settlement of mercantile debts. American gold coins had again virtually disappeared and would continue to do so from domestic circulation. The select committee in the House returned to the prior recommendation that the ratio be increased to 15.6 to 1 by decreasing the gold content of an eagle to 237 grains. They called for a short deadline to convert from old to new coins to prevent speculators from profiting.[22] The problem with this bill, having to compete for attention with the Missouri Compromise legislation, was that it was not introduced to the House until February 2, 1821, and the Fifteenth Congress would adjourn on March 3.[23] There was not a chance that action would be taken on this poorly understood topic in such a short time.

• • • •

Meanwhile more upheaval occurred at the Bank of the United States. Nicholas Biddle was no longer on its board, having retired at the end of 1821 in disgust over Langdon Cheves's decision to resume paying dividends to the shareholders. Cheves then announced in the summer of 1822 that he was stepping down as president of the Bank. Biddle returned to the fray as the dark horse to succeed the outgoing president.

Nicolas Biddle had been valedictorian of his class at Princeton at age 15. Born in 1786, he hailed from a Philadelphia family noted for its wealth and financial acumen. Biddle went abroad in 1804 as an unpaid clerk to John Armstrong, U.S. minister to France. While there, Biddle traveled extensively, ending his duties with a brief stint under James Monroe, the U.S. Representative to the Court of St. James in London. Returning home, Biddle married well and set up as a gentleman farmer and politician. He was particularly drawn to what he considered scientific farming.

Dark horse or not, Biddle had the necessary political connections. When the frontrunners knocked themselves

Fig. 14. Three survivors of John Reich's Capped Bust gold-coin design from this period of economic turmoil reside in the National Numismatic Collection. There are stunning Proof examples for the 1821 quarter and the 1821 half eagle. The 1822 half eagle has seen some circulation. Of the 17,796 half eagles minted in 1822, only three exist today; two can be found in the National Numismatic Collection.

out, Biddle easily gained the support of Monroe and Crawford. While short on experience in day-to-day banking operations, his theoretical knowledge stood him in good stead. His policies were hailed in the 1820s and the Bank of the United States became known by some as Mr. Biddle's Bank.[24]

• • • •

By 1823, the United States had come out of the Panic of 1819. The prior year's imports exceeded exports by $8 million. It was reported in the House of Representatives that not a single gold coin resided in the vaults of the New York banks. Likewise, the Spanish milled dollars had been swept up in the China trade. Businessmen were estimating that one-third of the specie in the country went to export in 1822 (fig. 14).[25] The specie reserve of the Eastern banks was entirely made up of French silver and American half dollars and lesser denominations.[26] The topics of gold valuation, legal-tender status of foreign coinage, and another extension for the Mint in Philadelphia were going to come up in this session of Congress.

The issue of the Mint remaining in Philadelphia was addressed first. The cost of moving the Mint to Washington was viewed as a major hurdle. In addition, the Bank of the United States supplied most of the bullion deposits and the prospect of separating the two institutions made little sense.[27] Philadelphia received five more years.[28]

Foreign legal tender was maintained for four years for the French crowns, five-franc pieces, and foreign gold was made legal tender for land purchases only.[29] Crawford agreed with the thinking in the House that, while there was no gold on the Eastern seaboard, scattered immigrant farmers still had gold coin stashes from their native countries with which they would pay for their land.[30] Totally unaddressed in this legislation, the South American colonies of Spain were in revolt. The Mint was already receiving silver bullion for coining from Mexico.[31] The Spanish milled dollar would shortly be no more as the new countries took control of the colonial Spanish mints.

Crawford now feebly pushed to change the gold valuation, calling for it to be increased to 16 to 1.[32] His half-hearted plea fell upon deaf ears. In fact the man was ill and would suffer a stroke in 1823. Without Crawford's leadership, the United States lurched a long way toward a silver standard. The average American, assuming he had specie and must use it as opposed to paper currency, would make a purchase with a French crown of Napoleon or a five-franc piece and receive his change in worn and therefore debased fractional Spanish coins or, on a rare occasion, smaller denominations of United States coins.[33]

• • • •

On November 1, 1823, 18 years after Robert Patterson had pronounced him feeble and unable to withstand the rigors of the engraver's job, Robert Scot died. John Reich had not been at the Mint since 1817. There was no backup.

Reich's work had been well enough received. At the end of 1814, in part because of his excellent execution of the Preble medal, the Navy Department had given him the series of naval medals authorized by Congress for heroic actions in the War of 1812. Reich's work on the first of the medals to Isaac Hull was slow but the execution was excellent. This was lucrative business; the statement by Patterson that Reich would assume medal work as part of his Mint duties was long since forgotten.[34] In addition, his Mint activity in 1815 with rampant bullion shortages was minimal. Reich finally started the second medal, for Stephen Decatur, at the end of 1816. In March 1817 Reich abruptly resigned from the Mint. In June he submitted his plasters for the Decatur medal to the Navy Department and his obverse was rejected. The likeness of Decatur was described as a mere caricature. Reich at this point had to admit that his eyesight had failed to the point that he could no longer execute fine medallic work.[35] His career as an engraver was virtually over.

Throughout this period, Robert Patterson had gradually withdrawn from the day-to-day supervision of the Mint. His signature rarely appeared on any correspondence. Thus, the decision of Scot's replacement was in the hands of the chief coiner, Adam Eckfeldt. Logic would dictate that the frontrunner was Moritz Fürst. Fürst had remained in Philadelphia, struggling to get by in the private sector. When the Navy Department grew frustrated at Reich's slowness on the Hull medal, they gave part of the work to Fürst. When Reich quit, Fürst stepped in to assume the entire naval commission. Working with Eckfeldt, he took on the Monroe Indian peace medal obverse and the commission from the War Department for the military medals from the War of 1812.

However, Fürst had competition. On December 1, 1823, Christian Gobrecht, another competent Philadelphia engraver, wrote directly to President Monroe seeking the engraver's position. Gobrecht had started his career apprenticed to a clock maker. He then taught himself engraving and diesinking. At this point, he was most noted for his portrait plates published in the *American Biographic Dictionary* of 1810.[36] More importantly, Gobrecht had performed some the engraver's duties at the Mint on a contract basis during the decline of Scot.[37]

Neither man got the appointment. Fürst had proved difficult to work with on the medal commissions. He had complained directly to Washington in 1823, when Adam Eckfeldt dragged his feet hardening the dies for the military medals. Eckfeldt was slow and overly cautious in doing this work, fearful that he would destroy the dies in the process. Yet he was even slow to strike the medals as well, indicating that Fürst was justified in his complaints. In addition, Fürst simply could not manage his money. He was making

Fig. 15. William Kneass's shortcomings as an engraver were painfully obvious almost from his first day as engraver at the Mint.

incessant demands for advances on his commissions and the medal work paid very well. Fürst simply spent more than he earned.[38] Gobrecht's problem was that Monroe was not going to make the decision on this appointment; Eckfeldt through Patterson would call the shots.

The man Eckfeldt chose was William Kneass (fig. 15). He had run an engraving shop on 4th Street above Chestnut that was a popular meeting place for cultured gentlemen. He had also worked as an engraver of plates for book illustrations. He was known mainly for his line engraving but also worked in aquatints.[39] Even though Fürst would not be threatened by the prospect of losing his medals business at the Mint to Kneass, he was still frustrated. At the end of 1824, with the military medals commission largely completed, Fürst presented a memorial to Congress seeking compensation from the government for its failure to employ him at the Mint in 1807.[40] It was promptly rejected.[41]

• • • •

There was a reason that Robert Patterson appeared out of the loop in the selection process for an engraver. The old man's health took a serious turn for the worse in December 1823. He actually went so far as to prepare a letter of resignation. In doing so, Patterson had also come to an unusual decision. He would attempt to designate his successor. He had a son, Robert Maskell Patterson, who was dutiful and had shown interest in the Mint. However the father did not recommend his son for the position. He chose instead his son-in-law, Samuel Moore, a fellow member of the American Philosophical Society.[42] When the elder Patterson suddenly recovered his health, this sensitive matter was put aside.

Circumstances would indicate that Patterson's decision of successorship was based upon political calculations. His son was a relative unknown, while his son-in-law had served in Congress from 1818 to 1822. Moore had gained his seat in a special election when Samuel Ingham resigned to tend to his ailing wife. More importantly, Samuel Moore had played a role in the Missouri Compromise, admitting Missouri to the Union in 1821 as a slave state.

Moore was, in principle, opposed to any extension of slavery.[43] When Henry Clay crafted his famous compromise in March 1820, he deliberately broke the contentious issues into two parts. The first bill called for the admission of Missouri as a slave state. Moore voted against but the bill carried by three votes. The second measure restricted the extension of slavery north of 36 degrees 30 minutes north latitude. Moore as an expressed restrictionist could vote for this bill that easily carried.[44] None of this proceeding was particularly remarkable in regard to Moore.

Over the following months restrictionists in Ohio and Pennsylvania began urging Congress to reject this compromise, putting Moore in the hot seat. Missourians unwittingly aided the effort by drafting a constitution barring freed slaves from entering the state. When Clay returned for the second session of the Sixteenth Congress at the beginning of 1821, he had to refight the battle. In this effort, Clay had the full support of the Monroe administration which sought to avoid sectional strife.

At issue was the wording of the House resolution, requiring Missouri to amend its constitution to remove this offending clause before it could be admitted to statehood. Samuel Moore was active both on the floor of the House and in a select committee with Henry Clay and others to work out the acceptable wording.[45] On February 26 Clay presented his "second" Missouri Compromise. With heated debate, the crucial motion that determined the sense of the House carried in Clay's favor by four votes, including that of Samuel Moore.[46] Although Samuel Moore resigned his seat in 1822, his support of Clay and the Monroe administration was not to be forgotten.

The first that Samuel Moore learned of the elder Patterson's decision was in late June of 1824. Patterson was again slipping and this time the end was definitely near. The resignation was made effective July 1. Moore headed to Washington on July 15 with the Mint director's testimonial. As Robert Patterson had suspected, President Monroe's decision in Samuel Moore's favor was prompt. Robert Patterson passed away July 22, 1824.

Samuel Moore was educated at the University of Pennsylvania. After graduating, he served as an instructor there for two years before studying medicine and becoming a doctor. When he came down with consumption-like symptoms in 1798, Benjamin Rush recommended a voyage to Canton. When Moore returned, he was both cured and hooked on the wealth to be gained from the China trade. He made four more voyages to Canton, using the profits to purchase a large tract of land outside Philadelphia. Here, he operated a farm and constructed a woolen mill during the War of 1812.[47]

Moore was reluctant to accept the appointment. It would compel him to give up a promising business venture in Georgia that would have been his preference.[48] However, Moore would not disappoint his father-in-law and put his personal desires aside. Robert Patterson had made a good choice.

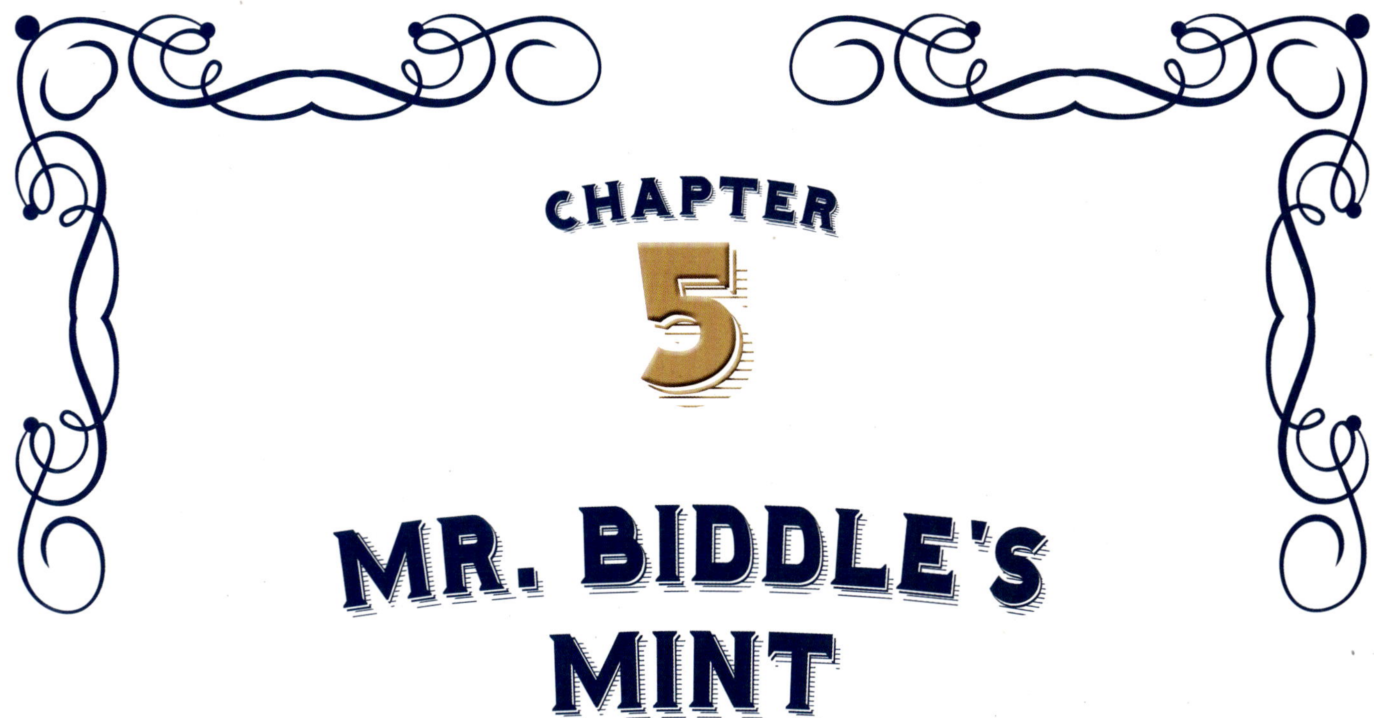

CHAPTER 5

MR. BIDDLE'S MINT

Samuel Moore (fig. 16) had his hands full. First and foremost, a cursory inspection revealed a seriously deteriorated Mint physical plant. The original building, actually two structures joined together, now housed the receiving and weighing rooms and one pressroom on the first floor. A dark, winding passageway that required illumination at all times led to the second floor, housing all of the officers except the assayer. Moore's office was on the third floor, along with the assaying furnace and necessary chemical agents. The basement held the Mint's vaults. Behind this building was a two-story brick facility erected in the 1816 expansion to house a ten-horsepower steam engine. Designed specifically for the purpose, this building was really the only structure deemed adequate on the property.

It went downhill from here. A former stable stored the coined and uncoined copper. Beyond that sat a two-story, brick building erected on a year-to-year leased lot in which the refinery was situated. The refining furnace was located in the basement resulting in a totally inefficient operation. A small two-story frame building, slightly constructed, contained the silver coining presses on the first floor and was in almost daily use. Nearby was an old, dilapidated, two-story brick building where the copper coinage was executed. In the upstairs of these last two buildings were the Mint's machine shops. Finally, there were two roughly boarded buildings that served as the Mint's blacksmith shop and coalhouse.

Fig. 16. As director of the Mint, Samuel Moore brought a full-time effort to the job of increasing the nation's specie supply.

In addition to these structures, the Mint leased a lot that served as a wood yard. However, its real purpose was to control the frontage along an alley that bisected the property. As long as the Mint controlled this frontage, they could close access to the alley, an absolute must for security.[1]

The poor condition of the site would have been of immediate and major concern had the Mint's ability to perform from inception not been hindered by congressional policy. Failing to decide on a permanent location for the Mint, refusing to address the flaw in the gold to silver ratio, making no appropriation for the purchase of bullion, and continuing to rely upon foreign specie in addition to federal coins as legal tender all contributed to this sorry state of affairs. In turn, in a simple act of survival, the Mint had allied itself with the Bank of the United States to assure an adequate bullion supply. It could be said with little exaggeration that the Mint now was Mr. Biddle's Mint. When the BUS and other banks demanded half dollars in exchange for their foreign coins, the Mint had no choice but to acquiesce. Many of these half dollars then sat in bank vaults as security against each bank's issue of paper currency. With gold disappearing overseas the minute it left the mint, the nation's economy subsisted on paper currency. The common man relied upon tattered pieces of paper from banks he most likely did not know, a few French five-franc pieces, and the debased Spanish fractional pieces.

Samuel Moore, a relatively young 50, brought vitality to the director's position. As Mint director, he must move methodically to put the Mint on firm ground. The curse of legal-tender status for foreign coins must be put to an end. He must drive the mint's output to practical capacity and keep it there. Final resolution of the location of the mint was a must for long-term stability. Most important, output at the mint of fractional silver coins must be upped to get these smaller pieces into the hands of the public. Long term, a new facility would be needed to replace the cobbled-together arrangement now in place. Finally, the gold to silver ratio must be legislatively corrected. It would take time and, as with any plan, it would need a little luck and a lot of timing.

• • • •

In his first full year at the Mint, 1825, Moore presented an improved picture. The Bank of the United States supplied only half of the Mint's silver bullion, in the form of foreign specie. The remainder came from Mexico, South America, and the West Indies in the form of raw silver as the former Spanish colonies worked to establish their countries financially. When bank deposits slowed down in October, Moore was able to put some of this raw bullion into quarters and dimes. The result was that in terms of numbers of coins struck, 1825 exceeded all previous years. Now Moore worried that the Mint was approaching practical capacity, particularly when bank deposits spiked and the pressure was on to minimize the wait time for these priority customers.

• • • •

Moore's attention was not focused solely on coin output. He firmly believed that the Mint director had an implied obligation to change the designs of American coins from time to time. These designs needed to reflect good taste and the improved state of the arts, while conforming to existing legal requirements.[2]

First, he investigated the law, going to the Journal of the Senate and other sources to see that the senators originally intended to put the head of the president upon American coins, much in the style of European nations that employed the heads of monarchs upon their coins. However the House insisted that a figure emblematic of liberty be placed on the obverse of the coins. The Mint director could find no record of the debates that would enlighten him as to the thinking behind such a figure.

Moore seemed particularly fixated upon the cap that adorned John Reich's designs for both the silver and gold coins. He turned to the one man still alive who had been present at the time and could shed some light on this issue, Thomas Jefferson. He had specific questions for Jefferson. At the time when the Mint was established, what figure or impression did Congress and the Washington administration consider as emblematic of liberty? Before 1792, did any state or national government adopt the liberty cap as such an emblem? What emblems or expectations of liberty were prevalent at the time? If the liberty cap was the emblem intended by the law or deemed a suitable American emblem, was it proper to create redundancy by placing an emblem of liberty on the head of the figure personifying liberty?

Then, Moore shared with Jefferson some of his thinking on the subject. When he was satisfied that a suitable impression of liberty could be obtained, consistent with the intent of the law, he would have a few pattern pieces struck for review in Washington. Supposing the female head to be an appropriate figure, Moore had three alternatives to Reich's design to consider. He could modify it so as not to create the appearance of any major changes. He could exclude the cap and adopt an easy disposition of the hair with no ornamentation but a band bearing an inscription *Liberty*. Or he could adopt a classical cap. The first option would be the easiest for his engraver to implement. Moore early on knew that William Kneass had real limitations. The second, if well executed, Moore preferred as being more true to life and nature. The third would have the advantage of being modeled after the exquisite classical works of Greece and Rome.[3]

In early 1825, Thomas Jefferson was an old man living in retirement at his home, Monticello. Since the end of his presidency, he had not returned to Washington. Despite his seclusion, his opinion still carried weight. He admitted to Moore that he had no memory of the issue. He had taken the time before answering Moore to check his papers, finding nothing on the subject. He could not remember a single circumstance of the debate concerning devices for the coinage other than that someone had proposed Washington's head as suitable. It had been objected to and the head of Liberty adopted instead. Whether it was with or without a pileus, Jefferson did not remember. As a pileus was a conical Roman hat conferred upon slaves after being freed, surely it ought to be without, for Americans were not emancipated slaves.[4]

With characteristic confidence, Moore moved forward, engaging Christian Gobrecht to prepare sketches and medallions for a new head of Liberty. He sought critical input, showing Gobrecht's work to the well-established Philadelphia artist Thomas Sully. He also sought input from Nicholas Biddle. Moore needed the approval of his financial partner. He even turned to his brother-in-law, Robert Maskell Patterson. All three highly commended Gobrecht's initial work.

Now Moore sought to solve two problems simultaneously. While Reich was still at the Mint in the mid-teens, he had prepared a large number of working dies. These dies had carried the Mint's operations throughout the period while Scot was in decline and again after the inexperienced Kneass came aboard. Moore badly needed an assistant engraver who knew something about diesinking. He contacted President John Quincy Adams with a proposal that he hire Gobrecht as that assistant engraver. He would gain a competent engraver, as well as the execution of his new designs.

In his request to the president, he pointed out that while dies were on hand for the current coins being struck, there were none for the half dime, dollar, or eagle coins. While the supply of working dies was still adequate, that situation would change should illness strike the engraver. He extolled Gobrecht's qualifications, including his interim employment at the Mint after Robert Scot's death. Gobrecht was also currently supplying the letter stamps used on the coinage. There was one hitch in the proposal. Moore alluded to the possibility that the job would not be full-time.[5]

Adams rejected Moore's proposal in an indirect bureaucratic manner. The president was against employing an assistant engraver at the Mint without first obtaining the approval of Congress. Moore, disappointed, asked the president through his secretary of the Treasury, Richard Rush, to reconsider. Pulling out all the stops, he told Rush that he planned to submit some new medallions and drawings for a head of Liberty for the president's review once the work was completed. In a spate of optimism, Moore stated that he hoped a new design would yet bear the date of 1825.[6] This forthrightness with Rush was understandable. The secretary was the son of Dr. Benjamin Rush, brother to the current Mint treasurer.

For four months Moore waited. On January 12, 1826, Rush gave Moore approval to hire Gobrecht, provided he could get a congressional appropriation.[7] Adams wanted to know the salary. Moore answered that it would not be more than Reich received, $600 per annum.[8] Part-time or not, Gobrecht was not going to work as an assistant to a man the likes of Kneass at that salary. While Moore swore that he had not told Gobrecht about his abortive attempt to employ him, the artist would have had to be deaf and dumb not to have caught wind of it.

Somewhere along the line, Moore's redesign effort died. Most likely the parsimonious Adams was at the root of it. It was a rare failure for the accomplished Samuel Moore.

• • • •

1826 was a problematic year for Moore. Bullion deposits from the banks requiring half dollars were up, with the Bank of the United States alone sending $1.6 million to be recoined. Moore struck the previously unheard-of quantity of slightly more than four million half dollar coins for the year. Even so, he was up to his ears in silver bullion by the year's end. Taking the time to strike dimes and quarters was out of the question. He was embarrassed to admit that old worn Spanish fractional pieces would have to carry the burden of providing change in commerce for the time being. In spite of this situation, Moore was not ready to propose resumption of dollar coin production in spite of the efficiencies that would be gained. He believed Jefferson's suggestion to halt their production in order to stop their export remained valid.[9] In 1827 Moore did get a respectable quantity of dimes struck within the total coin-

Fig. 17. Nicholas Biddle, shown in this 1826 painting by Thomas Sully, was active behind the scenes to secure congressional approval to expand the Mint's production capacity.

age of more than $3 million. Moore's timing was good, with record output going into 1828 when the location of the U.S. Mint returned to the front burner in Congress.

The agony over the ultimate location for the United States Mint ended during the waning days of the first session of the Twentieth Congress. President John Quincy Adams on May 21, 1828, signed an act into law for the continuance of the Mint in Philadelphia indefinitely.[10] It had been a long road. The last pull seemed simple by comparison. Yet there were nuances that were buried within the details.

From inception the Mint director had had to appear neutral in the congressional debates on the Mint's location. Thus, as 1827 came to a close, Moore was silent on the one subject that was foremost in his mind. Nicholas Biddle (fig. 17) was not. As the year closed, Biddle wrote Pennsylvania congressman John Sergeant, wanting to know Mint output for 1827.[11] It was all very circumspect, very much the way the politically adroit Biddle operated. He could have asked Samuel Moore directly for the number. One could have inferred anything from this innocuous request by the head of the Bank of the United States. But what it told Biddle was that no complaints could be lodged against the Mint's performance in Philadelphia. The time was right to settle the location issue once and for all.

John Sergeant (fig. 18) headed up the select committee on the Mint in the House where he had represented Pennsylvania off and on since 1815. He and Moore had been at the University of Pennsylvania together. Moore put three points to Sergeant and the select committee for consideration. The Mint could continue in Philadelphia either for a limited or indefinite period of time. Either way, there were certain legal enactments needed where existing statutes were either inadequate or silent. Regardless of the Mint's location, a new building was needed.[12]

On January 21, the committee met and decided legislation would be introduced authorizing the Mint to remain in Philadelphia for five years or until otherwise provided by law. The committee had specific questions regarding Moore's overhaul of the statutes.[13] However, they were silent on the issue of a new building. Moore was at least partway there.

With the introduction of H.R. 106, Moore carried two of his three objectives. In addition to essentially retaining the Mint indefinitely in Philadelphia, the bill encompassed some housekeeping items including establishing the troy ounce as the unit of measure for the Mint and allowing the director to appoint his own clerks.[14]

Fig. 18. John Sergeant played a leading role in the House of Representatives in gaining the appropriation for a new Mint facility in Philadelphia. He left Congress in 1829 to become legal counsel to the Second Bank of the United States and would go on to become Henry Clay's running mate in the presidential election of 1832. He was Nicholas Biddle's man through and through.

Debate on H.R. 106 took place on May 6. No objection whatsoever was voiced to leaving the Mint in Philadelphia. Moore had rendered the old criticisms moot by ratcheting up coin production and allowing Biddle to wield his influence behind the scenes. Gulian Verplanck of New York City raised the only question. He confusedly associated the fixing of the troy ounce with action to correct the undervaluation of American gold coins. Sergeant corrected him. The real problem with the undervaluation of gold, as had been correctly identified in 1819, was in the legally fixed ratio of value between gold and silver. In Sergeant's opinion there seemed no remedy but to confine the current coin of the nation to one metal. Sergeant sidestepped the controversy as to whether that metal ought to be gold or silver. A snag that could have stopped this bill cold had been avoided.[15] The bill moved over to the Senate where it encountered a similar lack of difficulty.[16]

The issue of the Mint's expansion, left hanging in this debate, came to a head on December 4, 1828, in a meeting between Biddle and Moore. Biddle had called the meeting as a result of a letter from Churchill Cambreleng, chairman of the House Committee on Commerce. He and Biddle were friends but more importantly, Cambreleng, a New Yorker, had strong political ties to the rising Democratic faction within the Democratic Republicans. Cambreleng wanted to know the possibilities of increased steam applications within the Mint. Moore had his opening. He told Biddle that the present configuration of the Mint's facilities prevented any additional productivity enhancements such as Cambreleng suggested. The conversation quickly evolved into a discussion of how to get the appropriation process for a Mint expansion back on track. It was resolved that Moore would write to Sergeant. Biddle alerted Cambreleng in turn.[17]

It fell again to the Select Committee on the Mint in the House in this second session of the Twentieth Congress to address the issue of a new building. In addition to Sergeant, the committee consisted of Richard Coulter of Pennsylvania, Thomas Chilton of Kentucky, Thomas Davenport of Virginia, and Thomas Mitchell of South Carolina.[18] While Moore could count on the two Pennsylvania votes, the Southerners were a question mark. His problem was that the second session was short, with multiple appropriation acts demanding the majority of the representatives' time. In a choreographed response to Moore's request, Sergeant asked for a report on the existing facility and any proposed actions to be taken. This gave Moore the cover he needed to get his case to the committee.

Samuel Moore was blunt in addressing the shortcomings of the existing Mint. South American silver bullion containing traces of gold had had to be turned away because of the Mint's inability to successfully separate the two metals. This bullion had actually been withdrawn from the Mint's vaults for shipping to laboratories in France and England. The chemical separation process could not be implemented in any of the existing Mint buildings, nor was there space on the property to construct the needed facilities.

Moore also was perturbed that private dwellings adjoined one of the Mint's coining rooms and specie vaults. While no problems had arisen in the past, the exposure was there. The Mint needed to be detached from any private dwellings.

However, the heart of Moore's argument was the simple inadequacy of the present buildings. They were in such decrepit condition that no repairs or rebuilding could bring them up to standard. The present location of the assayer's department was unsuitable. The introduction of steam-powered coin presses was out of the question.

To construct the new facility at the existing location would require land purchases for $15,000. The cost of the required new buildings would be $50,000 to $60,000. Much would depend on the architectural style of the front edifice. Moore wanted it to be in good taste. To secure the added production capacity, Moore wanted new machinery manufactured by Matthew Boulton in Birmingham, England. He had received a preliminary quote from Boulton in 1827 of £7,000, or $35,000, at Liverpool. Moore mentioned reports that machinery meeting his specifications originally intended for a South American mint was in New York for sale. Moore speculated that this machinery could be acquired for the same price quoted by Boulton before shipping expense.

Moore closed his report stating that in every department repairs had been postponed when possible in the belief that something more would eventually be deemed necessary. The roof of the front building was decayed. The steam boiler had been in operation since 1816 and its continued operation was in doubt. While coinage capacity was adequate at present, Moore could foresee constrictions in the not-too-distant future.[19]

However, Moore dodged a key issue in this report. Should the Mint rehabilitate its existing buildings or scrap the whole affair and move to a new location? A new location would eliminate production interruptions that were bound to occur in any remake of the existing operation. Perhaps Moore was concerned that he might get more than he wished when it came to a new location, such as a complete removal from Philadelphia.

The Select Committee met on the morning of January 5, 1829. They were in agreement to move forward in concept but they could not agree upon the sum to be appropriated. The total of Moore's estimates had been $100,000 to $110,000. Coulter wanted $150,000. Sergeant thought $120,000 was enough. However, the others felt it best not to ask for more than $100,000. Just as Moore had feared, Davenport raised the issue of the appropriateness of Philadelphia for the Mint. Easily enough, committee discussion seemed to satisfy him. Not wanting to risk disagreement and knowing that time was short in this session, Sergeant simply reported the bill leaving the appropriation blank. He would deal with this issue of location that he expected to hear again from other quarters when it arose.[20]

Meanwhile, Moore was second-guessing himself for raising the issue of a new Mint facility. The distribution of the report from the Select Committee on the Mint to the whole House shed too much light on his difficulties. If the Mint location was changed to another city, he knew there were those in Philadelphia who would never forgive him for initiating this move instead of allowing the Mint to slumber in seeming security. Moore believed himself vindicated by the dilapidated condition of the physical plant. Moreover, Biddle had approved of Sergeant's decision to distribute the report.[21] Biddle was up to his ears in this move to expand the Mint. Added capacity would provide the needed specie reserves for increased banknote circulation. However, too much capacity could stoke the fires of the bank's hard-money critics.

Moore had one more ace up his sleeve. The man who now held his old House seat, Samuel Delucenna Ingham (fig. 19), had just arrived in Washington. Ingham's support would hold more than normal sway. He had already accepted the position of secretary of the Treasury in the Jackson administration that would take office on March 4, 1829, one day after the close of this Congress. Moore did not hesitate to ask for Ingham's help. He played the Philadelphia card, saying that there were vague insinuations in certain quarters concerning the Mint's location.[22]

Fig. 19. Samuel D. Ingham took Moore's congressional seat at his resignation in 1822. Ingham then went on to become Moore's boss as secretary of the Treasury under Andrew Jackson.

The logjam broke on February 9, 1829, in the form of a letter from Churchill Cambreleng to Nicholas Biddle. Cambreleng spoke approvingly of the Mint appropriation and wished it well in the House. Moore relayed this support to Sergeant in a letter the same day it was learned by Biddle. Not wanting to let off the pressure, though, Moore told Sergeant that he had recently rejected a silver bullion deposit from the Bank of the United States because it contained too much gold. Yet he closed on a positive note. He had just sent quarter eagles struck by a close collar currently being employed on dime production to Treasury (fig. 20). He was really proud of the improved appearance of the raised rim.[23]

Action moved quickly now. On February 19, a line item of $120,000 for expansion of the Mint was added to the House appropriation bill. This move was necessitated because there was no hope of getting the bill passed on a standalone basis in the short session. There had been one hitch in this action. An amendment had been introduced to increase the appropriation to $150,000. It passed with a majority but lacked a quorum. Sergeant, fearing a snag, asked that the amendment be withdrawn. It was done and the Mint appropriation of $120,000 was on its way to approval in both houses of Congress.[24] Just this once, the aims of the Bank of the United States aligned with those of the hard-money Jacksonians. It would not always be thus.

• • • •

With the appropriation settled just before the inauguration of Andrew Jackson, Moore moved fast, lest minds change. He went to Philadelphia's leading architect, William Strickland.[25] Strickland had studied under Benjamin Latrobe and was one of the founders of the Greek Revival movement in the United States. Or course, it helped in Moore's eyes that Strickland had designed the magnificent building at Fourth and Chestnut for the second Bank of the United States.

If any of the congressmen voting for the appropriation had any misgivings about whether there would be a new building or expansion of the existing facility with attendant production disruptions, Moore quickly removed all doubt. Without any hesitation, he selected a site square in the city's financial district, on the northwest corner of Chestnut and Juniper streets, extending to Penn Square at Market Street. The cat came out of the bag when the comptroller of the Treasury, Joseph Anderson, wrote on April 20 asking for particulars regarding the buildings to be erected for the expansion of the Mint. In a straightforward manner, Moore told the comptroller that the structure would be wholly new, erected upon a vacant lot. No

Fig. 20.1. In 1828 Director Moore began striking coins with a close collar. He initiated this change with the dime and quarter eagle that year. While hampered by the thinness of the planchets, the close-collar coins, with their higher rims, generally exhibited superior details compared to the previous open-collar strikes. In a comparison between the 1827 and 1828 dime, the relief detail of Liberty's eye and nose are improved in the close-collar version (1828). Also the eagle's claws show better detail on the reverse.

Fig. 20.2. Both the 1825 and 1829 examples of the quarter eagle are Proofs. In the softer gold (1829), the improved detail from the close-collar strike shows in Liberty's hair and the eagle's feathers. However, real improvements in coin design from close-collar strikes would have to await the proportionately higher rims on the larger diameter coins yet to be converted.

part of the old machinery or any of the existing establishment was to be sold under the existing provisions.[26]

Moore, at this point, had plans in hand from Strickland's firm. The 120 feet of the building facing Chestnut Street were to be executed in top-grade, blue marble. The rear elevation, facing Market Street, was to be formed of Virginia "tru-stone" with marble steps. The angles of the east and west lateral walls were to be of free stone. The foundations of all of the walls as high as the water table called for "superb best" building stone. All other walls were to be made with good, hard, well-burnt brick. The marble and free stone portions were to be backed with brick. Brick archways in the main part of the building would provide floor supports. The flooring would be of yellow pine with oak joists. Double iron doors fronted each of the vaults. The design came with a piazza resting on cast-iron columns. Basement windows had strong shutters for security. There would also be strong entrance gates and a handsome iron railing extending along the fronts on Chestnut and Market streets. Porticos would have copper roofing and the main structure, slate.[27] It was Greek Revival done to the best of Strickland's ability.

Moore knew right away that he was reaching with this building. Regardless, he moved forward boldly. He would act as the general contractor to save money, employing an inspector in his absence to ensure quality. He was relentless in his dealings with the subcontractors. He would brook no outside interference as well. When John Sergeant recommended a friend for some of the business, Moore politely acknowledged the communication and gave the contract to another builder. Now all was ready.

While there were no notices in the newspapers and little public fanfare, it was the high point of Samuel Moore's term as Mint director. On July 4, 1829, ground was broken with the laying of a cornerstone for the new Mint building.[28] To mark the occasion, Moore struck half dimes, last issued in 1805 (fig. 21). They were struck with a close

Fig. 21. To celebrate the laying of the corner stone for the new Mint building, Moore authorized the resumption of half dime production, last undertaken in 1805. The problem of adapting the design to smaller denominations is apparent on this half dime. While the Capped Bust was suitable for the half dollar, it was increasingly awkward, particularly the reverse design, when applied to the smaller denominations. This desire on the Mint's part to apply the same or similar designs across the gold- and silver-coin series would hamper coin designs throughout the 19th century.

collar and raised rim. In conveying the new coins to Ingham, the president, and his cabinet, Moore praised them but admitted that they were not perfect.[29] The simple fact was the Capped Bust design with the perched eagle on the reverse did not reduce well to the diameter of a half dime. Moore badly needed new designs.

• • • •

Moore still had one large, looming issue to address—the machinery for the new Mint facility. In his communication with Sergeant initiating the whole process the previous December, he had not given the full details of his previous inquiries to Boulton. In the late summer of 1827, Moore had actually queried Matthew Boulton regarding horsepower requirements for a steam engine in anticipation of Congress's authorizing a new Mint facility. Moore wanted steam power for all the Mint's planned activities including four presses devoted to half dollars. Moore needed to know Boulton's terms and length of time required for providing a "system of machinery." He even asked if Boulton would sell such drawings and instructions that would enable the Americans to construct this machinery. That was a nonstarter for Boulton, as once these drawings left his control, they were forever gone since international patent protection did not exist at that time.

Here negotiations remained until Moore broke ground for the new Mint facility. Again he went to Boulton concerning the lead about minting equipment being available in New York City. Matthew Boulton confirmed the origin of this equipment but would go no further. The Mint director was now forced to open negotiations with the true owners of the machinery. Bad news followed. The equipment was actually at the dock in Liverpool. It would cost the Mint £3,824 at the pier. The owners would not pay transportation to the United States nor guarantee the performance of the equipment.

Moore was incredulous. He insisted that freight and insurance be paid by the sellers. Otherwise he would be in an embarrassing position should something adverse happen to the cargo. In reality, his construction budget would not allow him the luxury of paying this additional cost. He then made another try at gaining Boulton's specifications and drawings. Moore insisted that the sellers provide him with evidence or description of the adequacy of the equipment before a contract could be signed.[30] On this point, the sellers failed to extract the necessary plans from Boulton, the firm claiming they were just too complex and detailed to execute.[31] Here the negotiations fell apart. Moore was left with no alternative but to develop machinery of American design, of which there was none outside of the Mint.

Nevertheless, Moore optimistically stated in his annual report for 1829 that all went well that first construction season. Work would be completed by the end of 1830, with the Mint in full operation on the two-year anniversary of the ground breaking.

CHAPTER 6

A FLY IN THE OINTMENT

While Moore was having his way with the House of Representatives in the second session of the Twentieth Congress, the Senate put a fly in his ointment. They passed a resolution on December 29, 1828, charging the secretary of the Treasury with determining, as accurately as possible, the true ratio between gold and silver and to report back in the next session of Congress.[1] The outgoing Adams administration chose to take no action on this resolution. It would take the Jackson administration's Treasury Department 17 months to come to grips with this issue.

The Senate of the Twenty-First Congress in its first session did not wait on Treasury. Nathan Sanford (fig. 22) from New York City reported for the Senate's Select Committee on the State of the Coinage to the chamber on January 11, 1830.

Sanford wisely ducked the issue of the gold-to-silver ratio, deferring to the pending Treasury study. However, he did not hesitate to point out that other improvements were necessary. He argued that large coins were more frequently removed from circulation than smaller pieces; circulating coins were never entirely uniform in weight; and, small coins lost a greater proportion of weight by circulation. This disproportionate wear was a direct inducement to convert large coins into bullion when needed for export or manufacturing purposes. Furthermore, when a diminished coin could be used to obtain a coin of full weight,

Fig. 22. Senator Nathan Sanford, growing impatient with the Jackson administration for dragging its feet, argued that legal-tender status for foreign specie should be terminated after the new mint was placed in service.

the coin of full weight circulated no more. It was converted to bullion or treated as bullion and exported.

The senator was particularly disgusted by the circulating Spanish coins. Most were well-worn, the smaller pieces more so than the larger pieces. Many of the old Spanish dollars that remained were below legal weight and were filed or sweated. These coins legally passed by tail (face amount) in spite of their deficient intrinsic value. Spanish dollars were now coined only in Madrid and rarely made their way to the United States. The mints in the former Spanish dominions in South America had all come under the control of new governments. Consequently, the weights of their coinages were no longer as reliable.

Sanford presented some very telling figures. Since its inception, the U.S. Mint had coined slightly less than $34 million face value. Yet at this point the total specie in circulation in the United States was only an estimated $14 million in federal coins. To these were added $5 million of Spanish coins and $4 million from various other foreign countries. None of the American gold remained. Foreign gold coins were seen in commerce and were valued by weight and fineness, not by their varying face values. Metropolitan newspapers carried "Prices Current" columns giving exchange values. Almost all the early federal silver coins had disappeared. A large proportion of the federal silver coins now in circulation had been issued within the last ten years. At this point U.S. silver coins were, to a great extent, treated as bullion. Meanwhile, the Spanish coins in their worn state continued to circulate. Sanford reached a basic conclusion from these numbers.

> The silver coins issued by our Mint have exceeded the amount of all the coins now in the United States; and the portion of these silver coins which has disappeared, is a sum greater than the amount of all those foreign coins now in this country. An amount not less than $11 million of our silver coins has been withdrawn from circulation; the concurrent use of Spanish coins inferior to our own coins in weight and intrinsic value, but of equal value in currency by tale, has been the principal cause of this fact.

Sanford added that if these Spanish coins continued to circulate, diminished in weight as they were, they would to a great extent expel American coins from circulation. It was indispensable to the preservation of our own coins that the legal-tender status of the Spanish coins cease.

To further reinforce the recommendations that were coming, Sanford reviewed the state of the Mint. He noted that the Mint was satisfactory in spite of the fact that its operations were conducted in a facility extremely unsuited for this purpose. However, a new Mint facility was to open and be in full operation on July 4, 1831. Whereas the old operation had a production capacity of $5 million annually, the new facility was forecast to be able to coin $10 million, well more than the nation's needs.

Sanford closed with an emotional appeal. Without the regulations that the committee was proposing, dollars would not be coined or, if coined, would not circulate. The dollar, the largest silver coin authorized by law, would be known as a money of account only. The committee's recommendations were that U.S. silver coins of less than a dollar should not be legal tender for payment of any sum exceeding $10. No foreign coin whatsoever should be legal tender. In a nod to intrinsic value, the committee recommended that no U.S. coin diminished by wear more than a quarter of its full weight should be legal tender. The exclusion of foreign coins should coincide with the projected date for full operating capacity of the Mint. Restriction of legal tender for domestic coins would be immediate. The same would hold for coins with excessive wear.[2]

Sanford's select committee recommendations were reasonable. They would have enhanced the circulation of American silver coinage. The one failure was the omission of a seigniorage on the silver coinage, a debasement of the silver content below intrinsic value. If Treasury had been prompt in issuing their report on the valuation ratio, these recommendations in some form would have had a good chance of coming to fruition. It was not to be.

• • • •

The much-anticipated report prepared by Secretary of the Treasury Samuel D. Ingham arrived in the Senate on

May 29, 1830. It opened with a review of the legislation of 1792, which established the Mint and set the ratio at 15 parts silver equivalent to 1 part gold in value. The English system that had been established in 1816 was also assessed. Payments in silver as legal tender were limited to 40 shillings (two pounds), or the equivalent of $10. In addition the British Royal Mint did not charge for coinage. However, they debased the coinage by paying 62 shillings for standard silver received and coining it into 66 shillings. This amounted to a seigniorage of about 6.5 percent. On the other hand, gold taken in at the Royal Mint was not debased when converted to coin. The end result was a current gold-to-silver ratio of 15.8 to 1. In France the ratio was 15.5, however the Mint did not pay full market for its gold purchases. Had the French Mint paid fair-market value for its gold, the ratio would have been 15.8.

Ingham observed that the American market for gold and silver was in line with the legally mandated ratio up to 1820. It was only after that time that domestic valuations reflected the European market, resulting in American gold coins being undervalued. Yet he noted that gold had not circulated prior to 1820. What he failed to recognize was that the ratio had started to come unglued during the Napoleonic Wars. In his opinion part of the reason was that bank paper had superseded gold for large payments when that currency was sufficiently credit worthy. Thus, the United States had long subsisted without gold with little inconvenience—never mind the large amounts of paper currency circulating unrestrained. On the other hand, shortages of silver coins had proved intolerable. When silver was drained, it would be replaced, not by gold, but by small bank notes and paper tokens. It was extremely important that the Mint not value gold so low as to prevent the possibility of silver being exported in preference to gold.

In the end, Ingham had skewed the facts to favor his position: he was a silver man. He recommended fixing the legal ratio at 15.625 to 1. Gold was still undervalued. It was just not undervalued to the point that it would be openly melted for its bullion value because of the added charges to the broker amounting to 5.37 percent for transportation and insurance. At the same time, there was a very comfortable cushion to ensure that silver was not drained instead for export payments.[3]

Nathan Sanford took issue with the report in the Senate. He disagreed with the premise that gold had ceased to circulate with the introduction of paper currency. Exasperated, he stated that the Mint now coined gold wholly without public benefit and the public paid the expense of this useless coinage. In actuality, the U.S. Mint performed a service for the holder of gold bullion by assaying and weighing the bullion for free. If Congress would not rectify the legal proportion between the two metals, they ought to abolish the coinage of gold.

Still Sanford defended gold. While silver coins were useful when small sums were involved, gold coins would be eminently convenient for large payments and long transportation. For the two species of coins to circulate together, their relative ratio must reflect their relative market value.

Sanford had another reason to insist that gold be returned to circulation. In the Constitution, the power to coin money and regulate its value was retained exclusively for the federal government. No such control over paper currency existed. It was issued from a multitude of banks established by different authorities and under no common control, exposing the country constantly to the danger of inflationary speculation arising from excessive issues of banknotes.

There were approximately 500 incorporated banks in the country, with the number increasing annually. Approximately $77 million of the $100 million in total money circulating in the U.S. consisted of banknotes. Within those banknotes, half were for sums greater than $5, about one-fourth for $5, and the remaining one-fourth for less than $5 with the greater proportion $1 notes. Sanford believed that there would be less of a demand for paper currency in a country where the specie consisted of both silver and gold coins. By inference, a viable gold coinage would act to suppress that portion of the bank notes of $5 or less. To Sanford, this was enough justification to strive for a real gold coin circulation.

The senator strongly believed that the relative ratio of gold to silver must be the same as the relative value they bore in bullion. He rejected the Treasury Department's position that the ratio should be 1 or 2 percent less than the relative market of gold to silver. Sanford quoted Albert Gallatin that the premium on U.S. gold coins in the second half of the last decade had been 5.16 percent, equating to a ratio of 15.82. Sales of gold bullion in the New York market over the same period indicated a ratio of 15.912. Furthermore, the relative value of gold to silver in Spain, Portugal, and South America had for years been 16. The greater amount of gold bullion now came from Mexico, while gold exports went to Europe at 15.85. Sanford noted that the average between this buy-sell was 15.925, far from Treasury's position of 15.625.

In closing, Sanford argued that, by the use of paper money, gold was more removed from circulation than silver. In order to circulate, U.S. gold coins must be able to contend with the demand for export and the expelling influence of paper money at home. Sanford recommended that the ratio slightly overvalue gold to secure the circulation of gold coins and so that the resultant loss of silver coins would not be to an inconvenient level. Sanford assigned the high-end ratio of 16. He however believed that the ratio should reflect the relative bullion values of the two metals which averaged out to be 15.925. He then recommended the ratio of 15.9.[4] The Select Committee duly introduced a gold-coin bill, S. 6, which reflected this ratio. The eagle, if coinage of this gold piece were to resume, would be reduced from 247.5 grains of pure gold to 233.49 grains.[5]

It would be an absolute nightmare for Samuel Moore and the U.S. Mint to implement this weight for gold coins. He had recommended to Sanford an easily divisible number that reflected a ratio of 16 to 1 and employed alloy at 10 percent by weight in each coin.[6]

The man leading the House Select Committee on Coins, Campbell Patrick White, was also a New Yorker, and like Ingham, a staunch silver man. White took a more measured approach than Sanford, writing Ingham on January 5, 1831, to ask the Mint's present and expected capacity. White also wanted to know the Mint director's experience in regard to fineness and weight of the silver dollars coming from the mints in the former Spanish possessions in South America. Alluding to complaints from New York bankers, White asked the length of time that could be expected at the new facility from the receipt of bullion until the depositor took delivery of the coins. He wanted to know at what point the Mint issued the depositor a mint certificate for his bullion and at what rate the Philadelphia banks discounted those certificates.[7]

On January 14, the House received the Senate's S. 6.[8] This prompted more questions from White for Ingham regarding the silver content and valuation ratio for U.S. coins. The secretary dumped both letters on Moore for answers. Ingham's cover letter to White left the door open for continued legal-tender status for foreign coins. The secretary saw no issue with making Mexican dollars and French five-franc pieces legal tender for a limited time, provided the value set for them was low enough to make it worthwhile for their holders to have them recoined at the Mint. Ingham, in contradiction to President Jackson, was a supporter of the Bank of the United States, the probable beneficiary in this arrangement. Ingham had no problem with the American dollar being slightly lower in weight than the Spanish dollar, since that coin's presence in the country was negligible. The secretary wobbled on the issue of the silver-to-gold ratio. He wanted 15.625 combined with a standard 90 percent fineness because this lower ratio would not threaten the withdrawal of silver from circulation. However, he had no reasonable ground for fearing the export of silver at the higher Senate rate of 15.9. In fact, he was encouraged by the Senate's action.

It fell to Moore to provide specific answers to White's questions. The new Mint facility was not going to be in production by July 4, 1831. August now appeared the earliest that production could commence. Full production could not be reached until the beginning of 1832. Moore had just tacitly admitted that his construction project in Philadelphia had encountered problems. In discussing capacity, Moore brought up the dollar coin.

> Three thousand dollars, in dollars, most probably more, may be coined in the same time as two thousand in half dollars, with an equal number of presses; and the annual expense, wastage excepted, would be about the same. The wastage per cent, on dollars would be less than on the lower denominations, but the difference would be unimportant between dollars and half dollars.[9]

Moore repeated his estimate for the capacity of the new Mint of $10 million annually.

As to the new South American coins, they generally exhibited less careful workmanship than their predecessors, the Spanish milled dollars of the 18th century. The Columbian coin was of particularly poor quality. In Moore's opinion, extension of legal-tender status need only be done for the Mexican dollar. It was familiar to the people and maintained a satisfactory intrinsic value.

Moore also answered White's request concerning depositor delays. In a normal situation, assay of a bullion deposit took 24 hours. A mint certificate was issued at that point, which would be discounted at the Philadelphia banks by 0.5 percent if the depositor wanted his money immediately. The depositor could be expected to wait about 20 days at the new Mint for the conversion of his bullion into coin. Moore had not been asked directly about the wait at the U.S. Mint's present location and therefore discreetly sidestepped the question.

Moore closed optimistically, by saying so many Mexican dollars were expected to reach the Mint for recoining, shortages of U.S. coins should be totally eliminated within three years. It could be done even more rapidly if the government would adopt the policy of directly supplying bullion to the Mint.[10]

White's report from the Select Committee was made February 22, 1831. With adjournment scheduled for March 3, time was short for anything but an approval of the Senate bill. White's tenor was negative from the first. American currency differed from that of all other commercial nations in that it was effectively paper, secured by a specie fund held by the issuers of the currency, the banks. The public was deeply concerned over the safety of this specie fund, but it did not seem of any importance what it consisted of, whether gold or silver coins, or bullion. Gold and silver, whether coined or not, were viewed in the commercial world as bullion and valued according to their fine metal content. White could not understand how public convenience was promoted by the coinage of silver and gold, some of which passed temporarily into the vaults of banks and soon afterwards to the refiners in foreign nations to be melted.

The Select Committee recommended leaving the silver content at 371.25 grains for the dollar coin. However, the Spanish milled dollar should cease to be accepted as legal tender. The silver coins in banks should be viewed as the money of commerce, valued by their pure metal content. White noted that both Moore and Ingham were agreeable to making the Mexican dollar legal tender. The congressman rejected this discrimination against the other former Spanish mints and recommended the inclusion of Central America, Peru, Chile, La Plata (Argentina), and Brazil. White stated that the deposits of silver bullion for the preceding five years appeared to be increasing and were abundant for all useful and desirable purposes. There would be no bullion purchase fund. White also proposed creating a depositor fund for prompt payment in place of Mint certificates at a cost to the depositor of 0.5 percent. He saw no reason for the Philadelphia banks to enjoy this profit, created by their exclusive, cozy relationship with the Mint. In a positive move, White agreed that the alloy should be one-tenth part of standard coins.[11]

In regard to the valuation ratio, the Select Committee was dubious over the need to support the double standard of gold and silver. They did not feel that rejecting one or the other of the metals would be injurious. A double standard by its very definition required the necessity of occasional adjustments to reflect market fluctuations of one or the other metal. However, silver was the money to which the American people had become accustomed. Therefore it would be highly injudicious to risk the loss of American silver coins by placing the gold ratio even at its international market rate. White considered the Senate proposal above said market rate—thus, unacceptable. The committee reaffirmed Secretary Ingham's recommendation of 15.625.

White made one last observation. Gold and silver coins would not be sustained in circulation with banknotes possessing public confidence. If the national interest required the permanent use of the gold eagle and the silver dollar, the issue of bank bills of $1, $2, $3, $5, and $10 must be prohibited.[12]

White and Sanford were too far apart. There was no hope of finding common ground. The Twenty-First Congress adjourned without dealing with the undervaluation of American gold coins or any of the other systemic problems at the U.S. Mint.

• • • •

It was no accident that Moore mentioned in his report to White the capacity upgrade gained if the Mint resumed striking dollar coins. It was a trial balloon and White had not shot it down. In fact, silver imports had exceeded exports annually since 1825 and absolute exports had fallen almost to nil in 1830. Economic trends said the time was right to resume production of this coin. Moore fired off a letter to Ingham on April 13, 1831. He used as a trigger the receipt by the Mint of two deposits on March 28 of Spanish dollars from Canton. The flow that had condemned the American dollar to the melting pots had reversed.

Ingham was prompt in his response.

> Having submitted to the President your letter of the 13th inst., I am directed to instruct you, that, as there no longer exists any cause for suspending the coinage of Dollars, the directions which have been heretofore given for that object are to be considered as no longer in force.[13]

Samuel Moore was now free to resume dollar coinage at his discretion. Dies using the old design apparently were prepared. Yet nothing happened.[14]

In a December 1833 report to Congress, Moore gave his first official reason for not moving forward. He had postponed resurrecting the dollar until modifications to the alloy of the silver coinage were adopted so that the coin would be compatible with its European counterparts.[15] It sounded good but was hard to swallow given the enthusiasm with which he had pursued gaining permission. A much more likely reason was that silver exports had ultimately soared in 1831 and had only begun to decline significantly again in 1833. Moore simply had made a bad call in 1831 and did not wish to draw attention to it while keeping the option to resume dollar production open.

• • • •

The failure of the House and Senate to come to an agreement to fix the valuation ratio was not Moore's only headache in 1831. The preceding winter had been intensely cold and the construction season delayed as below-normal temperatures continued to linger into spring. The project was always going to be tight given the original appropriation. The money Moore had planned for equipment purchases was rapidly shrinking to feed the demands of the building itself. Moore had gone to Congress the preceding year to get authorization to sell the existing Mint building and apply the proceeds to equipment purchases for the new operation.[16] It was a slick way to get a supplemental appropriation without the political embarrassment of admitting an overrun. However, those funds would not be available until the new building was complete. Purchase of equipment in England from Matthew Boulton was out. There was simply not enough money.

1849

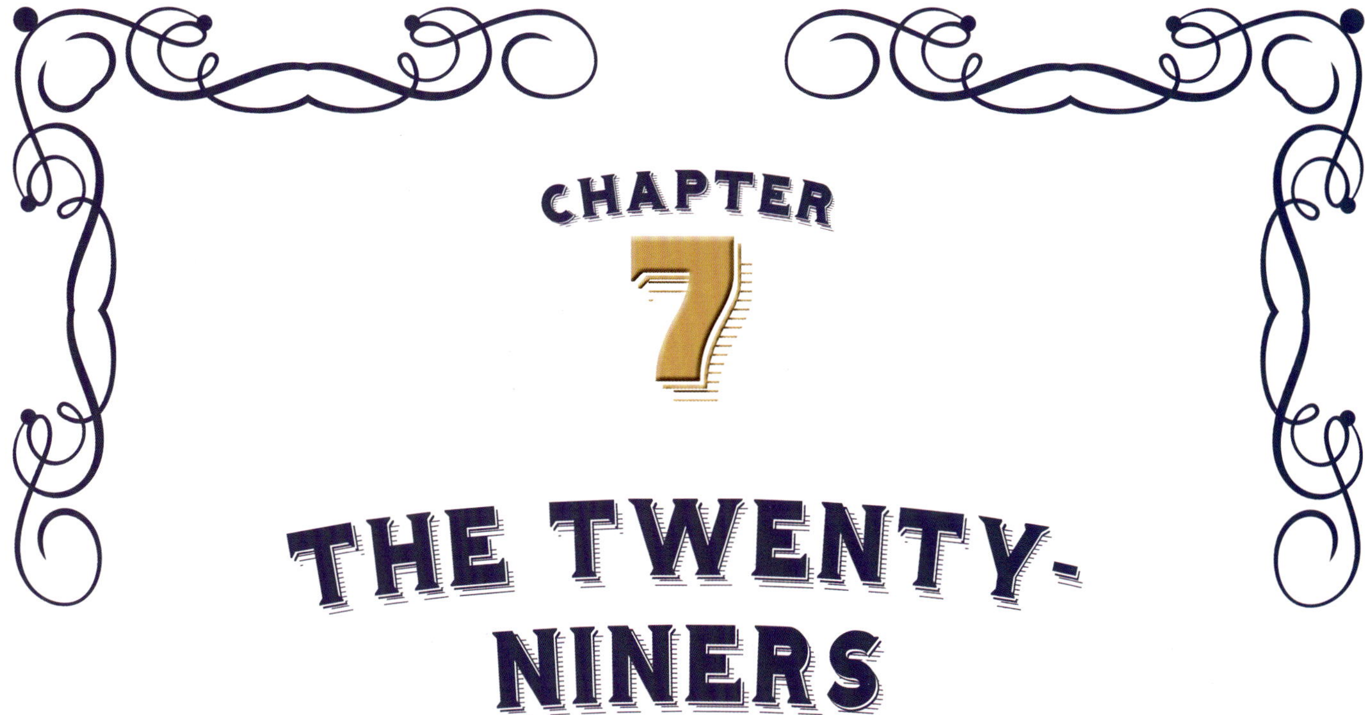

CHAPTER 7

THE TWENTY-NINERS

The Senate resolution for the Treasury study on December 29, 1828, was driven by more than just a desire to reform the gold-to-silver ratio in preparation for moving to the new and expanded Mint operation. Something else was astir. Native gold from North Carolina had been dribbling into the Mint in increasing amounts throughout the 1820s. However, the gold reaching the Mint was just the tip of the iceberg.

The first discovery had been by accident, on the farm of John Reed in Cabarrus County, North Carolina, in 1799. On a Sunday morning Reed and his wife had taken the one horse the family owned to attend church services. Their son, Conrad, was left to babysit and fend for himself. For amusement, Conrad went bow fishing along Little Meadow Creek, which meandered through the farm. A glittering yellow rock, about the size of a shoe, caught his attention in the water. The boy carried it home to show his father that evening. A week later, John Reed took it into nearby Concord to see if it had value, only to learn it was supposedly worthless. The yellow mystery served as a doorstop in the family's cabin for the next three years.

John Reed did not give up. When the opportunity arose to travel to Fayetteville, the farmer took the rock to show to a local jeweler. The jeweler identified the 17-pound rock as gold ore. He gave Reed $3.50 for it and Reed became the first American victim of a gold-field swindle. However, Reed was not without ability. Learning that he had been taken and the jeweler had profited handsomely

from his ignorance, he returned to Fayetteville and the purchase price was adjusted. Reed also took partners and began to prospect for gold on his farm, finding substantial placer deposits.[1]

News traveled slowly at that time. It was not until 1804 that widespread placer mining developed in western North Carolina and the first gold showed up at the Mint in Philadelphia. The question of the source of all this placer gold remained unanswered until 1825. That year Mathias Tobias Barringer, a farmer and part-time prospector, discovered the first vein of gold-bearing quartz. Shortly thereafter additional quartz veins were discovered in Mecklenburg County, near the little town of Charlotte. Now the rush was on, with thousands of treasure hunters pouring into North Carolina. Mecklenburg County became a prospector's paradise, with a mine on almost every farm.[2]

As it turned out, the gold veins were laid down in the Blue Ridge Mountains, forming an intermittent belt just east of the mountains that stretched southward from the Middle Atlantic States into North and South Carolina. It seemed to stop abruptly at the Georgia border. In truth the goldfield continued into Georgia, but these were lands deeded by treaty to the Cherokee Indian Nation. Everything changed on August 1, 1829, when gold was discovered on their lands and the "Great Intrusion" into the Cherokee Nation started.[3]

The story of the Cherokees and Georgia gold was actually much more complex. The state of Georgia had been actively trying to expunge its Indian population since 1802, when it ceded its claims to western lands, which would eventually become Alabama and Mississippi, to the federal government in exchange for a promise to remove all Indians from its remaining territory as soon as could be peaceably accomplished. The Creeks inhabiting potentially rich farmland in the south and central part of the state were the first to go. However, the situation with the Cherokees was not so simple. The federal government had guaranteed Cherokee sovereignty in two separate treaties prior to the 1802 agreement.[4] Legal expulsion of the Cherokee Nation was going to be much more difficult.

The Cherokees were determined not to cede any more land or to sign a treaty of removal with the United States. They even stopped granting rights of way for roads and canals. In addition, they decided to adopt the white man's ways, becoming farmers, merchants, blacksmiths, and carpenters. They built towns, established schools, converted to Christianity, and erected churches. They adopted a constitution modeled on the U.S. Constitution. They also established a newspaper, the *Cherokee Phoenix*, with a national circulation. Its editor was the Cherokee Elias Boudinot (fig. 23). His given name was Buck. As a young man, Christian missionaries had taken Buck to be educated in Connecticut. Along the way, he met the elderly former

Fig. 23. Elias Boudinot, also known as Buck Watie, was a member of a prominent Cherokee Nation family and became editor of the *Cherokee Phoenix*, the first Native American newspaper. Published in Cherokee and English, this newspaper showcased the achievements of these native people.

Mint director, Elias Boudinot. At that point Boudinot was president of the American Bible Society. Buck was so impressed with Boudinot that, following the recent Cherokee practice of taking the names of prominent whites and benefactors, he took the old Mint director's name.[5] The ultimate irony of this action would prove tragic.

In December 1828, Georgia enacted a law incorporating the Cherokee lands into the state of Georgia, effective June 1, 1830. After that date, all laws and customs of the Cherokee Nation would be null and void. However, the law allowed the Cherokees to retain title to their lands until the state could decide how best to dispose of them. Meanwhile the Indians would be subject to Georgia law—as people of color, they were not considered competent witnesses in court cases involving white men.[6]

In May 1830, President Andrew Jackson pushed a law, the Indian Removal Act, through Congress to encourage the relocation of all eastern Indian tribes to west of the Mississippi River. This law was subject to all previously negotiated treaties, basically leaving the Cherokees in place. Impatient with the expected slow pace of the federal government to negotiate a removal treaty with the Cherokees and fired by the discovery of gold on their lands, the governor of Georgia issued a proclamation on June 1, 1830, in accordance with the state law of 1828, implementing state control of the Cherokee lands. With scant protection under Georgia law for the Cherokees, the taking of their gold-bearing lands was now open to the more aggressive miners.

Gold flowed out of the Georgia hills with one newspaper estimating that nearly a quarter-million dollars of the yellow metal passed through Augusta, Georgia's largest inland city at the time, in the first nine months of 1830. It was now clear that the gold-bearing belt was richest in its southern portion. One of its highest concentrations was in the Dahlonega Belt, near the town of the same name in northeast Georgia. The name Dahlonega came from the Cherokee word, *dalanigei*, meaning yellow money.[7]

Most of the gold coming out of both North Carolina and Georgia was in a virtually pure state, assaying at 900 to 950 fine. As a result, this metal was in demand for jewelry. It also went into the more lucrative export market. This gold, in an economy fueled by paper currency, became a currency of its own. Businessmen carried their gold in quills, as the young Sherman had recalled some years later in California. Three-and-a-half grains (480 grains in a troy ounce) would buy a pint of whiskey. A pennyweight—24 grains or 1/20 of a troy ounce—was worth almost a dollar in country stores.[8]

There clearly was a need in the backcountry of North Carolina and Georgia for a viable and convenient currency. The small miners, unable to participate in the export markets and without access to jewelers, were taking a haircut of as much as 15 percent on their raw gold when forced to sell to brokers. Shipping the gold to Philadelphia for coinage was not an alternative either. The journey to Philadelphia was long. Insurance was needed to protect against the danger of robbery. Once in Philadelphia, this bullion went to the back of the queue behind the favored local banks and the Bank of the United States. The whole process to payment could take as long as three months. The alternative was to take the gold to a BUS branch in Charleston or Savannah. There the depositor would be given two-thirds of the value of the bullion, but would again have to wait for final payment until the bullion's value was fixed at the Mint. That would take two months. To add insult to injury, the price paid at the Mint reflected the gold-to-silver ratio of 15 to 1.

Development of a private mint would solve these problems for the miners. The first such operation was established in 1830 in Milledgeville, at that time the capital of Georgia, by Templeton Reid.

Reid was a bit of an eccentric, having dabbled in several manufacturing ventures. His forte was the building of cotton gins, but he had put in time as a jeweler and clock maker and then as a gunsmith. On July 24, 1830, the Milledgeville newspapers reported that Reid had coined $1,500 in quarter eagles, half eagles, and the eagle denomination that the U.S. Mint had discontinued in 1805 (fig. 24). The articles also quoted Reid as assuring readers that these coins would be accepted at face value by the Mint and most banks. Reid had managed to come up with a coin press, dies, and the means of making the necessary planchets—no easy task. However, he recognized that Milledgeville, 100 miles south of the gold fields, was too remote to the miners. He moved his operation in late July or early August to Gainesville, 20 or so miles from Dahlonega.

Trouble struck on August 16. In a letter to the editor of the Augusta newspaper, the writer stated that he had forwarded Reid's gold coins to the Philadelphia Mint and the assay results had been unsatisfactory. The coins had the correct weight, but their gold content was deficient by as much as 9 percent in the quarter eagle and 4 percent in the eagle. Reid reacted strongly but really failed to rebut the accusation. In the face of more adverse publicity, Reid closed his doors in the middle of October. The public had lost confidence in his coins.

Reid, in his process, had fluxed the gold to remove the extraneous material. However, he had not bothered to refine the raw gold to eliminate the mostly silver found with it. Reid had simply assumed his gold was in pure form. His mint remained in operation for only 70 working days. He had at least established the fact that a private mint could operate in competition to the U.S. Mint. The Constitution did not prohibit private individuals from coining their own money. The way it was worded only prohibited states. Yet whether such a venture could be viable remained to be proved.[9]

The reason behind Reid's failure spread through the gold region. The newspaper in Rutherfordton, North Carolina, pointedly editorialized that the Reid operation was the way things should not be done. It just so happened

Fig. 24. For a few short months in 1830, the private mint operated by Templeton Reid flourished in Georgia. Its production, primarily of quarter and half eagles, attempted to meet the miners' demands to efficiently convert bullion into specie and address the lack of circulating coinage from the U.S. Mint in the gold fields. When his coins failed to consistently meet the standard of intrinsic value, his operations quickly fell into demise.

Fig. 25. Christopher Bechtler, a German immigrant, set up his private mint in Rutherfordton, North Carolina, and would ultimately compete successfully with the U.S. branch mint in nearby Charlotte.

that Rutherfordton had a new arrival in the spring of 1831 who had the necessary skills. At age 48, Christopher Bechtler (fig. 25) had emigrated to the United States in 1830 with his two sons and nephew. His idea was to set up shop in Philadelphia. Bechtler, from Pforzheim, Germany, was an accomplished gun- and goldsmith. Arriving in Philadelphia and filing citizenship papers, he promptly caught gold fever and headed to North Carolina. He apparently chose Rutherfordton due to the large German population in the surrounding area.

Bechtler never struck it rich as a gold miner. Instead he established a private mint with its first output of quarter and half eagles in 1831. From the start, he was sensitive to the issue of integrity for his operations. He went to great lengths to assure his customers of a fair assay. He also avoided Reid's mistake of assuming a virtually pure fineness of the fluxed gold. Bechtler used a crude method termed a "fire ordeal" to determine the gold's fineness. Thus, his coinage gained a reputation for its accuracy.

From the first, Bechtler's business was successful (fig. 26). In 1832 he added to his coinage a $1 gold piece that proved popular. Over the coming years his private mint gold output rivaled that of the Mint in Philadelphia. In the Southeast, the circulation of his gold coins was frequently greater than those of the Mint. His coins were accepted in commerce as far away as Kentucky and Tennessee.[10] Even when his assays came up short on average by 2.5 percent at the Philadelphia Mint, people refused to accept the results. Where Reid had failed, Bechtler proved that a private mint could be successful.[11]

During this period pressure continued to build for the removal of the Cherokee Indians. Not surprisingly, Georgia proceeded with the tacit approval of the president to distribute the lands to be taken from the Indians. The gubernatorial election of 1831 turned on the mechanics of this distribution. The winning candidate supported a lottery, while the loser wanted to retain the minerals for the state. By election time, the Cherokee editor, Elias Boudinot, described the voters as "sick with the expectation of Indian land and gold." In preparing to implement a land lottery in 1832, the state surveyed the Indian holdings into lots. Citizens of the state who were not native Indians could then register for the lottery in which these lands would be raffled off. Most Georgians viewed this lottery as a chance to win a gold mine.

The Cherokee fought back, taking their cause to the Supreme Court. On March 22, 1832, Chief Justice John Marshall ruled that Georgia laws had no effect on the Cherokee Nation. Some supporters even urged the Cherokees to apply for statehood. President Jackson had another view altogether. He refused to enforce the court's order. He told the Cherokees directly that their only hope was to surrender their homeland and move beyond the Mississippi.[12]

By May 1833 the lottery was completed and additional thousands flooded into the gold region seeking out their newly acquired lands. In an effort to at least appear to be treating the Cherokees with respect, Georgia law forbade the lottery winners to occupy their lots if the Cherokees lived on them. They would have to wait until the Cherokees voluntarily moved or were forced to do so by the state. If the Cherokees vacated, they were to be paid for improvements on the land. To enforce this law, the state established a feeble 11-man force to patrol the Indian lands and expel any intruders. Even this restriction was wiped away when the legislature succumbed to pressure and passed a law allowing lottery winners to test their holdings for gold and operate thereon regardless of Indian occupancy. In spite of this encroachment, the Cherokees held on, hoping to avoid the expulsion.[13]

These lottery lands often changed hands several times and frauds were committed, all in the hope of acquiring wealth without labor. Amidst the wheeling and dealing, leases were given to prospectors. The rent ranged from one-tenth to one-half of the gold production from the property, with the average being one-fourth. Payment was

Fig. 26. Learning from Reid's failure, Christopher Bechtler built a thriving business attuned to his customers. To Bechtler goes the credit for issuing the first $1 gold piece in the United States. Bechtler was careful to stamp the standard weight of the coin and its purity, expressed in carats, on the reverse. The $1 gold piece marked A. Bechtler and the $5 gold piece were struck after the United States went to a gold-to-silver ratio of 16 to 1. This specific $1 gold piece was struck after 1840, when the elder Bechtler turned over operations of the private mint to his son, August. The $5 gold piece is a rare Proof example. The fine weight of all three coins, driving intrinsic value, is just slightly above that of their U.S. Mint–issued counterpart.

Fig. 27. This image of John C. Calhoun was drawn by J.B. Longacre in 1834; it appeared in his book of famous Americans.

a matter of the honesty of the miner. Some joked that they had left the landowner's rent in the mine. The owner could come get it himself whenever he wanted it bad enough.[14]

Capital flowed in to develop the mines surrounding Dahlonega. Gold challenged cotton as Georgia's most economically important industry. At the height of the gold rush there were as many as 15,000 miners within a 15-mile radius of Dahlonega.[15] One investor was John C. Calhoun (fig. 27) and another was his son-in-law, Thomas Clemson, a mining engineer. Calhoun, in spite of his governmental duties, first as vice-president and then as a senator from South Carolina, was a frequent visitor to his mine just south of Dahlonega, near Auraria. It was no small operation, employing 20 slaves at its peak.[16] In 1833 Calhoun sent gold to the Mint at Philadelphia valued at $603.93 to be coined.[17]

By 1834, the Southern gold fields had assumed an air of stability and permanence. Large mines fueled by foreign investment were coming into operation.[18] Capital also came from the American money centers. Samuel Moore was a member of one such charter company that invested in a Virginia gold mine.[19] The one outstanding issue was the need to improve the way this gold was monetized. It was only a matter of time before discussion would turn to a branch mint. If it were located in Georgia it would seal the fate of the Cherokees. It would serve as an affirmation of the politics of expulsion.

1849

CHAPTER 8

GRIDLOCK

The decision swirled around a few grains of gold. Twenty-four grains are in a pennyweight. Twenty pennyweights of 24-carat pure gold, or 480 grains, make up a troy ounce. A grain of gold is so light as to be indiscernible to the human hand. Perhaps that was why Congress could not come to grips with the necessary weight adjustment of American gold coins to make them circulate.

• • • •

Campbell White was an American success story. Born in Ireland in 1787, he gained only a limited education. In 1816 he immigrated to America, landing in New York City. Here he engaged in mercantile pursuits, successfully avoiding the pitfalls of the Panic of 1819. He reached a pinnacle upon being named cashier of the Manhattan Bank, a position that would resemble a chief operating officer in later times. During his tenure, he was accused of making fraudulent loans but was acquitted. In another context he served 15 days of jail time for assaulting a director of the bank. When the Democratic Republicans splintered in 1828, White ran as a Jacksonian for election to the Twenty-First Congress and won.[1] He was named president of the newly formed Chemical Bank in New York City in 1831. It could safely be assumed that when White spoke on the floor of the House, he spoke for the New York City financial community.

While the Twenty-First Congress had ended in frustration for White, the congressman did not back down. At the opening of the Twenty-Second Congress in December 1831, White moved that another select committee be formed to consider the state of gold and silver coinage and also to inquire into the expediency of extending legal-tender status to certain foreign silver coins. As expected, White chaired this committee composed of three other Jacksonians and two anti-Jacksonians. One of the Jackson men was Henry Horn of Philadelphia, who could be counted on to be an advocate for the Mint.[2]

On March 17, 1832, White took the offensive, submitting the written report of the committee and two separate bills to be considered by the House in a Committee of the Whole. The report made it clear that White was speaking for the Jackson administration, espousing the displacement of paper currency by hard currency through reform of the gold-to-silver ratio and returning to that old elixir of foreign coins as legal tender.

Behind the scenes, a confrontation was building over the rechartering of the Bank of the United States. The charter of the Second Bank of the United States was due to expire in 1836.

White dealt directly with the BUS issue in his report to the House. In two years, from 1830 to 1832, paper currency had expanded rapidly—from $38 million to $57 million. The majority of the newly issued paper notes came from a select few banks. In a nation with a population of 13 million people, this $18 million increase was unbelievable. To make matters worse, the Bank of the United States was the largest offender, having expanded the amount of paper currency it issued from $15 million to $25 million—an increase of 67 percent. The New York banks were the second-largest offenders, expanding the amount of their paper currency from $10 million to $14 million.

Competing factors were at work here. Nicholas Biddle had opened the loan spigots to curry favor in the looming battle with Andrew Jackson over rechartering. The New York banks, now in a winner-take-all competition for financial supremacy with Philadelphia, had responded in kind. The size and rapidity of the increase worried White. If unchecked, it would fuel excessive speculation, leading to another financial panic. To make matters worse, the banks had not increased their specie reserves in support of the increased paper-currency issues. Total reserves had actually dropped slightly. White put it another way in his report.

> The committee are convinced that the banks, during the last two years, have contributed greatly to inconsiderate overtrading, which has produced the present pecuniary distress and consequent depression of prices; injudicious discounts and loans have inflicted serious injury upon the circumstances of the borrowers and the facility thus given to an increase of notes has caused excessive issues, and great depreciation of the currency.
>
> . . . The committee cannot doubt, from the details exhibited of the excessive circulation of these important banks, that the currency has been suddenly, injudiciously, and injuriously degraded, to the prejudice of pending contracts, and to the subversion of the intrinsic value of the money unit, upon which the security and steady value of property essentially depend.[3]

White may not have had the word *inflation* in his vocabulary, but he certainly understood its pernicious effects. He went on to note that, had the United States been on a monetary system of hard specie during this period, the detrimental expansion fueled by paper currency would not have happened, as it nearly equaled the entire amount of gold and silver mined in the world during those two years.

Although White remained firmly committed to a silver standard, he had to admit that gold had a role to play, in spite of the inherent difficulties associated with fluctuating market values for the two metals relative to each other. He firmly believed that gold and silver would not remain in circulation unless bank notes from $1 to $10 were prohibited. Recognizing that the probability of obtaining this prohibition was unlikely, White had to acknowledge the role for gold. While silver was good for small transactions, in actuality it would displace little of the paper currency. Only the larger-denomination gold coins had a real chance to hold paper in check.

White mentioned only in passing extending legal-tender status to certain foreign silver coins. It was clear the committee had given this issue only a cursory examination. He justified taking this action as being consistent with the desire to limit the propagation of paper currency through increased circulating specie.[4]

In support of this report, White and his committee introduced two bills. The first pertained to the gold-to-silver ratio. It called for reducing the gold content of the eagle from 247.5 grains to 237.6 and thus raising the ratio to 15.625, unchanged from White's position in the preceding Congress. The composition of the silver coins would remain unchanged.[5] The second bill called for legal-tender status for the dollars from Mexico, Peru, Chile, Brazil, and Central America, and the French five-franc piece for a period of three years. These coins would only be valued by their intrinsic silver content.[6]

With the introduction of these bills, White had opened Pandora's box. Mischief was not long in coming. While limited by House scheduling constraints, the intense debate went on for four days. Richard Wilde of Augusta, Georgia, a man of nearly identical background to White's, argued that the committee's bill did not go far enough. With proximity to the southern gold fields, Wilde essentially spoke for the miners. It made no sense to go on coining this gold at the expense of the government only to have it immediately exported. American gold coinage was merely inspected for its value and then stamped for export. He offered a resolution, instructing the Select Committee on Coinage to make additional inquiries. Wilde was laying the groundwork for a higher gold-to-silver ratio.

Wilde wanted to impose a stamp duty on bank bills of small denominations to restrict or eliminate small-denomination currency in favor of specie. It would also protect the uneducated from losses by fraud or the forgery of banknotes. In addition, the Georgian complained about the delay at the Mint for individuals wishing to convert their bullion to coin. The interest associated with an average delay of 40 days was basically a seigniorage of 0.5 percent. He reminded congressmen that when bullion was brought to the Mint, a certificate to the bearer was issued based upon the assayed results that could be cashed at area banks at a discount of that same 0.5 percent.[7]

On the second day, Wilde modified his stance. His resolution now would ask the committee to inquire as to the actions necessary to make prompt payment to the depositors in exchange for a seigniorage not exceeding the expense of coining; consider imposing a duty on bank bills of small denominations; and restrict legal tender so that gold coins would be lawful for large transactions and silver coins for small payments.[8] No debate followed.

On March 22 there was pushback on the measure to tax small-denomination paper currency. Wilde would only agree to modify his resolution by prohibiting notes of less than $5 in payments of debts due the United States. There followed a long discussion of the gold-to-silver ratio. No new ground was plowed but there was substantial support for a higher ratio. The value of an eagle ought to pass at a rate above its bullion content, equal to the expense of coinage but not more than 16 to 1.[9]

Again there was resistance to the tax on small-denomination paper currency. Now the issue of states' rights was invoked in response to the tax. One wise soul noted that the United States could never retain its specie, no matter the legislative restrictions created, without maintaining a positive trade balance. Wilde lost the floor with his resolution in limbo.[10] He would have to lobby his colleagues for a second opportunity.

Throughout this debate, White had remained silent. He had made a tactical mistake in assuming what had been supported in the House in the previous Congress would still be supported in this Congress. His decision to emphasize the state of American paper currency in justifying a change in the valuation ratio had stirred up a hornet's nest. Debate on a tax or outright ban of small-denomination paper currency had turned emotional with the invoking of states' rights. White had to rapidly change course.

He opened correspondence with Samuel Moore. He wanted to know what proportion of alloy might be incorporated into the dimes and half dimes without lessening their durability in circulation. He was thinking of a substantial debasement of these coins in terms of silver content to ensure their presence in circulation. In addition, he was of the opinion that the French practice of using nine-tenths gold or silver and one-tenth base metal should be adopted. He asked Moore the cost of coinage as a percentage for each denomination. Also he wanted to know what charge per ounce of bullion would be sufficient to defray the expense of melting, assaying, and stamping the weight and fineness upon ingots of silver and gold. Clearly White, hearing the tenor of the debate over Wilde's resolution of inquiry, was taking aim at the two entrenched Hamiltonian principles of intrinsic value and free coinage. He was also toying with authorizing ingots in place of coinage to avoid adjusting the ratio for gold.[11]

Wilde reentered the picture at the end of April having quietly gained support for some form of his resolution in the interim. He again called for the Select Committee on Coins to consider prompt payment to bullion depositors in exchange for a seigniorage charge, and making gold legal tender for large payments and silver for small payments. He modified his call to tax small-denomination paper currency and now only wanted an investigation. The chairman of the Ways and Means Committee then called for an amendment, asking that the committee inquire into making silver the only legal tender and into issuing gold coins at fixed weights and pureness, whose values would be fixed from time to time. These gold coins would be receivable in payments of all debts to the United States but would not otherwise be legal tender. Here was White's idea in practice: to avoid the difficulty of fixing a specific value ratio between the two metals.[12] With this amendment, Wilde's resolution passed and White's committee was back to square one.

Moore's response to White on May 4 was subjective. Costs as a percent for coinage ran from a low of 1.25 percent for half dollars to more than 3 percent for half dimes. The numbers were dependent upon quantities struck with these percentages based upon current volumes. The costs per ounce for bars and ingots were uncertain. Moore had no real experience with varying the proportion of alloy on the smaller coins; nor did he have an opinion on adopting the French practice of using one-tenth alloy in the coins.[13] While Moore's response gave White some direction, it was not enough. White came to Moore a second time for his opinions on the issues bedeviling the Select Committee on Coins.

On May 25, 1832, Moore formally responded with a detailed study. He threw out several options in regard to the valuation ratio. He worked from the standard gold weight of 270 grains for an eagle. He wanted to avoid the operational headaches associated with the fractional grains that were appearing in all the proposed changes. If the eagle were set at 260 grains, no gold coin issued would suffer a fractional grain in its weight. Using the current alloy of one-twelfth would back into a fine gold content of 238.33 grains and a gold-to-silver ratio of 15.577. The Mint director then went a step further. Holding the standard weight of an eagle at 260 grains, he proposed increasing the alloy to one-tenth, leaving the fine gold content at 234 grains with a ratio of 15.865. Moore viewed the valuation as an experiment to be tried and judged, before setting a more permanent ratio that would be incorporated into a revised set of Mint regulations in the next Congress.

That said, Moore diplomatically opined that he did not think that the gold-to-silver ratio proposed by the committee was capable of disturbing American currency. He expanded, saying that he agreed that there should be one practical standard of value, and for this purpose silver was most fit in the United States. Therefore it was highly important that the ratio not be set so high as to displace undervalued silver from the currency when the state of foreign exchange required specie exports. Moore was hardly supportive of gold; it should play only an auxiliary role, as Americans denominated their currency in single dollar coins, not in eagles.

Moore was adamant that foreign coins should be entirely eliminated from American currency. It should be done over two years, starting with the smallest fractional Spanish coins and ending with the largest 24 months later. There would be expense to the government for those coins worn to the point that their intrinsic value was below their legal-tender value. Moore wanted no more foreign coins as substitutes for Mint production. If the committee felt foreign coins were necessary to maintain an adequate supply of specie in circulation, they should not be made legal tender at a rate that would forbid their coming to the Mint without loss. Moore did not want a windfall benefiting the bullion brokers.

The Mint director also supported seigniorage for two reasons. First, it would defray the costs of operating the Mint. Second, by reducing the silver and gold composition, the impacted coins would be more likely to be retained in the country instead of being exported.

The mechanics of this seigniorage mirrored the system in place at the British Royal Mint. Moore also noted that this seigniorage could be taken from the coin's weight, its fineness, or a combination of both. Moore expected that this seigniorage would have the beneficial side effect of expelling foreign specie of higher fineness. However, at some point American specie would have to follow to settle unfavorable trade balances that were the true cause of specie shortages in the United States. The Mint director then qualified his argument for seigniorage, saying it only applied to the subsidiary silver coins; applying it to a dollar coin would create some distrust in the international markets.

In the area of prompt payment for deposits, the Mint director noted that the banks had provided the largest share of deposits and had been ill inclined to suffer the 0.5-percent prompt-payment charge. For some years, delays in payment had averaged 40 to 50 days. With the new Mint coming into service, this delay should shorten appreciably. Moore estimated that requiring prompt payment at the 0.5-percent discount at the Mint would require a bullion fund of $150,000 to $200,000. However, the expense associated with a 0.5-percent discount in combination with a seigniorage charge would likely discourage depositors.[14]

White next made an unusual move. On June 30, 1832, with just 10 days until the adjournment of the first session of this Congress, he introduced a new coinage reform bill. This bill had virtually no chance of being considered. Some of it came straight from Samuel Moore's report and some of it certainly did not. In either case it was a radical departure from existing practices at the Mint. The depositor would pay a charge not to exceed $1 for every 100 ounces of bullion for melting and assaying. Prompt payment for deposits was to be provided at a discount of 0.5 percent. The secretary of the Treasury would be required to maintain on hand at the Bank of the United States or to have in the course of manufacture at the Mint $100,000 in coin to facilitate this requirement—much less than what Moore thought prudent. These proposals were straightforward and simple enough.

Next came the game changer. The weight and fineness of the eagle and dollar coins would remain unchanged. However, the $5 gold piece would be reduced to 112.5 grains of pure gold, a reduction of 10 percent from its existing content. The quarter eagle would be discontinued and replaced with $2 and $3 gold pieces with gold contents prorated from the $5 coin. Using a gold-to-silver ratio of 16 to 1, half dollars would contain 180 grains of pure silver with appropriate adjustments for the quarter, dime, and half dime. White based these numbers on a valuation of gold at four cents per grain and silver at four grains for one cent. The implied seigniorage on silver coins was 3.13 percent.

The bill would require that all gold and silver coins subsidiary to the eagle and dollar exhibit on their obverse their value and on their reverse their weight in grains. Subsidiary gold coins would be legal tender in amounts not exceeding $10 with an exception for the purchase of public lands to the amount of $200. Subsidiary silver coins would be limited in tender to $5.

Silver coins minted before the effective date of the changeover would be valued at a rate of $1.156 per ounce. No foreign coins would be legal tender for sums less than $100. That restriction was intended to curtail their use to large transactions, typically between banks. Practically, individuals would ignore this provision.

That the eagle and dollar coins remained unchanged from their existing weights made no difference since they weren't minted. However, if enacted, this law guaranteed that eagles would not circulate. Being undervalued and having no seigniorage, they would be held by banks and brokers to satisfy trade-balance requirements. On the other hand, the dollar coin, with slightly less silver than its South American and Mexican counterparts, had a better chance of passing in domestic commerce. The introduction of $2 and $3 gold pieces was aimed directly at expelling small-denomination paper currency and recognized that the quarter eagle, at a face value of $2.50, was an oddity. The bill was flawed in that it did not specify a redemption value for previously minted gold coins; nor did it specify which foreign silver coins were to be legal tender.[15]

The entire bill was destined for the graveyard at this late date in the session. Mint reform had been a sideshow to the raging battle between Henry Clay and Andrew Jackson over the Bank of the United States. No one would focus on specie reform while the fate of the Bank dangled in the wind.

• • • •

In his first message to Congress in December 1829, President Jackson had vaguely called for modifications to the charter of the Bank of the United States that would expire in 1836 in order to establish a sound and uniform currency. Now, two years later, Jackson called for BUS stock to be sold to the public and again for the charter to be modified. Henry Clay, with his party's nomination for the presidency secure, saw this issue as an opportunity to score points against Jackson. He convinced Nicholas Biddle that it was an appropriate time to request a new charter. Clay assured him that the request would pass both houses of Congress. Jackson dared not veto it; Clay would see that the veto was overridden. Clay sealed the deal by reminding Biddle that if he delayed and Clay lost the election, rechartering would only be more difficult in a second Jackson term.

As Clay was the strongest supporter of the Bank, Biddle had no choice. In January 1832, Biddle petitioned Congress for the early rechartering. As an enticement to draw support, the legislation modified the bank's charter by placing limits on its ability to hold real estate and establish new branches. The president would gain the power to appoint one director at each branch and Congress could act to restrict the issue of small bank notes.

An infuriated Jackson saw through this move by his hated political enemy, Clay, and vowed to destroy the bank. Daniel Webster handled floor management in the Senate of the recharter that passed in May. The recharter passed the House on July 3. A week later, Jackson vetoed the bill. An override attempt failed on July 13.[16] As both houses adjourned on July 16, 1832, Campbell White had to know that currency reform had just assumed a much larger importance to Andrew Jackson and his supporters.

• • • •

White held silent as the second session of the Twenty-Second Congress opened in December 1832. There was no support for the resurrection of the bill he had introduced the preceding June. Instead it seemed as if the House of Representatives wanted to restart the whole process. On December 14 the House passed a resolution calling for the Mint director to report on the relative values of gold and silver. In an added twist they also asked for an assessment of the degree of fineness and proportion of alloy best suited in gold coins to give durability without sacrificing the brightness of the metal.[17] Poor Samuel Moore was spinning his wheels writing reports to the House.

Moore provided detailed tables showing the ratio of value for gold and silver from 1821 to 1832. At the current American ratio of 15 to 1, gold coins valued at their bullion content were being exported occasionally to France but far more frequently to England. Moore observed that gold coins often remained in the vaults of the Mint unclaimed by depositors until the day of departure of one of the mail packets for Liverpool. Moore believed that on the whole, the relative value of gold and silver in Europe as it impacted the United States should be determined by the market rates of England and France. That equivalent market ratio in the United States was 15.65. Surely this was the last word on the valuation ratio.

The question of gold alloy and durability was much more in Moore's field of expertise. Pure gold was too soft to serve as a satisfactory material for coinage. The American experience of adding one-twelfth-part alloy composed of equal parts of copper and silver had provided a satisfactory remedy to pure gold's inherent softness, yielding a durable coin for circulating purposes.

Furthermore, gold never occurred naturally in its pure state, coming most generally with traces of copper and or silver. The expense of removing all of the silver was prohibitive with the Mint's separation process, making it more cost effective to retain a last portion as part of the alloy. Moore did note that copper was far more economical as an alloy, although its proportion to silver in the mix would impact the complexion of the gold coin.

Moore provided the committee with six quarter eagles for inspection. The first quarter eagle reflected existing practice at the Mint; the second example used only silver as the alloy; the third example contained an equal mix of copper and silver; the fourth used only copper as the alloy. Finally, the last two samples were Moore's attempt to point the congressmen where he wanted them to go. The pure gold was adjusted in both examples consistent with a gold-to-silver ratio of 15.625 with the alloy increased to one part in ten. The fifth sample contained equal proportions of copper and silver in the alloy. The last sample adjusted the alloy, using two parts copper to one part silver.

The Mint director dismissed the specimens with alloys that were either all silver or all copper. They were less attractive, exhibiting complexions respectively that were either too pale or too dark. The examples that contained an alloy of equal parts silver and copper looked more like fine gold, with the last sample with the greater mix of copper being only slightly impaired in comparison. He observed that an equal mix of the two metals in alloy, with that alloy being either one part in twelve or one part in ten, gave the best appearance. The refining department's capabilities for removing silver from raw gold were well within this requirement. The sixth example, using two parts copper, probably represented the upper limit for copper in the alloy while still minting an attractive coin.[18]

Nothing happened. From December 1832 to May 1833, the nation was preoccupied with the nullification crisis in South Carolina, triggered by a tariff act deemed unfair to the agricultural South. Monetary reform paled in comparison to South Carolina's threatened claim that a state had the right to nullify federal laws. The nation and Congress were in gridlock until President Jackson found a way to force South Carolina back into the fold.

With the second session of the Twenty-Second Congress in its final days, White knew he must start over once again. He moved that the director of the Mint communicate to the House at the commencement of the Twenty-Third Congress such amendments to the existing laws governing and regulating the Mint that he deemed necessary to the efficiency of the institution.[19]

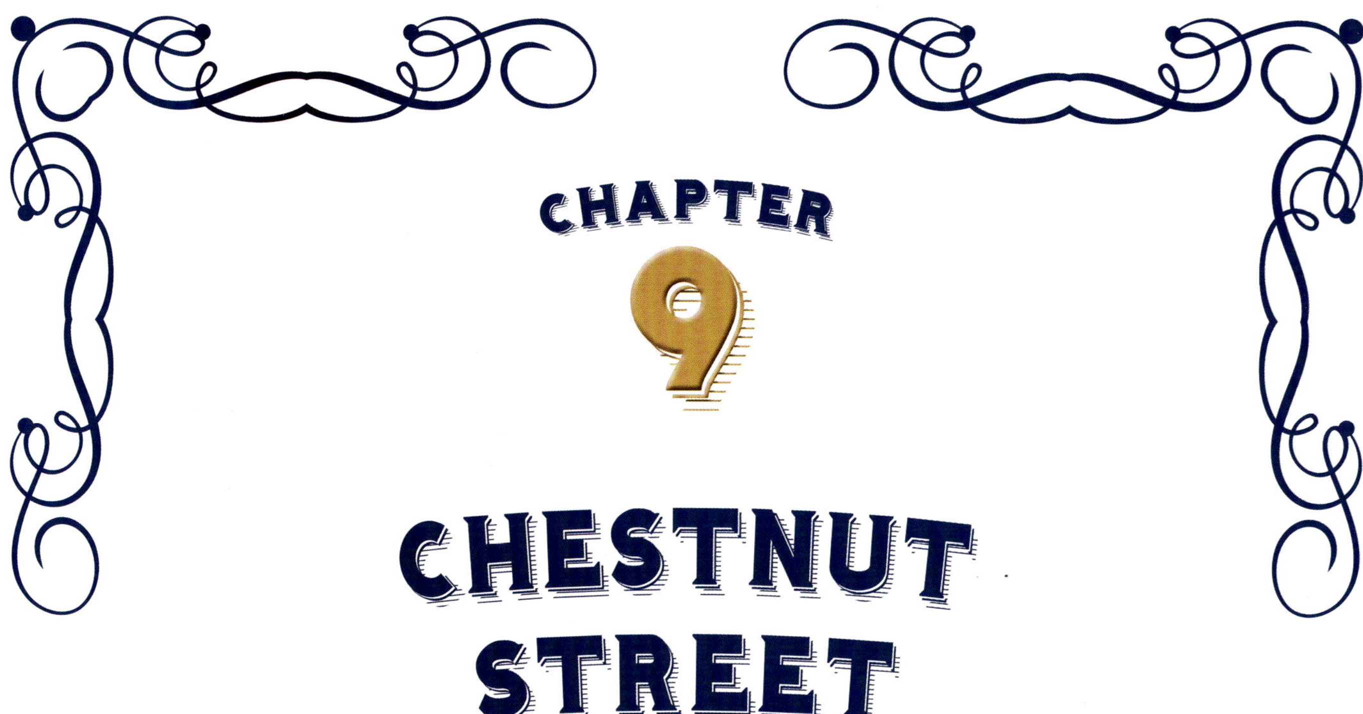

CHAPTER 9

CHESTNUT STREET

Chestnut Street runs west, from the docks of the Delaware River through the heart of Philadelphia. In 1833 it was home to the Second Bank of the United States and other large local banking institutions. This street lay at the center of the most densely populated, highest-rent district of the city. But it was no longer the street that Elias Boudinot had once walked. Much of the luster had faded.

To be sure, there was more to Chestnut Street than the banks. The American Philosophical Society still called the meeting hall just off Chestnut at Independence Square home.[1] For a time they had even rented out part of the building to house Charles Willson Peale's natural history museum. With Thomas Jefferson serving as president of its board of visitors, Peale's establishment had been the closest thing to a national museum in the United States. However, Peale had died in 1827 without achieving his dream of government sponsorship for his museum. This entity had since been managed by two of his sons, Franklin and Titian Peale.

The fate of the street kept coming back to its banks. Competition from New York City had been growing throughout the 1820s. The city had had a larger population than Philadelphia for some time, but that was not the driving factor—the Erie Canal had made the big difference. Agricultural products from the American West and upstate New York now flowed easily through the city's docks for export to Europe. To make matters worse, Phil-

Fig. 28. Andrew Jackson, painted by Thomas Sully (1845). This image would be used on the $20 bill.

adelphia was at a disadvantage geographically. Its access to the Atlantic Ocean was the Delaware River, which regularly froze over during the winter. In addition, it was separated from western Pennsylvania by the Allegheny Mountains that no canal had yet been able to breach. To the south, Baltimore captured the maritime-trade business. As a result, New York banks were threatening Philadelphia's financial dominance.

Not surprisingly, the nation's leading financiers up to this point had haled from Chestnut Street. Stephen Girard, a French immigrant, had thrived in this financial center. When Congress failed to recharter the First Bank of the United States in 1811, Girard purchased its assets. When the young country was on the verge of insolvency in 1814, Girard was one of the primary people who floated the bonds that allowed the United States to keep fighting Great Britain. In 1816 Girard converted those bonds into stock of the Second Bank of the United States. No one lives forever and Girard died of complications from a carriage accident on December 26, 1831. Perhaps it was only coincidence that Andrew Jackson (fig. 28) refrained from taking action against the BUS during his first two years in the presidency. Perhaps Henry Clay would have been successful regardless in persuading Nicholas Biddle to go for early rechartering. One thing was certain. Girard left the bulk of his fortune to charity, pulling this capital out of Philadelphia's financial markets at a time when competition with New York City was intense.

Jackson's destruction of the BUS was not a given when he captured the presidency. His secretary of the Treasury, Samuel Ingham, represented old-line Philadelphia through and through. Though a Jacksonian, he was a supporter of both the BUS and Vice President John Calhoun. When Jackson fell out with Calhoun and purged his cabinet in August 1831, Ingham lost his position. However, his replacement, Louis McLane from Delaware, was also a pro-BUS man. Even so, the political controversy surrounding the rechartering and subsequent veto in 1832 rendered McLane's support moot.

In May 1833, Jackson shuffled his cabinet again. During this change, McLane was promoted to the position of secretary of state. That summer, following the failed recharter effort, Jackson remained undecided as to whether or not he should leave federal deposits with the BUS or pull

Fig. 29. William Duane did not last long as Andrew Jackson's secretary of the Treasury when he refused to do the president's bidding regarding the Second Bank of the United States.

them for placement in state banks controlled largely by political supporters. McLane's successor, William Duane (fig. 29), another Philadelphian, had supported Jackson's policies on the BUS.

In August, Jackson learned that the BUS and Biddle had spent $100,000 trying to defeat him in the election of 1832. That was enough for the president. In mid-September he ordered the federal deposits removed. Duane refused, claiming that Congress must be informed, and was cashiered. Jackson immediately turned to Roger Taney, who was only too willing to do the job. Deposits were removed, effective October 1, 1833.

The BUS fought Jackson that autumn, allowing the money supply to contract. Biddle called in debts and reduced loan activity, throwing the country into a mini-panic. The stage was now set for one last battle in 1834.

The citizens of Philadelphia understood all too well what would happen if the Second Bank of the United States lost its charter. Without the bank, Philadelphia would lose its financial preeminence. Processions from all parts of Philadelphia and the surrounding countryside converged on Independence Square on March 20, 1834. Shops and businesses closed along Chestnut Street. There were at least 4,000 people in attendance to protest the removal of deposits from the BUS. The makeup of the attendees was unique in that it included both merchants and traders of Chestnut Street and laborers and mechanics from the city and its environs.

William Duane's house overlooked Independence Square. As the processions passed by, Duane could be seen standing at his window. He bowed repeatedly to the crowd and dabbed his eyes with a handkerchief. Mrs. Duane appeared at the window as well but was soon overcome by emotion and turned away.

A rostrum had been erected on the south side of the Independence Square. The speakers there whipped up the crowd with vilifications of Andrew Jackson. They protested that the removal of deposits was an assumption of power on the president's part. It was an act of usurpation dictated by passion to gratify Jackson's vindictive feelings. The crowd blamed the subsequent loss of commerce on this unlawful act and called for restoration of the deposits. The speakers were fully certain that another bank would be established at the expiration of the current charter. Without mentioning a specific address, they made it clear that the next bank probably would be located in New York City.[2] Totally unspoken was what would happen to Mr. Biddle's Mint once the Bank of the United States ceased to exist. Men in the know had to wonder, despite the Mint's new edifice on Chestnut Street.

• • • •

For Samuel Moore it had been no easy journey building a new mint. The weather delays of 1831 had been compounded by a cholera epidemic on the Eastern Seaboard in 1832. The death count in Philadelphia that summer was high. Many residents fled from the city to the countryside. August proved to be the worst month, with more than a hundred cases a day reported, many deadly. Production at the Mint was greatly impacted during the third quarter and Moore's expected opening of the new facility at mid-year was pushed back yet again. It was not until the end of January 1833 that the machinery had been transferred, set up and placed into operation.[3]

• • • •

In spite of the construction delays, Moore's performance up to this point had been above reproach. Since 1829, Mint output had consisted of more than the customary half dollars for the banks. Excepting the period of 1832's cholera epidemic, half dime production had exceeded one million coins each year. Dimes were not far behind. Even quarters began to make a consistent appearance.

After a three-year hiatus, Moore had resumed quarter production in January 1831. On the 29th of that month, he sent $10 face value of the new coins to the secretary of the Treasury, Louis McLane. He noted that the quarter (fig. 30) conformed in proportion to the smaller diameters set by the use of close collars for the half dime, dime, and gold coins. He promised a similar "improvement" would soon be available for the larger coins. That was odd word-

Fig. 30. It had been three years since the Mint had last struck quarters when Director Moore rolled out his close-collar specimen of 1831. He took the liberty of dropping the motto E Pluribus Unum from the reverse. This forced the engraver, Kneass, to enlarge the eagle. He botched it. The bird's left wing was lengthened without attention to perspective. Kneass also did away with the tail feathers just above the eagle's right claw, which had been visible in the earlier version.

ing, given that the only larger coin then being struck was the half dollar. It was another tip-off that Samuel Moore was serious about restarting dollar coinage at the beginning of 1831.

Throughout all these conversions to close-collar striking, Moore had remained largely mum in communications with Treasury over the benefits. The changeover on the dime and half dime were hardly noticeable; the same could be said for the gold coins since they did not circulate. For the quarter, this would not be the case.

Moore took the opportunity to make a radical change in the coin's inscriptions as well. He dropped the motto "E Pluribus Unum" from the reverse above the eagle. The law did not authorize its use. Moore assumed that it had found its way upon America's coinage via the employment of the Great Seal. The Mint director considered this addition unfortunate and unfit for coins. Putting it on a scroll above the eagle depressed the position of the bird, which impaired the symmetry of the reverse design. If approved, Moore wanted it removed from the smaller half dime and dime as well. For the gold coins, he was vague, saying only that it would take time.[4]

Moore had his way with the changes. Jackson personally approved the removal of the motto and all liked the close-collar striking.[5] However, the approval of the motto's removal was not a complete endorsement. It remained on the other coinage.

• • • •

Once the relocation of the machinery was completed, Moore could be proud of his accomplishment. The new building fit well with its financial companions on Chestnut Street. Using large, Ionic porticos in the front and rear, coupled with an interior court, Strickland had based the design on a celebrated Greek temple (fig. 31).

While a bright shining star from the exterior, Moore had a problem hidden inside. Not much had changed from the old mint in terms of equipment. To be sure, there was a new steam engine. However, that had come with a supplemental appropriation of $17,500 in May 1832.[6] The coin presses still operated without steam power. Other processes were unchanged since their conversion to steam power at the former mint. In 1833 Moore was again faced with a second supplemental appropriation of $11,000 for "carpentry and machinery."[7] The old Mint property, now vacant, sold for $10,000. This gave Moore some extra money, but far from what he had originally envisioned when he queried Boulton for a complete equipment package. In total, the Mint would cost $198,500, far more than the original appropriation of $120,000.[8]

Recognizing his problem early on, Moore's solution was unique. He gained approval for an assistant assayer with the stated purpose to send him to Europe to investigate and report on the latest, state-of-the-art minting technology. Moore wanted specific details on the newest process for separating gold and silver. Hopefully, this individual would also return with observations and drawings that could be converted into the new machinery needed to increase the Mint's capacity.

Moore consulted with his brother-in-law, Robert Maskell Patterson. One of Patterson's closest friends was Franklin Peale. The Patterson and Peale families had been friends since the Revolutionary War. Patterson knew that Franklin was mechanically gifted and recommended him for the job.[9] Patterson even served as the go-between in negotiating the terms of Peale's employment. Moore wanted Peale to improve his French prior to leaving for Europe. He told Patterson that he could pay Peale $800 to $1,000, plus expenses, but certainly no more.[10] The deal was generous, all the more so when Peale began submitting his expenses. Franklin Peale took the job and departed for Europe in May 1831.

• • • •

Moore had one problem that seemingly could not wait until Peale's return. Gold from the Southern fields was coming in to the Mint in greater quantities and from a wider area, including South Carolina, Virginia, Tennessee, and Alabama. The Mint received $520,000 in 1831, fueled by the expanding production in Georgia. In 1832 the number jumped to $678,000, and in 1833, it jumped again to $868,000. Moore knew that the Mint was not seeing even half of the gold mined in the region. He attributed some truth to the remark that an estimated $1.5 million had been produced in the region in 1833. That would be about one-fifth of all the gold produced from all other sources in Europe and the Americas.[11] If this gold suddenly showed up on his doorstep, Moore knew he could not refine it, even in its largely pure state.

The Mint's refining process had remained unchanged since Joseph Cloud took the melter refiner position in

Fig. 31. The second U.S. Mint, placed in service in 1835, graced Philadelphia's financial district on Chestnut Street.

1797. The method of refining gold was to melt the raw bullion with three times its weight of silver, run it through a cold-water bath to granulate, and then separate the two metals using strong nitric acid.[12] By any measure it was a cumbersome and extremely time-consuming process. It was also highly counterproductive in that it tied up a large amount of silver to process any increased flow of raw gold that could otherwise be coined. That was an unacceptable trade off.

Moore needed to take action. The Mint director was aware that there was a more efficient process that substituted sulfuric acid for nitric acid. Anticipating the results of Peale's investigation, he included $7,000 in seed money to acquire rights to this new process in his Mint appropriation. He went a step further, explaining to Secretary of the Treasury Roger Taney in person its critical nature and lobbying C.P. White for support in the House. In spite of this effort, the House cut it. Moore did everything but say that he believed that Roger Taney had not pushed hard enough to keep the appropriation in the budget.[13] He would just have to hitch up his pants and hope.

• • • •

For the first 10 years of his time as director, Moore's performance had been beyond criticism. He could only be faulted in his tendency toward allowing nepotism to influence his decisions about the Mint's staff. In April 1832, Jacob Eckfeldt, Adam Eckfeldt's son, was appointed assayer. Adam Eckfeldt now essentially had control of three departments, if one considered that the engraver, Kneass, owed his position to the chief coiner. Moore also appointed his wife's nephew, William DuBois, as his clerk in September 1833.[14] The Mint was beginning to look like a family affair for the Eckfeldt's and Patterson's.

1849

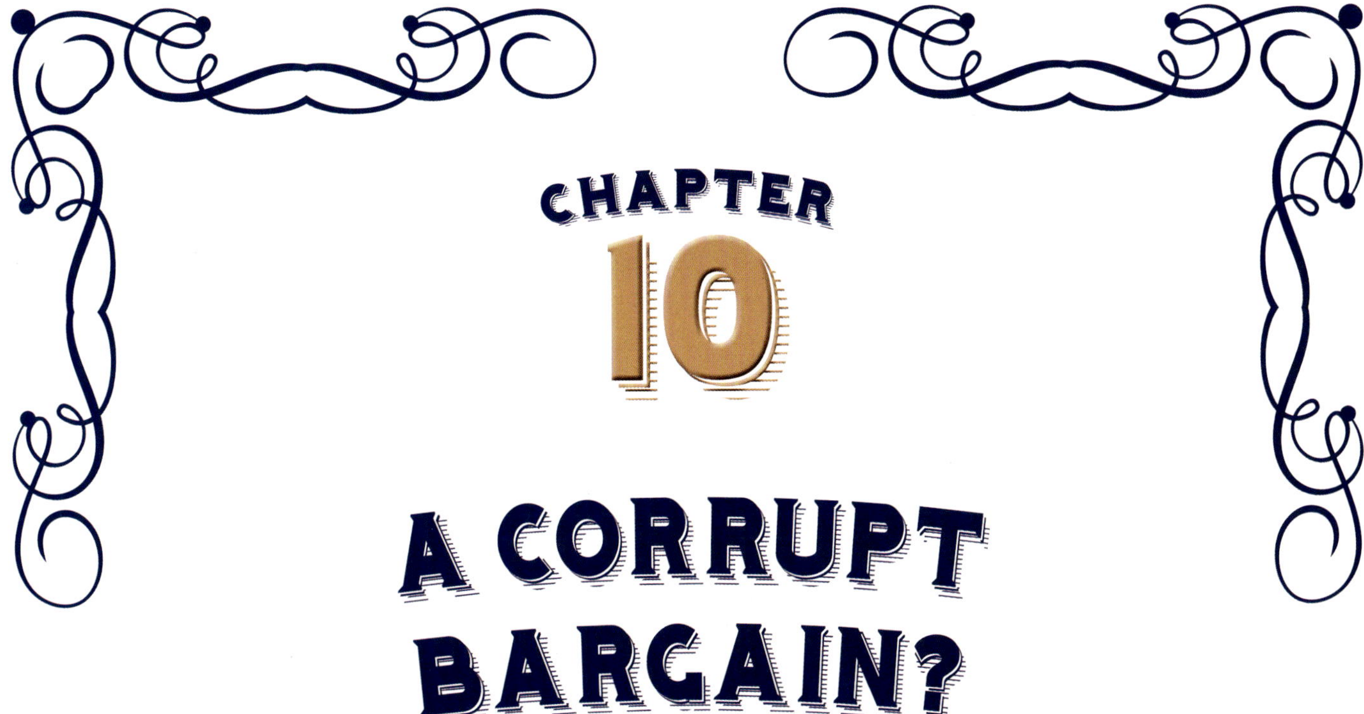

CHAPTER 10

A CORRUPT BARGAIN?

Samuel Moore was prompt in submitting his mandated congressional report at the beginning of the first session of the Twenty-Third Congress in December 1833. As he penned this document in draft form, he must have wondered if the effort would be futile once again. For his clerk, William DuBois, it was a completely different issue. Moore's handwriting was almost indecipherable.

No guidance on proposed changes to Mint regulations could be expected from the Treasury Department. For a year now, the secretary of the Treasury position had been a revolving door. Nevertheless, Moore did not shy from the task.

The Mint director was standing firm in support of a gold-to-silver ratio of 15.625 to 1, as recommended by former secretary Ingham in 1830. Silver, not gold, was the main currency of the United States. He did not want to fall into the trap of overvaluing gold, optimistically conjecturing that the continued development of the Southern gold fields very likely would restrain the increase in the valuation ratio. No limit had yet been assigned to the ultimate extent of this field.

Moore summed up the issue by saying that silver should remain the basis of American currency and the controlling standard of value. Gold also had a role to play and should be a legal tender for all amounts. However, it should be gold that was exported to settle trade balances, leaving silver to circulate in everyday commerce.

The Mint director did not want to change the fine silver content of the dollar in implementing a change in the ratio. However, he wanted 264 grains of standard gold in the eagle coin, of which 237.6 grains would be fine gold and 26.4 grains, or one-tenth of the coin's weight, would be alloy. Moore argued that it more nearly approximated the fineness of gold bullion delivered to the Mint. Relying upon the work he did for the previous Congress, Moore believed the proportion of silver should not exceed that of copper in the alloy.

Moore wanted the alloy changed to one-tenth on silver coins as well. The resulting standard silver would then, like gold, more closely conform to raw bullion. That meant the weight of the dollar would be decreased from 416 grains to 412.5 grains. This would adjust U.S. Mint practices to harmonize with those in Europe. It would also greatly facilitate weighing in decimals instead of fractions at the Mint.

Moore supported prompt payment of depositors at a charge of 0.5 percent and rescinding the option to decline this arrangement by receiving payment at the point of coinage. Moore feared continuing the policy of free coinage, if associated with prompt payment, because it would subject the Mint to those depositors who merely wanted their bullion in a more commercially convenient form. On the other hand, a higher charge might restrict the bullion being presented for coinage.

The Mint director believed the charges in place for refining metals too base for coinage and rendering ductile that which was too brittle were adequate. However, he wanted a separate charge for assaying. While not required, the Mint for all practical purposes did not turn away small depositors in spite of the inconvenience. On deposits under a specific weight limitation, Moore wanted the ability to charge for assaying and preliminary melting. In this manner, the fee would encourage small depositors to comingle their deposits. While the regulation would encourage the use of brokers, it would gain economies of scale for the Mint.

Next Moore addressed the lack of small circulating silver coins. To correct this situation, Moore recommended limiting the legal tender of all silver coins subordinate to the half dollar to $10, the face amount of the largest gold coin, to prevent their exportation.

To accelerate the distribution of small silver, Moore wanted legal-tender status for fractional Spanish coins to be rescinded in stages; July 4, 1836, for sixteenths and eighths of a real and July 4, 1838, for quarter and half reales. Moore was willing to grant legal-tender status to Mexican dollars and other like silver coins as a temporary measure, capped at five years. Treating them as equivalent to an American dollar even though their intrinsic value was slightly higher would ensure that they were used first to satisfy trade balances. Moore was silent on the profit that would accrue to the brokers and bankers should this proposal become law. The Mint director did caution that assays of these coins indicated wide and unacceptable fluctuations in their silver content, making it expedient to limit the value of their legal tender.

In Moore's opinion, the existing coins of the higher fine gold content should be left in circulation to fulfill the needs of jewelers or be sent abroad for payments. He just did not want to have to deal with a recall.

In closing, Moore revisited the call for prompt payment. Based on current and planned mining operations in the Southern gold fields, he expected that $2 million in gold coins would be issued per year from the Mint. He believed that this number had a good possibility of increasing further in future years. Given the expected volumes, Moore suggested that a limitation of $50,000 be placed as a maximum on any single deposit payable within a ten-day period. If there was no such limit placed, the capacity of the Mint must be increased to handle sudden surges in deposits or a large amount of public money must be held for payment to depositors in such peak periods.[1]

In principle, Campbell White endorsed Moore's report.[2] White chose to approach the issues this time in three separate bills. On January 29, 1834, he introduced legislation that would grant legal-tender status by weight for a period of three years to the dollars of Mexico, Peru, Chile, and Central America. It also extended this status to restamped dollars of Brazil and French five-franc pieces. To ensure these coins remained only in the banking system of the country and did not leak out into daily commerce, their legal-tender status would not apply to any debt less than $100.[3]

White began the real push for reforming legislation on February 19 with two bills. The first made certain foreign gold coins legal tender in the United States by weight without limit as to amount for three years.[4] Moore had not contemplated any foreign gold coins being legal tender.

For the second bill White pulled from the two versions that he had introduced in the Twenty-Second Congress, tempered by Moore's report. This bill called for the resumption of production of eagle and dollar coins at the Mint. It set the gold-to-silver ratio at 15.625 to 1 by reducing the fine gold content of the eagle to 237.6 grains. In conformance with Moore's recommendation, the alloy was set at 10 percent for both silver and gold coins.

White returned to his original concept of incorporating seigniorage by setting the fine gold and silver contents of the subsidiary coinage at a gold-to-silver ratio of 16 to 1. A $5 gold piece would contain 112.5 grains of fine gold and a half dollar would contain 180 grains of fine silver, with lesser denominations adjusted pro rata. On each of these subsidiary coins, the value would be shown on the obverse and the weight in grains on the reverse. To address debasing of the currency, legal tender of these subsidiary denominations was limited to $5. Gone was the concept of replacing the quarter eagle with $2 and $3 gold coins.

White recognized that no bank or broker would consent to have bullion coined into subsidiary denominations. Put another way, no depositor in his right mind would bring 237.6 grains of fine gold to the Mint and choose to receive two $5 gold pieces containing a combined 225 grains of fine gold, allowing the Mint to retain the difference as seigniorage. The same analogy held for silver bullion. The depositor would demand eagles and dollars. So White inserted a clause that instructed the secretary of the Treasury to furnish the money required to enable the Mint to supply the public with the subsidiary gold and silver coins. He was instructing the Treasury Department to acquire bullion at market for the Mint but allowing the Mint to profit from the resulting seigniorage on the subsidiary coins as an offset to operating expenses.

White followed Moore's advice on the recall of the existing coinage. The Mint would cease striking coins of the higher silver and gold fineness on September 30, 1834. However, gold would be legal tender by weight.

White seconded Moore's concept of charging for the melting and assaying of gold deposited with an inherent penalty for smaller deposits. Thus the way would be clear for the Mint to produce gold ingots in place of coinage. The congressman was more aggressive on prompt pay provisions. The Mint must pay within five days, deducting from the amount of the deposit 0.5 percent on gold and 1 percent on silver bullion. White ignored Moore's plea for a bullion fund should coinage demands of Southern gold come in surges. The inference here was that ingot production would be used in the case of large bullion deposits.[5]

This well-crafted bill was read twice and landed upon the speaker's desk with a dull thud to await consideration in a Committee of the Whole House. And wait it did as February turned into March and March stretched into April. The last gasp of the Bank of the United States was playing out to the attention of all in a bitter Senate debate.

• • • •

Because money was tight due to Nicolas Biddle's actions at the BUS, interest rates had doubled over the autumn and winter to 12 percent. Presentations of memorials and petitions for and against rechartering the Bank were a daily occurrence in the Senate. Calhoun, Clay, and Webster, the Great Triumvirate, were united more in their opposition to Andrew Jackson than in support of the Bank. The result was they were not united in their efforts to save the Bank. Clay spent his political chips gaining an unprecedented censure of President Jackson for the removal of deposits from the Bank without consulting Congress. Calhoun meanwhile was focused solely upon his hatred of Jackson.

As chairman of the Senate Finance Committee, Daniel Webster had the better approach. After failing to pick off any Jackson supporters with a committee report that was critical of Jackson's handling of the Bank of the United States, Webster moved without the support of Clay and Calhoun for a compromise. He brought forth a bill that extended the Bank charter for six years before requiring a replacement bank in exchange for restoring the public funds to that institution. In a bow to Jackson's hard-money policy, Webster proposed prohibiting the Bank from issuing any paper currency in denominations less than $20. This was aimed at gaining the support of Thomas Hart Benton, the leading advocate for hard money in the Senate. However, without Clay and Calhoun, Webster was forced to withdraw the bill. The Bank of the United States was dead and a legislative logjam cleared.[6]

• • • •

As if White needed more problems, Senator Benton muddied the waters on March 29, 1834, calling for a joint committee from the two houses of Congress to be formed to consider a suitable gold-to-silver ratio.[7] If White did not know where Benton stood on this issue, the senator removed all doubt in a long speech on the Senate floor; he wanted a ratio of 16 to 1.[8] Benton spoke for Andrew Jackson. White gained breathing room on April 9 when the Senate tabled Benton's motion.[9]

The first of White's bills to come up for consideration was the reinstatement of legal-tender status for foreign silver coins. The bill as drafted cleared the Committee of the Whole on May 2, 1834, and appeared to be heading for smooth sailing. It was not to be. When the bill came up for passage, Benjamin Gorham, an anti-Jackson man from Massachusetts, called for an amendment permitting foreign silver coins to be accepted by tale rather than by weight. The vote was 86 in favor and 82, including White, against. South American dollars would be accepted at a value of $1 and French five-francs at a value of 93 cents.[10] Also the three-year limitation of legal-tender status was removed.[11] The curse of circulating foreign silver was back and Campbell White's monetary reforms at the Mint were in trouble.

With the first session of this Congress set to end on June 30, White pushed successfully to have the Committee of the Whole finally take up the Mint reform bill on June 14. This legislation had sat on the speaker's desk for almost four months. With the recess looming, White was desperate to force a decision on the bill. Horace Binney, an anti-Jackson member from Philadelphia and a director of the Bank of the United States, took the floor. He approved the provision that fixed the relative value of gold to silver at 15.625 to 1 for the eagle and dollar. However, he could not support debasing the subsidiary coins. He invoked the name of Albert Gallatin, which still carried weight in Washington, in declaring debasement of the currency a bad thing. He noted that Moore was against debasement. White argued that limiting legal tender on these coins adequately addressed the fear of debasing the currency. He also reminded Binney that it would offset some of the cost of operating the Mint. Dudley Selden from New York City, a Jacksonian with White, agreed with Binney but wanted to see the bill carried into the House for debate.[12] Then Seaborn Jones of Georgia gave notice that he intended to amend the bill when it next came up for consideration. With this brief discussion, the bill was laid aside. Both sides of the political spectrum were against debasing the subsidiary coinage using the ratio of 16 to 1. Binney spoke for the Mint. Selden had served on the Select Committee on Coins with White. This bill was dead on all accounts and time was running out.

White had watched the country in the first four years of the decade go through the financial gyrations of unchecked currency expansion and boom times followed by the politically inspired currency contraction and resulting recession. In fact Biddle was still holding firm to this policy but, with pressure mounting from the business community, would soon relent. Without some kind of bill that placed gold back into the financial picture, the Jackson "pet" state banks, fueled by federal government deposits that had been removed from the BUS, would most likely start another round of paper-currency expansion, launching the United States yet again into a boom-bust cycle. No silver would ever check the issue of small-denomination paper currency, the worst offender. Only gold, and lots of it, had that chance. White had to do something radical to gain passage and time was against him.

White sat down with Seaborn Jones and the two men talked openly and freely. Jones told White that he intended to amend White's bill to raise the ratio to 16 to 1. Jones was well versed on the subject of gold-to-silver ratios worldwide. He emphasized that the ratio of 15.625 to 1 was too far below market. As the two men talked, Jones, echoing Benton's speech, made his point that adopting 16 to 1 was consistent with the other nations of the Western hemisphere. It would be a middle course, the course of prudence as well as safety. Jones acknowledged that silver would indeed become scarce if the value of gold was set too high. On the other hand, if the values of gold and silver were set equal to the market, gold would be selected for exportation because of the lesser transportation expense. The Mint must value gold a little more than silver to secure an equal circulation of both metals. Jones assured White that using a 16 to 1 ratio was not so great a difference as to produce a flight of silver.

White now had a dilemma. All the time he sat talking with Jones, there was a gorilla in the arena carrying a big club. Benton had signaled what Jackson wanted. White's bank was one of Jackson's "pets." Would White cave to the administration?

On Saturday, June 21, with just seven working days until the end of the first session, White gained the floor to take up his bill by obtaining the required majority of two to one. It was the first sign of support for White during the whole session. Something was up.

White immediately moved to amend his bill. The fine gold content of the eagle coin would be reduced to 232 grains of pure gold. The smaller-denomination gold coins would be reduced accordingly. A $1 gold coin was authorized. The effective date of the legislation would be July 31, 1834. White had just thrown all of his previous efforts to the wind. In effect he was calling for a gold-to-silver ratio of 16 to 1 and nothing more. It was no longer a Mint reform bill but was simply dubbed the gold-coin bill in the press. By including a gold dollar, he was hoping to check the issuance of paper dollars. White gave a justification for his actions but it was lost in the uproar he had caused.

Selden objected strenuously to White's amended bill. Its practical effect would be nothing short of banishing existing silver coins from the country. He immediately moved to amend White's amended bill returning the ratio to 15.625 to 1.

William Clowney of South Carolina spoke for the radical element within the Southern representatives. He was in support of 16 to 1 and this amended bill removed his objections. He was for sound currency to furnish a medium of exchange when the Bank of the United States ceased to exist in 1836. There was great evil in the disproportion of paper currency compared to specie. The first step to establishing sound currency was to reform the coinage of gold. White's strategy was now clear. By raising the ratio to 16 to 1, he gained the support of the South.

Selden stirred up a hornet's nest telling the chamber that he considered this increase in the valuation ratio a tariff on gold. Emotions from the Southern contingent rose. Feelings were still raw over the last round of tariff compromises, which the South generally viewed as favorable to manufacturing interests in the North and highly unfair to agricultural interests in the South. Jones emotionally stated that he saw the higher ratio in favor of the South as but a poor pittance to purchase the South and its support of tariffs.

Gorham deplored the introduction of gold dollars in this amended bill. They would easily "escape" from the pocket. They would never supersede the use of small bank bills because of their inconvenience. He too believed that this proposal made gold too cheap and that the country would have no silver as a result.

Finally Horace Binney weighed in. He noted that White, without any notice, had abandoned his whole bill, subsidiary currency and all, to come out with a simple call for making the gold-to-silver ratio 16 to 1. He took this action in spite of the final opinion of his committee that 15.625 was the utmost limit to which the value could be raised. Had this occurred at an earlier stage in the session, Binney would have moved to have the whole subject recommitted. The Philadelphia congressman did not agree that any change in the valuation ratio would materially increase specie circulation in the country. Gold, however valued, would not to any extent take the place of bank paper while bank paper was permitted by law to circulate as it did now. Gold would instead displace silver. No change in the valuation would produce any considerable increase of specie in the banks. Nothing would induce the banks nor could anything compel them to keep more of either metal on hand than was necessary to sustain paper circulation. He flatly stated that it was a delusion that this bill would give a specie currency to the country; neither would it give increased stability to bank paper. Binney had just delivered the newly forming opposition Whig party's response to the bill.[13]

The vote was not even close: 145 in favor to 36 in opposition. A loose confederation of Whigs, anti-Jacksonians, and reactionary anti-Masons voted against the measure. Two Democrats joined them, one from Missouri and Dudley Selden.[14]

White's other bill, making certain foreign gold coins legal tender, now came up for consideration. White moved to amend it, bringing values for coins from specific countries into conformance with a 16 to 1 ratio. He also eliminated the three-year time limitation on legal-tender status. It was routinely approved.[15]

As had been predicted in the House debate, these bills faced little dissent in the Senate. Benton would overwhelm any organized opposition. Furthermore, Henry Clay was not opposed to this legislation; he was familiar with the issues involved. Nathan Sanford had been his vice-presidential running mate in 1824. In fact the short time remaining in this session of Congress now worked in favor of this legislation. On June 28, two days before the recess, Webster brought up the gold-coin bill. Without explanation, he moved to strike the authorization for a dollar gold piece. There was some griping that the ratio of 16 to 1 was too high.[16] However, that argument failed to gain traction in the debate. It was all over but the shouting. The House approved Webster's amendment and Jackson signed the legislation, effective that same day.[17]

• • • •

Dudley Selden resigned from the House in disgust on July 1, 1834.

Public reaction to the bill's passage was immediate. News commentary favorable to the Jackson administration was laced with ridiculous optimism. They somehow made it the fault of the Bank of the United States that gold had not circulated for a generation in the United States. This accusation gained traction when it became known that the BUS had over $1 million of foreign and domestic gold coins in its vaults.[18] Pro-Jackson newspapers went on to say that gold in the form of "Benton's gold lozenges" in defiance of bank power to issue paper currency would diffuse itself and spread throughout the country, becoming the familiar money of every industrious man's pocket.[19] One newspaper editor, drunk with enthusiasm, went so far as to predict that by the time the Bank charter expired in 1836 there would be more gold in circulation than the current circulation of BUS notes.[20] While the Mint might be able to coin that amount of gold at the expense of any silver coins, the Southern gold fields were not capable of producing anywhere near that much bullion.

The Whigs jabbed hard at this ebullience over gold.

The *Globe* wrote: "Where is such a glorious glory of gold to come from? The gold region of Virginia and other states. Bah! It will require a Midas with an ass's ears to make a long bray about this!"[21]

Another Whig newspaper proclaimed that by the Jackson process every $10 was now declared $10.6675 and had consequently become bullion to be received and passed only by weight. The editor observed that American gold coins would be kept at home because they were intrinsically too poor to be received abroad at face value—not by pure metal, but by law.[22]

More disturbing were the accusations of unfair speculation and profiteering within the Jackson administration on the outstanding gold coins minted under the old valuation ratio of 15 to 1. It was alleged that the gold-coin bill was tabled in the House to give time for speculation by Jackson's group of informal advisers, known as the "Kitchen Cabinet," who held the real power in the administration. Supposedly the decision was made as early as January to change the ratio in the draft legislation and substitute in its stead 16 to 1. Upon this decision the "pet" banks in New York and the government brokers were directed to purchase on joint account all the previously minted gold coins they could find in the market. It was said those purchases amounted to more than $1 million.

Even more disturbing were the allegations swirling around Amos Kendall. Kendall, a graduate of Dartmouth, had tutored Henry Clay's children before moving on to publish a newspaper in the Kentucky state capital. Later, feeling Clay had not directed enough financial support his way, Kendall switched allegiance to Andrew Jackson. He went to Washington seeking a patronage job and in 1834 was fourth auditor in the Treasury Department. However, Kendall's influence extended far above this seemingly minor position. He wrote most of Jackson's annual reports to Congress and drafted the president's veto message on the Bank of the United States recharter. Kendall was also involved in selecting the "pet" banks to receive federal deposits. In regard to the New York banks chosen, he and Campbell White were acquainted with each other. In 1835 he would become postmaster general, chief dispenser of political patronage jobs, under Jackson.

It was claimed that Amos Kendall drafted the amended bill that ultimately became law. His firm, Kendall & Company, then received $40,000 as its share of the profits from the speculation in previously minted overweight gold coins.[23] Given the simplicity of the final legislation, there was no need for him to draft it. In addition, the profit from

$1 million of gold would be only $66,000, throwing into question the size of the payment to Kendall.

Campbell White successfully stood for reelection to the House that autumn. He returned for the rump second session of the Twenty-Third Congress in December. However, he failed to take his seat in the Twenty-Fourth Congress and retired from politics.

• • • •

For Samuel Moore the work now began. Theoretically the effective date of July 31 for the changeover in the fine gold content of the coinage was to prevent speculation. But the bill had been tabled for so long and the downside risk of speculating on its passage so slight that the deadline failed in its intent while causing implementation headaches at the Mint. Moore set the redemption at $10.66 for each $10 in overweight gold coins.[24]

The real problem was differentiating the new lighter gold coins from the old gold coins. There was not time for a complete redesign. Moore asked Levi Woodbury, newly on the job as secretary of the Treasury, for suggestions. Taney had lost the position when Clay influenced a hostile Senate to refuse confirmation of his appointment. Woodbury would end the revolving door at Treasury but his suggestions at this point were amateurish. He first proposed adding the abbreviation "Aug," the first month for striking the new coins. Then Woodbury realized that production would continue beyond August and suggested instead stamping "New" after the date on the gold coins. Finally he threw up his hands and left it to Moore to decide.[25]

With Washington out of the way, Moore's only restriction was the ability of his engraver, William Kneass. In addition, Adam Eckfeldt could not procrastinate with the die-hardening aspect. Production of half eagles commenced on August 1.[26] Moore had taken a unique approach to his problem. On the obverse, he had Kneass remove the cap on Liberty, which he had never particularly liked. Liberty's profile was updated as well. In his press release Moore even quoted Jefferson's derision of the use of a pileus from 1825.[27] On the reverse, he simply removed the motto "E Pluribus Unum," which had been on his agenda for some time (fig. 32). Moore understood the artistic concept, in regard to inscriptions, that less is better. Kneass had no problem with the motto removal but his substitution of curly hair for the cap on Liberty, copied from the Classic Head cent design of 1808 by John Reich, was artistically nothing short of awful.

The changeover went smoothly. Gold coinage in the last five months of 1834 totaled $8.5 million. Deposits for recoinage of the old gold coins amounted to $1 million, including one lot of $500,000 from a single depositor.[28] While some brokers, possibly including Amos Kendall, were involved, the large lot mostly likely came from the Second Bank of the United States.

Fig. 32. Even the beautiful frosting of the design elements on this Proof example cannot hide Kneass's inept design. The "classic" head of Liberty on the obverse is just plain ugly. It was taken from Reich's Classic Head design for the large cent of 1808. The eagle on the reverse might be an improvement over Reich's version but that is saying very little. Neither is much to talk about.

As 1834 closed out, Woodbury was not happy with the omission of the motto. He noted the new designs had been the subject of complaints. He suggested to Moore that with the coming year the designs be reworked and improved. The reverse should be such as to not preclude the return of the motto or alternatively it could be placed over Liberty's head on the obverse.[29] Moore now had a dilemma. He had turned away from William Kneass in 1825 when he last considered new designs on the circulating coins.

• • • •

Woodbury had a bigger problem. As fall bore in on Washington, a newspaper article appeared across the river in Alexandria. Gold had been coined but it was not circulating. The hated bank notes were holding their own. Not a single bill less circulated in the District of Columbia.[30] Uh oh!

CHAPTER 11

BRANCH-MINT FOLLIES

The concept of branch mints was not a new one. They had been successfully employed in France for some time. Now there were clamors in Congress for a branch mint to serve the Southern gold fields. Raw bullion from this source was subject to a discount to allow for risks of impurities. While the Mint might have estimated the wait time for bullion sent to Philadelphia to be 40 days for processing, that delay did not take into account transit time. The miners were of the opinion that the total wait time was seldom less than four months and often in winter a full six months.[1] The suggestion to construct at least one branch mint in North Carolina was made as early as 1831 in the *American Journal of Science and Arts*. A proposal for a mint in the Georgia region was drawn up at a meeting held at the Paschal Hotel in the little village of Auraria in November 1833. The idea immediately received the enthusiastic support of John Calhoun.[2]

The first attempt came in the second session of the Twenty-First Congress in the House of Representatives, concurrent with Campbell White's first tussle with the gold-to-silver ratio. On January 4, 1831, a committee was appointed with Samuel Carson as chair to investigate the feasibility of locating an assay office in the Southern gold region. Of the five congressmen on the committee, four, including Carson, were from the gold-producing states, making the recommendation a foregone conclusion.[3] On February 15 Carson introduced a bill to establish assay

offices in North Carolina and Georgia, under the supervision of the director of the Mint. These offices would assay and stamp or mark the purity and value of the gold without charge.[4] This opening salvo went nowhere.

Supporters waited patiently for almost a full year before broaching the subject again in the House. Once again Samuel Carson was in the lead with a five-man committee stacked in favor of the Southern gold region.[5] The bill that came out this time was more aggressive in that it called for the establishment of four assay offices, one each in Virginia, North Carolina, South Carolina, and Georgia.[6] The proposal in reality was not that expensive. The legislation called for only an assayer in each location. The largest equipment expense would be the balance beams for scales that would have to be imported from France.[7] This time there would be debate.

The first objection came in a form no one was prepared to answer. Erastus Root of New York rose to argue that the Constitution did not give Congress the power to establish assay offices. Under strict construction, it only granted the power to coin money. Root claimed that the bill would simply assay gold for the convenience of the exporter or the jeweler. This assayed gold would not go to the Mint for coinage. Carson defended his constituents saying that they wished to avoid the risk of transporting their gold to Philadelphia to have its value fixed. Then Thomas Foster of Georgia acknowledged that he had anticipated a constitutional objection and proposed amending the bill, adding the words "as branches of the United States Mint." The seed of branch mints was now planted in the minds of the legislators. However, the ensuing arguments that December 19, 1832, wandered from point to point on the constitutional issue with states' rights being the underlying driver. The Southern congressmen were faced with adhering to their principles on states' rights or backing away to get something they wanted. The end result was a tabled bill.[8]

The next day discussion resumed and Root, with the ongoing debates over the valuation ratio fresh on his mind, was much more direct. Here was an attempt to establish offices for the inspection of a commodity for exportation, and to render the measure constitutional by appending those offices to the Mint. If a law were passed to regulate the value of gold, gold enough would be taken to the Mint to be coined. Congress should make gold current in the country for what it was worth so that the assay offices would not have to attract gold to the Mint. No one refuted, nor could they, what Root had said. Again the bill was postponed.[9]

The issue simmered for another week. Then Foster took the floor to amend the original bill to make the assay offices branches of the assay office of the Mint in Philadelphia. That was splitting hairs but it enabled the Southerners to dodge the constitutionality of the assay offices while preserving their position on states' rights. However, Carson remained in favor of his original bill. It had the Mint director's support. Root took the floor and once more went to the heart of the issue. The transmission of gold by the Southern assayers to be coined at the Mint would be a useless expense because when coined, it would be worth more as bullion than as coin.

Again discussion was cut off. This time it was for lack of a quorum.[10] Erastus Root had killed this bill for the Twenty-Second Congress. Based upon the debate, any action must await resolution of the gold-to-silver ratio. Also, to avoid the issue of strict construction of the Constitution, the next attempt would involve branch mints for the Southern gold region.

• • • •

As the Twenty-Third Congress convened for its second session in December 1834, it was clear to those in control that there would be movement on the branch mint. The question really was whether there would be more branch mints once the floodgates were opened. Campbell White was first out of the blocks on December 10, gaining approval of a motion instructing the Ways and Means Committee to investigate establishing a branch mint in New York City.[11] James Graham from Rutherfordton, where the Bechtlers were already running a private mint, shortly thereafter called for a branch mint in North Carolina.[12] Right on the heels of this motion was another one calling for a mint in New Orleans.[13]

James K. Polk, chairman of the Ways and Means Committee, in an effort to bring order to the situation, called on secretary of the Treasury Levi Woodbury for a report on the situation. Woodbury tossed this political football to Samuel Moore. His report was factual yet deferential toward the lawmakers as to whether Mint branches were needed. He noted that maintenance of fineness and weight had not been a problem with the French branch-mint system. The decision really boiled down to a comparison of expenditures to implement the proposed system compared to the additional benefits to be derived from it.

Moore again estimated the recently opened Mint facility in Philadelphia would have a capacity to coin $10 million for the coming 10 years, assuming a 60/40 split in favor of gold over silver. He saw no reason under existing economic circumstances for a shortage of silver bullion that might restrain output. In fact, should the ratio be flipped with more silver than gold available, the present operation could easily handle the increased volume required to reach $10 million with only a small addition to the work force.

In regard to the proposed branch mints, New York and New Orleans should coin both gold and silver while the branch in the Southern gold fields should be limited to gold. He noted that at present, the cost of transporting bullion from either New Orleans or the Southern gold fields and back after coining amounted to about 3 percent of the value of the bullion. For New York, where the transit time to Philadelphia was never more than eight hours, the cost of transportation was about one-third of 1 percent. The facilities of New York as a receiving port and a center of distribution rendered it probable that, next to New Orleans, where substantial sums of silver entered the country, a branch mint would contribute the most good. Moore understood too well the situation in the Southern gold fields, saying that a branch mint would manifestly promote the interests of the locality selected.

Once again Moore attacked the concept of free coinage. These branch mints, if enacted, must be paid for, otherwise Treasury took on added expense for the benefit of the bullion dealers and miners. Moore recognized that the concept of seigniorage faced stiff resistance in Congress. Instead he again broached the issue of immediate payment from a bullion fund that would justify a charge for coinage.[14]

On February 12, 1835, a bill was reported out of Ways and Means. It called for three branch mints, one at New York, one at New Orleans and one designated by the secretary of the Treasury within or convenient to the Southern gold fields. In a unique twist the bill specified the mintmarks to be used. New York would be NM; Philadelphia, CM; New Orleans, SM; and the branch in the gold region would be GM. These mintmarks would provide accountability for quality control. New York and New Orleans would be authorized to coin gold, silver, and copper. In a move that could not have made Moore happy, each branch would have a director and full roster of officers, including an engraver, reporting to the secretary of the Treasury.[15]

This bill represented a departure from previous efforts and it would therefore sit until its sponsor gained enough support to get it before a Committee of the Whole for debate. As a result, not surprisingly, attention shifted to the Senate, where similar efforts were underway.

On February 3, 1835, Louisiana senator George Augustus Waggaman fired the first shot in that chamber, calling for a select committee to consider a branch mint in New Orleans. His motion was tabled.[16] Two days later, Waggaman made the necessary correction to gain broader support by calling for a select committee to evaluate branch mints at New Orleans and somewhere in the gold region. That resulting committee consisted of Waggaman, John Calhoun, John King from Georgia, Willie Mangum from North Carolina, and Thomas Hart Benton.[17] It only remained to be seen if the rest of the Senate would swallow what this committee was going to cook up.

The full Senate did not have long to wait; the committee reported a bill on February 20, 1835. It called for a branch mint at New Orleans for the coinage of gold and silver and branch mints at Charlotte and near Dahlonega, Georgia, for the coinage of gold. Appropriations were authorized for construction, officer positions established and employees capped at 20 for New Orleans and five for each of the Southern gold mints. Each of these mints would report to the director in Philadelphia.[18] In his accompanying discussion, Waggaman noted that the Georgia mint would be located at Auraria, 10 miles southwest of Dahlonega. John Calhoun had no shame, his mine being located at Auraria. Waggaman justified these three mints on the grounds that substantial transportation-cost savings would result when compared to the alternative of shipping the bullion to Philadelphia for coinage.

New York senator Nathaniel Tallmadge opened discussion of the bill by proposing an amendment to establish another branch mint in New York. Waggaman objected, saying the travel time to Philadelphia was so short that the cost savings would not justify this branch mint. Calhoun attempted to deflect the amendment, saying that the moment was not right. When the proper time came, he would support branches in New York, Boston, Norfolk, and Charleston, as well as any other central places of necessity. Benton reinforced Calhoun, saying that in the next session he would not oppose other locations. However, due to the lateness of this session and the immediate needs of New Orleans and the Southern gold fields, he did not wish to impede the bill's progress by adding other locations. Tallmadge took the bait and withdrew his amendment. The question of adoption was about to be called when Henry Clay rose to speak.[19]

Clay, nearing his 58th birthday, was at the height of his speaking powers. When he took the Senate floor, his smile, his bright intelligent eyes, and his incredible speaking voice animated his body. As he spoke he gestured constantly, nodded his head, and stepped back and forth, but it was his voice that constantly gripped his audience. The content of his words, the intellectual power of his argument, commanded the respect and admiration of his colleagues. Whenever he gave a major speech, the galleries were full and representatives deserted the House to hear the man.

Clay's style of debate was unique. His asides, spoken in an undertone, were often so clever, humorous, and sharp-edged that the audience listened to him all the more intently to not miss these tidbits. Frequently Clay tried to intimidate opponents. He could be exceedingly imperious in debate and show more than a touch of bad temper.[20]

On this day, Henry Clay (fig. 33) wanted nothing to do with branch mints. The senator started easily enough, saying that he wished the bill tabled so that it could be printed with amendments. Clay needed to be careful; Waggaman was a fellow Whig from a state that strongly supported his presidential aspirations. Clay stated that he was disposed to feel favorably towards the bill considering the friendly quarter from which it came. Nevertheless, John Calhoun asked Clay to withdraw his motion. Alexander Porter, the other senator from Louisiana, also asked Clay to withdraw his motion, stating the lateness of the session could cause

Fig. 33. This portrait of Henry Clay, by Samuel Osgood in 1834, shows the senator in middle age at the height of his oratorical powers.

the loss of this bill. Here Clay became testy. This bill established substantial government expenses in perpetuity to maintain these mints. While the importation of bullion in the form of South American and Mexican specie into New Orleans had been substantial for the last several years, it might cease altogether in the future. The senator wished to have a little time to study the situation. Clay would not withdraw his motion and Waggaman assented on the understanding that he could again call up the bill the next day.[21]

When Waggaman took the floor in the Committee of the Whole the following day, Henry Clay was prepared, stating emphatically that the Philadelphia Mint was adequate to the country's needs. The specie entering through New Orleans would find its way into the nation's commercial markets. Clay soft-pedaled his feelings about the proposed Southern gold mints. He supposed it would gratify the pride of North Carolinians and Georgians to have branch mints but the objections to the measure were so strong that he could not consent to yield his opposition. Clay moved for an indefinite postponement.

Both North Carolina senators rose in objection, both stating that the two mints in the Southern gold fields were necessary for the miners to achieve full value for their production and that this savings would easily offset the cost of these two facilities. Thomas Hart Benton picked up the debate, saying that the establishment of these branches was an act of justice to the people of the South and West. Philadelphia could coin but not diffuse the coin among the people. Much of the money attracted to Philadelphia from the South and West never returned. Only local mints could give specie back to the people. Carried away in his rhetoric, Benton declared there ought to be five or six branch mints including one at Charleston, Norfolk, and New York or Boston. Give the Mint five or six branches and no one would want the paper currency of the Bank of the United States when they could get gold from a regional mint.

The question of postponement was called and Clay lost soundly, 16 for and 27 against. In this vote he had strange bedfellows—the two Democratic Pennsylvania senators. One, James Buchanan, was a constant political rival of Clay. Clearly the Philadelphia Mint sided with Clay on the issue of branch mints.

Henry Clay rejected this defeat. He now set out to "test the opinion of the Senate." He moved to authorize one branch only. This motion likewise went down to defeat, 18 for and 24 against. Next Clay asked that the bill be postponed until the following Monday, February 23. There was hope; he lost this motion narrowly, 20 for and 22 against. Clay promptly moved that the bill be amended to establish a mint at Louisville, Kentucky. This proposal went down in flames without a division of the vote.

Now the bill was reported favorably out of the Committee of the Whole to the Senate proper. Here Clay again commenced a delaying tactic. Twice he attempted to reduce the $3,000 salary for the superintendent of the New Orleans Mint, first by $1,000, which was rejected, and then by $500, which was approved. The salaries of the treasurer, coiner, and melter and refiner of the New Orleans Mint were challenged but sustained against Clay's opposition. On the issue of the clerks' salaries at New Orleans, Clay was successful. Clay also went after the salaries of the superintendents at the two proposed gold-field mints without success.

At this point, the bill was engrossed and read a third and final time.[22] However, the hour was now late after the tedious maneuvering of Clay. The Kentucky senator had bought time to lobby against the branch mints.

The branch-mint bill did not return to the Senate agenda until Tuesday, the 24th. Clay had not been idle in the interim. Isaac Hill, a powerful Democrat from New Hampshire, argued that salaries at the New Orleans Mint were 25 to 33 percent higher than they would be anywhere else in the country. New Orleans had a "sickly season" from three to six months of the year that would require suspension of operations at the branch mint. Hill considered Louisville a far better point for a branch mint. Bedford Brown of North Carolina questioned why gold and silver entering the port of New Orleans needed to be recoined when they had just voted to make gold and silver from the Latin American countries legal tender. John Black, a Mississippi Democrat, thought the branch mints at Charlotte and at or near Dahlonega (Auraria was slipping out of the picture) not justified. He moved to recommit the bill with instructions to strike out all the branches and to locate just one branch either in North or South Carolina, Georgia, or Louisiana. Theodore Frelinghuysen, Clay's ally from New Jersey, cited a letter from Samuel Moore in favor of only one branch in the gold regions of the South. Frelinghuysen suggested the government pay the cost of transporting the gold mined in North Carolina and Georgia to Philadelphia. That would be cheaper than establishing branch mints in those states.

Now that his audience was warmed up, Clay rose to speak.

> Owing to the effective opposition which this measure has received from the honorable Senator from New Hampshire, I could have but little to add, for really it was unnecessary to say anything, as the honorable gentleman had spoken, and so well, too, to the purpose. It gives me pleasure to find myself co-operating with the honorable Senator, and I assure the honorable Senator that, if he always takes the same substantial, solid ground he has occupied this morning, we shall be in co-operation much oftener than heretofore. Sir, politics make strange bedfellows. Who would ever have imagined that the honorable Senator from New Hampshire and myself could have come together? But I assure him, on this occasion, I embrace him most closely, for I think he has a great deal of reason and propriety on his side. They give rise to some strange reflections. Who would have thought, after the able and eloquent report made the other day, and accompanied also by a speech not less distinguished for its ability and excellence, by the gentleman from South Carolina (Calhoun), against patronage – who, I say, would have expected that, in the course of three or four short days, the Senator from New Hampshire would have been opposing the extension of patronage, and the Senator from South Carolina espousing that cause? It is a singular world in which we live!

There was laughter on the floor at one point during this introduction. Without being specific, Clay had taken a shot at the Jackson administration and questioned Calhoun's motives for support of the branch-mint bill.

Now Henry Clay questioned the justification for the New Orleans Mint. He believed the specie importation of the prior year to be inordinately high. He called the freight rate savings into question. He asked why foreign gold and silver that was already legal tender needed to be restamped with an eagle. He hoped that the bill would be recommitted.

It fell to Waggaman to rebut. To recommit the bill at this late date would be to kill it. He accused Clay of coming down from his high ground to indulge in ridicule. The Kentucky senator's argument was disingenuous. Now Waggaman had to take Clay's arguments and refute them. The low transportation rate Clay cited was not for high-value gold and silver but ordinary freight. The high level of foreign silver reaching New Orleans was not a fluke. Commercial exports through New Orleans were growing faster than any other city in the United States, including New York. This fact alone justified a branch mint.

Waggaman could not let go of the offense he had taken from Clay's speech. He repeated that Clay had abandoned the high ground and that he had resorted to "other means of defense or offense." Next he defended the gold-region branch mints. Charlotte was a very thriving and increasing village of 1,000 or 1,500 inhabitants. Mecklenburg County, in which it was located, was one of the most populous in North Carolina. Besides, Calhoun had just informed him it was the first county in which American independence was declared. On these facts, Waggaman could not see the grounds for opposing the branch mints. He repeated that to recommit at this time would be to kill the bill.

Clay retook the floor. He stated he was very sorry to perceive that the gentleman from Louisiana was in danger of losing his good humor. Waggaman broke in to say that he had never felt in better humor in his life. However, he certainly was not disposed to approve of the honorable senator from Kentucky's sarcastic remarks.

Clay could not let that sit, noting that Waggaman had attributed to him disingenuousness. He now went back to Waggaman's justification for the New Orleans Mint. He noted that the business of New Orleans was in exports that were exchanged at the destination ports for goods to be imported. Those merchants were either paid in goods shipped or in bills drawn on New York and other large city banks. Clay was questioning just how much specie was going to return to New Orleans—a point that Waggaman had yet to refute.

Next came the bait.

> It is remarkable how the gentleman puts forward the pretensions of New Orleans, and how little he talks about those places in the South at which it is proposed to establish the two other Mints. New Orleans is the great steam engine which draws the cars through the two Houses of Congress. One of the places where a Mint is to be established is Talenega or Dahlohnega, I do not know which it is, and believe I never should get hold of the right name. Where is it? For I know not.

Waggaman said, "I believe it is in Muscat County, Georgia." Calhoun corrected, "No. Lumpkin County."

Clay continued.

> A place which has no existence (until by the authority of the general government the Indian title is extinguished) to do any act, the performance of which implies that the Senate pays no respect to it – that they do not regard the Indian title, which, so far as the general Government is concerned remains unextinguished? I think not. Honorable Senators know, from the proceedings in this and the other body, that it is probable that negotiations might be going on between the general Government and the State authorities on the subject to which I have adverted. Whether there are, or not, I am not authorized to say. But supposing there are, would it, I ask, be right that Congress should do any thing, which would imply an act of sovereignty, without reference to the rights of the aborigines? Certainly not. If the majority of the Senate is disposed to have three Mints – if they are determined to have them, despite all the arguments which have been urged against them – I hope that the motion of the honorable Senator from Mississippi, to commit the bill, will prevail, if for no other purpose than to remove the location of the Mint out of that part of Georgia in which it is proposed to establish it, to some other, within the jurisdiction of the State, acknowledged by the general government.

Henry Clay had just played his hold card, the real reason he opposed the branch-mint bill was the designation of Dahlonega, in Cherokee lands, as one of the branches. Henry Clay was a staunch supporter of the Cherokees if only to embarrass his archrival, Andrew Jackson.

On the arguments droned, rehashing each of the points Clay and his supporters had originally made. In exasperation Clay asked if anyone could tell him what sort of necessity there was for establishing the two mints in the gold region. One location was in the bosom of inaccessible mountains and the other's principal recommendation was that it was the burial place of a gallant Revolutionary War hero. Clay thought a monument more suited in that instance than a branch mint. John Calhoun, for his part, managed to inject sectional conflicts into the discussion. Clay, reacting, was astounded that branch mints should become a sectional issue. What were the sectional characteristics of mints in Charlotte and a remote corner of northern Georgia? With that last exchange with Calhoun, the debate exhausted itself.

The question to commit the bill back to committee was called. The vote was 21 in favor and 22 against. Henry Clay had lost by one vote. In the end Bedford Brown of North Carolina who had spoken against New Orleans defected, took the good with the bad and voted with the branch-mint supporters.[23]

It was all over but the shouting. Within minutes the Senate had passed the branch-mint bill and sent it to the House to be approved. It was in and out of Ways and Means without an amendment. On the last day of the congressional session, the House brought the bill onto the floor for consideration. Campbell White attempted to amend it to include New York. There just wasn't time; his amendment lost.[24] The bill was passed into law.[25]

• • • •

Henry Clay had lost the branch-mint vote but the real losers were the Cherokees. The senator from Kentucky was right when he alluded to the possibility that talks involving the Cherokees might be underway. A treaty of removal was signed between the federal government and a minority of the Cherokee leaders on December 29, 1835. Elias Boudinot was one of the Indian leaders signing, convinced it was the only way to save the Cherokee culture. Those leaders did so at the risk of death, the Cherokee sentence for making an unauthorized law. The new branch mint at Dahlonega commenced operations on

April 17, 1838. Georgians saw this event as a national affirmation of their policies over the preceding decade toward the Cherokee Nation. Not coincidentally, that same month President Martin Van Buren ordered the removal of the Cherokees to the Indian Territory west of the Mississippi River. The Cherokee Elias Boudinot, along with the other pro-removal leaders, was executed in the new lands as the last of the survivors from that tragic forced march arrived.[26]

• • • •

Campbell White's fears of a major panic came true. The speculative bubble for this panic was public-land sales. They increased from $3.9 million in 1833 to $4.8 million in 1834 in spite of the mini-panic. Then, with the Bank of the United States constraints removed, they jumped to $14.8 million in 1835 and to $24.9 million in 1836. Concurrently, paper currency in circulation increased from $61 million to $75 million. There was inflation across the board.

Levi Woodbury tried to stem the flood of paper currency. In 1835 he ordered state banks receiving federal government deposits not to issue notes worth less than $5. These were the notes that circulated most frequently in commerce and were the least likely to return to the issuing bank for redemption. Their issuance had been a gravy train for state banks. Meanwhile the Jackson administration achieved one of its goals: the elimination of U.S. government debt. Thus the deposits in the pet banks took on a much more permanent nature supporting additional currency issues. In April 1836, Congress enacted a ban on all notes smaller than $20, to take effect in March 1837. In addition, Woodbury issued a Treasury circular requiring land payments to the federal government be made in specie. Still the land speculation continued unabated, pulling specie out of the New York banks and putting it into the regional banks of the West. The American economy was on very treacherous ground.

• • • •

Samuel Moore had his own set of problems with the adjourning of the Twenty-Third Congress. Well before the branch-mint law was enacted, he approached Woodbury about hiring an assistant engraver. Additional dies would have to be prepared for the branch mints and these should be done at Philadelphia. He had in mind Christian Gobrecht once again, calling him an "artist of great merit." Moore was prepared to offer Gobrecht an annual salary of $1,500, hardly that of an assistant. Moore had even plowed old ground, talking to Gobrecht about preparing a new head of Liberty for the coins. Gobrecht was willing to come but needed some time to finish a current commission first. Even Kneass was comfortable with the arrangement. For Moore it would be the ideal situation. He gained a competent engraver to provide new coin designs without upsetting Kneass.[27] Woodbury dragged his feet.

For Director Moore, there was a bigger issue. He was ready to resign. He was 61 years old. He had an investment opportunity in coal mining. In addition he had to be realistic. While his political colleague, Ingham, had been secretary of the Treasury, he was on firm ground. However, if guilt by association was sufficient, his relationship with Nicholas Biddle was enough to taint him now in the eyes of the Jackson administration. The Philadelphia Mint needed a staunch Democrat at the helm to ensure its survival. Moore knew it was time to exit the stage but only upon the condition that he could designate his successor.[28] It was time to fix what had made him uncomfortable from the beginning about taking this job.

PART II

PHILADELPHIA'S CROWN JEWEL

CHAPTER 12

CHANGING OF THE GUARD

Robert Maskell Patterson took the seat of honor. It was October 3, 1835, at the upscale Mansion House Hotel in Philadelphia (fig. 34). The man stood five feet nine inches, weighed about 160 pounds, had dark brown hair and eyes, and was impeccably dressed for the occasion. Patterson's manner that evening was at once dignified, cheerful, and winning.[1] He was at ease among his friends; for Robert Maskell Patterson friendship was everything, and to his friends he gave absolute loyalty. Only a strong sense of duty rivaled this loyalty.

In attendance, among others, was Peter Duponceau, president of the American Philosophical Society. As Patterson looked across the room he saw a veritable who's who of the APS, all longtime friends. The occasion was his return to Philadelphia from his position as a professor at the University of Virginia to assume the post of director of the Mint, held in former times by his father.[2] Patterson had long wanted this moment; it had been worth the wait.

That Patterson was here came as no surprise to anybody who knew the man. His life had been full of stellar achievements. He was born on March 23, 1787. His father enrolled him at an early age in the preparatory department of the University of Pennsylvania, bypassing primary schooling entirely. His childhood was driven by academic pursuits, with no time and little affinity for games and sports. In 1804 at 17 he received his Master's degree. He then chose to pursue medicine, receiving his degree in 1808.

Fig. 34. This elegant hotel, located at Third and Spruce streets, was in the heart of upscale Philadelphia and had once been the home of Thomas Willing's daughter, Anne.

In 1809, to further his scientific knowledge, Robert Maskell Patterson left for two years in Paris to study medicine, chemistry, and natural philosophy under the leading French minds of the day. However, Patterson did not arrive in Paris as an ordinary student. He was armed with letters of introduction from his father's friend, Thomas Jefferson. His arrival carried such prominence that upon the departure of the American minister to France, John Armstrong, he was appointed temporary consul general to the court of Napoleon. This honor turned into embarrassment when he was snubbed by Napoleon on account of his last name, which, by happenstance, was the same as that of the American wife of the emperor's brother, Jerome, of whom Napoleon heartily disapproved.[3]

In 1811 Patterson left France for England to attend the last course of lectures by Sir Humphry Davy. When war with England became imminent, Patterson returned home carrying official dispatches aboard the American frigate *Constitution*. His intention was to practice medicine in Philadelphia. However, in 1813, he was appointed professor of natural philosophy in the medical department of the University of Pennsylvania. From here he became chair of mathematics and natural philosophy, succeeding his father in 1814. A month later he was elected vice provost.

On April 20, 1814, Patterson married Helen Hamilton Leiper (fig. 35), the daughter of Thomas Leiper, a staunch Jeffersonian Democrat and very successful businessman in Philadelphia. Leiper had been active in the Revolutionary War and afterwards served as a presidential elector and as a director of the first Bank of the United States.

Not only had Patterson gained a wife of great beauty and social accomplishments, he also gained added political exposure through his father-in-law. When Leiper was named a commissioner for the defense of Philadelphia during the British incursion that burned Washington, D.C., Patterson superintended the erection of the fortifications.

Early married life for Robert Maskell Patterson was a family affair. The newlyweds moved on campus into apartments occupied by Patterson's mother, father, and sister. At this point Robert Maskell Patterson met a young Yale graduate, John Kane (fig. 36), who was studying to become a lawyer. Kane would later remember it as a happy time. In the evenings Helen would sing for John at the piano. Patterson introduced him to the scientific wits of the city as well as to the "wits who were not scientific but merry instead." The most important introduction, however, was to Helen's equally beautiful sister, Jane. Kane passed the bar in 1817 and married Jane on April 20, 1819.

Fig. 35. This painting by Charles Willson Peale of Mrs. Thomas Leiper and her daughter Helen, the future Mrs. R.M. Patterson, was just one more link between the Patterson and Peale families.

Fig. 36. John Kintzing Kane by John Neagle. Kane and Robert Maskell Patterson would be lifelong friends.

Robert Maskell Patterson and John Kane would thereafter be linked not only by their many common pursuits but also by a common wedding-anniversary date.[4]

Doors opened to Robert Maskell Patterson. In 1820 both he and John Kane were involved in the founding of the Musical Fund Society to promote the performance of music and aid needy performing artists. This was the first society of its type in the United States. Patterson also assisted in the founding of the Franklin Institute in 1824, for the promotion of the mechanical arts, another first in the nation. He was an active participant in its educational activities, serving as a volunteer instructor in these first years. The one area that Patterson avoided was politics. When offered the nomination for a seat in the House of Representatives, at a time when nomination meant election, he declined.

Throughout this period, Patterson seemed content to follow in his father's footsteps at the University of Pennsylvania, making occasional forays of his own in pursuit of the arts and science. Throughout, the American Philosophical Society had his foremost attention; he rarely missed the biweekly meetings. All of this was about to change.

When the aged Robert Patterson, whose health was declining rapidly in December 1823, named his son-in-law Samuel Moore as his choice as successor at the Mint, it had to be a blow to Robert Maskell Patterson. Nevertheless he accepted the decision dutifully. Helen, however, did not. The matter simmered during the brief recovery of the elder Patterson. Then, with the end near, Thomas Leiper swung into action. In July 1824, he wrote to his old friend, Thomas Jefferson, asking for his endorsement of the younger Patterson to be Mint director. Jefferson quickly complied, giving a strong endorsement, but the old man wisely deferred to President James Monroe's judgment in the matter.

"Knowing as you do the infinite mischief that can be done to our circulating medium by ignorance of its director, this decision cannot be in juster [*sic*] hands."[5]

Monroe, on the other hand, was comfortable with Samuel Moore. Jefferson's efforts fell on barren ground. Six weeks later an embarrassed Leiper wrote to Jefferson explaining that he had not known the Patterson family had been in favor of Moore. He had also written to Monroe and John Calhoun and he mistakenly believed his letters were in essence the first application for the office.

Moore even felt it necessary to write to Jefferson to state the circumstances of the family endorsement that Leiper did not relate. Moore was much less specific as to whether Leiper knew of these circumstances in advance or not. Moore explained that Robert Maskell Patterson discovered Leiper's action after Moore had left for Washington to discuss the appointment with President Monroe. Patterson, ever dutiful to the wishes of his father, then had the onerous task of disavowing Leiper's recommendation

Fig. 37. Portrait of Robert Maskell Patterson, by Samuel F. DuBois in 1855. The family was never quite satisfied with this posthumous painting.

in a letter to Moore to be placed in Monroe's hands.[6] What Helen thought of this turn of events was left unsaid.

For the next four years, life seemed to move in slow motion in Philadelphia for Robert Maskell Patterson. He did cajole the American Philosophical Society into accepting John Kane for membership in its ranks. For Kane this membership had nothing to do with scientific achievement; it provided entry into the highest echelons of Philadelphia society. Patterson was also involved in the nascent canal-building effort as Philadelphia and Pennsylvania struggled to keep up with New York State.

By 1828 Patterson had been teaching at the University of Pennsylvania for 14 years. The position was certainly secure but the opportunity for advancement was minimal. When the University of Virginia offered Patterson the position of professor of natural philosophy, he was ready for the move. His parting from Philadelphia had been bittersweet. Just as he had been welcomed back with a dinner at the Mansion House Hotel, many of the same attendees now wished him farewell at a dinner there on August 20, 1828.

Patterson was only the third native-born professor on campus. He and Helen took up residence at the third pavilion on the West Lawn. Helen, whose father had bought tobacco from Virginia plantations, was in her element, throwing their living quarters open to both faculty and students. Patterson had a classroom dedicated strictly to him in the rotunda. His reputation built quickly; his lectures were noted for their lucidity and simple language. Patterson was a master of English, always finding the most appropriate words for any occasion.

During his tenure at UVA, Patterson served his time as chairman of the faculty. It was a position that could test the will of someone with Patterson's kindly disposition. Yet he dealt with the often conflicting and diverse faculty positions. By far Patterson's most important accomplishment at UVA occurred in 1829, when he was charged with the oversight of the construction and subsequent operation of a new astronomical observatory. For help in this endeavor, he turned to men from his Philadelphia roots: Isaiah Lukens, a vice president of the Franklin Institute and noted clock maker, and Franklin Peale.[7] Lukens was an obvious choice while Peale was not.

The record is not clear on where or when Patterson and Peale met. While the two families were close, the eight-year gap in their ages would argue that the friendship developed much later. Peale, with his excellent tenor voice, was a leading light of the Musical Fund Society. Also as a manager of his father's museum, he would have had ample opportunity to interface with Patterson when he became a trustee in 1827.[8] Regardless of the timing, the two men had become and would remain the best of friends.

After this initial burst of activity, matters for Patterson at UVA more or less settled into a routine. However, Patterson did not cut ties to Philadelphia and the Mint. In addition to recommending Peale to Samuel Moore as they talked over affairs of the Mint, he provided a letter of introduction for Peale to use in Paris.[9]

Robert Maskell Patterson's (fig. 37) academic career came to an end in 1835. Afterward Patterson would make much of the fact that President Jackson sought him out for the position of director of the Mint and not the other way around. That statement was certainly an oversimplification. The inquiry from Treasury secretary Levi Woodbury on behalf of the president was written on May 18, 1835.[10] Patterson, jumping at the chance to return to his native Philadelphia, accepted the offer three days later. He set the tenor for his term in office by saying he "embraced with great satisfaction" this position "so honorable and so allied both in its mechanical and chemical operations with the science to which he had been so attached."[11]

Moore had made no secret of his intention to retire from office and that Patterson was his choice as successor. As early as the start of 1835, Moore had openly acknowledged to Woodbury that he was having conversations with Patterson and that Patterson was aware of his intent to use Gobrecht to prepare a design for a new head of Liberty. Moore also made much of the fact to Woodbury that Patterson had recommended Peale for the trip to Europe.[12] In addition to Moore's promotion of Patterson, in all probability there was someone else just as involved.

John Kane had been a strong Jackson man since the presidential election of 1824 that ended up in the House, where John Quincy Adams won despite not gaining even a plurality of the electoral vote. In the 1828 presidential election, his pamphlets in support of Jackson circulated throughout the country. Kane was present in Washington during the nullification crisis and was appointed by Jackson in 1832 as one of three commissioners under the Convention of Indemnity with France to resolve claims arising from French spoliation of American vessels during the Napoleonic Wars. The French dragged their feet in cooperating, necessitating Kane's involvement throughout 1835 in Washington. That Jackson held Kane in high esteem was demonstrated two years later. As Jackson was leaving the White House in March 1837, he instructed that his inkstand and boxwood sand box be given to Kane.[13] Obviously Patterson's good friend had ready access to Andrew Jackson at the time the Mint director's position became available.

Patterson may not have actively sought the Mint position but he clearly had friends who would seek it for him. Waiting to greet him was the newly arrived from Europe assistant assayer, Franklin Peale.[14] Patterson now not only had the position he sought but also his close friend in place to help implement his directives.

CHAPTER 13

FRANKLIN PEALE!

Franklin Peale was born October 15, 1795, on the second floor of the American Philosophical Society hall into a unique American family. Charles Willson Peale, his father, had been a militia captain in Philadelphia during the American Revolution. He fought under George Washington at Princeton and wintered at Valley Forge. When the British left Pennsylvania, Charles Willson Peale entered politics as a radical Republican. His political beliefs did not conflict with his buying one of the nicer confiscated Tory homes readily available after the British retreat, giving him prominent visibility in Philadelphia society.

However, revolutionary politics were not Charles Willson Peale's calling. Before the American Revolution, he had studied painting in England and returned to the colonies as an accomplished portraitist. Like other English and American painters of his time, he maintained a small gallery where he presented mostly his own works, attracting visitors and enhancing his reputation. He built a large addition to his gallery in 1782 and began filling it with portraits of the American participants in the Revolution. In many cases, those images would define the faces of these men for later generations of Americans.

In spite of his painting success, Charles Willson Peale's finances were tight, pushing him to seek new ventures. The one he settled upon was a natural history museum, which opened in June 1784. His friend and fellow liberal politician, David Rittenhouse, advised against it on the grounds that, while the idea was good, it would force Peale to neglect his art. On the other hand, Robert Patterson liked the plan, hoping it would become a great national institution. He made the first gift, a preserved paddlefish that became the foundation of the collection.[1]

From this humble beginning, Charles Willson Peale aggressively promoted his new enterprise. Robert Patterson and Thomas Jefferson were on the first board of visitors which provided oversight for the museum.[2] When his gallery lease expired in 1794, Peale moved his museum to the American Philosophical Society Hall. The association of his museum with the society would lend more credibility to his collection. Ever the promoter, Peale was not content to just crate his collection and move it to the hall. For the larger items, he hired boys from the neighborhood. He lined the boys up and had them carry mounted animals over their heads. Then he marched them in parade style to the hall, attracting the attention of onlookers along the way.[3] His museum needed paid attendance to survive and this parade provided free advertising.

Home life for the Peale family was every bit as unique. Just keeping up with the family members was a chore. Peale fathered 17 children by two wives. Many of them were named after Renaissance painters. Franklin was the third of six children by his second wife. By this time, Charles Willson Peale had moved his family into an apartment above his exhibits, which explains why the birth occurred in the APS Hall. However, Franklin was not named Franklin at his birth. In keeping with his penchant for unusual names, Peale named the boy Aldrovand after Ulisse Aldrovandi, an Italian naturalist and collector from the 16th century. This time, the father had gone too far and four months later he asked the American Philosophical Society to come up with a name for the first child born in their hall. Thus, the boy became Benjamin Franklin Peale.[4]

Franklin Peale spent his childhood in a home devoid of discipline. His father objected to the use of the rod. The children had an unstructured education but benefited from exposure to whatever pursuit or endeavor their father was involved in at the museum. In that vein, they all learned more or less to paint, spoke French, read prolifically, wrote verses, and sang. They attended school but never in any regular fashion.[5] Franklin's formal education ended before he was 17, and consisted of a few years at a Bucks County school after his father bought a farm and moved to the countryside, a short stint at the University of Pennsylvania, and another brief stay at the Germantown Academy.[6] His domestic life was marred by the death of his mother during childbirth in 1804. Adding to this trauma was the fact that his father promptly married for a third time, although there would be no more siblings. In this environment, Franklin grew up doing largely as he pleased without the discipline that comes with accountability.

When it came time for Franklin to choose a profession, his interests gravitated toward manufacturing—the machinist's trade in particular. Franklin was moving in a different direction from the artistic or scientific careers of his brothers and half brothers. Charles Willson Peale considered this desire a foolish whim. In late 1812 or early 1813, he placed Franklin with William Young, the prominent owner of a cotton factory near Wilmington, Delaware, with the understanding that Young was to lead the boy away from this endeavor. Connected with the factory was a machine shop for making carding and spinning machinery, run by the Hodgson brothers. Franklin was soon drawn to their shop and within a year his work excelled over that of the Hodgsons.[7]

Young Peale was not content merely to learn the trade. He made drawings of the cotton spinning machinery that converted the cotton fiber into yarn within the factory. After a year's apprenticeship, he returned home and, with his father's financing, executed patterns for castings that could be used to make his own machinery. His dream was to open a cotton mill with advanced mechanical innovations.

Franklin had another surprise for his father. He had met a lady, Eliza Greatrake, whom he intended to marry in two or three years. Upon questioning, the elder Peale learned that Franklin knew little of the woman's background. In what must have come as a surprise to Franklin, his father did not take a permissive tone and pointed out that it would be necessary for the boy to be able to support a family financially before marrying.

Meanwhile, Franklin took a position with a Philadelphia firm operated by the husband of one of his half-sisters. This company made machines for bending and cutting wire into card teeth. Franklin soon distinguished himself on the foot lathe with hand tools. There were none better than he and few his equal. Clearly, he had an aptitude for machinery.

Not long after Franklin's initial discussion with his father about marriage, Eliza came to Philadelphia. She did not make a good first impression. One of Franklin's half sisters, upon meeting her, said she acted strangely and pronounced her crazy. The elder Peale noticed that she tossed her head from side to side at his first meeting with her. Franklin then asked his father to visit Eliza's mother, who was in town sick and confined to her room. Peale did so expecting to be asked to render some aid. Mrs. Greatrake on the other hand expected Peale to seek her permission for Franklin to marry Eliza. That did not happen.

At this point, Eliza was 26 years old and desperate to avoid spinsterhood. Franklin was 18 and uninitiated. Within a week of Charles Willson Peale's meeting the mother, the couple married without his consent. Nevertheless, Peale set them up in a house next to the family garden. Eliza made a mess of domestic work and soon dropped all pretense of maintaining the home. Three years later when they had a daughter, Anna, Eliza slipped over the edge. It was the end of their marriage. Eliza returned to her mother, who promptly committed her to an institution.

Ultimately, the Peale family had to pay for Eliza's incarceration. A marriage annulment was granted in 1821. Charles Willson Peale then employed Franklin at the family museum for just enough salary to maintain him and his daughter.[8] Gone were the dreams of a cotton mill. Franklin Peale would have to pick up the pieces from his mistake and start over.

Franklin made the most of his position as a "manager" of Peale's Museum. His name gave him entry into Philadelphia society. Gradually he pulled himself out of the ditch. After his father's death in 1827, he and his brother, Titian, took over management of the museum. In 1831 Franklin also began lecturing on machines at the Franklin Institute; he had been involved at its founding in 1824.

Franklin Peale had inherited his father's promotional skills. Shortly after the Rain Hill tests in Great Britain, wherein steam engines built by Ericsson and Stephenson competed against each other, Peale came up with the idea of building a model engine that would operate within the museum. This would help increase attendance. Franklin chose the losing engine by Ericsson as a model for his. He employed his friend Matthias Baldwin, who maintained a machine shop in Philadelphia, to build the engine. Once completed, the little steam engine pulled two miniature cars, seating four people, on tracks in a circuit within the museum.[9]

When the experimental engine had run its course in terms of popularity, Franklin Peale moved on to his next promotional gimmick for the museum. It was a fork in the road for Franklin. Matthias Baldwin made the little engine the start of what would become Baldwin Locomotive Works. Baldwin would, throughout his life, hold Franklin Peale in the highest esteem.[10]

When Samuel Moore, with Robert Maskell Patterson's approval, tapped Franklin Peale to be assistant assayer at the Mint, it was an opportunity for Peale to escape a growing problem. His father had failed, in spite of repeated efforts, to secure a national charter for the museum. Jefferson while president had not thought it a proper function of government. State and local support was intermittent and the museum was going through a long, slow decline, which began after Charles Willson Peale's death. Competition had sprung up in other cities for exhibits, specimens, and visitors. For Franklin, the Mint position was a new challenge with the added potential of immersing him in his first love: machinery.

On May 8, 1833, Franklin Peale set out on the greatest adventure of his life. He would have a completely free hand to investigate the latest technology in use at European mints. He left his 17-year-old daughter in the care of the family of Thomas Sully, his friend and a noted Philadelphia artist. Franklin, in a parting letter, admonished Anna to study her arts in his absence and consult with Sully freely, giving the utmost deference to Sully's experience and judgment.[11]

With his knowledge of the French language, Paris was both his destination and his base of operations. While Peale would investigate all minting processes, his focus was on refining.[12] He carried a letter of introduction to Robert Mushet of the British Royal Mint to study the use of sulfuric acid in the refining process, with the intent of introducing it to the Philadelphia Mint. However, when in London the following November, Franklin waxed eloquent in a letter to his daughter about superintending the making and transporting of an apparatus required for assaying using the new process, *voci humide*. He was silent about methods of refining with sulfuric acid. He also talked of the good weather he was encountering in London and of the numerous open-air amusements and recreation. He was becoming an expert at a variety of minting processes, but it was not all work and no play.[13]

On New Year's Day 1834, Peale wrote Director Moore with the news that he was out of money. He wanted to go to Rouen to study the process used there with sulfuric acid to separate silver from gold. However, the French were going to require a fee to allow him access to their knowledge. He was hard at work drafting up the information he had gained in London and was sending a new balance to Jacob Eckfeldt, the Mint assayer.[14] Joseph Saxton, a transplanted American, was actually making the balance. Saxton was an experienced machinist in his own right with knowledge of coining and engraving. In 1829 he had made significant improvements to a medal ruling machine, originally devised by Christian Gobrecht for copying medals, that would eliminate distortions,[15] Moore took Peale's request in stride, asking for the congressional appropriation to purchase rights to the French refining process that was subsequently denied.[16]

Peale stayed through 1834 and well into 1835. He observed the latest coin presses in use in mints in France and Germany. They were significantly more advanced than the screw presses at Philadelphia.[17] Finally, in the spring of 1835, Peale returned to America. Oddly, it coincided perfectly with the appointment of Robert Maskell Patterson as the new Mint director. In a letter to Patterson that he wrote immediately upon landing, Franklin called the voyage from Liverpool to New York a rough passage that took 46 days.[18]

Franklin Peale brought back more than just advanced knowledge of coining from Europe. At least as early as 1832, Franklin had involved himself in the design process of medals, seeking one for the family museum.[19] Now he brought back knowledge of the latest engraving technology from the Paris Mint, where he had seen a portrait lathe in operation. Up to this point, an engraver in the

United States prepared his design in a plastic material such as wax or clay. Then, he was forced to dig out of solid metal a reproduction of his design for the master die, taking impressions in soft metal as he progressed. This required long periods of time to complete.

In Paris a cast could be taken from the artist's model or it could be electrotyped in copper. From this mold, a copy could be cast in hard metal, bronze, or iron, and retouched at will by the artist. This copy could be placed in the portrait lathe to generate an exact reduction in steel of the major design devices for the master die. Subsequently, minor design devices and inscriptions could be added by hand.[20] This portrait lathe, specifically a Tour á Portrait de Contamin, was a machine capable of artistic output, the kind of mechanical improvement that most intrigued Franklin Peale.

CHAPTER 14

A DESIGN OF GREAT MERIT

There was no honeymoon period for Robert Maskell Patterson when he took the oath of office on July 15, 1835.[1] Samuel Moore had administered the Mint quite well; however, he still left Patterson with a problem. In Moore's zeal to entice Christian Gobrecht to come to the Mint, he had overreached.

Moore had given Patterson a heads up, telling him that Gobrecht would take no less than $1,500 as an annual salary, for which no money had been appropriated. Now Moore wanted Patterson, on his way from Charlottesville to Philadelphia via Washington, D.C., to talk to President Andrew Jackson about the funding.[2]

An anxious Moore had jumped the gun in his note to Patterson. Five days later, he received word from Secretary Levi Woodbury that there was great worry in Washington about the timeliness of die preparation. As a result, the salary named was acceptable for the assistant engraver position.[3] Now Moore had a different problem. Regardless of the money, Gobrecht would never consent to the title of assistant engraver.

Time was too short for Moore to resolve the issue properly. He told Gobrecht for the first time that he was resigning and that Patterson would be replacing him. At this point, everything must wait for Patterson's approval. He turned the problem of job title over to Patterson to address during his visit to Washington, D.C.[4] Patterson was amenable to all this maneuvering.[5] He was convinced that Gobrecht had the taste and skill necessary to perform this position.[6]

If Patterson did not fully realize the issues swirling around the Gobrecht appointment before he went to Washington, Levi Woodbury explained the situation to him in detail. William Kneass, the engraver, received an annual salary of only $1,200. This amount was fixed by law. Gobrecht's higher salary was bound to cause friction, but Woodbury was willing to accept that. Now, Patterson was asking for a title that made the lines of authority in the engraving department even murkier. Approval was not immediately forthcoming. Patterson was unperturbed. He still had until the end of December to smooth things out at the Mint before Gobrecht took the job.

If issues within the engraving department were not enough, on June 29, Moore alerted Patterson to a practice outside the strict confines of the Mint. In May Secretary of War Lewis Cass had requested that the Mint execute a gold medal authorized by Congress for a Colonel George Croghan for exploits during the War of 1812. Moritz Fürst had applied to execute the medal but Cass left it up to Moore's discretion.[7] Now, Cass was asking for a status report on the medal. Moore had procrastinated on this project, waiting for Fürst, who was usually brought in on such occasions, to appear at the Mint's door. However, Moore had absolutely no idea of the man's whereabouts. No money had yet been appropriated, but that would not be a problem provided Fürst could wait to be paid later. Moore then dismissed this issue, saying that the expense incurred at the Mint could "readily be adjusted." It was not probable that any other artist could be engaged who could execute the medal better than Fürst, who, through hard work, had developed a solid reputation in this field.[8]

What Moore left unsaid was that the medal would be struck at the Mint under the auspices of the chief coiner, Adam Eckfeldt, and that Fürst and Eckfeldt, as in the past, would split the appropriation between them. Before ever setting foot in the door of the Mint, Patterson learned that the Mint's engraving activity could be a real headache.

• • • •

In spite of these early issues, it was a joyous occasion for Patterson as he assumed the reins of the Mint. There were so many old and familiar faces from the times he had tagged along with his father that it was a homecoming of sorts. Only the buildings had changed. Of course, there was also his good friend, Franklin Peale, there to meet him. Moore had left the institution in good shape overall. Still there was some unfinished business such as Mint regulations, coin alloys, and coining equipment. In addition, there was the restart of dollar coin production and the ever-vexing issue of coin designs.

Patterson wasted no time. He wanted to be known as a reformer at the Mint. At the top of his list was a change in the coin designs to make them "more creditable specimens of taste and art." He and Peale talked extensively on the topic. Franklin laid out the conclusions years later at an American Philosophical Society presentation. The coinage of a high-ranking country, such as the United States, should bear evidence on its face of the condition and progress of both the fine and mechanical arts of the country. In addition, securing the high-level artistic talent in the design and execution of the finished coin would help guard against counterfeiting. In this vein, the government should seek the highest grade of skill regardless of the cost for the design of new devices. Furthermore, the search for such artisans should not be limited to the United States. Peale in particular believed that a mechanic of good skill could provide the coining dies and that it was not necessary that the artist employed to provide the new designs also serve as a diesinker.[9]

Fig. 38. A self portrait by Thomas Sully, composed in the decade preceding his work on the Gobrecht-dollar design.

Patterson did indeed go outside the Mint for the first design that he intended for the resurrected dollar coin. Soaring silver imports in 1834 and 1835 had made him confident that he could restart the coin.[10] While he left the confines of the Mint in his quest for an artist, he did not go far. On August 1, he asked Thomas Sully (fig. 38) to provide the design for the obverse. After setting out the legal requirements, he acknowledged that he ought to leave the issue of the design in Sully's hands. However, Sully should excuse him for making some suggestions.

> For the "impression emblematic of Liberty," you know that our coins have heretofore used a bust, etc. It appears to me that it would be better to introduce an entire figure. When a *likeness* is to be given, as in the European coins, the head alone is very properly used, in order that the features may be distinctly represented. But, when an *emblem* only is called for, it would seem rather desirable to avoid this individuality in the features. Besides there is certainly more room for a display of taste and beauty of form when the full figure is used.
>
> The round form of the coin, its small size, and the practical necessity of covering as much of the face as possible, seem to require that the figure be in a sitting posture, - sitting, for example on a rock.
>
> To be distinctly "emblematic of Liberty," I would propose that the figure hold in her right hand the liberty-pole surmounted by the pileus, - an emblem not unclassical, and which is universally understood.
>
> I would also suggest that the left hand be made to rest upon the United States shield, on which the word "Liberty," required by the law may be inscribed.

Patterson's description of a potential design was drawn directly from a rough sketch (fig. 39) that he had had Kneass prepare that same day.[11]

Patterson had certainly not consulted his brother-in-law. If he had, he would have known of Jefferson's objection in 1825 to the use of the pileus. Patterson also told Sully that, at least for now, he had specific design ideas for the reverse, for which he intended to use Titian Peale.[12] From this letter it is clear: Patterson was going to control the design process and Sully would be a mere tool in his hands. Politics and public art can never be separated. This added layer of hands-on control risked becoming a recipe for mediocrity.

Patterson was no less specific to Titian Peale. The law required a representation of an eagle on the reverse with the inscription "United States of America" And the denomination. The Mint director wanted to meet this requirement in an artistic manner but closer to nature than on the then-current coins. Patterson told Peale to prepare a sketch of a bald eagle in flight amidst a constellation of 24 stars, representing the states of the Union, dispersed around it.[13] The eagle's claws should clutch a scroll with the words "E Pluribus Unum." Despite leaving Titian no leeway, Patterson had struck upon an original theme with promise for success.[14]

The selection of Thomas Sully and Titian Peale was above criticism. Sully carried a national reputation as a portrait painter.[15] In fact, he had executed portraits of the Mint director and his wife. He was also a founding member of the Musical Fund Society with Patterson. Titian Peale (fig. 40), while a naturalist by training, was quite proficient in sketching wildlife, on a par with John James Audubon. While Franklin Peale might have reinforced

Fig. 39. A rough study by engraver William Kneass of Patterson's new obverse design concept, dated September 1835 (note that the date is in different handwriting, indicating it was postdated). Kneass quickly left the scene after suffering a stroke.

Fig. 40. A self portrait by Titian Peale.

Fig. 41. Levi Woodbury served as secretary of the Treasury during the first years of Robert Maskell Patterson's administration at the Mint. He survived Jackson's revolving cabinet door to extend his term into the Van Buren administration.

Patterson's decision, the final choice was clearly made by the Mint director.

As Patterson was kicking off this project, he had to confront an entirely different issue in the engraving department. William Kneass suffered a mild stroke in late August 1835.[16] He was unable to leave his home for several weeks. When he did return, Kneass was noticeably weakened in one arm. Patterson had no choice but to accelerate the hiring of Gobrecht and deal with the prickly issue of job title. On August 31, 1835, Secretary Woodbury (fig. 41) authorized Patterson to hire Gobrecht as "second engraver."[17] In finessing the issues of title and salary, no one seemed to focus on the fact that Gobrecht would need time to get fully up to speed on his new job requirements.[18] Moore's previous discussions with Gobrecht made it clear that, regardless of the Mint's needs, Gobrecht had private commissions underway that would have to be completed that fall before he could take up his position full time.

Thomas Sully took a full six weeks to answer Patterson in the affirmative. He would spare no pains to meet Patterson's views on the proper devices for the design. He also recommended Luigi Persico, a well-known neoclassical Italian sculptor, to execute the model in bas-relief.[19] In 1825 Persico, along with Gobrecht, had been part of Director Moore's redesign project for a new head of Liberty.[20] A model would help the engraver better understand the design than if he had to take it directly from a drawing.[21] Sully was recognizing that the engraving department at the Mint was in a state of flux. He was also, in an indirect way, introducing the issue of proper relief for the design. Patterson had not raised this aspect in his proposal letter.

Once started, Sully proceeded quickly, sending three sketches for Patterson's review. Of the three Sully had a favorite. The concept of employing a sculptor for a model had fallen by the wayside as Sully offered to make any corrections Patterson wanted and provide a copy for the diesinker. The simple fact of the matter was that Persico was no longer in the country and the few American sculptors in existence were several years away from any national reputation.

On October 15, Patterson related progress on the new design to Secretary Woodbury. Sully had consulted various classical engravings and medals to guide his work with one sketch (fig. 42) that, in Patterson's opinion, was clearly outstanding—preferable to the other alternatives. Gobrecht (fig. 43) had made an outline of this favored sketch, a seated Liberty holding a pole in one hand topped with a pileus and a shield in the other, on a dollar-sized copper planchet to judge the general effect of the design upon the coin itself; Patterson enclosed it for the secretary and the president to review. The Mint director stated that the intricate details would be carefully attended to in the final execution of the design and would materially improve its effect. At this point, Patterson wanted approval for the execution of a die to strike a specimen coin for Woodbury's final approval. This business of developing a new design had no real approval precedent, either administratively or by law, for Patterson to follow.[22]

Fig. 42. Thomas Sully's sketch, prepared at the request of Patterson, for the proposed new obverse design of the dollar coin.

Fig. 43. Christian Gobrecht was an accomplished artist whose time had finally come at the U.S. Mint.

Woodbury and President Jackson gave their assent to proceed the following day. However, the president noted that Liberty's pole was too short and wished it lengthened.[23] Here the written record goes cold. While Patterson had authorization to proceed, the Mint director was not yet satisfied beyond a basic concept of a seated Liberty and much work remained before he was ready to initiate preparation of a trial die. Titian Peale even entered the fray, with a rendering in oil on cardboard (fig. 45). Surviving sketches (fig. 44) indicate Gobrecht modified the design, changing the gown arrangement back and forth, and adjusting the drapery over the arms and shield. The tilt of the head, a forward lean to the figure, and placement of Liberty's right arm changed as well. This uncertain evolution of the female figure away from Sully's rendition and more toward that of Peale's continued through the end of the year and into January 1836. Likewise, Titian's numerous sketches in pencil and watercolor of the eagle (fig. 46) failed to gain the director's acceptance.[24] The project stalled.

• • • •

As Patterson was struggling with the evolving coin design, problems of a different nature arose at the Mint. On the evening of October 27, the Mint director heard accusations against the melter and refiner, Joseph Cloud. The claims were of such seriousness that Patterson addressed their existence without specifics in a letter to Cloud the next day. He gave the old man, who had been at the Mint 40 years, the option of retiring honorably rather than bearing the embarrassment of a public investigation. He knew that Cloud had talked of resigning to Moore. Patterson promised not to reveal the nature of the charges, only saying that rumors were afloat at the Mint and noting a circumstance involving the Mint treasurer, William Findlay. Without saying it, Patterson implied that money was involved.[25]

It took Cloud a full month to acquiesce to Patterson's demand. In announcing Cloud's resignation to Woodbury and President Jackson, effective at the end of the year, Patterson gave no hint that anything was amiss. It was, however, essential that he fill the position at once to maintain the efficiency of the Mint. In that regard, Patterson nominated Franklin Peale. Peale was up to date with the latest refining techniques in France, Germany, and England. Patterson was enclosing a letter from Samuel Moore endorsing the recommendation.[26] Woodbury promptly wrote back that the president had no objection to the appointment of Peale. Patterson had Woodbury's full confidence.

Andrew Jackson was as good as his word, nominating Peale without a hint of politics on December 21, 1835.[27] Patterson left nothing to doubt as Jackson's appointments did not always make it through the hostile Senate. He wrote Thomas Hart Benton, playing to the senator's hard-money obsession, saying that with Cloud gone, coinage "must stop" without a melter and refiner, despite millions in bullion in the vaults.[28] Fortunately for Patterson, Benton failed to ask the obvious—why was so much bullion sitting uncoined? Actually, Patterson had exaggerated. There was only about $800,000 in the vaults at year end.[29] The director also wrote to Senator Thomas Ewing, an old friend related through the marriage of Patterson's sister, stating that the position was of such a nature that it should be devoid of party politics.[30] Patterson had covered himself with both political factions in the Senate. Franklin Peale's nomination was approved in short order. He took the oath of office as a Mint officer on January 11, 1836.[31] On that same day, Patterson signed off on an audit of Cloud's bullion accounts showing no discrepancies.[32]

Patterson was not finished. With Peale's confirmation in hand, he asked Woodbury's permission to appoint his clerk and nephew, William DuBois, to the now vacant assistant assayer's position. DuBois had been pursuing a law career when he contracted a voice affliction, necessitating his acceptance of a clerical position under Samuel Moore. Since Peale's return, DuBois had been doing the work of the assistant assayer while Patterson used Peale to make improvements throughout the minting process.[33] Woodbury, in approving this request, did not ask why Jacob Eckfeldt suddenly needed an assistant when he had managed without one during Franklin Peale's absence. In one fell swoop, Patterson had effectively neutered Adam

These sketches, part of the National Numismatic Collection, give a glimpse at the evolution of Gobrecht's Liberty design. These first six sketches represent early work as Gobrecht's concept of Liberty evolved away from the work by Sully into a vision of his own. The final three sketches are pictured later in the chapter.

Fig. 44.1. This sketch is patterned after Sully's design with a slight modification in the drapery treatment over Liberty's arms. This work is likely the pattern for the outline on a dollar-sized planchet that Patterson sent to Secretary Woodbury and President Jackson for review.

Fig. 44.2. This sketch incorporates Titian Peale's treatment of the drapery about Liberty's left breast and midriff. The drapery treatment over the arms has returned to Sully's style.

Fig. 44.3. In this sketch the tiara is gone and Gobrecht has applied his own style to the drapery over Liberty's arms. This work is done on mica, an intermediate step at the time in transferring a design sketch into clay.

Fig. 44.4. Gobrecht has returned to Sully's drapery treatment over the arms in this sketch on mica. However, the figure of Liberty is starting to lean slightly forward.

Fig. 44.5. Gobrecht has moved Liberty's right hand to the back of the shield and removed the drapery from her arms. Liberty's hand now holds the ribbon containing the inscription. The trailing part of that ribbon is tucked behind the shield.

Fig. 44.6. In this sketch, Gobrecht has enlarged the rock upon which Liberty is sitting and pronounced the lean of her figure forward. He has also covered the now-empty corner of the shield with drapery to compensate for moving the hand.

Fig. 45. This oil on cardboard by Titian Peale of an ill-proportioned Liberty seated upon a farm implement provided a second model from which Gobrecht could base his sketches.

Fig. 46. These six sketches by Titian Peale are in rough form but exhibit an innovative approach. The first sketch (top left) shows an eagle rising with a crude outline of a scroll in its beak. The second (top right) is semi-finished, with the eagle rising in a field of stars and a scroll with "E Pluribus Unum" clutched it its claws. The third sketch (center left) again places the rising eagle in a field of stars but the scroll with "E Pluribus Unum" is at the bottom rim where one would expect to see the coin's denomination. The fourth sketch (center right) in polished form completes the evolution of the eagle rising amidst stars and the scroll at the base. The fifth sketch (bottom left) employs an eagle standing upon a rock. The sixth sketch (bottom right) places this standing eagle with 13 arrows and a crudely drawn olive branch at its feet in a field of stars; "E Pluribus Unum" appears on the rock.

Fig. 47. Several fusible-metal trial strikes survive at the Library Company of Philadelphia. In the mid-stage die trial, the shield is draped, the pole is shorter and the folds of Liberty's gown are over done. This design appears to have been the source of Patterson's criticisms expressed in his letter of January 14, 1836, to Secretary of the Treasury Levi Woodbury.

Eckfeldt's control of the Mint's operations. It had taken six short months for Robert Maskell Patterson to bring this institution under his total control.

• • • •

On January 8, 1836, Patterson was again focused on the new dollar design. He had approved a sketch by Gobrecht and authorized a trial strike with a brass die using a fusible metal. In a letter to Woodbury, he stated there were imperfections that would be corrected at the cutting of a regular die in steel. Nevertheless, the thin piece of metal offered a distinct impression. However, it was subject to bending and Patterson fretted that the general likeness, as it would appear on coins, might be more accurately presented using a less malleable metal (fig. 47). The director was only sending impressions to Woodbury and Jackson. He was not ready to have the design subjected to general criticism. At this point, Patterson wanted permission to proceed.[34]

Patterson got his permission but not without comment. The pole was still not long enough to suit Jackson. Woodbury also regretted that the right foot of Liberty was not visible so as to show more distinctly the design and character of the impression. Woodbury's eye was looking for an anchor point. Patterson responded to this criticism in a forthright manner, explaining why the pole had not been lengthened. He also went into detail on the problems he saw with Gobrecht's engraving work to date. The left arm was too prominent. The left shoulder was too low and distant from the neck. The right arm was too muscular. The index finger of the left hand was too much in the position of pointing. There was too much confusion of drapery at the left breast and near the right hand. The knees were too lumpy with their articulation not being shown with sufficient distinctness. In these comments, Patterson was referring to Liberty's proper left and right. These criticisms were well founded, not only showing Patterson a good judge of art but also indicating that his frustration level was growing.[35] What Patterson did not note to Woodbury was that, under Gobrecht's hand, the upper body of Liberty leaned slightly forward. That was the most fundamental of the deviations from Sully's sketch. Now Gobrecht had to address these criticisms.

Meanwhile, Robert Maskell Patterson approached Rembrandt Peale, Franklin's half-brother. The two men had been together in Paris and were close. Patterson, in a letter written February 8, asked Rembrandt to contact Charles Cushing Wright (fig. 48), a noted engraver in New York. Patterson wanted to know Wright's philosophy in regard to the art on coinage. More importantly, Patterson wanted help at the Mint. Wright told Rembrandt that he had so little leisure time he could not reflect upon the subject of proper coin art. However, he would send Pat-

Fig. 48. Charles Cushing Wright, pictured here in a self portrait in 1827, would go on to become one of the best engravers—if not the best—in America by the time of his death in 1854. He was also one of the original founders of the prestigious National Academy of Design.

terson some samples of his work, though they would not adequately reflect what he could do. Wright also offered comments constructive in nature but not necessarily to the point of addressing Gobrecht's difficulties.

Wright called the current American coin designs deficient, not worthy of a civilized country, and much below the standard of art available. The talent was sufficient to produce a good coin. Wright had no idea why the present coin designs were so inadequate. He pointed out that the dies for new designs must be executed in the best possible manner. Wright questioned why the engraving of American paper money was so much better than the coin work. Then he answered his question by stating no undisputed artist could afford to give the prime of his life for the engraver's paltry annual salary of $1,200. If Rembrandt had issued a feeler on behalf of Patterson to Wright about an engraving position at the Mint, he had his answer.

Wright had some advice as well.

> The devices of our coin being established by Law, the First Artist of our country should make drawings in black and white, and those most approved should be modeled large and finished properly before the die is commenced. The die should be well cut, a die of what is usually called a male or hub should be finished to correspond with the model then be again resunk and finished with the utmost care. Coins should be made so to pile or stand when placed upon each other, having a rim or border sufficiently raised to protect the work. Dies for coins are made in a manner different from medal dies, the work on coins should be well relieved for effect but still it would not answer to have them too bold or much raised above the surface. It requires on that account much skill to produce a good effect, much more then where more relief can be given.[36]

It was sage advice. Sully had wanted a sculptor such as Persico to model his drawing, while Gobrecht took a different tack, generating multiple sketches followed by a rough cut die to strike fusible metal specimens. Gobrecht's approach muddied the water and frustrated Patterson.

Unfortunately, Patterson did not receive this letter until the first week in March. Rembrandt offered his own advice in addition to Wright's letter.

> Would it not be well to get him to execute something for you—if such an operation is within your power. Mr. Gobrecht may be the best man in the world, without being much of an artist. But as the Mint is now under the direction of Taste, Knowledge and Energy and a total reform and improvement is to be effected (*sic*) in all its operations, ought you not to have the very best Artist the Country can produce? And ought not our coins to be equal to any in the world? Or is there any good reason why they should not be better than any?
>
> If Mr. Wright is not the most accomplished Artist—then he that is better should be employed—but I do not know of one more competent.[37]

Rembrandt Peale had pulled out all the stops to get Patterson to pull back and restart the process. He even appealed to Patterson's vanity—a reform-minded director would not hesitate to take this action.[38]

Rembrandt's letter could not have come at a worse time. Patterson was absent from the Mint and had been for several weeks due to family illness. He was not equipped emotionally to make such a radical call. Besides, he had become enamored with the seated Liberty design, having recently commissioned Sully to reproduce it in an oil portrait.

In the interim, Franklin had become, in all but title, the acting Mint director.[39] In fact, progress had been made in Patterson's absence. Titian Peale had acquired a recently killed eagle that either he or someone under his direction had mounted at the desired attitude for the coin design. Next, he used an optical device known as a camera lucida to give an exact reproduction in his sketch.[40] The result, in Franklin's view, was remarkable. Even Adam Eckfeldt had shown a rare level of enthusiasm over the sketch (fig. 49).

As to Gobrecht, there were more issues. Peale was concerned with one in particular. He strongly declared his

Fig. 49. This sketch of an eagle rising by Titian Peale is in a style that caught Patterson's fancy, allowing the reverse design to finally move forward.

feelings to Patterson regarding Gobrecht's artistic abilities.

> In the many conversations that I have had with Mr. Gobrecht, he has advanced positively a principal that must be combated to the death ere we can hope to see upon our coin such a specimen of the arts as shall satisfy you or anyone possessing a particle of genuine taste or judgment in such matters. It is that *in the reduction* of designs to the small size of dies etc. It is necessary to make *small* parts such as folds of small dimensions, nay called *features*, *larger* than the proportion calls for. Now I am sustained by Sully and *all* artists with whom I have conversed in the fullest conviction that this principal is utterly fallacious—it is the principal of caricaturists, of inferior artists, of anybody but a sound artist. I have not yet attempted to combat such a notion but feel it a duty to communicate it to you that when the time comes you may not have an idea presented for which we are unprepared.

In the context of the art of painting in the first half of the 19th century, Peale's position was correct. However, Gobrecht was trying to impart a sense of three dimensions in the coin design through exaggerations in the depth of the folds of Liberty's gown. To this point, the engraver was correct. Peale's fear that the figure would come to resemble a caricature was clearly unfounded and a misunderstanding of what Gobrecht was attempting to accomplish.

Meanwhile, Gobrecht, apparently unaware of the maneuvering around him, was moving forward with die preparation. Peale also stated that tests in steel had been conducted that proved much more curvature on the face of the die would be required to bring up the impression in a manner consistent with English and French coins. The pressure on the planchet must begin in the center and progress to the rim.[41] Both Peale and Eckfeldt knew this design was going to be difficult to bring up fully in the Mint's coin presses. It can also be inferred from this discussion that Gobrecht was trying to incorporate relief into his figure of Liberty.

At the end of the first week of March, Gobrecht had made progress. He had worked through more sketches, simplifying the drapery and addressing the criticisms of January (fig. 50). In fact Gobrecht had finished engraving his die (fig. 51), in this case the hub, and had decided upon the necessary convexity to bring up the obverse design satisfactorily. Tools, including a dish with a 24-inch radius, to produce the concavity on the hub were not available. Peale had ordered them on his own discretion. He told Patterson in a letter that he had no idea when Gobrecht would be done.[42]

On April 9, 1836, Patterson, back in command, sent two specimens of the obverse design from the second die to Woodbury, one for President Jackson's approval. He was pleased with the improvements, saying that artists and men of taste who had been unfavorable to the first version all approved this second attempt. Gone were many of the folds in the drapery, thereby avoiding the objections raised

The final three Gobrecht Liberty sketches reflect Gobrecht's work from the January 8, 1836, trial submittal to the final version that Patterson presented to the secretary of the Treasury and the president on April 9, 1836.

Fig. 50.1. Gobrecht has tucked Liberty's right calf under her left leg. The pole holding the pileus has been lengthened. This sketch in mica is closest to the die-trial splasher that survives at the Library Company of Philadelphia.

Fig. 50.2. The engraver has refigured and exposed Liberty's right foot in an attempt to better anchor the figure to the plinth in accordance with Secretary Woodbury's criticism.

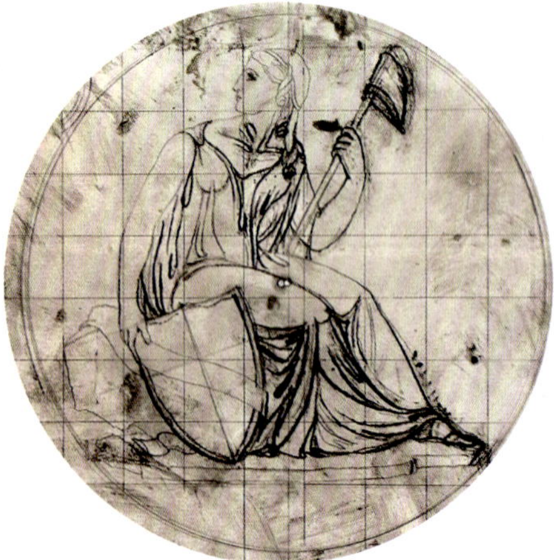

Fig. 50.3. Gobrecht has simplified his treatment of the drapery in this sketch on mica in response to Patterson's critique. Also the index finger of the left hand no longer points. While the pole remains extended, this rendition very closely resembles the final design. Note the hole in the center of the sketch where the mica was pinned into the clay.

Fig. 51. This late-stage die trial has the simplified gown arrangement of the final version, a longer pole, and the drapery is removed from the shield, although this looks to be an adjustment overlaid roughly in the die.

by Franklin Peale. The director also enclosed drawings for the reverse. The eagle was true to nature, flying, as was the country, in an onward and upward course. The absurdity of the shield on the eagle's breast had been avoided by incorporating that motif into the obverse. The arrows and branches clutched in the eagle's feet had been removed, being contrary to good taste. Gone also was the original concept of a scroll bearing "E Pluribus Unum." A constellation of stars for each state of the Union was scattered in the field surrounding the eagle.[43] In an original style, the sizes of the stars varied, imparting the sense of a third dimension.

Patterson hoped these designs met the approval of the secretary and the president. While intended for the dollar coin, it had occurred to him that it might be fitting to use these designs on the coins to be made from the indemnity gold to be received from France. It would be a shame if $6 million in gold were spread across the country with that thing on the back which courtesy might call an eagle. There might be a delay of three to four months in issuing these coins, but they could be issued before the next Congress by preparing the planchets in advance.[44]

Woodbury answered, preferring the sketch in which the eagle was, as he described it, "in flight on its prey." However, he thought perhaps the mouth should be closed.[45] Patterson was pleased that Woodbury had at least accepted the design. The objection of the bird's mouth being open, Patterson had also raised to Titian Peale. The change had been tried, but the effect had been detrimental. First, it took away the spirited appearance of the bird. Second, it required the smoothing down of the feathers on the neck. Those neck feathers were never ruffled except when the bird's mouth was open. No fewer than 30 sketches had been rejected and at one time Patterson feared the design concept would have to be abandoned.

Patterson inferred that Woodbury's silence on employing the design on the gold coinage was, in fact, a rejection of the idea. Woodbury had previously expressed concern that coinage production not be impaired in any way. Therefore Patterson was sticking to the plan to employ the design on the new dollar coins and would proceed with the dies.[46]

Progress was still at a snail's pace. A third obverse impression was sent to Woodbury in the middle of June. Patterson judged it even better than the previous attempt. Gobrecht was to commence work on the reverse die immediately. The design now centered on an eagle with its mouth not so obviously open and neck feathers smoothed back.[47] Samples of the reverse in soft metal were sent to Woodbury and President Jackson on August 27 and promptly approved.[48]

Finally, on September 22, 1836, Patterson notified Adam Eckfeldt that Gobrecht had sunk the dies and the impressions had been approved by Treasury. This final version bore the inscription "C. Gobrecht F" on the plinth.[49] Eckfeldt was to make every effort for an early release of the new dollar coin. In what was the accepted division of labor at the Mint, it was up to Eckfeldt to make the hubs and working dies. Patterson wanted the cutting and milling machines adapted for the dollar planchets in advance. The new dollars were to be struck in a close reeded collar on the large screw press. Use of this screw press would be temporary until its replacement could be put in service.[50] The confident satisfaction of Patterson seems to jump from the page of this letter. It was premature.

It was possible but not necessarily practical to produce a reeded edge with a screw press. These coins would have plain edges. In the greater picture, that was minor. Still there was delay. Eckfeldt must have struggled with hardening of the dies. This had always been more black magic than process for him. However, there was another more serious problem. It had been so long since the Mint had struck dollar coins that the existing screw presses were inadequate to the task. In November Patterson told Levi Woodbury without giving a reason that they were "engaged in making a press suitable for coining it."[51]

Production finally commenced in early December. There were difficulties almost from the start. The feed fingers were slamming into the reverse die. Die chips and rim nicks quickly developed. From this damage, numismatists have recently constructed an emission sequence that reveals even more about this striking. Initially, the obverse and reverse dies were paired 180 degrees from each other in what is known as coin turn, with the eagle

Fig. 52. Part of the National Numismatic Collection, this Gobrecht dollar was one of the first struck; its reverse is free of any small defects in the die caused by the feed mechanism.

on the reverse rising. Then, production was stopped and the reverse die rotated so that the eagle was soaring level and the dies were no longer opposite of each other, in what is known as medal turn. Then, the dies were again adjusted, retaining the medal turn but allowing the eagle to once again rise at various degrees. Apparently, Eckfeldt was rotating the reverse die in an effort to solve the problem with the feeding mechanism. It had been a long time since he had dealt with the 416-grain silver planchets. He then moved back to coin turn and ended with medal turn and the bird rising.[52]

On December 16, 1836, Robert Maskell Patterson proudly presented a specimen of the new dollar coin (fig. 52) to the American Philosophical Society.[53] He had been elected a vice president of the society at the beginning of the year.[54] This coin was one of 1,000 from this year-end production run.

This process had been a learning experience for Patterson. He would make process improvements going forward. However, the Gobrecht dollar, named for the engraver, was a decided improvement over anything that had come from the Mint since its inception. The engraver had given the figure of Liberty a respectable relief. In terms of simplicity, the coin was a masterpiece. In the opinion of the author, the reverse was easily the best coin design produced at the Mint in the 19th century. The obverse, however, had flaws that stemmed from Patterson's restrictive instructions to Sully. Placing Liberty upon a rock removed any opportunity to inject life into the figure. Hence Liberty, in part because of Gobrecht's altering her posture, appears to be looking over her shoulder with no object to draw her gaze. The coin designers of the next century would have solved this problem by turning Liberty's head to face a sunburst. However, this change risked impairing the simplicity of the obverse design. While this coin just missed being one of the absolute all-time greats, Robert Maskell Patterson had good reason to be proud.

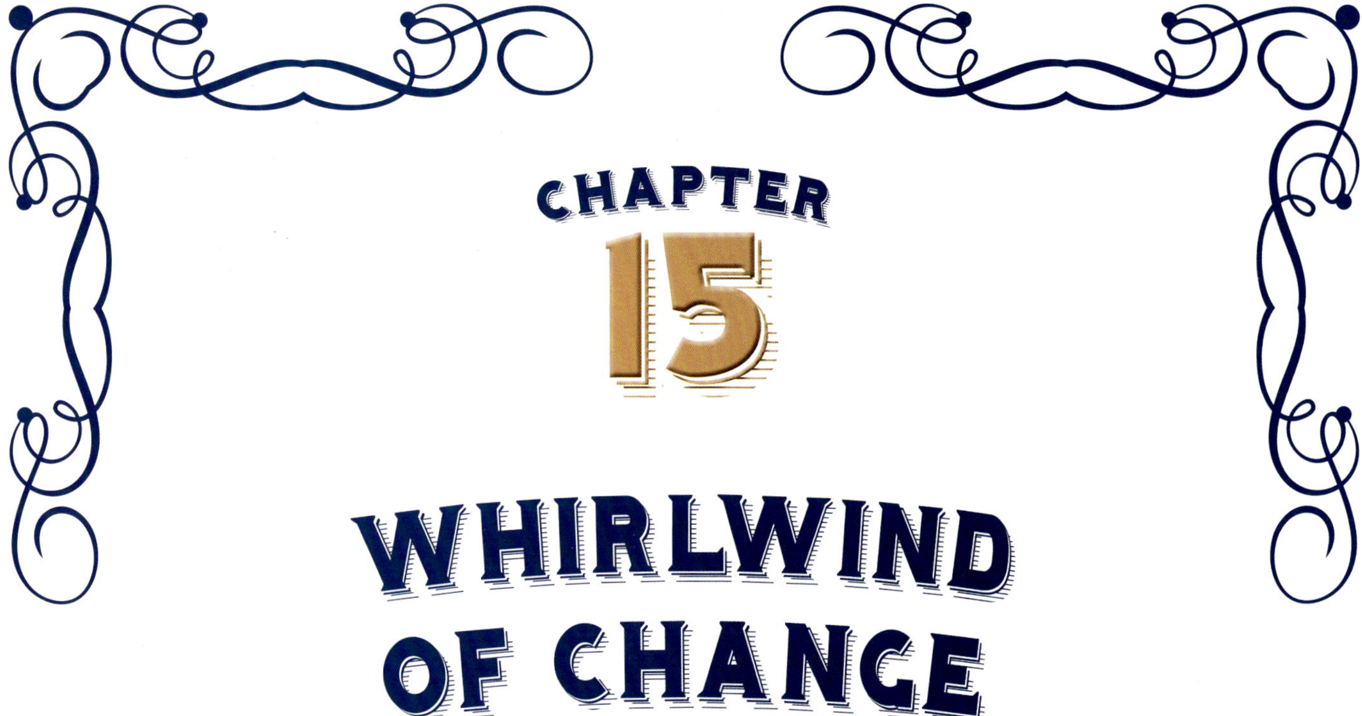

CHAPTER 15

WHIRLWIND OF CHANGE

Robert Maskell Patterson had more on his mind than new coin designs as he assumed the reins of the Mint. First on his list was harnessing the knowledge Franklin Peale brought back from Europe. Steam power was used throughout the Mint except in the milling and coining operations. It took three men to operate one of the old, large screw presses that stamped out the coins, just as it had since the beginning of the Mint. Some of the smaller presses only required two men, but productivity gains were certainly to be had regardless.

While in Europe, Franklin Peale had had the opportunity to observe a steam-powered coin press in operation at Karlsruhe in Baden in what would become Germany. In Paris Peale was able to examine in detail another press designed by M. Thonnellier. While at the Royal Mint in London, he saw screw presses adapted to steam power. It was a sight he dismissed, calling it one of the greatest curiosities in mechanics that he had ever seen. The German and French coin presses employed a toggle joint that Peale observed to be superior to any adaptation of the old screw press. The concept was not strange to Peale. His friend, Matthias Baldwin, had started construction of just such a press several years previously but had discontinued the project to complete other jobs.[1]

Peale was up for making changes. In the weeks before Patterson arrived, he had started work with Jacob Eckfeldt on a new method for assaying silver.[2] However, when Pat-

terson inserted Peale into Adam Eckfeldt's coining department, there was hesitation. The chief coiner was resistant.

> If Mr. Peale had full swing he would turn everything upside down; why he even talks of throwing away our costly coining presses that have done and are doing such good service, dispensing with the manpower, and yet he won't hear of applying steam power to our old screw presses which has been successfully done in the Royal Mint, London. He wants something better and no doubt he would have it if we were starting anew.[3]

By the last week of September 1835, Peale had a model of his proposed steam-powered coin press. At about that same time, Patterson, Eckfeldt, and Peale were guests aboard the first steam passenger train from Philadelphia to Lancaster. The timing was auspicious, as the conversation amongst the three men over the applications of steam power in the coining department must have been lively.

Patterson immediately sought permission to place a contract with Merrick & Company, a leading Philadelphia foundry. He would have done the work in house in the Mint's machine shop, but it was already occupied fabricating screw presses for the New Orleans branch mint. The director would give the press a trial in Philadelphia. If it was as successful as he expected it to be, he would use it as a model for the branch mints, including New Orleans.[4] Peale was going to have to move fast.

He first turned to his half-nephew, George Escol Sellers, who ran the machine shop in Philadelphia that had constructed the steam locomotive for the Lancaster trial run, pushing aside Merrick & Company for the time being. Peale provided drawings to Sellers from which the patterns, forgings, and castings were made. They were delivered to the Mint, where Peale put them together himself. At some point, he acquired the help of the same Joseph Saxton who had built the balance beam for him in London and had since returned to America. Work seemed to be coming toward completion in February 1836. Peale went so far as to have a special die prepared, probably by Gobrecht, with a radiated pileus on one side and wording commemorating the first steam-powered coinage at the Mint on the other. Copper one-cent planchets were to be used. The date Peale fixed and had engraved on the die was February 22, 1836, George Washington's birthday. He even had a few of the medals struck in silver, brass, and gilt.[5] That date came and went, but the press was not yet in operation.

Two weeks later, Peale seemed bogged down. In a letter to Patterson, while the director was absent dealing with the unidentified family illness, Peale wrote optimistically that the press was coming along nicely, but he could not even offer conjecture as to when it would be completed.[6] It is clear from this comment there were problems and solutions were not yet at hand. However, in two more weeks, all was ready. The date of March 23, 1836, was punched over the old date on the medal die.[7] First, a trial was run with Patterson, Peale, Sellers, and Saxton to make sure all was in order. Then, on this second date fixed, Baldwin, Merrick, and the other prominent Philadelphia mechanics were invited for the ceremonial first striking (fig. 53).[8] The new coin press was placed into service with the intention to strike one-cent pieces, quarters, and half eagles.[9]

Fig. 53. This medal, celebrating the successful introduction of a steam-powered coin press at the Mint, was engraved by Christian Gobrecht and struck using regular cent planchets.

Concurrently, Peale also began constructing a steam-powered milling machine. This machine was originally used to impress letters or ornaments on the edge of coins. More recently, it had been used to throw up a thickened edge upon the planchets to facilitate a better border on the coin in the striking process using a close collar. It had the side benefit of reducing stress upon the working dies, which added to their useful life. Again, Peale started with a model, from which a working prototype was fabricated in the Mint machine shop. The finished example was an art form unto itself. A classical-style tripod of cast iron supported the milling table with its adjustable edge dies. Peale would always bring a refined artistic eye to his finished machinery. Through this tripod rose the vertical steam drive shaft from below. In ideal conditions, this machine that operated in triplicate could process 200 planchets per minute, well more than needed for coining. Peale put it into operation in February 1836 without incident.[10]

• • • •

Simultaneous with this extensive overhauling of the coining operation, Patterson moved forward on another front. Over the years a hodgepodge of regulations, laws, and accepted practices at the Philadelphia Mint had evolved. It was time to codify them. Patterson used his friend John Kane to assist in drafting his proposed statutes. Once completed, he turned to Churchill Cambreleng to introduce the legislation in the House. Cambreleng, now serving as chairman of the Ways and Means Committee, was Martin Van Buren's man in the House of Representatives, and Van Buren was Jackson's heir designate.

However, Patterson's effort was sidetracked in early February 1836 when the issue of minting a $1 gold piece again came up for consideration in the House. For a second time, James Graham (fig. 54) called for the Ways and Means Committee to consider introducing this denomination that circulated freely in his home district courtesy of the Bechtlers.[11] Two weeks later, on February 13, Ransom Gillet of New York State moved that a select committee be formed to consider gold coins in the denominations of $1, $2, $3, and $4. The committee would also consider whether any additional branch mints were necessary. Here reappeared the suggestion of establishing a branch mint in New York City. The resulting committee included Gillet and Joseph Ingersoll (fig. 55) from Philadelphia.[12] That Ingersoll was a Whig made no difference. He and Patterson were friends and would work in unison. Without the power of Nicholas Biddle and the Bank of the United States, the Mint was going to have to stand on its own two feet to defeat the financial interests in New York City and remain viable.

Fig. 55. Joseph R. Ingersoll, shown in this engraving by Alexander Handyside Ritchie, assumed John Sergeant's seat in the House of Representatives. For many years, Ingersoll worked with Robert Maskell Patterson to support and defend the Mint at Philadelphia.

Fig. 54. A North Carolina representative from the district where the Bechtler private mint was located, James Graham was an indefatigable supporter of the $1 gold piece.

Ingersoll and Patterson talked on the evening of the 15th. The Mint director was unalterably opposed to a gold dollar, due to its small size. As was typical, he approached the argument from a scientific viewpoint. Gold was more valuable than silver by the proportion of 16 to 1 and heavier by a proportion of 13 to 7. Thus, a gold dollar would be approximately 30 times lighter than a silver dollar. That meant it would be one-third lighter than a half dime. In this argument, Patterson viewed weight as synonymous with size. Key to this analysis was the idea that the dollar gold coin would have the same thickness as a half dime. This was not necessarily the case. Patterson also argued that any sum in silver coin less than a quarter eagle could easily be carried without inconvenience. The director acknowledged that it appeared to be the policy of the federal government to substitute gold for bank notes. However, overstating his case, he believed "all but a few states" had forbidden paper notes in small denominations.[13]

Patterson's negative stance was not enough. Treasury secretary Levi Woodbury wanted to see examples. Patterson had to pull Gobrecht off the new silver dollar coin design in February and March to generate a pattern for gold dollars (fig. 56). Gobrecht used the same radiated pileus from the steam-press medal on the obverse and the denomination "1 D." surrounded by a palm branch on the reverse. Patterson sent samples to Woodbury on March 23,

Fig. 56. Director Patterson had to pull Gobrecht off his work on the silver-dollar design in order to provide congressmen with examples of a gold dollar and to reinforce his point concerning the small size of the proposed coin. To expedite matters, the same pileus design theme used on the first steam-press medal was employed on the obverse of this pattern piece. The engraving on both sides was roughly executed, detracting from the coin's appearance.

along with some copper steam-press commemorative medals.[14] He sent other specimens to congressmen to illustrate the small size of the gold coin.

Patterson and Ingersoll could not sway the Select Committee. Their report rebutted thoroughly the objection to the coin's smallness and the possibility of its being mistaken for a silver piece of lesser value.

> It is believed that the people have had no difficulty in distinguishing between silver coins now and heretofore in circulation when not defaced. We have now the half disme and the six and one fourth cent piece, the disme and the twelve and a half cent piece, and the six penny sterling: but they are not mistaken one for the other. We have, also, two pistareens, the one valued at about sixteen cents, and the other eighteen cents and a fraction: we have the English shilling sterling, and the Spanish and American quarter dollars but the one is never mistaken for the other. We have the half dollar and half crown, but they are never mistaken for each other, nor for the two and sixpence sterling: we also have the five franc piece, but it is not mistaken for the dollar, nor is either to be confounded with the crown.

While the report meant to address the $1 gold piece, it certainly gives a unique snapshot of the hodgepodge that made up American circulating specie in 1836. The report went on to castigate small-denomination paper money. Few could recognize counterfeit and spurious bank notes. The common man could not be expected to detect such notes, particularly those from distant banks. In conclusion, the committee directed their chairman to report out a bill authorizing the striking of $1, $2, and $3 gold coins.

Patterson and Ingersoll were successful on one point. The committee did not address the need for additional branch mints. The drive for a branch in New York City was blunted, at least for now.[15]

What Ingersoll could not get in the committee he subsequently gained on the floor of the House. On June 23, Gillet moved that the rules of the House in regard to priority be suspended to allow his bill to be considered. While the yeas on his motion exceeded the nays, the required two-thirds majority to suspend the rules was not there. His bill was dead for the session.[16]

On April 5, 1836, Churchill Cambreleng took the floor to introduce H.R. 529, a bill supplementary to the 1792 act establishing and regulating the Mint. Robert Maskell Patterson's moment had arrived on the House floor. It was the first time in the history of the Mint that a sitting director had taken a direct role in initiating legislation in Congress.

The bill set forth the duties of each of the officers. The director was responsible for the control and management of the Mint, and reporting to the president annually upon its operations, essentially as it had been from the beginning of the Mint. Additionally, the director reported to the secretary of the Treasury on a day-to-day basis. The melter and refiner executed all operations necessary to form ingots of standard silver and gold suitable for the chief coiner, from metals delivered to him from the treasurer. The chief coiner executed all operations necessary to strike coins, conformable in all respects to the law, from those ingots. Finally, the engraver prepared and engraved all the dies with the mandated devices and inscriptions for use at the Mint and its branches. The director retained the power to employ such workmen at the Mint from time to time as he deemed necessary.

The bill set forth bonds required of each of the officers as well as their salaries. The director's salary was placed at $3,500 per year. This figure included traveling expenses to the different branches and all other charges. This odd provision virtually assured that Patterson would minimize his travel as director, delegating it instead to other officers who could be reimbursed for their expenses. The other officers were to receive $2,000 each. Salaries for assistants and clerks were to be determined by the director, with the approval of the president.

The standard for silver and gold coins was to be set at 900 parts pure metal and 100 parts alloy. The alloy of the silver coins was to be copper. For the gold coins, an alloy composed of copper and silver was called for, with the condition that silver should not exceed one half the alloy. The Mint would now be able to work with a simple fraction for obtaining standard silver and gold. It also gave considerable flexibility to the Mint in refining gold bullion containing variable amounts of silver.

The bill set out the weights of standard silver and gold for the coins resulting from the change in the amount of alloy. A dollar would be 412.5 grains compared to the previous 416 grains. An eagle would be unchanged 258 grains of standard gold. However, its gold content would be adjusted ever so slightly from 232 grains to 232.2 grains to bring its fineness from 899.2 to 900. The resulting silver-to-gold ratio would decrease to 15.9884. No one would give this tiny tweak of the gold content a second thought, even if it did slightly devalue gold.

The other silver and gold coins were proportional with the exception of the dime and half dime. Patterson was debasing these two coins 3.2 percent, in line with earlier thinking prior to the act of 1834. The Mint had incurred substantial demand for the two coins since he had taken its helm. While he did not want to revisit the ratio of 16 to 1, he wanted to ensure that these coins stayed in circulation. Seigniorage resulting from this debasement would accrue to the Mint to defray general expenses. As further insurance, the Mint director called for limiting the legal tender of these two coins to $1. Patterson in making a seemingly small change was taking a big risk that the whole bill would derail. Debasement was, for whatever reason, controversial.

Patterson also addressed copper coins, calling for a reduction in weight for the cent from 168 grains to 140 grains, with the half cent reduced accordingly. He proposed the legal tender limit for copper coins be 10 cents.

The proposed bill reaffirmed the devices and inscriptions required on the coinage. The obverse was to have an impression emblematic of Liberty, the inscription "Liberty," and the date. The reverse of the gold and silver coins was to have the figure or representation of an eagle, the inscription "United States of America," and the designation of value. No mention was made of the motto "E Pluribus Unum," which now only survived on the half dollar. Patterson was wisely holding the inscriptions to a minimum. On the dime and half dime, due to space constraints, the eagle was to be omitted.

Patterson's draft legislation reaffirmed the principle of free coinage, but with conditions. The Mint had the right to refuse deposits of less than $200 or any bullion so base as to be unsuitable for coining. Also, when gold and silver were combined, if the value of either metal after deducting the expense of separation was less than $10, that metal would not be separated for the benefit of the depositor. When gold was combined with silver in such a small proportion that it could not be separated economically, the whole would be coined as silver.

The only charge to a depositor would be for refining bullion that was below standard, toughening when metals were contained that rendered the bullion unfit for coinage, using copper or silver as alloy in above-standard bullion, and separating gold and silver when these metals existed together in the bullion. These charges would be adjusted from time to time to reflect the Mint's actual costs and the resulting receipts would be applied against the contingent expenses of the Mint.

The bill enabled the secretary of the Treasury to maintain, at his discretion, a bullion fund at the Mint of not more than $300,000 to facilitate prompt payment without a discount. While Congress had previously ignored the need for a bullion fund, Patterson was on safe ground here. In February Senator Thomas Hart Benton had moved that the secretary of the Treasury report on the adequacy of the supply of bullion and foreign coins available to the Mint.[17] Secretary Woodbury promptly responded that the gold supplied to the Mint was inadequate to keep it constantly employed. In the secretary's opinion, a bullion fund as large as $100,000 was needed with the only charge to the depositor being for wastage.[18]

The remainder of the bill provided accounting rules for transfer of bullion between the treasurer and the operating departments. The bill also established acceptable standard deviations for coinage weights and wastage for the melter and refiner. The Assay Commission established to annually verify the fineness of the Mint's coinage would now be composed of the district court judge and the United States attorney for the Eastern District of Pennsylvania, the collector of the port of Philadelphia, and others appointed by the president.[19]

That same April 5, Thomas Hart Benton (fig. 57), the irrepressible hard-money advocate, was doing his own thing in the Senate. He had asked Patterson for the capacity of the Mint, no doubt in reaction to Woodbury's comment in his February report on the facility's idle capacity. In response, the director had stated that on a consistent basis the number was something like 12 million coins per year. However, with the improvements underway in steam-driven milling and coin presses and expected improvements in melting and refining, he felt Mint capacity would ultimately increase threefold over the next several years. Patterson was optimistic.[20]

Fig. 57. Thomas Hart Benton, depicted here in an early painting by Matthew Jouett, was a staunch Jackson administration supporter and an advocate for hard money throughout his political career.

Benton could do the math. If Mint capacity achieved Patterson's forecast of 36 million coins and there was no commensurate increase in the bullion available for coinage, the Mint would stand idle over 80 percent of the time. Benton gave notice of intent to file a bill that would demand prompt payment for deposits of bullion at the Mint and repeal refining charges. To support prompt payment, Benton would make the Mint and its branches depositories for public money instead of the deposit banks.[21] This proposal went well beyond anything contemplated by Woodbury or Patterson.

The effect of this conflicting legislation in the Senate was to gum up the works. Nothing went anywhere. Behind this inertia was the fear that the pet banks would lose their federal deposits. A frustrated Patterson told Woodbury that there was no hope in this session of Congress and no one could give him any encouragement for the coming short second session either.[22]

It wasn't a complete loss for Patterson. Congress appropriated $20,000 to the Mint for the introduction of new machinery and apparatus, including the application of steam power to coinage and improvements in the melting and refining department.[23] Patterson could now go ahead with Merrick for the construction of a steam-powered coin press for half dollars and dollars that would be placed into service the coming autumn.[24]

Changes in the melting and refining department were another matter altogether. Peale called the department "gloriously deficient," lacking even basic tools needed for its operations. With the appropriation in hand, Peale was ready. Well in advance, he had prepared patterns for ingot molds and the silver furnace. He had also completed drawings for the other furnaces and implements and placed them in the hands of his relative, George Escol Sellers, to be ready.[25] These changes would result in a doubling of capacity in his department.[26] However, that was only part of the story.

Franklin Peale also wanted to convert the refining activity over to the more efficient sulfuric-acid process widely used in Europe. Implementation of this new process would require dedication of corresponding space on two floors of the Mint. New equipment, including platina vessels, would be necessitated. Operation would be around the clock, requiring the Mint to stay open at night. Unaddressed by Peale, the resulting noxious sulfur fumes, more so than the existing nitric-acid fumes, would be unacceptable on Chestnut Street. The whole changeover would cost $30,000. Patterson saw the changes as totally impractical to implement and the cost unjustified, given the small amount of gold bullion requiring silver separation. Without a second thought, he killed this proposal.[27]

Patterson was better organized for the second session of the Twenty-Fourth Congress, even if doubts as to the passage of H.R. 529 existed. He left nothing to chance, traveling to Washington to work behind the scenes. He relied on Peale to keep him abreast of Mint operations. He also had the melter and refiner review the language of the proposed legislation.[28]

Fig. 58. Churchill Cambreleng, the powerful New York congressman and one-time supporter of the Philadelphia Mint expansion, now worked with Robert Maskell Patterson to push Mint-reform legislation.

Churchill Cambreleng (fig. 58) made the first move in the early days of this session on December 15, 1836, announcing his intent to amend the bill. The provision allowing the Mint to benefit when the amount of either silver or gold being separated in a bullion deposit fell below $10 was adjusted, substituting "cannot be removed advantageously" for the $10 threshold. Also, the clause allowing the Mint to coin as silver that bullion containing very small amounts of gold was dropped.

Patterson had picked up on Benton's efforts the previous spring, now increasing the bullion fund to $1 million.[29] Beyond another potential conflict with Benton, he had been forced into this action. The New York–based Bank of America had presented gold bullion received from the French indemnity settlement for coinage and had experienced delays. The bank also had a backlog of silver bullion on deposit. Perhaps Peale's new steam-driven press was not working quite as well as he claimed. The bank president, George Newbold, grew so frustrated with the Mint that he took his complaints to a New York newspaper. Secretary Woodbury read the article and sent it to Patterson's attention, an indirect rebuke.[30] Patterson, in turn, wrote an angry letter to Newbold stating that the bullion inventory numbers in the newspaper were exaggerated. Half of the silver bullion claimed had been in the Mint's vaults only a few days.[31] Still, Patterson could not allow this situation to fester.

The omens for passage looked good when Silas Wright of New York (Van Buren's protégé in the Senate) introduced a companion bill, S. 33, on December 19, 1836.[32] The next day, Graham again moved that the House Ways and Means Committee consider a $1 gold piece.[33] It would have been easy to tack this onto the Mint bill, but nothing of that nature happened.

On December 22, Cambreleng took the floor and asked that the rules be suspended to bring up the Mint bill that was intended to take effect January 1, 1837. He got his two-thirds vote to go to a Committee of the Whole and the debate was on.

Former president John Quincy Adams, now a member of the House, rose. Regardless of his harassing tactics on behalf of the abolition of slavery, he was much respected and his opinions held sway. Adams querulously asked why the bill needed to be passed by the first of the coming year. It was an important bill and should be carefully examined. Adams stubbornly refused to acknowledge that reducing the alloy and therefore the weight of the dollar did not alter its fine silver content. He used this opening to argue that the bill was debasing the specie—in his opinion one of the most immoral acts a government could perform. Adams also argued against the reduction in intrinsic value of the copper coinage. Such a reduction, in his words, was injurious to the poor people who used these coins.

Adams then argued that, if the change in alloy did not alter the value of the dollar, why change at all? The present dollar coin was of the same weight and value as many of the Spanish milled dollars. This was a convenience to all who dealt with dollars by weight. This change would seriously affect the country's commerce.

Cambreleng was surprised at Adams's opposition. He expressed frustration, saying that this bill was substantially the same as the one in the last session, which the House had not acted upon. Others came to his support over the change in weight. In reaction, Adams moved that the committee rise. It failed by only one vote.

Now Ingersoll entered the fray. The weight of the cent was being reduced because of the growing price of copper. Regardless, it was an immaterial decrease. Ingersoll made plain that only the alloy in the dollar was being reduced—the value expressed in fine silver was unchanged. The object of this Mint bill was to produce a complete organization, a system of arrangement, a plan of business so as to enable all who dealt with the Mint to have a distinct and clear understanding of what was to be done on the part of the public and of individuals employed by the public to superintend and conduct the Mint's business. It was spoken only as Robert Maskell Patterson could have worded it.

The Committee of the Whole was now deep in debates over the copper coins. There was a general consensus to leave the copper-coin regulations as they were. While the price of copper had increased by 25 percent in the last six to eight months, Ingersoll did not want the bill derailed over this issue. Still, there was no clear resolution. Then it was discovered that a quorum of the House no longer existed. Members had bailed out rapidly over this dry, technical bill. There was no choice but to adjourn for the day.[34]

The matter now simmered until after Christmas. The House resolved itself into a Committee of the Whole on December 28. All agreed to leave the weight of the cent and half cent unchanged. The minimum amount of gold and silver bullion receivable at the Mint was reduced to $100. Now came the real sticking point. Adams noted that a dime was one tenth of a dollar. However, he was against this new math that one tenth of 412.5 grains was 40 grains. Cambreleng was inclined to agree with Adams on this point. He weakly noted that the reduced weights were at the recommendation of Patterson to ensure that these coins stayed in circulation and were less likely to be exported or melted. Besides, it cost more proportionally to mint one of these small coins than it did the larger ones. These arguments fell on sterile ground. Adams had carried the day. Gone also was the legal-tender cap on dimes and half dimes. The bill, as amended, was passed.[35]

The Senate took up H.R. 529 on January 10, 1837, and passed it routinely. President Jackson signed it into law on January 17, 1837.[36]

Robert Maskell Patterson had just scored a trifecta. His dollar coin design had been struck and was now in circulation, much to his satisfaction. A steam-driven coin press had been successfully placed in service. He now had a revised set of statutes with which to conduct business at the Mint. In 18 months, Patterson had introduced some of the most sweeping changes at the Mint since its establishment in 1792.

There was just one dark cloud on the horizon. On December 31, 1836, Churchill Cambreleng presented a resolution of the Common Council of New York City soliciting the establishment of a branch mint in that city.[37] This branch mint issue was not going to die.

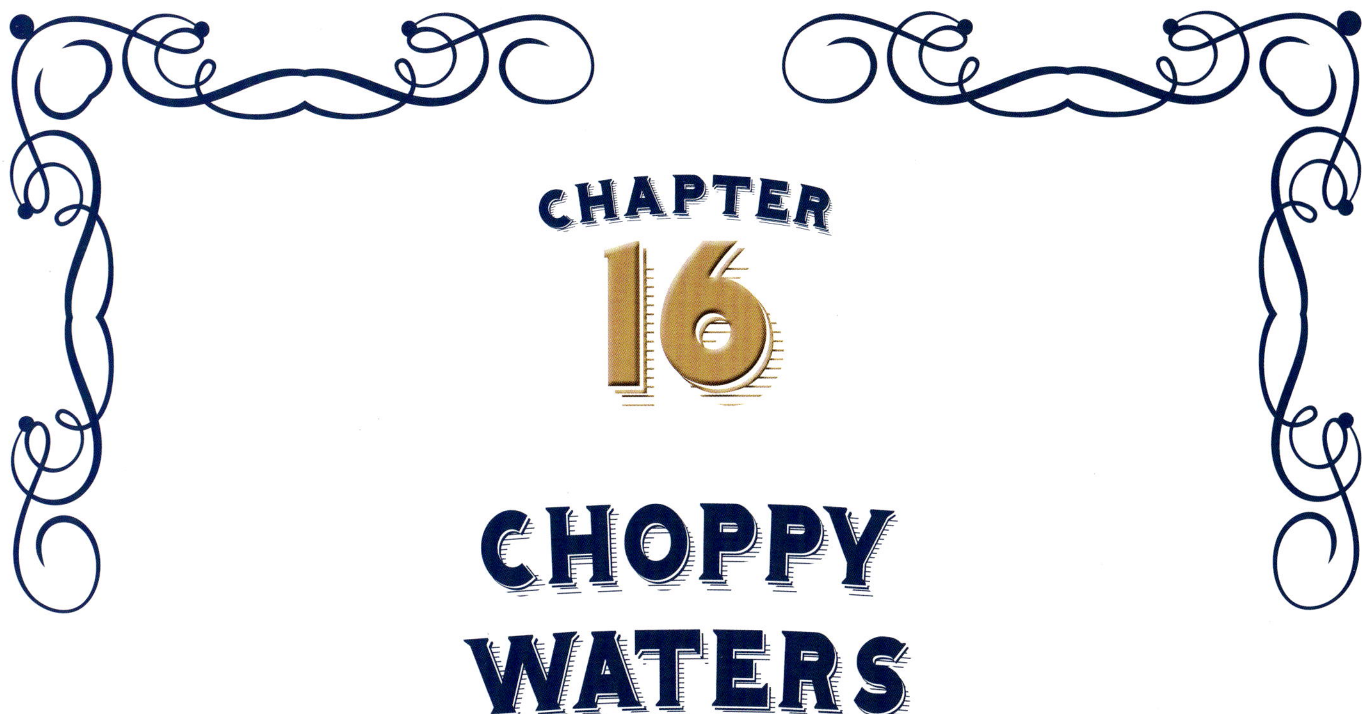

CHAPTER 16

CHOPPY WATERS

The ink of President Jackson's signature had hardly dried on the Mint Act of 1837 before Patterson had his hands full. Money was the root of the problem. While the officers had seen no salary increase since the inception of the Mint, the magnitude of the raises seemed large to the uninitiated.

Inequalities in pay among the workmen had been a bone of contention for some time, particularly in Adam Eckfeldt's department. The root of this trouble was Eckfeldt's payments to certain of the men who helped him with the medals business that he and Fürst had conducted on the side.[1]

The men beneath the officers sensed an opportunity and wasted no time in acting. On January 20, 1837, they petitioned Patterson for an across-the-board pay increase. They complained of the inflation of the past several years that had adversely impacted the price of all their daily necessities. Here was the real-world impact of the torrent of paper currency that was flooding the country. The men assured Patterson that they had been able to get by only by rigid economy and self-denial. If sickness were to strike any of them, they would be destitute. Thirty-two men, 80 percent of the workforce, signed the petition.[2]

Patterson seems to have taken no action. For an across-the-board pay raise, he would have been compelled to seek Secretary Levi Woodbury's approval.

The other issue was more vexing. Kneass, in his stroke-weakened condition, was now making $500 more than Gobrecht, an unacceptable situation. Patterson stepped in and split the difference. Kneass was to pay Gobrecht $62.50 per quarter so that each netted $1,750 per year. Patterson would claim in later years that it was Kneass who approached him about the injustice of his receiving more than Gobrecht under the new salary structure. The family would deny this in a messy affair after Kneass died. For the time being, the issue was quelled and Kneass and Gobrecht remained on good terms.[3]

• • • •

All this bickering and adjusting of salaries at the Mint was rendered moot in April when the economic house of cards crumbled. A crop failure in the North caused agricultural prices to increase. Great Britain, faced with a poor harvest at home as well, shifted its food purchases to Europe. The Bank of England, short of funds for these purchases, began curtailing loans to British firms heavily invested in the United States. At the same time, cotton prices in the south took a plunge from over production, primarily from the newly acquired Indian lands. The international cotton brokers were the first to fail as a result of the Bank of England's credit contraction. These failures in turn started a run on the banks in New York City. With specie pulled west to fund land purchases, they began to fail. Specie payments in New York were halted on May 10, 1837, and quickly spread throughout the country. With no specie available, the land speculation bubble burst, wiping out the equity of both farmers and planters.

When a bank failed not only were its depositors hurt but its currency was suddenly of no value to the holder. In this panic literally wagonloads of paper currency became worthless overnight. The only sure safety was specie, and the public began widespread hoarding, which only worsened the sudden and drastic currency contraction. In reaction, merchants began issuing their own unofficial currency—hard times tokens. With no central bank in place to counteract the economic contraction, the Panic of 1837 plunged the nation into a deep and ultimately unnecessarily prolonged depression.[4]

• • • •

While the issuance of the dollar coin with its new design occupied the limelight at the Mint in the closing months of 1836, Patterson was faced with addressing the half dollars. Merrick & Company had delivered their new steam-powered coin press that autumn on schedule. Patterson decided to make a statement with the initiation of half dollar production from this press, using a close collar in combination with a reeded edge. He also wanted to dress up the designs on both the obverse and reverse, to take advantage of the raised rim. Patterson told Secretary Woodbury that the close collar would give a mathematical

Fig. 59. At the end of 1836 Gobrecht quickly modified Reich's Capped Bust design to take advantage of the close collar being implemented on half dollars. These were to be struck on a new steam press. Its resulting raised edge allowed him to increase the relief. Gobrecht also took advantage of the situation to update the image of Liberty, slightly altering the cap. On the reverse, he removed the motto and simplified the appearance of the olive branch.

equality to the half dollar's diameter. It was a vague explanation. However, it would certainly give a consistent, improved look across the silver coinage.

With the year rapidly coming to a close, Gobrecht had limited options. For the half dollar, he simply retooled Reich's Capped Bust design (fig. 59), introducing only slight improvements. With the raised rim, the engraver was able to add relief to the facial features of Liberty, imparting some life into the old design. Overall, the face seemed thinner and the cap less frumpy. On the reverse, Gobrecht removed the motto "E Pluribus Unum." This was no surprise, given Patterson's predilection. It also brought this design in line with the quarter dollar. These modifications were easily made and with little fanfare.

How did Gobrecht respond so quickly? Most good artists never discard any old work, regardless of how it is received. What were the designs and "models of dies" that Gobrecht had supplied Mint director Samuel Moore in 1826? Moore had several approaches to redesign under consideration at the time. The easiest and least intrusive option had been to stick with Reich's dress cap and modify it so as not to create the appearance of any major design changes. Gobrecht's work in 1826 had earned him a fee of $100, hardly an amount appropriate for a complete new design. The likelihood was a simple rework of Reich's Capped Bust Liberty. It would not have been practical, because without raised rims it would not have stacked—a necessary prerequisite. With "models of dies" available, Gobrecht was in a position to promptly respond to Patterson's request.

While the design and dies were forthcoming, the coins were not. On November 8, 1836, Patterson belatedly conveyed samples of the new half dollars to Secretary Woodbury, proudly stating these were the first silver coins to be struck by steam.[5] Patterson was pleased with the way this design struck up in the new press. Still, there were more delays. Gobrecht did not receive permission to prepare the working dies for this new half dollar design until Christmas Eve. With Patterson in Washington pushing his reform legislation, permission came through Peale.[6] Over the final five working days of 1836, a set of working dies was placed in service with Mint records indicating 1,200 coins struck. However, that number may be understated, with more than 4,000 half dollars issued with the 1836 date. The recorded output represented less than an hour at rated capacity for the steam-powered coin press, a disappointing performance given that ample planchets had been available.

Patterson's November communication to Woodbury skirted another issue. No half dimes, dimes, or quarters had been struck on Franklin Peale's original steam-powered coin press, contrary to Patterson's expectations. While copper-coin production had been reasonable, output from Peale's steam-powered coin press in 1836 was hardly indicative of the expected tripling of capacity. Applying steam technology to the minting of coins was still more art than science.

With the passage of the Mint Act in January 1837, Patterson returned to the Mint to face another problem. The initial press run for the Gobrecht dollar had been distributed, with 400 given to dignitaries and 600 held at the Mint for payout to banks and the general public. However, the public response had been tepid. The description of the design motifs and the fact that the design would be adopted for other coins (subsidiary silver pieces) had been duly reported in the *Philadelphia Public Ledger*.[7] Yet the paper also complained about the weight of the dollar coin. It was argued that 20 of these coins were an encumbrance and would induce a man to regard silver as he would an iron wedge or a brick. He might travel for five years and carry enough gold in his pockets to pay his expenses for the entire period, while the same amount of silver would require a yoke of oxen. The newspaper had no problem with a silver dollar if it would supersede paper, but a gold dollar would be so much better.[8] Patterson would have expected better treatment from a Philadelphia newspaper.

Even more unsettling had been a letter Franklin Peale sent to Patterson while he was still in Washington. The new dollar design, for want of a better argument, was coming under much criticism for looking too medallic. The clean obverse and Gobrecht's signature "C. Gobrecht F(ecit)." certainly supported that comment. However, Peale singled out the fact that the coins had been struck with a "*smooth edge*." He suggested to Patterson that the perception could be corrected with an "ornament" to surround the edge. One point that Peale failed to make was that these pieces exhibited a fair amount of relief, much more so than any of the other coins issued at the Mint, adding to the medallic look. Gobrecht had been successful in giving these dollars more than standard coin relief. Likewise, Eckfeldt's screw press had fully brought up the features. Peale closed by saying these pieces would have to be struck by hand until the steam-powered coin press was ready.[9]

Fig. 60. Director Patterson's solution for preserving the Gobrecht dollar design in 1837 was to employ the obverse on dimes and half dimes. It was a stopgap measure that put Titian Peale's beautiful flying-eagle reverse design in jeopardy. It also should have told Patterson that the Liberty Seated design was too complex to employ on small-denomination silver coins.

What happened next with the Gobrecht dollar design is undocumented in Mint correspondence. Another production run of 600 coins was undertaken in March. The coin press used was never revealed. However, there exists one Gobrecht dollar from the end of the die-emission sequence of 1836 that bears a reeded edge.[10] If this coin were struck on a lighter-weight planchet in conformance with the law change, it would be compelling proof of its identity and indicate the use of the steam-powered coin press. Unfortunately, this surviving example weighs 414.36 grains, leaving the question unanswered.[11]

The production run was a failure. Three years later, a brief press report stated that the dollar coins looked so bad that the die was broken up.[12] That brief snippet left more questions than it answered. Ultimately, these coins were melted in November 1839.[13] Also, the die was not broken up but was used for restrikes of this design in 1859.[14]

Patterson now faced a dilemma. He was in danger of losing his Liberty Seated design. Once approved, it needed to reach the public, lest destructive criticism develop. His solution was quite simple. He introduced the Liberty Seated design on the dime (fig. 60) and half dime; this did not require an eagle on the reverse. For the reverse, Gobrecht employed a simple laurel wreath encircling each coin's denomination. The quarter and half dollar would have to wait until Patterson solved his problem of the coinability of the flying eagle reverse paired with the Liberty Seated obverse.

• • • •

As if all these issues were not enough, the branch mints took their place in Patterson's spectrum of difficulties in August 1837. The Mint director had devoted considerable attention to the equipment procurement for the three branch mints. He, Eckfeldt, and Peale were in constant contact with the fabricators in Philadelphia as the work progressed.

Patterson's initial approach had been to push the envelope of technology in equipping the branch mints. A few days after the demonstration train ride to Lancaster, Patterson sent a note inviting George Escol Sellers to drop by the Mint. Upon arriving, Patterson gave Sellers a call for bids for the machinery to be placed in service at Charlotte and Dahlonega. Time was short. The specifications for the bids included no drawings or plans, only written descriptions based upon the machinery in operation at Philadelphia. Sellers wanted to employ a design for a horizontal steam engine in line with his experience with locomotives. Eckfeldt was adamantly opposed to this innovation. A long conference with Patterson and Eckfeldt ensued, followed by a visit by these two men, plus Peale, to Sellers's shop. When all was done, Patterson took the radical course, giving Sellers the contract for the steam engine, rolling mills, and milling machinery and their erection, as well as construction of the melting and refining furnaces. Merrick got the business for the steam-powered coin presses.[15] It did not bother Patterson that Sellers and Peale were related. Nor was he concerned that Sellers's father had been close to Adam Eckfeldt and his own father. Sellers had the best technology. How that technology was going to work in the backwoods of North Carolina and Georgia was another question.

Trouble came where Patterson had almost no control—the construction of the buildings to house the equipment. He had used William Strickland, the architect for the Philadelphia Mint, to provide a single plan for both Charlotte and Dahlonega.[16] Thereafter, commissioners appointed by President Jackson to oversee the contractors for each building had charge of the proceedings. Ignatius Few was responsible at Dahlonega. In March 1837, Few reported to Woodbury that in spite of the contractor having been on the job for nearly a year, the building was nowhere near completion. Much of what was completed was poorly done. However, Few himself was not exempt from criticism. He spent very little time in Dahlonega. This intolerable situation came to a head on August 6, 1837, when a weight-bearing outer wall buckled from the lateral thrust of the masonry arches providing fireproof floor support.

Progress was no better at Charlotte, but for different reasons. A severe drought had crippled water transportation, stranding the heavy equipment en route from Philadelphia. The steam engine was in place but little else.

Patterson naturally turned to Franklin Peale, seeking Woodbury's permission to send him south. Peale had not a clue what he was getting into. As if on holiday, he took his daughter, Anna, with him. They arrived in Charlotte on September 23, 1837.

Franklin almost panicked. In spite of having worked with Patterson in Charlottesville, Virginia, some years previously, he was not prepared for this small crossroads-mining town. The bricks used to construct the building, while acceptable in North Carolina, would be regarded as poor quality in Philadelphia. He called Charlotte "this fag end of creation where the only active beings are the hogs." That was minor; Peale had real problems.

A shipment of castings and copper vessels for the melting furnace had disappeared after landing at Charleston. Brickwork for the furnace could not be started until this shipment was found. Consequently, he put the masons from Philadelphia to doing other work around the building. In addition, the contractor wanted more money and the branch superintendent was having problems meeting his payroll.

Two weeks in, Peale threw up his hands. The furnace castings were still missing. Peale was considering sending his brick masons on to Dahlonega. Then, he walked away from it all, taking time out to visit the area mines.

Peale returned more in control of himself. Perhaps the real problem was the hotel accommodations for his daughter, as by now they had moved into the home of the Mint superintendent. Two weeks later, the castings were found in Columbia, South Carolina. Now the clouds parted and Peale made progress. Yet he was pessimistic and thought that the men selected to run these branch mints did not have the necessary knowledge to oversee the work required.[17]

Peale left Charlotte on November 10, finally giving that location a clean bill of health, and arrived in Dahlonega four days later. The mint building was easily seen as it was on a hill in full view of the town square. No one was there to meet him. The same shoddy workmanship on the building as at Charlotte greeted him. The contractor was ignorant and the workmen drunken. Peale reported back to Philadelphia that the men at Dahlonega were certainly deserving of diplomas for botching.[18]

At least Peale had the Philadelphia men sent over from Charlotte to rely upon. He set the men to correcting the deficiencies in the building design as best they could and began overseeing the construction of the melting furnaces. Still, he was quick to blame Few for the work, saying that it really could not be completely corrected without a new appropriation from Congress. He warned Patterson to set aside money in future appropriations for building repairs here. He did lay some blame with the Philadelphia Mint, ordering a brick building in a country where there was no clay but an abundance of granite instead.

Before leaving Dahlonega at the end of December 1837, Peale took time to observe the surrounding gold fields. Every hill was filled with gold-bearing quartz and every valley and gorge with debris. He called the gold supply immensely inexhaustible. The problem was that the workings were extremely inefficient, so that operations at that moment, in the depth of the Panic of 1837, were languishing. Peale thought there was a great opportunity for improved mining technology and capital investment that would restore the mines to productive operations.[19] However, the opposite was also true. If capital did not come into play, or the economically minable reserves were not as large as previously thought, production had peaked.

Both mints went into operation in the first half of 1838, striking half eagles and quarter eagles. Patterson had specified the smallest of the steam presses for the two gold mints, eliminating the possibility of their striking the larger eagle coin.[20] Subsequently, the Mint director gave credit where credit was due, mentioning Peale's work in his annual report to the president.[21]

Toward the end of his stay at the Southern gold mints, Peale suggested that he visit the New Orleans branch. Patterson vetoed this idea outright. Perhaps he knew Peale too well. However, Patterson had good reasons to want Peale back. The New Orleans melter and refiner, James Maxwell, had been working Peale's furnaces in his absence and would soon have to report to the branch mint. Patterson feared that wastage would skyrocket in the interim if Peale did not return.

• • • •

The director had another reason for wanting Peale in Philadelphia. He had had a talk with Eckfeldt. Patterson had decided upon yet another new steam engine for the Mint and wanted Peale's advice. Furthermore, there were to be changes in the coining department. The medal press was to be moved to the lower pressrooms. There it would be out of the way but not retired. In addition to the government medals of Eckfeldt and Fürst, Gobrecht had brought his private medal business, including commissions from the Franklin Institute and the New England Society for the Promotion of Manufactures and Mechanical Arts, with him. The old half dollar screw press was to be put in limbo and the other old screw presses would be taken out of service. Now Eckfeldt was pushing for a colossal press for dollars.[22] Here the evidence was clear that the Mint could not strike the Gobrecht dollars. Patterson's forward-looking design was still in limbo.

In November 1837, Patterson received from Woodbury a letter sent by Moritz Fürst to the secretary of war. The letter has not survived, but that it went to the secretary of war meant that its purpose involved the military medals commissioned by Congress and, given Fürst's notorious inability to manage his finances, money. However, much can be inferred from Patterson's reply to Woodbury. Charles Cushing Wright's name had come up again for possible employment at the Philadelphia Mint. Patterson acknowledged that he came strongly recommended by Rembrandt Peale. If a position ever opened up in the engraving department, the director would consider him. However, he had two engravers, Kneass and Gobrecht, whose work at sinking dies was satisfactory at the present time.[23]

Patterson was looking at his engraving department through rose-colored glasses. Peale had brought innovations back from Paris—a modification to the process of transferring the coin designs from the hub to the working dies for the coin presses. Previously only a partial transfer was possible, requiring additional handwork from the engravers. In 1836, using Peale's method, the entire design was transferred from the hub to the working dies, saving much time and yielding uniform working dies.[24]

Still, in reality, Kneass was of almost no use, simply serving out his time according to the custom established by his predecessor, Robert Scot. Gobrecht was not without his problems. Coin engraving was not the same as banknote and print engraving. At least Patterson was realistic when he described both men as diesinkers. Their body of work left questions about both men's capabilities as designers.

There was another reason that Patterson looked askance at adding a third engraver. He had purchased a Contamin portrait lathe. No doubt the dollar design's travails in 1836 had convinced Patterson of the need. Franklin Peale, having seen a lathe used in Europe, would have been a strong backer. The Contamin machine had gone into service in either March or April 1837. This lathe could, by means of a tracer and graver, reproduce an exact copy from a model into a soft steel hub blank of smaller diameter. The model and the hub blank were rotated with equal motion counterclockwise. The tracer and graver moved in unison from the center to the outside edge. The process took at least several passes to accomplish, with the tools set closer and closer to the model and hub. The results were not perfect, requiring a good deal of hand finishing. Its real value to the engraver was in the mechanizing of the rough early work. Also, the lathe only dealt with the design motifs. The lettering was hand-punched into the master die made from the hub. The date and mintmark were then punched into the working dies.

That lathe was used to prepare the obverse dies for the 1837 Liberty Seated half dimes and dimes—very likely from a hub for the dollar coin. For whatever reason, Gobrecht did not like the new portrait lathe.[25] Peale, on the other hand, with his early experience working with lathes and his love of innovation, pushed for it.

Patterson's belief, in lockstep with Peale, was that there would come a time when the engraving function would be marginalized by machines. When new designs were desired, he could go to outside artists.

• • • •

The uncertainty surrounding the implementation of new designs on the silver coins intensified in 1838. The effort focused on the half dollar, given that the Mint did not yet have a steam press capable of producing acceptable dollar strikes. Gobrecht started with an obverse design taken

Fig. 61. Lacking a suitable coin press for dollars, Patterson directed Gobrecht to redesign the half dollar. His first attempt was a modification of Reich's design with the eagle facing to its left without a shield. The eagle's left leg failed to strike up on this pattern piece.

Fig. 62. Gobrecht also paired his obverse with the eagle from his 1836 modification of Reich's design. In this case the eagle on the reverse struck up fully.

Fig. 63. Before progressing to pattern strikes, Gobrecht prepared heraldic-eagle sketches for possible use on the reverse of the half dollar. The engraver appeared undecided about the use and placement of the shield.

loosely from his Capped Bust of 1836 and 1837 (figs. 61 and 62). He removed the cap, replacing it with a coronet and a ribbon inscribed with "Liberty." The hair fell in curls over Liberty's shoulder somewhat like his earlier version. In description, the design bears a striking similarity to one of Samuel Moore's options from his correspondence with Thomas Jefferson. Moore had proposed dropping the cap and adopting an easy disposition of the hair with no ornamentation except a band with "Liberty." Gobrecht was reaching back to 1826. In the second attempt, Gobrecht employed the seated Liberty from the dollar coin with "Liberty" on the ribbon both raised and incused. In both cases, 13 stars surrounded Liberty, a departure from the original dollar design.

For the reverse, Gobrecht started with a series of sketches, some or all of which still survive (fig. 63). One actually made it into a large bronze cast using Titian Peale's rising eagle with arrows and laurel branch in its claws (fig. 64).

Ultimately, Gobrecht employed three different reverses. He returned to the discarded design of a flying eagle with beak open, modified to remove the stars from the field that were now redundant. The engraver also reworked Reich's old design of a standing eagle with shield (fig. 65) and added a standing eagle of his own without the shield (fig. 66).[26] Patterns were struck in varying combinations of these obverse and reverse designs. Gobrecht was looking at both the design and the striking characteristics exhibited by the various combinations.

No correspondence exists that gives insight into Patterson's decision-making process. However, if striking capability was the criterion, the seated Liberty paired with Gobrecht's modification of Reich's reverse won hands down (fig. 67). Patterson's actions show his conclusions. By mid-year, the half dimes and dimes had been modified by adding 13 stars to the obverse, making this consistent with the seated Liberty of Gobrecht's half dollar patterns. In September 1838, Patterson sent 20 examples of a quarter design he proposed to Woodbury for approval. The seated Liberty, surrounded by 13 stars, with Reich's retooled eagle for a reverse, went into production later that month.[27] Still, nothing developed with the half dollar. Patterson was hoping against hope that the flying eagle might still work on the larger silver coins.

With the quarter out of the way, Patterson turned to Gobrecht for the gold coins. Again it seemed that

Fig. 64.1. This casting shows markings indicating that it was used in the Contamin lathe to produce a die.

Fig. 64.2. This restrike from the late 1850s shows the Titian Peale reverse that Gobrecht considered but never took beyond the die preparation phase. The detail on the eagle is far short of that exhibited on the bronze casting used to produce the die. This flying eagle was just not going to coin up in combination with the seated Liberty obverse given the coin-press capabilities in place at the Mint.

Fig. 65. Gobrecht even went back to an earlier version of Titian Peale's flying eagle with beak open paired with the seated Liberty, ribbon lettering incused. With the stars employed on the obverse, the reverse stars were removed. In this case the eagle's breast and wingtip failed to strike up, a hint of the problem that Patterson must have been fighting on the dollar coin.

Fig. 66. Gobrecht paired his Liberty Seated with stars obverse design with his reverse of the eagle facing left. "Liberty" on the ribbon is incused. In this case the eagle's leg struck up fully but badly needed detail was lost on its breast.

Fig. 67. The combination that must have given Director Patterson a premonition of the future matched the starred seated Liberty with raised lettering on the ribbon, with Reich's reworked reverse. Seated Liberty's shield was fully struck on the obverse where it had given problems on the other examples. The eagle on the reverse was sharp and well struck. But placing shields on both the obverse and the reverse was a design flaw.

Gobrecht returned to that earlier time with Moore, reinforced by their discussions in 1835. In a situation where a classical cap for Liberty was desired, Moore called for Liberty to be modeled after the exquisite ancient works of Greece and Rome. With Patterson, the cap was a non-starter. *Walter Breen's Complete Encyclopedia of U.S. and Colonial Coins* states that Gobrecht took his model of Liberty from the painting by Benjamin West titled *Omnia Vincit Amor* (Love Conquers All) (fig. 68). The head of Venus does bear a striking resemblance to Gobrecht's head of Liberty. For the reverse, Gobrecht retooled Reich's eagle on the gold coins as he had with the quarter. On December 6, 1838, samples went to Woodbury and then circulation strikes for the eagle gold coin commenced for the first time since 1804 (fig. 69).[28]

With the half dollar on hold, Patterson returned to the silver dollar coin. He raised the issue first with Woodbury.

Fig. 68. One can see a relationship between the female image on the left of Benjamin West's *Omnia Vincit Amor* to Gobrecht's profile of Liberty used on his gold-coins design.

Fig. 69. After a hiatus of 34 years, the eagle gold coin reappeared with a facelift and a rejuvenated eagle on the reverse, courtesy of Gobrecht. Patterson was passing on the opportunity to offer a totally revamped design for gold coins.

Fig. 70. Perhaps it was inevitable that the stars must migrate to the obverse of this design. The result does not compare to the 1836 version. The design has lost all of its uniqueness.

In an exchange of correspondence that lends credence to the pedigree of the reeded-edge dollar, Patterson sent his most recent strike. If he were trying to offset the criticism that the design looked too much like a medal, his choice would have been the reeded-edge coin from the March 1837 production run. Woodbury asked for fifty more coins, wanting peer opinions. Patterson answered that he could not comply. He had only those coins from December 1836 available.[29]

Patterson then ordered a new pattern using the obverse die from 1836 with stars punched around the rim. This is evident by the tool marks removing Gobrecht's name from the plinth in the hub. A new die was required for the reverse removing the stars from the field.[30] Everything had been done to counter the criticism that the design looked too much like a medal (fig. 70). Yet Patterson held off. Washington was balking. His beautiful flying eagle was dying.

CHAPTER 17

PARTY POLITICS

Adam Eckfeldt would be 70 on June 15, 1839. He had been a fixture at the Mint since its beginning; it was in his blood. Still, the stresses of being chief coiner were wearing on him. He had talked to Mint director Robert Patterson before about resigning but had not fixed a date. This time, it was different. When he told Patterson he intended to resign, he meant it. Eckfeldt did not need the money; he had gotten rich beyond his expectations, in part from his lucrative side business in medals. In fact, he would be ranked among a who's who of wealthy Philadelphians in the 1840s.[1]

For Robert Maskell Patterson, Eckfeldt's resignation was an opportunity—but one that had to be managed carefully. The spoils system ushered in by President Andrew Jackson had been perpetuated to a much fuller extent under Martin Van Buren. While politics at the Mint had hitherto been largely restricted to the appointment of the treasurer, there was no assurance that its grip would not be extended to the skilled positions. For Patterson, it was a matter of timing. Franklin Peale was his choice, but Peale was once again in Georgia attending to problems at the Dahlonega branch mint. The resignation must not become public until Peale returned and was in position to take over Eckfeldt's responsibilities. If the resignation became public before that time, the agitations of the politicians might upset Patterson's plans.[2]

Patterson was successful in his efforts to manage the transition. On March 11, 1839, he notified President Van

Buren of Eckfeldt's resignation. He wasted no time in promoting Peale to Van Buren for the position.

> The situation thus to be vacated is the most difficult of the practical offices in the Mint to fill; and I should almost despair of its being supplied satisfactorily were it not that our Melter and Refiner, Franklin Peale, Esq. has consented to a transfer to this office, if such should be your pleasure. The qualifications of Mr. Peale are of the highest class. He is an excellent mechanician—was sent by the government to examine the principal Mints in Europe, and made himself thoroughly acquainted with the improvements in their mechanical and chemical operations;—and has since had the executive part of the duty of introducing them into this Mint. In his own department and that of the assayer, these changes are completed, in the coining department, they are still going on, under his immediate care. Even when completed, he is certainly the most proper man to conduct the operations: indeed he is the *only* man known to me, who is competent to fill the place in the manner in which so important a situation ought to be filled. I strongly and unhesitatingly recommend, therefore, that when Mr. Eckfeldt's resignation is accepted, Mr. Peale be transferred from the office of melter and refiner to that of chief coiner.[3]

If Patterson was successful in *transferring* Peale to the chief coiner's position, that left the melter and refiner position open. In the same letter lauding Peale's accomplishments to Van Buren, the Mint director also recommended Philadelphian James C. Booth for the empty position. Booth was a graduate of the University of Pennsylvania and a European-trained chemist. He had also taught at the Franklin Institute. More importantly, Booth had been elected in January to membership in the American Philosophical Society. Patterson had previously considered him for the assayer's position at the New Orleans Mint, in 1837. He was well qualified for the melter and refiner's position, but the problem was that Patterson was going to spend all his political chips for Peale's appointment.

The next day Eckfeldt followed through with his formal resignation, taking the opportunity to recommend Peale.[4] Treasury secretary Levi Woodbury immediately conveyed to Patterson the president's desire that Democrats be considered for the two positions.

Patterson was now faced with potentially losing Peale and gaining two political appointees. The Mint director had anticipated this response. He had enlisted Henry Gilpin to approach the president through the back door. Gilpin had been U.S. attorney for the eastern district of Pennsylvania, studied law under Joseph Ingersoll, and was a member of the American Philosophical Society. Now, he was solicitor for the Treasury Department. Gilpin relayed Van Buren's assurance that no appointment would be made without carefully considering the fitness of the individual for the position. However, he was adamant that the individual must be of "firm democratic principles."[5]

Patterson remained confident of Peale's appointment. In a confidential communication to Woodbury, he made his case that the persons appointed should have the essential requisites of skill and science combined with personal character that would command confidence. He acknowledged a strong desire that they be of the political party and philosophy into which he was born and had been a conscientious supporter. Patterson reemphasized that he was proposing a transfer of Peale, not a promotion. Peale was a member of the party and supporter of party principles in regard to the relations of the Treasury Department and the banks—the all-important litmus test of loyalty.

Professor Booth was another story. Politically, he was neutral and brought no bias to the table. This appointment must be made on the basis of scientific knowledge and personal character alone. Patterson knew this nomination was on shaky ground and suggested several alternatives.

Van Buren was closing no doors on his options. Gilpin wrote Patterson that the president had had an interview at the White House with an accomplished, well-recommended machinist for Eckfeldt's position.[6] That was enough to make Patterson go to Washington to consult with Van Buren directly. That trip resolved the situation for Peale but not Booth. Even as an apolitical Whig, he was doomed. Jonas R. McClintock, a medical doctor turned politician and current mayor of Pittsburgh, was offered and accepted the melter and refiner appointment.[7] McClintock had enlisted the support of two former governors of Pennsylvania.[8] Both men assumed their new positions under recess appointments with formal approvals coming from the Senate in the first two months of 1840.

• • • •

On May 1, 1839, in his new position as chief operating officer at the Mint, Franklin Peale announced his marriage to Caroline Eugenie Girard Haslam, a widow.[9] It had been 18 years since the annulment of his first marriage to Eliza Greatrake. This one promised to be on much better footing. Caroline was a niece of Stephen Girard, who had left virtually no money to his family. Unfortunately, that meant she came with no dowry, only her social connections and resulting obligations. She could also be willful. In later years, during a vacation at Cape May, the Philadelphia watering hole on the Jersey shore, she insisted that Franklin extend his stay because she had been sickly and the weather was bad.[10]

On June 7, 1839, Patterson informed Adam Eckfeldt that, in appreciation of his long and meritorious service to the Mint, he would receive a medal (fig. 71).[11] Odds are

Fig. 71. Perhaps it was fitting that Fürst cut the obverse die for the medal honoring Adam Eckfeldt and the 25 years he served as chief coiner. It was presented to him by his fellow officers at his retirement.

Fig. 72. Patterned after the gold-coin design, this right-facing image of Liberty was an improvement over the existing Capped Bust. However, Director Patterson rejected it in favor of the Liberty Seated design, maintaining a single obverse for silver coins. He accepted the reverse eagle, creating a design in common with the quarter.

Fig. 73. The beautiful Proof eagle of 1840, along with the quarter and half eagles, employed Gobrecht's Liberty, facing left this time, from his pattern half dollar of 1839. Compared to the gold-coin design of 1838, Liberty's hair around the ear has been modified and the truncation of the neck has been softened.

Fig. 74. In a last attempt to save this design, Patterson followed the 1838 pattern and took the stars off the reverse. It was a futile effort and only hurt the design.

that Eckfeldt supervised its striking. From the effective date of his resignation, the former chief coiner had continued to come to the Mint as if nothing had changed. Eckfeldt was doing the work he loved without the stress of responsibility. That he received no pay was not a concern. Peale thereby gained an assistant, allowing him to avoid the drudgery of a daily routine and make the social rounds with his new wife. It was a partnership that would continue until Eckfeldt's death.

• • • •

With Peale in place, Patterson turned to the vexing issue of the Gobrecht designs. He pushed a decision on the dollar coin back, dealing with the half dollar first. There were more pattern coins produced. Engraver Christian Gobrecht even tried a stylish head of Liberty facing right (fig. 72). On August 15, 1839, Patterson bit the bullet and opted for conformity with the quarter. In his conveyance of two strikes to Secretary Woodbury for review, he noted that approval of this design for the half dollar would complete the new series for silver coins using the seated Liberty figure.

Patterson also addressed the gold-coin designs in this letter. He intended to retain Gobrecht's head of Liberty (fig. 73) from the half dollar patterns for the gold coins—an evolution from the $10 coin adopted in 1838. Still stuck on design continuity across a single metal, Patterson was lucky that the simplicity of Gobrecht's head of Liberty fit as well on the quarter and half eagles as it did on the eagle coin. Patterson was silent on the reverse design for the dollar coin.

In a postscript, the director called Woodbury's attention to the appearance of the two examples sent to him: one was bright and the other exhibited frosted devices.[12] Peale was experimenting with Proof finishes.[13]

Patterson had one last go at the flying-eagle reverse on the Gobrecht dollar in December 1839 (fig. 74). There were 300 pieces struck in medal turn and duly recorded in the Mint's account books. The eagle soared on these coins without the stars in the field, consistent with the pattern strike of 1838. Then the design quietly faded into oblivion. The production run was consigned to the Mint's melting pot in April 1840.[14] Patterson's daring eagle concept brought to life by Titian Peale would fly no more, except for a spate of restrikes beginning in the late 1850s and, for three years on the Flying Eagle cent. Coins from the 1836 issue became a curiosity. Andrew Jackson used one as a pocket piece. Later, many specimens came into the numismatic market holed; they had been used as watch fobs.

The problem could not have been over the strikeability of the design this time. A third, more powerful, steam-driven press was to come on line in early 1840. It was to be the pride of the Mint, written up in the prestigious *Franklin Institute Journal.* Designed by Peale, this press would exhibit his standard trademark of graceful lines and liberal applications of brass to the moving parts. The heavy cast-iron arch that provided the striking pressure had been provided again by Merrick. Unlike Eckfeldt, Peale would actively promote his handiwork, bragging that the press could strike 5,000 coins an hour and could sustain operations for a full shift without maintenance. In giving tours and showing off the machine, Peale would be described as the "urbane gentleman."[15]

If it was Patterson's hope that the new coin press would prove that it was feasible to strike the Gobrecht dollar on a standard production run, he was not to get the opportunity. Almost three years later, he provided a vague explanation of what had happened. The flying eagle without heraldic appendages "did not satisfy the public and it was abandoned."[16] This statement is reinforced by the existence of Gobrecht sketches of heraldic eagles for a dollar coin (fig. 75). By making the incremental changes in the quarter and half dollar using a reworked version of the Reich reverse, Patterson had sunk his own ship. The desire to retain the custom of uniform designs across the silver coinage, coupled with acceptance of the heraldic eagle reverse, had doomed his flying eagle. Had the technology of the steam-powered press been capable of producing the force necessary to strike up this design in 1837, its adoption might never have been questioned.

Fig. 75. Pictured is one of Gobrecht's heraldic-eagle sketches, proposed and rejected as a replacement for the flying eagle. The faint outline of a shield is visible on the eagle's breast.

• • • •

With the branch mints in operation, Patterson turned to flaws at the gold mints of Charlotte and Dahlonega. The mints were woefully underutilized. Patterson needed to control costs by removing the authority of the branch superintendents to hire hourly employees, thereby transferring branch-mint authority to himself. Additionally, he wanted the two branches to coin small silver obtained from the refining of the gold bullion. It made no sense to ship this silver in ingot form to Philadelphia for coining. Given the limited capabilities of the small coin presses in place at both mints, he could strike denominations no larger than a quarter and even that might be pushing the presses.[17]

Patterson chose Van Buren's man in the Senate, Silas Wright, to introduce the necessary legislation, signaling that it had the support of the president. The bill sailed through the Senate with no debate.[18] However, it was late in the session. Any resistance in the House would kill the bill until Congress reconvened. Perhaps Patterson knew it was best to initiate his legislation in the Senate. In spite of the bill's seemingly innocuous provisions, it ran into trouble in the House. Churchill Cambreleng was still chairman of the Ways and Means Committee. Regardless of his party politics, he was a New Yorker first. He was not about to strengthen the existing branch mints at the expense of New York's chances for its own mint. He reported the bill out of committee on July 4, 1838, with the recommendation that it not pass.[19] The House adjourned July 9, taking no action on Patterson's bill.

With the opening of the third session in December, Patterson picked up where he had left off, with Bedford Brown of North Carolina reintroducing the bill in the Senate.[20] After a cursory review in Wright's Finance Committee, the bill passed the Senate on January 25, 1839.[21] Patterson had no better results in the House this time around. Cambreleng reported the bill out of committee, with a minor amendment subjecting Patterson's power of hiring to the approval of the president.[22] In the House discussion, information was called for on the expenses of the Charlotte branch mint and the additional cost to implement silver coinage. Patterson estimated that it would cost $1,500 for assaying equipment to handle the silver and two additional men in the operations. Backed into a corner, he now admitted that only dimes and half dimes could be coined under this scenario.[23] Patterson's report raised too many questions. Even a resolution passed by the General Assembly of North Carolina urging passage of the bill fell upon deaf ears.[24] Patterson's bill was dead again.

As 1840 was a presidential election year, politics were most intense in the newly seated Twenty-Sixth Congress. Senator Brown introduced the branch mint bill for the third time.[25] Again, it sped through the Finance Committee. However, the action suddenly shifted to the House. Charles Ogle, a Whig from rural Somerset, Pennsylvania, gained the House floor. He had Patterson's Mint report for 1839 that talked of a Mint capacity of $12 million, far in excess of current output. Ogle noted that the cost of production from the three branch mints in 1838 and 1839 far exceeded that of Philadelphia. Ogle wanted a select committee appointed to inquire into closing the branch mints. It failed miserably, 61 yeas to 104 nays. The hard-money Democrats and Southern congressmen easily carried the day. However, within the Philadelphia delegation that could be counted to vote the Philadelphia Mint position, two Whigs voted for the resolution. One Whig and two Democrats did not cast votes.[26] Had Patterson given up on the branch mints?

The action in the House was a precursor to what was coming in the Senate. Henry Clay had voted against the branch-mint bill in 1839 but had not spoken against it. This time would be different. Clay opened with his trademark sarcasm, stating he hoped some reason would be given why this bill should pass. However, he was not buying into the assumption that costs would be negligible should the gold mints be allowed to strike minor silver coins. Clay took the position that, instead of acts involving the government in additional expense for these branch mints, the only proper act would be to abolish them. He considered their establishment a mere wasteful expenditure of public money. The silver obtained from refining the raw gold bullion brought to these mints could be sent to Philadelphia, coined, and transported back again at less expense than if coined at the Charlotte and Dahlonega mints. Clay announced his opposition and that he would ask for the yeas and nays on its passage.

Wilson Lumpkin, the former governor of Georgia who had played a leading role in the expulsion of the Cherokees, spoke in opposition to Clay. He called the expenses to date distorted by startup costs. There was gold enough in this region to support inexhaustible mines that would sustain these branches for generations to come. However, he did admit that the placer deposits, the easy mining, were largely depleted. Still, he was certain that gold production would rebound, given an adequate supply of labor that currently was being drained away by railroad construction and the strong agricultural markets. Lumpkin even went a step further. He flatly stated there was enough capacity and gold bullion at all the mints to replace foreign gold coins circulating in the United States.

Senator Brown now took the floor in favor of passage. His support for his own bill was hardly resounding. He admitted that in retrospect he might wish to reconsider the building of these mints, but now that they were up, it made no sense not to permit them to strike silver coinage.

William Preston, the Whig senator from South Carolina, took issue with Lumpkin's optimistic assessment of future gold production from the region. The gains initially seen had not perpetuated themselves, as many mines decreased their output or were abandoned. Preston moved that the bill be recommitted to the Finance Committee, with instructions to inquire into discontinuing the branch mints. John Calhoun then rose, naturally in favor of the branch mints. The South Carolina senators were going to cancel each other out in any vote.

Finally James Buchanan, entered the debate. He was on the same side as Henry Clay. He pointed out to the senators that, under the existing law, the superintendent was obliged to employ a separate class of laborers for each particular function at the mints. For Philadelphia, this was not an issue. For the smaller branch mints, it represented an unnecessary burden. The express purpose of the first clause of this bill was to reduce expenses at the branches. As for the coinage of silver at the gold mints, the bill provided no appropriation. There was no additional cash out-of-pocket cost. Under these circumstances, Buchanan was willing to give his vote for the bill. But if Senator Preston would introduce a resolution to inquire whether it was necessary to keep these mints, he would vote for that measure as well. The Pennsylvania senator believed there could be strong arguments as to why there should be no other mints than at Philadelphia. Buchanan had a reputation as a political sneak. He was having it both ways. Was Patterson trying to play that same game? The motion to recommit failed with only 11 yeas against 27 nays. The bill was then read a third time and passed.[27]

Upon arriving in the House, this bill was promptly referred to the Judiciary Committee, as opposed to the Ways and Means Committee which had oversight on mint issues, guaranteeing its burial.[28] Debate in the House on this subject for the remainder of the session centered on striking the appropriation for the Charlotte Mint. The dispute involved local issues in Charlotte.

• • • •

The presidential election of 1840 was never really in doubt. The country remained mired in a deep economic decline, a hangover from the Panic of 1837. The Whigs gained the presidency for the first time, with their apolitical former military chieftain, William Henry Harrison. They had turned their backs on their leader, Henry Clay, believing, as one upstart delegate from Pennsylvania, Thaddeus Stevens, succinctly put it, that the senator from Kentucky could not win. It was a grand time for the Whig party, which had never before held the levers of power in Washington. For Democratic office holders, it was an entirely different emotion. Would there be political retribution when Harrison was inaugurated on March 4, 1841?

Robert Maskell Patterson felt reasonably confident; his old friend and distant relative, Thomas Ewing, was the new secretary of the Treasury. Still he left nothing to chance, permitting the American Philosophical Society to petition President Harrison for his retention at the Mint.[29] For the time being, it was enough.

Tragically, Harrison contracted pneumonia and died on April 4, 1841. Vice President John Tyler took his place and initially signaled that the Whig agenda would remain unchanged, keeping Harrison's cabinet in place. Political appointments would continue apace.

In May Ewing quizzed Patterson hard about the duties of the melter and refiner. Surprisingly, Patterson, while deferential to Ewing's position, was defensive of McClintock. He even noted that McClintock's department had reduced wastage compared to the last eight years, a rare, though backhanded, criticism of Peale. McClintock's performance was above reproach. Patterson had always been anxious to keep partisanship out of the Mint. There had been an accusation that Patterson had made a political speech on the steps of his home before the presidential election. He now took the opportunity to strongly deny it. In fact, Patterson made it a point never to attend political meetings.

If Ewing felt he must make a change, Patterson pushed hard again for James Booth. Booth had not applied for the position because he knew it to be ably filled. Patterson believed there could be no cause for the removal of McClintock that did not invariably point to Booth as his successor.[30]

Ewing backed off. However, the treasurer's position was in the administration's crosshairs for replacement. Patterson would have expected this action, but the person they put forth was repugnant.

The man Tyler appointed was the anti-Mason, Whig-allied, former governor of Pennsylvania, Joseph Ritner (fig. 76). A farmer with a rural education, he was the opposite of the urbane Patterson. Ritner had been defeated in a bitter reelection contest in 1838. Outrageous Whig vote frauds in Philadelphia were well known at the time. Unfortunately, the vote in the remainder of the state was such that whoever carried Philadelphia carried the General Assembly. The situation degenerated with Ritner, whose term had ended, refusing to vacate his office. The competing factions each elected speakers of the General Assembly, and the Whigs attempted to unseat Democratic senators. A riot ensued in the lobby outside the Senate chamber, forcing Ritner's mentor, the club-footed Thaddeus Stevens, to vacate through a window. Ritner proclaimed a state of insurrection and called for federal troops. His request was refused. Patterson's close friend, John Kane, was selected by the Democrats to negotiate with the Whigs to defuse the situation. Kane quickly succeeded, and the Democrats gained their rightful seats.[31] The affair became known as the Buck Shot War.

Ritner entered Mint employment on a recess appointment. Once Patterson learned of the presidential action, he fought it. Ritner was virtually blind in both eyes from cataracts. Patterson told Treasury secretary Ewing that

Fig. 76. Joseph Ritner, political ally of Thaddeus Stevens, was a thorn in the side of Robert Maskell Patterson.

Ritner could not find his way across a room, could not see to read, and could not sign his name without having the place marked for him. In fact, surgery had been performed on one of his eyes since the appointment and it was unsuccessful. Patterson prognosticated that, with the man's advanced age, there was little hope that Ritner's vision would return. To make matters worse, Ritner had brought along a son who handled all the counting for the old man. Ritner wished his son to remain as long as he was incapacitated with the cataracts. That was okay with Patterson until he learned that Ritner really wanted his son to be employed as his clerk—the present clerk would have to be discharged to make room. Nothing would be gained here and, in fact, experience would be lost.[32]

The situation for Patterson deteriorated during the third week of July 1841. On the evening of July 21, Ritner called in the clerk and gave notice that he would be terminated at the end of the month. When the clerk questioned Ritner as to the cause of his dismissal, Ritner told the man he had no complaint against him. Patterson felt the clerk distinguished in every qualification and shuddered to think what would happen when Ritner's son, who was untrained and unqualified as a bookkeeper, took the position. In the Mint, there were checks and balances to prevent errors. There were no such checks in the treasurer's office. As the termination of a clerk's employment must be approved by the secretary, Patterson immediately wrote to Ewing about this miscarriage of justice.

Patterson had more complaints to add in his letter. Ritner, since his appointment, had been to the Mint only once—the previous day, to dismiss the clerk. Once accomplished, he left the Mint, intending to return to his farm for several weeks. Since the appointment, all papers requiring his signature had to be taken to his boardinghouse. Patterson, in his frustration, even pronounced Ritner's cataracts case as nearly hopeless, although he admitted that he had not examined Ritner or consulted with the man's physician.[33]

The normally cautious Patterson was out on a limb. Ritner's vision was not incurable. While surgery on the left eye had not succeeded due to postoperative inflammation, the right eye was still in question. In February, Ritner's physician had operated on that eye with satisfactory results. Then Ritner insisted on traveling to Washington against his doctor's advice. This caused complications with a secondary membranous cataract forming on the right eye. Another surgery would have to be performed and promised a good chance of success.[34]

Patterson's first letter was enough. President Tyler presented Ritner's name to the Senate for confirmation on June 17.[35] His name, with others, was duly referred to the Finance Committee, chaired by the embittered Henry Clay. On June 29, Clay reported for confirmation all those names except Ritner.[36] On July 15, James Buchanan, in an effort to embarrass Clay, ordered that when the question of Ritner's nomination was taken, it should be by vote and not by voice.[37] Clay would now have to openly vote against his president's nominee. Clay was far too smart for Buchanan. When the question of Ritner's nomination came up for vote on September 10, the Senate rejected the nomination, seven yeas against 31 nays.[38] Clay had soundly killed the nomination behind the scenes, no doubt with the information provided by Patterson, and then voted with the yeas. It was pure retribution, aimed at Thaddeus Stevens for his maneuvering against Clay during the 1840 Whig presidential nominating convention.

Tyler immediately nominated Isaac Roach, a veteran officer of the War of 1812, in place of Ritner.[39] Roach, who had married into large wealth, was the former mayor of Philadelphia and a Whig.[40] Ritner would openly blame Clay for his removal. In the ultimate irony, however, the sight in his right eye had been restored by the time of the Senate confirmation vote. At the same time, Ritner also should have known who had provided the information concerning his blindness.

All that summer, relations between Henry Clay and John Tyler deteriorated. Clay had initially judged Tyler as someone junior to him—someone to whom he could dictate action. Clay wanted a newly chartered third Bank of the United States to control national monetary policy. Tyler balked and ultimately killed the effort. On the day after Clay killed the Ritner nomination, Thomas Ewing, along with all but one of the cabinet secretaries, resigned. Only the secretary of state, Daniel Webster, remained. Patterson had lost his man and now must deal with a secretary of the Treasury who was potentially hostile to him.

• • • •

In the Mint Act of 1837, Patterson had not gone far enough in one area: legal-tender status of foreign specie. He first raised the issue in his annual report for 1838. The law of 1834 setting legal tender for foreign gold coins had been too liberal. The fineness of these gold coins had proven to be consistently less than the stated fineness used to calculate their values in the act. Consequently, these coins were being overvalued in commercial transactions. Just as importantly, the Mint would not purchase them at their legal-tender value because it would lose money in the recoinage. Given that the Mint coinage capacity was sufficient to provide all the gold coins necessary for domestic use, Patterson now wanted their legal-tender status repealed. On the other hand, the foreign silver coins did not pose the same problem and Patterson was neutral on their legal-tender status. What he did not say in his report was the slight increase in the gold content of American coins called for in the Mint Act of 1837 widened this valuation disparity.[41]

In his report for 1839, he repeated his plea for congressional action, again to no avail. Congress seemed more worried about preventing counterfeit foreign coins from entering commerce. He appealed directly to Thomas Hart Benton for action. He admitted that the 1837 law aggravated the situation. In addition, he noted that, when the fineness of the foreign gold coins was above the American standard, as in the case of the British and the French, there was added cost to the Mint. The alloy used by these foreign mints was only copper. Therefore, the Mint incurred expense to add silver to reduce the fineness and comply with American law. He got nowhere with the champion of hard money, who was clearly leery of the Mint's claims of the productive capacity sufficient to replace these coins.[42]

As the Van Buren Democrats were leaving office, Patterson made a concerted effort in the second session of the Twenty-Sixth Congress for repeal. He pushed Silas Wright in the Senate Finance Committee to take action.[43] He followed with an identical appeal in his annual report for 1840, which outgoing President Van Buren highlighted in his annual message to Congress.[44] Again, nothing happened.

Patterson had more luck with the incoming Whigs. George Evans, Wright's Whig replacement as chair of the Senate Finance Committee, introduced Patterson's legislation on April 13, 1842. It set new values for the gold coins of Great Britain and France and reset values for the Spanish Pillar dollar and the dollars of Mexico, Peru, and Bolivia. Legal-tender status for all other foreign coins would be repealed.[45] The bill struggled in the Senate, finally coming up for consideration at the end of the session. Benton moved that it be tabled. Once again Patterson was thwarted.[46]

In reality, Benton had valid concerns about the specie supply. Coinage was down substantially in 1841, silver by half. Silver bullion was not appearing at the Mint for coinage in the same volumes as it had previously. People were petitioning Congress to legislate changes in the postal rates to coincide with the coins issued from the Mint. Change, in spite of continued production emphasis on dimes and half dimes, was becoming difficult for vendors to make. As the depression dragged on, people were hoarding their silver coins and spending paper money that might depreciate overnight should the issuing bank close its doors.

Patterson's relationship with the Whigs in Congress was not all that rosy either. During the Twenty-Seventh Congress, a Clay supporter introduced a bill to abolish all three branch mints.[47] The New Orleans Mint was adding fuel to the fire; there had been management issues at the branch. Frequent yellow-fever epidemics had forced the closure of that mint for extended periods of time. The chief coiner and melter and refiner had died in the epidemic of 1839.[48] While operations were now on an even keel, the past problems were enough to tip the scales of sentiment in this Congress against New Orleans.

Resistance came immediately from Representative James Graham. He emphasized that, should the Charlotte Mint close, this gold would not go to Philadelphia. It would go to the Bechtlers' mint in his home district. Bechtler would then coin it or cast it into bars for export. It was an unacceptable alternative in either case. Patterson had previously railed against the Bechtler mint and accused it of consistently substandard coinage. He openly wondered why Congress prohibited the private minting of copper but not gold and silver.[49] However, his real problem had been that Bechtler diverted gold that would otherwise have gone to the Charlotte Mint. Using the Bechtler mint as the stalking horse, Graham's appeal, aimed at the hard-money Democrats, was successful in stopping the bill dead in its tracks.

With the branch-mint issue out of the way for the time being, Finance Committee chairman Evans reintroduced the foreign-specie legislation at the opening of the third session in December 1842. Benton tabled the bill again.[50] Patterson immediately wrote to Benton stating that advocating a change in the 1834 act reflected no intention of driving foreign coins out of the country. His wish was to keep them in the country by encouraging recoinage. As for the silver currency, there was no change except the exclusion of the fractions of the Spanish Pillar dollars.[51]

Evans and Benton finally reached an accommodation. If Evans would drop the fourth clause withdrawing legal-tender status for those coins not named in the legislation, Benton would stand aside. With the deal cut, the bill sailed through Congress.[52] The victory was hollow. Patterson was furious—foreign currency in the United States was now a mess. The old Spanish Pillar dollars and their fractions were by that time all worn below legal weight. The gold coins of Portugal remained legal tender at an overvalued amount under the 1834 act. The gold coins of Spain, Mexico, and Columbia were so inconsistent as to be incapable of valuation but remained at their fictitious value set by the 1834 act.[53] With that salvo, Patterson threw up his hands in exasperation. Part of the pie was better than nothing.

• • • •

The politicians were not through with Patterson. By 1843 Tyler had openly broken with Henry Clay and was seeking a political base from which to run for the presidency again. The moves would be sweeping, and the battle lines quickly drawn. Clay had resigned from the Senate in March 1842 in order to devote himself full time to running for president in 1844. Yet he was still powerful enough to work his magic in the Senate against Tyler. On February 27, 1843, the Senate rejected Tyler's nomination of a supporter for minister to France. Furthermore, on February 28, 1843, Walter Forward, a solid Pennsylvania Whig who did not cooperate with Tyler, resigned as secretary of the Treasury. Tyler transferred his secretary of war to that position and nominated a Pennsylvanian for secretary of war to maintain his support in that state.

Tyler also moved to strengthen his position in Pennsylvania, a state deemed key to his election chances.[54] As Mint director, Patterson controlled considerable patronage jobs. Behind closed doors, Tyler nominated Joseph Ritner to take Patterson's position. Ritner would get his revenge. However, it was not to be. The long arm of Henry Clay. from his Lexington, Kentucky, home, saved Patterson. His lieutenant, John Crittenden, killed the nomination in the Senate.[55] Clay was going to put up a fight over Pennsylvania and it served his purpose to leave Patterson in place.

CHAPTER 18

AN AMERICAN SIR ISAAC NEWTON

In the 1840s, the Philadelphia Mint was a showplace. The engine room was as clean as a parlor floor, seemingly perfectly noiseless, free from all the hissing leaks, oily smells, and other nuisances that one would expect when visiting such an operation in those days. Every part of the steam engine, including the flywheel, was turned, with no sharp or abrupt edges, and polished. The journal bearings were supplied with oil by siphon cups that regulated the flow of the lubricating oil so that not a drop of excess was seen.

Beauty was not overlooked in this dazzling display of mechanical accomplishments. The cylinder, pump, and other parts of the engine were mounted on an entablature, supported by eight Grecian Doric columns. These columns were arranged to contain the pipes for egress and ingress of steam and water, keeping the overall profile of the engine clean and simple. The stop-valve of the engine was in the form of an Etruscan vase, placed on a pedestal between the end columns under the cylinder. The floor of the engine room was paved with colored tiles similar to those found in the ancient palaces of Carnac. The machinery in the coining department was equally as artistic, yet noted for its accelerated movements. Those who visited remarked upon the marriage of efficiency and beauty of form in these operations.[1]

For the laborers who worked at the Mint, this mechanical beauty made little difference in their day. It started

and ended at the sound of a bell rung by a doorkeeper. The men worked 10-hour shifts through the week, except for Saturdays, when their work ended two hours early. During the warm months, work commenced at six in the morning and ended at four in the afternoon. The men were allowed to bring both their breakfast and lunch to be eaten in place. From the beginning of October to the end of March, the day started at seven and the men were expected to eat breakfast before starting work. They received three days off without pay during the year—Christmas, the Fourth of July, and Election Day. To operate the mint took 40 workmen, 2 doorkeepers, and a watchman. Within the operations there were 31 men in the coining department, 8 with the melter and refiner, and 1 in the assayer's office. Daily pay ranged from $1.40 to $2.00 for the top skilled mechanics and $2.50 for the coining-department foreman. The men were docked for absences regardless of the reason and were paid at straight time rates for overtime work. The average daily wage was $1.68. That translated into an annual payment of about $500, assuming there was no lost time.

The men complained about the pay structure and petitioned from time to time for increases in the hourly rates for what were essentially skilled positions. The tradeoff for the men in this situation was job security. There were no layoffs at the Mint. Also, there were periods of idleness brought on in part by the intermittent flow of bullion for coinage and in part by the segmentation of the work activities. The men in each department had a particular skill that was not transferrable to another department. In addition, the functions in each department required that the men work in gangs. Thus, cross-training had little benefit. For the men, work was often routine drudgery with periods of intense activity fitted around periods of idleness or make-work.[2]

The activities of the officers were in stark contrast to the laborers. Including the clerks and assistants, their wages were ample. Office hours were from nine to four, except for the chief coiner,and the melter and refiner, who had to be with their men in the early morning.[3] Of course, with Adam Eckfeldt still working in the coining department, there was little need for chief coiner Franklin Peale to be an early riser. None of their daily jobs were arduous, particularly that of the engraver.

• • • •

Mint Director Robert Maskell Patterson found this arrangement distinctly to his liking. With time on his hands, he could indulge himself in multiple scientific pursuits. Consequently, he was able to play a leading role in the American Philosophical Society, as well as participate in community philanthropy.

Patterson's activities tied to the American Philosophical Society started immediately upon his return to Philadelphia from Charlottesville with his observation of Halley's Comet.[4] In 1836 the secretary of the Navy asked Patterson and other members of the society to recommend books, instruments, and materials needed for the Wilkes South Seas Expedition of Discovery.[5] Titian Peale would accompany this expedition as a naturalist when it set sail three years later. Patterson formed a society committee to observe the eclipse of the sun on September 18, 1838. He also reported to the society that year on a study of Earth's magnetism, aimed at aiding ship navigation.[6] Later that same year, he embarked on the brig USS *Washington* in New York City to observe experiments to determine ocean depth by echoes, a concept well ahead of its time.[7] It came as no surprise to anyone with knowledge of the American Philosophical Society that Patterson was chosen to give the principal address at its 100th-anniversary celebration in 1843.

Patterson's scientific endeavors were not always external to the U.S. Mint. In 1840 he and Peale successfully reproduced at the Philadelphia Mint experiments conducted in England dealing with the generation of electricity from steam. Helping with that work was Joseph Saxton, who was assuming the role of Peale's go-to guy. Patterson even set up a library at the Philadelphia Mint consisting of the leading scientific journals of the day. It was a place where Peale could frequently be found.

Undoubtedly both a high and a low point of Patterson's scientific pursuits involved the Wilkes Expedition. Patterson had maintained his board seat in Charles Willson Peale's museum continuously since the death of its founder. Subsequently, John Kane joined the board, along with Franklin Peale and Escol Sellers. The business, now called the Philadelphia Museum, moved into its own building in 1838. At this point, the institution still enjoyed a reputation as the finest, if not the only worthwhile, museum in the United States. In fact, it was equal to many of the best in Europe.

The tie-in with the Wilkes Expedition came in an offhand manner. A Philadelphia engraver of some repute, James B. Longacre, was engraving a portrait of Secretary of War Joel Poinsett for inclusion in his great endeavor, *The National Portrait Gallery of Distinguished Americans*. As Longacre worked, the two men talked. They found themselves in agreement that the Philadelphia Museum would be the best depository for the expedition collections. Upon returning to Philadelphia, Longacre passed this information along to John Kane. Kane, with his Democratic political connections, acted quickly. Just in time for the order to be transmitted to the ships before they set sail, Van Buren's secretary of the Navy, John Paulding, ordered all collected items to be sent to the Philadelphia Museum. With Titian Peale heavily involved in gathering the specimens, the arrangement could not have been better for the museum.

As the ensuing depression from the Panic of 1837 deepened, the museum, with its added burden of a new building, delegated much of its day-to-day activities to the directors in an effort to hold down expenses. Patterson and Peale took over the natural-history and miscellaneous collections. Thus, they were in charge of the shipments from the expedition as they arrived. Crates began to appear at the Mint, where the two men carefully unpacked and cataloged the contents.

All went well until February 5, 1841, when John Paulding, in one of his last acts before the Whigs took office, ordered that all items on deposit at the Philadelphia Museum be forwarded to the national Cabinet of Natural History—the forerunner of the Smithsonian Institution—in Washington. When the first crates arrived from Philadelphia, they were only half full, using wood shavings, unobtainable in the South Seas, to fill the voids. Wrongdoing was denied. Subsequent crates delivered directly to Washington revealed that one-quarter of the items coming in—the most choice—were marked private by Titian and destined for the museum. Others on the expedition did the same but not to the extent that Titian did.[8]

Removal of this depository status, in combination with the depression, marked the beginning of the end for the Philadelphia Museum. It could not compete with this forerunner to the Smithsonian Institution. It was ironic that the American minister to Great Britain, Richard Rush, son of old Benjamin Rush, played an important role in securing the bequest of James Smithson that funded this government cabinet. When the Philadelphia Museum's imminent collapse was apparent, Patterson tried unsuccessfully to take it over for the benefit of the American Philosophical Society. For Patterson, the museum was the one enterprise with which he was associated that met with failure.

Patterson did not confine himself only to scientific activities. He was president of the Musical Fund Society, an officer of the Franklin Institute, and a guiding light of the Pennsylvania Institution for the Instruction of the Blind. He involved himself in finding methods for the blind to read writing and musical notations using wax and transferring these symbols to sheets of lead.[9] Patterson was also active in business affairs, serving for a time as president of the Pennsylvania Life Annuity Company. With such a wide variety of interests, Patterson maintained a very high profile in Philadelphia society. Not surprisingly, years later, it would be said by friends and acquaintances that Robert Maskell Patterson was an "American Sir Isaac Newton."[10]

••••

Amidst the successes of his outside endeavors and the showpiece of innovative equipment at the Mint, one area seemed to cause Patterson nothing but difficulties—the Mint's engraving department. William Kneass's medical problems and his inability to perform many of the engraver's functions are well documented. However, Christian Gobrecht seemed to gradually drop from the equation after the completion of the half dollar designs for 1839. He was nearing his 54th birthday. Health should not have been an issue; yet it might have been. His absences from the Mint were not yet noticeable, but they would become so later.[11] Otherwise, there is only conjecture.

In searching for a solution to his dilemma, it is not surprising that Patterson turned to Franklin Peale. In January 1840, to demonstrate the technology of the day, the chief coiner used a medallion portrait head of Benjamin Franklin in burnt clay about five inches in diameter as his model. From this model, a pattern casting was made in Boston using Berlin steel. This casting was then placed in the Contamin portrait lathe to produce a hub that only needed a slight retouching by the engraver. The hub, made of hardened steel, could then be used with the powerful screw press to produce any number of working dies from which medals could be struck. Patterson sent two of the resulting Franklin medals to Treasury secretary Levi Woodbury, proudly proclaiming that a new era in making medals was at hand that dispensed entirely with the difficult art of diesinking. All that was required was a good model in clay or any other plastic material. The rest was purely mechanical.[12]

Franklin Peale knew Berlin steel was not the best casting material. The chief coiner was aware of the use of voltaic electricity, which produced a simple electro-chemical reaction in which a solution of copper sulfate was made to precipitate metallic copper upon another metal. Experiments were underway in London using this process to produce a facsimile in copper of a medal from an impression of that medal made in lead. The patent holder claimed the copy produced was a "most *exact impress* of the original."[13]

Peale, with the help of Joseph Saxton and others, began to experiment in an effort to improve upon this electrotype process. Using a simple voltaic circle consisting of zinc and copper plates connected by two copper wires and placed in a corrosive liquid, they placed copper sulfate next to the copper plate but separated from the corrosive liquid by plaster of Paris. As a result, copper was precipitated onto the copper plate, producing an exact impression in reverse on the deposit of any etchings on the copper plate. The same held true for any copper medal. Thus, the engraver could work in the more malleable copper, as opposed to the more durable steel, and be able to produce an electrotype copy for use in the Contamin lathe.[14]

In the middle of Peale's experiments, William Kneass died on August 27, 1840, just shy of his 59th birthday. In keeping with Mint tradition, Patterson had allowed Kneass to stay "on the job" until the bitter end, without regard to his ability to perform. However, the director got little thanks from his family. Kneass's widow raised the issue of the salary sharing with Gobrecht to Secretary Woodbury, saying that Kneass had been given no choice by Patterson but to agree to the arrangement. Her demand that Gobrecht reimburse her for the amounts taken went nowhere.[15]

Without addressing Gobrecht's health, Patterson wasted no time in nominating the man to be engraver. The job was one in which the politicians had no desire to interfere. Gobrecht was formally nominated by President Martin Van Buren on December 16, 1840, and confirmed by the Senate the next day.[16] In making the nomination, Patterson noted that a replacement for Gobrecht would not be necessary, saving the government $1,500 in annual salary. Gobrecht would have the aid of a mechanic and the benefit of Peale's improvements to the mechanical process for making multiple working dies, greatly diminishing the workload of the engraver.[17]

By inference, Patterson's offhand reference to a mechanic aiding Gobrecht implied little skill was required for this activity. That was far from the case. In an employee census the following year, Patterson described this individual as a very superior mechanician employed in making dies, etc., at a compensation of $83.33 per month. An annual salary of $1,000 was hardly normal. In fact, it was extraordinary.[18] Just who was this mechanic?

This man was Ball Hughes (fig. 77) and he was certainly no mechanic when he went on the Mint's payroll in late 1839. If Patterson was not already familiar with Hughes's work, he undoubtedly became so in early 1839 with the American Philosophical Society purchase of a bust of Dr. Nathaniel Bowditch executed by Hughes.[19] Ball Hughes was an accomplished, well-known sculptor, far more comfortable modeling the human form than Gobrecht.

Fig. 78. The changes executed by Ball Hughes to the Liberty Seated design in 1840 are apparent in this comparison. Here, a dollar coin from 1840 is compared with Gobrecht's seated Liberty from the 1839 aborted dollar striking. Also included is the reverse from Gobrecht's half dollar pattern of that same year.

Fig. 77. Robert Ball Hughes's short stay at the Mint was followed by a long and distinguished career as a sculptor of national repute.

There is considerable speculation as to what adjustments in Gobrecht's designs Hughes made during his time at the Mint. Hughes possibly prepared the dies for the Liberty Seated dollar design of 1840 (fig. 78), which formally adopted the heraldic eagle reverse of the half dollar and quarter. On the obverse, drapery over Liberty's left arm is a departure from Gobrecht's original design. Probably in an effort to enhance the design's strikeability, relief was lowered on parts of Liberty's torso while rounding her arms more fully. In addition, the rock upon which the figure of Liberty sits was reduced in size. The eagle on the reverse is slightly different from Gobrecht's version on the half dollar as well, with its feathers rougher and unevenly spaced, which would have reflected Hughes's naturalistic style.[20]

Still Patterson was not satisfied. Perhaps he had come to realize too late that one design does not necessarily fit all coins, at least not this one. The seated Liberty was satisfactory on the half dollar and dollar. However, its complexity left much to be desired artistically on the dime and half dime.

Seeking improvement, the Mint director invited Horatio Greenough (fig. 79) to visit the Philadelphia Mint in

Fig. 79. Robert Maskell Patterson enlisted the services of Horatio Greenough, shown here in an 1829 painting by Rembrandt Peale, in an abortive attempt to replace the Liberty Seated design in 1842.

1842. Greenough, an acquaintance of Rembrandt Peale's, was one of the best-known American sculptors of this era. While there, Franklin Peale took the opportunity to discuss with Greenough his mechanical processes for dispensing with the diesinker. All that would be required now, according to an enthusiastic Peale, was a medallion from an artist in some form of plastic material. Patterson talked of his ongoing desire to make the art on American coins more creditable. In spite of the implementation of the Liberty Seated motif, he was not satisfied. Although Philadelphia artist Thomas Sully's design had much merit, it was not without its faults. The eagle had given them infinite fits. Resignedly, Patterson was now of the opinion that they must abandon a naturalistic representation of the bird and return to an eagle with a shield nailed to its breast and with branches and arrows in its claws. Perhaps the best solution was to adapt the eagle from the Great Seal of the United States. Patterson believed that with the proper exercise of taste, something of this character could be designed that would be satisfactory. He pushed Greenough to consider taking a shot at a new design.[21]

Greenough was intrigued by the challenge. Yet he readily admitted in communicating with Patterson after the meeting that, while it was easy to find fault with the existing coin designs, it was no easy matter to make great changes. He had toyed with coin designs for the United States in the past. The objects of his designs were nationality and simplicity, with each part having a distinct and palpable meaning. Any images that were forced by vagueness to have their names written upon them should be avoided. Greenough questioned Patterson on whether the coin ought to have a prominently placed denomination in Roman numerals and if the design should be applied across several coins of varying size. The sculptor was sure, given the Contamin reducing lathe, that his designs could be effectively executed at the Mint.[22]

Patterson encouragingly wrote back to Greenough, explaining that the law mandated that certain types of coins have an eagle on the reverse. The idea of showing the denominations was one that he had considered. However, it would take a change in the law to implement. Nevertheless, Patterson was confident that Congress would make the necessary changes when shown the improvement in coin recognition that would result. Considering that Patterson was, at this same time, having difficulties getting a technical fix on foreign-coin valuations through Congress, this was wishful thinking. Patterson went on to say that he wanted Greenough not to be bound by existing laws or by instructions or suggestions from Patterson in formulating his designs. It was an artist that he wanted, not a mechanic. Patterson had come a long way in that regard from his first attempts with Thomas Sully and Titian Peale. However, he did caution Greenough that there were many practical points relating to the coinage process that would have to be addressed once the designs were completed.[23]

As optimistic as Patterson was, there were too many hurdles for Greenough. It was clear from Patterson's letter that the process would be long and drawn out, which would keep the sculptor away from Italy, where he had established a studio some years before. Their correspondence stopped and no models or sketches exist that would indicate that Greenough seriously considered taking the commission. However, it was clear that Patterson was dissatisfied with his Liberty Seated design and was ready to restart the process with an outside artist, bypassing the engraver entirely in favor of the Contamin reducing lathe.

• • • •

During these first years of the 1840s, a changing of the guard occurred with regard to striking medals. Moritz Fürst died in 1840, effectively removing his partner, Adam Eckfeldt, from the equation. With Gobrecht increasingly ailing, it left a clear field for someone to take over this lucrative side business. Franklin Peale gladly stepped into the role. The generous remuneration would allow him to maintain a high-profile lifestyle in Philadelphia society, befitting of both the Peale clan and his wife's Girard relatives.

Peale was barely in office before he was executing medals for the Franklin Institute (fig. 80). A hitch developed

Fig. 80. As Gobrecht's health failed, Franklin Peale aggressively picked up the medals business from the Franklin Institute. Gobrecht had engraved dies for these medals in 1825.

when Peale was faced with striking an Indian Peace medal with President John Tyler's likeness. He and Patterson turned to Ferdinand Pettrich to do the modeling. While Pettrich's work was satisfactory, Patterson had reservations about the artist. Complaining that his work was apt to have a European influence, Patterson disqualified Pettrich from consideration for any improved coin designs at the time he decided to approach Greenough.

Peale almost pushed the medals business to the brink in 1843. The event that triggered the problem was the request from the Smithsonian forerunner for a set of American medals struck to date. At this point, the issue of presidential Indian Peace medals was discussed and it was noted that none were ever struck bearing the likenesses of the first two presidents. Patterson saw this omission as a chance to bring Greenough into the fold before he left for Italy, by commissioning him to provide the necessary models. Peale would cut the dies with the portrait lathe. Patterson proposed it to Secretary of the Treasury John Spencer. As to the small expense involved, he argued that all the other Indian Peace medals had been struck under contingent fund appropriations from the War Department. He did not see why in this instance it should be any different.[24] However, matters did not proceed as Patterson expected.

Secretary of War James Porter asked for details. Patterson put him off, explaining that preparing the necessary dies was the responsibility of the chief coiner. Peale was vacationing at Cape May in New Jersey with his wife, and some sort of accident delayed his returning to Philadelphia.[25] When Peale's estimate of cost did come, Porter balked. He noted that the cost was moderate if the dies were to be prepared outside the Mint. However, it was his impression that the work would be done at the Mint and that there would be little if any cost outside of the models and material.

Patterson's reply was the first official response to the outside activities of the chief coiners at the Philadelphia Mint.

> Permit me to observe that the business of making dies for medals and of striking medals is nowhere prescribed by law as a function of the Mint, or a duty of any of its officers, and that it has never been heretofore so considered by the Departments of War and Navy, for which all the public medals have been made. The numerous medals voted by Congress to the officers distinguished in the last war were not executed ever under the care of the Director, but under contracts made by the honorable Joseph Hopkinson,[26] who received a commission on the money expended. It is true that a part of the work was done at the Mint, and by one of its officers, the Chief Coiner; but the work was always looked upon as extra-official, and he was remunerated for it accordingly.

That certainly was true as far as it went. However, Patterson's next comments raised questions as to the appropriateness of that remuneration. Given the "anxiety" of Spencer and Porter that these medals be executed, Franklin Peale was willing, in this instance, to overlook any personal remuneration. Only out-of-pocket expenses would be included in the cost of the medals. How far below the original estimate that might be, Patterson could not say. Still, Patterson defended the original estimate, saying that it would be much greater without the use of the Mint's machinery.

Attached to Patterson's file copy of this letter were notes clearly in Peale's handwriting. They are enlightening as to the chief coiner's thought process.

> The keeping and preservation of dies for medals is confided very properly to the Chief Coiner of the Mint but cannot be considered as included with his official duties under the law.
>
> The striking of medals has always been confided to the Chief Coiner of the Mint but considered and paid for as a private matter. The engraving of dies for medals has never been considered an official duty of the Engraver of the Mint. The Director alone has control & agency as the representative of the sec. of War or Navy.
>
> The estimate furnished by the Chief Coiner is such as barely to cover the expenses and labour for which he becomes responsible. The advantage which the U.S. derives from the use of its machinery employed in the operation is the great reduction as the cost of these [unreadable] compliments or rewards—and this reduction of cost grows out of the observations and skill of the present Chief Coiner, Mr. Peale from which the Mint operations have [unreadable] [unreadable] and important advantages.[27]

Patterson knew better than to quote directly from what Peale had supplied. It was clearly self-serving. Peale's description of the duties of the chief coiner in regard to medals can only be described as manipulative. It also sought to cut the engraver out of the process entirely.

Spencer was subtle in his reply to Patterson.

> It would seem from your letter that the Chief Coiner executes such work *at the Mint*. If so, it is not perceived by the department how he can with propriety make it the subject of private emolument. At all events, in the present case, the authority of the department to the work is sufficient to justify the employment of his time and services in it.
>
> From the anxiety expressed by the C. Coiner & yourself that the work should be executed, it is hoped and expected that all the aid and every facility within the power of your establishment will be cheerfully furnished for its completion.[28]

The anxiety that the project be undertaken was not Spencer's. It was Patterson's and Peale's. Spencer covered himself in regard to the appropriateness of payments to the chief coiner for medal work undertaken at the Mint. While Spencer approved the project, his approval was a veiled warning to Patterson that he was on his own if adverse reaction developed. Having just saved his job by the skin of his teeth, Patterson was not about to move forward on his own. The project to strike Indian Peace medals depicting Washington and Adams was dead.

Peale was fortunate that he had completed the Indian Peace medals with President Tyler's image the previous February. Luckily for him, no new medals would be required until there was a change in the presidency. If Tyler lost the coming election, Spencer would be gone, as would the issue of Peale's profiting privately through government medals. The issue of using Mint equipment for private medals remained a dirty little secret, yet to be exposed to outside scrutiny.

• • • •

On July 26, 1844, the funeral of Christian Gobrecht was held at 4 p.m. at his home on Walnut Street. In accordance with his wishes, the officers and all people connected with the Mint attended. The engraver was 58.[29] Barely two weeks later, Peale took on Gobrecht's private medal work for the Massachusetts Charitable Mechanic Association. Now all medal work was consolidated under the chief coiner.[30]

CHAPTER 19

NEW FACES

The year 1844 was a presidential election year and John Tyler was still seeking a base, any base, to help him win the presidency. Texas annexation had, from time to time, flared into the national consciousness since that republic had gained its independence from Mexico. Senator John Calhoun saw annexation as essential to the well-being of the slaveholding Southern states. When rumors of possible British intervention surfaced in late 1843, Tyler took a political risk. He would gain the support of Southern Democrats and either force Northern Democrats to heel or he would form his own party in the South. Consequently, Tyler permitted his secretary of state, Abel P. Upshur, to restart annexation negotiations. Upshur, a Virginian and Calhoun protégé, was only too happy to move forward.

Annexation discussions with Texan authorities proceeded smoothly until February 28, 1844. A presidential party including Upshur was aboard the battleship USS *Princeton* in the Potomac River to observe the firing of the largest naval gun ever built. It exploded, killing Upshur. Tyler turned to John Calhoun as his replacement. Calhoun wasted no time in completing the treaty and presenting it to the Senate for ratification in April. However, he did it in such a manner as to inflame sectional feelings and polarize national politics.[1]

Henry Clay had the Whig nomination sewn up. Since leaving the Senate, he had traveled the country, garnering

support for his presidential nomination. He had no need to take a position on the current discussion of the annexation issue. His opinion was known, having spoken out against annexation some years before. Still, against the advice of his political friends, he reiterated his position in a way that it could not be misunderstood. Clay thought annexation would inevitably lead to a costly, dishonorable war with Mexico over a territory that many people did not want to see join the Union.

The maneuvering of Tyler aside, Martin Van Buren had the best chance for the Democratic nomination in 1844. Pressed by his Northern supporters, Van Buren likewise stepped to the plate over annexation. He asserted that the acquisition of Texas would be an act of aggression against Mexico that would stain the honor of the nation, already well stained by the recent Trail of Tears.

The Democratic Party required a two-thirds majority for nomination. Van Buren could muster only a majority. The other contenders who were close behind, Lewis Cass, James Buchanan, and Levi Woodbury, now assumed a greater role. The convention deadlocked. On the ninth ballot, they nominated James K. Polk, former Tennessee governor and two-term speaker of the House. Polk was moderately pro-annexation and had former president Andrew Jackson's backing.

The race was on. Clay, with his opposition to annexation, had totally lost the South. Only by carrying the Border States, New England, New York, and Pennsylvania, could Clay win. New York and Pennsylvania would be ground zero in this election.[2]

• • • •

Robert Maskell Patterson felt little pressure to replace his deceased engraver, Christian Gobrecht. With Franklin Peale's support, the Mint director had downgraded the position in practice if not in fact. He had terminated the services of Robert Ball Hughes the year before. When the issue of gold dollars cropped up in Congress the preceding January, Patterson had had Peale strike additional dollars from Gobrecht's old design of 1836 for the review of the House Ways and Means Committee. He had even pulled out a warmed-over version of his 1836 objections to the coin for Treasury secretary John C. Spencer's benefit.[3] When Patterson wished to reinforce his objections to the coin by adding fears of counterfeiting, he again turned to Peale. He had the chief coiner produce an electrotype silver gilt dollar coin for the committee's review.[4] In Patterson's mind, there was little need for an engraver other than for mechanical day-to-day chores. Even these, Peale's men did on a regular basis.

Patterson was distracted from the search for a replacement for Gobrecht. The day after the funeral, there was a fire at the Charlotte Mint. It had occurred early that Saturday morning, starting small. It should have been easily containable. However, no one took the initiative to tap the second-floor water supply for the steam boilers. What should have been a minor event ended up destroying the building and damaging much of the machinery.[5] Patterson had inherited these branch mints. Their output, driven by diminishing gold production, was far below the original rosy expectations of their proponents. Meanwhile, the Philadelphia Mint remained well below its practical capacity. With the hard money Democrats out of power, there was no driving force in Washington to push for repairs. Besides, the issue of a branch mint at New York had come up again in the recently concluded first session of the Twenty-Eighth Congress.[6] It had gone nowhere but was the wildcard in the political mix that could determine the action to be taken at Charlotte. Against this backdrop, Patterson took the path of least resistance: he did nothing.

Meanwhile, the chore of finding Gobrecht's replacement would not go away. Recommendations and applications for the job came quickly. Thomas Sully recommended Thomas Welch, a skilled engraver and an excellent draftsman. Welch had assured Sully that he was well acquainted with the business of diesinking.[7] In former years, Welch had studied under James Longacre and had prepared an engraving of James Madison for inclusion in Longacre's book of famous Americans. Still Patterson took no initiative in filling this position. He made no contact with Charles Cushing Wright, who had earned his earlier praise. For a man who had proactively sought well-qualified men to fill vacancies within the Mint officers, Patterson's actions seemed out of character. That is, unless Patterson was only looking for a proxy who would stand by while Peale continued his push to mechanize the function.

James Barton Longacre (fig. 81) did not know what he was getting into. He had initially not even considered the appointment of engraver. However, Robert Bald, a Philadelphia banknote engraver and friend, had pressed him to consider it. Longacre had married in 1826 and now had five children; the youngest was four years old. His life's work, the *National Portrait Gallery of Distinguished Americans*, had been a victim of the depression. His partner in the venture had dropped out in 1839, and Longacre had struggled to complete the work to meet his existing subscription commitments.[8] A devoutly religious man, Longacre recognized that the $2,000 annual salary would allow him to comfortably provide for his family.[9] Still he hesitated. He had no political connections other than John Calhoun. Bald argued that Longacre's standing within the country as an artist gave him a superior claim. Besides, Bald correctly pointed out that John Calhoun had more influence within the Tyler administration than anyone else.

Longacre took the plunge, speaking directly with Calhoun. The secretary of state told him point-blank that

Fig. 81. James B. Longacre, in a self portrait in water color (1845).

politics would not be considered in gaining his recommendation. Calhoun would only be swayed by the highest qualifications. While the appointment of the engraver was within the confines of the Treasury Department, Calhoun would take pleasure in laying Longacre's testimonials before the secretary of the Treasury.[10]

It was enough. Longacre accepted the engraver's position under an interim appointment. President Tyler officially presented his name to the Senate for confirmation on December 18, 1844.[11] For Patterson, it was a dual disappointment. The president had appointed Longacre before he had presented his own recommendation. In addition, Longacre was a recognized engraver and artist, putting in jeopardy Patterson's efforts, in conjunction with Franklin Peale, to downgrade the position. However, one factor would work in Patterson and Peale's favor: Longacre was not a diesinker. With his knowledge of the engraving process, Peale would still hold a trump card.

• • • •

For Patterson, there was more political interference to fend off involving personnel at the Mint; after all, it was an election year. The newspapers were full of speculation that Tyler intended to replace the treasurer at the Mint. Worse, there was talk that the assayer, Jacob Eckfeldt, was out too. Patterson took a politically discreet route to argue against these changes. He approached Robert Walker, a senator from Mississippi, who had Tyler's ear in spite of being a Democrat. Patterson was most concerned about the rumor of Eckfeldt's termination. Using the same argument that he had when he gained Peale's appointment as chief coiner, he emphasized that the assayer's position was "*the* place that should be touched with the greatest of caution." Eckfeldt was respected both as an assayer and as a metallurgist.[12] Once again he was successful.

Patterson was not so fortunate in October. He wanted to appoint his son, Bob, to the position of director's clerk. Bob Patterson had graduated from the University of Pennsylvania and read law in the office of John Kane. Young Patterson gained admittance to the Philadelphia bar in 1840. However, his career had been cut short by a sudden hearing impairment.[13] Robert Patterson's motives in seeking this appointment were driven more by chance than by any grand scheme. His clerk was leaving and it was an opportunity to put his son in a position where his hearing impairment would not hinder his performance. However, Patterson had to be thinking in the back of his mind about the long term. He was within months of reaching his 10th anniversary at the Mint. If the line of succession within the Patterson family was to be maintained, what better position was there for young Bob?

Regardless of Patterson's motives, the secretary of the Treasury rejected the nomination. However, there was nothing personal in the rejection. President Tyler in general opposed nepotism in this type of situation.[14]

• • • •

The presidential election was hard fought that year. While much was at stake for the nation, the politics were personal. The Democrats worked to cement the tie between Jackson and Polk by calling their nominee "Young Hickory." However, in Pennsylvania this simplistic election strategy needed help. The state had become increasingly industrial as the nation emerged from its economic depression, driven by its deposits of coal and iron ore, making tariffs a keystone political issue. With the Whigs associated with protective tariffs, Polk had an uphill battle to win the state. Patterson's close friend and political ally, John Kane, fixed that.

Kane had known Polk from his days in Washington, when he negotiated the French indemnity claims. Upon Polk's nomination, Kane wrote the candidate advising him to release no letters to the newspapers (as Henry Clay was doing indiscriminately and to his own detriment). Polk wrote at once to Kane, promising him he would follow his advice. Some weeks later, Polk sent a draft letter to Kane which laid out his position on tariffs, saying that he sanctioned reasonable protection for home industry.[15] Kane advised against release and Polk adhered to his promise. The issue heated up in Pennsylvania, as Polk's votes in Congress on the issue had been all over the board and people began to suspect Polk was against the tariffs that were so thoroughly despised in the South. Then Kane, on his own initiative, released the letter.

This was the story related by Kane in his autobiography. Rumors at that time in Philadelphia had Kane authoring this letter for Polk and releasing it at the point when it would do the most good.[16] The Whig press responded at once but to little avail. Clay, while carrying Philadelphia, lost Pennsylvania by 6,332 votes. Afterward, Clay claimed that Kane's sleight-of-hand statement of Polk's position on protective tariffs stole Pennsylvania.[17]

With Pennsylvania taken from him, Clay had to have New York. However, it was not to be. Clay lost New York by 2,106 votes, suffering from the candidacy of a third-party abolitionist. The dark horse James K. Polk had beaten Henry Clay, the heart and soul of the Whig party, in an extremely close election.

It was one of the most momentous elections in American history. However, that possibility was of little concern to Philadelphia Democrats because one of their own, George Dallas, was now the vice president–elect. There was heady talk that both Dallas and Andrew Jackson supported John Kane for a cabinet post in the upcoming Polk administration.[18] Robert Maskell Patterson now seemed in the catbird's seat. His position at the Mint would be secure with Kane in such a position of influence.

Patterson did not have long to wait to exact his revenge upon the outgoing Tyler administration. An applicant for the director's clerk position appeared out of the blue. The man had the strong support of Tyler's secretary of the Treasury and Tyler too. Tyler would find it very agreeable if Patterson could see his way clear to recommending the young man for the position.[19] Given Tyler's treatment of Patterson, the Mint director could be forgiven if he thumbed his nose at this request.

• • • •

Patterson still had the second session of the Twenty-Eighth Congress to deal with in December of that year. The legislators promptly forced his hand on the Charlotte branch mint, requesting an estimate for the cost of repairs. The number was $35,000. Buried in that amount was an appropriation for only one new press.[20] Patterson saw no point in expanding this Mint's capacity beyond what it was already coining. Besides, what he did for Charlotte, the Georgia congressional delegation would insist he also do for Dahlonega.

Petitions flowed into Congress. Support from North Carolina for rebuilding at Charlotte came as no surprise. A memorial from the citizens of Charleston praying for the removal of the Mint to that city was not unexpected.[21] However, quickly on the heels of the Charleston memorial was another one from New York City requesting a branch mint for their city.[22] All the branch-mint issues were now on the table that would have stayed submerged, at least for a time, had not the issue of rebuilding the Charlotte Mint come to the fore.

Patterson finally got off dead center in his annual report to the president on February 5, 1845. He came down squarely in favor of rebuilding the Charlotte Mint. He reasoned that the region in which the Charlotte and Dahlonega mints were positioned contained gold mines as numerous and as rich as any in the world. They were presently less productive due to the diversion of labor away from the gold fields. Patterson was sure that this condition was only temporary.[23] He really had little choice; any other position would have led to branch mints at Charleston and New York. In this case, he was on safe ground. Congress took the least expensive route, electing to appropriate the money to rebuild Charlotte.

• • • •

With the closing of the Twenty-Eighth Congress, the Polk administration took office. Patterson's new boss at Treasury was none other than Robert Walker, who had resigned his Senate seat to come on board. Walker was originally a Pennsylvanian, having graduated from the University of Pennsylvania in 1819. He had practiced law briefly in Pittsburgh before migrating to Mississippi in 1826. While he lived in a Southern state, his point of view was not restricted to Southern positions. Unhappily for Patterson, he would prove to be a strong voice for the financial institutions in New York City.

Patterson was thorough this time in proposing his son be appointed as his clerk. Shortly after Polk's inauguration, Patterson attended a dinner party hosted by A. Dallas Bache and his wife in Washington, D.C. He was in high company. Bache was one of Benjamin Franklin's great-grandchildren. Also in attendance was Vice President George Dallas, Bache's uncle. These two families were political powerhouses in Philadelphia as well as forces to be reckoned with at the national level.[24]

Two months later, Patterson went to Dallas Bache for the recommendation.[25] Bache was a fellow officer in the American Philosophical Society. He was presently the superintendent of the Office of Coastal Survey and the Office of Weights and Measures in Washington. Beyond George Dallas, Bache had one more connection to offer—his sister, Mary, was Robert Walker's wife. Robert Maskell Patterson was not to be denied. If Patterson had not focused upon succession the previous October, the firepower he called in from Bache to support his son's appointment made it clear that he was currently considering the issue.

• • • •

Amidst these events, James Longacre settled into his engraving position. It was a rocky start. As soon as he arrived at the Mint, Patterson asked him to resign his elected position on the council of Spring Garden, a separately chartered entity within Philadelphia. The Mint director considered it inappropriate for Longacre to hold this office at the same time he was an officer of the Mint. While Longacre complied, it irked him. Patterson seemed brusque and unfriendly.[26]

There were other signs that indicated to Longacre that some considered his position inferior to others at the Mint. Patterson told him that standard operating procedure when Longacre needed assistance was to call on the coining-department foreman.[27] Yet Eckfeldt was subject to the dictates of his boss, Franklin Peale. As a result, Longacre occasionally had trouble finding qualified men who were available to work for him. When the workers were available, the screw press used for making hubs and working dies was often in use by Peale for making his medals, further impeding Longacre. Even Longacre's workplace was substandard. His single-room office had a northern exposure and an overhanging piazza that blocked direct sunlight. At times, his light was further restricted by chimney smoke coming from the refinery on one side and the steam-engine boiler fire on the other.[28]

Longacre had to know that Franklin Peale looked upon his position with disdain. Peale made no secret of the fact that he considered the engraver's job a sinecure.[29] Over time, Longacre grew defensive and began finding fault with Peale. While Peale considered the engraver's daily work menial, Longacre observed that the chief coiner had to go to an outside engraver to place the inscriptions upon his medals. The Contamin reducing lathe was also under Peale's control. Longacre knew that Peale's skills were better than his on this machine. However, Peale no longer operated this lathe, using instead one of his subordinates to do the work. Longacre, in a sarcastic but telling comment, observed that the skill to adjust or watch the revolution of a steel point driven by steam offered feeble stimulus to his ambitions as an artist.[30]

Some of Longacre's animosity also centered on the profitability of Peale's lucrative medals business. Longacre was the only professional artist and engraver among the Mint officers. Yet all the government work for medals and their profits went to the chief coiner. Longacre would eventually attempt to enter this business as well with the aid of C.C. Wright.[31]

Years later Longacre would express his frustration with the situation using this metaphor:

> The birds that I had expected to display their plumage in the atelier of the engraver have flown over my head preferring it would seem the more spacious apartments of the chief coiner to be caged.[32]

Still Longacre persevered. He would not make waves, just meet the daily requirements of his job. However, his feelings simmered below the surface, with his frustrations centered upon Franklin Peale.

Longacre had been on the job officially for almost six months when the opportunity presented itself to Patterson to replace him. Allen Leonard, a Philadelphia silversmith and diesinker, had talked to Secretary Walker and

President Polk. They, in turn, had kicked the issue down to the Mint director.[33] Patterson interviewed Leonard, who brought an example of the work upon which he had built his reputation: a medal displaying the head of John Adams. Patterson told Leonard that he did not consider that single medal satisfactory evidence of the man's ability to place American coins on an equal footing with those of Europe. He would not support Leonard's application to be engraver. In response, Leonard volunteered to prepare a die in coin relief.

Here the matter sat until Walker pressed Patterson for an update in the middle of August 1845. Patterson provided an honest assessment of Longacre's abilities. The man was a highly regarded gentleman in the community, an important attribute in Patterson's eyes. He had some reputation as an engraver in copper. However, he was not a diesinker. To Patterson's knowledge Longacre had made no attempt at this art. The routine of the Mint at this point did not require it. So long as there were no changes in the present coin designs, the sinking of dies for the Mint was a mechanical operation and the office of the engraver was little more than a sinecure.

Patterson frankly admitted to the secretary that he was not content with U.S. coins as works of art. If he knew of an individual with the talent and skill to bring forth new designs for the circulating coins, Patterson would not hesitate to recommend him for appointment to the engraver's position. However, Patterson did not think such a person existed in the United States.[34]

Leonard delivered his coin-relief die to Patterson on September 22. He made excuses that the press of business had prevented him from doing his best. Given the necessary time, Leonard was confident that he could cut a die infinitely better.[35] Patterson immediately had a splash impression in a fusible alloy made. That could only mean one thing: Franklin Peale was in the picture. The two men and Peale met the next day in what must have been a disappointment for Leonard. Patterson was not pleased with the design; he did not consider it an original work. Even though it was not intended, the design bore a strong resemblance to a likeness of Louis Philippe from a French five-franc piece. However, the Mint director did feel the diesinking was creditable enough.

In reporting the results to Walker, Patterson made the point that there were others more qualified than Leonard if Longacre were to be replaced. He brought up Thomas Welch, using the same methods as when he had continued to push for Booth when the Tyler administration was considering replacing McClintock as melter and refiner. Welch had the blessing of Sully, close friend of the Peale brothers. In fact, Patterson had gone a step further. Welch was now working on a trial of his own. Patterson wished to wait until Welch had completed his effort before making a decision on Longacre. Patterson was prepared to do what had not been done at the Mint since its establishment: fire the engraver.

In spite of the rough interview, Leonard refused to give up. Two months later he sent a die and two impressions, one each for Patterson and Peale, of an image of a noted professor in Philadelphia. He also addressed Patterson's complaints from the first meeting, attempting to turn the negative into a positive. French engraver Joseph-Francois Domard had designed the five-franc piece that was in question, and Leonard unabashedly stated that his quick grasp of the masterly style of Domard was a point in his favor. Leonard also addressed Patterson's objection to the design, falling back upon his reputation as a competent designer for the preceding 17 years in Boston and Philadelphia. He pledged to the Mint director that, if appointed, he would become a master at design. Leonard was confident that he could produce a coin as good as any in Europe.[36]

Getting no response from Patterson, Leonard went around the Mint director to Walker, cooking his goose in the process. Leonard sent Secretary Walker a much-improved second impression of the image of Louis Philippe. An irked Patterson pointed out that Leonard's work was nothing more than a copy, although he acknowledged it displayed mechanical skill in diesinking. However, its merits as a work of art drew from the excellence of Domard's original design. The skills shown by Leonard were not what they wanted at the Mint.

In Patterson's rebuttal to Walker, he set out his view of the requirements of the engraver.

> We require an artist of taste, judgment and inventive talent; a man who can design as well as execute. Nay, the mechanical skill of the die-sinker [*sic*] is even a subordinate qualification with which we could almost entirely dispense. If the artist, after making his design be able to model it in wax, so as to make a medallion of three or four inches diameter, in bas-relief, all the rest can be done by ordinary workmen. A cast of the medallion is made in iron, and from this, by the aid of the "portrait lathe" a die is cut, which is a perfect facsimile of the original, reduced to the size required. Some of the medals executed at the Mint, one of Franklin, and the Indian medals of President Tyler, were struck from dies made this way. The original dies of our dime and half-dime were also cut by the portrait lathe, set in motion by the steam engine.

This certainly spelled out where Peale, with Patterson's cooperation, wanted to take the engraving function. It was a short step from here to employ an outside artist for the designs and modeling, with the diesinking done under the auspices of the chief coiner.

Now Patterson expressed a complete turnabout in his assessment of Longacre.

> The present incumbent in the office of Engraver of the Mint—Mr. Longacre—has shown, as I think, more taste and judgment in making devices for an improved coinage here than have been exhibited by any of his predecessors. He has shown that he is quite competent to make the required models from his drawings, and he is now engaged in this work. I think that it will be successful, and that he will be able, if not interrupted in his labors, to accomplish the improvement in our coins which is desired. I hope, therefore, that his tenure in office will not be interrupted until I am able to lay [*sic*] before you, and through you the President, the evidence of his skill and taste.[37]

Clearly, Thomas Welch's work had proved unsatisfactory. Longacre had stirred himself to step out from the daily confines of his job. The process with Leonard had gone on too long, with too many different people involved. Surely Longacre had gotten wind that his position was in jeopardy. However, the engraver quickly ceased his effort. Later he would only state that the conflicting views of those who had asked, if not demanded, to be heard—meaning Peale and Patterson—were so widely varying as to discourage him from pursuing new designs.[38] However, Longacre had bought some time. It was enough; by now the United States was embroiled in a war with Mexico over Texas.

• • • •

President Polk correctly interpreted his victory as a mandate to bring Texas into the Union. However, Polk had more in his sights than Texas. He also wanted Alta California. That region had actively rebelled with Texas when the Mexican government moved to centralize power in 1835 and 1836. Mexico, regarding Texas as the more serious challenge, chose conciliation with Alta California. The result had been an enfeebled local government, with weakened ties to the distant central government in Mexico City.

Before Polk could take action in regard to Mexico, he moved to settle the dispute with Great Britain over the partition of the Oregon Territory, where the two nations held overlapping claims. In spite of strong political rhetoric to the contrary, Polk opened conciliatory talks with the British consul in Washington, D.C. The resulting settlement deflected the westward American migration away from what would later become British Columbia.

Congress passed legislation enabling Texas to join the Union as a state in March 1845. In February 1846, the new state government assumed power. With control came an inherited problem with Mexico: the disputed southern boundary. The boundary of the old Mexican state had been the Nueces River. However, many Texans considered the territory between the Nueces and the Rio Grande, farther to the south, to be part of Texas.

In June 1845, Polk ordered General Zachary Taylor and 4,000 troops into Texas to secure the southern boundary. At first, Taylor stopped at Corpus Christi by the mouth of the Nueces River. This was not good enough for Polk. His secretary of war, William Marcy instructed Taylor to treat any incursion of Mexican forces north of the Rio Grande as an act of war. The Mexicans, with an empty national treasury, offered to negotiate. In the fall of 1845, a diplomatic mission to Mexico City was organized with instructions that the annexation of Texas was non-negotiable. However, the United States was prepared to offer to pay $5 million for New Mexico and $20 million for Alta California. In addition, the commissioners were to seek payment of American citizens' claims against Mexico, which were badly inflated.

It is clear from these instructions that Polk highly valued the acquisition of Alta California. He began to pursue alternative options for taking that territory should his purchase offer fail. The president ordered his Pacific naval squadron to be prepared to seize Yerba Buena, the settlement later known as San Francisco, in the event of a war with Mexico. He instructed the U.S. consul in Monterrey to encourage disaffected Californians to seek U.S. annexation. Furthermore, he ordered a topographical expedition under Lt. Colonel John Frémont to march west from St. Louis toward California. Its numbers were too large for a simple topographical survey but large enough to support an uprising in California should the opportunity occur.

In January 1846, the failure of the mission to Mexico was apparent. Polk ordered General Taylor to advance to the Rio Grande. Taylor moved cautiously, as the territory was entirely occupied by Mexican citizens who regarded Taylor's move as an invasion. The Mexican military at Matamoros, blockaded at the mouth of the Rio Grande by the U.S. Navy, was ordered by its government to take defensive actions. The local commander considered the blockade sufficient provocation and notified Taylor that hostilities had commenced. The following day, April 25, 1846, the two forces clashed.

For the Americans, it was a splendid little war. Against superior numerical forces, Taylor was victorious in the north. But personal tragedy lay buried in his triumph. Henry Clay, who had not wanted the war, paid a terrible price. His favorite son, Henry Jr., fell on the battlefield at Buena Vista. Meanwhile, General Winfield Scott landed at Veracruz and, in a well-coordinated march, captured Mexico City. Less likely was the success of Frémont and the Navy in Alta California. Frémont's men banded together with a small group of American settlers and declared an independent republic at Sonoma. Given that the population was overwhelmingly Mexican, it was a brash move. The timely arrival of the Navy at Monterrey and Yerba Buena staved off what almost assuredly would have been a complete defeat for Frémont once the Mexican forces of Alta California organized. Polk had his plum.

• • • •

Jonas McClintock had been a short-term player at the Mint since the death of his father in March 1844. His extended absences necessitated that Patterson appoint Jacob Eckfeldt as acting melter and refiner in addition to his duties as assayer.[39] At the beginning of 1846, McClintock gave Patterson the heads-up that he would resign. With the Democrats in, Booth was once again out of consideration. Wanting to be proactive in determining McClintock's successor, Patterson held off announcing the resignation while turning to Dallas Bache for a recommendation. Bache had a young man under his supervision, Richard Sears McCulloh, in mind.

Bache described McCulloh as a gentleman with a solid background in chemistry and mathematics. While his experience was in sugar refining—having just been dispatched to Cuba—Bache assured Patterson that McCulloh was just as adept with metals. He held a professorship of mathematics, philosophy, and chemistry at Jefferson College in Philadelphia. Just as important to Patterson, his father was J.W. McCulloh, comptroller at Treasury. This man ran the audits of the Mint, which could be extremely fastidious.[40] It would be nice to have some leverage with the auditor.

Sight unseen, Robert Patterson took the liberty of designating Richard McCulloh as his desired replacement for McClintock. Bache smoothed the way in Washington; but the nomination was never really in doubt. Walker was highly in favor of the appointment from the beginning.[41]

McCulloh's nomination was approved in the Senate on April 1, 1846.[42] The operation he was inheriting from McClintock was virtually unchanged from Peale's time in the position. Patterson had again considered making upgrades in 1844, but he had summarily dismissed the option to switch from nitric acid to sulfuric acid in the processing of the precious metals. His objections were the same as when he rejected Peale's proposal. The Mint would require an expensive reconfiguration and the resulting sulfuric-acid fumes would be noxious to the surrounding community. Patterson knew he had let the Mint fall behind the times, but with the limited refining requirements, the older nitric-acid process was just as economical.[43] His fault was in not investigating the improvements in the sulfuric-acid process in the intervening years.

McCulloh seemed to fit right in at the Mint. He gained admittance to the American Philosophical Society in October 1846, no doubt with Patterson's sponsorship.[44] That same fall, McCulloh and Peale worked together in the manufacturing of gun cotton for the war effort.[45]

Fig. 82. To mark the occasion of President Polk's visit to the Mint, Franklin Peale struck inaugural medals for the presidential party; he had them plated and placed in individual presentation cases.

The first sign of friction came after President Polk's visit to the Mint on June 24, 1847. Franklin Peale presented gilt presidential inaugural medals (fig. 82) to the Polk party. Peale was particularly proud of this medal. It had come entirely from his hand without any assistance from Longacre. The chief coiner had taken a large portrait medallion in wax provided by the well-established American artist John Gadsby Chapman, used the electrotype process to form a mold, and prepared a cast in fine iron.[46] From this cast, he had used the portrait lathe to cut a reduction in a softened steel die. The die was then retouched and hardened. Patterson called the resulting medal beautifully finished and comparable to those made by a diesinker.[47]

Peale struck the medals in Polk's presence. He then sent them out for plating and had presentation cases made for them. That completed, Peale applied, through a worker, for reimbursement of this expense from the Mint's contingency fund. The treasurer's clerk objected—it was inappropriate to pay for this activity with public funds. Peale grudgingly accepted this rejection but asked the officers and clerks for contributions to make up his shortfall. Though the amount involved was only $17, this offended McCulloh's sense of what was appropriate for a Mint officer.[48]

Peale also called upon McCulloh from time to time to supply silver for the chief coiner's medal business. The melter and refiner complied, believing this was customary procedure at the Mint. Peale had always promptly reimbursed McCulloh for these silver advances; however, in one instance, he was late by several weeks. McCulloh began to research under what authority Peale was requesting bullion from his department. Finding none, McCulloh went to Patterson. Patterson acknowledged that the melter and refiner had no duty to advance bullion to the chief coiner for the creation of medals. McCulloh then suggested that Peale requisition the bullion from the War Department. Peale rejected this idea entirely. Finally, a compromise was reached whereby McCulloh advanced the bullion with Patterson's knowledge.[49]

The next issue to color McCulloh's thinking came from an unlikely source. Randall Hutchinson, the pay clerk who had rejected Peale's reimbursement, embezzled $23,000 from the Mint and fled to the Virgin Islands in December 1847. This case was particularly embarrassing for Patterson and the Treasury Department. Although the clerk was captured in early 1848 and returned to Philadelphia for trial, only $2,350 was recovered. Forfeiture of the clerk's $5,000 bond eased the shortfall only somewhat.[50] Patterson was forced to cut expenses to the bone in the ordinary fund from which the money was stolen. Otherwise, he would have had to go to Congress for a supplemental appropriation.[51] This action directly impacted McCulloh. He had made requests to overhaul his department in 1847 based upon his experiences in his first year. Patterson had approved a new furnace for melting silver and additional laboratory items. As a result of the defalcation, he had to suspend all alterations indefinitely. The furnace, while virtually finished, did not draw properly, leaving it useless.[52]

• • • •

The last change in personnel came as no surprise to Robert Maskell Patterson, yet he resisted it vigorously. No sooner had Polk taken office than James Buchanan, his secretary of state, contacted Patterson about Isaac Roach. Buchanan was handling patronage in Pennsylvania and wanted to know if Roach had displaced a Democrat when he took the treasurer's office. Patterson reminded Buchanan that Roach replaced Ritner and Ritner had been appointed after a resignation. Technically the answer was no, which seemed sufficient for the time being.[53]

In March 1847, Patterson got wind of a move by Harrisburg Democrats to turn Roach out of office in favor of James Ross Snowden. Snowden had been speaker of the Pennsylvania House of Representatives in 1842 and 1844. He assumed the treasurer's position for the state in 1845 but had been recently sacked when the Whigs gained control of the governorship. Now the Democrats wanted revenge. Patterson went overboard in his defense of Roach to Secretary Walker. He called Snowden an unexceptional treasurer. He complimented Roach in the performance of his burdensome duties. Most bothersome to Patterson was the fear that a party test would now become a condition of office at the Mint. Patterson had really shaded reality in this defense of Roach. Perhaps it was not the defense of Roach but the desire to prevent the appointment of Snowden that had brought out this combativeness in Patterson. He even pleaded to Walker that the secretary should not yield to a feeling of sympathy for Snowden as a meritorious and ill-used man.[54]

Patterson's protest was in vain. Walker removed Roach in favor of Snowden in April. It is impossible to pin down what exactly stirred Patterson against Snowden. There had been others with political backgrounds in the treasurer's position. However, the Mint position had come at the end of their respective careers. That was not the case for Snowden.

Regardless of the animosity, Snowden moved into his position without difficulty. Smooth and polished, he soon took on the function formerly held by Franklin Peale of giving tours of the Mint facilities to outsiders. Much of Peale's handiwork was certainly on view: the milling machine, the steam presses, and the large scales used to weigh lots of $5,000 in $5 gold pieces. However, by far the visitors found the bagging of the *yellow boys*, or newly struck gold coins, the highlight of the tour.[55] The Philadelphia Mint was striking gold pieces that year, both half eagles and eagles, in quantities never before even dreamed of.

As with Longacre, Patterson seemed to settle down in his relationship with Snowden. The defalcation by the pay clerk the following December did not stop Snowden's confirmation in the Senate on February 16, 1848.[56] With his future now relatively stable, the 39-year-old Snowden married 25-year-old Susan Engle Patterson, daughter of Major General Robert Patterson, on September 13, 1848. (General Patterson had been a power in Pennsylvania Democratic politics for some time. He had performed admirably in the War with Mexico before returning to Philadelphia to enter private business. The general was no relation to the Mint director, having emigrated from Ireland in 1798. Ironically, however, the two men lived within three blocks of each other on the same street.) This marriage cemented Snowden in Philadelphia society and augmented his already substantial position in the Democratic Party.

• • • •

In this changing of the guard, Patterson lost one man he could ill afford to lose. John Kane did not get the much speculated upon position in Polk's cabinet. He instead went to Harrisburg as state attorney general in 1845. However, Polk owed him. When the position of federal judge for the eastern district of Pennsylvania opened in 1846, Polk appointed Kane. That was a problem for Patterson. Kane believed firmly that a federal judge must avoid politics.[57] Patterson had lost his political ally and, for the first time since assuming the Mint position, he was on his own.

1849

CHAPTER 20

PHILADELPHIA VS. NEW YORK CITY

On August 6, 1846, Robert Walker's (fig. 83) constitutional Treasury system was enacted, establishing a regional Sub-Treasury network to replace the bank deposit system. It was another nail in the coffin of Philadelphia's once formidable financial community along Chestnut Street. The deterioration so feared in the local demonstration of March 1834 had accelerated with the final demise of the Second Bank of the United States. Upon the failure of the Whigs to charter a new bank during the Tyler administration, the shift of the financial power to New York City became a foregone conclusion. Walker's removal of deposits from the banks took away their ability to jack up their growth rate through risky currency expansions. With a level, commercially driven playing field, New York City easily beat Philadelphia.

The system was put in place on January 1, 1847, just in time for a trial by fire. Over the course of the year, Treasury had borrowed $49 million, including considerable amounts from Europe, to finance the war with Mexico. The Sub-Treasury system restrained the inflation that a war-driven economy would have been expected to produce. It also enabled the country to weather the effects of a distant European recession in 1847 and 1848. The system was judged a success.[1]

There was one more piece in the puzzle for New York City's financial district. Massive amounts of foreign gold

Fig. 83. As Treasury secretary, Robert Walker was an unabashed supporter of a branch mint in New York City.

flowed into New York City from the proceeds of the war bonds and British purchases of foodstuffs to counteract the Irish potato famine. This gold was transported primarily to Philadelphia but also to New Orleans for recoinage. Philadelphia produced a record $13 million in gold coins in 1847.[2]

With foreign specie flowing into the young metropolis in increasing amounts—never mind that 1847 was an exceptional year—the New York City financial community clamored for a branch mint. Left unsaid, a branch mint in New York City would virtually starve the original mint in Philadelphia of the needed bullion for coinage. It was clear to Mint director Robert Maskell Patterson that any such operation in New York City would rapidly kill the Philadelphia Mint. That was unacceptable both to him and to the surviving banking industry in Philadelphia.

• • • •

When Director Patterson opened the letter from J.R. Ingersoll in December 1845, he knew he had to be on top of his game. Ingersoll, the Mint's voice in Congress, warned him that the New York delegation was once again going to push for a branch mint in New York City at an early date.[3] When it came to the Mint, these two Philadelphians were of the same mind. They would stop at nothing in the defense of their institution.[4] Patterson begged off of an immediate reply. He needed to do some research.

Patterson tackled this issue on December 26, 1845. First, the Mint in Philadelphia had never reached its capacity of $12 million in equal parts gold and silver. The coinage of all four mints combined fell short of the capacity of the Philadelphia Mint alone. Second, the capital cost of a facility would be in the neighborhood of $500,000, given the costs incurred at New Orleans (where the land had been provided free of charge by the city). The annual operating costs would approximate $50,000.

A mint at New York City would have to be justified by the savings accruing to its depositors. The two cities were between five and six hours apart. The cost of transporting silver between the two was $1 of transport cost per $1,000 of silver. For gold, it was from $0.25 to $0.38 per $1,000. From 1839 to 1844, $3,761,879 in bullion came from New York and $14,404,141 from Philadelphia and points south. Clearly, the transportation savings to the depositors at a hypothetical New York branch mint would be insufficient, based upon these historic volumes.

Patterson recognized there were holes in this argument. He had no idea how much bullion was held back by the New York banks instead of submitted to the Mint for recoinage. Given that silver was undervalued at the Mint on the basis of the 16-to-1 ratio of silver to gold, this amount was most likely significant. What he did not address to Ingersoll was the shifting trend in trade from a negative balance to a positive balance. Also, New York was gaining the upper hand as the preferred port of call for ships carrying immigrants with their nest eggs from Europe. Thus, his historically based statistics were flawed.

Levi Woodbury and others in the Van Buren administration had wanted a New York branch mint for years but had been unable to get it seriously considered by Congress.[5] Patterson knew a battle royal was only a matter of time.

Next James McKay, chairman of the House Ways and Means Committee, sent Patterson a list of questions.[6] They were identical to the points Patterson raised in his letter to Ingersoll. The Philadelphia congressman must have shown the letter to McKay, who was now pushing to get those answers on the record.

Petitions were presented in both houses of Congress in favor of a branch mint at New York City.[7] On April 22, 1846, legislation was introduced in the Senate to establish the branch mint, appropriating $200,000 for its erection. This estimate was way too low.[8] In a counterbalancing move, identical legislation to establish a branch mint at Charleston was introduced.[9]

Patterson knew that this companion legislation would be a killer. When the Charlotte Mint burned, there was a compelling argument to replace Charlotte and Dahlonega with a single mint at Charleston that would benefit from easy access to foreign bullion coming through the port. Now, just adding another mint at Charleston made no sense economically.[10] Yet with sectional feelings running high, the New York City branch mint stood little chance without a companion branch mint somewhere in the South.

The first session of this Congress adjourned without any action taken on either branch-mint bill. Patterson breathed a sigh of relief. However, before 1846 ended, the problem came back—and this time with force. On December 8, 1846, in President James K. Polk's annual message to Congress, he called for a branch mint at New York City. Two-thirds of the customs revenue of the United States came through New York City. The ability to immediately convert that revenue to U.S. coinage would greatly facilitate the transaction of public business while enlarging the circulation of gold and silver.[11]

Now Patterson would have to be careful in how he fought to kill this proposal. Indeed, he was already crosswise with Robert Walker. The secretary had rejected Patterson's candidates for the annual Assay Commission, a surprising action for what were really perfunctory appointments. He appointed in their stead four of his own, including two whom Patterson had previously tapped for the commission. Worse, he had not bothered to consult with Patterson on the matter.

Patterson wrote to Dallas Bache (fig. 84) asking what he had done to incur the secretary's wrath.[12] That was a mistake on two counts. He was asking Bache to betray any confidences that Walker might have shared with Bache's sister and within his family circle. Second, Patterson didn't need to ask. He should have known that his opposition to a New York City branch mint was going to become known by the Polk administration and acted upon.

Legislatively, it came down the same way it had in the first session. On December 17, 1846, companion bills were introduced in the Senate calling for branch mints in New York City and Charleston.[13] As expected, nothing moved in the Senate following that flurry of activity. Little more was accomplished in the House.

The action all occurred on the last day of the congressional session. The House was in Committee of the Whole discussing a bill to modify the Sub-Treasury system. Suddenly, Horace Seaman of New York moved to amend the bill with the Senate bill from the last session authorizing a branch mint in New York City. At this point, the time had been reached for the House, in a previously agreed-upon move, to adjourn until the evening session at five o'clock. There was no time to talk about the surprise amendment.

When the House reconvened, Seaman's amendment carried. Then Isaac Holmes of South Carolina moved a new section be added to the bill establishing a branch mint at Charleston. The House rejected this amendment. John Rockwell, a Connecticut Whig, moved the bill be tabled.

Fig. 84. Great-grandson of Benjamin Franklin and related through his mother to the politically powerful Dallas family in Philadelphia, Alexander Dallas Bache wielded power well beyond his modest position in the federal government.

This too was rejected by a sound majority.[14] New York City had a chance if the Senate would act in the eleventh hour.

The bill came over from the House that night with a request that the Senate suspend its rules, as the House had, to take up this legislation. George Badger, a Whig from North Carolina, objected. After debate, Badger's objection was overridden as it would be a discourtesy to the House. The bill was read a first time. It was then to be read a second time when Badger again objected. No bill could be given its second reading on the same day as its first. There was no motion this time to suspend the rules. The bill was lost.[15] The Senate had managed to preserve decorum while killing the bill.

• • • •

A new Congress did not ease Patterson's problems. In his annual message, President Polk again strongly called for a branch mint in New York City. The president took a more populist tone in his argument this time. Foreign coin, especially foreign gold, would not circulate extensively as a currency among the people. Extending the circulation of hard currency and diffusing it among the people could only be accomplished through recoinage at a branch mint in New York City, the seat of the influx of foreign coins.[16] Three weeks later, on December 30, 1847, Ingersoll warned Patterson that the Polk administration was going to push hard and the congressman was afraid that they were going to succeed. Ingersoll wanted Patterson to supply him with facts and figures to refute any claims of cost savings accruing to a hypothetical New York City branch-mint operation. He assured Patterson that he would protect the Mint director.[17]

In spite of Ingersoll's fears, moves in the Thirtieth Congress to comply with Polk's call for a New York City branch mint appeared to fizzle. Senator John Adams Dix from New York introduced the necessary legislation on December 14, 1847, appropriating $225,000 for the proposed New York City branch mint. His measure was sent to the Finance Committee, where it stalled.[18] Meanwhile, petitions and resolutions flowed from South Carolina in favor of a mint at Charleston. It was clear that Southern legislators thought that if they applied enough pressure, they could ride on the coattails of New York City.

Dix's bill came out of the Finance Committee without amendment on March 28. That it did not suffer the addition of Charleston in committee was a good thing. Now it had to work its way to the floor. Two weeks later, a companion bill was introduced in the House and referred to the Ways and Means Committee. The amount appropriated in this bill for New York City was $200,000.[19] The stage was set.

The Senate bill came up first for consideration in a Committee of the Whole on July 14. Andrew Butler of South Carolina immediately moved to amend the bill to include Charleston, bringing the total appropriation to $425,000. Badger, who had killed the branch-mint bill in the last Congress, raised the point that the two proposed branch mints would more likely cost $1 million. In addition, annual operating expenses would be in the $70,000 to $80,000 range. Besides, he could not understand why the specie arriving in New York City could not be sent to Philadelphia. The only cost was transportation and insurance. The distance between the two cities was only five hours and the cost therefore could not be that great. Badger added sarcastically that this bill would enable New York City to erect a new and splendid public building to increase its magnificent array of marble edifices and bring it to close approximation with a city of palaces. Badger asked rhetorically where the system of branch mints was to end. Applications could come from all quarters of the country—Boston, Norfolk, et cetera, until the entire seacoast would be dotted with branch mints.

An attempt to recover from this emotional slapdown was made by John Niles of Connecticut. A branch ought to be built in New York City. It was the source of two-thirds of the nation's customs revenues, payable in specie only. Dix added that the cost of insurance and transportation based upon shipment value for gold alone to Philadelphia was 0.75 percent and gold and silver in combination, 1 percent. There was currently $8 million in specie in New York, of which only $3 million was in U.S. coin. Badger quickly retorted that the reason so much foreign specie was retained in New York City was that the brokers profited from keeping it there. Badger was partly wrong. In the case of gold, it wasn't overvalued enough at the Mint to offset the cost of recoinage. Why would bankers bother to recoin their gold when the foreign gold coins were legal tender?

Senator Dix also pleaded with Butler to offer his amendment for a Charleston branch mint as a separate bill. He stated he was favorable to the amendment but wished that the two actions not be bound together. Butler knew better than to take this bait and refused to withdraw his amendment. There also was skepticism from some of the Northern senators toward the Charleston mint proposal. They could only be persuaded if the branch mints at Charlotte and Dahlonega were abandoned.

First to be considered was Butler's amendment adding Charleston. It passed with 27 yeas against 21 nays. Now the question was called on the amended bill. It failed with 22 for versus 27 against. The senators present from Georgia and North Carolina both voted against the bill, knowing full well that its passage would kill their branch mints.[20]

Ingersoll gloated. Should the issue now be brought up in the House, it would be burdened by a Charleston amendment as it had in the Senate, and thus destroyed.[21] They made strange bedfellows. Patterson now needed the votes from the two Southern gold-mint states to hold the forces pushing for a New York City mint at bay. As long as this delicate balance held in the Senate, Philadelphia was safe.

CHAPTER 21

SHERMAN'S GOLD

Lieutenant Lucien Loeser departed California on September 1, 1848, with Sherman's oyster can filled with gold. Loeser had graduated from West Point in July 1842 and he had been stuck in California with Sherman while many of his classmates had gone on to fame in the Mexican-American War. Now he was headed back to Washington with this tin of gold—menial duty indeed but it provided him with a chance to reunite with his family. While in Washington, D.C., Loeser intended to marry Sarah Eaton, the daughter of an Army surgeon.

Loeser boarded a chartered sailing vessel destined for Paita, on the northwest coast of Peru. Time was of the essence; he must reach Peru in time to catch the October steamer for Panama. Luckily, he was able to make the connection. After 40 days, Loeser arrived at Balboa, Panama's port on the Pacific Ocean. Now, the Army officer faced the most arduous segment of his journey: he must traverse the central spine of mountains and hills by horse to the headwaters of the Chagres River. From there, he would complete his 50-mile journey by boat through the jungle terrain to Colón on the Caribbean Sea. It typically took travelers a week, but it was not as simple as that. This region had been known as a pesthole from its earliest days as a Spanish settlement. Malaria and yellow fever were rife. Fortunately for the lieutenant, the peak time for malaria was in the summer months, at the beginning of

the rainy season. By November, at the end of the wet season, the rains had destroyed the mosquito breeding grounds. Still, for Loeser the trip through the lowlands of the Chagres River was nothing but misery, hot and steamy the entire time. Reaching Colón, he connected with a steamer bound for Jamaica and then secured passage to New Orleans on a small sailing vessel.[1]

• • • •

For Mint director Robert Maskell Patterson, 1848 marked a return to more familiar patterns. Coinage requirements had settled back to former levels after the heavy inflow from the bond issues of 1847. However, there was one issue that should have gone better in 1848.

The saga started the prior August, when Patterson had been forced to divert his attention to the preparation of two medals honoring General Zachary Taylor's military victories at Palo Alto, Resaca de la Palma, and Monterrey. The authorizing legislation for the first medal had passed Congress in 1846, but nothing had been done in the interim. In August 1847, Secretary of War William Marcy finally began to move. An artist, William G. Brown, had returned from Mexico with a likeness of Taylor that met the general's approval. Marcy asked that Patterson use this portrait for the medal. While Patterson had suggested a design for the reverse in December 1846, the secretary now promised the reverse design from Brown would follow in a couple of weeks.[2]

For six more weeks, nothing happened. Brown did not appear at the Mint with a portrait. Marcy was silent on a reverse design. On October 2, 1847, Marcy wrote Patterson, informing the Mint director that he had reviewed his suggestion of the prior December and now found that reverse acceptable. Because Congress had appropriated no additional money, there would be no accompanying bronze issue. After having delayed for so long, Marcy was now in a hurry for Patterson to finish the work.[3]

Three days later, Brown appeared at Patterson's office in the Mint. He would make the necessary portrait of General Taylor for $200; or, if the Mint would provide a pair of dies and the right to strike a limited run of bronze medals for his own benefit, he would provide the portrait at no cost. Patterson was favorable to this request. It would require that hubs be made at the Mint, but this was a small expense and would give the Mint the flexibility to strike these medals for substantial public distribution at a later date.[4] Unsaid, it left more of any forthcoming congressional appropriation on a net basis for Franklin Peale. Marcy approved.[5]

Patterson's instructions to Brown were explicit. He was to complete the portrait as soon as possible and deliver it to John Battin, a sculptor, who would prepare the wax model. All went well, but there was much to do on Brown's part. Ultimately, the first gold medal commemorating General Taylor and his victories at Palo Alto and Resaca de la Palma was not struck until March 1848.

The obverse of this medal was remarkable for its mediocrity. Peale had used the Contamin portrait lathe to prepare the obverse hub from the wax model. The beauty of the Contamin device was that it generated an exact reproduction from the model. Unfortunately, this was also its weakness, as it could not improve upon the original. In this case, the wax model did not compare to the one Peale had used for the Polk inaugural medal. This hub badly needed the skilled hands of an engraver to bring life to the model.

There were worse problems with the medal's reverse. It was an exact copy of the reverse of the medal honoring General Winfield Scott in the War of 1812, engraved by Moritz Fürst and struck in 1824. While it had been proposed by Patterson, this duplication had to have been suggested by Peale, who had possession of the old original dies. Making the sin all the more deplorable, Scott had been the other victorious American commanding general in Mexico. To use an identical design for the reverse of the medal commemorating General Taylor was unthinkable. Both Peale and Patterson should have known better. There was absolutely no excuse.

Patterson corrected this fault on the second Taylor medal that was struck in May 1848. However, in its own way, it was just as bad as the first. He could have gone to Longacre or outside of the Mint, but he did not. Instead, Patterson utilized the reverse of the Polk inaugural medal for this medal commemorating Taylor's actions in Monterrey.[6] The only plausible excuse was that the War Department had dragged its feet for so long, perhaps Patterson did not think he had the time to generate a proper reverse (fig. 85). Nevertheless, the whole affair reflected poorly upon Patterson, while Peale appeared to slip by with no recognition for his part in the process.

• • • •

Lieutenant Loeser landed in New Orleans on November 23, 1848. His arrival was major news for the *New Orleans Picayune*. The tight-lipped Loeser said little to the publication. However, David Carter, who had traveled with him and was returning from the gold fields, had plenty to say. The extent of the find was 150 miles in length and 50 miles in breadth, although Carter was a bit skeptical of this point. The gold was not confined to the streams; men also mined it by digging up the dirt and washing the soil from the metal. Gold fever in California was at epidemic proportions. Crews of whaling ships and other commercial vessels deserted for the gold fields. As soon as it was disbanded, a New York volunteer regiment headed to the region en masse. Money that had been plentiful before the strike was now in short supply. The economy was running on gold dust. Perhaps the most important nugget con-

Fig. 85. When Congress approved two gold medals for General Taylor's military victories in 1846 and 1847, the Mint faced a difficulty—no one could produce an acceptable likeness of the general. A creditable image did not surface until October 1847. Peale generated the obverse die from a wax model by John Battin using the Contamin portrait lathe. Because time was short, Director Patterson authorized the employment of the reverse from the 1812 Winfield Scott medal for one medal. For the other one, he had Peale use the reverse of the Polk inaugural medal. It was a bad decision, compounded by Peale's mediocre work on the obverse.

tained in the article was that, as of yet, capital was not necessary to recover this gold. All one needed after arriving at the gold fields was a strong back, a willingness to work under rugged conditions, and a bare minimum of necessities.[7] A week and half later, the *National Intelligencer*, a newspaper with a national circulation, reprinted this article, fanning rumors already sweeping through the country.

The Army officer arrived in Washington just in time for Polk's annual message to Congress. Ahead of this message, Philadelphia was abuzz. However, it was not the content of the message that stirred speculation; it was its method of delivery. The postmaster general had issued instructions for the conveyance of Polk's message by express train to Philadelphia, New York, and Boston. At the exact time that the written message left Washington by locomotive, the same document would be telegraphed to Philadelphia and points north. The *Philadelphia Public Ledger* guessed that the locomotive might win the race to Philadelphia, but it was questionable regarding New York and it would surely lose the race to Boston. The newspaper did hazard a prediction that this would be the last time the locomotive won any segment of this race.[8]

Robert Walker delivered the presidential message for Polk. Upper California, irrespective of the vast mineral wealth recently developed there, held as much value and importance to the United States as Louisiana did at the time of its purchase from France in 1803. A great commercial city was destined to speedily arise on the California coast, somewhere on the bay of San Francisco, that would serve the Pacific Basin.

Having first glanced over the gold discovery, Walker now returned. It had been known for some time that precious metals existed in considerable quantities in the newly acquired territory. Recent discoveries rendered it probable that these deposits were more extensive and valuable than anticipated. The extraordinary accounts of the abundance of gold would have been difficult to believe had they not been corroborated by the reports of military officers visiting the gold-producing districts. The report of the commanding officer, Colonel Mason, confirmed that the supply of gold was remarkably large and that this gold could be found in various places over an extensive area.

Now, the practical side of Walker surfaced. To speedily avail itself of the undeveloped wealth in these gold fields, in this session Congress should authorize a branch mint. Gone for the time being was any thought of a branch mint in New York City or Charleston. This California mint would convert into coin both the gold mined in California and the bullion and specie from western Mexico and Peru that were being diverted annually by ships to Great Britain for the benefit of that nation's financial system. Output from a branch mint in California would flow to New

Fig. 86. Intended to be a signboard for what President Polk considered the key accomplishment of his administration—the annexation of California—this quarter eagle would grow to represent much more. With the impetus of the gold discovery in California, the industrialization of America proceeded at a rapid rate, allowing the young country to assume an expanded position on the world stage after the Civil War.

Orleans, New York, and other Atlantic Coast cities. Walker pointedly did not mention Philadelphia. The quantity of specie would greatly increase in the United States and its circulation abroad would be promoted, giving American merchants greater leverage in China and the west coast of North and South America, where U.S. coins were not current at their face value. Walker hoped that the great distance between European nations and the Pacific Basin, combined with this influx of new gold, would give the United States a competitive trading edge.[9]

It is doubtful that the average American reading this message got past the initial discussion of gold in California. Sherman's gold had put to rest the doubts about the rumors. The rush was on!

While Walker had accepted the gold as it was presented, Secretary of War Marcy was more cautious. Three days after Walker's presentation to Congress, he conveyed Sherman's gold samples, now in a tea caddy, to the Mint for analysis. He noted to Patterson that there was some doubt that it was genuine. Marcy wanted an answer to that question as soon as possible.

However, there was more to Marcy's instructions. He wanted one pound, twelve troy ounces, returned via his messenger. If the metal was found to be pure, which Marcy did not expect, he wanted enough of it reserved for two additional medals ordered by Congress for generals Taylor and Scott. The remainder, with the exception of two small bars, he wanted coined. Expecting many to desire coins struck from California gold, Marcy suggested striking quarter eagles with some distinguishing mark. Marcy also sent a quantity of cinnabar that he wanted analyzed as well.[10]

On the same day that Marcy wrote to Patterson, David Carter showed up at the Mint bearing the first Californian gold to appear in Philadelphia. It was entirely composed of grains and dust.[11] Marcy's samples arrived the next day. The two batches combined weighed 1851.8 troy ounces.

Patterson reported that gold in nugget form from the dry diggings averaged one to two pennyweights or 24 to 48 grains. Gold from streams was in flake form, requiring six or seven flakes to make a grain, and by far made up the greater proportion of the sample. When the gold was melted, its weight was reduced by 2.3 percent through the burning off of extraneous materials that were bonded with it. Assay results for this gold showed a fineness of .892 to .897—nearly coin grade. The value of the gold per troy ounce was $18.053 in its raw state and $18.50 after melting.[12]

Patterson gave the cinnabar to Jacob Eckfeldt and James Booth to analyze.[13] Patterson was once again bringing Booth back into the equation. In speaking out against Peale, had McCulloh cost himself in Patterson's eyes?

Patterson had another problem that he did not divulge to either Marcy or Walker. While the gold was nearly coin grade, the remainder was composed almost entirely of silver. That was slightly more than twice as much as was permitted by law and four times as much as was customarily used by the Mint as an alloy in its gold coins. Immediately, there were delays in refining this gold, to the point that on January 5, 1849, Patterson was forced to write to Marcy and admit the problem. Patterson also blamed the delay in part on applying the distinguishing stamp that Marcy had required on the gold coins. The Mint had to contract to an outside source for a punch to place the letters "CAL" on the reverse die above the eagle.

From Sherman's sample of gold were struck 1,389 quarter eagles (fig. 86).[14] Did Peale apply the "CAL" mark on the quarter eagles or was Longacre entrusted with the task? Three of the "CAL" quarter eagles, in Proof condition, appeared in the January 21, 1870, auction of Longacre's estate.[15] The engraver would not have collected Peale's work.

Some have called this quarter eagle the first commemorative coin struck by the United States. In actuality, it was a political signboard for President Polk. He was not seeking the presidency in 1848. On the other hand, he considered the acquisition of California one of the great accomplishments of his term. This politicizing of an American coin was nothing more than Polk seeking to establish a permanent legacy.

For Robert Maskell Patterson, the problem encountered in refining Sherman's gold was a fire bell in the night. His refining department was not equipped to handle any great influx of this bullion. Furthermore, Patterson's relationship with McCulloh was deteriorating. There were serious storm clouds on the horizon for the U.S. Mint.

PART III

THE GREAT MELTDOWN

1849

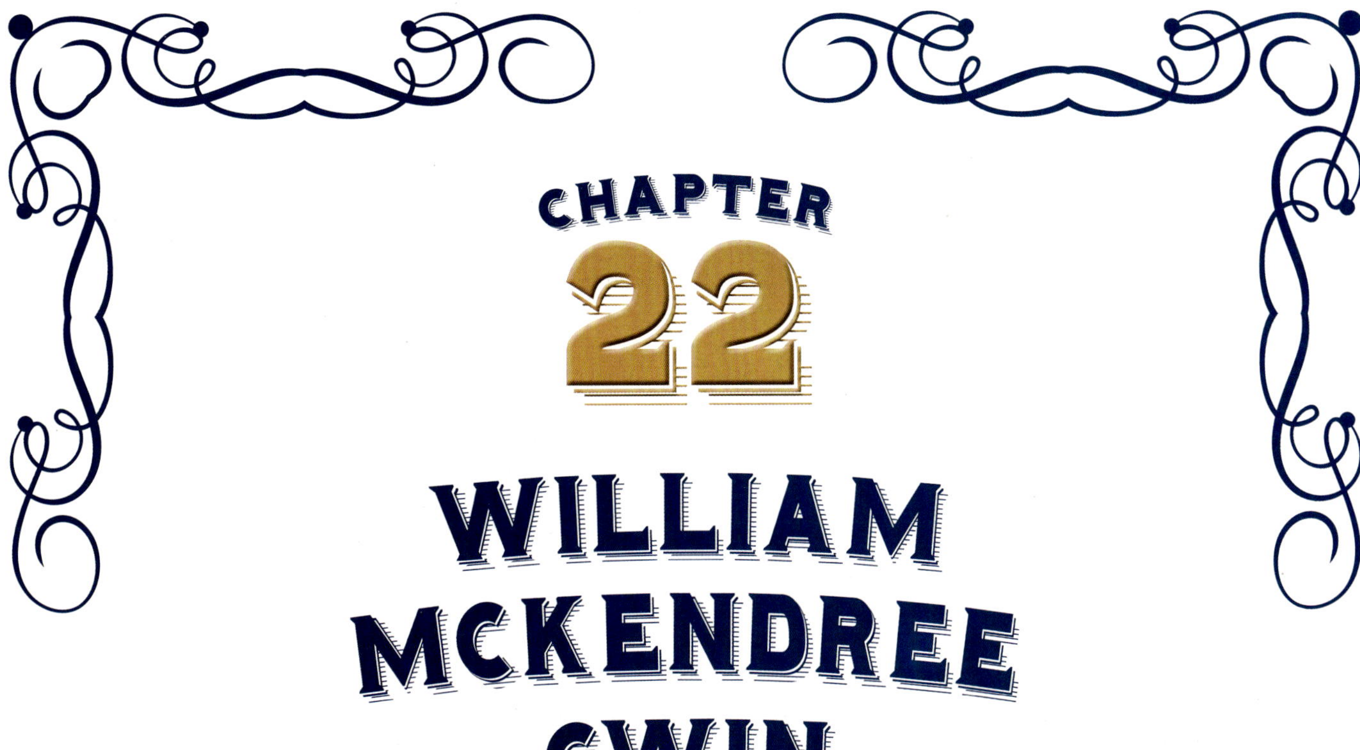

CHAPTER 22

WILLIAM MCKENDREE GWIN

Two men stood watching the inaugural parade—a celebration of Whigs giddy with the thought that they were about to grasp the levers of patronage in the federal government. Eight years before, Harrison had failed them, dying just weeks after his inauguration and leaving them with a half-hearted Whig in John Tyler. At their convention, the Whig Party had once again thrown party principles to the wind and rejected Henry Clay in favor of a military hero. Zachary Taylor had easily bested his Democratic opponent, William Cass, who had the added burden of Martin Van Buren running in opposition on the Free Soil ticket. Democrats now faced four years out of power.

It was a wet, cold winter day that chilled to the bone. Sleet would change to snow as the day wore on, but the Whig merrymakers hardly took note. The official date for the inauguration had fallen on a Sunday; so, the parade and parties were postponed to Monday. However, for the Democrats, the weather only deepened their gloom.

At first glance, these two men standing on the steps of Willard's Hotel seemed an odd couple. One was short and stocky, the other tall and stately. Their common bond, besides being Democrats, was ownership of plantations in Mississippi. Stephen Douglas, in his first term as the senator from Illinois, had inherited his holding through his first wife, Martha Martin.

Douglas turned to his companion and asked what he would do. William McKendree Gwin (fig. 87) did not hes-

Fig. 87. The sheer power of William McKendree Gwin's personality is captured in this daguerreotype.

itate in his answer. He was going to California. That statement would not have completely shocked Douglas. Others were doing the same. But, what followed must have seemed an absolute long shot to the Illinois senator. Gwin was not going to seek his fortune in the gold fields. The just-adjourned Congress had failed to organize California even as a territory. Gwin was going to advocate that Californians organize their own government and seek admission to the Union. Then he turned to Douglas and predicted he would be presenting the Senate his commission as a senator from the new state of California within a year. No matter the odds, Douglas knew his man and wished him well. If anyone could pull it off, it would be Dr. Gwin.[1]

• • • •

Gwin essentially retraced the path of Lieutenant Loeser. From his plantation outside of Vicksburg, Missisippi, he hurried to New Orleans. From there, he traveled by steamer to Colón, up the Chagres River by pongo boat, and over the hump by mule. He reached Panama City on the last day of March but he found steamship service to San Francisco had been suspended; Panama City was overrun with gold seekers. Gwin waited amidst malaria and cholera outbreaks. It was mid-May when the steamer *Panama*, on her maiden voyage around the Horn from New York, appeared. There was a stampede to get on board, with tickets scalped at astronomical prices. Gwin, of course, managed to find a place on a ship now crammed with triple her normal passenger capacity. On June 4, the *Panama* arrived in San Francisco Bay, out of coal and burning the ship's woodwork to maintain steam. The men lining the rails were greeted by fog and then, as the sun burned through, by barren dunes and hills dotted with the scruffy collection of buildings and tents that was San Francisco. These men came from all walks of life: there were military officers coming to their postings; a presidential emissary, T. Butler King, instructed to encourage

California statehood; and, of course, those coming to seek their fortune in the gold fields.[2] Of those fortune seekers, many were looking for a fresh start, an escape from the past. If one had asked Gwin his reasons for coming, he would have restated his desire to be senator. And yet, Gwin had a past.

• • • •

On October 9, 1805, William McKendree Gwin was born into a plantation family in middle Tennessee. He grew up almost in sight of Andrew Jackson's home, the Hermitage. James and Samuel, Gwin's father and older brother, went to New Orleans with Jackson. James served as a chaplain to the Tennessee volunteers. However, Jackson knew James as an accomplished Indian fighter and placed him in a significant command post during the Battle of New Orleans, despite his noncombatant status. Likewise, Samuel was an officer with the volunteers and was wounded at New Orleans. He went on to follow Jackson into the Indian wars and fought at Pensacola. With this kind of family résumé, the younger Gwin was marked for success.

Gwin was a well-educated man, despite the frontier conditions at that time in Tennessee. He studied with tutors and read law at nearby Gallatin, where he passed the bar at 21. At this point, Gwin made a career change. Feeling he had no public speaking skills, a must for a lawyer, he enrolled in medical school at Transylvania University in Lexington, Kentucky. He graduated with honors, earning his medical degree in 1828.

Everything changed with Andrew Jackson's assumption of the presidency in 1829. Samuel, his health broken from campaigning with the general, took a job with the Jackson administration as a clerk in the Post Office Department in Washington. With an annual salary of $1,000, he was hardly on easy street, but he was at the center of power. A year later, his father also tried to place William in the Post Office. Jackson rejected the idea; there was a rule stating that only one family member could be employed in that department. James then asked for a position for his son in the surveyor-general's department in the newly acquired Indian lands of Alabama and Mississippi. William had, at one time, gained practical experience surveying land.[3] Nothing came of that request, but the die was cast. Dr. William Gwin headed to Mississippi to establish his medical practice.

His choice of location was no accident. Located on the Natchez Trace, Clinton was a promising little town. The capital was to be moved inland from Natchez and Clinton had yet to be overshadowed by the town of Jackson in that contest. The town's most important attribute was the federal government's Mt. Salus Land Office. Here, applications to purchase government land and subsequent payments were taken in. It was a center for land speculators. The public land boom was just gathering a head of steam in 1830 and there was real money to be made here. Dr. Gwin was soon attracted, and this activity rapidly overshadowed his medical practice.

Meanwhile in Washington, his older brother Samuel had taken an active political role in support of President Jackson. The year 1830 found Samuel at a testimonial dinner for Jackson, rubbing elbows with Martin Van Buren and Amos Kendall.[4] On July 4, 1831, Samuel was at another exclusive celebration where toasts were made accompanied by music and the thunder of cannon fire. Samuel's toast was to the eventual running mate of Martin Van Buren; the man was astute.[5]

Back in Mississippi, a seemingly minor event was about to hit the national scene. On October 15, 1830, George Poindexter (fig. 88) was appointed by Mississippi's governor to fill the senatorial vacancy caused by the death of Robert Adams. Poindexter was subsequently elected to serve the remainder of Adams's term. Upon arriving in Washington, Poindexter's enemies warned Jackson not to trust the man as he was a friend of Henry Clay. Both Jackson and Van Buren felt it was only a matter of time until Poindexter allied with opponents of their administration.

The break came over senatorial privilege in local presidential appointments. Soon after Poindexter took his seat, Jackson appointed Stokely Hays, a Tennessean and the

Fig. 88. Both Andrew Jackson and the Gwin family viewed George Poindexter as a mortal enemy.

nephew of his deceased wife, to be surveyor-general of public lands in Mississippi. Poindexter took offense that Jackson had usurped his patronage privileges. The senator then submitted a motion on February 3, 1831, stating that it would be inexpedient to appoint a citizen of one state to an office in another state without some evident necessity for such an appointment. In the anti-Jackson–dominated Senate, the motion carried. Poindexter and the president ultimately compromised with Poindexter's man getting the surveyor-generalship position and Hayes receiving an appointment as register in the Mt. Salus Land Office. All would have been settled and done if Hayes hadn't died before he could take the position.[6]

Andrew Jackson turned to Samuel Gwin with a recess appointment on October 3, 1831. Now the two brothers would be together, with Samuel in a position to feed intelligence to the doctor that would assist in his land speculating. However, the appointment hit a snag. Jackson formally nominated Samuel Gwin three days into the first session of the Twenty-Second Congress. Two weeks later, the Senate soundly rejected the nomination, heeding Poindexter's position on the unsuitability of out-of-state appointments. The Gwin brothers took this rejection personally.

Samuel had expected trouble. He wrote a public letter to Senator Poindexter immediately after his recess appointment, pleading for approval. While he was not a resident of Mississippi, he had been with Jackson in the Indian campaigns and against the British at New Orleans. In fact, he had shed his blood on Mississippi's soil in defense of the country. Now he and his wife both suffered ill health and needed to move to a warmer climate.[7] The letter was pure theater and a play for support—but not from Poindexter.

The fact was the two men hated each other. After Gwin had been wounded at the Battle of New Orleans, he encountered Poindexter at the hospital. It seemed that Poindexter's health had failed him just as the British landed. This was a topic of conversation among the officers, with Gwin and others questioning his courage. The accusations got back to Poindexter, who patiently bided his time, waiting for a payback. When the nomination came up for a vote, Poindexter made a deal with the Jackson opposition. Clay and Calhoun needed Poindexter's vote to stop Jackson's nomination of Van Buren to be minister to England. The deal was made and Samuel Gwin was the loser.[8]

Andrew Jackson could be tenacious, particularly when crossed. He attempted to have the motion regarding out-of-state appointments rescinded in January 1832. It was tabled. In June, Jackson asked the Senate to reconsider Gwin, forwarding letters of recommendation from prominent citizens in Mississippi. Poindexter countered with letters of his own against Gwin. The issued was tabled in an effort to freeze Jackson's hand.[9] On the last day of the session, Poindexter moved that Jackson be informed that the Senate did not intend to take any action on the nomination of Gwin. Jackson ignored them and gave a second recess appointment to Samuel Gwin immediately after the Senate adjourned.

Meanwhile, all of this back-and-forth action was causing havoc in the Mt. Salus Land Office. Without a register, no one could apply to purchase public lands. With his recess appointment in hand, Samuel Gwin began taking applications. There was a rush; the settlers, who had never read law, still understood the tenuous nature of a recess appointment. To make matters worse, the receiver for payments, J.B. Damron, was terminally ill. There were days when he did not appear at the office. On the days he was there, Damron would accept land payments and put the money in a strong box without recording the transactions. Under the avalanche of applications, he fell hopelessly behind.

There were other problems as well. The settlers would often take out an application on a tract of land and not have the necessary funds to pay for it. They were chronically short of money, and the receiver was not going to take a cow in settlement. Sometimes the application lapsed. Other times, they went to William Jones. Jones, a former schoolteacher, was a lender of last resort. He was also a "shaver," purchasing banknotes of distant banks at steep discounts and then flipping them at a profit. Gwin often found himself sending the settlers to Jones. It was an absolutely chaotic time in the land office.

Samuel Gwin also had to deal with his brother. Dr. Gwin, in addition to his speculative activity, was pulling together a large block of land for himself on the Mississippi River just outside of Vicksburg. Another individual had a similar area of interest adjacent to his. There was an understanding that each would stay out of the other's land position. When the other man poached with an application in Dr. Gwin's area, Gwin went into the land office and insisted his brother take out similar applications for tracts in the offending individual's domain, as well as competing applications upon those tracts wrongly claimed in his land block. He promptly paid for them. Samuel complained that this action would show him in a bad light within the community, but William held fast. Dr. Gwin drew a liberal line when it came to business versus family. He would brook no double crosses.[10]

With the convening of the second session of the Twenty-Second Congress, Poindexter went on the offensive, submitting four resolutions that were read and considered by unanimous consent. They were aimed at the constitutionality of Gwin receiving a second recess appointment from Jackson. However, Poindexter had lost his leverage now that the Whigs had scuttled the Van Buren appointment. When Poindexter moved that the Gwin proceedings be taken to the public Journal of the Senate, Henry Clay tabled the motion.

Jackson moved on February 19, 1833, nominating Gwin formally yet again. A week later, the Senate considered the nomination and rejected it with a margin of only one vote: 19 yeas to 20 nays. For Jackson, this vote was a show of weakness in the opposition.

Gwin's appointment came to a head on the next-to-last day of the second session. Senator George M. Bibb of Kentucky tried to pass a resolution that the second recess appointment of Gwin should not be allowed to pass in silence, as it deprived the Senate of its oversight of executive appointments. The resolution was soundly trounced. Then Senator William R. King from Alabama moved that the resolution of February 3, 1831, respecting out-of-state appointments to federal positions, be rescinded. The resolution passed. Meanwhile, Jackson announced to the Senate that, given their rejection of several nominations to positions in Mississippi, he would make no further attempts to fill the offices in question. It was a threat with teeth. If the land offices failed to function, Mississippi's economic growth would come to a screeching halt. Compromise was quickly reached at four in the morning with a quorum barely present.[11] The register's position at the new land office at Chocchuma, being opened to handle the disposition of Choctaw lands gained in the 1830 treaty of Dancing Rabbit Creek, was given to Gwin and a second individual received the Mt. Salus position.[12] Poindexter was bitter over this political defeat.

With the new register in place at Mt. Salus, discrepancies came to light from Samuel Gwin's administration. Damron had died and John Black, Mississippi's other senator, had taken funds held by the deceased receiver and placed them in a bank for "safe keeping."[13] Accusations flew, with Gwin unjustly bearing the brunt of them. The low point came on August 23, 1833, with William Jones's published call for testimony of any person aware of official misdemeanor conduct by Samuel Gwin. In the broadside, Jones called Gwin an Algerian pirate and a Botany Bay convict. Samuel Gwin still maintained his home and his family in the Clinton area in spite of the new appointment. He took personal offense and laid the attack at the feet of Poindexter.[14]

Jackson was not done with Poindexter. He proceeded to rub salt in the wound by naming Dr. Gwin as U.S. marshal for the district of Mississippi after the Senate had dispensed with Samuel Gwin and adjourned. This was an extremely lucrative appointment. Although a marshal received no salary, his fees for serving as a collection and disbursal agent for the federal courts could reach the staggering sum of $150,000 annually, with half of this amount given to the appointee himself.

William Gwin knew he had a fight on his hands to gain Senate confirmation. He met with the governor, a Jackson man, and Senator Black. Black promised to defend Gwin on the floor of the Senate and push for the confirmation. Gwin optimistically dropped his medical practice.

Dr. Gwin had another iron in the fire at that point. In his land speculations, he had formed a firm friendship with Robert Walker, a Natchez lawyer from Pennsylvania. Public sales of Indian lands totaling 1 million acres in northwest Mississippi, acquired from the Choctaws, were slated for the last part of October 1833. The two men hired a surveyor to inspect the lands for the best holdings. Gwin and Walker then set up a land company to bid on this federal acreage at rock-bottom prices. They would have to be careful to allow settlers already on the land—who were basically squatters—to either bid individually for their holdings or acquire them from the company at cost. This action was designed to retain the support of the local people. Stock would be sold in the company at the price of $1,000 per share. No one individual would hold more than one share and the ultimate subscription numbered some 150 investors. By bidding aggressively early on, the company hoped to squelch competitive bidders. After the public sale was completed, the lands obtained by the company would be resold to the public in an open auction. The profits would then be divided among the shareholders and the company terminated. The shareholder agreement stated that there would be no favoritism given to shareholders at the reselling of the lands at public auction. Many large planters were involved. Yet the return on an investment of $1,000, no matter how great, was hardly worth their trouble.[15]

The land sales kicked off on October 21, 1833, with Samuel Gwin in charge of the auction. That first day, there was a competing land company from Alabama. There had been earlier discussion between the two entities about combining. The Alabamians had not wanted to give squatters preferential treatment. Now the two parties met in earnest and Walker was insistent that that preference be given. The Alabama company agreed and the two parties combined to form the Chocchuma Land Company.

The next day, Samuel Gwin could see what had happened. He was helpless. Senator Black was on hand and he asked the senator to give a legal ruling. Black's answer was that there was no prohibition. The sales went on with competing bidders dropping out. Whenever an outsider bid, the price on that tract would be run up. He would then be forced to pay it or default and wait for the tract to be auctioned a second time or negotiate with Walker and company to gain the tract at cost plus a markup.

The sales went off like clockwork. The company returned a dividend to the investors of slightly more than $300 per share. The local settlers gave a testimonial dinner for Robert Walker, who had acted out front as one of the company agents during the bidding. Walker had purchased, for his own account or in partnership, 77,000 acres, including 26,000 acres for assignment to squatters.[16] Although no one would admit it, the federal government benefited as well. Far more land was sold than would otherwise have been the case, opening vast tracts to development.[17]

Dr. Gwin, on the other hand, stayed in the background. The problem was that the company acquired from two-thirds to three-quarters of all the land put up for bid, a massive amount with an attendant public profile. There were rumors; it was alleged that company shareholders had had a first look at the lands acquired. There was real potential for trouble here, and it fell on Samuel Gwin, not his brother.

Soon the rumors turned into accusations. The Mississippi legislature called for an investigation. Samuel Gwin welcomed it as an opportunity to get rid of the black cloud attached to his name. Then, William Jones published another accusatory handbill, further stirring up the situation. Finally, the legislature adjourned without taking action. It was the worst scenario for the register. He now had no opportunity to clear his name in a public forum. The Gwin brothers took out their frustration on Jones. Dr. Gwin gave him a public beating—a sound flogging, in the words of one observer. Jones countered; he challenged William Gwin to a duel but then backed out.

The action next returned to the floor of the Senate. Andrew Jackson submitted William Gwin's name to be Mississippi's marshal on January 20, 1834.[18] The nomination was referred to the judiciary committee against the backdrop of accusations against Samuel Gwin of fraud. On March 3, 1834, Poindexter offered a resolution that the Committee on Public Lands, of which he was chair, be authorized to investigate allegations of improprieties surrounding the public sale of the Choctaw lands at Chocchuma.[19] For good measure, he also asked for the authority to investigate the activities of the registers and receivers at any land office which violated the law. Thus, he pulled Mt. Salus into the equation.

Meanwhile, the nomination sat in limbo until May 29.[20] To Dr. Gwin's consternation, Senator Black did absolutely nothing to either push the nomination or, which was more egregious, to defend his brother. Henry Clay's colleague from Kentucky, George Bibb, reported the nomination to the floor where Poindexter immediately moved it be tabled.[21]

On June 28, Black finally rose in favor of Dr. Gwin, asking that consideration of the nomination be resumed. The Senate promptly adjourned for the day.[22] Two days later, the nomination came up for a vote. Gwin's opponents had chosen their time carefully. Vice-President Van Buren was not in the chair, leaving it to the president *pro tempore*, George Poindexter, to preside over the Senate. The vote was a tie, 17 yeas and 17 nays. It was up to Poindexter, who, in respect for his anti-administration politics, had been voted into that position that month. Jackson and Gwin were defeated.[23]

With all the rumors circulating, Andrew Jackson could not stand behind William as he had Samuel. Instead, he nominated General Thomas Hinds that same day and the Senate unanimously approved. Just as suddenly, the scene in the Senate shifted again. Senator King of Alabama pulled John Calhoun aside. King told Calhoun he was sure that Hinds would not serve. Furthermore, the statements that Poindexter had made against Gwin, swaying the senator to vote against the doctor, were simply not true. John Calhoun immediately rose to the floor and stated he wished to change his vote on William Gwin.[24] The Senate reconsidered and Gwin was approved. Congress promptly adjourned for the session.[25] Dr. Gwin had used up one of his nine lives to get this appointment.

If Samuel Gwin had any illusions that he would be vindicated in the Senate investigation he was soon disavowed of those thoughts. Poindexter appointed Isaac Caldwell, his former law partner, and William Jones as commissioners to investigate the Mt. Salus Land Office. James and Samuel Marsh, of whom Samuel Gwin held no better opinion, were in charge of the investigation at Chocchuma. From the beginning, their depositions were suspect. The deponents were restricted to answering specific questions that limited the range of their responses. Some deponents were not given an opportunity to review their testimony. One was plied with alcohol to loosen his tongue. When the reports were finished on December 15, 1834, Samuel Gwin was infuriated. With Robert Walker's help, he set about finding all those who testified in order to cross-examine them. While some had left the country, a clear image of partiality emerged, cultivated through the work of Caldwell and Jones.

The Gwin brothers had been incensed with Poindexter from the start of the investigations. Poindexter was up for reelection in the fall of 1835. In an extremely candid letter to Jackson, Dr. Gwin claimed that this investigation was the most fatal step that Poindexter had ever taken. Gwin confidently predicted that he would be beaten by a majority of two to one either by Walker, Samuel Gwin, or himself. However, Dr. Gwin was opposed to his brother running because he had not been a resident of the state long enough. Walker was one of the most talented men in the South, but Gwin brought up the one weakness of Walker: he had wavered on the removal of deposits from the branches of the Bank of the United States. This action threatened the viability of the Natchez branch needed by Walker to support his land speculation. Walker was unsure if a state bank would be an adequate alternative. Jackson could be expected to easily take offense at this action, given his strong emotions against the national bank. Gwin smoothed this over by stating that Walker supported Jackson and hated Poindexter. Yet the letter seemed to be leaving a back door open for William Gwin to step into the nomination if Jackson had second thoughts about Walker. Dr. Gwin closed the topic with an ominous threat.

> If elected he [Poindexter] will have to walk over the dead bodies of *three* persons before he takes his seat. Mr. Walker, my brother and myself, he has used every effort to destroy. If we cannot disgrace him by beating him he shall atone for his attacks upon us by his blood.[26]

The depth of President Jackson's personal feelings toward Poindexter became public knowledge on January 30, 1835. An assassin attempted to fire two shots at point-blank range into Jackson's back as he was leaving a funeral service in the Capitol. Both pistols misfired and Jackson immediately shouted to bystanders that Poindexter must be behind the attempt. A subsequent Senate investigation cleared Poindexter beyond a doubt. However, the breach was now in the open.[27]

In Clinton, Samuel Gwin finished his rebuttal depositions at the end of June 1835. He had foolishly sent some of the earliest work to Washington; it promptly disappeared and he would have to retake some of the testimony. At the same time, he gave the responses to Walker to edit. At this point, Gwin intended to quit his job as register as soon as he was cleared of wrongdoing. He had acquired enough land to call his home a plantation and had purchased an interest in an area sawmill. His children were being schooled in Nashville. He had done okay as a land register. In a letter to President Jackson, he expressed his gratitude for the president's kindness at a time when he had been unable to support his young family. He also frankly told Jackson that he had wanted to issue a public retort to Poindexter, designed to draw the man into a duel, but discreet friends had dissuaded him. His health troubling him, he closed, saying that if he lived, he wanted to travel to Washington to resign in person.

Poindexter seemed finished in Mississippi. He did not contest the senatorial selection process. He even considered a race for the state legislature but saw that he had no chance there either. All but conceding defeat, he left the state with his young wife for watering holes in the Virginias.[28] Walker, on the other hand, now had to be sure that he would face no Democratic challengers. With Poindexter gone, he dragged his feet over the editing of Samuel Gwin's response to the senator's charges. When he returned them to Gwin, they were far more inflammatory than anything Gwin would have submitted. Gwin had to find a cooler head and restart the editing process.[29]

Andrew Jackson saw to it that Robert Walker gained the Senate post. The Whig opposition was using Poindexter's fraud allegations and an old letter that Walker wrote to Senator Black questioning deposit removal against him. In response, Jackson weighed in strongly on Walker's side by putting the praises in Dr. Gwin's letter into his own words. Walker was among the first in talents, attainments, and integrity. However, what counted most in Jackson's mind was that Walker had been a victim of Poindexter's malice. The letter, written in July, was published in October.[30] Of course, it did not hurt that Walker had a solid base of support in the northwest counties, formed from the Choctaw land dealings. The Senate seat was now Walker's to lose.

If it could have ended there, the Gwin brothers would have had a victory. However, George Poindexter returned to Jackson for the elaborate inauguration celebration of the newly elected Whig governor, Charles Lynch, on January 7, 1836. Lynch gave a levee in his office in which Poindexter got quite drunk. Egged on by his friends, Poindexter climbed upon a table to deliver a furious political speech. He excoriated Jackson for his appointments in Mississippi. Samuel Gwin, who was present, could not contain himself, hissing at Poindexter. Isaac Caldwell came to Poindexter's defense and the two men exchanged angry words. Gwin, afterward, consulted with a friend from Clinton, Henry Foote, who counseled him not to challenge Caldwell to a duel. On January 9, the legislature elected Walker on the fifth ballot as senator, further embittering Poindexter.[31] A day later, a challenge arrived from Caldwell in Poindexter's handwriting. If accepted, the duel would take place on the outskirts of Jackson at daybreak the next day.

For Samuel Gwin, his health failing, there was nothing to lose. Getting Caldwell would be almost equivalent to shooting Poindexter, who was not going to fight anyway. Gwin had the right to propose terms. They were deadly; the combatants would have four pistols each and take their places thirty paces apart with the right of advance.[32]

At the appointed time, Gwin's second, Foote, gave the word to commence. Both men advanced, exchanging the first shot without effect. Caldwell's second shot hit Gwin in the left breast. Gwin braced himself, took careful aim, and hit Caldwell in the abdomen. Both men fell to the ground.[33] Caldwell was taken to his home, where he died several hours later. Caldwell's wife was unforgiving toward Poindexter, present at the man's death.[34] Samuel Gwin, likewise, was carried from the field with what many considered a mortal wound. Twice in the coming months there would be reports of his demise.[35] Still he held on, not signing his final statement in response to the Senate Committee of Public Lands investigation until March 1836. The full report was submitted to the Senate on May 1, 1836. Sadly, with Poindexter gone, the issue was simply dropped from the Senate's agenda. There would be no hearing for Samuel Gwin and there would be no closure, only rumors swirling around both Gwin brothers.

The year 1836 went well for William Gwin. His 20,000-acre plantation near Vicksburg was progressing nicely. In mid-September, Gwin accompanied President Jackson back to Washington from Tennessee when Jackson's personal secretary, A.J. Donelson, was forced to remain behind to tend his sickly wife. Gwin most likely stayed at the executive mansion and may have served as Jackson's secretary until Donelson's return three weeks later.[36]

The tide turned in 1837. Samuel, after a year of agony, finally succumbed to his wound. Then, financial disaster rained down upon all of the land speculators in Mississippi. The 1836 Treasury circular requiring payment for all land purchases in specie burst the land bubble. Gwin saw his land, which had had values as high as $30 per acre, suddenly decrease in worth to as little as $0.65 per acre. His equity base was virtually wiped out. Worse, the cash-flow machine of marshal's fees suddenly turned sour. Gwin found himself forced by the courts to accept worthless notes and bank script for escrow accounts in his name. However, when it came time to pay the claimants from those accounts, the courts insisted on payment in specie. Gwin was caught in the middle. Paper losses were one thing; losses of this sort were real and immediate. Robert Walker was hit even harder, with his senatorial wages at one point being attached.

Still Dr. Gwin persevered on the political front. He ran to replace Black in the Senate in 1837.[37] However, in a precursor to the next presidential election, the legislature picked a Whig candidate instead. Gwin continued at his marshal post until 1840, when he ran for one of Mississippi's two congressional seats, winning election to the Twenty-Seventh Congress. While Gwin accomplished little during this term in office, he did use it to overcome his fear of public speaking.

Upon completion of his term in office and still plagued by debt, Gwin returned to Mississippi. In addition to his plantation holdings, he had helped set up commission houses in 1839, including Halsey and Gwin in Vicksburg and Claiborne and Freeman in Natchez, to finance and supply planters.[38] With the nation starting to recover from its depression, it was time to nurture these investments. He also took on the claims of the Chickasaw Indians over the federal government's negligent investment of their funds from land sales. It was an unpopular case with Mississippians, who resented any money going to the Chickasaws, regardless of the reason. Gwin successfully pursued two claims. The first, on interest due on money deposited with the Agricultural Bank of Mississippi, was for a little less than $8,000. Gwin received payment from the federal government in January 1845. He took as his fees 50 percent of the payment, raising no eyebrows. The second claim, of $112,000 arising from an accounting error, ran into heavy opposition when he claimed half of the settlement. Payment was prohibited by an act of Congress and would not ultimately be settled for years. It was during this process that Dr. Gwin first became acquainted with J.W. McCulloh, first comptroller of the Treasury Department.[39]

Politically, Gwin was going to pay a high price for these fees now hanging in limbo. He went to Washington in early 1845. Walker was in line for a cabinet appointment, given his key support in helping Polk defeat Van Buren at the Democratic convention. Gwin would later state that Polk offered Walker the less significant position of attorney general. That much certainly was true.[40] Walker viewed the attorney general position as a political dead end. Instead, he wanted to be secretary of the Treasury because he considered it the most important post in the cabinet. Gwin claimed to be instrumental in gaining it for him, although there were others who made the same boast.[41] In return, Walker maneuvered to gain Gwin a seat in the Senate. He wrote to Governor Albert Brown, asking that the appointment be made immediately because of an important pending vote in the Senate. Gwin was in town and available. Brown surprised Walker by rejecting Gwin out of hand. The doctor was "in bad odor" with a number of Democrats in the state; his appointment would divide the party.[42]

Still, Dr. Gwin would not accept defeat. Fearing that he might not have Andrew Jackson's support, he wrote the old man in April 1845, seeking his blessing for either the Senate or the House.[43] His concerns were unjustified, as Jackson promptly and warmly endorsed his old family friend.[44] However, if by now Gwin still did not know how some Democrats felt about him, the proceedings of the Warren County (Vicksburg) Democratic convention to name delegates to the state convention that year should have lifted the veil from his eyes. The county convention passed a resolution stating that anyone associated with the Indian claims, meaning Gwin, was unfit to represent Mississippi in the federal government.[45]

Regardless, Gwin pushed to be nominated for his old seat in the House at the state convention in Jackson, Mississippi. Here he met his match in Jefferson Davis, who had gained the support of the Warren County delegation. Even so, on the first day of the convention it appeared that Gwin would gain the nomination. Aware that Gwin's momentum needed to be slowed, the Davis supporters forced an early adjournment that day. Davis had some fifty Warren county supporters, well in excess of the county's delegation numbers. They now had the evening to work the back rooms to gain the nomination for Davis.[46]

The following day, there were demonstrations both for and against Gwin. The doctor mounted the rostrum to demand a specification of any charges against him. He also defended his actions in the Indian affair. No one rose to confront him directly and the voting commenced. There was a lesser candidate in addition to Gwin and Davis. In the first vote, Gwin and Davis tied. In the second vote, the third candidate dropped out and the majority of his voters turned to Davis.[47]

Bested by Jefferson Davis in his first time out, Gwin was finished in Mississippi politics. In 1847, he would try once more to gain a seat in the Senate. This time he was defeated by Samuel Gwin's second, Henry Foote, for the

Democratic nomination.[48] However, Robert Walker threw Gwin a bone. He appointed him one of three commissioners to oversee the construction of the customs house in New Orleans. This job was a sinecure, just like those for the two Southern branch mints. However, Gwin refused to accept this condition and took an active role in purchasing the land, approving the design, and negotiating the construction contract.[49] It was in this position that he found himself at Zachary Taylor's inauguration in 1849, far from his former achievements and aspirations.

• • • •

To describe the atmosphere that Dr. Gwin encountered when he disembarked in California on June 4, 1849, as chaotic is an understatement. The good news was that none of the observations in Sherman's report were close to the truth regarding the extent and richness of the gold region. New discoveries were made daily, and it seemed that every river or stream had gold in abundance.[50] A letter writer from Monterrey seemed to sum the situation up nicely.

> At present the people are running over the country and picking it out of the earth here and there just as a thousand hogs let loose in a forest would root up ground-nuts. Some get eight or ten ounces a day, and the least active one or two. They make the most who employ wild Indians to hunt it for them. There is one man who has sixty Indians in his employ—his profits are a dollar a minute. The wild Indians know nothing of its value, and wonder what the pale faces want to do with it; they will give an ounce of it for the same weight of coined silver, or a thimble full of glass beads, or a glass of grog. And the white men themselves often give an ounce of it, which is worth at our Mint eighteen dollars or more, for a bottle of brandy, a box of soda powders or a plug of tobacco.
>
> . . . Our grain gold, in exchange for coin, sells for nine and ten dollars an ounce, though it is well known to be worth at the Mint in Philadelphia eighteen dollars an ounce at least. Such is the scarcity of coin here. We want a Mint.[51]

With unheard of numbers of men working the gold fields, inflation was rampant. Flour, which sold before the influx for $4 per one hundred pounds, sold at the end of 1848 for $16. Merchants with access to manufactured goods from the East could make a killing selling them to the miners.

The bad news was that San Francisco was a miserable little collection of tents and flimsy shelters (fig. 89). Its July 1849 population of 5,000 would grow to 15,000 in October and to 30,000 by year's end. Open fires were necessary for cooking and warmth, and, not surprisingly, fires

Fig. 89. Abandoned ships in the San Francisco harbor in 1849, with the scattered, ramshackle buildings that constituted the community in the background.

Fig. 90. The first double eagle—if it could be called that, given its deficient gold content—was struck using California gold by the Mormons at Salt Lake City.

repeatedly swept through the shantytown. And yet, like mushrooms, new dwellings sprang up after each fire to take the place of those destroyed. In this atmosphere, with mostly male inhabitants, crime was pervasive.

Congressional failure to organize the territory meant there was no applicable law other than the martial law administered by the military. However, it was inadequate for policing the civilian population and there was virtually no rule of law. A gang flourished in San Francisco until the people, organized as vigilantes, rose up and put it down.

The peace treaty with Mexico bound the American government to continue to enforce the laws in place until a permanent government was established. However, in many instances these laws were vague and inadequate in addressing the conditions being encountered. The large land grants given by Spain and then Mexico had never been properly surveyed, throwing land titles into question. Boundaries were disputable and establishing titles could be a nightmare. The miners, on the other hand, cared little for legal niceties. They took what they found—royalty payments to a landowner were few and far between. Mining on public land without any form of payment for that right was now the norm.

There was another problem that was just as vexing. With no laws, no banks could be organized. Therefore, there was no local paper currency. Any bank notes from back east had little or no value because of the impossibility of presenting those notes for payment. Legal-tender coinage was hoarded by importing merchants to pay customs duties. If the merchant was short the needed specie, he could deposit raw gold at the rate of $10 per troy ounce. While the customs officer would take raw gold for import duties, the importing merchant must redeem that gold with specie, half in three months and the remaining half in six. If he failed, his bullion would be sold at auction to a broker at an even lower rate of $6 to $8 per ounce. Oftentimes, the merchant would be put in the ludicrous position of having to pay a premium for Mexican silver coins to avoid a bigger loss on his gold bullion on deposit.[52]

At the time Gwin took up residence in San Francisco, private gold coinage was just making its appearance. At first, these coins were deemed a boon to commerce. While the government would not accept them in the payment of debts, they were better than trade centered on raw gold bullion, steeply discounted to allow for discrepancies in fineness. However, the coins made in California soon came into disrepute, as their intrinsic values varied from the face amount stamped upon them. The worst of these were the Mormon $20 gold pieces struck in Salt Lake City from California gold. They carried an intrinsic value that fluctuated around $17 (fig. 90). None of these private mints refined their raw bullion to produce a .900 fine coin. They were all struck from raw gold straight from the placer mines, leaving the inherent silver in place and yielding a fineness of .884 to .887. The situation was intolerable. It was also a speculator or broker's dream.

Against this backdrop, Gwin wasted no time in advocating state government, giving speeches at Sacramento and Stockton, supply hubs for the miners. His timing was good. On the day before Gwin arrived in San Francisco, the military governor had issued a proclamation calling for the election of delegates to a constitutional convention. Drawing from his early days in Mississippi, Gwin was comfortable in this setting. On August 1 he easily won election to the constitutional convention to be held in Monterrey on September 1, 1849.

There were 48 delegates elected from throughout the territory. Those participating in the convention were assigned specific committees. Gwin, however, initially had no assignment. Questionable rumors that he had embezzled $70,000 from the federal government while marshal and that President Jackson had shielded him from prosecution had followed him to California. Thus, the other delegates were leery of him. Some even whispered that Gwin's role at the convention was to ensure the acceptance of slavery in the Constitution.[53]

Gwin took his position in stride. His ostracism did not last long; there were too many issues to be resolved. He argued to outlaw dueling and prohibit state banks. He was soon placed on the Boundary Committee with Henry W. Halleck, an Army officer sent by the military governor to participate in the convention. The thorny issue was the delineation of California's eastern border, to which there seemed as many opinions as there were delegates. The issue of a U.S. Assay Office was raised but voted down as not germane to a constitution.[54] Slavery was the number one problem. The miners simply did not want to compete with slaves in the gold fields, as had been the case in Georgia and North Carolina.[55]

Gwin owned slaves at his Mississippi plantation. However, he had supported the proposition of the Democratic presidential candidate, Lewis Cass, in 1848 that each territory had a right to make its own choice regarding this issue.[56] As the convention wore on, it became apparent that slavery was not going to carry. The option to divide the territory into two states by extending the eastern border to the Rocky Mountains with slavery in the south was considered but rejected after strong debate. How far Gwin went to pursue slavery is an open question. At some point, he had to see that if he pursued slavery in the territory, California's admittance into the Union would be greatly delayed, frustrating his Senate aspirations.[57]

When the drafting committee was constituted, the convention president named Gwin the chairman *pro tempore*. However, once fully formed, the committee voted him out of the chair. Gwin came out of the convention with what seemed to be two entirely different reputations. On one hand, he was proclaimed as having made the compromises necessary to bring the convention to a successful conclusion with a draft constitution acceptable to the population. On the other hand, one delegate called him a "California Machiavelli."

Gwin could not seem to rise above his past. A newspaper article quoted from a letter stating that none "stood higher or fell harder than Dr. Gwin, who came out here for the purpose of superintending our political affairs for us. There is no person more capable of contending with a powerful opposition than himself, but I very much doubt his success in the present instance."[58] The quote could only be alluding to Gwin's ultimate quest for a Senate seat.

Indeed, Gwin did have competition. John Frémont was considered a shoo-in for one of the seats. Henry Halleck, the Army officer at the convention who had served as military secretary of state, was also a strong candidate. The president of the convention, Robert Semple, promised to give Gwin stiff competition. Finally, Taylor's man, T. Butler King, was running as a Whig. It was a crowded field.

King lost momentum early, holding a poorly attended rally in San Francisco in spite of support from the local newspaper, the *Daily Alta California*. Meanwhile, Gwin canvassed the gold fields, using liquor to seek votes from the miners for state legislators he hoped could be influenced to support him. When the statewide elections produced a strongly Democratic legislature, King's chances narrowed. Halleck seemed the frontrunner; Gwin and Semple were completely disregarded.[59] No one seemed to think Gwin had a chance until just before the legislature met.[60]

The legislature convened at noon on Saturday, December 15, 1849, at the *Pueblo de San Jose* (township of San Jose). Unfortunately, the legislators promptly adjourned until the following Monday for lack of a quorum. It was the rainy season in California. They complained of the mud and the lack of any decent accommodations in the little village. The town was already overrun with the various candidates and a strong contingent of their friends and allies.[61] Gwin certainly was among that number, having been on the receiving end of that ploy in Mississippi.

The vote for senators came the following Thursday at five in the afternoon. In the first vote, Frémont carried a majority of the 46 votes cast, gaining election. With Frémont out of the equation, Gwin held on with 22 votes in the second ballot; however, with five legislators not voting, no one claimed a majority. Now Gwin had to scramble to gain support from the legislators who had abstained. This he did, getting 24 votes, the exact number needed on the third ballot. Gwin was now a senator from an unrecognized state. It had taken him seven months to make good on his word to Stephen Douglas.[62]

On January 1, 1850, William McKendree Gwin boarded the steamer *Oregon* bound for Panama.[63] Ironically, the man who had indirectly focused his attention on California was also aboard; Lieutenant W.T. Sherman was carrying dispatches to General Winfield Scott in New York City.[64] Crossing the isthmus, Gwin took the steamer *Falcon* to New Orleans for a brief stay before departing for Washington, D.C.[65]

CHAPTER 23

LAME DUCKS

January 1, 1849, was a red-letter day for Robert Maskell Patterson; he was elected president of the American Philosophical Society. It was the only honor that his father had held that had escaped him. In actuality, he had been elected to the position once before at the beginning of 1845. However, that election bucked longstanding tradition at the APS, which allowed an individual to retain office until death or voluntary resignation. That was not the case in the 1845 election and he refused to serve. Now with the death of the sitting president, his turn had come. It was an honor of national proportions.

Patterson did not feel that way about his position at the Mint. He would later say that he had long since accomplished all that he had set out to do at that institution. He would soon be 62 and had to admit to himself that he was slowing down. His son, Bob, had been playing an increasing role in the day-to-day operations of the Mint and it was Patterson's desire that he succeed him. However, with the Whigs coming into office, any thought of establishing that succession must be postponed for four years.

On this first day of the new year, Patterson had before him two immediate issues at the Mint. The congressional authorization of gold medals for the military exploits of generals Scott and Taylor remained to be executed. After Peale's pedestrian effort on the first two medals commemorating Taylor, Patterson had made a change. He did not even consider giving the work to Longacre. Instead, on

January 4, 1849, he sought permission from the War Department to send Peale to New York to interview Charles Cushing Wright and Augustus Mitchell.[1] It was an easy decision for Peale, given Wright's outstanding ability and Mitchell's limited experience in the field.[2] Two weeks later, Wright had the commission. He requested faced dies from the Mint. After the engraving, he would turn the border. He would prepare the likeness of Taylor from a bas-relief by Salathiel Ellis (fig. 91). The portrait of Scott would be modeled from life.[3] The War Department was to provide the reverse designs. The medal commemorating President-elect Taylor would be completed first.

The second issue involved a request by Patterson's melter and refiner, Richard McCulloh, to modify and improve the furnace that had been on hold since the defalcation by Hutchinson. The furnace's air supply needed to be increased. The draft also needed to be enhanced, by either adding height to the chimney or increasing the fuel-circulating device. At present, it took several hours of firing before the heat was sufficient to melt silver. In addition, McCulloh wanted to change accounting procedures between his department and that of the treasurer and to hire a weigh clerk to weigh silver ingots coming from the treasurer. McCulloh's reason for requesting this change was the high wastage of silver in his department. Patterson tossed this report aside.[4] He had no intention of making any changes in McCulloh's department. Perhaps the incoming Whig administration would alleviate the thorn in his side that Richard McCulloh was fast becoming.

Fig. 92. James McKay came to the second session of the Thirtieth Congress determined to overcome Director Patterson's opposition to striking $1 gold pieces at the Mint.

Fig. 91. Congress authorized additional gold medals for major generals Zachary Taylor and Winfield Scott on May 9, 1848. The Taylor medal, given obvious political precedence and engraved by Charles Cushing Wright, was struck on July 4, 1849.

• • • •

Patterson soon had a bigger thorn to deal with: James Iver McKay. McKay was the ranking Democrat and former chairman of the Ways and Means Committee in the House (fig. 92). He had been the favorite son of the North Carolina delegates to the 1848 Democratic convention, but he came in a distant fifth in the balloting for the vice-presidential nomination. He had not stood for reelection to the House that fall. With the adjournment of the Thirtieth Congress, his 18-year career as a representative would come to an end. McKay had one last objective. He meant to see Congress authorize the striking of a $1 gold coin.

McKay knew that the coins would circulate. After the fire at the Charlotte Mint, much of the gold region's bullion was diverted to Bechtler's private mint in Rutherfordton. Here, August Bechtler, having taken over for Christopher, converted a substantial portion of the Carolina gold into $1 gold coins that moved freely into regional commerce. McKay had an ally in the effort, Senator Stephen Douglas (fig. 93). When Douglas was in the House with McKay, he introduced motions in the Twenty-Eighth and Twenty-Ninth Congresses to instruct the Ways and Means Committee to report on the issue.[5]

Patterson had appeared cooperative enough in 1844. When he had sent nine specimens, restrikes from

Fig. 93. In 1849, having just transferred from the House of Representatives, Stephen Douglas pushed behind the scenes in the Senate for legislation authorizing the $1 and $20 gold pieces.

Gobrecht's 1836 dies, he suggested the design be changed to incorporate a head of Liberty on the obverse and that the legislation not require an eagle on the reverse.[6] In March 1844, McKay was able to report out a bill authorizing a $1 gold piece incorporating Patterson's reverse recommendation with a standard weight of 25.8 grains.[7] However, Patterson had aggressively sought and obtained the support of the Whig administration to kill the bill.

In 1846 McKay in the Ways and Means Committee had discussed the possibility of a $20 gold piece. Patterson was equally negative regarding this concept. He believed the coin wholly unnecessary. He pushed his creditability stating that no other country in the world had had success with a larger-denomination gold coin. In fact the Spanish colonies in South America had minted an 8-escudo piece or doubloon with a value of about $16 for a number of years. Patterson went on to state that these pieces, if coined, would not find their way into circulation.[8] In the face of that opposition, McKay did not even attempt to report out a bill.

The discovery of gold in California changed everything. McKay was ready to take on Patterson. He turned to Douglas to fire the first shot, a resolution that the Senate Committee on Finance inquire into the striking of $1 and $20 gold pieces. It passed unanimously.[9] That things might be different this time around became apparent when Representative James Pollock introduced a petition from Union County, Pennsylvania, praying for the authorization of $1 gold coins.[10]

Gauging his support, McKay had a bill authorizing only the $1 gold piece reported out of the Ways and Means Committee on January 25, 1849. Just as before, it would be exempt from the requirement of an eagle on its reverse. But that was not all; McKay supplemented his bill with a public relations campaign to drum up support. Even before the bill was introduced, the *Daily Globe* published an article calling for an experiment with such a coin. In support of its position, the newspaper opined that quarter eagles were inconvenient because of their fractional value and their monetary size. Nine times out of ten, their face value was too big for an ordinary purchase. The silver dollar was too heavy and large, while the competing paper dollar was too light and subject to depreciation, if not outright counterfeiting.[11]

Once the bill was on the floor of the House, McKay went to the editors of the *Washington Union* to push for adoption. He pointed out that a $1 gold coin would replace some of the ragged banknotes. It would also be a convenient way to send money by mail. McKay showed the newspaper a "made for coining" $1 coin, the size of a half dime with a square aperture in its center. This piece had been hand engraved with an incused design. On one side were 13 stars and the date. On the other was the imprint "United States of America" surrounding a wreath. Not employing a die, the coin had a thrown-together, crude look. The square hole, while permitting a thicker and broader coin, also had the advantage of making the gold piece easily distinguishable from other pocket change.[12]

McKay then sent Patterson the article in the *Washington Union*, asking for his opinion. He also raised the issue of a $20 gold piece. Once again, Patterson sent six trial $1 coins, three gold and three gilt. Patterson felt the form as described in the article, with a square hole in the center, would be very objectionable. Obviously, McKay had used a Washington jeweler to gin up that example. Patterson admitted that he had no objection to a double eagle other than that it was not needed. It would be between a half dollar and silver dollar in size with the potential to be a handsome coin.[13]

On the Senate side, the Democrats were in the majority, with Charles Atherton of New Hampshire as chair of the Committee on Finance. Atherton reported out S. 414 on February 1, authorizing both the $1 and $20 coins. The double eagle, the name of the new denomination, would have a standard weight of 516 grains and a fine gold weight of 464.4 grains (note that there are 480 grains in a troy ounce). The majority of Democrats guaranteed the double eagle would get a receptive audience in the Senate.

On February 20, McKay reported his bill out of Ways and Means, amended to include the double eagle. The act had a sunset provision of March 4, 1851, to support billing this proposal as an experiment. Experiment or no, he had less than two weeks to get the measure enacted before the final session of this Congress expired. Upon the completion of the required reading for this bill, Ingersoll, the Philadelphia congressman, objected to the bill being put on its way to passage. The debate was on.

McKay proceeded to attack the long-standing objections voiced by Patterson. One was that the piece was too small and would be easily mistaken for a half dime. McKay had some sample pieces and thought that anyone seeing them would be satisfied that there was not much weight in that objection. McKay acknowledged that the $1 coin could easily be counterfeited and that it would be subject to unacceptable wastage through wear from circulation. McKay curiously let these two claims stand without rebuttal. Instead he raised two more points. The Mint Act of 1837 required the Mint to deliver to depositors the coins they specified for their bullion. If they did not want the $1 coin there would be no demand. Furthermore the authorization for the two coins expired on March 4, 1851. If there was sufficient demand for the two gold coins, Congress could extend the act. McKay's argument was not the most forceful presentation. He closed by stating that if it met the pleasure of the House, he would call the question.

Ingersoll blurted out that he hoped not. Another congressman asked that McKay withdraw his motion to allow for more debate. McKay conceded, giving Ingersoll his opening. Ingersoll noted that the proposal to coin gold dollars had been around since 1836 but had always met with little favor. It owed its current support and favor to McKay, who had brooded over this project for so long. The director of the Mint had heretofore opposed the whole scheme. It was his fear now that something might be put forth that would swing support toward this gold coin. This measure was now before the House with little explanation and no argument. The House was to guess as well as it could the reasons supporting the passage of the bill.

Ingersoll was only warming up to his topic; he had more to say. There was no precedent or example that would justify the introduction of so small a coin. Looking to the civilized world, there was not another example currently circulating. This coin was a toy! It had no true purpose.

> A little piece of precious metal, scarcely perceptible to the eye or touch, may be a plaything for the idle, a counter for the card table—perhaps a light addition to a lady's purse in her morning's shopping, or a medium of fraud upon the post office laws, by lurking concealed under the seal of a letter. Beyond these fanciful purposes, it has none.

Then Ingersoll, with a skillful play on words, took a shot at both coins.

> It seems great coins are to be issued as well as small ones. If eagles' wings are to be clipped down to a standard so small that they will fail to perform their office from their insignificance, they are, as the bill proposed, to be doubled into a ponderous and unparalleled size.

Ingersoll also made a more serious strike at the gold dollar. If gold became more plentiful, its price would drop in relation to silver. (Ingersoll was on solid ground as this was in fact already taking place.) Should that happen, no one would want the little gold dollar when the more valuable silver dollar was available. There was one flaw in this line of thought. If the gold-to-silver ratio undervalued silver, that silver dollar would no longer be in circulation; it would have already left the country in satisfaction of foreign obligations.

Next, an East Coast Whig took the reins from Ingersoll to argue against the double eagle. There was no demand for a $20 gold piece. The director of the Mint himself had declared that there was no utility in $20 gold coins. They were not desired and they would contribute nothing to the economy. This congressman then returned to the issues of identification and counterfeiting. A Democrat from Tennessee quickly countered him. Who could distinguish in the dark between a $1 bill and a $100 bill? As to counterfeiting, who could determine a genuine banknote? It seemed to the gentleman from Tennessee that every argument urged against these gold coins could be applied tenfold to banknotes. And so the discussion went back and forth.

Finally Henry Nicoll, a New York City Democrat, gained the floor and called the question on the original bill. There were calls of "that's right" from congressmen who were exasperated by the endless arguments over a seemingly simple issue. But just as quickly, there were calls of "hold on" from those opposed to the measure. There was an immediate appeal to Nicoll to withdraw his motion. He refused. Then there was a move to table. It fell, with only 37 yeas to 127 nays. A coalition of Midwest Whigs had joined with Democrats to defeat the East-Coast Whigs. McKay's bill was on its way. Now came the vote on Nicoll's motion. It carried with 110 ayes; no one bothered to count the nays. Next, the amendment adding the double eagle was approved. A third reading of the bill was ordered, tantamount to its passage. Ingersoll objected on a technicality and was overruled by the Speaker. The bill promptly passed.[14]

In the end, when the Whigs split their vote, the bill's passage had been a foregone conclusion. McKay had not pressed his arguments because there was no need. Westerners, regardless of their political affiliation, were in support of a gold dollar. Silver dollars were not circulating to any great extent and the values of small-denomination banknotes were as suspect as ever. On the other hand, the double eagle got a free ride on the groundswell of support for the $1 coin.

In the Senate, amendments from the Finance Committee were offered on February 22.[15] The measure passed and went back to the House for reconciliation. The end product that passed on the last day of the session dropped the 1851 sunset date.[16] Now Patterson had to put two new denominations that he opposed into production.

• • • •

With the Whigs back in power due to the election of Zachary Taylor, Patterson's removal was a distinct possibility. However, circumstances conspired in the best of ways for the Mint director. Taylor, seeking a member of the Philadelphia Whig establishment for his cabinet, chose William Morris Meredith as secretary of the Treasury. Meredith certainly fit the mold; he was the former U.S. attorney for eastern Pennsylvania and the acknowledged leader of the bar in Philadelphia. He was also a close friend of Joseph Ingersoll.[17] More importantly to Patterson, Meredith was a member of the American Philosophical Society. He was not going to cashier the president of the society.

Still, Patterson served at the will of the president and there was a move to gain his dismissal among Philadelphia Whigs. In Patterson's favor, Zachary Taylor was a military commander first and foremost. When the "Committee of Seventy-six," formed by the original Taylor supporters in Philadelphia, questioned Taylor's appointment of Meredith, the president asked the nature of their objections. They had none; they simply wanted their man in the position. Taylor then stated that if that was the case, he would keep Robert Walker as a holdover.[18]

• • • •

With the active support of the press for the new $1 gold coin, Patterson had no option but to quickly develop designs for the coin. Peale urged him to go outside the Mint for this work. He even stated that the oversight obligation rested with the chief coiner.[19] McCulloh knew of Peale's efforts and went to Longacre, spurring the engraver to action. Uncharacteristically, Longacre went to Patterson and told him he was ready to commence the work. He made the additional point that the coinage laws charged the engraver with the duty to provide the dies for all coins. Surprisingly, Patterson gave in to Longacre.[20]

Patterson instructed the engraver to give precedence to the small gold coin. Consistent with his desire for the application of one design across several coins, an obverse would be developed for use on both coins. The reverse of the dollar coin would be simply a wreath enclosing the denomination and date of the coin with "United States of America" around the rim. Longacre, with strong guidance from Patterson, quickly chose as his model for Liberty *Venus Accroupie* (Venus Crouching) (fig. 94) from a collection at the Louvre.[21] Patterson sent a resulting sketch to Secretary of the Treasury Meredith, keeping him in the loop (fig. 95).

Fig. 94. Longacre used *Venus Accroupie*, most likely under instructions from Robert Maskell Patterson, as the model for Liberty's head on the $1 gold piece.

In that same letter to Meredith, Patterson also relayed the diameters to be implemented. They were proportional to the cube roots of each coin's volume and, when the metal was the same, to their values. The double eagle would have a diameter of 1.32 inches and the $1 coin, 0.5 inches. Patterson could not help taking one last shot against the dollar gold piece, knowing that East Coast Whigs were generally against it. The diameter of the dollar coin would be less by one-sixth that of a half dime. This was necessary, given that volume of the coin was one-third that of the half dime. If the diameter were to be increased, the planchet would be so thin as to cause a problem bringing up the obverse and reverse designs when struck.[22]

The engraver started immediately to make a model in wax of the head to be used on the obverse. In many ways this engraving was more difficult than that of a larger coin because of the minute nature of the work. Sensitive to criticism coming from art circles, Longacre had decided

Fig. 95. Two slightly differing versions of Longacre's rendition of *Venus Accroupie*, adapted for use on the obverse of the $1 gold piece. The necklace would ultimately be eliminated.

on a higher relief. He intended to try to give an expression and character to the design more consistent with approved standards of art than had been utilized to date on American coins. Longacre firmly believed that the idea of beauty or grace in the art of design without a convexity of line was impossible.[23]

Through the remainder of March and into April, Longacre labored at his first real engraving attempt. Seeking to put his work above criticism and ensuring its adaptation to the coin press, he made the obverse master die and hubs for the working dies twice over.[24] By the beginning of May, work was progressing rapidly. He acquired his "Liberty" punch for the figure's headband, a finishing touch. He had a working die ready for the obverse on May 3. Four days later the hub for the reverse was ready.

On May 8, production began. Longacre proudly scooped up one of the little gold pieces from the first day's run and put it in an envelope for John Calhoun.[25] He wrote Calhoun that this coin represented his first opportunity since his appointment to execute a design from start to finish and he wanted the senator to have this piece as a token of his gratitude.[26]

In reviewing Longacre's diary entries for that first week in May, there is no question that he was rushed at the end. The reason was Patterson. McKay's public-relations campaign had been more successful than need be. Coupled with enthusiasm generated by the California gold strike, public anticipation for the new coins was now at a fever pitch. Patterson had received an anonymous letter on May 4 that rattled him.

> You will be removed in consequence of your hostility to the Gold Dollar Coin and you will only be able to save yourself by an immense issue of that coin. Two months! To get one die struck is absurd and if the diesinkers won't work or can't work better remove them. The President has said this day "he holds you responsible and the laws must be carried out."
>
> We are strangers to each other but I think it proper that you should know the President's opinions and intentions.[27]

The *Washington Union* waded into the fray on May 6. Their article alleged the delay had been caused by the time consumed making the master dies and hubs. The chief coiner had $100,000 in gold planchets and strips ready to support production. It had been rumored that Patterson had held back on issuing the new coin because he was opposed to its authorization. Patterson would never stoop to such an action nor would he condescend to defend himself from such slanderous claims.[28] This article had too much inside information; it was a Mint plant. The real question was how was it planted: Franklin Peale on his own or with Patterson's acquiescing knowledge? In either case the conduit would have been Titian Peale, now employed as an assistant examiner in the U.S. Patent Office. One thing was certain: Longacre was expendable if the criticism heated up.

Longacre had hurried the reverse, drawing heavily from Gobrecht's design for the reverse of the half dime. No previous engraver had been asked to turn out work that quickly. In a questionable move, Longacre left the wreath open at the top, giving the effect of deemphasizing that element of the design.

The heat quickly evaporated with the issuance of the new $1 coin (fig. 96). The *Washington Union* proclaimed it a little bijou, beautifully executed. The newspaper positively glowed over the obverse design, a bust of the goddess of Liberty encircled by her brilliant stars. There was such taste and prettiness about the gold piece's looks; it was so much more beautiful than the ragged $1 banknotes.[29] Still, from other papers there was a grumble about the

Fig. 96. James Longacre's first attempt at designing and engraving a coin at the Mint turned out reasonably well. The engraver would go back and adjust the wreath on the reverse, closing the gap between its ends and the numeral 1.

Fig. 97. Rembrandt Peale painted Benjamin Franklin Peale in 1849. The stylishly bewhiskered but slightly balding chief coiner was at the height of his power. For many years this portrait hung at Baldwin Locomotive Works until it was gifted to the Pennsylvania Academy of the Fine Arts in 1925.

coin's small size. They compared it in diameter to Bechtler's dollar and found it wanting.[30] That was not a fair comparison; the Bechtler dollar bore only inscriptions; no design devices complicated its strikeability, allowing for a thinner planchet.

Patterson was now off the political front burner. On May 26, a presidential conversation leaked into the press. Josiah Randall, a leading trial attorney in Philadelphia, was meeting with Taylor with the objective of following through with Patterson's removal. The president asked if Patterson had ever meddled in politics. The answer was no. Then Taylor asked if the office had been in the hands of the same family for more than forty years. Yes, it had. Taylor asked if Patterson was competent and a gentleman. Both, Randall answered. Then if that was the case, Taylor did not care if the office had been in the family for five hundred years.[31] The case against Robert Maskell Patterson was closed.

After the dust had settled, Longacre went back to the reverse design to modify the wreath. He closed it up around the numeral 1, a small but significant improvement. He did this without complaint, meaning that if Patterson originated the change, Longacre agreed with it. It was all done quietly with no release to the press and no internal communication to the Treasury Department. In fact, official notification to Treasury only came in March 1850 when Meredith sent Patterson a closed wreath $1 gold piece and asked if it was a counterfeit.[32]

Now Longacre's stock was up with Patterson. The *Washington Union* reported at the end of May that the new head of Liberty was due to the genius of the engraver at the Mint.[33]

• • • •

Significant quantities of gold began arriving at the Philadelphia Mint in early April 1849. The flow was not even; it came in unpredictable torrents as the steamers landed at New York City. Once ashore, it went straight to Philadelphia. The Mint, tied to the ratio set forth in the acts of 1834 and 1837 that overvalued gold, was paying a higher price in terms of silver than London or Paris. Not only individual Americans but also the brokers were going to gravitate toward Philadelphia. Gold bullion deliveries through the end of June 1849 amounted to $2 million, a volume that the Southern gold fields never approached, even at the height of their production.[34]

The problem for Patterson was the antiquated refining process at the Mint. Throughput capacity to remove the excess silver from this raw gold bullion was only about $100,000 per month. Franklin Peale (fig. 97) wanted to go outside the Mint to augment the refining activity, using a third party as he had seen the English and French mints do. McCulloh opposed this move.[35] By the end of May, Patterson recognized his problem was serious and that working the men overtime was not going to fix it.

McCulloh knew James Booth, who had been his professor in school. The two men talked, with Booth pointing out that the introduction of steam into the refining process had been successfully applied in other chemical processes. McCulloh gained Patterson's permission to try injecting steam into the water bath that was part of the silver recovery process. It involved a partial shutdown in June and July to implement. Some of the officers, certainly including Peale, doubted that McCulloh could make the modification work. On the other hand, Patterson really had no alternative. He had no clear-cut legal authority to take the work outside the Mint. Besides, he trusted Booth and respected his judgment.

In the meantime, the gold flow kept coming, and prompt payment of depositors became a thing of the past. McCulloh claimed that the steam injection system increased his refining capacity to $1.5 million per month. However, in the succeeding months his men were consistently working until ten, twelve, and one at night, trying to surmount the backlog that stubbornly increased in spite of the improved refining capacity. At the same time, Patterson, seeing the skyrocketing wages for the extra hours, was not happy on any account.[36]

To make matters even worse, the relationship between McCulloh and Peale deteriorated to the point that the two men could no longer be civil toward each other. The flash point involved the striking of the gold medals for Taylor and Scott. Wright had finished his work on the Taylor medal in time for the ceremonial striking to be held on July 4, 1849. In advance, Peale requested 20 ounces of refined gold from McCulloh for this semi-official activity. McCulloh did so with the express understanding that the gold medal should remain in Peale's custody until he had delivered to McCulloh a like amount of gold. Meanwhile Patterson, sensitive to the politics in Washington, was anxious to get the gold medal to the president.[37] Peale expediently overlooked his promise to McCulloh and released the medal. When McCulloh asked Peale to restore the gold bullion, Peale blithely replied that it would inconvenience him. McCulloh strongly insisted, and Peale complied that day.[38]

Another incident of a more personal nature pushed McCulloh closer to the edge. Whether it happened before or after the Taylor medal incident, McCulloh never revealed. McCulloh had hired a friend, Professor Joel B. Reynolds, with the promise that he would seek for Reynolds the appointment of assistant melter and refiner. This was no shot in the dark for McCulloh; the 23-year-old Reynolds was fluent in French and had distinguished himself at the University of Pennsylvania and the Franklin Institute.[39]

Triggering the dustup, Franklin Peale had called for a delivery of ingots from the melter and refiner. The usual procedure was for McCulloh to deliver them to the treasurer, whose clerk would then record the ingots and issue them to Peale. McCulloh sent Reynolds instead. Peale refused to accept them. He condescendingly insisted McCulloh should deliver the ingots in person and never through someone of an inferior rank. Worse, Peale made a scene, angering Reynolds and embarrassing the treasury clerk.

Peale did not stop there, going straight to Patterson. He complained that by not delivering the ingots himself, McCulloh had committed a breach of decorum. Peale believed he deserved respect and that McCulloh should conduct himself in a particular manner. Much to McCulloh's consternation, Patterson backed Peale and stood by protocol, noting that Reynolds was only a workman.[40] The real issue was Peale's jealousy; McCulloh might get an assistant while Peale had none. Petty as this incident was, Peale was going to do nothing that might enhance Reynolds's implied stature in the Mint hierarchy.

On another front, C.C. Wright made progress toward completing the dies for the Scott medal in July. However, he struggled with the multiple intricate battle scenes, each enclosed in a wreath on the reverse. The reverses of both the Taylor and Scott medals had been designed by staff officers in the War Department, as was the custom for military medals authorized by Congress. It was not until August 11 that Wright completed the dies and forwarded them to Peale. In his note to Patterson, he regretted that he did not have different designs that would have enabled him to better show his skills.[41] That was putting the issue diplomatically; the War Department reverses were atrocious.

The arrival of these dies set up yet another confrontation between Peale and McCulloh. On August 17, 1849, Peale requested gold from McCulloh for use in the Scott medal. McCulloh refused, not only for the Scott medal but also for any other gold or silver medal.

The matter festered for a whole week until McCulloh wrote formally to Patterson. He stated that his position on advancing Peale metals for his medal work was devoid of personal considerations. Creditable individuals outside the Mint had informed him that the medals business as it was now conducted in the Mint was viewed in the community as doubtful, if not outright illegal. Within the Mint, the workers, with few exceptions, believed it wrong that they should be required to work for the monetary benefit of an officer of the institution. If the activity were legal, McCulloh doubted whether the manufacture of medals in the Mint was expedient or right, especially when executed for the Franklin Institute or the Worcester

County Mechanics Association of Massachusetts. In addition, private artists looked with displeasure and jealousy upon this competition. McCulloh made it clear in his letter to Patterson that he was not proffering charges against Peale for official misconduct. McCulloh asserted that if he was wrong, he would cheerfully admit his mistake.[42]

Continuing the formality, Patterson replied by letter the following day. His statement was significant for what it did not say. Patterson acknowledged that McCulloh was responsible for the bullion placed in his keeping. If it was his will, he had a perfect right to decline an interchange of any part of it, even for other bullion of equal value and even if it was required for government use.

McCulloh was determined to have the last word in this affair. On August 25, he took on Patterson directly. He noted the director's narrow reply to his letter. He correctly noted that it implied McCulloh's actions might have been caused by an unwillingness to facilitate the work of the government. That was certainly not the case. Had he had any indication that Peale's work was according to custom, he would not have refused the bullion. Furthermore McCulloh's position in the matter was reinforced by Peale's subsequent action. When refused by the melter and refiner, Peale obtained his gold from the treasurer. However, he used part of it for a gold medal commissioned by an association in Massachusetts. McCulloh then stated that he objected only to giving aid to an officer involved in a transaction of profit using the labor of Mint workers and the machinery of the Mint. There was nothing Patterson could say on this point.

That same day, Patterson sent the completed Scott medal to the secretary of war (fig. 98). He also enclosed a bill from the chief coiner that was substantially reduced from its June estimate.[43] McCulloh could at least take comfort that he had inflicted a financial blow upon Franklin Peale. His actions had raised a flag that Patterson could not ignore.

Shortly after this correspondence, McCulloh talked directly to Patterson. He wanted the director to understand that he had nothing personal against Peale in his refusal to supply the metal. In fact, if Patterson had not already done so, McCulloh wished him to feel free to share their correspondence with Peale. McCulloh then delved deeper, dredging up the Polk medal affair from 1847. He asserted that Peale either did not have a proper sense of right and wrong in monetary matters or was not always governed by that sense. By way of a rebuttal, Patterson asked McCulloh whether the dinner given to Polk later that day at the Navy yard had been paid for out of the public purse.[44] McCulloh stubbornly answered that it ought not to have been if it was.[45]

Fig. 98. The second of the two military-medal commissions from the Mexican-American War executed by Charles Cushing Wright for the U.S. Mint. The gold supplied for the presentation medal set up the final showdown between Richard McCulloh and Franklin Peale at the Mint. The messy reverse design came from the War Department.

Fig. 99. James Booth, shown in this 1845 daguerreotype, vacillated between accepting or rejecting the melter and refiner's position at the Mint. He subsequently fell under the influence of Franklin Peale and Robert Maskell Patterson.

On October 26, 1849, Patterson notified Secretary Meredith that McCulloh had resigned. He was leaving to take a position at Princeton College as a professor of natural philosophy. Excepting the treasurers, McCulloh's stay at the Mint had been shorter than that of any officer. Patterson's words of praise for McCulloh were so brief as to be damning. The director now recommended James C. Booth (fig. 99), the man he had sought ten years earlier. Of course he was careful to point out that Booth was a Whig.[46] McCulloh's resignation sounded so clear-cut, but it had not been that simple.

As McCulloh began to reduce his inventory of unrefined bullion in September after the process modification, the steamer *Empire City* arrived with $520,000 in California gold. At the same time, Treasury presented a demand draft upon the Mint for $200,000. It was all too much, the straw that broke the camel's back. Patterson was forced to admit to Meredith that McCulloh's changes in the refining department were not yet obtaining planned results. Coinage was far in arrears of deposits, with the amount due depositors then exceeding $1 million. With a little more time, Patterson hoped McCulloh would work the kinks out of the refining process and eliminate the backlog of payments to the depositors. Even so, it would be helpful if the draft could be voided, allowing these funds to flow to the depositors.[47]

On October 8, in response to Meredith's further inquiries, Patterson expressed confidence that difficulties in the refining department were abating. Patterson had added four workmen to the eight already employed in the department and the work was moving rapidly now. If he found more men were needed, he would hire them.[48] It was at this point that McCulloh resigned.

Now the intrigue began. McCulloh had such a tin ear when it came to his relations with Patterson that he thought he might influence the selection process in favor of J.B. Reynolds. Upon learning that Patterson's preference was Booth, McCulloh went to Booth, declaring that the hostility of the other officers to McCulloh would also be exhibited toward him. He also showed Booth his exchange of letters with Patterson involving Peale's medal activity.[49] Although Booth knew the other men well, McCulloh's assertions convinced him to decline the nomination.

At this point, Patterson was forced to appeal personally to Booth to take the position. He explained that Reynolds had a background in physics, making Booth the better candidate. Booth asked Patterson if the duties of the position would prevent him from further experiments in general chemistry in his personal laboratory. Patterson answered that although the duties of late had been more onerous then previously, he believed that Booth would have ample time for experimentation. Patterson also encouraged Booth's outside laboratory activities, believing them to be the duty of any chemist interested in advancing his skills. This said, Booth set aside his concerns and agreed to seek the appointment.[50]

McCulloh, with intentions not altogether pure, wrote a letter of recommendation to his father at Treasury on behalf of Booth. He also wanted Booth's support in seeking an assistant melter and refiner position for Reynolds. McCulloh's accounts balanced on December 1 and he left the employ of the Mint. Booth took over in November, posted his bond on December 4, and started work under a recess appointment.

Before leaving, McCulloh made one last attempt to make good on his promise to Joel Reynolds. However, Patterson rejected outright the promotion of Reynolds to assistant melter and refiner. Patterson felt it inappropriate to create a new position within that department, stating that Booth should have the opportunity to make that determination. McCulloh's parting advice to Reynolds was to accept nothing less.

Booth, being the new man on the block, did not go directly to Patterson on behalf of Reynolds. Instead he asked the other officers for their opinions. The consensus was that the work of the melting and refining department did not justify the position. The office of melter and refiner would be a mere sinecure with an assistant.[51] One could be reminded of Franklin Peale's use of that term to describe the engraver's position.

In subsequently relating Reynolds's rejection to McCulloh, Booth stated that Peale was behind Patterson's refusal. If Booth was to have an assistant, Peale believed that he should as well; however, Patterson was not amenable to that as long as Adam Eckfeldt was still pulling the load for Peale. The unanswered question was to what degree did Peale harbor jealousy toward the professionally trained Reynolds.

A short time afterwards, Reynolds resigned from the Mint. He was elected a member of the American Philosophical Society on January 17, 1851.[52] Patterson had at least retained an open mind toward Reynolds. Tragically, the young man died horribly on May 16, 1851, from burns he received when a new steamboat boiler he and others were pressure-testing just outside of Philadelphia accidentally exploded.[53] Right or wrong, upon learning of the death of Reynolds, McCulloh became embittered toward Peale.

Booth faced another issue in that first month at the Mint. There was a move to convince him to remove McCulloh's steam injection system. Clearly this diversion of steam was hampering the performance of the coining department. This time he stood his ground.

Total deposits of California gold for 1849 were $6,147,519; deposits to New Orleans were $666,080, and deposits to Philadelphia were $5,481,439. Patterson closed his annual report for the year on a note of optimism, stating that the Mint's refining capacity was now deemed adequate and that he hoped henceforth to make prompt payment to depositors.[54]

Patterson and the Philadelphia Mint had absolutely no idea of the magnitude of raw gold that was going to hit them in 1850. A golden tsunami of unimaginable proportions was headed their way.

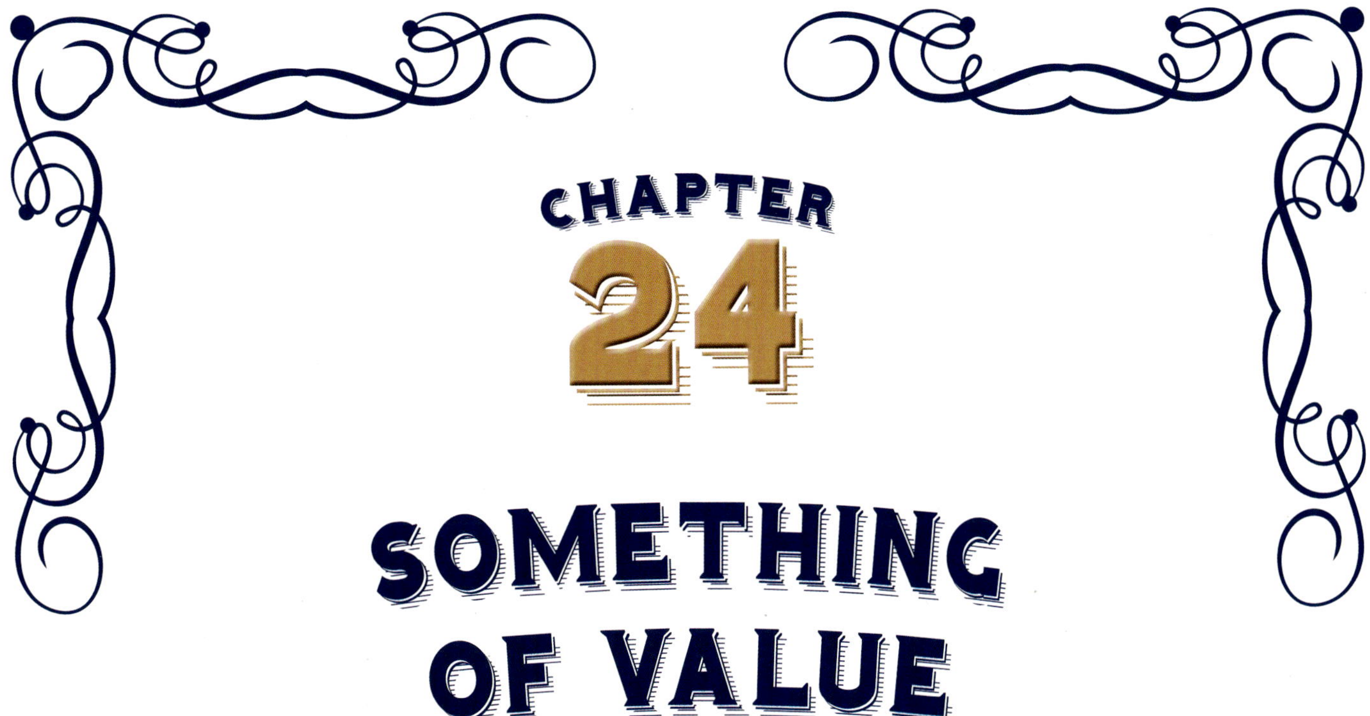

CHAPTER 24

SOMETHING OF VALUE

James Longacre found himself totally done in by the effort to get the $1 gold piece design into production. He had taxed his body too severely and now feared for his health. He shrank from the thought of the $20 gold piece design that stared him in the face. Consequently, he went to Patterson to seek approval to hire an assistant as the little "Mint drops," the nickname for the dollar coins, were just going into circulation.

To Longacre's surprise, Patterson would have none of it. Still stung from criticism due to supposed delays in the dollar coin's reaching circulation, Patterson had a different idea. He had no objection to having the engraving done outside the Mint to ease Longacre's burden. If it could not be done in Philadelphia, it could be done in another city, or even in Europe for that matter. Longacre understood; he was getting no help.[1]

The design concepts for the double eagle were relatively straightforward. For the obverse, Longacre would follow the original intent to carryover the Liberty head from the $1 gold coin. Also, it did not hurt that by now public approval of the dollar-coin design was universal. The reverse would incorporate a variation on the Great Seal, reflecting Patterson's opinion that nothing else would meet with approval in Washington. Longacre's early attempts produced a reverse entirely too complex (fig. 100). From there, Longacre refined his design, clearing the field and adding a double scroll that joined over the

Fig. 100. Longacre's early study for the reverse of the double eagle.

Fig. 101. Longacre's late-stage simplified sketch for the reverse of the double eagle.

eagle's shield. This double scroll alluded to the name of the coin—the double eagle—and contained the motto "E Pluribus Unum." The eagle's wings were now outstretched and the halo of 13 stars and above that, sunrays in an arc, were sharpened (fig. 101).

Next, Longacre made a fateful decision; he would try for high relief. With the double eagle, Longacre felt he had a perfect opportunity to answer critics of the Mint's low-relief coinage.[2] To set his relief, he proportionally scaled up the head from the gold dollar, which had been coined easily enough.[3]

Modeling first commenced on the reverse. Following established procedure, Longacre asked Peale's foreman, George Eckfeldt, to prepare a metallic disc to commence the work. George was the son of Adam's half brother.[4] Nothing happened. When he queried Eckfeldt, he learned that Peale had forbidden the work, saying that it would be of no use to Longacre. The engraver immediately went to Patterson and forced the issue of Peale's compliance.[5]

Peale had good reason for his refusal. The curvature specified for the disc was a forewarning that Longacre intended high relief. Peale knew instantly that he did not have the necessary steam power to strike up this design. He also doubted that the working dies could withstand for any length of time the repeated stress when placed into production. What Longacre was proposing was a die for a medal and not for a coin. He was standing his ground as chief coiner and the only officer competent to judge proper curvature and depth for coinage production. While high-handed in his approach, Peale was on firm ground.

Longacre did not see it that way. Was the problem want of sufficient power or an improperly executed die? It reminded Longacre of a story about a barber unable to fit Benjamin Franklin with a wig. The wig was not too small; the head was too big.[6] This analogy oversimplified the issue, as Longacre would shortly learn, much to his grief. Regardless, Patterson sided with his engraver over his friend and Peale had to supply the disc prepared to Longacre's specifications.[7]

Longacre proceeded to complete this high-relief first reverse model in copper only to encounter more trouble from Peale. The plan called for Peale to prepare an electrotype mold that would serve to make a cast in steel for the reduction. The process, using a galvanic battery in the apartments of the chief coiner, failed, destroying Longacre's model. Longacre had only a backup in plaster. It was not perfect and would require the engraver to make corrections at the completion of the reduction process in the master die.

Once the die was completed, it went back to the coining department to be hardened. Disaster struck again. The die split during the hardening process and Longacre could do nothing but start over. It was now October and the engraver still had the obverse master die to complete as well as the hubs.

By now a personal element had entered the equation. Longacre's 42-year-old wife, Eliza, was pregnant with their fourth child. The due date was the following April. Devoutly religious, Longacre would have taken solace in his beliefs. Both husband and wife knew that a pregnancy this late in life could be fraught with complications.

Fig. 102. This undisputed king of the U.S. Mint Cabinet, which became the National Numismatic Collection, owes its rarity as a single coin to its unsuitability for mass production. Its relief would not efficiently coin up. Yet the design clearly had merit; with subsequent adjustments to lower the relief of the obverse, it would take its place within the circulating specie of the realm and become an icon of newfound U.S. economic wealth.

Feeling overwhelmed and dismayed at his lack of progress, Longacre again asked Patterson for help. This time the director gave in. But with no more progress than had been made since the summer, Patterson must have doubted whether Longacre was up to the task.

Longacre approached C.C. Wright in New York, who directed him to Peter Cross. Sometime during this process, whether it was through Cross or more likely the highly accomplished Wright, Longacre came to the realization that he must compromise his expectations for the relief on the double eagle. He was adamant that the obverse stay true in scale to the relief of the $1 gold piece. However, he was going to have to remove the relief from the reverse. The Greeks could only maintain relief on one side. The Romans made no improvements. Even the Italian Renaissance masters could not produce relief on both sides of their magnificent medals. If he did not make this change, his design would never strike properly.

Cross commenced working at the Mint on November 6, 1849, at a weekly salary of $16.[8] With an experienced diesinker on board, progress was steady. However, there was frustration of another kind. The days were short and the light deficient in Longacre's work area. Now more frequently than ever, what light existed was blocked by the smoke from the steam engines and the melting and refining furnaces struggling under the backlog of gold bullion.[9]

As work was drawing to a close, Longacre took a moment to give the departing Richard McCulloh a gift, a plaster cast from his first reverse of the double eagle. McCulloh, wishing to make this memento of their friendship less fragile, had a copy made in metal that Longacre later touched up with his graver.[10]

Peter Cross returned to New York on December 20.[11] A trial for the new design with a high-relief obverse was set for December 22, 1849. Longacre was not present for the test.[12] As the trial was being set up, the workmen involved noted the hardness of the alloyed gold to be used. It seemed as hard as the steel die with which it was to be struck. Jacob Eckfeldt, the assayer, made the same observation, questioning the amount of copper used in the alloying. At least one coin was struck using the screw press (fig. 102).[13] Peale reported the results in a letter to Patterson on December 24, 1849. Patterson immediately sent a sample to Meredith for the secretary's approval. In a most perfunctory and detached manner, the mint director absolved himself of any responsibility for the delay and asked Meredith's prompt approval that as many of these coins could be struck in the remaining few days of 1849 as possible. He was passing no judgment on this coin, particularly its coinability since it had not be struck on a steam-powered production press.[14]

Franklin Peale had a different opinion expressed in a letter to Patterson on December 24. The impression of the new double eagle could not be brought up on the standard coin press. The depth of the head on the obverse was such that the steel of the die could not sustain the degree of pressure necessary to give a full impression. In addition, there was also the minor disadvantage that the head projected above the rim of the coin, preventing the coin from being stacked for counting purposes at banks and unnecessarily subjecting it to abrasion that would cause intrinsic-value issues over time.[15]

The chief coiner's letter galvanized Patterson to action. On Christmas Day he explained in a letter to Meredith that the sample before the secretary had not been struck on the ordinary steam press. A number subsequent to the trial strike of December 22nd were produced on this press with unsatisfactory results. Patterson enclosed Peale's letter for good measure. Patterson told Secretary Meredith that the relief of the obverse die was too high for coinage. He inferred that given the time taken by Longacre to prepare the first die, the delay to correct this mistake would be very considerable.[16] That was a gross exaggeration. Patterson was setting forth his defense should criticism develop over this delay, as had been the case with the one-dollar coin in the spring.

Peale delivered the bad news personally to Longacre in the presence of Patterson on December 26. Longacre was chagrinned that the head of Liberty projected above the coin's rim. He afterward called the test striking a failure and referred to it as little as possible. He admitted after the fact that he had overestimated the ability of the coin press to fully bring up the details of the obverse. The power of a coin press was specific and fixed. However, the striking force was also a function of the surface area to be struck, and it diminished in proportion to the diameter of the planchet used. Thus what worked on a gold dollar coin became problematic on the double eagle. Longacre had no option but to recommend that relief of the head of Liberty be reduced on those elements that did not strike up.[17]

While the failure of the trial was not an issue, questions remained. The observation of the men involved that the hardness of the gold was exceptional has merit. Copper alloyed with gold in use at the Mint since 1795 certainly does make for a harder metal. McCulloh was gone from the refining department and Booth would not yet be effective. Yet J.B. Reynolds, who no doubt prepared this refined gold, was competent enough. There is one other option. Excessive rolling, bending, or stretching of gold will cause it to harden as well. Preparing planchets of a new size and thickness from the gold bars provided by the refining department was the responsibility of Peale. This was the more likely source of the excessive hardness.[18]

Was there only one coin struck in the December 22 trial? That piece has survived in the Mint Cabinet and has become unique in American numismatic lore. However, a single striking goes against simple logic. The December 1849 wastage report for double eagles showed a loss of 2.34 troy ounces; that translates into 1123.2 grains.[19] The specifications for the new double eagles called for a standard gold weight of 516 grains. Clearly, the wastage report supports the striking of a second double eagle from these dies. In addition, Longacre later spoke to the injury of the

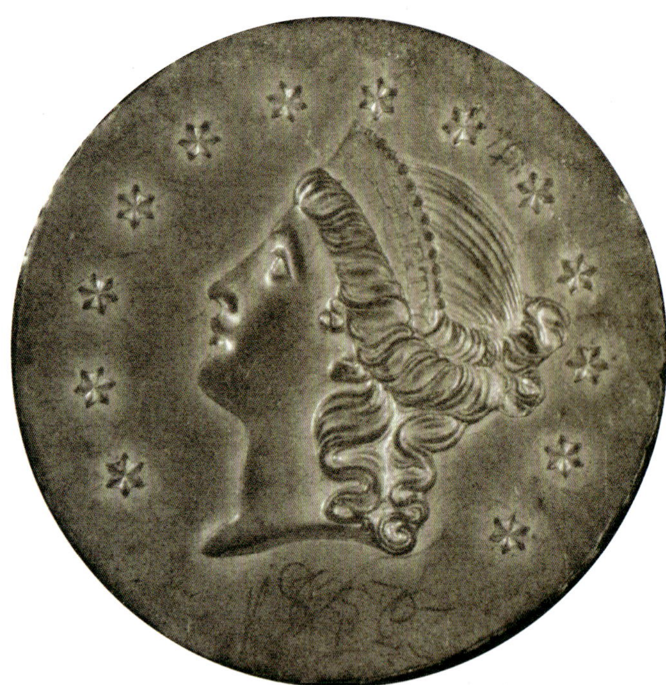

Fig. 103. A splasher, probably from the January obverse die, showing a weak strike of "Liberty" on the coronet, indicating that additional reductions in relief would be needed. However, the hair lines are sharp.

dies used in this first trial.[20] It is clear there was no failure in striking the first trial specimen on December 22. The failure must have come during the multiple strikings with the ordinary steam press attempted before Peale's report of December 24. Substantiating this conclusion, Peale in later testimony stated that for all intents and purposes, the dies were destroyed within an hour.[21] No wastage was reported from this activity leading to the conclusion that these pieces went to the melting pot.

To say that Robert Maskell Patterson was disappointed by the results would be an understatement. He sought and obtained Meredith's permission to replace Longacre. After all these years, Patterson was finally turning to Charles Cushing Wright, the preeminent American medal engraver. Patterson sent a feeler to Wright on December 29.

> Let me ask, in perfect confidence, whether you would, if appointed, accept the office of Engraver at this Mint. The salary is $2,000 per annum. The duties occupy but little time, except when original dies are to be made. I beg you to give me an immediate answer.[22]

There was much left unsaid in this letter. Since, at this point, Patterson was not traveling, it is highly likely that a personal visit was made by Peale to seal the deal. The circumstantial evidence supporting this assumption is that Wright accepted, began to wind down his business, and started work on a new reverse model for the double eagle.[23]

Longacre, unaware of this vote of no confidence, called Cross back to the Mint. The assistant arrived on January 9 and started work the next day, putting the finishing touches on Longacre's efforts to reduce the obverse relief (fig. 103). The following day, Longacre finished the hub for the obverse.[24]

Longacre went to Peale to set up another trial strike. To his amazement, Peale declined. The chief coiner had no gold in readiness for the trial.[25] Peale was obviously stalling. More importantly, Patterson's silence on the matter was deafening. Longacre had no option but to sit and wait. Two weeks later, on January 26, Peale announced he was ready. Again the test was conducted in Peale's apartments using the screw press. Again the piece did not meet Peale's approval. The only defect that Longacre could see was a slight flatness in the center of Liberty's head. At this point, the chief coiner told Longacre that the position of Liberty's head on the obverse must be moved in order for the design to strike up. Longacre was frustrated that Peale would wait until this late date to mention this option. Had it been mentioned earlier in the process, Longacre would have objected only as a matter of taste.[26] Given the near absence of relief on the reverse, it is hard to understand how Peale's suggestion of moving Liberty's head would have improved the results of the trial strike. It certainly would have further delayed the project.

Longacre then asked Peale for one of the newly struck trial pieces from which to make further adjustments in the relief. Again to his amazement, Peale refused. The chief coiner declined on the grounds that he would have difficulty with his accounts. Longacre offered to make up the difference from his own pocket. Peale absolutely refused a second time. In frustration, Longacre asked what he was to do. Peale then suggested an impression in silver. The hardness was hardly comparable but Longacre felt he had no alternative.[27]

Peale later defended himself for what was really an indefensible position. He attached no particular importance to having an impression in gold. A diesinker did not require Proof impressions in gold before he completed his work. On the contrary, the only impression in gold a diesinker saw was that of the completed coin. He believed that Longacre's real objective was to exhibit the pieces as triumphant evidences of his success and to refute to ignorant parties the unfitness of his dies for coinage. It was a well-known fact that a few single impressions from dies with the depth and characteristics of a medal could be made using excessive power from the coining press. To the eyes of the public these special strikes would present a bold, effective, and attractive appearance. However, those experienced in the process of coining knew that the dies would fail and the machinery suffer under the stress of the excessive pressure used to repeatedly strike up the high-relief design. As Peale had legal custody of the piece, he refused to let Longacre have it to induce snap judgments from the uninitiated.[28] In other words, Peale was covering in order to give his boss time to maneuver Longacre out of the Mint.

Now the jockeying began. Longacre tried to see Patterson for a personal interview but each time it seemed that Peale would appear, thwarting Longacre's efforts to defend himself privately to the director. Finally, on January 30, Longacre penned a long missive to Patterson.

The engraver did not discuss the early difficulties with the reverse die. He acknowledged that more work remained after this second trial striking. However, he lambasted Peale for not giving him the trial strike in gold upon which to base his adjustments in relief. He went on to state that he had compared the silver impression to gold coins currently in production. The lack of a full strike on Longacre's double eagle was no worse than what was coming off the production line at that time. Longacre still had not fully grasped the concept that a trial on a screw press did not constitute a fair test of how the coin would strike up in full production. He also excused the length of time he had taken to reach this point, blaming the newness of the size of the double eagle and his lack of any gold coin of comparable size upon which to base his relief. At least Longacre was acknowledging that scaling up from the dollar gold coin to determine relief had been a mistake.

In closing, Longacre couched his words carefully, but there was no mistaking the underlying intent.

> It is not my wish to trouble you with a multiplicity of issues at this juncture—my object is to contribute what I can to secure and elevate the interests and credit of this branch of the public service; but should my intercourse with the coining department encounter in the future the impediments I have recently experienced, I shall be compelled to ask for a striking press to be placed under my direction for the purpose of proving my own work independently of any adverse interference and for the protection of my feelings as a gentleman.[29]

These words captured Robert Maskell Patterson's attention but not in the way that Longacre intended. It could be inferred that Longacre was building a case in his defense should the government seek his removal. It forced Patterson to act.

Patterson did not formally respond with an answering letter. Several days later he dropped into Longacre's workspace to talk. The conversation was general, almost banal in nature, concerning the trial and the direction in which Longacre was headed. Patterson never brought up the issue of Peale's seeming lack of cooperation. Then, a couple days later, Patterson returned. He had "painful intelligence" to communicate; the executive authority of

Fig. 104. Secretary of the Treasury William Meredith protected Patterson's job at the Mint but also refused Patterson's request to terminate Longacre.

the government had determined that Longacre should be removed from office. Patterson called the decision imperative and he urgently advised Longacre to resign.[30]

The engraver was stunned. His first inclination was to fold his tent and leave, given the obvious animosity of both Peale and Patterson. But as the shock wore off, he realized that his actions were not cause for termination; any decision for his removal had to have been based upon misrepresentations. Longacre dug his heels in, requesting an interview with the secretary of the Treasury. He was not walking into this meeting completely cold. One of his earliest and more agreeable engravings for his book of great Americans was that of Gouverneur Morris, Meredith's great uncle. At the time of its execution, Longacre gained the friendship of Meredith's father. Still, Longacre was leaving no stone unturned; he also mentioned in his note to Meredith that he was probably the only Mint officer who voted for Taylor.[31]

Longacre did not wait for a reply, taking the train to Washington on the same day he penned the note.[32] The two men met the following day, February 13, 1850. Meredith (fig. 104) appeared much pressed with business and he only gave Longacre a brief interview. The engraver initiated the discussion by mentioning that he had just learned of the government's dissatisfaction with his work and he wanted to understand how he had given offense. Meredith commented that he had been told the engraver was no diesinker. Longacre responded that the job called for an engraver and in that regard his qualifications could not be disputed. In his words, not one of his predecessors had been a diesinker by trade either. He had been in office for five years without complaint.[33]

The next exchange cemented Longacre's belief that the dissatisfaction with his performance was not in Washington but was of a homegrown nature. Longacre brought a silver impression grudgingly provided by Peale on January 26. Meredith showed surprise, wanting to know what had become of the dies used to strike this specimen. Longacre now knew that Meredith was operating from knowledge provided by Patterson after the failure occurring between December 22 and 24. Longacre told the secretary that the dies were in perfect order.[34] Longacre asked permission to make a statement of facts to Meredith and to be directed to finish the work on the double eagle.[35] Meredith concurred and Longacre now had breathing room.

Longacre's letter to Meredith set out in detail the problems he had encountered in the development of his design. He spared no detail, discussing the ruined electrotype casting mold and the split die, the poor light in his workroom, and even his mistake in assuming the level of relief achievable on the obverse. He provided details of his confrontation with Peale on January 26. He noted that at the Royal Mint in London, the engraver had the final say on the fitness of the dies and not, Longacre inferred, the chief coiner. He addressed his lack of qualification as a diesinker. For an engraver to discharge his duties he must be a designer, a modeler, and have a general knowledge of numismatics. Diesinking was but a minor part of the duties of the office.[36] With the letter complete, Longacre proceeded to prepare what he would call his second model of the obverse, dismissing the December 22 trial as a complete failure.

Fig. 105. This splasher—assuming it was done with the final obverse die—shows full details, indicating the design was nearly complete. Here the hairlines are not as sharp as in the earlier splasher. Longacre had softened the detail to facilitate the strike.

What Longacre did not know was that Meredith had taken the engraver's letter with the silver trial strike to President Taylor for his review. The president, with the uninitiated eye that Peale so feared, told Meredith that Longacre should not be concerned about his position as long as Taylor was in power.[37] It had another impact as well. Wright had written Patterson on February 12 asking for direction. Was the job his or not? He must renegotiate his shop lease by February 20 or terminate.[38] This last delay took Wright out of the picture.

The engraver now kept Meredith apprised of his progress, realizing that he had no other supporter. On March 1, he sent the secretary impressions in fusible metal from his second set of dies (fig. 105). They would demonstrate for Meredith the relief now being applied to the obverse. Based on a newly completed trial, Longacre believed that the relief was strikeable with the existing coin press. However, he was not happy with the flatness of the reverse as he felt it would not stand up to public scrutiny. In defense of his work, given the constraints of the coin presses at the Mint, he told Meredith that he had sent Congressman Moore, the Whig representative from Longacre's district, a metallic cast of his original high-relief reverse. Meredith was free to inspect it at his convenience and it would provide a more exact measure of Longacre's skills as an artist. It was also a subtle way of conveying to Meredith that the engraver had additional connections to the Philadelphia Whig establishment.[39]

The new double eagles were struck from Longacre's second die on March 12, 1850. Patterson sent two to Meredith, one of which was to be forwarded to the president. Patterson could not help criticizing the design one more time. These double eagles had been struck with all the force that could be applied and to such a degree as to injure the die, yet the impression was still not perfect. The face of Liberty was still too much in relief.[40] Longacre did not feel that way about his design. He even managed to get his hands on one of the double eagles from the first obverse striking on January 26 for his personal collection.[41]

The public began to see these coins in Boston, New York, and Philadelphia over the final two weeks of March. The reaction was lukewarm at best. The *Boston Transcript* called the coin simply ugly.[42] The *New York Tribune* considered the design awkward; the eagle of the reverse was out of proportion with the head of Liberty on the obverse.[43] Others were more complimentary. Adams Express showed the new coin to the reporters of the *Philadelphia Inquirer*, who called it truly beautiful.[44] The lesser-known *Philadelphia Sun* stated that it far exceeded the other gold coins in elegance as in value.[45] A cute turn of phrase, this report appeared in a number of papers and constituted what passed at the time for a Mint press release. It was stingy in its praise. There were no reports of interest about the new coin coming out of Washington. In fact, most newspapers hardly took note. This coin had had Patterson's disapproval from the start and now he would do no more than was required in promoting its issuance.

Patterson had lost Wright but he had not given up the fight to rid himself of Longacre. On April 1, he wrote to Meredith. The extension of time that the secretary had granted Longacre was over and he wished to know where the matter stood. If the office of engraver was to be vacated, Patterson proposed that a replacement not be appointed at least until the next session of Congress. In the meantime Patterson would engage the assistance of the best artists in the country to execute a new series of designs for American coins that would meet with Meredith's approval. This would justify Patterson's recommendation for the abolishment of the engraver's position.[46] Patterson meant to do away with Longacre's double eagle design, decidedly the best to enter general circulation from the Mint to that point and one that would stand the test of time.

On April 6, Eliza Longacre went into labor and delivered a daughter. Three days later, she was taken seriously ill with a fever. She appeared to make progress by mid-April to the point that Longacre was able to travel on business. However, she took a turn for the worse and died on May 1, 1850. The child—Longacre never did refer to the girl by name in his diary—died on June 2, 1850.[47] At this juncture, Patterson mercifully ceased pushing for Longacre's removal; yet their relationship remained strained.

• • • •

Patterson had more to keep him occupied than coin designs. Franklin Peale wanted a sweeping overhaul of the coining department. Now that he had lost the fight to coin a low-relief double eagle, he had to acknowledge that Longacre's complaint of insufficient power had merit. The boilers and engines might be shiny and clean but some had been in service since 1832. In addition, the practical consequences of diverting steam to the refining process meant idling the largest steam engine and constricting the rolling and cutting operations in Peale's department for two-fifths of each day. In Patterson's defense, there was little reason to spend money on the power plant while the Mint puttered along through the early and mid-1840s at nothing close to capacity.

Franklin Peale was never guilty of dreaming small dreams. He wanted to replace three sets of boilers with one new, larger boiler, a powerful steam engine, and a new rolling mill with enhanced gearing. Here was the answer to Longacre's complaints about the lack of striking power and the hardness of the gold. Peale never touched on these subjects. He claimed that while the coinage heretofore had kept pace with the refinery and the other departments of the Mint, now he would have four times the power, giving him ample capacity to handle any influx of California gold. In addition, he would add a seventh coin press that would be dedicated solely to the new double eagle, and he would relocate the new steam engine, providing more room for the expansion of refining activity.[48]

Patterson had his back to the wall. Besides, with the large amounts of California gold rolling in, his operating expenses for the current fiscal year were well over budget. Even so, he sat on Peale's request for a full month before forwarding it to Meredith on February 26. On May 15, Congress approved a $12,000 operating deficiency appropriation and $20,800 for Peale's improvements and the extension of the chimney.[49] Meanwhile in Washington, Meredith was taking no chances concerning the Mint's ability to handle all the California gold. A bill was passed in the House and referred to the Senate Finance Committee to increase the bullion fund to $2 million.[50] Meredith asked the committee to amend the bill by giving the president full latitude to designate whatever sums were necessary for the bullion fund at Philadelphia.[51] Now both Philadelphia and Washington were bracing for the worst as the gold continued to roll into the Mint.

CHAPTER 25

BAD CHEMISTRY

From day one, James Booth was overwhelmed in the refining department. McCulloh's expansion, completed the previous fall, was turning out to be nothing but a stopgap. Booth had a backlog of $1 million with incoming gold in January 1850 pegged at $1.5 million.[1] The reality of McCulloh's capacity estimate of $1.5 million per month was much closer to $1 million. The Mint was drowning in gold. Worse, depositors were finding it advantageous to send their gold to London, selling bills against it at 9.5 percent in order to receive their money immediately rather than wait at the Mint.

With Patterson's full cooperation, Booth set out to immediately expand refining capacity. After tinkering, he gained $500,000 more capacity in January. When February deliveries hit $2 million, Booth took major action, adding six new furnaces that month.[2] Another $500,000 in capacity was added in May and then again in September, to bring total throughput to $3 million per month.[3] Over time, he would also increase employment from 14 men to 31.[4] As spring turned into summer, Booth gained some breathing room, but there was little capacity to spare. Any more California gold and the Mint would be right back where it had started at the beginning of the year.

Amidst this backdrop, a letter arrived for Patterson with familiar handwriting dated February 11. It was from Richard McCulloh (fig. 106). If Patterson thought he was free of McCulloh, he now knew differently. The former melter

Fig. 106. Richard Sears McCulloh continued to do battle with Franklin Peale after leaving the Mint. In the end Peale would weather this storm but in a greatly weakened condition.

and refiner had merely moved across the Delaware River to his new position at Princeton College. In the letter, McCulloh told Patterson that he had perfected the process of using zinc in place of nitric acid during refining and was offering to sell it to the government. With the construction of the furnaces underway, Patterson, in a fit of overconfidence, did not bother to respond to McCulloh.

McCulloh had been experimenting with the refining process in 1849 while he was still at the Mint. He had tried chlorine in the form of hydrochloric acid. It was the talk of the Mint at the time, as the fumes from the process overcame his men; McCulloh quickly dropped that approach. Then in the final weeks before he left, he and Reynolds hit upon the option of using zinc. They set up a small furnace in the basement of the Mint to test the process on a bench scale. As McCulloh left, he knew the method had promise; he even showed it to Patterson. He continued to improve the process at Princeton.[5] However, the one kink in the plan was his failure to place Reynolds as his successor. Now he must deal with Booth and that complicated matters. All he could do was sit and stew, waiting for a reply from Patterson that never came.

• • • •

For months it was rumored that Henry Clay was coming back to the Senate. Whigs worried that he might try to encroach upon President Taylor's agenda. The betting from Democrats was not whether but how much.[6] Rumor turned into fact with the convening of the first session of the Thirty-First Congress on December 3, 1849. The issue of California statehood colored everything. In his annual message to Congress on December 24, President Taylor called for a branch mint in California.[7] Yet how could the political establishment that had failed to organize California as a territory in the previous Congress rise above itself to give California statehood and authorize a mint? This would be especially difficult with all the entangling side issues involving slavery swirling around. All eyes looked to Clay to once more craft a compromise that punted the issue of slavery down the road.

It was only natural then that Dr. William Gwin went straight to Clay when the former arrived in Washington in February 1850. The Kentucky senator greeted Gwin warmly. If Clay had his way, he told Gwin, he would admit California immediately. However, Southern hotheads thought otherwise. Discreetly, Gwin and the California congressional delegation withdrew to New York City to wait while the struggle over slavery played out.[8]

In spite of the focus on finding a compromise that let California into the Union as a free state, there was time for other congressional issues that impacted the Mint. Taylor's call for a branch mint in California had opened a Pandora's box. What flew out first was not a mint for San Francisco but another bill in the Senate to establish a branch in New York City. Daniel Dickinson, New York Democrat and chair of the Finance Committee, led the charge.[9] Not to be outdone, the South Carolinians again introduced a petition calling for a branch mint in Charleston.[10] However, their case was not nearly as strong as before. A rail line had been completed between Charleston and Charlotte that permitted easy movement of gold for coinage. North Carolina was not going to support South Carolina. Southern unity quickly broke down and no companion bill materialized, clearing the way for New York City.

A second issue swirled around a scarcity of silver specie. Imports had exceeded exports for several years and undervalued silver was leaving the country in preference to gold in settlement of these debts. Whereas the year before, newspapers had crowed about the ability to purchase a copy of the daily paper with one of the new gold dollar coins, now little was said about that coin's convenience. That same gold dollar could not purchase a newspaper in 1850 because the newsboy could not make change.

The congressional solution to the coin shortage was to authorize more coin denominations. First came a call in the House to issue silver coins valued at one-third and one quarter of a dime.[11] Subsequently a bill was introduced in the House calling for the introduction of a double dime, or twenty-cent piece. It also provided for the redemption of fractional foreign specie as a means of providing the silver for this new issue. The bill had some merit in that the quarter dollar, as with the quarter eagle, was worth an odd amount, necessitating more and different denominations to make change when used for a purchase. However, the bill did not provide for the suspension of quarter production, a fatal flaw.[12]

Debate on Henry Clay's compromise omnibus bill dominated Washington politics throughout the late winter and early spring of 1850. It was not until a lull in the slavery debate in May that the opportunity arose for issues impacting the Mint to reach the floor of the Senate. First out was a call for the Finance Committee to consider amending the Mint Act of 1837; this amendment would allow silver alloy in gold coinage to be increased to match the content of silver alloy in California gold. The New York bullion brokers were looking for a quick fix to drastically cut their wait time at the Mint. The resolution also asked the committee to report on the expediency of establishing a mint in California, or one or more depots for assaying gold bullion.[13]

The first action in the House on a New York City branch mint came on May 22. New York Whig J. Phillips Phoenix introduced a bill appropriating $225,000 for the proposed facility. He asked that the House set aside a date to debate the bill in a Committee of the Whole. Objection was promptly made, stopping Phoenix.[14] In addition, J.R. Chandler (fig. 107), Ingersoll's successor from Philadelphia, gave notice that he would move to amend Phoenix's bill. His amendment would allow the assistant U.S. treasurer in New York to accept gold and silver bullion. This bullion would be sent to Philadelphia at government expense to be assayed and a certificate of deposit would be issued, payable by the assistant treasurer in New York City. Chandler had designed a mechanism that tore the heart out of the economic justification for the branch mint.[15] This scheme would give the New York banks speedy access to gold coin for their bullion and foreign specie and shift to the government the transportation expense to Philadelphia. Chandler's action was enough to stop the New York forces in the House for the time being.

Fig. 107. J.R. Chandler succeeded to the House seat of J.R. Ingersoll, with its implied responsibility to protect the Mint at Philadelphia, in 1849.

Two days later, Dickinson picked up the fight in the Senate for the branch mint; this debate would extend over the period of a week.[16] There were solid arguments in New York's favor. One of the leading bullion houses in New York estimated that four-fifths of the coinage at Philadelphia was for the account of New York banking institutions. In addition, immigration into the United States was booming, with the vast majority of these peoples flowing through the port of New York, bringing with them considerable specie from their home countries. This specie now either went to brokers at a discount or was carried with the immigrants to their ultimate destination. A branch mint would capture this specie for recoining.[17]

Solid economic arguments were not going to carry the day for New York—this issue was too emotional. Opponents of New York City derisively asserted that the branch mint would become the exclusive instrument of the merchant princes of the city. Proponents countered that merchants, whether they were princes or not, could ill afford to have their money lay idle for the 40 to 60 days it took for Philadelphia to recoin it. The New Yorkers noted that half the receipts coming into the Philadelphia Mint for recoinage were for the account of the federal government. Philadelphia was the mint of the government; New York would be the mint of the people. Against this emotional backdrop, debate opened with the Senate constituting itself into a Committee of the Whole to thrash out the issue.

Immediately, Thomas Hart Benton hijacked Dickinson's agenda, introducing an amendment to include a branch mint at San Francisco. Now the floodgates were open and Jefferson Davis (fig. 108) stepped into the breach. He argued for two assay offices, one at Sacramento and one at Stockton. These two settlements were situated on the two rivers that drained the gold fields of California. Dr. Gwin may have based himself in New York while waiting for statehood for California but he was hardly idle. The words Davis spoke were Gwin's words. Davis went on to argue that the nation needed three mints only: one in New York, another in New Orleans and a third in San Francisco. Through this statement, Gwin was now on record opposing the Philadelphia Mint. In closing, Davis stated that if a branch mint was placed in San Francisco, an assay office must either be at the mint or in the gold fields to ensure that miners did not have to go through brokers to monetize their gold bullion.[18]

Fig. 108. Even though they were former political rivals, Jefferson Davis spoke in support of William McKendree Gwin, giving the yet-to-be seated California senator a voice on the Senate floor.

R.M.T. Hunter from the Finance Committee took the floor to state that a Mint in California should only plan to coin what was demanded regionally. This suggestion of restricted capacity seemed at odds with what others were advocating. Hunter was more in tune when he argued that the export of gold bullion from California would be as important as the export of cotton from the South. This much was Gwin's thinking. While Gwin's methods deserved questioning, his vision for California was an asset. He saw San Francisco as the great commercial hub for the Pacific.

Dickinson sensed the situation getting away from him when George Badger, a North Carolina Whig, moved to substitute San Francisco for New York in his original bill. Dickinson told the Senate that while he preferred action on California be kept separate from the New York City bill, he was willing to let them be linked. Benton took the floor to explain his amendment. It was to establish a mint at San Francisco as soon as a building and machinery could be readied. Assuming it would take two years to accomplish, his amendment authorized an assayer be appointed immediately to enable miners to obtain full value for their gold. This office would then be absorbed into the Mint when that facility was placed in service.

At this point, Henry Clay (fig. 109) rose from his seat. All eyes focused on the acknowledged leader of the Senate.

> I have risen merely to express the hope that we shall come to a vote on this subject as soon as we can.
>
> With regard to the Mints proposed to be established, I do not mean to go into any argument as to their propriety or desirableness. Before I left home, and while in conversation with distinguished men, I came to the conclusion—which has been strengthened rather than weakened—that a Mint at San Francisco was necessary, was highly proper, and should be established without delay. This is still my opinion.
>
> Now with respect to the other Mint, proposed to be established in New York, I am also satisfied that it ought to be established. When I was last in New York I went to the Sub-Treasury office and saw the amount of gold there, and talked with the merchants and men of most intelligence, on this subject; and I think it is necessary. But while I say this, I would say that there are two Mints in existence that ought not to be in existence. One of them is in North Carolina and the other is in Georgia. I make no proposition to discontinue them. But I shall go for the New York Mint, and for the San Francisco Mint. I think both are necessary, and I have merely risen to express that opinion.

Clay obviously wanted to get debate back on track for his compromise bill. However, if he saw that branch mints at San Francisco and New York could peel away opposition votes to his compromise, he was willing to incorporate them into his legislation. Also it was clear that Dr. Gwin had advocated for a mint during his meeting with Clay.

Henry Clay did not get his way. In fact mentioning the existing branch mints just added fuel to the fire. George Badger regained the floor and noted tongue in cheek that the strongest opposition to the New York mint came from those with mints in their own neighborhoods. The most strenuous advocates of the branch mint at New York City were the senators and representatives from that state. Badger did feel the cost savings were strong enough to justify taking action. As for the Southern mints, at least the one in North Carolina, he believed, had turned out to be a humbug establishment without necessity or value. Badger then got down to a basic reality. Adding a branch mint at New York would effectively replace the mint at Philadelphia.

Dickinson called for a vote. From his seat, Henry Clay called out to "now move the special order of the day"—in effect calling for the vote. It did no good.[19] It would be two more days before the Senate could organize itself to come

Fig. 109. His face showing the ravages of time and his body racked by tuberculosis, Henry Clay came back to the Senate one more time to forge the framework for the Compromise of 1850.

to a vote. On May 31, 1850, with only 35 of the 60 senators present—barely a quorum—S. 24, authorizing mints at New York City and San Francisco, passed.[20]

Everything changed on July 9, 1850. Zachary Taylor opposed Clay's compromise. He was no supporter of slavery, preferring that California be admitted under the terms of its state constitution, which banned slavery without any offsetting concessions to the South. On July 4, Taylor had participated in celebratory festivities on the grounds where the Washington Monument was to be erected. Reports commonly indicate that the president ate a large quantity of raw fruit and iced milk during this event. He died of resulting gastrointestinal causes on July 9, and Vice President Millard Fillmore, a Whig politician, became president. William Meredith was out as secretary of the Treasury; he was succeeded on July 20 by Thomas Corwin, a Whig senator from Ohio.

S. 24 languished in the House until July 22 when it was read twice and committed to a Committee of the Whole; but no date was set for the debate.[21] Also, in a little-noted event with profound implications, Dickinson reported to the Senate that the Committee on Finance refused to consider relaxing the alloy requirements for gold coinage to accommodate the larger amounts of silver found in California gold.[22] Dickinson's stated reason was that the miners would not be paid for the silver left unrecovered in the gold.[23] In reality, New York City was giving no quarter to Philadelphia.

Meanwhile Clay's compromise omnibus bill failed on July 21. The aging senator immediately left for Newport, Rhode Island, to recuperate. In his absence, Stephen Douglas broke the omnibus bill into its separate sections and succeeded in gaining the passage of each section individually, saving Clay's compromise. The California statehood legislation then passed on August 18. Dr. Gwin, courtesy of his friend Douglas, had achieved his dream; he was a United States senator. He officially took his seat on September 10, 1850.

Even though it was late in this congressional session, Dr. Gwin wasted no time. He had three overarching goals: he wanted a coastal survey to facilitate the shipping trade; he wanted an intercontinental railroad to tie the West to the rest of the country; and he wanted a way to monetize the gold bullion in order to make California a leader in international financing.

On September 19, 1850, Dr. Gwin took to the floor of the Senate. He introduced a bill to establish assay offices at Sacramento and Stockton.[24] Gwin clearly saw that the branch-mint bill was dead on arrival in the House. Tying San Francisco to the New York City bill had been a mistake. Now something must be done or the chaotic money situation in California would only grow worse.

Senator Gwin also introduced a second bill, authorizing the coinage of large rectangular gold ingots in the denominations of $100, $250, and $500. The fineness would by .980 with 20 parts alloy of copper and silver in any mixed proportion or either alloy alone. The weight of these ingots would be adjusted to contain the same proportional amount of pure gold as contained in the circulating gold coins of the country. The bill was ten pages in length and contained language and provisions consistent with the Mint Act of 1837. It addressed such issues as acceptable tolerances for variances in weights and fineness and charges for toughening the gold when the bullion contained metals that rendered it brittle or unfit for coinage.

Gwin even addressed the appearance of these gold ingots. On one side would be stamped the year, weight, and fineness, and an impression emblematic of liberty with the inscription "Liberty." The ingot would also have some distinguishing mark to designate by whom it was assayed and where. On the other side of the ingot would be stamped the value along with an impression of an eagle and the inscription "United States of America." On all six surfaces, tracery of fine curved lines would be added to prevent sweating or shaving of the gold. This work would be the duty of the engraver.[25]

Where in the world did Dr. Gwin get the details to craft this legislation?

• • • •

Richard Sears McCulloh had had enough of waiting on Robert Maskell Patterson. On July 1, 1850, McCulloh wrote to Secretary Meredith, setting forth the merits of his process for refining gold and offering to provide any additional information that might be desired. McCulloh was proposing to replace the old system, which combined nitric acid with two pounds of silver (improvements over the years had cut the silver requirements by a pound) for every pound of gold to produce pure gold while recovering the silver.[26] McCulloh's process substituted zinc for the nitric acid and silver. Meredith forwarded the letter to Patterson. In this manner, McCulloh was forcing Patterson to respond. The Mint director replied to Meredith that neither he nor any of the officers of the Mint were acquainted with the results of the process. Since Patterson had been aware of McCulloh's experiments while the latter was still at the Mint, he was walking a fine line in this response. Patterson had no opinion of the merits of the process until its details were known and it had been tried on a large-scale basis. Patterson showed no intellectual curiosity about the process in this letter to Meredith. He was going to take no initiative, limiting his actions to only those required by his superior officer.

Unaware of this exchange, McCulloh moved to protect his process and further advance its commercial prospects. He filed a caveat with the patent office, an official notice of intent to file a patent within one year. It required a description of the process without an examination for patentable subject matter and without a requirement for patent claims. He also retained legal counsel, who advised him that special legislation would be required to permit the government to acquire the rights to use his process. Accordingly McCulloh petitioned both houses of Congress, offering to sell his process. Senator Dickinson received this petition on July 6, 11 days before his Committee on Finance recommended that the Mint law regarding gold coin alloys not be altered.[27]

Just because Patterson was not seeking information from McCulloh about his process did not mean that he did not want to know about it. Franklin Peale wrote to his brother Titian in the patent office for those details on July 9. He also let the cat out of the bag in that letter to Titian, alluding to the possibility that the Mint had been working on a similar, if not identical, process as McCulloh.[28] This explains Patterson's coy behavior.

At this point, James Booth met with McCulloh. Booth told him that he believed he was working on a process along the same lines as McCulloh. He had actually worked a few hundred pounds of gold with zinc in various ways. Patterson had shown Meredith's letter to Booth and he had told the director that he was pretty sure what the caveat would contain. Patterson speculated that McCulloh would ask a large amount for the rights. Booth responded that he thought the process would be worth it. Booth told McCulloh that they should combine forces and proceed ahead jointly.

After the meeting, McCulloh wrote a letter to Booth, stating that he had succeeded on a small scale with his process. He was encountering difficulties with the brittleness of the recovered pure gold but he soon expected to overcome them.[29]

En route to Washington, McCulloh called on Patterson at the Mint on July 28. He explained details of the process and showed Patterson a draft clause that he was seeking to have inserted in the all-encompassing civil and diplomatic appropriation bill that would be passed by Congress before adjournment in September. Patterson had no objection to the legislation but remained noncommittal about what course he would take in its regard as director of the Mint. Patterson suggested that McCulloh write to him from Washington so that he might formulate an official reply to be shown to the congressional committees. Upon arriving at the Capitol the next day, McCulloh altered his approach; an official letter from Patterson against his process would kill the deal. Instead, McCulloh wrote to Patterson privately; Patterson refused to respond.

McCulloh's plan of attack suffered a major setback on August 21, 1850. In a vote of four to three, the House Ways and Means Committee decided not to consider purchasing McCulloh's process. The decision was purely due to personal politics. McCulloh's father, in his official capacity as auditor at the Treasury, had opposed a claim arising from land that Georgia took from the Creek and Cherokee Indians in the 1830s. Robert Toombs of Georgia, who sat on Ways and Means, killed the measure as personal payback. There was hope in the Senate but the odds were now against McCulloh gaining the appropriation.[30]

Meanwhile, Booth was working the kinks out of his process. He had a partner; Henry Morfit, a well-connected Washington attorney, was fronting for his son, Campbell, an established chemist and former student of Booth's. Now aware, due to McCulloh, of the brittleness issue within the process, Booth backpedalled from his proposition to McCulloh that they proceed jointly. He casually told McCulloh that there was no hurry in forming a partnership. In fact, Booth was on vacation at the beach, free from the concerns over the growing bullion inflow at the Mint. He was buying time to advance his process; he would then be in a better position to negotiate with McCulloh.

In August Booth filed an application for letters patent, a step beyond McCulloh's caveat. Patterson promptly wrote the commissioner of patents asking for an expedited review. On September 9, Booth and Morfit petitioned the new secretary of the Treasury, Thomas Corwin, to instruct the director of the Mint to compare the process of Booth and Morfit to any other used or known at the Mint and to report the particulars of that comparison to the Treasury Department. The study would also estimate the value of the process with a view toward acquiring its rights from Booth and Morfit. They were not bashful in this petition, extolling the virtues of their new process. It would eliminate the need for silver in the refining process. It would increase the Mint's monthly refining capacity to more than $10 million without the requirement of additional space. Also, the process was safe, easily executed by the workers, and produced no noxious fumes.[31]

From this position of strength, Booth informed McCulloh that they would proceed in competition with him if he did not accede to forming a union in which they shared equally the rights of each other's patented process. Outmaneuvered, McCulloh agreed. However, when the agreement was signed, there was one more partner on McCulloh's side: Samuel F. Butterworth. Butterworth had been the U.S. attorney for Mississippi under Van Buren. It was no leap of faith to conclude that Butterworth was fronting for Gwin in this deal. Gwin, for his part, would have assured McCulloh that he could get an appropriation through Congress. How had Dr. Gwin gotten involved in this deal?

• • • •

The deal done, Booth suggested that McCulloh refrain from contacting Patterson for his endorsement of the process. Officers of the Mint, meaning Peale and Patterson—although probably less so in the director's case—were hostile to McCulloh. Booth would handle gaining the director's support.[32] What Booth did not tell McCulloh during these negotiations was that the patent examiner had questioned some of Booth's claims and he was going to have to modify his application.[33]

Amidst all this jockeying for personal gain, the roof fell in on Robert Maskell Patterson. In July 1850, bullion receipts matched the refining capacity of the Mint. In August they hit $3,275,000 and continued to climb in September. Another expansion of the refining department was necessary just to stay abreast of the gold influx.[34]

To make matters worse, J.R. Chandler wrote Patterson from the House of Representatives on September 7, 1850. The bill authorizing the New York City branch mint was before the House for consideration. Delays in paying certificates for bullion deposited at the Philadelphia Mint were increasing. Chandler knew that vast amounts of California gold were in the pipeline. These circumstances were providing the House supporters of the branch mint with new strength. Chandler pleaded; two good facts were worth a whole day's argument. Chandler was going to stall and delay, hoping the press of adjournment might save them. Yet he asked in thinly veiled frustration what had caused the delays and why had the Mint not surged forward in production? Could the Mint handle the great influx of California gold and still meet the new demand for small coins? Chandler had not a clue that refining was the problem.[35]

Patterson panicked; he had no idea how to respond. He showed Chandler's letter to Jacob Eckfeldt and William DuBois, the assayers. They said what Patterson could not admit; for more than a year the Mint had been falling further and further behind in processing the raw California gold. That being the case, it would seem best that Chandler waive all opposition and allow the New York City branch mint to move forward. The trick with that strategy was to ensure that the appropriation truly restricted the New York facility to a branch mint and did not serve as a foundation for Philadelphia's replacement. Once the gold flow from California abated—as it surely would over time—there was always the risk that New York would replace Philadelphia, to the dishonor of those loyal to the main mint. As an alternative they suggested that Chandler make the point that the contest ought to be between San

Francisco and New York City. No one really opposed a mint at San Francisco; it posed no threat to Philadelphia. With San Francisco in place and Franklin Peale's expansions near completion, a New York City mint would be superfluous.[36]

The advice was logical. However, Patterson did not for a minute trust the New York congressional delegation to leave well enough alone if a branch-mint appropriation was restricted. Once they got their foot in the door, he believed Philadelphia was doomed. He prepared a letter detailing the expansions that Peale and Booth had implemented, hoping this would give Chandler the ammunition he needed to stall S. 24. He also took advantage of Booth's being in Washington—he was lobbying for an appropriation to fund the purchase of his process—to have the melter and refiner meet with Chandler to provide details and insights into the expected capacity improvements.[37] Chandler even asked that Booth stay in town to be on call for any questions that might come up concerning the Mint's operations. All this time, Booth was mum about his negotiations with McCulloh.[38]

It turned out that Chandler and Patterson had little to worry about over the New York City branch mint in this session. Phoenix from the Committee on Commerce made the report in favor of the New York location. He argued passionately that New York, as the premier American port, needed a mint to more effectively compete in world markets. That point was totally lost on congressmen from the rural interior of the country. The financial section of the report merely repeated the points presented during the Senate debate.[39] On September 28, two days before adjournment, the floor manager for the New York City Mint, George Briggs, moved that the rules be suspended so the Committee of the Whole could take up consideration of S. 24. The vote was overwhelmingly against him. The measure would be held over to the second session.[40] Before adjourning, Congress did appropriate $25,000 for the purchase of the process for refining gold currently being patented by McCulloh and Booth.[41] Gwin had upheld his part of the bargain.

• • • •

After he had arrived in Washington the previous February, Dr. Gwin began to make inquiries into the scientific aspects of the California gold being mined. He went to Joseph Henry, secretary of the Smithsonian, and to Dallas Bache at the Coastal Survey. With Bache he also wanted the California coast surveyed to establish lighthouses and to better delineate harbors. When it came to coinage questions, both men recommended Richard McCulloh. Here was the connection between Richard McCulloh and Dr. Gwin. From Bache this was a bit out of character. However, he had recently become irritated at Booth for poaching one of his assistants for Booth's private laboratory.[42] As for Henry, there was no love lost between the Smithsonian and the Peale family after the shenanigans of the South Seas expedition.

McCulloh had been only too willing to help Gwin. Over time, the two would become confidants when it came to matters of the Mint. For starters, McCulloh reinforced Gwin's idea to promote the production of gold ingots in California. All European nations except Great Britain used ingots. Most of the California gold would eventually end up in Europe. Would it not make sense for it to go there in the form of bars, avoiding the expense and delay of coinage? For California, a mint was indispensible, but the depositor should have the option of asking that his bullion be either coined or cast into ingots.

Once the branch-mint bill appeared bogged down in the House, Gwin had switched strategies, seeking assay offices authorized to make ingots only. The mechanics of the legislation authorizing the production of ingots could only have been prepared with McCulloh's help. That fact would have been immediately discernible by Robert Patterson.

When Gwin's two bills reached the Finance Committee, he learned that Patterson was hostile to the establishment of a large mint and assay office in California. In effect, R.M.T. Hunter spoke for Patterson. The Mint director had never been for any branch mints, feeling their production capacity was redundant. Nor was Patterson in favor of Gwin's bill for the production of ingots.

In an unusual move for him, Patterson wrote directly to Gwin, stating that the senator's ingot bill was fatally flawed. The Mint director aimed his criticism at the bill, section by section. Some sections were ambiguous, others were not expedient, and the remaining sections were impractical. As time in the session was short, Patterson would not give detailed reasons for his judgments. His principal problem was preparing ingots of specific uniform values as opposed to using individual weights and fineness to determine each ingot's value. He took issue with any engraving on the ingots. The particular character of the exterior of a cast ingot would be such as to prevent theft by shaving.

Patterson hoped that Gwin would receive the criticisms in the candid and courteous spirit in which they were intended and that the experience of the Mint in such matters would be considered important. In that regard Patterson offered a substitute bill. The whole tone of the letter infuriated Gwin; the letter stopped his bills dead in their tracks. Yet what Patterson was offering—the ability of any mint or assay office to make gold ingots of values less than $10,000 receivable as legal tender for government debts—was a better solution.

On the last day of the session, Gwin had no choice but to accede to the will of the Senate. The secretary of the Treasury was authorized to contract out the duties of assaying with the proprietors of some well-established assaying works in California who would be placed under the supervision of an assayer appointed by the president.[43] Augustus Humbert was promptly nominated by the president and just as promptly approved in the Senate.

It was better than nothing. California had lost before its representatives ever took their seats when the branch-mint authorizations for New York City and San Francisco were linked together in one bill. The resulting last-minute fix addressed the needs of the California miners but not the needs of the population in total; it would only serve to delay their acquisition of a fully functional mint.

• • • •

With the California economy fueled by gold dust, the need for assayers at the start of 1849 had been critical. Hand in hand with the assayers were the private mints. Coins of any type were thought to be an improvement over little bags of golden flakes. However, just as the people of North Carolina and Georgia learned, Californians were soon to discover that private assayers and mints were not all created equal, nor were they the answer to their problems. First to lose the faith of the people were the Mormon gold coins, but there were others.

F.D. Kohler and David Broderick set up the Pacific Company in the second half of 1849. They had come out together from New York, where they had been members of volunteer fire companies. These organizations were only a step or two above the notorious gangs of that city. Kohler was a jeweler by trade and Broderick a denizen of Tammany Hall. Colonel Jonathan Stevenson, who had commanded the unruly 1st New York Volunteer Regiment sent to California during the war with Mexico, bankrolled their operation. The Pacific Company immediately began purchasing gold worth $18 an ounce on the East Coast for $14 an ounce. They in turn coined the bullion, on a contract basis for various other entities, into $5 and $10 gold pieces with intrinsic values of $4 and $8 respectively.[44] When Broderick was voted into the state senate in the election of December 1849, they sold the operation to Baldwin & Co.[45]

Baldwin expanded the business, issuing $5, $10, and $20 gold pieces throughout 1850. While they were not nearly as aggressive as their predecessor company, their pieces were still short of intrinsic value by 2 to 3 percent. When independent assays confirmed this fact in April 1851, the owners took the first steamship available for the East Coast.[46]

Most private mints were not swindle operations. Theodore Dubosq, a Philadelphia jeweler, began his operation sometime in 1849. He used dies designed by James Longacre and cut by Peter Cross.[47] Unlike Baldwin, Dubosq coins came much closer to intrinsic value.[48] However, none of these mints operated a refinery, resulting in varying silver content across their coinage and making intrinsic value a hit-or-miss affair.

By far the most reputable of the private mints was Moffat & Co. John Moffat, a New York assayer, came to California in early 1849. He arrived armed with testimonials, the most important being from Robert Walker, the former Treasury secretary.[49] He set up a gold brokerage business in partnership with his former employees, Joseph Curtis, Philo Perry, and Samuel Ward. At first shipping their gold dust to the East Coast, they hit upon the idea of opening a private mint. The first issues were small rectangular gold bars stamped with their value. With the arrival of Albert Küner, a Bavarian cameo cutter, in July 1849, the firm began producing $5 and $10 gold pieces. The reverse of these coins bore an image of an eagle identical to those on similar denominations from the U.S. Mint. However, instead of the inscription "United States of America," these coins contained the abbreviation "S. M. V.," or Standard Mint Value. It was such a simple addition and yet it was a marketing masterpiece. While the coins suffered the same intrinsic-value problem as the Dubosq pieces, they were close enough to gain the public's confidence. Their coins held up reasonably well in assay tests run by DuBois and Eckfeldt at the Mint. Their fineness was a hair light, but the two Mint assayers failed to give a credit for the extra silver contained in their alloy. Moffat & Co. pieces quickly became the preferred medium of exchange for San Francisco merchants.[50] Still, they were not legal tender, preventing their use in paying debts to the government.

In an effort to improve the chaotic monetary system in the state and gain full value for the miners for their gold bullion, the legislature created the state assay office through a law enacted on April 20, 1850. No one was particularly surprised when Frederick Kohler was named the state assayer. Broderick, quickly accumulating political power, would go on to lead a faction of the California Democratic Party in opposition to Senator Gwin.

Two state assay locations were maintained, one in San Francisco and one in Sacramento. In spite of the political nature of this beast, the office functioned as it was intended, issuing ingots accurately in a range of values that held up when tested at the Philadelphia Mint. Among the brokers, the state assay office was an object of scorn for obvious reasons. It gave fair market value to the miners at the expense of the brokers.[51] However, there was one large problem: these ingots were still not legal tender. They were not accepted at the U.S. customs house in San Francisco for payment of import duties.

Thus, the situation that Augustus Humbert walked into in January 1851 was little improved from the early days of the Gold Rush. The Treasury Department had contracted with Moffat & Co. to perform the assaying work. That should have come as no surprise to those in the political mainstream. Gwin knew from his Mississippi days how

Fig. 110. This $50 gold piece, issued by U.S. assayer Augustus Humbert in 1851, used the eagle design developed by Charles Cushing Wright. Struck in Proof, this specimen still shows significant points on the eagle that failed to strike up. Had this design been used on the double eagle instead of Longacre's, there would still have been a serious issue with coinability.

important it was for a senator to control appointments in his state. He had gained the upper hand in this regard when his colleague, John Frémont, in a Senate lottery to determine the terms of the two senators, drew the short term ending with the adjournment of the Thirty-First Congress on March 3, 1851. To boot, Frémont, in spite of being married to Thomas Hart Benton's highly accomplished daughter, Jessie Anne, was too idealistic and politically inexperienced. The assaying contract was a political plum of the first rank that Gwin would not have overlooked. With the Walker connection in hand, Moffat had the inside track.

Humbert brought with him one die provided by C.C. Wright. Its image was a stylized eagle standing upon a rock holding a shield.[52] Wright was no exception to the rule about never discarding good design concepts. This eagle can only be what Wright intended for the reverse of the double eagle had he gained the engraver's position in February 1850. But it did not hold a candle to Longacre's eagle. The die itself was octagonal, intended for a $50 gold piece. For the other side, Humbert drew upon his jeweler's background, using an engine-turned device typically found upon watchcases. As these pieces were issued (fig. 110), they were quickly accepted and became commonly known as *slugs*. Once Humbert was in operation, the state assay office closed down.

Moffat & Co. immediately began advertising in the *Alta California* that they would be receiving gold dust for smelting and assaying, and forming the same into ingots and bars under a contract authorized by the Act of Congress of September 30, 1850. The presence of the supervisory U.S. assayer meant that the ingots and bars would have the United States stamp affixed to them.[53] This advertisement did everything but outright declare these bars and ingots to be legal tender. That much of this gold dust came out in the form of $50 gold pieces bearing the inscription "United States of America" only added to the misconception.

By mid-February 1851 another article claimed that by order of the secretary of the Treasury, these ingots and coins were to be received for duties and other dues by the U.S. government. Local bankers had also stated that the coins and ingots would be accepted at their establishments at their stamped value.[54] The perception of their legal-tender status was further enhanced when Butler King, now collector of the port, stated that he would accept them in payment of government duties.[55]

In fact, the authorizing legislation was silent on their legal-tender status. The contractor under the supervision of the U.S. assayer would "perform such duties in assaying and fixing the value of gold in grain and lumps, and in forming the same into bars, as shall be prescribed by the Secretary of the Treasury, and that the said United States assayer shall cause the stamp of the United States, indicating the degree of fineness and value, to be affixed to each bar or ingot of gold that shall be issued from the establishment."[56] There was nothing about legal-tender status here. There was really nothing authorizing the issue of the facsimile coins, the $50 slugs.

Every effort had been made to give the impression that this operation was a government-approved mint. While better than a private mint, it was still only an assay office. It put an end to the gouging of miners by unscrupulous brokers. It brought stability to local merchant transactions. However, it was only a matter of time until these slugs arrived at the Treasury in the East, causing an order to be issued forbidding their acceptance for government debts. The people of California in total were only marginally better off with this assay office than before and when that reality set in, there would be anger and increased pressure for a full-fledged mint.

CHAPTER 26

BESIEGED

James Ross Snowden, treasurer of the U.S. Mint since 1847, was the first to go. It should have come as no surprise. The new president, Millard Fillmore, was a politician first. His Treasury secretary was from the same mold. In spoils politics, believe it or not, there were rules. If you replaced someone from the opposition party, you could expect to be replaced yourself if the opposition party regained power.

The man behind this removal seemed to be Congressman Joseph Chandler of Pennsylvania, the liaison for Patterson and the Mint in Congress. Snowden knew he was in the crosshairs and tried to muster support where he could. J.B. Trevor, longtime cashier at the Philadelphia Bank and former state legislator, was the most influential Whig supporter of Snowden.[1] He cited the fact that Snowden had remained aloof from politics while at the Mint. Others pointed out that he had maintained good relations with the Whigs of Philadelphia and New York who had dealings with the Mint. In the end, Trevor said it best: if they removed Snowden they would convert him into an efficient opponent. Furthermore the Whigs gained nothing by replacing him.[2] Unsaid was the fundamental reason that Trevor, as a Whig, was supporting Snowden. Snowden's father-in-law, General Patterson, had been a longtime director of the Philadelphia Bank, resigning in 1847 to fight in the Mexican-American War.[3] However, these pleas to reason did no good; Snowden was dismissed.

Fig. 111. Without the Philadelphia ties of his predecessor, Secretary of the Treasury Thomas Corwin was free to deal with Robert Maskell Patterson as he pleased.

Treasury Secretary Thomas Corwin (fig. 111) was not finished. Throughout the summer, Longacre had been in limbo, waiting to see if the other shoe would drop, costing him the engraver's position. Corwin wrote confidentially to Longacre asking for details of the attempt to remove him the previous winter. Answering on October 3, 1850, Longacre minced no words, accusing Peale, based upon the technical nature of the complaint against the engraver, of being behind the conspiracy to remove him. Longacre offered to make available to Corwin his formal written rebuttal of that complaint, prepared at Meredith's request in February.[4]

Matters began to boil immediately after Longacre's communication and Richard McCulloh seemed to be in the thick of things. On October 12, McCulloh asked that Longacre query George Eckfeldt for details surrounding the medals Peale had made for generals Taylor and Scott, including how much Peale had been paid for this work. McCulloh cautioned Longacre not to tell anyone that the information was for him.[5] Then, Longacre received a hand-carried note from Secretary Corwin on October 16, asking for any information regarding the business of the Mint that he should know. He wanted facts in relation to the proper conduct of the Mint and he wanted copies of any correspondence with Meredith.[6]

Longacre recognized he was now in an extremely delicate position. He wrote the secretary the next day asking for an appointment in Washington.[7] Two days later McCulloh sent Longacre his copies of his correspondence with Patterson complaining about Peale's medal activity and refusing to advance the necessary gold.[8] The coordination between the two men was all too smooth. The messenger of the hand-carried note had to have been McCulloh. Regardless, Corwin now knew he had a problem at the Mint.

Perhaps Robert Maskell Patterson knew what was going on behind his back or maybe he just had a sixth sense. He caused a petition to be drawn up, addressed to Corwin, urging that he be retained as director of the Mint. In addition, the petition made the somewhat questionable point that none of the officers, excepting the treasurer, had been subjected to change on political grounds. Nine prominent Whigs signed it, including J.R. Ingersoll, the man Chandler had just replaced in the House.[9]

• • • •

In the middle of this brewing storm, Patterson received a letter that promised to have serious consequences. Dr. Gwin had been infuriated by Patterson's opposition to his bill to make ingots of specific values. Before he left Washington at the end of the first session of the Thirty-First Congress, he sat down with Richard McCulloh to review Patterson's letter and his suggested substitute bill. Still he waited before responding. With the short time between sessions, he was not returning to California, journeying instead to his plantation outside Vicksburg. In Gwin's eyes, Patterson had stepped out of his bounds in opposing Gwin's bill as well as the branch mint for San Francisco. Gwin felt that Patterson had crossed him. His reply now to the Mint director needed to firmly defend his position.

The senator flatly rejected Patterson's proposed substitute bill authorizing ingots of specific fineness but varying weight. He called it a limited system for European bankers designed chiefly for international exchanges that Gwin considered antiquated and, on the whole, inadequate and inadvisable. Gold was a staple production of California. Given that the Constitution prohibited states from coining money, it behooved the United States to extend every facility to California for the inspection of that gold, to certify its weight and quality and to stamp it to that effect.

Gwin was absolutely not buying that the Mint would have difficulty maintaining the weights of the ingots necessary to produce them in specific amounts. It was a matter of arithmetic, whether it was a coin of $10 value or an ingot of $10,000 value. Furthermore, Gwin doubted that Patterson would assert that it was more costly to produce a single ingot of $10,000 compared to one thousand $10 gold pieces or ten thousand $1 gold pieces. He also noted what was to become a major issue for the Mint: Patterson had found it both expeditious and economical to convert the gold pouring into the Mint into double eagles as opposed to $1 gold pieces.

Gwin took an indirect shot at Peale in rebutting Patterson's rejection of engraved scrollwork on the proposed ingots. While they might seem impractical to the chief coiner, he firmly believed that the ingenious and skillful artisans of Philadelphia could contrive machinery adapted to this purpose and that it would be neither very complex nor very costly. The mechanical skill of the United States was fully adequate to the fabrication of rectangular ingots or coins covered with impressions and tracery with a degree of beauty and perfection far surpassing that of any of the coins previously struck at the Mint. It was work that could readily be done in New York if Patterson could not accomplish it at the Mint or in Philadelphia.

Dr. Gwin did not stop there. He tore into flaws in the Mint Act of 1837. In his bill, Gwin had proposed that the assayer verify the weights as well as the fineness of the ingots. Presently the treasurer handled that job. Gwin pointed out that the law left the allotment of work assigned to each Mint officer undefined and subject to the administrative regulation of the director. Gwin was utterly opposed; it should have been prescribed by law. When an officer took an oath to perform the duties of his office, he had the right to know definitively what those duties were. Any conflict between officers with unclear or overlapping duties could give rise to embarrassing difficulties unless fixed by law. That statement had to jump out at Patterson. Clearly Gwin knew of the recent goings on with McCulloh and Longacre.

Gwin also dissected Patterson's complaint that the standard deviations of allowable weight and fineness were too tight in his proposed bill. The senator simply stated that in large ingots the great advantage of numbers of pieces to compensate for errors was lost. The skill of the officers therefore had to be tasked to the utmost to secure a rigid uniformity in compliance with legal standards. On the other hand, an overly generous deviation limit exempted the officers from exercising their highest skill and fidelity; it could also tempt them into dishonesty and criminal activity.[10]

It is highly doubtful that Robert Maskell Patterson had ever been addressed on such blunt terms. Furthermore, Gwin's arguments came from a firm foundation and understanding of the Mint's operations. The gentlemanly Patterson was no match for Gwin's iron fist within the proverbial velvet glove. There was simply no answer to Gwin's powerful objections.

• • • •

Richard McCulloh had been stung by Booth's assertion that Patterson was only slightly less hostile toward him than Peale. Peale he understood, as the feeling was mutual. Of the director however, he had expected more; at the least, Patterson should have maintained his objectivity. As a result, McCulloh felt isolated from the Mint.

Booth, now understanding that his observation had pushed McCulloh too far, tried to backtrack in a letter dated September 21. All the officers were desirous to see the two men's processes carried out. Booth did not expect them to throw any impediment in the way unless it would be the manner of determining the cost of the present and the new processes. Patterson's reluctance really stemmed from not wanting to do anything unless officially required, lest he give umbrage to others. However, if officially required, the Mint director would give a true and honest reply. If the secretary of the Treasury was to contract with Booth and McCulloh, he must be satisfied with the quality of each process based upon information provided by the Mint. Booth closed by volunteering that there was no room at the Mint at this time to run the necessary experiments to meet this requirement. The melter and refiner blithely stated that he could make the trial anyway in a few days.

This communication did not assuage McCulloh's feelings. He did not understand why Patterson continued to drag his feet in testing the processes, given the obvious pressing need to enlarge the Mint's refining capacity. McCulloh dismissed the need to assess costs until after the trials had been completed. He saw this issue as a wedge used by Peale to delay and derail their efforts. In fact, he closed the door on Booth's efforts to soften his attitude about the Mint. McCulloh knew each of the officers; he stated with finality that he had correctly estimated and justly considered each of them.

Nothing happened in October at the Mint. There was correspondence between the two parties discussing whether to sell their processes to the government and take the $25,000 appropriated. McCulloh's father got into the mix, negotiating on behalf of his son. Campbell Morfit wanted to take the money and run; however, none of the other partners were ready to sell out yet. J.W. McCulloh, in relaying these negotiations to his son, noted that the bullion fund at the Mint and its branches had now reached $5.5 million. He could not understand why somebody at the Mint was not moving more aggressively to procure a rapid and cheap refining process.[11] That comment from his father seemed to set Richard McCulloh off, bringing his hatred of Franklin Peale to a boiling point. In fact, McCulloh wrote his friend Longacre that month that he regretted having anything to do with Booth's appointment. He believed that Booth had deceived him; Booth was a weak man and a tool of Peale.[12]

• • • •

At this point Richard McCulloh went off the deep end. Yet it was premeditated. His brother, John, was an attorney in New York City. This was becoming a family affair. An anonymous letter was sent to the editor of the *New York Express* and was printed on November 1, 1850. The *Express* was a Whig organ and its editor had strong ties to Washington. This missive was for the president's eyes.

To the Editor: Our National Medals.

Medals struck in honor of our heroes in war are monuments of their fame and our country's history. Upon such the highest skill in art is usually exercised and no labor or expense is spared. The medals of Napoleon are exquisite and served to improve not only the fine arts in France but also in Europe. The medals of our Revolutionary War were struck in France. Those of the War of 1812 were executed in this country by artists under the supervision of the mint. They were well done but they did not compare to those of the French for the Revolutionary War heroes.

The first medal of the Mexican War, ordered by Congress, was presented to General Taylor for the battles of Palo Alto and Resaca de la Palma. It was executed at the mint, or rather by some of the officers of the mint in a style too inferior to be worthy of criticism. The head is said to have been reduced in a copying lathe such as is used for turning gun stocks, etc. from a rough model; the reverse is merely an impression from one of the old dies prepared originally and used for a medal from the War of 1812 with the letters of the inscription being crudely altered. The second medal to honor General Taylor for the battle of Monterrey was manufactured in a similar manner. Both are reported to have been made without the assistance or cooperation of the engraver of the mint or any other artist and by machinists only.

Such work, so mismanaged by incompetent persons for the selfish pecuniary gain was an outrage upon the military glory and the arts of our country. The wretched style in which it was done seems to have opened the eyes of some of the military gentlemen at Washington. When the succeeding medals were ordered, the task of preparing the dies was taken from the mint and confided to C.C. Wright, Esq. the accomplished die-sinker and engraver of our city.

Of the medals engraved by Wright, we will now speak only of the first two, the others we may hereafter describe and criticize. They were ordered about the same time, one for General Taylor for the battle of Buena Vista and the other for General Scott for the battles of Vera Cruz and Mexico City. They both are medals of workmanship far superior to anything executed in this country but still falling short of the best French style. The heads of Taylor and Scott are both admirably executed; on the reverse the battle scenes are well done but the small horses are rather stiff and even with faulty anatomy. Still the effect of the whole is very good and the touch excellent. Of the Scott medal, the design is highly ingenious, perfect and beautiful. It is said to have been devised in the Bureau of Military Engineers by Dr. Humphreys; a wreath or chain of ovals encircles the center piece, representing the capture of Mexico city, and each oval is itself a wreath marked with the name and enclosing an engraved relief of its proper and successive battle. This medal is certainly the most magnificent and the most honorable ever presented by our country for it commemorates not a single battle but an entire campaign.

That of General Taylor represents only the action of Buena Vista. When the dies were finished they were sent to the mint and the original medals were struck in gold; they were of equal size and about four times as large as any previous medal executed by order of our government.

This matter is worthy of attention as furnishing evidence that the boasted superiority of the mint at Philadelphia and its arrogant contempt for the skill of our city, must be abandoned by the government for the latter, whenever it requires anything to be done of more than ordinary perfection and merit. It also serves to show how official relations may be perverted and the abuse rewarded instead of being exposed and punished.

"An Artist"

Wright immediately saw the article in New York and clipped it for Patterson. He was more than willing to correct the inaccuracy concerning the dies being taken from the Mint and confided in him. Patterson had only to tell Wright what he should write to the newspaper. Wright also observed that no artist wrote that letter. Wright might not know who wrote the letter but there could be little doubt in Patterson's mind.[13]

Outside of Wright, it was as if McCulloh's letter had fallen upon deaf ears. There was no official reaction, no official inquiry. McCulloh was prepared, releasing a second letter to the *Express*, published on November 14.

To the Editor

An article appeared in your evening paper a short time since setting forth the disgraceful manner in which the medals ordered by Congress to be presented to General Taylor were executed in the Mint. The writer of the article has foreborn to inform the public of the full extent of the abuses practiced in the Mint at Philadelphia with reference to the manufacture of medals.

For some time past the *Officers of the Mint* have been in the habit of making medals not only for the

> Government to be distributed to the Indian tribes or presented to our victorious Generals, but also for *private firms* and *corporations*; and this business is said to have been carried on for their *profit* and to an extent which has added largely to the compensation of their offices.
>
> It does not appear by the published laws of the United States that Congress has ever given authority to persons employed in the Mint thus to convert it into a *workshop for their gain*, nor even that medals may be made in the Mint for the Government, as a source of pecuniary benefit to its salaried officers. But, however that may be, there certainly can be no sufficient valid excuse offered to justify those officers in employing the facilities of the Mint at the expense of the United States to make medals for private persons and institutions, and for their own gain thereby interfering and competing with the legitimate art and industry of the country to the disadvantage thereof. Such protection if protection with a vengeance! The whole business is corrupt, and the officers engaged in it deserve the severest censure. And if the President has overlooked such official misconduct, the Congress should see to it, and deal with those who have thus abused the responsible stations they occupy as they just merit.[14]

Against this backdrop of indirect attack, Patterson was once again overwhelmed by the incoming gold bullion. This time he flinched. The capacity of the refinery was inadequate; the bullion fund was too high for comfort. Politically he did not feel he could take many more hits. On that same November 14, he authorized the melter and refiner to take the silver content of the gold ingots prepared for coining to the maximum legal limit of 5 percent.[15] With a stroke of the pen, so to speak, Patterson had added $1 million to the Mint's refining capacity.[16] It would buy him time that he desperately needed. Once Peale's capacity expansion was completed, there would be additional space for more furnaces. It would cost the depositors the value of their unrecovered silver but that was small change in Patterson's eyes versus the cost to the government of the interest on the ever-climbing bullion fund.

This time McCulloh's letter hit home. Fillmore queried Corwin for details three days later. Patterson's answer was a defense of the activity. It had evolved over time in response to congressional acts authorizing medals. At first the work was done in France; then it was shifted to the Mint using outside artists. More recently attempts had been made to accomplish the work through mechanical means, using electrotypes and the portrait lathe. Beyond procuring suitable dies for the work, the mechanical means of striking the medals outside the Mint were completely lacking. Consequently, the department always put this work in the hands of the chief coiner and paid him for the extra work. At various times that officer obtained permission to do the same things for states, corporations, and individuals.

Over the past three years this branch of the art had advanced, particularly in New York and Boston, and there were engravers doing admirable work. Patterson suggested that instead of complaining, friends of the anonymous author should apply to the department at once for the next job of this kind. A medal was now due for President Fillmore and Patterson suggested that the preparation of a die and, by inference, the design be given over to a competition among outside artists. Then the die could either be utilized at the Mint or at an outside facility to strike the medal. The department could judge, as a result, whether a change in practice should be considered.

Patterson pointed out that the secretary of the Treasury held the power to forbid or restrict the striking of medals at the Mint. In regard to the charges that the chief coiner profited from his position, Patterson held a letter from Franklin Peale stating that the use of machinery, meaning the screw press, was the only advantage awarded to him and that it did not in any way interfere with Mint operations. Longacre would certainly have taken issue with that statement had he been consulted.

Patterson added that there was no predisposition within the Mint to retain the business. C.C. Wright had been used for the most recent Taylor and Scott medals. Had he been known to the Mint earlier, he would have been used for the first Taylor medals.[17]

Patterson's use of the term *department* in his response was vague. He failed to address the aggregate amounts paid to the chief coiner for his medals work, dwelling only upon the smaller issue of the use of the screw press to strike the medals. The use of Mint laborers in the process was omitted. In short, Patterson addressed only the tip of the iceberg, there for all, including Corwin, to see. Also he had suffered a complete memory lapse in his assertion that Wright was unknown to them before 1849. Nevertheless the response was enough to tamp down questions for the time being.

• • • •

Meanwhile anger and suspicion continued to well up in McCulloh's breast. Booth let slip in an offhand manner that Patterson would prepare a report for the president and secretary of the Treasury once the refining experiments were completed. However, he stated, the experiments progressed slowly due to the burden of increased amounts of bullion arriving from California. Booth still hoped to get to the experiments in a week or two. This excuse was to become a refrain. The experiments were always just a week or so away and bullion backlog was always the excuse for the delay. It did not help that, now in November, Booth also wanted to sell out to the government. He was concerned, and rightly so, that once the Mint had enough capacity in hand with the old process there would be no incentive to purchase their processes.

This was the first that McCulloh had heard of Patterson preparing a report. He would not comment on anything that Patterson would propose or state until he could see that report. As to selling out, McCulloh wisely pointed out that the existence of an appropriation did not mean that there was a willing purchaser on the other side, regardless of capacity in place. McCulloh also reminded Booth that having the capacity in place was only part of the equation. Their process was much cheaper than the Mint's. What he overlooked was that this savings would not accrue to the government, given that refining costs were born by the depositor.

McCulloh pressed again in mid-November for progress on Booth's experiments. As an aside, he told Longacre that there was something brewing; the studied evasive replies of Booth indicated trouble was coming. He intended to go to Washington in the middle of December for six weeks to "attend to affairs."[18] To this query, Booth responded he had found a way to finish McCulloh's processed gold—in other words, to toughen it. So far it was successful but he needed another two weeks. At the end of the month, Campbell Morfit again pressed McCulloh to consider selling their processes to the Mint. Time was of the essence as improvements in competing processes were constantly being made. The group should be prepared to sell as soon as the Mint report evaluating the two processes was issued. McCulloh countered that the Mint report had not been made and would probably never be made. If made, the report would be adverse. Peale's wishes would outweigh other matters at the Mint. The chief coiner had neither any interest in its success nor any love for McCulloh.

In the first week of December, Booth was more forthcoming to McCulloh on the status of his experiments. He had set aside $100,000 in bullion during the summer on which to experiment using McCulloh's process. He had just depleted that stock. Patterson had been present whenever Booth informed him that experiments were going forward. Only once had the zinc process yielded a toughened gold; all other results had produced gold too brittle for the coining process. Booth was now running 1,000 ounces of gold with 2,000 ounces of zinc, trying to toughen the gold directly in the melting pot. Booth's process had worked well except that given the press of his daily refining requirements, the time he had for "making solution" was never enough. Booth was now experimenting every day except when repairs were going forward. He was not prepared to take any action until either or both of the processes had been shown to be successful.

There was a reason for this sudden burst of energy on Booth's part. Secretary Corwin was including in his annual report to the Congress at the end of December a statement to the effect that testing of a new refining process was underway and, should results equal expectations, the Mint's capacity to refine gold bullion would double to $8 million per month, well more than future probable receipts.[19]

However, Booth's failure to resolve the brittleness issue was enough to raise concerns in McCulloh's mind. He turned to the melter and refiner at the New Orleans branch mint. McCulloh had recommended Dr. M.F. Bonzano, a friend, for this position. Bonzano, at McCulloh's request, refined 29 ounces of bullion with zinc. The New Orleans melter and refiner enthusiastically wrote back that the resulting gold was perfectly tough and all was satisfactory. That was enough for McCulloh; he would bypass Booth, whom he now suspected of being unduly influenced by Patterson and Peale.

On December 23, 1850, McCulloh wrote to Secretary Corwin relating the delays to date. He expressed frustration that the Mint had not diligently pressed forward with an evaluation of the two alternate methods. McCulloh also related the successful results using his process at New Orleans. He asked Corwin to instruct Patterson to try each process under someone designated by the secretary, who would then report the results to Patterson for transmittal to Corwin. That same day, Bonzano reported to McCulloh that four more experiments, each using thirty ounces of gold, had been successfully completed at New Orleans. Yes, the process was satisfactory but Bonzano did not calculate the wastage, absolutely necessary for its comparison to other methods of refining gold.

With these added results in hand, McCulloh again pressed Corwin at the beginning of the new year to take action at Philadelphia. Booth had every facility at hand for trying McCulloh's process on a large scale, and yet he had taken no such action.

McCulloh's frustration with Booth appeared in full view in a letter dated January 4, 1851. McCulloh had heard nothing from Booth since December 5. He had been expecting a report from Booth at any time on the melter and refiner's experiments. McCulloh now curtly requested that report. Again he got excuses. Booth had been preoccupied with the year-end closing of his accounts. At the same time, deposits in December had hit $5 million. Booth could make a report now but it would not be satisfactory. He was erecting a test furnace with a 3.5-foot-square hearth to test McCulloh's process. Booth stated that he had not erected this furnace earlier because it would have interfered with the work of the Mint. The furnace was nearly complete and Booth expected that he would be able to try it at the close of the next week.

Once again Booth had delayed and once again results were just a week away. With thinly veiled anger, McCulloh pointed out that instead of pursuing experiments that would validate either or both of their refining methods, Booth had, over the previous three months, engaged in expanding the capacity of the old system. If, in fact, Booth's process was attendant with difficulties, Booth owed it to McCulloh to inform him of such. As for McCulloh's process, he had waited expectantly for Booth to pronounce it superior, as he had done the previous summer before the two men had entered into their agreement. McCulloh was now prepared, with 48 hours' notice, to demonstrate his process.

Booth took great exception to this letter. McCulloh was fully aware that Booth had a duty to the government as an officer of the Mint to perform his tasks using the process at hand. McCulloh was also aware of the difficulties associated with experimenting in a confined space. In spite of these obstacles, Booth had persevered to the best of his ability. Booth flat-out questioned McCulloh's assertion that in 48 hours he could demonstrate his process; it could not be done on a working scale in that time frame. Booth, now reduced to making transparent excuses, asserted to McCulloh that prior to the mint expansion just completed in December, there was no place where such a test could be done. The test furnace was now nearly complete, and Booth expected to be able to report back favorably on both processes the following week.

On January 11, 1851, McCulloh got what he wanted. Corwin ordered that the gold refining processes of McCulloh and Booth be tested by skilled workmen in the presence of McCulloh and Booth. The delays associated with testing McCulloh's process had already been the cause of many complaints. Therefore, the work should be completed as soon as practicable. Patterson was to report to Corwin, stating when the tests could be conducted and the time they would take along with any observations.

Patterson was defensive in his reply to Corwin. The experiments had been pursued. They had not been successful. McCulloh's process had yet to produce an ingot fit for coinage. It can be inferred from that statement that Peale would be the judge of whether an ingot was suitable for coinage. Patterson attached a letter from Booth detailing the efforts to date. Again, Booth took note of the problems associated with toughening the gold using McCulloh's process. The modification that McCulloh suggested to deal with the brittleness issue required a large cupel furnace for which there had been no space at the Mint until the completion of the expansion project. Patterson quoted Booth, who once again promised that the questions involving McCulloh's process would be resolved in a week or two. Booth prognosticated that McCulloh's process was better than the Mint's but that his process was better than McCulloh's because it required less acid. In closing, Patterson pointed out that while he certainly was obligated to seek out more efficient refining methods, he hardly could have suspended existing operations in pursuit of that goal given the influx of California gold bullion. However, in the end, Patterson could not contain himself, pointing out that Treasury had never referred McCulloh's process to him for examination and the work to date on that process had been prosecuted under the director's own authority.

Meanwhile, McCulloh was back on Booth's case. McCulloh could not understand why Booth continued to keep him in ignorance of the difficulties Booth was encountering with his own process. It irritated McCulloh that Booth had veered from McCulloh's patent as he saw fit without heeding McCulloh's views. He took issue with Booth belaboring his claim; it would only take 48 hours to validate his process. The two men also sparred over who recommended what to correct the brittleness of the gold in McCulloh's process. In his note back to McCulloh, Booth cautioned that using a cupel furnace ran the risk of volatilizing the gold, giving unacceptable wastage. However, Booth closed his comments on an optimistic note; he was warming the new furnace as he wrote and would test its melting capacity next in preparation for starting the experiments on a large scale.

Matters between Booth and McCulloh finally took the ultimate nasty turn when McCulloh, in a very long letter recapping their relationship dated January 27, requested that a trial of both their processes be conducted in his presence. McCulloh ended the letter by enclosing a dollar gold piece that Booth might use to pay for a copy to be made of a letter from McCulloh of the preceding year, a copy of which McCulloh had failed to retain for his records and that Booth had repeatedly promised. In a stilted letter on January 30, Booth replied that his duties as melter and refiner were superior to his private interests. The tenor of McCulloh's recent letters was interfering with Booth's discharge of his official obligations in regard to both his regular duties and his special duties of examining the alternate refining processes. As such, Booth now requested that their correspondence cease and any further communications in relation to the operations of the Mint be made through an official medium. Booth also returned the gold dollar; he would get around to providing a copy of the missing letter at his leisure. Needless to say, the partnership was over in all but legal formalities.

This letter infuriated McCulloh. In typical fashion, on February 5, 1851, he fired a letter off to President Fillmore. It was tedious in nature, detailing each and every step leading up to the formation of the partnership with Booth and the subsequent disintegration of that partnership. Only in the final paragraphs did McCulloh get down to the real purpose of his missive: Patterson's hostility toward McCulloh—and therefore his process—had been caused by McCulloh's objections to Peale's illegal medal business. A fair trial was not to be had, resulting in a gross wrong to McCulloh and a heavy loss to the bullion depositors, who must reimburse the Mint its cost of refining. While an injustice had been done to McCulloh, he left it to the president to take such action consistent with Fillmore's sense of justice.

McCulloh wasn't finished. That same day he wrote to Corwin, revealing that the instructions given by the secretary of the Treasury for a test of each process in the presence of Booth and McCulloh had been ignored. Because of that action, McCulloh had laid the whole subject before the president for his consideration. He suspected that Booth's process was a failure. However, should tests of the two processes now be implemented, McCulloh would be unable to attend as classes had resumed at Princeton.

Corwin now pulled back from McCulloh. It was Assistant Treasury Secretary William Hodge who wrote a week later to convey Patterson's report on McCulloh's process. Patterson stated that McCulloh's process was a success in terms of practicality. It would produce malleable gold satisfactory for coining. However, its feasibility in relation to other competing processes was yet to be tested. Another experiment would be conducted within the next several days to assess the expense, labor, time, and wastage associated with using this zinc process. An objection to the process had been "suggested": the hazard of loss of gold through volatilization. When melted with other metals, zinc had a property at a certain temperature of escaping into the atmosphere.

For McCulloh, this report only reinforced his belief that he would never get a fair trial and that Patterson was behind the delays. Again writing to Corwin, McCulloh correctly pointed out that Booth had at length found McCulloh's process satisfactory for refining gold. Why Booth had not come to this conclusion sooner, given his initial positive reception of McCulloh's process, was a source of frustration. As to Patterson's *hypothetical* assertion that zinc might escape into the atmosphere, carrying gold with it, McCulloh agreed that that could be the case if the process was carried out with gross carelessness or willful mismanagement—but not if done with skill and care. Furthermore McCulloh had had a conversation with Campbell Morfit and he had learned that Booth's process was a failure. McCulloh considered their partnership at an end.

Corwin waded in one more time, calling Patterson to account for McCulloh's lack of presence during the tests. On March 18, Patterson wrote that his excuse was supposing McCulloh to be entirely in Booth's confidence and knowing that Booth also had an economic interest in the process. It was very far from Patterson's thoughts that McCulloh harbored suspicions that the tests would be conducted in an unfair manner.[20]

Two years later, Booth related what had happened at the Mint during this period. He had reported to Patterson on February 6 that both processes had overcome the problem of brittleness. In turn, he recommended the adoption of McCulloh's process at Philadelphia and that his process, which was more flexible, be held for use in California if a refining operation were established there. The existing process generated a "very large noxious and disagreeable vapor." It was largely unavoidable, injurious to the workers, and objectionable to those living in the vicinity of the Mint. The process was labor and fuel intensive. On the other hand, McCulloh's process—substituting zinc for silver—saved time, fuel, and labor.[21]

Patterson then requested that Booth test both processes, and particularly McCulloh's, for wastage. Having a financial interest, Booth excused himself from the supervision of this experiment. Instead, Patterson and his son, Bob, supervised the men. On May 9, 1851, four trials were conducted using McCulloh's process; they generally showed an unusual loss of gold. The metal had been toughened in a reverberating furnace, where air current might have caused loss through volatilization, so a fifth trial was conducted. This time the zinc combined with gold was melted in a covered black lead crucible; however, it again showed the same incidence of wastage.[22]

Now McCulloh had three problems to overcome: he needed to terminate his partnership with Booth legally; he needed clarification of the $25,000 congressional appropriation that had been earmarked for methods of gold refining being patented to McCulloh and Booth together; and he also had to focus on wastage.[23]

McCulloh had his work cut out for him. Yet the biggest obstacle was Patterson. The Mint director was going to continue to stonewall McCulloh to avoid having to purchase the process. Given the additional refining capacity coming on line at the Mint, time was on Patterson's side. With refining costs passed through to the depositors, there was just not any political impetus to push McCulloh's process on the basis of cost savings.

In his annual report to the president on January 27, 1851, Robert Maskell Patterson put a positive spin on his problems in the refinery. Very extensive enlargements had become necessary. Now on the point of completion, the capacity for refining was expected to reach $6 million to $7 million per month using the current separating process. This large increase had been obtained with many delays and interruptions, while the stream of deposits was constantly on the rise. Although the changes indicated were prosecuted with the greatest of energy, the Mint had not been able to avert a large accumulation of uncoined bullion. However, Patterson had no reason to doubt that the means were now at the Mint's disposal to work down the accumulation and provide prompt payment of all future deposits.[24] The usually cautious Patterson had just contradicted Corwin's statement in the secretary's report to Congress.

How Robert Maskell Patterson must now have wished that he had followed Peale's recommendation to outsource refining in 1849. Instead, much to his regret, he had followed his natural inclination to seek a scientific solution to his problem.

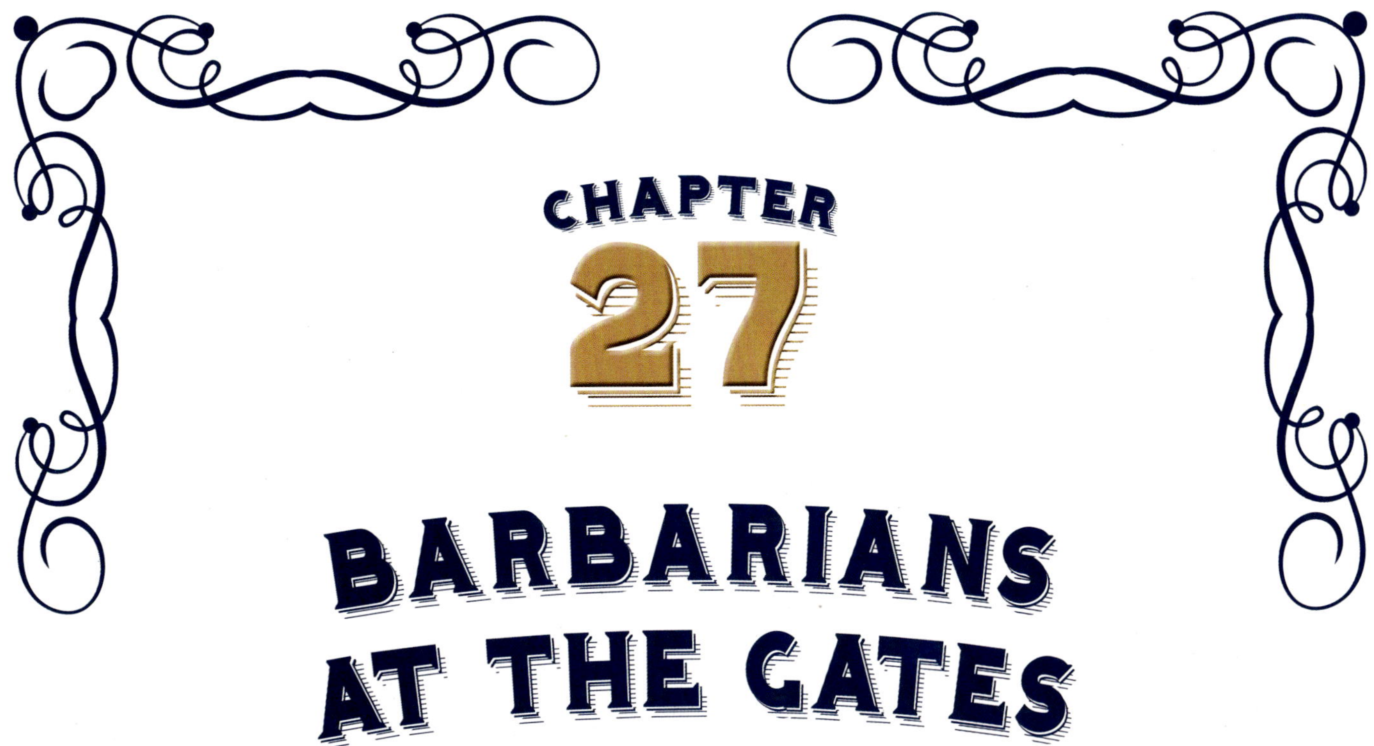

CHAPTER 27

BARBARIANS AT THE GATES

On December 2, 1850, the second session of the Thirty-First Congress convened, and S. 24 was back with a vengeance. Since the adjournment of the first session, backers of the proposed branch mints had been actively mustering support in the House of Representatives. For Patterson and Chandler, the only good news was that this bill must be passed in the House before the abbreviated second session adjourned on March 3, 1851. If it did not pass during this time, it would die.

The issue acquired additional urgency when President Millard Fillmore, in his report to Congress, repeated the call for the establishment of a branch mint in California at the earliest possible date. A bit late to the party but feeling the heat nonetheless, Fillmore noted that the miners were being compelled to sell their gold at a large discount. Until this mint was established, he asked that Congress authorize ingots issued by the assay office in San Francisco to be accepted in payment of government dues.[1]

George Briggs (fig. 112), a New York City Whig, was again the floor manager in the House for S. 24. He was a hardware dealer whose only political experience, apart from the first session of the Thirty-First Congress, had been one term in the Vermont legislature. In mid-December he made his first move, asking that S. 24 be made the order of the day for January 13, 1851, and that it remain so until disposed of. His motion carried.[2]

January 13 came but S. 24 was not on the agenda. Instead, J.R. Chandler took the floor to seek a resolution

Fig. 112. A freshman representative from New York City, George Briggs was an unlikely choice to lead the charge against the Philadelphia Mint.

of inquiry. In consequence of the increased supply of gold from California and Australia, the valuation ratio between gold and silver was rapidly diminishing. Silver was becoming an article of merchandise rather than currency, with the result that the nation's silver coins were once again exported in large quantities. Chandler wanted the Commerce Committee to take up the issue of reducing the value of U.S. silver coins by either diminishing their weight or increasing the proportion of alloy to stop this outflow.[3] Patterson had always been in favor of divorcing at least some of the U.S. silver coinage from intrinsic value. In the European market, silver was selling at a 2.5 to 3 percent premium over gold. However, the timing of this motion was certainly suspect. The *New York Herald* called it a strange proceeding.[4] Its intent appeared to be aimed at taking the silver-coin shortage off the table in the coming debate. Even better, if the attention of the House could be diverted to the still-thorny issue of the valuation ratio, that debate would sink any consideration of branch mints in this session.

Chandler gained a suspension of House rules to allow consideration of his resolution. Surprisingly, discussion turned to changing the composition of the gold dollar to allow for a larger diameter. Several members protested and Chandler refused to allow his resolution to be amended. It then carried the House.

Chandler did not have long to enjoy the fruits of his delaying tactic. Briggs gained approval on January 29 for the House to form a Committee of the Whole to consider S. 24. The fight was on. Briggs opened with a stinging criticism of the Philadelphia Mint's performance in 1850. Receipts of gold bullion coming into the port of New York that year had been $30 million. Philadelphia had coined almost $28 million in gold, of which more than $23 million had been double eagles. Bullion on deposit at year end in Philadelphia was more than $5 million. Had the Mint struck a sufficient amount of small coins to meet the nation's needs, the backlog of bullion would surely have swelled to $15 million. The Mint simply did not have the necessary capacity to meet the country's needs. What Briggs missed in this argument was the simple fact that any additional small coins, meaning silver, that the Mint struck would have promptly left the country to capture the valuation disparity with gold.

Briggs then switched gears. Two-thirds of customs revenues were collected at New York City. At the present rate of growth, New York City would become the financial capital of the world in 25 years. Briggs expected bullion receipts in 1851 to approach $50 million. The secretary of the Treasury had offered to establish an assay office in New York and pay the cost of transporting the bullion to Philadelphia for coinage. Given that the flow of bullion was expected to continue to increase, this transportation expense would be sufficient to pay for the establishment of a branch mint in New York in two years' time. Briggs believed that the construction of a branch mint in San Francisco would not much impact this bullion flow as that facility would coin gold otherwise destined for foreign mints. Plausible or not, that was the reasoning Briggs was applying to a potential San Francisco branch mint.

Briggs closed by asking that the bill be passed with no amendments; otherwise it would have to go back to the Senate where the press of time would likely prevent it from being reconsidered. As Briggs took his seat, Chandler stepped forward to submit a substitute bill. Clearly Chandler was going to push for the assay office solution. However, the chairman of the Committee of the Whole ruled that the amendment could not be considered until the original bill was perfected.[5] Chandler now must fight the bill on its merits.

The next day, Chandler still held the floor. He had no problem with a branch mint at San Francisco; it was necessary to the region and would be advantageous to the country. However, the justification for a mint in New York City must be for public necessity. Either the capacity of

Fig. 113. While Robert Maskell Patterson told Congress that the Mint stood ready to coin any and all gold, the Forty-Niners waiting at its front doors in Philadelphia had a different story to tell.

the Philadelphia Mint must be insufficient or the loss and inconvenience of transporting the bullion from New York to Philadelphia too great.

Chandler acknowledged that the Philadelphia Mint had not kept up with demand in 1850. However, the work of enlarging the Mint did not commence until the necessary money was appropriated in late May. Over the summer, Mint production had been suspended from time to time to permit the expansion work. Refining did not recommence until October. In December the Mint coined slightly more than $4 million. Chandler felt capacity was now at $75 million to $100 million and could easily be increased with little to no expense, aside from the cost of melting pots and furnaces.

A now better-educated Chandler admitted that the problem at Philadelphia had been separating the silver from the gold in the refining process. However, the Philadelphia Mint had overcome that difficulty and was ready to separate and coin gold bullion from anywhere in the world. Chandler also went to great lengths to point out that the delays were not the fault of the coining department. Their machinery had not been at work one-quarter of the time. The congressman quoted a letter from Patterson: "Whether we shall coin one million or one hundred million; whether double eagles or an equal proportion of all pieces, is simply a question of more or less hands. We have machinery enough, steam enough and room enough." (fig. 113) That argument put the onus on the secretary of the Treasury, since Patterson must get his permission to hire those additional hands.

Chandler also noted that a large last-minute deposit while the Mint was down for its annual account reconciliation had distorted the amount of unrefined bullion at year end. A backlog of $2.6 million on December 10 was more realistic.

Chandler acknowledged that most of the gold bullion was received in New York City. Why shouldn't it be? The federal government spent millions subsidizing steamer lines based in New York to compete with the British. As a consequence, these steamers sailed right by Baltimore and Philadelphia. While Chandler was not questioning the reason for this subsidy, he was against having it used to gain leverage against Philadelphia. As to the issue of transportation, Chandler questioned Briggs's economics. Adams & Co. would transport $20 million to $30 million in gold both ways for $15,000. A branch mint in New York would cost $1 million to $2 million, with annual operating expenses of $160,000. There was no way the transportation savings would justify that expenditure.

Chandler also attacked the weakest point of Briggs's argument: the San Francisco Mint would have no impact on New York's branch. Why would anyone transport gold bullion by steamer to New York when he could have it coined in San Francisco? The very idea of a mint in New York was ridiculous.

Chandler even reached across the aisle to notoriously tight-fisted Democrats. Current demands on the Treasury Department were high and the money proposed for a New York branch mint was an unneeded drain. Capacity was sufficient at Philadelphia. Corwin had recommended that owners of bullion in New York be paid promptly at an assay office that would issue Mint certificates receivable for all dues to the federal government—in essence, paper currency. Where was the need?

With this last point made, Chandler took his seat. He had countered each argument made by Briggs. The real debate would now begin.

First up was John Van Dyke, a New Jersey Whig. He proposed an amendment to move the New York mint to Jersey City across the Hudson River. It would cost only one-quarter as much. Moreover, the "densely thronged" population of New York might, at some unguarded moment, attempt to assail the mint during a time of public disaster or difficulty. Additionally, New York was already overrun with patronage. Locating the mint in Jersey City would remove the idea entertained by some about government establishments of corruption. It should be located in the incorruptible state of New Jersey. Laughter echoed in the chamber of the House at this comment. With that note of levity, the energy of the debate drained from the antagonists. The House agreed to extend the debate for three more hours the next day and adjourned.

On January 31, James Gore King delivered an emotional rebuttal to Chandler. A Whig from New Jersey, he was well suited to the task. He was a Harvard-educated Weehawken banker and railroad investor. His father had been a Federalist senator and a presidential candidate in 1816. King began with a bit of history. The permanent establishment of the Mint at Philadelphia occurred in 1828 and was very much driven by its proximity to the Bank of the United States. It was King's belief that the two entities would have been more useful to the country and subject to fewer objections had they been located in New York City.

King did not buy Chandler's estimate of the Mint's capacity. He could only judge the institution by what it had done, which was coin double eagles that were comparatively useless for general commerce. These coins did not displace paper currency and did not enter into circulation. King took a passing shot at the curious timing of the expansion; he would not say that these improvements had taken place—or had been hurried on—for the purpose of affecting this debate. King's point should have been to question how a mere $20,800 could produce such an increase in capacity. In the matter of the transportation quote from Adams & Co., King was quite sarcastic. He suspected the quote's purpose was to keep the Mint in Philadelphia and that the ultimate charges would approximate what the market would bear.

Next King artfully waded into the numbers from a New York point of view. Allowing interest on the coinage delay, he calculated that the annual transportation charge would approximate $135,000 to $225,000—and there certainly would be delays. Differing with the numbers Chandler had provided, King stated that the Mint had started 1850 with a deposit backlog of $1.5 million and ended up with $7 million based upon receipts of $27 million. King noted that Chandler said the New York Mint would cost $2 million. A voice in the back of the chamber cried out that it would cost only $1 million. King now weighed in that the $225,000 appropriation in the Senate bill was reasonable. He had returned to the transportation charges and backlog when Chandler foolishly interrupted. The Philadelphia representative had just learned from the Mint that the backlog was down to $4.7 million. King jumped on this, belittling Chandler's data. A mint that boasted an annual capacity of $75 million to $100 million in one month of "extraordinary effort" had made hardly a dent in the backlog.

Now King switched to the issue of depositor delays at Philadelphia. A depositor had a choice when bringing gold bullion to the Mint. He could have double eagles in 20 days or he could have dollar gold pieces, which would pass easily in daily trade, in 40 to 60 days. King had heard of instances where silver was sent to the Mint and small-denomination coins asked for in return, invoking a delay of two to three months. In fact, in 1850 only two-thirds of the silver deposited at the Philadelphia Mint had been coined, and this occurring at a time when silver coinage was in drastic short supply. What King did not understand was that this silver had been diverted into the refining process for gold bullion.

King's argument was weakest when it came to the San Francisco mint. He flatly stated that a mint at San Francisco would not render one needless in New York. A branch in San Francisco would coin only what was needed in California. The remaining gold would be melted into bars and transported to the East Coast. This volume would add greatly to the business of a branch at New York.

King's argument against the Treasury scheme to establish an assay office in New York and issue certificates receivable in payment of public dues for gold deposits was strong. The amount of funds available to Treasury would depend upon the influx of gold and not upon the revenue of the country as collected in coin, primarily from customs duties. Millions of dollars of government paper money would be issued without restrictions, receivable at every point where a debt to the government was payable. These certificates would in effect become a federal paper currency, something the government had avoided since the Revolutionary War.

Again, Chandler made the mistake of interrupting King, this time to ask him a question. Did the representative suppose that coining could be done any faster in New York than Philadelphia? King believed 10 or 12 days delay was enough, especially under the improved mode of parting gold from silver. The invisible hand of Richard McCulloh, now domiciled in New Jersey, had been at work here. King noted that in a letter written to him on January 4 by Patterson, the director stated that it took 29 days to return coin for bullion deposited there. King observed that the Philadelphia Mint seemed to have awakened from her long sleep since 1792, and had brought forth a large coinage in December and January, stimulated perhaps by the fear of a branch mint in New York.

At one point during the debate King asked, "Is it worthwhile for the country to be put to the inconvenience of having insufficient mint when our golden age is just commencing?"

Now the debate degenerated into attacks on both sides and an extensive back and forth of amendments and counter-amendments. A South Carolina representative asked whether it would be a mint in California or New York City. If California was preferable, establish it there; if New York, establish it there. But establish it where it would do the most good for the country. However, he exhorted them to not aggrandize one place, and to not concentrate all the means of the country in one location. J. Phillips Phoenix, a veteran in the sparring to gain a New York mint, even accused Patterson of using the double eagle to lessen the strain upon the Mint's capacity.

A Pennsylvania representative noted that the travel time between Philadelphia and New York was down to four-and-a-half hours. Did it make sense to erect a mint in New York to save nine hours and $15,000 in transportation costs? It would take three years to build a mint in New York. By that time the gold mines in California might be as dry as the gulches from which the gold was gathered.

Thomas Bayly, a Democrat from Virginia and chair of the Ways and Means Committee, now stood to make a statement. To him, the debate had dwindled down to an unseemly scramble between New York and Pennsylvania as to which would have the public patronage connected with the mint. Ways and Means members had discussed this question and were opposed to making any appropriation for a mint in New York City; the condition of the public treasury would not support it.

Sensing that the tide was turning against New York, George Briggs moved that the Committee of the Whole rise, stopping the debate. His motion failed. There was a motion that the bill not pass and a counter motion that it pass. The chair ruled both motions out of order. There was an amendment on the floor to move the New York location to New Jersey. It was considered and failed.

Joseph Cable then took the floor to offer an amendment. The Ohio Democrat was in over his head. He wanted the act to instruct the mint in New York to strike gold pieces in specific proportions to one another, limiting double eagles to one quarter of total gold production. He declared that the "scoundrelism of the mint in Philadelphia at this time is very proverbial." There were roars of laughter in the House, releasing the tensions that had built up over the two-day debate. Unfazed, Cable plowed on. The Mint had issued double eagles at the expense of all other coins. Their design was to draw away gold coins from circulation among the people. It was the plan of the bankers, stockjobbers, and speculators to withdraw gold coin from circulation so that it would not compete with their shinplasters. Laughter again erupted. The country and its politicians had moved beyond the rhetoric of Jacksonian populism. Cable bulled to a conclusion, saying he was finished with their system of plunder. Laughter followed but the amendment passed.

There was also an amendment to establish a branch at Charleston. It was ruled out of order. Bayly rose to say that Ways and Means had a solution that would require no new branch mints. They would authorize bars and ingots of gold, from $50 to $1,000, at the assayer's office. They were more convenient for commercial purposes than coins. The committee had agreed to the proposition almost unanimously.

Confusion swirled around the discussion. Finally the Committee of the Whole rose. Debate on S. 24 was now terminated. They had come to no conclusion and the House adjourned for the day.[6]

Four days later the House again convened as a Committee of the Whole to consider S. 24. James Brooks, another New York City Whig, had a motion on the floor to strike out the words *branch mint* and insert *mint* in S. 24 where it pertained to the proposed New York facility. It failed—a bad omen. Seizing the opportunity, Chandler offered a substitute for S. 24 that would establish a mint and assay office at San Francisco to strike gold, silver, and copper. In line with the Treasury's recommendation, it would also authorize the assistant treasurer in New York City to accept bullion deposits. Bayly immediately offered an amendment that gold bars and ingots issued by the assayer in San Francisco be accepted in payment of all government dues in California and Oregon at the value stamped upon them, for a period of five years. The chairman ruled that Bayly's amendment was a substitute for Chandler's substitute, and he again refused to allow a vote until the original bill was perfected.

There was a motion to strike the sections of S. 24 dealing with a branch mint in New York and instead insert that the mint be moved from Philadelphia to New York City. A point of order was raised that this amendment created a whole new bill and could not be acted upon in the Committee of the Whole. The chairman agreed and ruled it out of order. Brooks then asked if the bill could require that the equipment at Philadelphia be removed by January 1, 1853. That, too, was ruled out of order.

Brooks next moved to raise the appropriation from $225,000 for the New York branch mint to $500,000 in order to call attention to Chandler's ridiculous claim that the New York City operation would cost $2 million. Chandler rose to argue that the accounting numbers at Philadelphia did not capture all the expansion expenditures over the years. King then returned to the floor to amend Brooks's amendment, lowering the appropriation to $260,000. Chandler took the floor to rebut and was informed that he must limit his remarks to the two amendments, which were in turn rejected.

Isaac Morse, a Louisiana Democrat, now moved to amend the appropriation to $1 million. The needs of the country indicated that a mint should be located in New York and the mints ought to be placed where they were needed. The mint at New Orleans would deal with Mexican silver and California gold. If introduced, Morse would vote for the abolition of the mints at Philadelphia, Charlotte, and Dahlonega. It was the duty of the government to coin bullion in the places where it arrived in the country. The government had no right to force bullion owners to carry their bullion to the Mint at Philadelphia. An amendment to this amendment was then put forth to reduce the appropriation to $900,000. It was rejected.

Another amendment was made reducing the appropriation to $1—a backdoor way of reopening debate on the numbers justifying New York. In time this amendment was also rejected. Then Morse's original amendment failed, and more maneuvering followed. However, one amendment stayed on the floor for consideration: striking out the entire first section of the bill as it regarded a mint in New York City.

Fig. 114. Thaddeus Stevens showed his political acumen when he effectively called the question that killed the move to gain a branch mint for New York City.

At this point Thaddeus Stevens (fig. 114), having moved from the spoils politics of Pennsylvania to the national scene, took the floor for the first time in the debate. He was smart; opponents who underestimated him did so at their own peril. Stevens believed the House had made up its mind on this subject. To test that view, he offered an amendment to the amendment striking the first section. His amendment struck out New York and inserted San Francisco in the section to be stricken. It was absolutely bizarre. It was the only way to get around the arcane rules of the Committee of the Whole and to allow the House to vote down the New York branch mint.

Stevens argued that the country had four times the number of mints that it ought to have. The government had established the mint in Philadelphia and it was the responsibility of the individual to bring his bullion to the mint for coining. This was not an expense that the government ought to pay for. The Stevens amendment squeaked through: 79 ayes to 77 nays.

The amending went on for some time but the issue was settled as Thaddeus Stevens had foreseen. In the end,

Bayly won approval for his amendment, giving currency status to the bars and ingots coming out of the San Francisco assay office. However, when S. 24 finally passed, it was a skeleton of its former self. Senate reconsideration was out of the question.[7]

Throughout all the maneuvering in the House, Gwin had stood by helpless in the Senate. With the House decided, Gwin had little time to lose. On February 8, he introduced a bill to establish a branch mint at San Francisco; it was read twice and referred to the Committee on Finance. The committee reported back on February 19 with an amendment that was strictly a technical fix.[8] Henry Foote, Gwin's old colleague from Mississippi, wanted to know if there would be any debate. Gwin held his breath. Ewing stated that he thought not. Foote said he had important business yet to be considered by the Senate and would object if there was a debate. Senate rules required that a bill have no objections for it to be advanced and considered. Then the roof caved in. Isaac Walker, a Wisconsin Democrat, asked if this bill varied from the one passed in the first session. Gwin stated that the section pertaining to a mint in New York had been dropped. Walker cut him off, saying simply that it was not the same bill. The Senate had been engaged for several days on another topic of importance and this bill would interfere.[9] Walker objected. Gwin had run out of options to gain a vote for San Francisco. Additionally, there was no legislative authorization making the $50 gold slugs from the San Francisco assay office legal tender for government dues. Gwin would get the blame twice over.

• • • •

Not everything went Patterson's way in the Thirty-First Congress. In May 1850, during the first session, Senator Dickinson introduced legislation authorizing a three-cent piece. The idea was not new; it had been broached in the Ways and Means Committee of the House in 1849. The concept at that point involved a "silver" coin with a fineness of less than .500. Patterson had some patterns hastily ginned up but expressed concern that a coin of so little silver content would be easily counterfeited.

The bill that reached the floor in 1850 was well thought out. In a radical move, it broke from the requirement of intrinsic value. The coin would weigh 12.375 grains, proportional to the other silver coins, but would be composed of three-quarters silver and one-quarter copper, giving it an intrinsic value of 2-and-a-half cents.[10] In this manner the coin would circulate instead of being shipped to the melting pots of Europe. It would be legal tender for debts up to 30 cents. The Mint would pay out the three-cent piece in exchange for fractional foreign silver coins. Thus, once production began, the silver necessary to maintain output of the three-cent piece would come from the retired foreign fractional pieces. To promote the retiring of the foreign coins, the Mint would be authorized to pay reasonable freight to the depositors. Seigniorage profits would go toward defraying the Mint's contingent expense.[11]

Adding a new circulating coin at a time when the Mint was still struggling to coin the gold bullion being delivered was out of the question. In addition, the legislation called for a controversial companion one-cent piece of 75 percent copper and 25 percent silver. Still, Patterson had another pattern quickly prepared based upon the pileus designed by Gobrecht for Peale's commemorative medal, issued as the first steam-press coinage in 1837 (fig. 115). The bill never gained traction in the Senate, holding over to the second session.

The picture brightened considerably for the three-cent piece in 1851. In its second session, the Thirty-First Congress took up consideration of a law to reduce the postal rate from five cents for a one-sheet letter to a destination of under 300 miles to three cents, extending the destination distance to 3,000 miles in a move designed to subsidize communication throughout the vastly expanded country. At this point, support for a three-cent piece took hold. Deficient in intrinsic value, the piece was expected to stay in circulation and it would help facilitate the implementation of the new postal rate. As a result, a clause authorizing the piece was folded into the legislation. However, excluded from the language was the retirement of the foreign fractional silver and the section pertaining to the allocation of profits from the seigniorage.[12] The bill became law on March 3, 1851, the last day of the session.[13]

• • • •

James Longacre was still under close scrutiny at the Mint. There must be no repeat of his experience with the double eagle. He was ready, having anticipated the legislation in February. The law required the new coin be sufficiently different in design from the other American silver coins and that it contain the denomination, the date, and the inscription "United States of America."

Longacre's work progressed well. For the obverse, he settled upon a shield—his favorite motif—within a six-

Fig. 115. This design, taken from Peale's original steam coin-press medal, was simply a knock-off from the pattern $1 gold piece of 1836. So little effort was made on the design that the poorly punched "Liberty" was not even cleaned up.

pointed star. On the rim surrounding the star was "United States of America" and the date. The reverse held a large ornamental "C" encircling the Roman numeral III surrounded by 13 stars. This design for this tiny coin was simple and clean. However its size would soon earn the nickname *fish scale* from the American public.

Patterson had more worries than the design; the mechanics of implementing the new denomination had not really been addressed in the legislation. The Mint director's first concern was finding the silver to mint the coins. With silver coin leaving the country, Patterson was seeing only trifling amounts at the Mint. Furthermore, he knew that no one in their right mind was going to bring in silver coin at .900 fine to exchange at par for the new .750 fine three-cent pieces. How would he get them into circulation?[14]

By early March Patterson had settled down enough to make recommendations to the Treasury. He now had enough silver stock to initiate production. What he did not tell the Treasury Department was where the silver was going to come from. Effective April 1, Patterson ordered that silver alloy be cut back in gold coins to the prior levels used before the previous November. He had enough refining capacity now and if this stopped the Mint from working off the backlog of bullion, so be it. He did not really care.

At this point, he recommended that the treasurer of the Mint have the authority to purchase silver bullion for use in supplying the three-cent piece on an ongoing basis. The treasurer would exchange three-cent pieces for their legal equivalent in other U.S. coinage in bulk sales of no less than $30 and no more than $150. The Mint would pay transportation for up to 3 percent of the amount sold. Profits from the sales of these coins would go toward bullion purchases and transportation expenses.[15]

In this same communication, Patterson asked for guidance as to where these coins would be struck. The law merely specified the Mint and its branches. New Orleans could implement it but the branches at Charlotte and Dahlonega were not authorized by law to strike silver coins and had no bullion on hand. He also mentioned that the dies for the new coins were nearly ready and that specimens would be sent in a few days. Patterson received no definitive answer from the Treasury regarding his dilemma; they were taking his recommendations under advisement. In the meantime he was to prepare for a prompt and large issue of the three-cent piece. Patterson did get one answer; New Orleans was the only branch mint that would issue the new coin.[16]

Again the specter of Franklin Peale overshadowed this project. Longacre was preparing one set of designs. Yet Patterson intended to submit "specimens." The chief coiner wanted the pattern from 1850, which was associated with him as much as with Gobrecht, to be considered. Patterson consented, requiring Longacre to strike several of these pieces to be included for review by Corwin and the president. Patterson was giving Peale a shot at getting a design on a circulating U.S. coin. Longacre steamed at what he considered pure interference. What Patterson did not tell Longacre was that he had recommended that, given Longacre's official position as engraver, Longacre's design be chosen as long as no inferiorities were found. It was a weak endorsement of Longacre's work.

The president and the secretary of the Treasury decided on Longacre's design (fig. 116). Still, implementation questions remained in Patterson's mind. Secretary Corwin had not given him the authority to accept gold in exchange for the three-cent pieces. In his frustration, he reminded the Treasury Department that no one was going to trade silver for the little coin.[17] However, it really didn't matter anyway.

Fig. 116. Longacre's three-cent piece kept the design simple for the tiny tondo, resulting in a functional appearance.

CHAPTER 28

SACKED!

In February 1851, Dr. William McKendree Gwin was frustrated. The failure to gain a mint for San Francisco, as well as no authorization of legal-tender status for the output of the assay office, would cost him support of the miners and merchants at home. He laid the blame for this directly at the doorstep of the Philadelphia Mint.

Director of the Mint Robert Maskell Patterson had paid lip service to the supporters of a San Francisco mint, stating that California needed a mint—albeit a small one. Yet Patterson was also willing to see San Francisco go down in defeat in order to ensure that a branch in New York did not happen. There was also the issue of Patterson's clumsy handling of Gwin's legislation to authorize ingots in large denominations for financial transactions, including international trade.

Just as unsettling for Senator Gwin was the stonewalling and ultimate rejection by Patterson of McCulloh's improved gold-refining process. He should not have been surprised. An embittered McCulloh had come to Washington over the Christmas holidays of 1850, willing to share his anger with any and all who would listen. Now, Gwin's sweetheart deal with McCulloh looked worthless.

Indeed, Richard McCulloh had pulled out all the stops for his visit to Washington, going straight to Secretary Corwin to attack Franklin Peale. McCulloh detailed all of Peale's side business in the manufacturing of medals at the Mint during the former melter and refiner's tenure. It was a long litany—the Polk medal, the medals commemorat-

ing the Mexican-American War, and the private work for the Massachusetts mechanics' organization and the Franklin Institute. Corwin asked for details in writing. McCulloh obliged, backing up his assertions with copies of correspondence between Patterson and himself on the matter. He summed up the situation in a way that could hardly be argued.

> In extenuation, it may be stated, that the business of making medals in the mint originated many years since, in applications by the government to the coiner of the mint to prepare those needed by it, to be presented to the Indian tribes, or awarded by Congress to officers of our army and navy. A twig engrafted may be healthy at first, but it may grow to be a branch full of morbid excrescences, and poisonous to the whole tree. And certainly, the Government never could have designed that the Mint should become a factory, for the fabrication and sale of premiums to be awarded at agricultural fairs and industrial exhibitions.[1]

McCulloh's testimony was detrimental to Peale and highly unflattering to Patterson. Still, Corwin remained silent on the subject. Put simply, McCulloh did not have the political clout to affect changes at the Mint. Gwin did.

At this point in time, Gwin was negotiating with Corwin and Assistant Secretary Hodge over his Chickasaw Indian claims, which had been dormant since 1845. Gwin had used a go-between for some of the talks, while others had taken place directly between the three men. In the surviving correspondence, his tone with Corwin in achieving settlement and payment of his fees had been dictatorial.[2]

Had Gwin taken the opportunity to reinforce McCulloh's accusations and add some of his own? Had the two men coordinated their efforts? Gwin certainly had the temperament. There is no paper trail; Gwin would never have allowed that. Yet it is almost inconceivable that Gwin would not have taken advantage of a direct conversation with Corwin to attack the Mint and Patterson in particular.

McCulloh issued a memorial to Congress on February 24; it laid out the Booth correspondence as well as his own correspondence to Corwin pertaining to Peale's medals. Ostensibly, this memorial was in support of McCulloh gaining another congressional appropriation to purchase his refining process. But its revealing correspondence was there for anyone to read; it directly questioned activities at the Philadelphia Mint.

There was one fact that Corwin would not have divulged to Gwin. Much to his dismay, Corwin had learned through a communication from J.B. Trevor in Philadelphia that the bullion backlog at the Mint was vastly understated. As a prominent Whig and lead dog, so to speak, of the Philadelphia financial establishment, Trevor had the administration's ear. He was writing as chairman of the board of cashiers of the Philadelphia banks, which met twice weekly to function as an informal clearinghouse. In addition to the unrefined gold bullion held by the government at the Mint, which amounted to $4.7 million, there was another $6 million held by the banks on deposit at the Mint. Trevor said that Patterson intended to inform Corwin of this situation. Consequently, the banks were loaded down with Mint certificates issued to depositors against which they had advanced cash weeks previously. Moreover, much of their hard specie was flowing to New York in exchange for certificates issued there. The Philadelphia banks were badly short of coin. Clearly something had to be done.[3]

Sometime in late February 1851, Corwin determined that Robert Maskell Patterson had to go. The rumors of this possibility reached the Whig establishment in Philadelphia at the beginning of March. George Eckert (fig. 117), a Whig representative in the Thirtieth Congress and an ironmonger, jumped at the opportunity. His family company, later to be called Eckert and Brother, owned the Henry Clay, an iron-smelting furnace in Reading and one of the largest anthracite-fired furnaces in the United States. Eckert, like Patterson, had trained in the medical sciences, graduating from the University of Pennsylvania in 1824. He had briefly practiced medicine but, again like Patterson, his affinity was for the natural sciences.[4]

J.B. Trevor started the ball rolling with a recommendation supporting Eckert on March 5. If a decision was to be made between Patterson and Eckert, Eckert should be the choice. Eckert was well qualified, with knowledge of chemistry and metals. Trevor definitely felt a change ought to be made.[5] He followed up a week later, stating

Fig. 117. George Eckert and his brother-in-law pulled out all the political stops to gain the nomination over Stephen Colwell. Yet in the end, it was Colwell's reluctance to serve that threw the nomination to Eckert.

there was no question that Patterson should be replaced. He was behind the times. A man was needed that would infuse some vigor into the operations. This Mint, managed as it ought to be, should be ample to meet the needs of the depositors of gold bullion, rendering unnecessary the expenditure for another branch mint in a "neighboring city."[6] Here, in plain English, were the issues that had made Patterson vulnerable to the attacks of Gwin and McCulloh. Of course, it helped that Trevor was George Eckert's brother-in-law.

The bandwagon seemed to be rolling for Eckert. A petition in his favor was sent to the president. This petition included, among many others, the signatures of Ingersoll and Chandler, the two men in Congress who had worked closely with Patterson to thwart the New York mint legislation. It also included the signature of Stephen Colwell, a prominent Whig in the iron business.[7] He had been on the most recent assay commission, which met annually to verify that coin production adhered to legal specifications and tolerances for metal content. He had also just been made a member of the American Philosophical Society.

With a petition circulating, Patterson would have had to be a hermit not to know that his days were numbered. He tendered his resignation to President Millard Fillmore on March 15. Patterson did it with the gentlemanly grace that his peers would have expected of him.

> I have the honor to announce to you that in pursuance of a purpose long since matured, it is my intention at an early day to resign the office of Director of the Mint.
>
> The time which I have fixed on my retirement is the 30th of June next, at which day I shall have completed an official term of sixteen years. While, however, it would be a satisfaction to me to remain at my post for that period, my movements will be controlled so as entirely to meet your convenience, and if my resignation at any earlier day should seem desirable, it would be presented immediately upon an intimation to that effect.
>
> Considering the importance and responsibility of the duties devolving upon the head of the mint establishments, particularly at this time, I have thought it my duty by this communication, to afford you an ample opportunity for deliberation on the choice of my successor. Influenced by the same motives, I shall endeavor to withhold from the public any knowledge of the intended vacancy since you will doubtless prefer to be relieved from the importunities of the many incompetent applicants who would otherwise obtrude themselves upon our attention.[8]

Although Fillmore would have preferred Patterson leave the Mint sooner, he found these terms acceptable.[9]

Patterson now had time to influence the selection process. He knew that Eckert had the backing of the area banks. Under Patterson, the Mint had maintained its independence from these institutions. Would Eckert be able to stay out of the banks' back pockets? Also, in spite of the initial strong support behind Eckert, the man had baggage. For Eckert, tariffs came before party politics. In the elections of 1850, he opposed a Whig running for Congress because his opponent was stronger on tariffs that would protect Pennsylvania's iron interests. The Whig was defeated by 250 votes and Eckert shouldered the blame from the party regulars.[10] There was room here for Patterson to maneuver.

Patterson had another reason for staying involved. Eckert had competition from the former mayor of Philadelphia, Colonel Jonathan Swift. Swift was the epitome of a person Patterson did not want in the position—a politician with a reputation for hard drinking. However, Patterson had a personal reason for ensuring Swift's defeat.

Patterson had run afoul of Swift in his position as president of the Musical Fund Society. At the end of 1846, the Singing Hutchinsons performed at the society's Musical Fund Hall. These performers were noted for their abolitionist songs. During the performances, African Americans came into the concert hall. Though they were well dressed and conducted themselves appropriately, some members of the audience took offense. Citizens went to Mayor Swift to complain. He caved in to their demands, telling the Musical Fund Society officers that if a riot ensued, he would be unable to keep the peace. He prevailed upon the society's officers to take action. In reality, Patterson had no choice but to submit to the mayor's underhanded maneuver. The society was planning an important community fundraiser in the coming spring for major renovations to the hall. As vice president of the society, Franklin Peale sent a letter to the Hutchinsons stating that no African Americans would be admitted into their remaining performances.[11] The group promptly cancelled and left town. Worse for Patterson, the whole embarrassing story was picked up by the *New York Tribune* a week later.[12]

Patterson knew it was futile to advance his son, Bob, for the nomination. He had been hanging on in the hope of a Democratic administration in 1853, which would have greatly improved the chances of keeping the director's position within the family. He now turned to Stephen Colwell (fig. 118), a Whig he felt had the qualifications. Colwell was reluctant, given his early support of Eckert. Patterson called in his two brothers-in-law, the token Whigs in the family, to help with the Colwell nomination.

It might have only been a coincidence, but at this point, J.B. Trevor sent another letter that was forwarded to Fillmore. He complained that the Mint had been a family affair for more than 40 years. If Patterson had ever had any efficiency, he now lacked the energy and tact for the proper administration of the establishment. It was one last effort to diminish what remained of Patterson's political influence in Washington.[13]

Fig. 118. Stephen Colwell was the front-runner for the job of Mint director but he turned it down when he became subject to political infighting.

At this point, Colwell took a position. Others were putting his name up for the director's slot. They had done this without any encouragement from him, as he was not seeking the office and did not desire the position. He had a rule not to be a candidate for any office. He had endorsed George Eckert and still felt that Eckert was the best man for the job. However, others had put forth considerations that induced him to make an exception and allow his name to be used.[14] This was the opening Patterson needed. Samuel Moore, by now a leading anthracite coal miner, presented Colwell's name to Fillmore.[15] William Harris, Patterson's other brother-in-law, communicated with Corwin.

Patterson also called in American Philosophical Society members to support Colwell. Former secretary of the Treasury William Meredith signed a petition; Ingersoll switched sides; Professor Joseph Henry of the Smithsonian Institution and Dallas Bache wanted Colwell. A Colwell delegation went to Washington to confer on the nomination. Eckert even graciously recommended Colwell.[16]

The momentum swung to Stephen Colwell. He had the approval of both Corwin and Fillmore. By the first week in May, the nomination was his. Then, he unexpectedly withdrew his name in favor of George Eckert.[17]

Colwell had traveled to Washington to confer with Corwin on May 8. In spite of Eckert's public support of Colwell, there had been a whispering campaign by Eckert's friends against him. The most general complaint was that his nomination would hurt the Whig Party; Colwell did not believe a word of it. There was worse slandering, involving accusations to Fillmore's secretary of state, Daniel Webster, against Colwell. He found these particularly stinging since he held Webster in the highest regard. It hurt Colwell that Webster might be influenced to think less of him.

As Stephen Colwell returned to Pennsylvania, he made up his mind. He would have none of this politics of defamation. Most of all, he did not want to contribute to bringing the directorship of the Mint into the political arena. He cautioned Corwin that, while he supported Eckert, he could not condone the doings of his friends. This affair had been an infringement upon his rule; he could never again be a candidate for office.[18]

It took another letter from Trevor, pointing out that the leading Whigs in Philadelphia all supported Eckert now that Colwell had withdrawn, to swing a reluctant Corwin to support Eckert.[19] The nomination, in the form of a recess appointment, was made public June 9, 1851.[20]

• • • •

Among Patterson's last acts as director was dealing with damages to neighboring buildings from the acid fumes emitted from the Mint's refinery. Damp winds from the river were causing the acid vapors to precipitate upon nearby rooftops. In the case of the Presbyterian church next door, this acid rain had damaged the metal roofing to the extent that it needed to be replaced. The long-term fix at the Mint was even worse. They must either divert the vapors into the taller stack serving the steam boilers or acquire ground adjacent to the Mint to erect works that would capture the vapors. They opted for a short-term abatement, diverting the vapors and hoping for the best.[21]

Robert Maskell Patterson served his 16 years at the Mint with distinction and quietly stepped aside on June 30, 1851 (fig. 119). For the sin of staying too long for the sake of his son, Patterson had been cast aside. His family would always maintain that he retired due to failing health. That was the ending he really deserved.

Fig. 119. As a fitting tribute to a man who had left his mark upon the Mint, the officers and clerks gave Patterson a handsome medal recognizing his service. The medal had Peale's fingerprints all over it. Charles Cushing Wright engraved the obverse, an excellent likeness of Patterson. The reverse came once again from the reverse of the Winfield Scott medal arising from the War of 1812. Peale just would not let go of that design; the problem was that it was the only suitable reverse design in his inventory of medal dies.

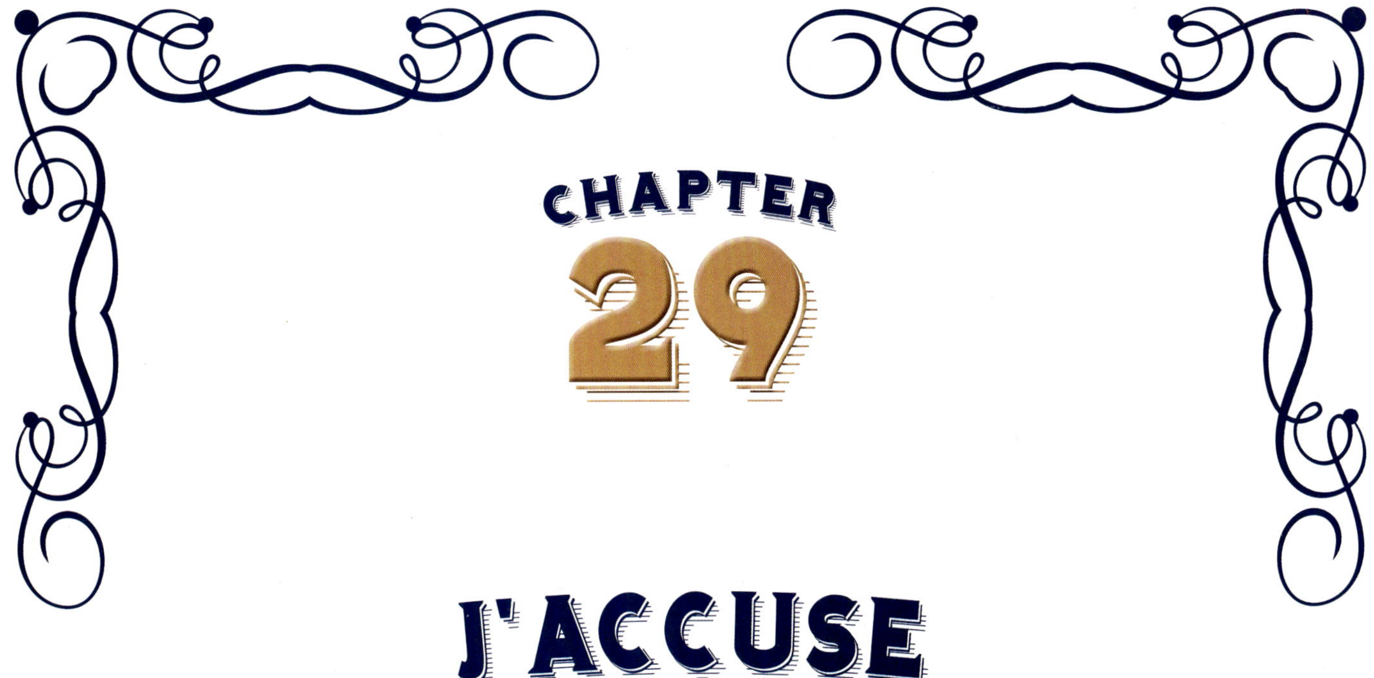

CHAPTER 29

J'ACCUSE

George Eckert was a wounded duck from the start. Reports would state that within weeks of his appointment, a personal tragedy left him adrift.[1] His brother-in-law, J.B. Trevor, had invested funds from the Philadelphia Bank in mining and transportation companies formed to exploit undeveloped coal reserves in upstate Pennsylvania in which he held a controlling interest. These advances were then secured by highly questionable bonds issued by the companies. None of these transactions had been posted in the bank's accounting records. This defalcation rocked the bank to its very foundation. Trevor had been awarded a bonus of $700 by the bank's board the preceding January; that same board was forced to demand his resignation on August 28, 1851.[2] Besides the personal trauma of the event, it left Eckert shorn of his political powerbase. Colwell's cautionary observation to Corwin proved to be prophetic.

Eckert's situation was also unique in that he shuttled back and forth between Reading and Philadelphia. The family iron operations were too important to completely divorce himself from their management. It was an ideal situation for Bob Patterson, the son of Eckert's predecessor at the Mint. If anything, he gained more authority because Eckert grew to depend upon him. Likewise, Franklin Peale felt no threat from the change. It helped that he seemed to have changed his political stripes and was now supporting the Whigs.[3]

Once again, Richard McCulloh entered the scene. His efforts of the preceding February to gain a separate congressional appropriation to purchase his refining process had been pigeonholed in the Ways and Means Committee.[4] He had no option but to wait out the changeover to Eckert before delivering his accusations of bias against Peale and the Mint to President Fillmore on August 1, 1851. He complained bitterly about the unfairness of the tests conducted at the Mint the previous winter. Booth had been absent for long periods from the Mint to attend to his personal affairs. Workmen who were not proficient in the new refining methods had conducted the trials. They had no working knowledge of his new process.

However, he reserved his harshest vitriol for Franklin Peale, citing Peale's animosity toward him. He called Peale's relationship with Patterson mysterious. He accused Peale of lavish and unnecessary expenditures without adequate appropriations. McCulloh also alleged that Peale meddled in the duties of other officers at the Mint and appropriated to his own gain that to which he was not legally entitled. Broad as these accusations were, there was more here than McCulloh had claimed heretofore in his diatribes against Peale. In concluding, he told Fillmore that he believed Peale had created many of the obstacles that had stood in the way of testing his process at the Mint. McCulloh now asked the president to order a trial of his process, to be conducted in his presence.[5]

McCulloh was awarded the action he sought. Eckert was chosen to investigate the charges of malfeasance against Peale and to report on the expediency of testing McCulloh's refining method in his presence. The Treasury Department asked that McCulloh cooperate with Eckert in this effort, to which he promptly agreed. It took Eckert, who was away from the Mint, a week to respond to McCulloh, asking that he detail the charges against Peale and provide testimony. McCulloh immediately came to the Mint to discuss with Eckert how to proceed. The Mint director wanted details in writing so that he could decide how the charges would be addressed in a hearing. McCulloh wanted Peale to have a chance to cross-examine, to present witnesses in his defense, and to have the benefit of counsel. Eckert deferred, saying that Treasury would make those decisions.

McCulloh immediately set about collecting the necessary documentation to support his charges from his sources within the Mint. This included asking James Longacre to provide details of Peale's interference in 1849 with his double eagle design and the subsequent meetings with Patterson and Meredith. Longacre complied, also providing copies of pertinent correspondence. This action revealed to Eckert and Peale that Longacre was a leak within the Mint. However, it soon became apparent that he was not the only one.

On September 4, to document his charges, McCulloh asked Eckert to provide cost details associated with the recently completed Mint expansion. He asked for the cost of the new steam engine and boilers, the tall chimney and its supporting flues, the new coining press for double eagles, and the new turning rolls and draw benches. It was clear that Peale's expansion had mushroomed well beyond its original scope and McCulloh was after the overrun against the appropriation. McCulloh also sought the accounting details behind the Polk medal of 1847. James Ross Snowden and William DuBois were the original sources of this leak. Finally, McCulloh asked for copies of all official correspondence relating to his refining process or matters at issue with Booth. That was a fishing expedition; McCulloh had already meticulously collected any correspondence that he got wind of on this subject.

There was enough information here to spur concerns by Eckert over Mint operations. On September 22, 1851, he implemented controls for the purchase of Mint supplies. While it went to all officers, the two most impacted were Booth and Peale. A purchasing requisition would be required on all supplies. When possible, items were to be purchased under special contracts through competitive bidding. Through his investigation of McCulloh's initial charges, Eckert had found something that he did not like.

McCulloh set out the details of his charges on September 24. Three could have been deduced from the broad charges: the Polk incident, the interference with Longacre, and the medals side business. The point about lavish and unnecessary expenditures of public money was new. The expense for the expansion had greatly exceeded the congressional appropriation. In addition, Peale's experimental streak had gotten the better of him. He had authorized new equipment that was inefficient and useless. Then McCulloh threw in two more specific examples from out of the blue. He knew about the trumpet-blowing sofa Peale had Mint workmen construct as a practical joke to play upon female visitors and the excessively ornamented balance case and stand made for the chief coiner's office.

McCulloh provided Eckert with the specification of charges on September 25. He stated that he would have been more prompt, but he had delayed, waiting on Eckert to provide cost details for the expansion and the transactions swirling around the Polk medal.

This missive put Eckert on the spot. He pleaded ignorance regarding the equipment costs. The steam engine, an expenditure of considerable size, had not yet been paid for. As it had been in service for something like nine months, that meant there was a performance issue. Additionally, the charges for many of the other items on McCulloh's list were included with bills that covered multiple items furnished by the same party and could not be easily separated. Eckert would provide these numbers as soon as they were available. He told McCulloh that the charges against Peale would be administrative, and he now wanted the names of persons that McCulloh wished examined. In other words, Eckert wanted to know McCulloh's sources within the

Mint. Poor Longacre was in the crosshairs. An administrative hearing would not necessarily entail cross-examination, nor would it require representation by counsel. Not surprisingly, Eckert also could not supply correspondence regarding the refining process that McCulloh did not already have. The Mint director also asked for time to consult with Treasury officials regarding additional tests of the refining process in McCulloh's presence.

Eckert and McCulloh met around October 20 to discuss the new trial of the zinc process. McCulloh wanted to conduct this test first, separating it from the charges against Peale and, by inference, Booth. By agreement at that meeting, McCulloh was to provide additional details on Peale's activities to Eckert.

Eckert was not forthcoming in this meeting with McCulloh. Once he had McCulloh's specification of charges in hand, he had a decision to make. The Mint director could either clean house or cover up. In reality, he had made that decision a week before his meeting with McCulloh.

On October 14, Eckert communicated with Thomas Corwin. If proven true, McCulloh's charges against Peale would make the chief coiner flagrantly unfit for duty. McCulloh had also charged Booth with being habitually away from his job at the Mint and biased in his testing of McCulloh's refining process. With regard to the charge against Peale, Eckert was unprepared to make a report. With his powerbase gone, he would have to be cautious in dealing with Peale, whose standing in the community was above reproach. Regarding Booth's absences, Eckert could not say whether Booth had been absent more or less than the other officers. Given that Eckert was going to split his time between Philadelphia and Reading, he had no intention of addressing this issue. However, Eckert went on to say that the melting and refining department's operations were conducted efficiently, with wastage within legal limits. That was as weak a defense of Booth as Eckert could give without condemning the man. As to the fairness of the experiments on McCulloh's process, he had not witnessed them and was reluctant to draw conclusions from those who had been present. However, Eckert did state that it was the desire of all those involved with the test to fairly assess the merits of McCulloh's process.

In moving forward with the trial, Eckert told Corwin that it was critical to assess if the gold melted with zinc was prone to loss through volatilization in such a manner that the conclusions would be beyond controversy. It was well established that melting these metals together at high temperatures did just that. The question was whether it was avoidable at a lower temperature while still permitting the process to work as intended. Fearing trouble, Eckert asked who would bear the loss of gold bullion should volatilization occur. Eckert wanted that burden placed upon McCulloh.[6]

Meanwhile, McCulloh immediately complied with Eckert's request for additional details concerning the Peale charges. It was the opening that he needed to put his accusations on record. The support that he submitted indicated that he had been active over the summer building his case. Particularly damning was the fact that, while Eckert could not provide details of the cost overrun for the Mint expansion, McCulloh thought he could.

McCulloh had stumbled upon a letter of Patterson's discussing the original appropriation. He had then mistakenly assumed the deficiency appropriation that covered estimated operating expense shortfalls for the 1850 fiscal year was the overrun on Peale's expansion project. It was one of the rare times that McCulloh factually erred.

Still, his gut instinct that money had been wasted on the project was correct. Under Peale's direction, the Mint workshop had fabricated a steam-driven draw bench for gold and silver strips. Its design was novel but it was doomed from the start. It dispensed with the horizontal pulley, drawing the ingot strip through a collar by means of a piston rod. Once the metal was extruded, the piston, free of resistance, was driven against the end of a cylinder, resulting in a violent explosion of noise.[7] The men called it Peale's steam gun. Peale said it was unmanageable. Parts were sent to Charlotte to make an ordinary draw bench; the remainder was useless and it was placed in the Mint's loft. The workshop also built a large lathe for turning chilled rolls; it failed in its trial. Peale ordered molds and pouring apparatus for casting large ingots from his nephew, Escol Sellers, in an attempt to expedite the refining process. The molds and pouring apparatus were based upon those in use at the British Royal Mint. However, they were not adapted to the rolling machinery, rendering them useless. Peale attempted to absolve himself of all responsibility for these boondoogles. Perhaps worse, Peale had prepared drawings and specifications for this machinery for which he was paid above and beyond his salary. Peale was an inventor with an artistic flair; his mind simply lacked the disciplined training of an engineer.

McCulloh went on to attack Peale's professional competence in the building of the balances in use at the Mint. Joseph Saxton, the man involved in the building of the original steam-driven coin presses, built these balances under Peale's direction. Saxton was perfectly capable of doing this work unsupervised. He went on to work for Dallas Bache at the coastal survey in Washington, making and repairing balances. However, Peale interfered with Saxton's design for the silver and gold balances in use in the Mint's assay room to the detriment of their performance. For his personal balance, Peale had gone so far as to attempt to have it gilded, set on a stand, and enclosed in an ornamental case.

McCulloh reserved the most serious allegations for Peale's personal conduct as chief coiner. He again brought up the Polk medal and the circumstances surrounding Peale's reimbursement. However, the personal chores that Peale used his men for were the most egregious. A number of men had been employed on the trumpeting sofa in

1846 or 1847. The copper trumpets were made in the rolling room and the springs came from the machine shop. One of the skilled mechanics spent two weeks making the mouthpieces and valves, and the exposed wood was painted to imitate rosewood. That was just one instance. Peale's house was virtually maintained by Mint workmen. They performed odd jobs, repairing window sashes, kitchen utensils, shower bath fixtures, and furniture. They built a trellis for the front of the home and constructed cast iron parlor tables. Mrs. Peale had a tambourine converted into a parlor drum. The men also built a folding music stand out of rosewood for use in musical performances. To rub salt into the wound, Peale seemed to have appropriated all of the undervalued old silver plate turned in at the Mint for himself, in contradiction to the past practice of allowing the other officers to benefit as well from this windfall.

There was also the question of Peale's extracurricular activities. Peale played an important role in supporting Robert Maskell Patterson's fundraising drive for the Musical Fund Hall expansion in 1847. In doing so, he freely used the Mint's workforce. The fundraising culminated in a great fair. Peale's men spent two days building an apparatus for jugglers' tricks. On the appointed day, Peale, dressed as a Turk, performed juggling tricks with the apparatus. Patterson was in the front row of the audience. For weeks in advance of the fair, Peale and his men were busy making kites of various sizes and shapes and flying them from the Mint's roof to advertise the fair. These kites were then sold at the fair for the benefit of the Musical Fund Society. After the fair ended, Peale made a wax medallion of himself as a juggler. It would have been acceptable for a private enterprise to support the Musical Fund Society in this manner, but it was not acceptable in the slightest for a government entity to do so.

Additionally, there were petty things that Peale did that antagonized his workers. One man was assigned to drive Peale and his daughter, Anna, around in their carriage on private errands. Another did plaster repairs at the house and spent a half-day shaking out rugs. In 1847 two Pennsylvania counties ordered copies of the United States standard weights and measures held at the Mint. Facsimiles were made by a Philadelphia firm and then returned to the Mint, where workers adjusted their weights and put the seals of the Commonwealth of Pennsylvania in brass upon them. Peale was paid $50 by each county. Although he was not involved in the project, he kept the money.

The list went on. Peale was a member of an archery club, and he had his men making bows and arrows and fixing tents before each outing of the group. There was a brass mirror needed by Rembrandt Peale that required three days of polishing at the Mint. Peale, on a whim, had medals made up for the leading pupils in a music class.

But Peale's worst transgression by far was his side business selling medals produced at the Mint. He pocketed the proceeds from the government medals. While this practice was in existence when Peale assumed the chief coiner's position, he pushed the activity to its natural limits and beyond. Once the official medals had been struck, Peale would strike additional copies in copper for his own account. This activity applied not only to medals that were current, but also to past medals whose dies he had meticulously gathered. Peale took this activity to a much greater level than had Adam Eckfeldt. Furthermore, his profit margin was almost total—the men and machinery were free. It wasn't just the screw press and its operators that were involved; the gold and silver bullion had to be worked from its raw state through melting and cast into ingots. Those ingots then had to be rolled into strips from which the metal discs could be cut. For all this activity, Peale had only to reimburse the Mint for the metal used in his medals. However, he would occasionally pay gratuities to the men who operated the screw press.

Peale did not stop with government medals. While a handful of private customers had been serviced by the Mint before Peale assumed his position, this activity greatly expanded under his aggressive self-promotion. He annually furnished gold, silver, and copper medals to the Franklin Institute, the Mechanics Institute of New York, and the Horticultural Society of Massachusetts. The Franklin Institute in particular considered Peale's charges for this work exorbitant.

McCulloh backed all these details with written statements from the men involved. Now, Eckert would have to decide how to proceed, given the messy politics of the situation.

Immediately on the heels of McCulloh's detailed accusations against Peale, Eckert received an unwanted letter. The Franklin Institute was holding its 21st annual exhibition of American manufactures in Philadelphia, which would close on November 1. Since the first exhibition, the Mint had struck the medals awarded to the recipients placing great value upon their prompt distribution. The president of the institution now wrote Eckert, stating that striking the medals elsewhere was not an option at this late date. It was important that these medals were done right and the Mint was the appropriate place for this to happen. They had had no previous difficulty making these arrangements and respectfully requested that Eckert authorize the striking of the new medals. Clearly this was standard operating procedure between the Franklin Institute and the Mint. It put George Eckert in a real vise.

Eckert was forced to go to Corwin for permission to strike the medals. He noted that McCulloh had taken exception to this practice and that it was the subject of a charge by him against Franklin Peale. As Eckert had not finished his investigation, he did not feel he had the authority to approve this work.

Eckert now squirmed around the issue. He did not deny that striking medals for private gain had been done at the

Mint. There was nothing obligatory in the defined duties of the chief coiner that involved striking medals without compensation. This fact was tacitly recognized by the government through their payment for medals authorized by Congress. In such cases, the chief coiner made a private contract with the government entity requesting the medals; this contract included payment for his private benefit. Eckert had no opinion of this practice other than to state that use of government machinery in this process had not been detrimental to the Mint's primary charge of coining money for general circulation. However, the use of workmen for private gain could not be justified. That issue was open to further examination by Eckert. On the contrary, use of workmen on their own terms when not engaged in Mint activities was acceptable to Eckert. He hoped that his inquiry into the chief coiner's activities would show this to be the case in past medals activity.

Eckert closed by kicking the issues into Corwin's court. Could Peale strike medals for private corporations or individuals? Could he use the old screw press for this purpose? Could he employ workers at the Mint? Eckert needed an answer quickly to accommodate the Franklin Institute. This letter reached Corwin on October 28, giving him no time to lose before the institute's deadline.

Corwin came back with answers two days later. Treasury approved striking the medals for the Franklin Institute. There was no problem employing the chief coiner in this work or for using the coin press. The work should be done outside of the usual business hours of the Mint or in such periods as to not interfere in any manner with the regular operations of the Mint. However, the letter was absolutely silent on compensation. Corwin was not going on record on that thorny issue.

For Peale, the situation was clear. He could strike the medals during slack time or after hours. If he took any compensation for the work, he did so at his own risk. Corwin had said no without saying no. For the second time, Richard McCulloh hit Franklin Peale where it hurt—his wallet.[8]

• • • •

By now, Californians knew that the assay office was no solution to their monetary problems. Both their grievances and their anger were genuine.

At first, reaction to the $50 ingots—or slugs, as they were called—was favorable. These pieces forced out of circulation all the debased private mintage that had been marked down to intrinsic value. Also, the price of gold dust firmed up and approached fair market value. However, there was a downside. Moffat & Co., acting as the contractor, by fiat now held a virtual monopoly on coin production, and their 2.75-percent seigniorage charge to the miners was deemed excessive.[9] In reaction, in March 1851 the state repealed its act preventing individuals from minting coins, although it still retained the requirement that they redeem their output in U.S. gold or silver upon demand. This necessary self-policing severely restricted the law's intent: to provide competition.

Once the substandard gold was pushed out of circulation, Californians began to realize assay office slugs were far from a perfect solution; they were cumbersome in commerce.[10] These $50 gold pieces actually aggravated the coin shortage when it came to making change. Moffat asked the Treasury Department for permission to issue smaller-denomination coins. Assistant Secretary of the Treasury William Hodge rejected this request, calling it inexpedient. Soon, slugs were discounted while foreign silver coins passed at a premium. In November 1851, Moffat renewed its request to mint smaller denominations, noting that slug production had fallen precipitously.

Falling output gained Corwin's attention. On December 9, 1851, he authorized $10 and $20 gold pieces. However, on December 10, he changed his mind. By now, Moffat's business had fallen to the point that they could not cover their fixed expenses. But Wass & Molitor, a new private mint, had opened its doors in November and they began coining the smaller gold pieces in January 1852. Once again, Corwin changed his position. The assay office adjusted their seigniorage fees and began striking the smaller gold coins in February 1852.[11]

Beyond these local issues, there still existed the problem of legal-tender status for the assay-office coinage. By law it was not legal tender, yet the customs collector received these $50 gold ingots in payment of duties. However, the illusion of legal-tender status was abruptly ended by the Mint; Eckert[12] refused to accept these gold ingots at their stated value. They were utterly unrecognized by any law and the United States had no obligation to accept them. The close imitation of the national coin devices by the private mints of California was inconvenient and in contravention of the law, but the officers of the Mint had no power to interfere.

In the mint debates of February 1851, Congressman Bayly had only aggravated the situation. As chairman of the Ways and Means Committee, he had stated in the debate that a mint was not necessary in California. All Congress had to do was grant legal-tender status to the assay-office production. Obviously, he had not thought out the issue of gold coinage with differing fineness standards. Californians saw his comment as a double-edged sword. With legal-tender status they would solve some of their immediate needs. However, they could rest assured that they would never get a branch mint.

In the end, Californians had no use for the assay office. They called it a swindle shop for its high seigniorage. Its benefit primarily accrued to a few persons, who could be expected to make a fortune and return home.[13] They wanted a mint.

CHAPTER 30

MR. WIZARD

In 1851, the Mint's melting and refining department was anything but the spit-and-polish that epitomized the rest of its manufacturing processes. Gold ore seemed to be lying around in heaps. Bars of refined gold passed through multiple hands. The heat of the place was insufferable, particularly in the sweltering summer months. Fires glowed with the intensity of a foundry. Crucibles were handled with iron tongs and cotton gloves. The faces of the men were smudged and dirt begrimed. "There was a suffocating sensation of hot air, steam and perspiration penetrating the atmosphere, which was anything but pleasant to experience."[1] Here in the press to process the deluge of gold from California, it was as if Dante's inferno really did exist.

The Mint's process of refining gold bullion consisted of melting the gold with two times its weight in silver, a process called silver quartation. The combined metals were then run into cold water and allowed to granulate. Next they were separated through the use of strong nitric acid, producing the fumes that plagued the Mint and its surrounding neighborhood. Finally, the silver was recovered through the use of zinc. The process was time consuming and used considerable fuel in the initial melting of gold and silver.[2] To proceed with this process, it was necessary for the Mint to carry about $200,000 of silver in perpetual inventory (fig. 120).

McCulloh's refining method pivoted on the substitution of zinc for silver in the initial separation process, eliminat-

Fig. 120. This rendering of the Philadelphia Mint in 1852 shows the newly extended chimney, yet the rooftop flag is obscured by smoke from the furnaces. This tranquil scene of the mint's exterior belies the turmoil within.

ing the perpetual need for silver. Using a low temperature, the gold bullion and zinc were melted. Next, cold and diluted sulfuric acid was used to remove the zinc, leaving the gold and silver in a pulverulent—or powdery—state. Finally nitric acid was used to remove and recover the silver. The gold was then toughened for casting into ingots in the hearth of a reverberatory, in which heat was radiated downward from the roof onto the gold. The avoidance of heating the additional silver saved time and therefore labor, to say nothing of fuel usage.[3]

Now the negotiations for the trial of McCulloh's process began. On November 13, 1851, McCulloh accepted the precondition that he must indemnify the government for any wastage above customary levels that might occur from his process during the experiments. However, he wanted any profit that might accrue from the experimental process to be for his account. The testing would be under McCulloh's exclusive direction and control. He also wanted control of observers. The bullion would be under the joint custody of McCulloh and the treasurer of the Mint; it was to be kept separate from the bullion of the melter and refiner. McCulloh, distrustful of Booth, wanted his former partner in the process to have absolutely no involvement in the trial.

Before starting the tests, McCulloh wanted to process several small batches of $1,000 to $2,000 each to familiarize the workmen with his process. He wanted the test broken into two phases. The first phase of refining bullion was not to exceed $250,000. If waste and expense did not appear to cause the government loss, the trial would continue to establish the applicability of the process to large quantities of gold bullion. McCulloh expected the full facilities of the Mint to be extended to him; any apparatus not available should be ordered, constructed, and modified under McCulloh's direction and at McCulloh's cost.

Assistant Treasury Secretary William Hodge sat on this proposal until the day after Christmas, at which time he instructed Eckert to proceed. From the tone of the communication, Hodge had apparently met with McCulloh before drafting his instructions. Hodge wanted no grounds for complaint on McCulloh's part. To prevent errors, the tests would be conducted under McCulloh's direction. While McCulloh had agreed to indemnify the government against losses, expenses such as erecting furnaces that would prove useful to the Mint beyond the trial were to be exempted from the indemnity. However, there was one slight and yet significant modification to McCulloh's proposal: the experiment was to be carried out on $200,000 to $300,000 of bullion, and if no serious loss occurred, Eckert could continue the test on a larger scale as Eckert and McCulloh deemed necessary or advisable until

McCulloh was satisfied. The department wanted Eckert to test the process to an extent that would enable him to report fully and definitively upon its merits. Eckert now had a say in whether the second phase would or would not be undertaken.

There was further discussion of a legal nature between Eckert and Hodge concerning who should have possession of the gold bullion for the trials. This was resolved in early January 1852, and McCulloh promptly arrived at the Mint to start his preparatory work. McCulloh and Eckert jointly decided to tear down the cupelling furnace that had been built by Booth the preceding February during his attempts to overcome the brittleness issue in McCulloh's process. In its place a new cupelling and reverberatory furnace would be constructed, which would be used after the trial for refining silver.

Upon tearing down the cupelling furnace, McCulloh found 17 ounces of gold in the dirt of its floor. He immediately jumped to the conclusion that this was gold that was "lost" when his process was tested by Patterson for volatilization. Booth rebutted that Patterson had used a different furnace for his tests in May 1851.

In addition to the new furnace, Eckert allowed McCulloh to use the silver-melting furnaces. McCulloh rebuilt two of these and tore down the third. This one he replaced with a new furnace for alloying and granulating the zinc and gold.

Anxious to start and no doubt remembering his claim to Booth that he only needed 48 hours to prove that his process worked, McCulloh pressed forward in January with a trial using 303 ounces of gold and zinc. Meanwhile, Eckert began an investigation of the wastage from the Mint's current process to provide a baseline for comparison using the two rebuilt silver-melting furnaces. Not wanting to bias Eckert's tests through spillage, McCulloh decided to melt zinc in one furnace and gold in the other, and then combine the two in a crucible outside the furnaces. Still McCulloh must have been staggered by the fact that the Mint really did not know the wastage from its current process. How could Patterson have rejected his process out of hand the preceding year without this critical knowledge?

McCulloh would afterward say that this improvised combining of the molten materials resulted in spillage, discrediting the results of the trial. Booth, however, had much more to say on the subject. Gold melted at 2200°F, while zinc melted at 700°F.[4] As a workman poured the melted gold into the melted zinc, the alloy appeared to be chilling, a hardening of the surface. McCulloh directed the workman to pour the gold faster, but the temperature differential was just too great. A series of small explosions took place, projecting hot metal from the crucible and scattering drops or grains upon the floor and surrounding objects. Worse, at least one of the grains came in contact with a beam in the 15-foot high ceiling. This beam, saturated with niter from the refining operations, caught fire.

It gave Booth satisfaction to smugly relate what happened next. The beam was quickly doused with water. However, two hours later, fire again flared up. In order to extinguish it, holes were bored in from the floor above and water was freely applied.[5] McCulloh had egg on his face even before the real tests had begun.

Egg or not, McCulloh had ammunition with which to fire back at Booth. Eckert's tests for baseline wastage using the existing process were a flop. When all was said and done, Booth calculated that he had more gold at the end of the test than when he started. That dissolved into finger pointing, since the furnaces had just been rebuilt, eliminating the possibility of gold residue from prior usage. Eckert dismissed the issue as a rounding problem. McCulloh knew better. The problem had to be with the initial assay work, where, as with the melting and refining department, green hands had been hired to deal with the influx of gold bullion.

On February 4, the third—or granulating—furnace was finished and was dry enough to kindle a fire. A test was conducted using only zinc. When it had sufficiently cooled, a valve was opened and eight streams of molten zinc flowed into a large copper kettle containing water in the basement below. It worked well. The advantage for the Mint was that this system worked equally well for silver. It would eliminate the Mint's existing system, which relied upon dipping to remove the molten silver and gold bullion—a source of spillage and therefore wastage.

All was ready. On February 5, McCulloh commenced the process of granulating 5,000 ounces of zinc with 1,973 ounces of gold. When the zinc was melted, the gold bars—heated to redness to prevent their chilling the alloy—were placed into the zinc. They easily dissolved without the temperature elevating past that of redness. Eckert, who was observing, and McCulloh could see no evidence of volatilization. However, a problem quickly ensued. The pipe passing down into the water-filled copper kettle was inexplicably elevated above the water. Consequently, a draft of cooling air chilled the metal at the bottom of the crucible so that when the valve was opened, only four of the eight openings allowed streams of the molten material to flow through them. Three of these four soon became blocked, and the fourth flowed at a diminished rate. The granulation was successful but the piping was hopelessly clogged.

McCulloh then modified the arrangement, using only four openings. To prevent another displacement of the tubing, he fixed an iron bedplate in the furnace below the crucible to prevent movement of the piping. Also, he ordered a larger kettle to ensure that all of the molten gold and zinc was captured.

On the morning of February 6, McCulloh was ready to restart the test. Before commencing, one of the workers gathered a scoop of several ounces of the alloyed gold and zinc in grains from the previous day's run. McCulloh ordered the man to place the scoop on top of one of the melting furnaces behind a number of large crucibles. McCulloh left the room for a few minutes. When he returned, the scoop was gone. There were many curious onlookers at this point. No one seemed to know what had happened to the scoop. McCulloh was upset but there was little he could do. This test was certainly compromised. McCulloh asked Eckert to order everyone without a work assignment out of the area.

At noon that day, and with his modifications completed, McCulloh commenced another trial using 1,964 ounces of gold bullion and about 5,000 ounces of zinc. At dusk the metal was all melted and the granulating process begun. All went well, with the four streams easily flowing. However, the kettle was not large enough. While the kettle was being replaced, a pan was held in place to capture the molten alloy. As the first kettle was removed, the piping was knocked from its place, causing the workman to drop the pan. Molten alloy momentarily poured onto the cellar floor, splashing widely and finely upon the clothing of the workmen and spectators. The hot metal went right through the men's pants and burned their legs. McCulloh was once again frustrated. The spectators had ignored Eckert's order to clear out. Worse, wastage numbers were going to be suspect. All day on Saturday, the 7th, McCulloh and his men tried to gather what metal they could from the basement floor.

McCulloh spent February 9 and 10 modifying his granulating system. Alterations were made to accommodate a new bedplate. Simplified valves were created to produce a single stream of molten metal. Hogsheads capable of receiving all the metal from the crucible were substituted for the copper kettle. McCulloh now had a system that was pretty much foolproof. While this activity was underway, McCulloh put all the granulated material collected on February 5 and 6 into sulfuric acid to separate the gold and silver from the zinc.

On February 11, another granulation using 1,995 ounces of gold bullion with about 5,000 ounces of zinc went smoothly. The granulations were smaller, thus increasing the surface area, which allowed the sulfuric acid to work faster. Two successive zinc granulations were completed. The goal was to clean out the crucible used in the initial combining of the gold and zinc with melted zinc to ensure that all the gold from the three batches of bullion was captured. This process failed to remove all the embedded gold, requiring the wrought-iron crucible to be bored out at a machine shop.

McCulloh knew that these two trials were not indicative of how efficient the process could be. He had insisted that no work be done using any part of the process without his presence. So no work was completed on the day he was having the crucible bored out. When he was working with the granulating process, no concurrent work took place with the acids. He was also forced to constantly tinker with the valves, losing time. Consequently, any analysis of time, labor, and materials used was of questionable value.

Next, the three batches of granulated gold were combined and refined, first with diluted nitric acid and then with strong nitric acid. The refined gold was subsequently toughened in the same black crucible that Patterson had successfully used for this part of the process. In all, 18 bars were cast. The metal was perfectly soft and free from brittleness. McCulloh then submitted the bars for assay, asking that each bar be assayed individually. Jacob Eckfeldt complained. February 1852 was the peak period for gold bullion flowing into the Mint and he resisted this added work burden. McCulloh yielded.

On February 16, McCulloh granulated 7,874 ounces of gold bullion, the last for the agreed-upon first phase. While all proceeded well, the work was not done with dispatch. Again, the question of cost savings was left open. By Saturday, February 21, refining was nearly completed. During the process McCulloh had learned by trial and error, and by the end he had successfully reduced his zinc usage to a two-to-one ratio.

Since February 12, an independent observer had been present at McCulloh's trials. The man was Woods Baker, and he worked for Bache in Washington. Corwin instructed Eckert to extend Baker every courtesy of the Mint. Until February 17, Baker was only able to spend afternoons and evenings at the Mint, but for three days thereafter he was available full time. Essentially, Baker saw the third trial, which proceeded unimpeded until after his departure. He was not there for the granulating incidents during the first two trials.

At this point McCulloh proposed to Eckert that with the Mint director's approval, he would granulate $750,000 in gold bullion on the coming Monday and Tuesday and then complete the refining by week's end. McCulloh wanted to demonstrate the speed and cost efficiency of his method, something that he had been unable to accomplish up to this point.

Eckert refused. A controversy had development from an unexpected quarter. The previous fall, Eckert had suggested to Booth that he should consider a cullendered crucible along the lines of the one used by McCulloh in his granulating process. With his characteristic tardiness, Booth did not get around to trying this modification of the Mint's silver-quartation process until he saw McCulloh successfully apply it in his setup.[6] McCulloh then formally wrote to the Mint director on Thursday, February 19, to protest both an infringement of his patent and a violation of their agreement that experimentation touching on any aspect of McCulloh's process be conducted in his presence. On Friday Eckert replied to McCulloh by letter, stating that he would suspend Booth's activity until he had reviewed McCulloh's patent application. He then promptly applied for a copy of the application at a cost of $2.50.[7] Their relations at this point were stiffly formal at best.

Personal feelings aside, Eckert gave McCulloh an official reason for the denial. The backlog of unprocessed bullion had reached intolerable levels during the two weeks of McCulloh's trials. Furthermore, the Mint's inventory of specie was severely depleted, hampering the treasurer's ability to pay depositors. It seemed nothing had really changed since Eckert took over from Patterson. In addition, Eckert needed the separating apparatus that McCulloh had been using for his refining, starting that Monday. That meant that McCulloh would have to do the final bit of refining with heat rather than chemicals to compensate for the loss of the separator.

This song was not what Eckert was singing in Washington. In his annual report to the president, penned a week before the test started, Eckert noted that the previous year, Patterson had laid out the problems associated with refining the bullion received from California. The former director had stated that the difficulties would be temporary in nature. It now afforded Eckert satisfaction to state that the impediments existing at the time of that report were soon removed. All deposits of bullion were now promptly paid and manufactured into coin with but a trifling delay. The Mint had never been in a condition of greater efficiency.[8]

So, McCulloh was not going to get a fair test, much less one complete problem-free trial. Eckert was flatly unwilling to move forward with the trials under any condition until it was demonstrated that McCulloh's refined gold would coin up. However, Eckert was willing to resume the tests at some undefined point in the future. Peeved, McCulloh said he would be glad to conduct those future trials once the government had purchased his patent rights. Calming down, he attempted to call what he perceived to be a bluff from Eckert. He would ask the Treasury to advance the Mint money sufficient to maintain current payments to depositors while McCulloh refined $1 million of gold bullion. Eckert hedged. He personally did not think that the Treasury would consent and he was unwilling to support it until he knew the coinability of the gold ingots that McCulloh had already refined.

McCulloh now had another barrier to knock down. George Eckfeldt was given charge of the ingots. The gold was found to be superior for coining. First, double eagles were made from it to test the perfection of the die impressions. Then gold dollars were coined to ascertain the workability of this metal. McCulloh requested a test of the gold's ductility. One of the strips for gold dollars was rolled multiple times, with the rolls screwed closer together each time until they could be tightened no more. There was not the slightest problem, nor were any imperfections apparent in the metal. Once and for all, the brittleness issue was dead.

With the coinability issue resolved, McCulloh had nothing to do but wind down his operations. The granulating furnace was torn down and the silver-melting furnaces were restored to their previous condition. It was apparent to McCulloh that a future date for the resumption of the test was never going to be named.

The last communication between the two men on the subject of the trials only added to McCulloh's consternation. On April 23, McCulloh asked for the result of the sweeps from his trials. Eckert was in Reading and did not reply until May 1. He wrote that those sweeps had been combined with the sweeps for the other operations in the refining department, preventing his compliance with McCulloh's request. Eckert gave an amount recovered based upon the average from all the sweeps. This action appeared to be simple sloppiness on the Mint's part.

It now boiled down to who would write their report of the test results first. McCulloh wisely deferred, wanting to see what issues Eckert addressed. The lot to write the first report inappropriately fell to Woods Baker. He had no axe to grind in this affair. However, his report went directly to McCulloh and not to Secretary Corwin.

Baker noted that the third trial was understood to be the first of a set of workings on a large scale. The melting and granulation took place without volatilization. McCulloh experienced trouble with one of the valves but had corrected it within the hour. The grains produced were remarkably uniform and finer than those yielded by the Mint's process. Baker went on to detail the subsequent activity. When the trial was completed, Baker found the bars of gold sufficiently malleable when struck together. They showed no evidence of crystalline fracture when pieces were clipped off the corners. Based upon the results in hand, Baker believed McCulloh's process superior in terms of cost, but that further improvements could be had through economies of scale and worker productivity.

Baker went on to state that, from conversations with Mint workmen, he learned that all small gold coins at that time were made from ingot clippings or remelted metal, taking time and causing more wastage. McCulloh's process would eliminate that inefficiency. The process also dispensed with precipitating, washing, reducing, and melting the large quantities of silver used in the Mint's silver-quartation process. Baker closed by observing that converting to McCulloh's process would require little initial capital expense and would be easier to maintain.[9]

Meanwhile, McCulloh successfully outlasted Eckert. The director wrote to Corwin on June 21, 1852. He assured the Treasury secretary that no facility was withheld from McCulloh. In general terms, Eckert detailed for Corwin the steps involved in the three trials undertaken.

He did not mention the difficulties that McCulloh had encountered. In assessing wastage he noted that the results of the individual trials seemed to give distorted numbers. The loss for the second trial was abnormally large and the third trial actually exhibited a gain. He was not forthcoming that some of the gold was misplaced or deliberately stolen in the first trial or that only an erroneous initial assay would have produced the false gain in the third trial. Eckert dealt with these questionable numbers by simply aggregating the trial results into one large sample. Eckert also made adjustments for an unexplained variance in the fineness of the bars without stating that McCulloh had been denied his wish that each individual ingot be assayed. Also, there were the sweeps that Eckert averaged back in on an allocated basis. Eckert then determined that the wastage was 19.969 ounces or 1.60 ounces per 1,000 ounces of pure metal. In contrast, Eckert claimed that the Mint's experience for calendar year 1850 was 0.22 ounces per 1,000 ounces, an outright distortion of the facts. Perhaps Eckert was not yet aware of Patterson's November actions, in which he bypassed the refining process for considerable volumes of gold bullion. However, Booth certainly was. Eckert chose to make no mention of the results from Booth's efforts to accurately fix the wastage number in February.

Eckert felt that care was taken at every step in McCulloh's process to minimize wastage. If the Mint adopted his process, the wastage result would not be expected to vary much from the test results. Eckert had expected to find that McCulloh's experiments produced a more desirable wastage in proportion to the Mint's experience. It was Eckert's opinion that the adoption of McCulloh's process would be "inexpedient."[10] The report was a masterpiece of deceit, yet it read smooth as silk. There was not an inkling of controversy to be found in it. To the uninitiated reader, Eckert's recommendation to reject McCulloh's process seemed the height of sanity.

McCulloh responded with a vengeance—if a bit late—on August 3, 1852. With his characteristic thoroughness, McCulloh detailed every event except the initial disastrous shakedown operation in January. The report of Woods Baker and testimonials of the men who had worked with McCulloh in the refining department were appended to the report. Contrary to Eckert, McCulloh placed his emphasis in his evaluation on the third trial, trouble-free until the very end when Eckert took away his use of the separator. There was no net gain but instead a loss of 6 ounces of standard gold. The wastage on that lot was 0.77 ounces per 1,000 ounces. Since the Mint had no real wastage benchmark, McCulloh used the one obtained by Robert Patterson in his trials of May 9, 1851: 0.60 ounces per 1,000 ounces. McCulloh called this difference statistically insignificant. He was also not bashful about pointing out that the Mint's wastage figures for 1850 and 1851 were distorted by the California bullion that bypassed the refining process. He noted that the Mint charged the depositors as if that gold had been refined. Thus McCulloh totally impeached Eckert's comparable numbers.

He then went to great lengths to prove that his method was superior in terms of costs and ease of execution.[11] However, no one at the Mint was disputing this fact; they simply did not care. The depositor paid the cost of refining. As long as they had the capacity in place to refine the deposits with an acceptable wastage, there was no incentive to acquire McCulloh's process.

Eckert could not allow this report to stand without a rebuttal. On August 17, he wrote to Corwin, explaining that Booth had tried McCulloh's process again and he had failed to improve upon the wastage exhibited in the silver-quartation process.[12] By now, Eckert also had in hand a recommendation from Peale to improve the silver separation. He proposed to melt the raw bullion and pour it in a thin stream into strong sulfuric or nitric acid.[13] If there was any doubt that Peale was not deeply involved in this controversy, this recommendation cleared up that question.

Corwin let Eckert's rebuttal stand. Eckert then billed McCulloh $9.50 on September 4, 1852, for the expenses of the trials attributable to him.[14] McCulloh waited until after the presidential election results were known to respond to the Mint director. He paid the amount but proceeded to point out the billing statement was both erroneous and an act of injustice.

> And in conclusion, I would observe that you seem strangely slow to learn, that experiments tried in the melting and refining department of the Mint, under charge of Prof. Booth, concerning the relative merits of my zinc method of refining and that now employed, have proved to have been grossly inaccurate and unworthy of credit. Nor can I admit, therefore, that the result of any late experiment, performed in said department and without my concurrence, could be a proper basis for that conventional determination of the ordinary gold wastage, stipulated with the Treasury Department to be made between you and myself, —notwithstanding that I have acceded to the corresponding pecuniary demand made by you.[15]

The bad blood as it pertained to Booth and McCulloh did not end there. McCulloh took his dispute to the *Scientific American* in October 1852. The magazine opined that it was certainly not only the height of folly, but blank stupidity not to adopt McCulloh's method. It asked what in the name of common sense was the reason his improved process was not employed at the Mint.[16] Booth published his letter of rebuttal addressed to President Fillmore on January 17, 1853, asserting that the test of McCulloh's process had been fully and fairly conducted and the wastage found unsatisfactory. *Scientific American* published this letter and then called for a commission of knowledgeable individuals under the authority of the Treasury Department to superintend a suitable trial at the Mint of McCulloh's process.[17] This demand went nowhere.

• • • •

George Eckert still had the vexing issue of the charges against Franklin Peale to address. He had not been inactive on this issue during the run up to the refining trials. In November 1851, the Mint director had asked Longacre for details of Peale's interference in the engraver's duties. Acting on McCulloh's advice, Longacre had insisted that his response to the inquiry be in writing. Out came all the details of the double eagle design difficulties and the interference with the design for the three-cent piece.[18] Longacre had company; Eckert also sought the testimony of William DuBois concerning the Polk medal. DuBois had forgotten the details and had to go to the records to refresh his memory. The only information Eckert received from DuBois was a regurgitation of what he could have seen for himself had he gone to the accounting ledgers. Eckert then interviewed one of the workmen; however, he took no written testimony from him.

At this point, Eckert sat on the investigation. However, matters did not cooperate with the Mint director's desire for a low profile for his chief coiner. Outside requests flowed in for medals. There was the medal for the Worcester Mechanics Institute and C.C. Wright wanted to have a special gold medal for Henry Clay struck at the Mint.[19] Permission was granted in each case, provided Mint operations were not disrupted and that costs were borne by the outside parties.

When in early January 1852 it became apparent that the venerable Adam Eckfeldt was at his end, Peale pushed for an assistant. He argued that his title, chief coiner, implied that he was entitled to an assistant. In Peale's words, Adam Eckfeldt had previously filled this position, acting in the chief coiner's absence. Seeing an opportunity, both Booth and Jacob Eckfeldt had already asked for help. It was clear the three men were acting in concert.[20] There was no way that Eckert could act on this request, even if he wanted to.

Eckert had shared the full range of McCulloh's charges with Peale; however, he had not shown him the supporting testimony. It was to these charges that Peale addressed his defense in a letter dated April 15, 1852. In this communication, Peale stated that the mysterious influence he had upon Robert Maskell Patterson was nothing more than an enduring friendship of 25 or 30 years. Peale's esteem for Patterson was unbounded and undeviating.

Peale denied that he had influenced the trials of McCulloh's refining process conducted by Booth during Patterson's tenure. There was no deferential relationship between Peale and Booth. Booth was competent enough to judge the value of McCulloh's refining process for himself. He called this charge malicious and vengeful since McCulloh had a patent and a large pecuniary interest in his process. In making this allegation, Peale threw up a smokescreen against one of McCulloh's accusations—that Peale harbored personal hostility because McCulloh had refused to furnish material for his medals operation.

Peale hid behind technicalities regarding lavish expenditures. The director of the Mint gave a warrant for every bill; no expenditure could be made without his authority. Mint expenses were subject to review by the auditor and comptroller of the Treasury. As to the overrun of the $20,800 expansion appropriation, Peale admitted that the estimate made by him was low. The expenditures were "lumped" into the contingency fund and Peale did not think it important to separate them. An overrun was not an official misdemeanor. The estimate was not made dishonestly and Peale failed to see why he must defend himself on this charge.

Peale had a defense for each piece of failed equipment that he had designed. Invariably, unforeseen circumstances had intervened to render each innovation of no benefit to the Mint. Perhaps the most questionable of his defenses involved the steam draw bench. According to Peale, it had been made at the request of the superintendent of the Charlotte Mint. It had proven "unmanageable," but it was successfully modified and was now in use at Charlotte.

Peale reserved special attention to his trumpeting sofa. It had been made of white pine and painted; the sofa was as plain as possible. He had made the upholstery and "appendages" principally, if not entirely, by his own hand. The alarm that sounded might or might not be considered an important safeguard for the premises. The sofa was now in Eckert's office. The Mint director could judge whether or not the matter was worthy of a misdemeanor charge.

Perhaps sensing that his defense of the sofa was over the top, Peale shifted to the offense. He claimed credit for the productivity improvements he had brought back from Europe and implemented at the Mint. In each instance his labors had been given freely to the Mint. In this context, he addressed the issue of the balance, of which he had constructed many over the course of his time at the Mint. McCulloh just happened to highlight the one time when Peale had tried to make an ornamental balance.

Like DuBois, Peale suffered from a loss of memory regarding the Polk medal. The records showed that the bill for the medal was made out in the name of George Hall, the man Peale had advanced to Eckert as his choice for assistant coiner. It appeared the bill had been withdrawn and the amount made up by a contribution from the officers. Eckert would have to determine if Peale's actions were "unofficerlike" and demoralizing.

Peale reserved special attention to the charges made by Longacre. He had extended every effort to cooperate with Longacre on the design of the double eagle to ensure no delays occurred. The acts that Longacre claimed were interference were, on the contrary, required of Peale in his official capacity. Peale regretted that Longacre misconstrued these actions but, under similar circumstances, Peale would feel constrained to act in a similar manner. He particularly defended his refusal to allow Longacre to take possession of a trial strike in gold of his double eagle design at the end of January 1850.

Peale was pointed in stating that as chief coiner he was the only official and competent judge of the proper depth and curvature of the dies. He was therefore bound to exercise his judgment and give his opinion. It was Longacre's place to conform to the exigencies of the coining operation and the restriction imposed by the materials of which the dies were made. Contrary to Peale's advice, Longacre set the relief of the dies for the double eagle too great. They were medal dies rather than coinage dies. As a consequence, these dies gave way within an hour under the excessive pressure used to bring up details of the design. Peale also noted that after the second trial, the dies had to be cut down to reduce the relief on certain high points before they could be put into production. As a result, the relief of Liberty was injured in some parts, while it remained too great in others. On the whole, the coin remained very far from creditable to the country.

At this point Peale became downright nasty toward Longacre. He claimed the engraver had had almost uninterrupted leisure since the issuing of the double eagle. It was well known that since Peale introduced the reducing lathe to the Mint, the office of engraver had become a sinecure except when Congress ordered a new coin. Since the double eagle, the only work required of the engraver had been the design of the three-cent piece. For this, Longacre had used the services of a trained diesinker from New York. Peale denied any knowledge of a supposed attempt to substitute a different three-cent piece design for that of Longacre's. Peale summed up his opinion of Longacre by stating that the engraver had had ample time to improve the double eagle with new dies as well as time to rework the entire series of U.S. coins, a task any good artist would have undertaken.

Peale admitted that he had used the workmen at odd times for chores around his house. It was a well-known fact that before the California Gold Rush, there were periods of considerable length when it was impossible to find work at the Mint for the men to do. Activity was dependent upon the intake of precious metals, which was impossible to predict. Peale would accept volunteer services, always of a trifling nature and never at a time when they would impede the Mint in the slightest.

Peale saved the most egregious accusation for last. The business of striking medals at the Mint had been practiced before he became chief coiner. Eckfeldt, appointed by Washington, did it; McCulloh, by inference, was attacking Eckfeldt. While nothing in the law permitted the Mint to strike medals, the government had had need of the services of the chief coiner to prepare national medals from the beginning. In doing so, the government always treated the chief coiner on a private footing and compensated him for his work. Most times, consent was sought to strike these medals and it was never refused. Since McCulloh's complaint, consent had been sought every time. The monetary gain of the chief coiner was not at the expense of the government, which must pay to have the medals struck regardless of who performed the work. The only advantage to the chief coiner was the use of the old screw press, no longer necessary in Mint operations. Peale conveniently omitted that this press was still used to make working dies from the hubs. Peale stated that the materials and compensation of the workmen were the charge of the chief coiner.[21] Had Peale seen the testimony of the workmen to McCulloh, he might have modified that last statement.

Peale tried to close on a positive note. He had gone to much effort to collect the dies for the previous federal, state, and private medals struck at the Mint. Without his effort, they might have been lost or destroyed. In France there was a museum of such French medals. He hoped that one day the same would be established at the U.S. Mint. In the meantime the chief coiner would take custody of them and strike copies when required. It was one final bit of effrontery given that the Mint cabinet had been in existence since 1838.

Peale presented no corroborating testimony from others aside from one letter of support signed by Robert Maskell Patterson. McCulloh would claim that while Patterson might have signed the letter, he certainly did not write it. McCulloh considered Peale shameless in his pursuit of Patterson's statement for the record that the chief coiner had always expressed a favorable opinion of McCulloh's refining process. Indeed, Patterson's health had deteriorated rapidly since resigning his position at the Mint. He suffered from heart disease and had retired from his position with the American Philosophical Society. He would shortly decline to stand for reelection as president of the Musical Fund Society.[22] In fact, he had withdrawn completely from Philadelphia society.

With the evidentiary portion of his investigation over, Eckert had to choose a course of action. It was a full 90 days before he filed his findings with Assistant Secretary Hodge on July 13, 1852. His excuse for the delay was his wish to see the refining trials through to their conclusion. With due formality, Eckert quoted the charges directly from McCulloh's submission. He cited his own activities, taking interviews and receiving Peale's written response. In conclusion, Eckert found that with one exception, Peale's conduct was not amenable to censure or inconsistent with his governmental duties. That exception was Peale's use of workmen to perform repairs to his house and furniture. However, there were extenuating circumstances. Prior to the influx of California gold, there was a great deal of downtime at the Mint. In such circumstances, the use of workmen in performing private services was not an interruption of their duties at the Mint; it was simply the use of time that would otherwise have been idly spent. It was as if Peale had ghostwritten Eckert's reply to Hodge.

Eckert did himself no favors when he continued by asserting that no such work had gone on since the arrival of the California gold. Eckert was also convinced that the time freely given by Peale in preparing drawings for the new machinery necessary to the capacity expansion of 1850 should be taken into consideration. This statement directly contradicted McCulloh's claim that Peale was paid for his drawings. Eckert believed that while, strictly speaking, the chief coiner was in the wrong, no public interest suffered as a consequence. Eckert believed Peale was eminently qualified for the position of chief coiner and he considered the investigation complete.

> It is proper to add that I have acted, in the course of the inquiry made by me in reference to these charges, upon the presumption that the Department has wished for a report of my *opinion* only, as the chief officer of the Mint. I have therefore purposely avoided a dry recital of evidence or documents, or any argumentatious commentary thereupon, as these would be tedious, and, I suppose, superfluous to the Department.

In all of these proceedings, the charges against Booth had been ignored.[23] Limited competence and a lack of fortitude were not impeachable offenses.

McCulloh was not happy and he was far from finished with the Mint. In a letter to Longacre, who was angry with him for publicly releasing some of his correspondence, McCulloh set forth his intentions. Eckert had been sleeping on his charges against Peale. If Eckert attempted to vindicate Peale, Corwin could expect another printed letter reviewing the matter in public. At this point, McCulloh was not aware of Eckert's whitewash. McCulloh naively believed that Eckert would hesitate before again falsifying facts in his official report to Corwin. Regardless, in a few months, McCulloh hoped to consign Eckert, his confederates, and the powers that sustained them in Washington to the walks of private life.[24]

• • • •

On June 29, 1852, the lion of the Senate died. Henry Clay's body was placed in state in the Capitol Rotunda. He was the first person in the United States to be accorded this honor. He had inspired the Whig Party for a generation. Now without its leader and pushed by the forces of abolition, the Whig Party was disintegrating on the eve of the presidential election of 1852. Waiting on the sidelines to pick up the pieces were the Democrats. McCulloh's hopes had a very real chance of becoming a reality.

PART IV

TO THE BRINK AND BACK

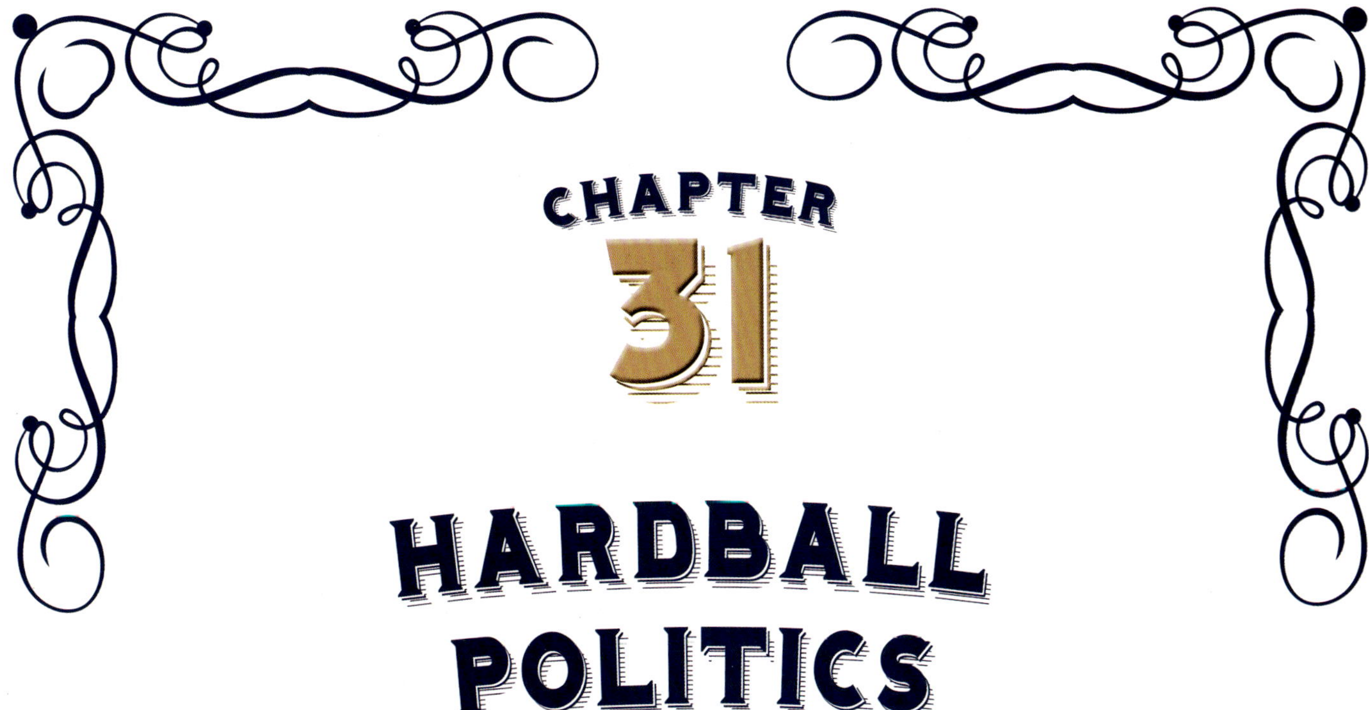

CHAPTER 31

HARDBALL POLITICS

Dr. William Gwin had learned the levers of power in the Senate during the Thirty-First Congress. To accomplish what he needed for California, Gwin gained a position on the powerful Finance Committee when the Thirty-Second Congress convened on December 1, 1851. It also placed him in the catbird seat for matters involving the Mint. The branch-mint proposals of New York and San Francisco would not be linked in this Congress.

Senator Gwin wasted no time advancing the San Francisco branch-mint proposal. He introduced bill S. 6 on December 4.[1] This bill, authorizing the mintage of silver and gold coins, was given its two readings and was then referred to the Finance Committee. As branch-mint authorizations went, the bill was pretty much standard fare. It called for the officers to be appointed by the president, with operational supervision vested in the director of the Mint. As with all Mint officers, removal for nonperformance rested not with the director but with the president.[2]

S. 6 was not the only bill that Gwin dropped in the hopper that day. He filed two more bills; one dealt with the survey of public lands in California and the other with the creation of a board to review payment claims against the United States arising from the takeover of California. Later in the session, Gwin would also press to fund monthly mail service between San Francisco and Shang-

hai, and to establish a naval base at Mare Island near Vallejo, California. Most importantly, he was actively seeking a transcontinental railroad to tie California to the rest of the nation. Gwin needed to dominate this Thirty-Second Congress, and the branch-mint bill was but one part of his legislative agenda.

The bill came back from the Finance Committee on December 15 with two amendments. The branch mint was to be empowered, if requested by the depositor, to provide bars or ingots from gold bullion rather than coins. In addition, the original bill abolished the assay office immediately upon passage, which was consistent with the desires of Gwin's constituents. The amendment kept the assay office in operation until the branch mint was placed in service. The Finance Committee chair, R.M.T. Hunter, pressed the Senate to form a Committee of the Whole, which promptly approved the amended bill.[3] Dr. Gwin had worked his magic.

The New Yorkers were almost as quick in the Senate, with Hamilton Fish introducing their bill on December 9.[4] The Finance Committee sat on this bill until February 25, 1852, when it was reported back with one amendment: New York City would be required to provide the site for the construction of this branch mint. The branch mint would be authorized to strike copper, silver, and gold coins, with $225,000 appropriated for its construction and the purchase of equipment.[5] Here the bill sat.

The real action was going to take place in the House regarding both these branch-mint proposals. The California branch-mint bill was given its two readings and sent to Ways and Means on December 18, 1851.[6] Quick on its heels was a resolution from the New York City common council tendering a plot of land for its proposed branch mint, even though no legislation was before the House.[7]

Counter-resolutions now came to the House and Senate floors. The board of trade in Philadelphia was opposed to a branch mint in New York.[8] The chamber of commerce from Charleston, South Carolina, wanted a branch mint.[9] The New York Chamber of Commerce applied to Fish in the Senate to have the mint in Philadelphia moved to their city.[10] Every indication pointed again to a bitter fight between New York and Philadelphia. Charleston, on the other hand, was out of the picture this time around.

Just as the New York branch-mint bill was tied up in the Senate Finance Committee, the San Francisco bill sat in Ways and Means. On April 12, San Francisco resident Joe McCorkle tried to force the San Francisco branch-mint bill onto the House floor for consideration. It required unanimous consent and failed. He then moved for a suspension of House rules. This motion, which required a two-thirds favorable vote, also failed.[11]

On June 12, Edward Marshall (fig. 121), the other member of the California delegation in the House, again asked for unanimous consent to move that Ways and Means report back to the House on the San Francisco branch-mint bill. George Briggs remained the floor manager for the New York branch-mint bill. He rose to delay the bill once again. Marshall turned in exasperation and said, "Oh Briggs, keep quiet!" That brought forth a burst of laughter. Briggs could have objected to Marshall's motion; however, he at once saw it as a losing proposition. The New York delegation's strategy had been to delay the San Francisco branch-mint bill so that their bill might first be passed. They knew—but would not admit—that a branch mint in San Francisco hurt their chances. However, it was clear that sentiment in the House was such that if they persisted openly with this delaying tactic, they would lose their support. Briggs sat down.

Fig. 121. Edward C. Marshall, shown in this 1851 engraving by Louis Truly, was a determined advocate in the House of Representatives for a branch mint at San Francisco.

The chairman of the Ways and Means Committee, George Houston from Alabama, asked if the House should be reconvened as a Committee of the Whole to consider this legislation. Tom Clingman of North Carolina then made the call. Marshall objected. His frustration was now near its boiling point. The bill had been in the House for seven months and for seven months the House had essentially done nothing. Clingman judged that it would only take a day or two more to pass. Marshall was not budging. The House calendar was crammed; unless the bill was taken up now, it would not see the light of day during this first session. It would take only a half hour to pass. Marshall was determined to overcome the New Yorkers' delaying tactics.

McCorkle now moved that the bill be put upon its passage. The bill was read, along with the proposed amendments from Ways and Means. The first nine amendments were minor, if not piddling. The final two were anything but piddling. At the urging of Treasury, Ways and Means wanted a seigniorage of 1 percent, or the actual cost if less, for all gold coinage at all the mints as a tax to cover the cost of operating these facilities. This amendment, if allowed to stand, did away with the principle of free coinage and would kill the bill.

The next amendment required the secretary of the Treasury to receive bids for the branch mint. However, he could not proceed unless these bids were below $300,000 in total. This amendment severely restricted capacity. San Francisco's mint would be able to meet regional demands and nothing more, ensuring that gold bullion would continue to move to New York. In fact, Corwin, anticipating authorization, had previously commissioned Theodore Adams, a government building contractor, to work up an estimate for a mint in San Francisco in March based on plans prepared by George Eckert and Franklin Peale. Typical for Peale, this was no mere regional mint. The building was estimated to cost $876,000 and the equipment another $260,000. This appropriation would barely purchase the equipment for the mint.[12]

Houston also added a final amendment of his own. He wanted the assay office in San Francisco abolished immediately. The office was minting half eagles and eagles, contrary to the original intent of the legislation that limited output to gold bars only. Houston understood these coins were being discounted at 3 to 5 percent of tale.

There was now some maneuvering to keep this bill on the House's legislative calendar for the next day. James Brooks, a New Yorker on Ways and Means, rose to question the propriety of this bill going through the House without being printed. The Speaker overruled him.

The next day debate began in earnest. Brooks wanted to discuss the seigniorage charge. Both Marshall and McCorkle were okay with that provision since the miners were already paying a charge of 2.75 percent to the assay office. Brooks droned on about the history of seigniorage, getting in occasional digs at the Philadelphia Mint. He wanted this amendment defeated. He pointed out that New York was in a contest to gain superiority over London as the financial center of the new world order. The holder of gold bullion, having crossed the Isthmus of Panama, would opt for London to avoid the seigniorage. With silver scarce as well, it was the "error of the moon" to impose this charge.

Brooks's statement diverted the House from the main principles of the debate. Others noted that silver had for some time been shipped from South America to London rather than the United States because the bullion holder could get more for it there. Houston gained the floor to dispute Brooks's statements on the proposed seigniorage charge and to defend Ways and Means. However, his efforts were in vain. He moved to recommit the bill to committee. It failed. He then moved to adjourn; this too was rejected. But in taking the vote, the count showed there was no quorum. The members had bailed rather than listen to a discussion of seigniorage.[13]

On June 22, the branch mint again gained a position on the House calendar. Houston read a well-prepared letter from W.L. Hodge, as acting secretary of the Treasury, defending the proposed seigniorage charge. It did nothing to stem the onslaught against this provision. McCorkle, sensing the sentiment in the House, switched sides on this argument. This amendment was defeated.

Houston's amendment to terminate the assay office at once had McCorkle's support. The miners were against the assay office, while the bankers and bullion brokers wanted it to remain. McCorkle believed that unless this amendment was passed, there would be nothing but delay regarding the branch mint from the Whig administration to appease the financial interests. When asked how the miners would get their gold processed before the mint was operational, his emotional answer was that they would wait. That was weak. McCorkle noted that assay-office gold coins were discounted 0.5 percent in New York, even though they were accepted at face value at the customs house in San Francisco by order of a Treasury Department circular.

As McCorkle closed, the Speaker interjected. He ruled Houston's amendment on the assay office out of order on a technicality. The assay office gained a reprieve until the mint could be placed in service. The bill was read a third time, the amendments engrossed, and then it was passed.[14]

The Senate accepted the House changes to its bill and on July 3, 1852, the San Francisco branch mint became a reality. That is, it would become a reality once the secretary of the Treasury obtained contracts for the construction of the building and the purchase of the necessary machinery in an amount not exceeding $300,000. Not contingent upon this cost requirement, the act had been expanded to grant any U.S. mint the authority to cast gold into bars or ingots if so demanded by the depositor. Now Corwin had to figure out how to construct anything resembling a mint in San Francisco with this paltry appropriation.[15]

Two more events of significance occurred in the waning hours of the first session of the Thirty-Second Congress. Throughout the session, Secretary Corwin had not pressed for the submittal of Eckert's nomination to the

Senate for approval. No doubt, the defalcation of J.B. Trevor had blunted any effort on Eckert's part to push this issue. For Eckert, the problem was that if the nomination was not submitted, his recess appointment terminated at the end of the session. Eckert had delayed the Peale findings until mid-July. That was just time enough for the report to be dealt with at Treasury but not long enough for it to be leaked into the public domain. Eckert's name was submitted to the Senate on the next-to-last day of the session. On August 31, Eckert, with others, was presented on the Senate floor for approval. Gwin had just moved to table an individual from the preceding group of nominations. If he stood up now, his move to table would be automatically approved and Eckert would be finished, just as Gwin's brother had been in Mississippi. Gwin let it pass; Eckert was confirmed. With Gwin silent, it was clearly Corwin who had delayed.[16] Had dealing effectively with McCulloh been part of the bargain between Corwin and Eckert? It really did not make any difference. With the Whigs in total disarray for the upcoming presidential election, Eckert had only months left before he would be unemployed.

The General Appropriation Act was winding its way through the Senate, heading for an August 30 approval. This was the vehicle for backroom last-minute deals. This act routinely spelled out the mechanics of the cap in the $300,000 appropriation for the branch mint at San Francisco.[17] However, there was a second, more important clause that impacted California in the appropriation act for which Gwin claimed credit.[18] The secretary of the Treasury was authorized to contract for a term not to exceed one year with one or more assaying establishments to perform the duties of an assay office at a fee of no more than 1 percent. Gwin had cut the assay office's seigniorage. In addition, the act required debts due to the United States to be paid in U.S. or foreign gold coins of "standard fineness"; this meant coins that were .900 fine with no more than 5 percent silver alloy. Up to this point, under the Treasury circular, duties had been payable with assay-office gold coins, .884 to .887 fine and containing no copper. If Gwin could not terminate the operations of the assay office to ensure that the construction of the branch mint was expeditiously pursued, he would do the next best thing.[19]

That Gwin was able to take either of these actions showed a man with a will of steel. He had lost his 11-year-old daughter on August 9 to "swamp fever." Named for her mother, Mary had been his favorite.[20]

• • • •

Senator Gwin was in a foul mood with the opening of the second session of the Thirty-Second Congress on December 6, 1852. He and McCorkle had returned to San Francisco after the first session only to discover that Gwin's plan to undercut the assay office had been subverted. At first, the firm of Curtis, Perry, and Ward, successor to Moffat & Co., sought to resign its position as contractor for the assay office.[21] Then the firm came up with a workaround. They could produce .900 fine gold ingots but the alloy would be strictly silver. There was not copper enough in San Francisco to bring the ingots into strict conformance with the gold standards defined by the provision. The customs collector was willing to cooperate if the merchants would indemnify him from loss should the federal government countermand his actions. It was a tenuous temporary fix.

Word reached Corwin that upon their return, Gwin and McCorkle intended to arraign the Treasury secretary before Congress for refusing to enforce the law regarding assay-office ingots containing only silver alloy in payment for government dues at the customs house.[22] Fortunately, the long journey back to Washington gave Gwin time to cool down and temper his reaction.

Still, Gwin had to respond. He had been the object of a letter-writing campaign attacking the standard-fineness provision; memorials had been sent to Congress assailing him and calling for its repeal. There were not enough circulating U.S. coins in the region to implement the law. It maddened Gwin that all these memorials were originating out of the San Francisco assay office, which had been instrumental in finding the workaround.

In a speech to the Senate, Gwin defended himself, stating that the object of his provision had been to restrain the exercise of the legislative power of coinage that had been usurped by the secretary of the Treasury. Corwin would get a little rough treatment but not an arraignment. Gwin pointed out that the original intent of the legislation establishing an assay office was to prepare gold bars for commercial purposes; it was never to provide circulating coinage receivable for government dues. Public dues were to be paid in silver and gold coinage only. It had, in effect, deferred passage of legislation to establish a California branch mint.

Splitting constitutional hairs was going to win no points for Gwin in the California business community. The California papers called the provision reckless and oppressive. Gwin understood that. He also knew that the miners wanted a mint with its free coinage—and that he must have their political support to remain in power.

Dr. Gwin was not finished. He complained that from the time he took his seat in the Senate he had had to contend with the Philadelphia Mint. He now declared that he was opposed to the manner in which the Treasury was proposing to construct the San Francisco mint. It is a virtual certainty that Gwin knew Theodore Adams's construction cost estimate. Adams had done a stint as a contractor in Vicksburg and was working with Gwin on the transcontinental railroad project.

The senator called for the Treasury to submit the plans and specifications for the branch mint.[23] The world had changed since the Philadelphia Mint was planned and constructed. A new state of affairs had arisen in the world bullion markets. However, Gwin would wait on this issue until March 4. He was alluding to the fact that the Democrats had returned to power in the fall elections, capturing the presidency for Franklin Pierce.

In case the Mint did not understand that it was payback time, Gwin announced his intent to ask for an investigation into certain abuses that defrauded depositors. More importantly, he stated that in one year the Mint had actually issued debased coinage that should have been withdrawn from circulation.[24]

The other shoe fell a week later, on January 6, 1853. Gwin submitted a resolution that was unanimously agreed to calling for the secretary of the Treasury to provide certain information for an investigation when the Mint's annual appropriation came before the Senate Finance Committee. Gwin wanted to know the method by which the Mint received gold coins minted before 1834. He wanted copies of assay-commission reports for the ten preceding years. He wanted to know under whose authority the Mint declined to separate silver and gold for the depositor when the net product of either metal was under $5, and whether the gold and silver were actually separated with the Mint's contingency fund thereby benefiting; what amount of silver was being left unextracted in the gold coins leaving Philadelphia; and why depositors were fully charged for separating silver from gold from November 14, 1850, to April 1, 1851, when significant amounts of this bullion were not refined. In addition, he noted that the depositors were deprived of nearly half the value of their silver that was in fact charged to the depositors as alloy. Finally, Gwin wanted to know under whose authority the Mint used the profit from the three-cent piece to defray contingent expenses.[25] Only Richard McCulloh had this kind of in-depth knowledge. It was payback time indeed.

George Eckert drew the difficult chore of answering this inquiry. If anybody could put lipstick on this pig, it was Eckert. While most of the practices had occurred before his time, it was still an embarrassment for the Mint and therefore to him, even if he was a lame duck.

At the heart of Gwin's request concerning the pre-1834 gold was the fact that prior to 1832, the Mint had ignored the requirement that each coin be 22 carats, yielding a fineness of .9167. In actuality, these coins had a fineness of .911 to .912. After the law change of 1834, which reduced the standard fineness to .900, the Mint had to decide how to value these older coins when presented for recoinage. It had been decided to value them at a fineness of .914, thereby splitting the shortfall equally between the depositor and the government. Eckert pointed out that the impact was small, as only $1,634,953 up to the close of the 1852 fiscal year had been presented for recoinage.[26]

Eckert cited the Mint Act of 1837 as the authority for withholding payments to depositors for small amounts of silver not deemed economically recoverable. It had been determined that $5 would be the cutoff, information which had been published in tariffs approved by the Treasury Department. Even before the influx of California gold, small deposits were batched together or lumped with larger ones for refining. Therefore, the Mint really did separate this silver, gaining the economic benefit. Originally this gain had been credited against the melter and refiner's wastage. However, in some instances, wastage actually showed a positive balance, which masked the actual wastage and therefore the performance of the melter and refiner. After McCulloh came on board, Patterson made the decision in October 1846 to credit the profit and loss account of the Mint for this gain. The account was then netted against Mint contingent expenses. Eckert was not forthcoming with the amount gained over the years by the Mint from this activity.

Eckert was defensive about the decision to bypass refining with a portion of the bullion in the winter of 1850 to 1851. He stated the obvious, that refining could not separate all of the silver from the gold. The Mint, while required to leave no more than 5 percent silver in the refined gold bars, by practice left on average 1 to 2 percent. During the period in question, the Mint ramped up the silver alloy to the full 5 percent permitted by law. The depositor received full credit for the absolute quantity of silver in the deposit; then the Mint charged the depositor for that portion left in the coin as alloy. The rate charged for refining, fixed by the secretary of the Treasury, was five cents per ounce of gold. The silver used as alloy was valued at $1.29 per ounce. Eckert calculated that the amount of additional silver used as alloy and charged to the depositors was $12,760. He justified the action as necessary in order to shorten the wait time for depositors to receive payment for their bullion. The interest that was avoided, which would have been incurred with this delay, easily offset the loss of the silver. Eckert even suggested that long delays forced many small depositors who could not afford to wait to sell their gold bullion at a markdown to brokers. Not a word was mentioned that the Mint would have drowned in gold bullion during this period if this action had not been taken.

Eckert admitted that profits on the three-cent piece were applied against contingent expenses. His defense was simply that if Congress wished these profits returned to Treasury, appropriations for contingent expenses at the Mint would have to be increased by an offsetting amount. While true, that position did not sit well.

In the matter of the debased coinage, Eckert submitted Patterson's correspondence. When the assay commission for the year 1847 met in Philadelphia on February 16, 1848, they found that gold coins struck at New Orleans the prior year were outside legal tolerances, with a fineness of .8978. The committee met again the next day to inspect gold bars made from melted coins at New Orleans. One bar was substandard. They duly reported this problem to the president the following day.

Patterson reported to the president the following April that the melter and refiner had inexplicably set his target at a fineness of .899 rather than .900. The entire source of gold coinage in 1847 for New Orleans was coins of Great Britain and France, already at a fineness of .900. Therefore, there was no explanation or excuse for the shortfall. Patterson closed the report stating the course to be taken was, by law, in the hands of the president. Indeed it was, and James Knox Polk replaced the melter and refiner. Patterson made no proposal to recall New Orleans gold coins, and for several years reports came out of Britain—vigorously denied by the American mint—that U.S. gold coins were substandard.[27]

It was all there for Gwin. However, his use of the report had nothing to do with establishing the Mint's operating appropriation for the coming year. What were pardonable actions before the onslaught of the California gold had now become abuses of an unacceptable magnitude. It was easy to see from these actions where the money had come from to fund Franklin Peale's overrun in the 1850 expansion and James Booth's furnaces, and how it was hidden. Gwin had a solution for this situation.

On January 26, 1853, Dr. Gwin introduced S. 596, a bill to better regulate the mints and secure the conformity of coins to their respective standards. It was read twice and referred to the Finance Committee. The bill called for a bureau within Treasury to oversee the four existing mints and the one to be built in San Francisco. There would be a director, an inspector, an engraver, and two assayers, to be appointed by the president. Each officer under the director would have an assistant. A superintendent would be appointed in Philadelphia in place of the present director. All records, standard weights and balances, and the coin cabinet were to be transferred to Washington.

The office of engraver was to be removed from Philadelphia by its present holder to Washington. The engraver was charged with preparing and engraving the legal devices and inscriptions for all dies used in the coinage of the various mints. He was to have custody of the dies and tools required for their manufacture and keep a detailed register of dies. It would also be his duty to examine the impressions of coins struck at each mint and report his findings to the director. Unfit dies were to be destroyed by the coiner in the presence of the superintendent at each mint. McCulloh had seen to his friend; if passed, it was everything for which Longacre could hope.

The bill reconstituted the assay commission. It would not be so easy for the director to put his close friends on the commission. If coins were found to be substandard, that fact would be reported to the president and the officers involved would be dismissed from office.

The next clause was aimed specifically at Franklin Peale and the nepotism in Philadelphia. All contracts for the purchase of supplies, all expenditures of money, and all estimates for appropriations were to be submitted to the director for approval. Relatives of the officers in Washington were barred from working at the mints. Those of the superintendents were barred from the respective mints of each superintendent. No clerk or officer would be allowed to carry on a side business or trade. Likewise, they were prohibited from activities within the mints that generated personal profits.

Finally, specific jail terms were spelled out for embezzlement at the Mint. This clause stemmed from the Hutchinson case where the crook was caught and convicted but could not be sentenced because the law made no such provision. Hutchinson had avoided jail time.[28]

Gwin's arguments for reform were compelling. But was it too much to digest too late in the session?

• • • •

J.R. Chandler had been waiting to pounce as soon as any New York branch-mint bill came out of the Ways and Means Committee. On January 18, 1853, New York congressman James Brooks made the first move (fig. 122), bringing just such a bill out of Ways and Means. At the end of the routine first reading, Chandler jumped up to object to the second reading. This triggered a vote to reject and turned the discussion into a debate over proper legislative procedures. Much to the disgust of Brooks, this exhausted the scheduled time that day for the presentation of new legislation.[29]

Chandler had gotten wind that the New Yorker's legislative strategy was to spring the bill on the House by moving for immediate action and calling the previous question to cut off debate and any amendments. Chandler had stopped that approach and now the battle was on.

Chandler controlled the floor the next day and set the tone for the debate, which was nasty. He reminded members from the last Congress that the outcry then had been the incompetency of the Philadelphia Mint in supplying gold coinage and its inability to process the gold bullion flowing in from California. Chandler pointed out that the expansion of the Philadelphia Mint was now complete and it could coin $100 million a year in various denominations. "All the demands upon the mint had been met. But no man, no set of men, not even the government itself, would be able to meet the everlasting wants of those who with the horse-leech cry 'give, give, give' to the great metropolis of the Union."

The time between the deposit of gold bullion and payment in coin was now down to five days. It could not be done any better in New York. Besides, the transit time

Fig. 122. In his attempt to gain a branch mint for New York City James Brooks came out swinging with an attack clearly supported by Senator Gwin.

from New York to Philadelphia had been reduced to three and half hours. The costs associated with a delay in monetizing the gold bullion were simply no longer there.

Of course, Chandler brought up the issue that the New York delegation did not want to discuss. With a mint at the very door to the gold fields in San Francisco, the source of bullion for coinage at New York was significantly reduced. The San Francisco Mint was authorized both to coin gold and cast ingots. Gold dust traversing the Isthmus of Panama would slow to a trickle.

If he had ended his discussion here, he would have made his point and kept the debate focused. But he did not. Chandler pointed out that no one in New York outside of the banking interests cared in the least about a branch mint. However, these same people cared about beating out Philadelphia. If they could not do it by debate and voting, they would buy it. That statement, implying the purchasing of votes, created a furor of denial in the House and distracted debate from the core issues.

At this point the chairman of Ways and Means called for the House to convene as a Committee of the Whole to debate the bill. It failed, 79 yeas to 82 nays. The three key players, Briggs, Brooks, and Chandler, all voted against.[30] Neither side was ready for a debate.

Chandler still held the floor on January 20, but he yielded it to Amos Tuck, a fellow Whig from New Hampshire. It would not do for a Philadelphia congressman to offer a compromise on this issue.

Tuck believed that no question had come before the House in the previous four years that had such a sound argument against it. The country did not need a mint at New York. The land and building for such a branch mint would cost about $250,000. He reminded the House that a recent newspaper article noted that land was more expensive in New York than in London. Machinery and fixtures would cost another $200,000, and a bullion fund of $2 million would be needed. He estimated that the branch mint's annual cost of operation would be $200,000 plus another $147,000 in interest on the bullion fund and capital costs. Also, there was the question of the impact of the upcoming branch mint at San Francisco.

Now Tuck threw out a compromise proposed by George Eckert. If, after constructing the mint in California, the government determined that additional facilities were needed at New York, they could be attained without the large expense of a branch mint. Tuck explained that mint operations were composed of two broad but distinct departments: the receiving department took in the bullion and paid out stamped coins in exchange, and the manufacturing department assayed the metal and converted it into coinage. These two departments did not need to be in the same building or even in the same city.

In Tuck's view, all that was necessary in New York was an office for receiving deposits of bullion in exchange for coinage of equivalent value. Labor would be held to a minimum by placing this office under the direction of the assistant treasurer for New York City. Tuck estimated an annual cost of $3,000 with no need of added building space. He estimated the cost of transporting the raw bullion to Philadelphia for coinage and the return trip to be $22,500, based upon annual volume of $30 million. This economic argument was compelling.

David Seymour from upstate New York delivered the counterproposal. He stated that this question was of national interest, not a miserable scramble between two rival cities. Originally it was thought that the mint should be located at the seat of government. Yet branch mints had been established in the United States by the dictates of trade, commerce, and population. Let Philadelphia remain the main mint. All New York City was asking was that the needs of her commerce not be neglected. In spite of any laws that might be passed, the commerce of the country was going to center upon New York. The greatest portion of the immigrant flow came through New York City, bringing large amounts of foreign specie for recoinage. Seymour estimated this amount was not less than $60 million per year. Proponents of a branch mint were on firmer ground with Seymour's argument.[31]

Here the kettle boiled until January 25. James Brooks was still smarting over how Chandler had stolen the march on him by moving to reject the bill before its second reading. Now it was his turn. It was no coincidence that Brooks was speaking the day before Gwin introduced his bill in the Senate for sweeping reform of the mint. He had access to McCulloh's computations of the full cost to depositors and to the public of the Mint's various dealings and he was prepared to share it with the House.

He went right to the heart of the matter. The Philadelphia Mint was a mere bauble to that city. It was not a bauble for New York; it was indispensible. Coinage was as indispensible, to a seat of commerce and exchanges, as a hammer was to a shipwright or carpenter. Brooks was now burning with anger. He called Chandler's address full of pointless declamations. He accused Chandler of exciting the passions of the House with his veiled charge of intended bribery. Chandler stood and interrupted Brooks, wishing to read a New York City newspaper article on the subject. Brooks interrupted back, stating that Chandler should expect no such courtesies from him, having taken the floor with his motion to reject. Chandler retorted that he asked for no courtesy. Brooks then refused to yield the floor.

With that exchange setting the tone, Brooks waded into the adequacy of the Philadelphia Mint. He denied that Philadelphia had the competency to coin all the California gold without resorting to tricks and creating extraordinary costs at the depositors' expense. Brooks then examined the decision to bypass refining a portion of the bullion deposits; it was simply throwing away the depositors' silver. To acquire a reputation for quick and efficient work, the silver of the depositor, worth $1.29 per ounce, was left in the gold. Yet the depositor was charged five cents for refining it. The total cost to the depositors was $34,760 and Brooks had tables from McCulloh to support this number in contradiction to Eckert's calculation. Worse in the eyes of Brooks was the fact that the Mint did not deny this claim. At this point the time for discussion expired.

The House reconvened at noon on January 26. The Reverend James Gallaher opened with a prayer. That was the last civil word spoken that day.

Brooks continued with his scathing indictment. He pointed out that the Mint was bound to return payment in kind to the depositor for his bullion. This meant that he should receive both silver and gold coins in proportion to the ratio of the two metals in his deposit. However, the Philadelphia Mint did no such thing. They paid out only in gold, keeping for themselves the silver valued 4 to 6 percent below market.

Next he exposed the accounting at the Mint for the seigniorage from the three-cent piece. Gains from 1851 and 1852 amounted to $93,317, which were applied against contingent expenses, making the Mint look much more efficient than it really was. If the Mint coined some 30 million of these pieces in 1853, as newspapers had stated, the gain would be $150,000.

Brooks then moved to the issue of not paying the depositor if the metal separated was less than $5. Again he had numbers from McCulloh. If a depositor brought in 62 ounces of bullion, the silver separated would be less than $5 in value. Given that the Mint lumped deposits together for refining, they actually recovered this silver. Brooks had a Mint memorandum in front of him that stated for the 12 months preceding June 30, 1851, the gain to the Mint from this practice was $46,750. It was another large sum to offset contingent expenses. Unlike Eckert in his report to the Senate Finance committee, McCulloh had laid out the full impact of the Mint's actions for Brooks.

As had Gwin, Brooks addressed the issues of coin debasement in New Orleans and the release of the embezzler, Hutchinson. Brooks also pointed out that in the preceding year, the Treasury had maintained a bullion fund at Philadelphia of almost $7 million to facilitate prompt payment to depositors. He quoted Secretary Corwin, calling this dead capital. He castigated the Mint for coining $41 million of double eagles out of a total coinage of $51 million in 1852. The country needed quarter eagles, yet the Mint had only coined a little more than one million of these pieces.

There were calls for Brooks to yield the floor so that questions might be asked. He refused. He talked about side issues that had little bearing on the decision to be made. He finally closed with one more dig at Chandler and the Mint. New York was asking for a mint and felt restive under the heavy tax paid to enable Philadelphia to keep her plaything of a mint.

At this point, Chandler's question was called to reject the New York branch-mint bill. It was soundly defeated. According to procedure, the bill was read a second time. Sensing victory, Brooks attempted to force the bill to a vote. Chandler, scared from the results of the preliminary vote, attempted to stall, moving that the bill be considered by a Committee of the Whole. This failed. Chandler was really in trouble.

The Speaker of the House now ruled that the question of the bill's passage could be called. It looked like Philadelphia was going down to sure defeat. As the roll was called, the votes were tallied and it was apparent that it would be close. When it came time for Edward Marshall to vote, he took the floor. Over objections, he explained why he was voting against the New York mint bill. The whole New York delegation had voted against the California mint bill. His vote was simple payback. The final tally was 87 yeas and 90 nays. But it was closer than that. Briggs changed his vote to a nay in a last-ditch effort to save the day. He could then move to have the vote reconsidered. Recasting Briggs's vote as it should have been, Marshall killed the mint bill. Defeat had been snatched from the jaws of victory by the New York delegation.

It was all over. For George Briggs it was a bitter pill to swallow. For two Congresses, over four sessions, he had labored constantly to gain this legislation in the House. He now stood to say, "Mr. Speaker I bow with submission to the defeat of the mint bill." Thomas Florence from Philadelphia replied, "There is nothing like Christian resignation and humility."

In the final vote, Democrats and Whigs were split. This was a pocketbook issue, not a party issue. Most of Maryland voted against the bill in support of the port of Baltimore. The regions of the country were split, although the Midwest tended to support New York, which exported their farm goods.[32]

• • • •

As the session drew to a close, the Senate began working on the deficiency bill. The backroom maneuvering had begun. Much of the work was done in the Finance Committee, with the California branch mint coming under additional scrutiny. Secretary Corwin had requested authorization to rent or lease space with a term of no more than three years for the continued operation of the assay office in San Francisco. Moneys for any necessary purchases of equipment would come out of the original mint appropriation. The amendment authorized the receipt of gold bullion to be exchanged for ingots or bars of gold. It also set the salary of the officers and enabled the hiring of the necessary assistants and workmen and the payment of their wages. If allowed to go forward, the assay office would no longer be a contract operation. In regard to the mint, no contract for the erection and establishment of the branch mint could be executed until a further order of Congress. Corwin was in a tight spot, doing what he could with an impossibly low appropriation.[33]

This amendment opened up a can of worms in the House revolving around the failed New York City branch mint. The chair of Ways and Means had requested a nonconcurrence with the Senate's amendment to the deficiency bill. Harry Hibbard, a representative from New Hampshire who had voted for the New York bill, moved that a clause repealing the San Francisco branch mint be tacked on to the Senate amendment. An assay operation had proven to be sufficient. No contract had yet been entered into for the construction of the branch mint. This amendment basically put them in the same situation as before. Hibbard could not understand why the money for a branch mint should be spent when an assay office would suffice.

This position brought Edward Marshall to his feet instantly. He admitted that the assay office was as busy as ever. But the viability of the assay office was far from Marshall's point. He called it one of the grossest and most oppressive frauds ever perpetrated upon any people. Now, as a consequence of the secretary of the Treasury's request, that office would remain as constant and injurious an operation as ever.

There was more discussion centering on the diversion of the branch-mint appropriation to the assay office. The general view was that it would take much more than this amount to establish a proper mint in San Francisco. If California would be content with an assay office in its stead, let the state have it. Marshall saw the diversion as squandering the already too-limited funds for the branch mint on the assay office. It would have the same effect as repealing the branch-mint act.

Marshall perceived the New Yorkers behind this amendment, attempting to reopen the entire branch-mint question. Emotional, he let his frustrations erupt. California had applied to Congress for two years for the establishment of a mint. What the state got from the House was a mutilated and insufficient version but it was better than nothing. The bill stipulated that the mint must be constructed for less than $300,000. What that would buy, Marshall could not prophesy. It must be some sort of blacksmith shop but it would prevent the miners from being swindled by the fees charged at the assay office. Moreover, Marshall was willing to bet that should this amendment become law, not one cent of the $300,000 appropriation would be left for the branch mint. Under this scenario, Marshall declared that his grandchildren would not see a mint in San Francisco. He closed by saying that he was told under good authority that Treasury had bids for constructing the branch mint in hand. He called for Ways and Means to reject the Senate's amendment.[34]

Marshall carried the day; Hibbard withdrew his amendment and the House rejected the Senate amendment. Where was Gwin in this affair? What was so apparent to Marshall would have been instantly obvious to the senator. Gwin would put up with an assay office in the interim in exchange for a much larger mint. The risk that New York would try to piggyback on any future appropriation made for San Francisco was a tradeoff he was willing to make. All along, he believed the nation needed two mints: San Francisco and New York. Just as importantly, the financing for an intercontinental railroad must come from New York. A deal could be made in this fertile atmosphere.

• • • •

Senator Hamilton Fish (fig. 123) was taken ill in February. After the Finance Committee stalled his New York branch-mint bill, he had let the House action take precedence. Recovering from his illness, he drafted a compromise amendment for the civil and diplomatic appropriation bill that would establish an assay office at New York City.

Fig. 123. Senator Hamilton Fish outmaneuvered Philadelphia Mint supporters in the waning hours of the Thirty-Second Congress to gain an assay office for New York City.

He dropped it in the legislative hopper on Saturday, February 26. The office would be authorized to receive bullion for assaying, melting, refining, and parting for the preparation of ingots, bars, or discs of either standard or pure fineness. No bar of less than ten ounces would be cast unless at the specific weights of one, two, three, or five ounces. All gold and silver bullion and all foreign coins to be converted into coinage would be transferred to the Philadelphia Mint at government expense. A sum of $100,000 was appropriated for this office.

On March 1, with two days remaining before adjournment, the proposal came up for discussion. Senator Richard Brodhead from Pennsylvania hoped that a question of order would be raised as he ventured that not five members of the Senate had reviewed this amendment. There was also a question over the validity of the estimate used for the appropriation. The appropriation was taken out. At each turn, R.M.T. Hunter, the Finance Committee chair, supported Fish. Finally, Brodhead, in desperation, argued that the amendment had not been printed until the preceding day. William Seward came to Fish's defense. Seward had been in the Senate for four years and he opined that there was not an issue that had been more fully before that body than the branch mint for New York. The point was made that a branch mint was not an assay office. Seward rebutted that the greater included the lesser. The amendment passed with strong support outside of Pennsylvania and the slaveholding agricultural areas.[35] In the House, the Pennsylvania delegation largely acquiesced in allowing Fish's amendment to pass.

Chandler had reviewed the draft legislation in advance. It appeared to him just what Eckert had proposed earlier as a compromise, although the assay function was an additional activity. In consequence, Chandler did not ask senators to oppose it when Fish introduced it. Fish had told Chandler that this assay office would satisfy New York and that the issue of a branch mint would be a thing of the past. Chandler had conveyed this information to Eckert on March 1, indicating that Fish had worked behind the scenes to gain support in advance.[36]

Reviewing the language of the legislation, Eckert saw it very differently from Chandler. The assay office contained a refining department and was authorized to cast bars or discs. The New Yorkers had everything that belonged to a mint except the right to make coins. In his mind coinage as a matter of course would eventually come. The truth of the matter was that Fish and company had effectively outmaneuvered Philadelphia. Eckert fumed that the bill with which he had furnished Chandler differed critically from Fish's amendment. The Mint director cynically observed that Chandler thought the two to be the same. That was a shocking mistake.[37]

In the final hours before adjournment, the $100,000 appropriation for the New York assay office reappeared.[38] In the matter of the San Francisco branch mint, the deadline for receiving bids was extended to April 1, 1853. The $300,000 appropriated was to be applied only to making the mint operational, and was not to be applied to the purchase of a building.[39]

• • • •

George Briggs went home to New York City with the close of the session. He had not stood for reelection to Congress. As soon as he arrived there was a call for a public dinner celebrating his return to private life and to honor his labors on the New York branch-mint bill "against the jealousy and parliamentary tact of a neighboring city." Briggs was humble in his response. Credit went to New York's senators and to his colleagues in the House. Their actions resulted in the bill introduced by Hamilton Fish, which would answer the practical purpose of a full mint. "The great object so long contended for has at last been achieved in spite of the opposition of our sister City and State to that meritorious measure." Briggs declined the dinner.[40]

In San Francisco, the site of the assay office became the branch mint. The building was 60 feet by 60 feet and 3 stories high. It incorporated the old offices of Curtis, Perry,

Fig. 124. The former assay office, this building hardly looked the part of a United States branch mint. Even Dahlonega had rated better.

and Ward, plus an expansion of the west side of 20 feet at a cost of $239,000. It was far from what Gwin had envisioned. In fact it had a look of a storefront operation (fig. 124). It went into service on April 3, 1854.[41] The miners did not share Gwin's vision; they were simply happy to have a mint two years sooner than what would otherwise have been.

Senator Gwin's mint-reform bill died in the Finance Committee. The impetus for passage dissipated when the New York branch-mint bill failed in the House. Support for the two issues were tied together. Moreover the Finance Committee was preoccupied in the latter stages of the second session by the issue of the silver-coin scarcity that had reached intolerable proportions.

1849

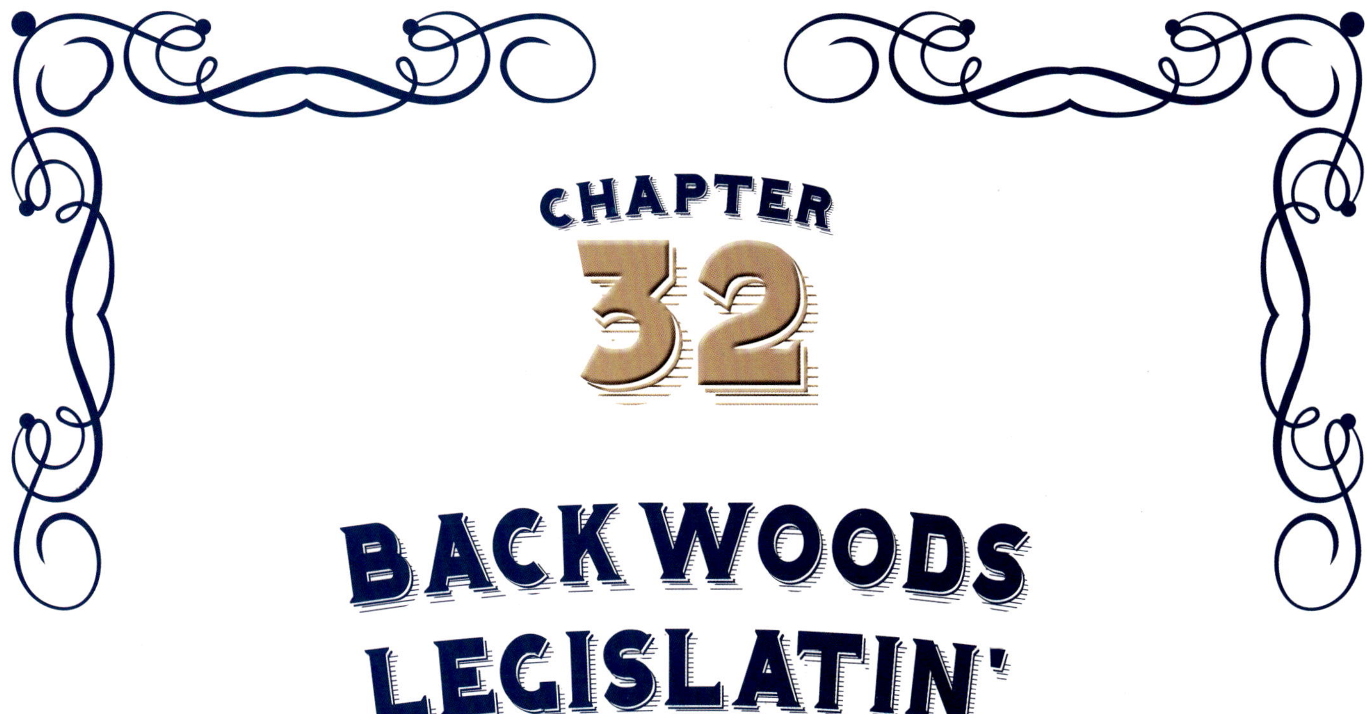

CHAPTER 32

BACKWOODS LEGISLATIN'

The issue of the scarcity of silver specie in the United States had been bubbling away, slowly building up pressure. This time around, the ratio of gold-to-silver values was reasonably well understood in economic circles. At one time gold had been rated too low, and now it was rated too high. In each instance, the undervalued metal was drawn out of circulation by being exported, hoarded, or melted. This was the present case with silver.

In designing a fix, opinions differed. Immense supplies of gold from California, Australia, and Siberia were anticipated in the market. If the ratio was adjusted downward from the current approximate value of 16 to 1, it would undoubtedly bring the relative values of the two metals back in line for a time. However, no one expected gold to hold its value in the face of excess supplies coming from the big new strikes. Hence, once on the path of adjustments, more would be required, leaving the value of American specie in flux. That scenario was unacceptable.

Some economic circles called for the United States to go to a silver standard. The world's silver supply had been stable for some time. Gold could be minted by weight with values reset periodically.[1] This suggestion ignored what legislators knew well the last time the ratio was reset: silver was fine for making change but extremely cumbersome in large quantities. But the current financial writers could be forgiven; it had been too long since some of them

had carried a single silver dollar, much less two or three, in their pants pockets.

Treasury Secretary Thomas Corwin had a different take on the subject. Substantial volumes of gold and silver coinage had been added to the country's circulating media. In addition to the California gold, silver was flowing into the country through immigrants. Given the rates of increase that the country was experiencing from these two sources, Corwin could foresee the day when the United States would be awash in hard specie. Bank issuance of paper currency could be dispensed with and the country could achieve a silver and gold currency contemplated in the Constitution.[2] Thomas Hart Benton, that old Jacksonian hard-money advocate, could not have spelled it out better. (A fixture in the Senate for some 30 years, Benton was gone. He had swung over to the Free Soil wing of his party and as a result lost his reelection bid.) Corwin was going to focus on keeping silver coinage from exportation.

In fact, as early as November 1851, Corwin had requested a report from George Eckert on the situation, particularly as it was addressed in Great Britain. At that point the market ratio of silver to gold was 15.675 to 1 in the United States versus a legal ratio, after the rounding adjustment, to weights of 15.988 to 1 in 1837. Eckert noted that the British were not plagued by silver leaving their domestic economy. The silver in their coinage was reduced 10 percent from intrinsic value. In other words, they had debased their silver coinage. The British were able to affect this monetary policy by restricting the legal-tender amount for their silver coins. Gold was applied for sums larger than 40 shillings, approximately US$10.

In making a recommendation to Corwin, Eckert turned to a letter written by Robert Maskell Patterson to Representative Phoenix the preceding February. It came too late in the Thirty-First Congress to get anything done. Patterson proposed reducing the metal content of the subsidiary silver coins while holding the dollar unchanged. Legal tender on these pieces would be limited to $5. Also, the treasurer of the Mint would be authorized to purchase the bullion necessary for these coins. The half dollar would be reduced from 206.25 grains of standard silver to 192 grains. The adjusted silver-to-gold ratio for the subsidiary silver coins would be 14.884 to 1, 5 percent below the market rate of 15.675 to 1. In Eckert's opinion, the British system cried out for adoption as soon as possible. Beyond that he had nothing more to add.[3] In reality, Eckert was in over his head and had he not had the director's clerk, Bob Patterson, to guide him to his father's letter, he would have been lost for a response.

Corwin was cautious as he moved forward. In February and again in November 1851, Secretary of State Daniel Webster sent private notes to the U.S. minister to Great Britain, Abbot Lawrence, instructing him to investigate the British system and the gold ratios in place in Europe. In response, Lawrence made the point that in limiting the legal-tender amount of these coins, the government must still redeem them in gold to prevent their depreciation domestically. In Lawrence's opinion, silver coins would have to have from 10 to 12 percent less bullion to prevent their being shipped to Europe.[4]

At the beginning of 1852, Corwin was ready to recommend changes to the subsidiary silver coins, which he placed in the hands of the Senate Finance Committee. In moving forward, the committee members adopted most, but not all, of Corwin's recommendations and added some of their own. S. 271 was introduced in the Senate on March 8, 1852, with an accompanying report.

The bill incorporated the recommended reduction in weight for the half dollar to 192 grains of standard silver. Pro rata reductions would be made to the quarter, dime, and half dime. These coins would be legal tender in private transactions up to $5; however, to prevent the depreciation of these debased coins, there would be no such limits for payment of public dues. In case this provision for the payment of public dues might induce artificial demand, the bill provided that the secretary of the Treasury was empowered to set production levels.

The committee chose not to develop or determine a relationship between gold and silver values. Just as Gwin had expected, gold had become an article of export, moving from country to country not as coins but as bullion. For purposes of trade, the bill would authorize the government to cast bullion into bars of either fine or standard gold at the request of the depositor for a small fee. Thus the government was spared the expense of coinage for which no fee was charged.

The committee observed that the coins used most in commerce were those capable of making the most payments and that could be transported and counted with the greatest convenience. The gold piece most used in the country was the half eagle. Of the small silver coins, the dime had the highest mintage. On the other hand, the double eagle was used solely for bullion. To the committee, it made the most sense to coin pieces of $1, $2, $3, $5, and $10 in value and to scrap the double eagle. However, the committee was not ready to take that radical step. They did call for a $3 gold piece with the idea that a $2 gold piece could be substituted for the quarter eagle at some time in the future.

To offset the expense of the Mint, the committee called for a charge to depositors of 0.5 percent in addition to the charge for refining—essentially, an end to free coinage. Profits from seigniorage would be transferred to Treasury. The treasurer of the Mint would acquire the necessary silver bullion for the subsidiary silver coins. No deposits of subsidiary silver coins would be accepted at the Mint. Such coins would be paid out at the Mint in exchange for gold coins at sums no less than $100. The effective date of the changeover was left blank.[5]

The bill routinely came up for consideration in the Senate on March 29. Finance Committee chairman R.M.T. Hunter moved for an effective date of May 1, 1852.[6] Somewhere in the process the date slipped to June 1. The bill passed and was sent to the House on March 30.[7] As structured, S. 271 was a masterpiece in simplicity; yet each clause played a significant role. It was like a finely crafted watch in which each moving part contributed to the success of the whole. The only flaw was the failure of the committee to call for the termination of the quarter eagle in favor of a $2 gold piece. The problem was that any amendment, if not carefully considered, could undo the intent of the legislation.

Once in the House, the bill went to Ways and Means where it sat and sat and sat. It sat through the entire remaining time of the first session. It sat for another two months of the second session while the issue of the New York City mint was thrashed out. It had been said in the House debate on the New York branch mint that coinage was a species of the occult to which few in Congress were willing to bend their minds. In the case of S. 271, nothing could have been closer to the truth.

The man from Ways and Means chosen to lead the drive to finally pass this bill in the House was Cyrus L. Dunham from Indiana. A more unlikely and less prepared individual would have been hard to find. There was nothing in the man's background from which to draw; he had no college education and no financial experience, being basically a frontier lawyer and legislator. George Houston, the committee chair, had the House experience. Another member, James Brooks, had the contacts with the New York financial markets but, being in the Whig minority, was precluded. Of the nine members of Ways and Means, Dunham was eighth in terms of seniority.

Nevertheless, on February 1, 1853, Dunham rose to deliver a prepared speech in favor of the amended bill coming out of Ways and Means. He had hardly begun before he was interrupted with a question. The committee had amended the Senate version to expand the legal-tender status for the proposed subsidiary silver coinage to include all debts due to the government. This served to highlight to the other members the disparity in legal-tender status between private and public debts. Willard Hall, Yale-educated from Missouri, wanted to know why. Dunham stumbled. He failed to address the need for these coins to not depreciate in purchasing power. Instead, he talked of the desire of Ways and Means to have gold as the standard currency, with these silver coins subservient. They would be tokens rather than currency, although the government would stand ready to redeem them at their nominal value.

Hall could not grasp why these coins would have unrestricted legal-tender status in one case and not the other. It seemed to give the advantage to the individual over the government. Dunham testily accused Hall of catechizing him on a subject to which Hall had given no previous attention. Hall rose to the occasion, saying he was extremely gratified at the lecture Dunham was delivering. Dunham was losing his audience.

On the man went, often arguing in the negative, explaining why certain actions were not taken in the bill. In other cases his logic in defense of the bill was flawed. He touched upon international monetary flows, showing he had not the slightest understanding of their mechanics. It actually made little difference as, judging by the comments and questions raised by the other representatives, they were just as ignorant on the subject. Then he raised the issue of the 0.5 percent coinage charge to defray Mint expenses, an end to free coinage.

James Brooks interrupted to asked what Dunham wanted done with his bill. Brooks was no friend, in that Dunham had just voted against the New York branch-mint bill. One member asked if Dunham had the least idea of putting this bill on its passage without a discussion of the important issues involved. Dunham rebutted that the bill had been before Congress for nearly two whole sessions. He was promptly corrected; it had been before Ways and Means, not the House. Brooks regained the floor to remind Dunham that the issue of seigniorage—the 0.5 percent coinage charge—had been soundly defeated the preceding June in the House. Therefore the bill needed to be examined.

Stopped by a member of his own committee, Dunham blustered that he was not proposing to recoin all the silver coinage in the country. He was not changing its nominal value. Once again he had been sidetracked.

Dunham got back on task when he stated that the expenses of the mints were substantial. Those who benefited from this activity should pay the expense. The country had an immense coinage at a great expense but a deficiency of specie for circulation. His closing shot was a swipe at the double eagle so beneficial to the financial institutions.[8]

Then Dunham went over the amendments proposed by Ways and Means in detail. Most were minor. With the law now becoming effective upon passage, the effective date obviously needed changing as it was unrealistic for Mint compliance. In another twist, the secretary of the Treasury was empowered to regulate the sizes and devices of the silver coins impacted by the act. Here was an opening not only to redesign the coins, but also to depart from the standard devices—a figure emblematic of liberty and the eagle—mandated in previous laws.[9] Dunham was now done. Yet just when you thought the discussion could not get any worse, it did.

On February 2 Andrew Johnson took the floor. Self-educated and apprenticed to a tailor, Johnson was even less prepared to debate this bill than Dunham. That did not stop him. The East Tennessee legislator focused on the dollar, which was not involved in the changeover. He asked why it was necessary to reduce the dollar from 412.5 grains of standard silver to 386 grains. Congress was depreciating the currency. They were defeating the very object contemplated in the Constitution: a sound currency. The nuanced provisions of the bill were beyond Johnson's ability to comprehend.

Charles Skelton from Trenton, New Jersey, quickly joined the debate, interrupting Johnson. Educated at Jefferson College in nearby Philadelphia, he was more than a match for either Dunham or Johnson. Skelton asked that Johnson recognize the practical difficulty the country was suffering under from the lack of circulating silver coins. The increase in the relative value of silver to gold had driven it out of circulation. The question of the day was how to keep this silver in circulation. Did Johnson have a better remedy? Johnson replied testily that he was coming to that if Skelton would allow him to continue. Skelton stated that he did not care about a particular remedy; he just wanted a remedy.

Johnson retorted that if Skelton would allow him to continue, he would get to his point much faster. Johnson now returned to his overriding theme. If they could, by law, make 107 dollars out of 100 dollars, none of the problems that had been solved from the time of alchemists to the present could compare with that solved by this modern Congress. It was all a bunch of quackery.

Johnson asked rhetorically where was the power to fix the value of a dollar? It was in the commercial world. These new coins were limited in payment to $5. Dunham jumped up at this misstatement. These coins were receivable for all dues of the U.S. government. That only egged on Johnson. Here was a coin that was legal tender for all debts and another that was only legal tender for public debts. Dunham wanted to ask Johnson a question but Johnson refused to yield. He would not allow Dunham to consume his time.

Johnson now expounded upon his developing theme. A man who owes the government would be obliged to pay 7 percent less than one who owed an individual. That was the worst sort of shinplaster legislation. Therefore, if one made this coin legal tender for all private debts, the obligations of contracts would be impaired. On the other hand, passage of this bill would create a two-tiered currency. This silver specie would take the character of depreciated paper. Mercifully, Johnson's allotted time to speak ended as he sputtered to an inconclusive end.[10]

On February 3, the first order of business was again S. 271. Johnson was on his feet instantly. He refused to admit that the remedy proposed was the right one. It would be better to do nothing than to make a change that only worsened the disease. In his remarks, Skelton had seemed to think that Johnson was duty-bound to offer an alternative. In Johnson's mind, that was only more evidence of the quackery of the times. Johnson now uttered the one intelligent comment that he had made so far in the debate. He would prefer to retire since he did not understand the case and was unwilling to minister to the disease.

However, Johnson continued talking without making a point. He circled back to the proposal that silver act as legal tender for government debts but not private debts. Dunham rose to protest that it would be legal tender up to $5 for private debts. Dunham would have been better served to let Johnson run his course. He said that Dunham's comment only served to show that those pushing this matter toward passage had no understanding of the law they were putting in place. The fact remained that those who presumed to know the defects in U.S. currency could not agree upon a proper plan to remedy them. Upon what Johnson based this statement was a mystery. Johnson finally opined that the bill ought not to pass as the Speaker hammered him to his seat.

Skelton, it seemed by default, was now the defender of S. 271. He obtained the floor, this time not to rebut Johnson but to renew the general arguments in favor of passage. He pointed out that the bill did not try to change the commercial values of these two metals; it could not. The country did have a disease; however, the bill was the remedy. In this case, increasing the weight of the gold coinage was not an option. Debasing the subsidiary silver coins as proposed took nothing out of anybody's pocket. Skelton did make one erroneous statement. He thought lightening the silver coinage included the dollar and that it would then circulate on an even basis with gold coinage. He had a point.

Johnson got back into the argument, stating obstinately that he had a remedy and that remedy was to do nothing, to let the patient alone. At this point another Tennessee legislator, who must have been dozing during the debates, added that he thought they should reduce the weight of gold coins and let silver remain as it was. That statement just fueled more skirmishing from both sides.

At the risk of repeating himself, Skelton retook the floor to try to clarify matters. They were not legislating a single cent out of anybody's pockets nor into anybody's pockets. They aimed to furnish small change for small transactions of business and gold for larger ones. This bill accomplished all the objects needed without doing injustice to anybody. With that, the morning hour for discussion expired; the House had exhausted itself with no progress made whatsoever. Over the three days not a single motion had been made.[11] This bill was in danger of dying on the legislative table.

Once more, on February 14, S. 271 came up, with Skelton leading the charge for passage. But now he had a problem that he wanted remedied. The bill called for a change in the devices of the coins. This amendment had been inserted so that the lighter coins could be easily distinguished from the heavier ones. This was not really necessary, as the heavier coins would be driven from circulation, finding their way into the bullion market. Even if a heavier coin remained in circulation, it would cause no loss to the individual receiving it in commerce.

There was an additional problem. Skelton had been informed by an officer of the Mint that new designs would require six to eight months to implement and it would necessitate the hiring of an additional engraver. That officer was Bob Patterson, sent by George Eckert to do what he could to aid the passage of this bill. Skelton's solution was to return to the original bill received from the Senate. He therefore recommended that the amendments from Ways and Means be voted down and the bill be put on its way to passage.

In support, Skelton repeated the arguments of the Senate in favor of seigniorage on bars and ingots but not on coinage. He knew this was a troublesome subject for Brooks and others in the House. Skelton then demanded the previous question, which in effect called for a vote on the bill without the proposed amendments from Ways and Means. To his frustration, he instead received a motion to table. Fortunately, it was soundly voted down.

Opponents to the bill now asked the Speaker if the morning hour for discussion had expired. The Speaker ruled that once the previous question had been ordered, it must be considered. Dunham asked to make a motion that the three-cent piece be adjusted in line with the other silver coinage. Hall, who had been quiet since the first day, objected. In his mind, this bill only had a chance of passing in its original condition as it came from the Senate. He was opposed to all amendments. A vote was then taken, defeating the amendments.

Finally, after more last-minute maneuvering and a move by Dunham that only muddled the situation, the vote was taken. Andrew Johnson demanded the yeas and nays. After 20 ayes, it was apparent there was no quorum. Tellers were ordered to round up the members. Nobody wanted to have to deal with this issue again, even less so to listen to Andrew Johnson. The votes were then tallied again. There were 94 ayes; no one bothered to count the nays. The bill passed.[12]

And so it was, with several stumbles and a lurch, the United States made a sweeping change in monetary policy. The concept of the intrinsic value of U.S. coinage had been challenged, and a long, slow slide away from this principle commenced. Free silver coinage was gone with the wind. Most importantly, the United States was now on the gold standard. The law did one other thing; it gave the power to strike ingots—at that point confined to the San Francisco Mint—to each of the U.S. Mint facilities. This opened the door for Senator Hamilton Fish to gain what New York needed in its assay office.

The silver dollar was retained as a fig-leaf token to a bimetallic standard that existed in name only. The Mint would continue to exchange these coins for the silver in the California bullion deposits. The depositors would then, in most cases, send them to the bullion dealers and hence back to the melting pot.

Somehow, when S. 271 came back to the Senate, the clause authorizing the secretary of the Treasury to regulate the size and devices of the new coins had reappeared. The Senate signed off and the president signed it into law with an effective date of June 1, 1852.[13] Clearly there were going to have to be corrections incorporated into the deficiency bill.

The necessary changes were made in the House. Dunham insisted that the seigniorage charge for casting the bars or ingots be the actual cost capped at 0.5 percent. Otherwise the charge for high-end bars and ingots would be too high. The effective date was changed to April 1, 1853.[14] Interestingly, Houston, as instructed by the Ways and Means Committee, added a section on the implementation of design changes on the subsidiary silver coins. To procure such devices, the director of the Mint was empowered, with the approval of the secretary of the Treasury, to temporarily engage the services of one or more outside artists distinguished in their respective fields. These artists would be paid to provide molds, models, and original dies. Their fees were to be paid from the contingent fund. Also, the three-cent piece was included in the bill; it became .900 fine, at a weight pro rata to the other silver coins. At the last minute, another move was made to make the debased silver coins legal tender for all debts, public and private. This amendment was voted down.[15]

There was one more action taken by the Thirty-Second Congress in its waning days. While in Washington, Bob Patterson met with Senator Hunter (fig. 125). As a student at the University of Virginia, Hunter had taken Professor Robert Maskell Patterson's courses and he greatly admired the man. For the father, he would do what he could for the son. Bob Patterson wanted the refining function gradually phased out at the Mint, with the work assumed by private contractors.[16] Patterson got his clause in an amendment to the appropriations for civil and diplomatic expenses bill.[17] That was all it took to effectively finish off McCulloh's zinc refining process as far as the Mint was concerned. If it was so much better, McCulloh could go into the contract refining business. What Booth thought about it, if he knew, was another thing.

Without a doubt, the actions of the Thirty-Second Congress were the most far reaching in regard to the Mint since the establishment of that institution in 1792.

• • • •

Now the pressure was on George Eckert to get the conforming subsidiary silver coins into circulation as fast as possible. Fortunately for him, some of the heat caused by the influx of California gold was off; incoming bullion had

Fig. 125. R.M.T. Hunter, chairman of the Senate Finance Committee, had been Robert Maskell Patterson's student at the University of Virginia and was a supporter of the family.

peaked during 1852, and volumes for the year in comparison to 1851 were actually down ever so slightly.[18] The unknown in the equation was how to respond to the congressional mandate for new devices to distinguish these coins from their heavier counterparts. Eckert would have to work with Longacre to find an acceptable way to comply without completely redesigning the affected coinage.

In early February, Longacre had approached Eckert about restructuring his department. The engraver had been called upon to testify in a gold-coin–counterfeit trial. Seeing the quality of the counterfeit coins, Longacre was determined to renew his efforts to gain control of the production of working dies. It was important that coins emitted from the Mint were error free to better distinguish them from counterfeit pieces. He told Eckert that to accomplish this goal, he would have to reorganize his department, which would involve increases in labor and operating costs. The machinery necessary for making the dies also had to be placed under the engraver's control. By inference, Longacre was criticizing the quality of the working dies prepared by Peale's men.[19]

Eckert formally approached Longacre for suggestions about the new coins on February 23. While it might be necessary to introduce entirely new designs, Eckert was, at the present, not expecting that from Longacre; he was looking for minor changes. Eckert suggested changing the reverses of the quarter and half dollar to make them conform to the reverses of the dime and half dime, which both showed a wreath encircling the appropriate denomination. He thought arrows at the date would suffice for the obverses of the four coins. If there was not a punch for the arrows, one could easily be purchased.[20]

Longacre agreed that the time was too short for elaborate changes. Temporary help would not contribute meaningfully in the short term. Elimination of the eagle on the reverses of the quarter and half dollar would, at the very least, require approval from Treasury. Longacre agreed with Eckert that arrows flanking the date would be the best option for the obverses. For the quarter and half dollar, he suggested covering the space between the eagle and the inscriptions with rays, termed a *gloryia*. For the half dime and dime, Longacre wanted to add a wreath or garland at the top of the reverses in the form of an oval containing a six-pointed star. However, he was afraid that there was not enough time to properly do the work on the reverses of the two smaller coins. He expected that models and molds would be required to make this change. Neither man addressed the three-cent piece, as it was not yet part of the equation.[21]

On the same day that Longacre replied, Eckert, in a formal communication, somewhat gave in to the engraver's request to gain control of working-die production. Longacre could draw upon the men and machinery necessary. The change would most likely involve a general reorganization of the engraver's office; certain men would have to be under Longacre's control to accomplish the tasks required. Then Eckert revealed the terms attached to this agreement. As exclusive control of the dies would devolve upon Longacre, he would be responsible for supplying the chief coiner with the dies at the time they were needed.[22] This arrangement was guaranteed to bring Longacre and Peale into open conflict.

With Longacre's reverse-design suggestions now in hand, Eckert asked how much time would be required to apply the rays and wreaths. He also wanted to know how long it would take if the rays were only applied to the quarter and half dollar, with the other two coins remaining unchanged. Did Longacre need assistance?[23]

On the following day, March 4, Longacre wrote to Eckert, but not about the designs. Instead, he was pleased with Eckert's position regarding the reorganization of his office. He recognized that using men from Peale's department might be the best solution. However, on principle, he objected. He would prefer to hire people with skills more suited to his requirements. He repeated that at all times, the machinery used ought to be under his control.[24]

At this point Longacre wrote to McCulloh concerning the proposed new designs. In his reply, McCulloh enclosed a clipping from the *National Intelligencer* that stated that the secretary of the Treasury was empowered to seek outside artists for new coin devices and that the effective date of the act would be April 1. McCulloh believed that it was Bob Patterson who had caused this clause to be inserted. He was wrong on that account, as Patterson had left Washington well before this clause found its way into the act. The extremely short implementation time was the work of Ways and Means. McCulloh told Longacre to stand by and do nothing. It was the Mint director who must take action in accordance with the law. Also, any communication between Longacre and Eckert should be in writing.[25] McCulloh had let his suspicions color his advice to his old friend.

Meanwhile, Eckert picked up Longacre's letter expecting answers to his pressing question of the time required to make design changes. Instead he found carefully couched words aimed at negotiating the separation of engraving activities from the coining department. In that regard, Eckert curtly told Longacre that he had no remarks to make at that time. The issue of the coin designs had been before Longacre since February 22 and Eckert needed answers. In providing these answers, Longacre should first assume no outside help. Then, for each activity, he should provide the time savings that an assistant would generate.[26]

That communication snapped Longacre back to reality. Eight working days would be required for the master dies and hubs of the quarter, assuming no interruptions. The half dollar would require the same amount of time. In Longacre's view, interruptions for the routine duties of his office were a major factor, as such work cropped up almost daily. An assistant could not be in place in time to work on the master dies, but one could cut the time for the hubs in half.[27]

That was enough for Eckert. Longacre could proceed with both the obverse and reverse changes on the quarter and half dollar (fig. 126). For the half dime and dime, arrows flanking the date would be sufficient. There was so little difference in silver for the smaller denominations that a sharp differentiation was not really necessary. There then remained the three-cent piece. For this coin, Longacre raised the rim of the star on the obverse and added two outlines. On the reverse, he added an olive branch above and a bundle of arrows below the roman numeral III.

With the design modifications set, Eckert was faced with one last problem: how to implement the new law. The director proposed publishing a fixed payment price list for foreign coins and silver bars. The payment schedule was based upon a price of $1.21 per ounce of standard silver.

Fig. 126. With the enactment of the 1853 law reducing the weight of the nation's silver coins, Congress mandated a design change with practically no time allowed for implementation. Longacre responded with the addition of arrows at the date for the half dime and greater denominations, and rays on the reverse of the quarter and half dollar. It maintained the integrity of the design while providing an expedient solution.

Eckert was concerned that the Mint procure an immediate supply of silver for the new coinage. With the specter of the New York branch-mint issue and Gwin's proposed Mint reorganization hanging over the head of the institution, Eckert wanted this changeover to go quickly and smoothly. However, Eckert's bullion-supply scheme subverted the law's control mechanisms, whereby the treasurer of the Mint supplied the bullion and the secretary of the Treasury had the authority to set production limits. It virtually ensured too much silver coming in and a flood of debased silver coins going out. It did have one positive side effect: foreign legal-tender silver dropped out of circulation. With legal tender limited to $5, these debased subsidiary silver coins would bounce around the financial system with nowhere to go for the rest of the decade.[28] Two years later, they would be called a drag on the market, and orders would finally be issued to temporarily suspend the production of quarters and half dollars.[29]

• • • •

Franklin Pierce was inaugurated on March 4, 1853. Eckert knew immediately that he was out. Rather than be booted, he resigned, preserving the fiction that the Mint director's job was not political. As a parting favor, he gained presidential approval for assistants for Booth and Peale. John Taylor would be the assistant melter and refiner and George Hall, the assistant coiner.[30] However, the incoming Democrats stopped these promotions cold.

CHAPTER 33

END OF THE LINE

It was late fall of 1852. Robert Maskell Patterson lay helplessly bedridden at his home at 1531 Locust Street. A stroke had felled him, paralyzing his right side. Now, with Franklin Pierce ascending to the presidency, George Eckert would surely be removed as director of the Mint. With the opportunity finally at hand to gain the succession for his son, Bob, that they both desired, he could not even lift his hand to write a recommendation letter.

However, Bob still had his mother, and Helen could be more formidable than his father. She drafted a letter to Mrs. Pierce on behalf of her son, and she finessed the politics like an old pro. Bob had first served as his father's assistant. When the elder Patterson's health began to fail and he determined that he must at some point resign, Bob took up the burden. In this manner, the father stayed on until the Mint expansion, necessitated by the California gold influx, was completed. Bob remained under the new director, George Eckert. Now Eckert, who operated a large iron works in Reading, had decided that he too must leave or suffer monetarily. Eckert knew of no one with equal claims to the position. He wanted Bob's friends to know that he was leaving the Mint so that they could make the necessary recommendations.

Helen Patterson went on to mention friends that would support Bob, including Judge John K. Kane, Supreme Court justice Robert Cooper Grier, former vice president

George Dallas, former attorney general Henry Gilpin, and General Robert Patterson. These were all good Democrats, but Helen had not approached any of them; she could not, given the circumstances of her position. She closed by saying that her husband's shattered powers and broken health prevented his making any effort to help his son.[1] Helen was ready to mail this letter when the death of Pierce's son stopped her. Out of decorum, she would wait.

At the other end of the state, in Pittsburgh, James Ross Snowden opened a letter from an old friend, Richard McCulloh. He had written to McCulloh the previous summer, commenting on his plans and aspirations. McCulloh approved of Snowden seeking a legal career in western Pennsylvania. He offered what help he could, but acknowledged he was neither a political potentate nor from the area. When Pierce took office, Snowden had his sights set on the position of U.S. attorney for western Pennsylvania.

That said, McCulloh asked what was to become of the Mint.

> Are you and I to look passively on and see the abuses of Peale, Booth, Eckert & Co, go unchecked or unpunished? Have we no duty to perform to the public, no friends there to protect or to serve, no evils to remedy? Where shall we find the right sort of a man for the Directorship? He should be a man of integrity and nerve—independent of and not be influenced by John K. Kane and his "old fogey" clique.[2] He should also know enough of men, of affairs, and of mint proceedings to be free from the necessity of learning everything from the subordinates he may find in office.

McCulloh thought that they would both be asked for recommendations for officers at the Mint. McCulloh believed it would be well if the two of them worked somewhat in concert.[3]

In Philadelphia, Helen Patterson held her fire until February. This time she penned her letter directly to the president and enclosed her first draft with an explanation for the delay to Mrs. Pierce. She minced no words with the president-elect. While it was unusual for a lady to write a letter such as this, her husband's circumstances dictated that she take this action. But she felt, as a mother, she had that right. Her husband's public duties obliged her to have more to do with the early training and education of her children than most mothers. She took pride in presenting one of her own to Pierce for a very responsible office.[4] Helen Patterson was the exception for her time.

It was at this point that George Eckert sent Bob Patterson to Washington, ostensibly to lobby for the debasement of silver coins. However, it also gave Patterson an opportunity to gain the support of R.M.T. Hunter. His support both within the administration and in the Senate confirmation process would be crucial.

Now came the avalanche of recommendations. The Pattersons pulled together a formidable list. It included Adams and Company, the express agency that handled the bullion transfers from New York; there was George Leiper, a former Democratic congressman from Delaware and a nephew of Helen's. The American Philosophical Society submitted a petition for Bob; it included the signatures of Henry Gilpin and Matthias Baldwin. It did not include Franklin Peale's signature. There were recommendations from Abraham Van Nest from the New York financial community and Thomas Allibone of the Bank of Pennsylvania. Patterson was covering all his bases. His father's friend George Dallas also signed on. However, this signature had a risk to it; Dallas was at odds with James Buchanan for the leadership of the Pennsylvania Democrats. One person missing from Helen's earlier list was Robert Patterson.[5]

Snowden was just as active seeking the U.S. attorney position in Pittsburgh. However, Snowden had a problem with some of his petitioners; more than one thought they were recommending him for the position of director of the Mint.

In fact, Snowden was having a tough time with that one. He wrote to James Buchanan on March 2, asking for a general recommendation. Buchanan had twice come to his aid when he was down and out. After being unceremoniously removed as Pennsylvania state treasurer by the Whigs in 1847, it was Buchanan who had secured for Snowden the position of treasurer at the Mint.[6]

Snowden laid it out for Buchanan. Friends were considering advancing him for the Mint position. In the meantime, he had learned that Eckert would resign in favor of Bob Patterson. However, echoing McCulloh, Snowden noted that there were Democrats in Philadelphia who would like to see an infusion of new blood at the Mint. Still, Snowden had not made up his mind. He was going to go to Washington and decide when he got there.[7]

That trip refocused Snowden on the U.S. attorney position. He now put in play his strongest supporter, his father-in-law. General Robert Patterson was not bashful. From 1300 Locust Street, just over two blocks from the "other" Robert Patterson, went out pleas for help. To Secretary of War Jefferson Davis, Patterson addressed his letter to "My Dear Colonel." He asked Davis, as an old brother soldier, to use his influence with the president. It was a personal favor and he did not forget favors.[8] He also wrote to Secretary of State William Marcy with the same pitch; he would not be slow to reciprocate this obligation to Marcy.[9] General Patterson did not overlook the president, asking for a personal favor to appoint his son-in-law.[10]

Neither man got their job. The Mint position went to Thomas Pettit. Pettit had been the U.S. attorney for eastern Pennsylvania under Polk. As such, he served on the assay commission at the Mint. In asking Pierce for the position, he said his association with the Mint had allowed him to learn something of its supervision and management. He admitted to having been temporarily impaired, healthwise. It was his foot. However, he was now fine and anxious to be honorably employed.[11] The only recommendation of merit came, ironically, from General Patterson.[12]

Thomas Pettit was completely in over his head. He was an object of pity, limping about the Mint, totally bewildered by all that was going on around him. The new secretary of the Treasury, James Guthrie, pressured Pettit, wanting to know what regulations Pettit proposed for issuing the new silver coins.[13] Bob Patterson resigned. Pettit begged him to stay on. Patterson acquiesced, running the Mint as he had for the past eight years. By mid-May it was obvious to everyone that Pettit was seriously ill; he could not perform the job for long. In fact, he died on May 31 at the age of 51. The process to find a new director started all over again.

Helen Patterson tried a different tack this time. She had had the support of Secretary Guthrie the last time but that had not been enough.[14] This time around, she went straight to James Buchanan (fig. 127). This move had no guarantee of success. Buchanan's influence with the administration was under a cloud. Pierce had asked him to be minister to Great Britain and Buchanan waivered.

Fig. 127. James Buchanan, the wily rival of President Pierce, came to the aid of the Patterson family.

He did not want his acceptance to cost Pennsylvanians patronage jobs, and thereby damage his power base. Pierce seemed determined to do just that, as he believed Buchanan to be a threat to his possible second term. Cutting off patronage and getting Buchanan out of the country would blunt this threat. In addition, Buchanan did not want to depart for England on an interim appointment. The British would treat that as what it was—only half a minister.

Against this backdrop, Buchanan left for Washington, arriving on May 18. The following day he met with Pierce to thrash out Pennsylvania appointments. Buchanan did not get a good feeling from these and subsequent discussions with the president; the man seemed less than straightforward in their talks.[15] Nevertheless, on May 30, there was agreement on one topic. When Buchanan brought up Bob Patterson's name, Pierce remarked that the place of director of the Mint seemed made for Mr. Patterson and Mr. Patterson made for the place.

The papers were made out appointing Patterson to the position that his father and grandfather had once held.[16] Buchanan left Washington on the evening of May 31, believing the appointment made. On June 1, the fact was announced in the newspapers. The family rejoiced—but then the roof caved in. The nomination was withdrawn in favor of James Ross Snowden (fig. 128). Helen Patterson was devastated. She blamed the state of American politics and she called Snowden a county-court lawyer. She suspected underhanded dealings. The mail of the two Patterson families was frequently confused by the post office, with their mail sometimes opened by the general by mistake. Helen would go no further but the implication was easy to see: General Patterson had learned in this manner of her efforts on behalf of her son and had taken action to gain the edge for his son-in-law.[17]

James Buchanan wrote to Mrs. Patterson on June 7. He had left Washington perfectly satisfied that Bob Patterson had the appointment. Why the president had changed his mind, Buchanan did not know. He had never heard Snowden's name mentioned in connection with the office until his appointment was announced. That was true in the strictest sense of the word, but Buchanan could hardly have been surprised that Snowden got the appointment. Buchanan told Helen Patterson that he should write her at greater length but every moment of his time was now occupied in preparation for his journey to Great Britain.[18] Again, Buchanan was being less than forthright. His acceptance of Pierce's ministerial appointment was up in the air after this last-minute switch at the Mint. In actuality, there was simply nothing more that Buchanan wished to confide in the family.

Bob Patterson was understandably bitter over the whole affair. He resigned on June 20, only to be persuaded by Snowden to reconsider. Snowden promised to approach

Fig. 128. James Ross Snowden seemingly came out of nowhere to snatch the Mint director's position away from Bob Patterson.

Fig. 129. Franklin Pierce proved difficult to predict when it came to presidential appointments. He had a bias toward military men and their influence. On the other hand, he distrusted James Buchanan as a potential rival in his bid for a second term.

Washington with the idea of creating an assistant director's post specifically for Patterson. Patterson hung on to his hope. Yet he could not avoid coming to a conclusion over what had happened to him when he saw Pierce come to town on July 11 at the head of a military procession. Actually, it was General Patterson at the lead, with President Pierce (fig. 129) on his right.[19]

Still Bob Patterson stayed on. In September rumors began to circulate that Patterson would be named superintendent of the New York assay office. The speculation could have come from the fact that he and Franklin Peale had traveled to New York in May to report on possible building locations.[20] He was not pleased with what he saw.[21] In fact, he was vindicated in this observation when the location was finally leased. The offices were in the former Bank of the United States building on Wall Street. However, the work was done in a six-story building directly behind and separate from the former bank building. The basement contained the boilers, the steam engine, the zinc-granulating furnace, and the crushing mill. The refining and melting rooms were housed on the third, fourth, and fifth floors.[22] The setup was a productivity nightmare.

The newspapers alluded to the possibility that Patterson was leaving because some Philadelphians had opposed his appointment to the directorship. They conjectured that it would be ironic if Patterson took his skills to the New York assay office so as to reduce the volume at the Philadelphia Mint and reinforce calls for its removal to New York. However, they reported that Bob Patterson declined, preferring to remain in Philadelphia for private reasons.[23]

The newspapers had it wrong. Guthrie did want Patterson to be superintendent. A vague one-liner from Washington said it all: Mr. Patterson Jr. had not been appointed to the New York assay office.[24] The president had overruled Guthrie again.[25] Perhaps the truth was that influential New Yorkers blackballed the nomination, thinking Patterson would be too partial to Philadelphia and would therefore sacrifice their interests.

Bob Patterson stayed at his post until November.[26] When nothing happened with the assistant-director appointment, he once again quit. The family accused Snowden of using him to learn the workings of the Mint. However, that was unfair; as the former treasurer, Snowden had the requisite knowledge to run the Mint. While Patterson would return for a stint as a clerk in the treasurer's office, it was the end of the line for the Patterson family at the Mint. As a consolation, Guthrie appointed him to the annual assay commission for 1854.[27] Regardless, Helen Patterson would nurse a grudge against Snowden for years.

• • • •

On July 11, 1853, Richard McCulloh published a pamphlet titled *The Proceedings of the Late Director of the Mint in Relation to the Official Misconduct of Franklin Peale, Esq., Chief Coiner, and Other Abuses in the Mint*. McCulloh had already met with Guthrie.[28] He certainly had no beef with his friend, Snowden, who had barely been on the job a month. This attack was aimed directly at Franklin Peale. By printing Peale's weak defense and Eckert's ridiculous conclusion to the investigation, McCulloh undercut the chief coiner and gave Snowden ammunition with which to rein in Peale.

Snowden's first resulting action was to raise objections on July 30, 1853, to the compensation over and above his salary as an officer that Peale received for striking medals. At Guthrie's order, medals were thereafter struck with no compensation given to the chief coiner or the workmen.[29]

• • • •

Looking back, he could say that it all started to unravel with the duel. At the close of the Thirty-Second Congress, Dr. William McKendree Gwin was at the height of his political power. With Pierce assuming the presidency, Gwin expected to completely control the federal patronage in California. After the Democratic president was inaugurated, the Senate convened in a special session to ratify executive appointments. Among others approved was Dr. Lewis Aiken Birdsall as the superintendent of the San Francisco branch mint.[30] While a practicing medical doctor, he had the prerequisite background in the natural sciences. When the session ended on April 11, Gwin headed to California in what could be described as a triumphant return.

Shortly after arriving home, Gwin chanced upon former California representative Joe McCorkle at the racetrack. Words were exchanged, and McCorkle accused Gwin of mishandling the federal patronage. Gwin's fiery temper got the better of him and he challenged McCorkle.

For Gwin, it was a matter of honor. For McCorkle, the reason for his outburst was personal. The man was certainly frustrated. He had wanted a second term in Congress but had failed to gain the Democratic nomination—tantamount to election—in 1852. It had gone instead to Milton Latham. However, there was a woman at the root of this trouble. McCorkle had been courting Sophie Birdsall, the daughter of the newly coined superintendent. She was described as a woman of magnificent mind and vigorous character. Just as important, she was marriage material in a frontier state where respectable women were in short supply. When McCorkle came back to California, he discovered that his congressional seat was not all he had lost; Sophie Birdsall and Milton Latham were to be wed that fall. In responding to McCorkle's taunts, Gwin had walked into a hornet's nest.

McCorkle sent a letter of grievance to Gwin on May 29, 1853. The place for the duel was the location of choice for such affairs, a spot near the Santa Clara county line where law enforcement was not a threat. Since Gwin issued the challenge, McCorkle had the right to name the weapon; he chose rifles. On June 1, the two men met. McCorkle won the choice of position and the word. They would stand with their backs to each other at thirty paces, wheel at McCorkle's word, and fire. Three times they fired without hitting each other. Gwin, at least, managed to graze McCorkle's hair. At this point, friends of the two parties halted the duel. They had discovered that their principals "were fighting under a misapprehension of facts." Explanations were given, Gwin denied the cause of McCorkle's allegations, and McCorkle withdrew his offensive language uttered at the racetrack.[31]

As relief flooded the field of conflict that no blood had been spilled, a farmer approached. He had a dead donkey and wanted to know who was going to pay for it. The two men flipped a coin and Gwin lost. However, he lost far more than the coin toss that day.

Gwin had a political challenger. After a short stint as a private minter, David Broderick (fig. 130) had become a

Fig. 130. David Broderick was Senator Gwin's bitter foe. He ultimately brought Gwin down, heckling him over a pointless duel. Broderick gained a seat in the U.S. Senate in 1857 only to lose his life two years later in a duel.

power in California politics, serving as president of the state senate in 1851. He took the lessons he learned as a Tammany man in New York and applied them at will in San Francisco. By 1853 he was the undisputed boss of the city. However, his political favors to cement that power were limited. Without Gwin's support, the real political plums were unavailable. Broderick wanted to be a senator, and Gwin, with his control of patronage, stood in his way. No quarter was going to be given in this battle.

A Broderick-subsidized newspaper took the duel and turned it into front-page entertainment. A large group of spectators had accompanied the two men. They supposedly came to the dueling field with picnic lunches and beer. In this account, no one remembered to bring the ammunition, so the neighborhood had to be scoured for the powder and ball. The paper claimed that Gwin winged a crow flying overhead and that McCorkle narrowly missed one of the seconds. Gwin had, if only momentarily, become a laughingstock.

Broderick made his move in January 1854. The fall elections had eroded Broderick's support in the California legislature. The lame-duck legislature had one more brief session before the new legislature convened. Under normal circumstances, it would be the purview of the new legislature to consider, in the fall of 1854, the re-election of Gwin for a second term. However, nothing in the law stated that the outgoing legislature could not hold that election. The battle was fierce and the bribes were plentiful. Still, the legislators were deadlocked. They neither elected Broderick in Gwin's place nor re-elected Gwin. The battle lines were now drawn; Broderick and Gwin would go at it again in the fall of 1854. No longer did Gwin have a clear playing field.

Gwin had better success with the Thirty-Third Congress. It read as a terse one-liner in the newspapers: on May 16, 1854, Samuel Butterworth was named superintendent of the New York assay office.[32] This was the same Butterworth who had fronted for Gwin in McCulloh's refining scheme. He was acceptable to New Yorkers because he was also a friend of Robert Walker, who had championed a New York branch mint before it had become a cause célèbre. When the assay office went into service on October 10, 1854, Gwin would control the two most important arms of the Mint—New York and San Francisco.[33] If his reform bill moving the bureau of the Mint to Washington and naming a new director became law, Gwin would have complete control going forward. It would be only a matter of time before an enlarged mint at San Francisco, coining facilities at New York, and the elimination of the Philadelphia Mint were achieved.

Back home, Broderick refused to back off. One point of contention was the swirl of questions surrounding the San Francisco branch-mint funding discussed by the Thirty-Second Congress at the end of the second session in February 1853. Gwin's position had been hard to fathom for anybody not present and involved at the time. Broderick, with his private-mint background and insider's knowledge, now orchestrated a campaign against Gwin directed at the mining districts in the legislature.

The shots were fired in the fall of 1854 under the pen name "Interior." In the first letter, the unknown author asserted that Gwin had sold his constituents out to the assay office and then stood by, allowing the mint bill to be effectively repealed in the funding bill. In each case, the letter accused Gwin of acting for corrupt purposes.

These initial claims were general in nature and Gwin responded. The first mint bill had linked New York and San Francisco, ensuring its defeat in the House. Gwin had taken his seat too late in the session to get a standalone San Francisco mint bill passed. An assay office was the best that could be done. Here Gwin finessed the truth by claiming that the bill required the secretary of the Treasury to contract for these services at the lowest possible rate; the secretary, a Whig, did not. By inference, it was Corwin's fault that the ensuing rate was too high. The enacting legislation was actually silent on this point.

In his defense, Gwin mentioned that he had inserted a clause in the appropriation bill of August 30, 1852, requiring the secretary of the Treasury to contract with one or more assaying firms upon the most reasonable terms, which were not to exceed 1 percent. It had had the desired effect of reducing assay rates, even if Corwin had not acted. Gwin neglected to mention the part of the amendment that had so infuriated San Francisco merchants, requiring private-mint issues to conform to Mint standards to maintain legal-tender status.

Gwin pointed out that in the following Congress, he had shepherded a bill through the Senate establishing a proper mint in San Francisco. However, the House sat on this bill for seven months. What came out was so mangled by amendments as to be absolutely worthless. The restriction of the appropriation to $300,000 was the equivalent to defeat; no complete mint could be established for this sum. It was R.M.T. Hunter who had brought forth the amendment in dispute. The California senators did nothing but agree to what was being called a corrupt bargain to maintain the assay office.[34]

Gwin's vigorous defense of his actions elicited a second accusatory letter from "Interior." From the statements contained in this last letter, it was clear the anonymous author had access to the internal dealings of the House and Senate during the Thirty-Second Congress.

The writer took Gwin's statements and twisted them to their maximum negative effect. The original law establishing the assay office did not cap or control the fees charged for assaying gold. Gwin was to blame; he had written the law. Gwin had not taken action against these rates until the clamor from the miners grew unbearable.

However, Gwin's accuser conveniently forgot that the assay fee was originally a godsend compared to the gouging of the bullion brokers.

In regard to the legislated cap on assay fees, the accuser was less than truthful, stating that Gwin pretended to pass a bill to reduce assay rates. The bill did authorize the secretary of the Treasury to contract with new assayers at reduced rates but it never repealed the existing contract; it was left in place. This accusation was false. Had Corwin followed the law, the new contracts would have effectively forced a reduction in rates across the board. "Interior" did bring up the issue of standard fineness for assay-office coinage, but only in passing. It was a topic better left alone and a tipoff as to who was behind these scurrilous letters.

The anonymous letter accused Gwin of introducing the amendment to the deficiency bill in the Senate Finance Committee that gave the assay office a three-year lease on life at the expense of the branch mint. He quoted from a debate in the House when Edward Marshall stopped this move in its tracks. After the House rejected this clause, Marshall and Robert Toombs of Georgia were appointed, with R.M.T. Hunter, to the conference committee to resolve the issue. The clause in question was called a "corrupt job," and Hunter offered no resistance to its being stricken. Gwin was caught here. Californians uniformly believed that any mint, no matter how inadequate, was better than no mint. No one wanted to focus on the three-year cap contained in the legislation that gave Gwin time to revisit the cost issue. With the New York assay office established, there would have been no objection the next time around for proper funding for the San Francisco branch mint. However, explaining that strategy in the heat of a political campaign was never going to fly.

The final accusation revolved around the purchase of the assay office to form the basic core of the new mint. The price paid for the building was more than twice its market value. Secretary Guthrie had violated the intent of the amendment appropriating $300,000 for the creation of the branch mint. Gwin had to be behind this move. He was the only one of the California delegation still in Washington at the close of the Thirty-Second Congress when Guthrie authorized the purchase. A word from Gwin would have killed this deal. This part of the political smear had a real ring of truth to it. "Interior" added fuel to the fire, saying that those who knew Gwin's relationship with the contract assayer would always believe that Gwin approved the rates and shared in the profits.

The writer closed by calling Gwin a political pirate—or, at best, a privateer—attached to nothing, regarding nothing but his own advancement.[35] No one speculated as to who "Interior" was. However, McCorkle was the most likely suspect. In good conscience, he could not attack Gwin for requiring standard fineness for legal-tender issue. He had been as much a part of that strategy as Gwin. McCorkle had gone over to Broderick, and he was running as a dark horse against Gwin for the Senate seat.

There is little doubt that Gwin had some involvement early on with the assay office, and with his connections, Broderick would have known the details. Gwin most likely extracted something from John Moffat in return for the original assaying contract; a minority interest in Moffat & Company would not have been out of line. However, when John Moffat sold out to his active partners Curtis, Perry, and Ward in February 1852, Gwin most likely exited as well. Gwin's aggressive stance against the assay-office fee structure can be dated to this point in time. However, it is less likely that Gwin received a cut of the assay-office purchase price. Gwin's support of Guthrie's purchase of the Curtis, Perry, and Ward building was based on political expediency. Past strategy aside, Gwin needed a mint as soon as possible or his bid for reelection to the Senate was dead.

These accusations were damaging. Gwin would later acknowledge that he had lost the miners' support. In an effort to regain some of that favor, he introduced a bill in the Senate to authorize $50 and $100 gold pieces.[36] It passed the Senate and made it out of committee in the House, but it failed to reach the House floor for debate prior to the adjournment of the session on August 8, 1854.[37]

When Broderick attacked Gwin's reelection that fall, the state legislature was again deadlocked, giving neither man the necessary majority of its votes. The Senate seat would sit empty until 1857, when Gwin had to compromise himself to regain his seat. By the time he returned to the Senate, his handpicked superintendents at New York City and San Francisco were gone. In addition, James Buchanan was now president, and he had tightened the presidential grip on patronage. The control that Gwin had in place within the Mint at the time he left the Senate was gone. Philadelphia had dodged another bullet.

1849

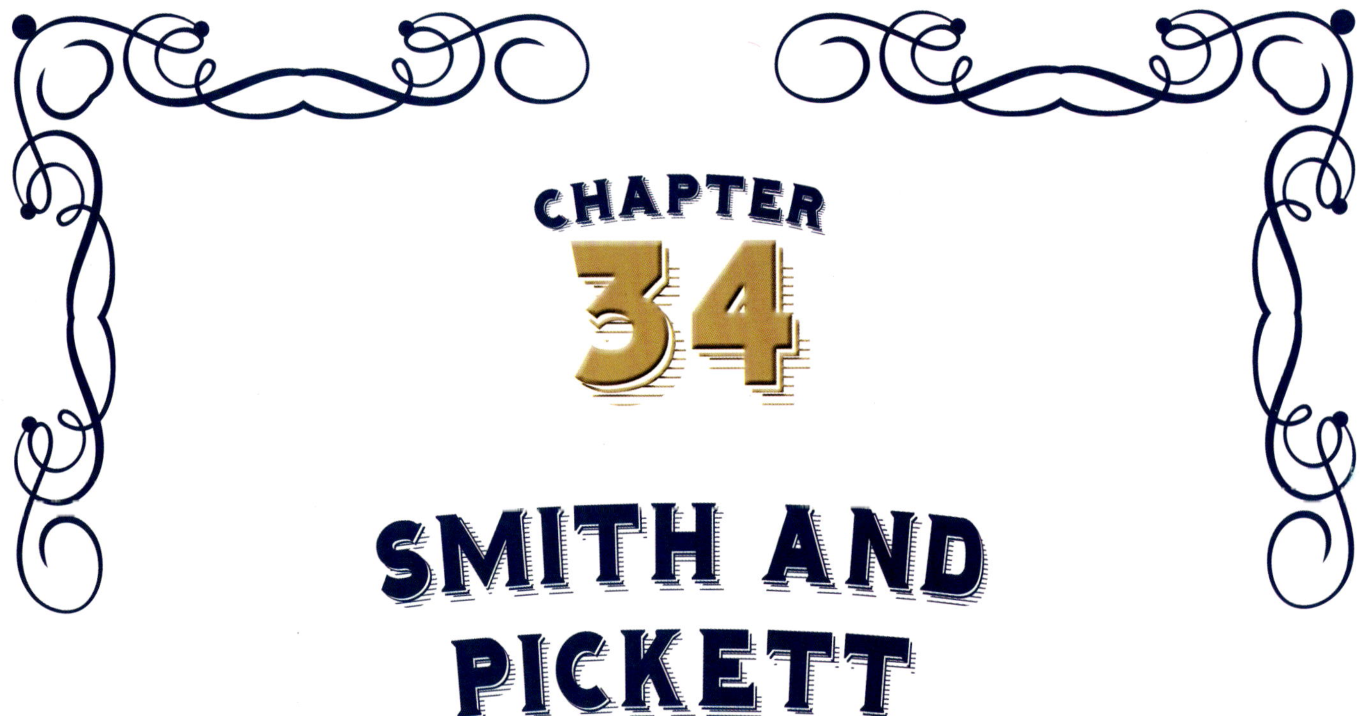

CHAPTER 34

SMITH AND PICKETT

James Ross Snowden's first job upon returning to the U.S. Mint was to coin enough silver to meet demand. He had to both replace and augment the existing silver coinage in circulation. As a consequence, the men in the coining department worked 12-hour days during the hot summer months of 1853. To alleviate the onerous conditions, chief coiner Benjamin Franklin Peale offered to augment the shift length during the cooler months by two or three hours. In a less-than-helpful suggestion, he also gave Snowden the option of adding a second shift. However, it would take 35 men and expose the Mint to security issues.[1]

An unexpected effect of the silver bill, as the law was now called, was a new demand for gold bars. As a result, layoffs were under consideration for the first time in the Philadelphia Mint's history in the adjusting department. It was here that the gold planchets were checked for the correct weight.[2] Snowden was never going to consider adding a shift while simultaneously terminating female employees in the adjusting room.

The fact was that no second shift would be necessary. Overtime hours were sufficient to flood the country with half dimes, dimes, and quarters from the bullion coming into the Mint. Even better for the Mint, there was so much subsidiary silver coinage in the system that Congress demonetized foreign specie in 1857. This change had been a long time coming.

It was probably inevitable that Snowden and Peale would come into conflict. Peale did it with style, combusting an annealing furnace in the refinery. It started, naturally enough, with an experiment. Peale wanted to specify that anthracite coal, instead of wood, be used for the two annealing furnaces to be employed at the San Francisco Mint. He had been at work testing his theories when Snowden arrived on the scene. In December 1853, Peale reached the point of a full-scale test using an annealing furnace in the refinery at Philadelphia.[3] Here Snowden got to experience Peale's lack of practicality firsthand. The heat content of anthracite coal is at least twice that of wood. While anthracite coal might be more heat efficient, the results in a boiler box constructed for wood combustion were predictable; it burned up. Faced with the $1,600 expense of rebuilding the furnace, Snowden put a tight rein on Peale, forbidding any more experiments.[4]

Why did Peale press forward when failure was assured? Franklin Peale was the president of a concern, inherited in part by his wife, that held 1,700 acres of anthracite coal lands. Whether he expected to burn coal at the Mint from his holdings or was just promoting anthracite coal, hoping for an indirect benefit, was never documented. However, one fact was indisputable: no director had sat on Peale like Snowden just had.

The issue of striking medals boiled up again in the spring of 1854. The Association for the Exhibition of the Industry of all Nations, headed by P.T. Barnum, had requested the Mint strike 118 silver medals and 1,150 bronze medals from dies prepared by C.C. Wright. Snowden went directly to the Treasury Department for approval. The approval came back with the stipulation that the Mint be reimbursed for all materials and that no officer should benefit from the arrangement. Snowden, in turn, formally asked Peale if the Mint could strike these medals and to provide a timeframe for their completion.

Peale answered Snowden with the same formality.

> [T]o promote the art of medal engraving and aiding in any way in the diffusion of medals as permanent records of remarkable events has always been an object of higher ambition to which I have bestowed much time, labour and my best activities, and is therefore an acceptable duty.

However, with the continuous press of California gold and the added burden of silver coinage, Peale did not believe he could strike so many medals during normal business hours. The material required was $500, and it would take three men working overtime for two months to execute this order—for which the men should be compensated. Of course, Peale would willingly give his best service at any and all times without profit, gain, or any other consideration.[5]

On the subject of making medals, Peale was now communicating to Snowden in writing. Peale's answer necessitated another round of letters between Snowden and Guthrie. With the added hours came added labor expense. Snowden pointed out that C.C. Wright now had a press that could strike these medals for the association if Guthrie wanted to pass on the business. Guthrie was willing to move forward as long as the costs were covered. Medals were going to be a volatile subject at the Mint.

• • • •

In May 1854, Snowden had more on his plate than Peale's medals. That the source of his troubles had not happened sooner was a godsend for the Philadelphia Mint. In fact, it would have swung the tide in the branch-mint debate to New York City.

As the gold-bullion flow took effect in the first year following its appearance at the Mint's doors, unprecedented hiring took place. Prior to that time, employment was largely by word of mouth. Relatives and friends had first dibs on any job that came open. Everybody knew everybody. That collegial atmosphere fell by the wayside in 1850.

Typical of the new clerks was J. Engel Negus, whose first day on the job was June 12, 1850. With Whig credentials, he took a position as a weigh clerk in the treasurer's office. His job was to receive the bullion from the depositors, weigh it, and register it in a book of deposits. He then placed the bullion in an open box with a slip of paper listing its number and weight. Prior to the arrival of California gold, a deposit was almost always sent immediately to a waiting crucible in the melt room. With the backlog of deposits that quickly developed from 1849 onwards, deposits were no longer directly sent to be melted. Instead these open boxes were placed unsecured in a vault to wait their turn.

The weakness in this system was that, after sitting in the vault for days or weeks, these raw deposits were not weighed again in the melting room. As long as the melted weight fell within reason, no questions would ever be raised. Given that bullion impurities could range from 0.5 to 7.0 percent, this was no check at all. Once the bullion had been cast into bars, the gold was again weighed and the bar was stamped with the deposit number and the weight. It was then returned to the treasurer to await assaying and refining. From this point, the depositor was protected.

Negus drew suspicion as early as December 1851. His assistant, Henry Cochran, noted that a deposit had Negus's name on it. He questioned Negus, who told him that the deposit actually belonged to his servant woman. Cochran also noticed some changes in the parcels of deposits after they had been weighed. He began to keep a record of these changes, taking them to George Dunning, the former director's clerk and now back in the employ of the Mint, and other officers not named. They told him to keep a watchful eye but nothing more was done.

In the fall of 1853, Negus purchased a fine house in a fashionable part of Philadelphia for $19,000, an astronomical sum for those times. When he hosted a party, attended by almost all the officers of the Mint, the handsome furnishings of the home were there for all to see. Still no eyebrows were raised.

Finally, in April 1854, suspicions were so glaring that Cochran and others went to the treasurer, Daniel Sturgeon. They decided to set a trap for Negus. After the arrival and weighing of a new deposit of California bullion, Sturgeon came back that night and checked the weights in the presence of other officers of the Mint. They discovered that 16 boxes were short almost 72 ounces of gold. They then searched the surrounding rooms and found almost that exact amount in a private closet in the vault where Negus kept some of his personal effects.

Snowden was immediately called in. The director ordered Negus to the Mint and confronted him with the evidence. Negus admitted the act but denied any wrongdoing, saying it was an experiment to show the treasurer how easy it was to steal from the open boxes of bullion.

Negus was allowed to come to work the next morning, May 11, and open the vault. During the day and after "forcible appeals," Negus confided to another clerk that he had taken $10,600, and he provided a list of the deposits that had been shorted. The following day, Negus returned to the Mint with $5,000; the day after that, he brought the remaining $5,600.

Snowden immediately sent a communication of the facts of the defalcation to the Treasury Department. He also sent melter and refiner James C. Booth to Washington to relate the situation verbally. Snowden then waited for instructions to take out a warrant for Negus's arrest. They finally arrived on May 31, and Snowden turned the case over to the district attorney. However, there was a problem. Negus's family had left from New York for England on May 17, and Negus had departed for Europe on May 20. The Mint now had egg all over its face.

Meanwhile, Snowden left no stone unturned. He wrote to Richard McCulloh to see what the former melter and refiner knew. McCulloh, who had sifted through seemingly all of the Mint's dirt, was taken completely by surprise; he was no help.[6]

Secretary Guthrie (fig. 131) was certainly slow in ordering the arrest of Negus. It is clear in hindsight that the secretary of the Treasury did not want Negus tried. The liability to the depositors could not be calculated; it could be astronomical. However, Guthrie was prompt in ordering an investigation. On June 1, he gave instructions to his investigators. He had chosen Richard Smith, the cashier of the Bank of the Metropolis in Washington, and J.C. Pickett, a Treasury auditor. Choosing a nongovernment investigator and chief operating officer of a bank was highly unusual. Smith would call the shots on the investigation and Pickett would do the work.

Fig. 131. As Treasury secretary, James Guthrie presided over the great defalcation at the Mint and the downfall of Franklin Peale.

Guthrie defined the scope of their investigation. It was much broader than just the defalcation. Guthrie wanted to know the system of accountability between the weigh clerk and the melter and refiner, and between the other officers involved in processing the bullion and converting it to coin. He wanted the men to examine the general condition and management of the Mint, the accounting procedures, the security of the bullion and coin, the attendance and vigilance of the officers, and the admission and access of visitors to the Mint. Guthrie was also suspicious of the actions surrounding Negus. He wanted to know how the amount deemed stolen was determined. He also wanted to know if any promise or agreement was made as an inducement for restitution, and whether his escape from the country was known in advance by any of the officers. Guthrie meant business on this point, empowering the men to consult with the district attorney if necessary. Clearly, Guthrie was building a defense to avoid any blame for the delay in charging Negus. On the surface, this investigation had all the makings of a witch-hunt. Yet the two men knew that the very integrity of the Mint was at stake and every possible effort must be made to preserve its good name.

Smith and Pickett were on site by June 2. Snowden was in Washington consulting with Guthrie, which delayed the start of the investigation until June 3. The two men almost immediately focused on the potential loss. They questioned people outside the Mint and learned that Negus had sold $10,000 in $50 slugs from the assay office and private mints to a city jeweler over the preceding 18 months. It also appeared that Negus sold gold to another jeweler who then skipped the country, carrying bills of exchange, shortly before the clerk fled. With annual deposits of at least $50 million in 1852 and 1853, and assuming 0.25 percent of this amount was taken by Negus, the loss in those two years amounted to $250,000, or almost 14,000 ounces of gold. Both men indicated in their resulting report that this amount represented the bare minimum that Negus could have taken. The loss could have been as high as 1, 2, or even 3 percent. At 3 percent, the loss in gold would have reached 168,000 ounces, a truly staggering amount. In follow-up work requested by Smith and Pickett, discrepancies in the weights reported by Negus seemed to conform to the higher of these percentages. Yet the investigators believed that if Cochran had not acted as he had, the losses ultimately incurred would have been of "stupendous magnitude."

The two investigators cleared the officers of any wrongdoing after the defalcation. They had properly notified Treasury and awaited instructions. There was no evidence of promises made to Negus that he would not be prosecuted. The two men concluded "that every step was taken, with due precautions, to prevent a premature explosion before the facts were sufficiently strong to ascertain and fix guilt upon Negus." That was odd wording that could only mean that Snowden had managed to control the flow of information to the press and hence limit the inflammatory speculation.

That was the easy part of the investigation. Smith and Pickett quickly reached one basic conclusion about the Mint: none of the departments kept adequate documentation. The system in place accounted for disbursements and receipts in the treasurer's department. Bullion was logged in and out. Gold ingots were returned from the melter and refiner and logged out to the chief coiner. The chief coiner returned coinage. It was simple, but it did not give departmental details. Only the chief coiner kept any kind of separate books. Peale represented these books as being only for his private satisfaction and not properly appropriate or belonging to the Mint. Unsaid, these books must have documented Peale's medal activities for private concerns. The investigators recommended that these books be public property. In addition, a more detailed set of journals and ledgers needed to be instituted within the various departments to improve accountability and the reconciliation of activities.

The Mint's security came under strong criticism from the two men. The heavy inflow of California gold had totally overloaded the existing vaults. The treasurer's vault, containing $140,000 in silver coins, was paid special attention in the report. It was really just a room with a common brick wall of ordinary thickness and a single door. That door consisted mainly of layers of board nailed together with sheet iron in between. Like all the others in the building, this door had a single lock of a very common variety. Even after accounting for the reduction in bullion flow with the opening of the New York and San Francisco operations, they recommended the bullion and coinage be more strongly secured. They also recommended that the boxes containing bullion waiting for melting and refining be cast iron and equipped with a spring lock.

Smith and Pickett raised real questions about the attendance of the officers. Snowden told them that the officers were at the Mint from nine o'clock in the morning until three o'clock in the afternoon, while the men worked ten-hour days. However, Booth seemed to contradict his boss. In his department, the men were occupied for ten hours if the work required it, and longer in emergencies. Booth and his assistants attended in proportion to the requirements of the business. Peale was more evasive, saying that he recognized no particular hours. He considered it proper to attend whenever duty demanded his presence, day or night. Smith and Pickett could plainly see that the attendance of the officers was not always regular. In their absence, the clerks opened the vaults and ran the Mint.

The two men devoted special attention to Franklin Peale's activities. Snowden told the men that no "for profit" medal activity had been undertaken by Peale while he had been director. Peale readily admitted that investigations of a scientific nature had been undertaken at the Mint and were still permitted. He stated that this activity was not restricted to projects that directly benefited the Mint. Smith and Pickett found that identical activity was carried on during idle hours in the assay department. One of Peale's men went so far as to accuse the coining-room foreman, George Eckfeldt, of using the mint's machinery on government time to execute work for outside parties. However, when the two men tried to verify this accusation, Peale and others circled the wagons in defense of Eckfeldt, claiming that there must have been some misunderstanding of the foreman's actions.

In spite of their experience in dealing with George Eckfeldt, Smith and Pickett seemed to come under the spell of Franklin Peale's persuasive ways. Peale had not lost his salesman skills from his museum days. The investigators paid Peale a compliment for introducing women to the workforce. They performed their duties as well as men. Peale even brought up the issue of the women's pay. They received less than half that of the men, and the two investigators recommended that they be given raises of 25 and 35 cents, to bring their pay to at least $1 per day.

In another telling comment, the investigators observed that a good deal of the machinery and apparatus of the Mint was more highly and expensively finished than absolutely necessary for working purposes. However, they did not consider this practice an extravagance; finished machinery lasted longer, looked better, and was better maintained than ordinary equipment. This was pure Franklin Peale.

While in Philadelphia, someone gave Smith and Pickett Richard McCulloh's indictment against Franklin Peale. This put them in a corner; if they recognized the charges, they would, in effect, be trying Peale a second time. It was something they did not wish to pursue, but they deferred to Guthrie for instructions. They went so far as to meet with McCulloh on June 15. After some back-and-forth regarding the testimony, the two men were able to discern that McCulloh really had nothing firsthand to add beyond his experiences as melter and refiner at the Mint. Receiving no instructions from Guthrie to engage further, they broke off contact with McCulloh. They submitted their report to Secretary Guthrie on July 8, 1854.[7]

• • • •

Change came to the Mint before Smith and Pickett had even commenced their investigation. Snowden knew that the opening of the San Francisco branch mint in April would impact bullion volumes at Philadelphia, and that this level would drop even further when the New York assay office opened in the fall (fig. 132). Notwithstanding the fact that San Francisco output was impaired by a shortage of parting acid, Snowden put his officers on notice on June 1, 1854. The men on hourly wages were to be paid only for the time that they were reasonably engaged.[8] There was more. Snowden had originally been unwilling to lay off the women in the adjusting room. Now he had to, telling Peale to reduce his force there to 28. In addition, Snowden ordered 15 men terminated from the coining department, providing specific names.[9] The workforce was about to take on a decidedly Democratic flavor.

Snowden was also operating under a legislative stricture. The silver-coin bill required the profits of the Mint

Fig. 132. Except for a few hairlines, this Proof 1854 double eagle is in near-perfect condition. It was the first coin struck at San Francisco and it resides in the National Numismatic Collection.

to be paid annually into the treasury. There would be no more offsets against contingent expenses. For example, the gain from bullion separation where the amount separated was under $5 went to Washington.[10] The small depositor was the loser either way.

The body blow came in September. Guthrie came down hard after having reviewed the investigative report with the president. The secretary wanted public confidence restored in the Mint. In that regard, he saw three areas for focus: greater caution needed to be taken in securing the bullion and coinage of the Mint; there needed to be better attendance and accountability of the officers and men; and Guthrie wanted greater economy in the expenses of the Mint.[11]

First and foremost, Snowden ordered all of Peale's failed or impractical equipment and useless implements cleaned out of the attic; they were to be sold at absolute auction. In addition, on September 4, 1854, Guthrie issued preliminary regulations that Snowden implemented immediately, with the provision that changes could be made if certain elements proved unworkable.[12] It was clear that Guthrie and Snowden had consulted; the proposed regulations went beyond the scope of the Smith and Pickett report.

First on the list of new regulations, the treasurer was to maintain a monthly report of the officers' attendance at the Mint. They were expected to be present at the stated hours of operation. Casual outsider visits to the Mint were to be discouraged; they interrupted the workflow and the attention of the officers. Such visits were to be limited to Wednesdays from nine to two.

In a shot across the bow for all the officers, Snowden stated emphatically that the number of workmen employed would be regulated by the amount of work to be performed. The focus of the Mint in the future would be balanced between the need for economy and the requirements of public service. A second general regulation stated clearly that beyond salary, no officer could profit from the operations of the Mint.[13]

Regulations in the coining department certainly had Snowden's input. In addition to rekeying and double-keying the vault doors, windows were to be closed at night. Other regulations were addressed directly to Peale and his personal conduct. Newspapers, pamphlets, and books were not to be received at the Mint except those belonging to the director's library. The chief coiner and all others employed in the coining department were prohibited from using their time during working hours to read such books or papers. They were also prohibited from any private work, transactions, or business during Mint hours.

Snowden, like Eckert, was concerned about the purchase of supplies in Peale's department. The new regulations stated that supplies could only be obtained by contract after advertising for 60 days, or by purchase in the open market. Records were to be kept, comparing purchase orders to actual quantities delivered and prices billed. In addition, supply purchases would still require a requisition signed by the director.[14] Snowden had left Franklin Peale with no wiggle room here. However, Peale's response was predictable. Everything was being done to purchase supplies at an advantage. Nothing came to mind that would help purchase supplies at lower costs. He pointed out defensively that the director had for some years negotiated the coal-supply contracts.[15]

The other officers received regulations for their respective departments and there was little variation in general terms across the departments. However, unique problems came to light that had to be quickly addressed. For engraver James Longacre, the prohibition of personal tools for his engraving raised an issue. When he took the position, the department had been bereft of any tools. He had been encouraged to bring his own rather than purchase new ones. In addition, his assistant, Peter Cross, was not temperamentally suited to working regular long hours.[16]

Snowden codified these regulations in a final document attached to the report of Smith and Pickett. The report was issued November 14, 1854, and one of the worst defalcations in the history of the Treasury Department to that point was put to rest.

• • • •

The record is completely blank concerning Franklin Peale's termination. To this day there remain rumors that the medal dies that Peale had so diligently collected through the years were removed from the Mint. That action would have benefited no one but Peale. Upon being discovered, the dies were recovered by Peale and returned.[17] The story has a ring of truth to it. Peale's outside income had been eliminated, and a side market for collectors of medal restrikes would have been lucrative. This is pure conjecture. However, there can be no doubt that Snowden's regulations put a straitjacket on Franklin Peale's activities, which he would have found suffocating. Some time that fall, Snowden preferred charges. Guthrie appropriately passed them on to President Pierce. As an officer appointed by the president, only the president was able to remove Peale.

On September 5, 1854, Robert Maskell Paterson quietly passed away in his home on Locust Street. He was 67 years old. It was the end of an era at the Philadelphia Mint.

• • • •

Peale did not go quietly. On April 22, 1856, he petitioned Congress for $30,000 in compensation for extra services performed at the Mint. Ever the promoter, Peale threw in every possible improvement at the Mint that he could possible claim during his tenure. While melter and refiner, he had introduced the procedure of using nitric acid to precipitate the silver out of solution and recovering the metal using zinc and sulfuric acid. He had also directed the construction of the steam-powered coin press. He was particularly proud of the engine used to power that press. Since the introduction of that coin press, he had made continuous improvements to its design, resulting in a machine far superior to those employed in Europe. Peale claimed primary credit for the mints at New Orleans, Charlotte, and Dahlonega. Their construction and operational shakedowns had occurred in great measure under his advice and direction. Peale also rightly took credit for the steam-driven milling machine. He was more careful in claiming credit for the balances used at the Mint, stating he had given them his devoted attention.

Foolishly, the former chief coiner took credit for his work done during the capacity expansion in 1850. While he restricted his claims to the steam engine and the rolling mill, he opened the door for a rebuttal against his other efforts at that time.

To back up his petition to Congress, he enlisted testimonials. George Eckert praised Peale's "extraordinary inventive genius" and his ability to overcome any and all mechanical difficulties as they arose. In the substitution of steam for hand power with the coin presses alone, Peale had saved the government thousands and thousands of dollars. As chairman of the assay commission, John Kane observed that Peale's mechanical improvements, not to mention the processes that he had introduced, had saved the government hundreds of thousands of dollars. Peale even pressed George Eckfeldt into service to support his claims of coining-process efficiencies.[18] Peale had his bases covered with both Whigs and Democrats.

The Senate bought into Peale's claims, although they reduced the amount to $10,000 before forwarding his petition to the House. At this point, James Guthrie had to get serious about stopping Peale's memorial. He asked Snowden to comment on Peale's supporting documentation. Guthrie specifically asked Snowden to determine the circumstances of Peale's trip to Europe while an employee of the Mint. Were experiments leading to improvements done while he was receiving a salary? Were workmen and Mint materials used? What were the exact times devoted by Peale to his duties at the Mint? While at the Mint was Peale engaged in activities for which he received compensation from third parties?[19] It read like a list of charges.

Snowden now had the chance to speak against Peale and he did not waste his opportunity. He pointed out that Peale had been hired to go to Europe for the express purpose of bringing the most up-to-date technology back to the Philadelphia Mint. As for the steam-driven coin press, Peale brought back several models for presses that served

Fig. 133. Executed posthumously by George Starkey in 1871, this dignified likeness of Franklin Peale was given to the Mint by his widow Caroline two years later. It was later housed at the Pennsylvania Academy of the Fine Arts in 1876.

as guides for his press. He inroduced nothing new or revolutionary; he copied and refined what already existed. The current presses were nothing more than evolutions from the first press based upon operating experience.

The improvements that Peale instituted in the refinery were in use in London and were simply a transfer of knowledge. However, this rebuttal gave Snowden an opportunity to give McCulloh credit for introducing steam to heat the stoneware and porcelain vessels in 1849. This improvement, coupled with the construction of additional furnaces in 1850, enabled the Mint to process the raw bullion from California.

Snowden gave credit for the construction of the balances to Joseph Saxton. How many, if any, improvements in the design were the result of Peale's input, Snowden could not say.

In summary, Snowden believed it was particularly difficult to determine the originality of design and execution for these improvements, and therefore it was difficult to assign value. This was more particularly the case where persons had been employed by the government and improvements were introduced in consequence of their official positions. Snowden recommended a commission to sort out the value of the various claims.

Snowden was not done. He took the opportunity to attack Peale's actions in the 1850 expansion. Peale's machine draw bench was useless and cost $2,000. His pouring machine for making ingots was never used and cost $7,000 or $8,000. His lathe for turning chilled rolls, which cost between $2,000 and $3,000, was cumbersome. Snowden had sold this equipment for scrap. The Mint director also used the opportunity to bring to light Peale's failed experiment with anthracite coal in the annealing furnace.

Snowden could not say what Peale's hours at the Mint were. He could not estimate Peale's medals activity. He instead stated that Peale had refused to provide his accounts, papers, and correspondence on this matter, regarding them as his personal property. That action was condemnation in itself.[20]

Snowden's report was enough. The move to legislate $10,000 to Franklin Peale was stopped dead. When Peale pushed again in 1858, he failed once more. It was not until Franklin Peale died on May 5, 1870, that feelings began to soften. With a different administration in power at the Philadelphia Mint composed of men who had been clerks in Peale's time, Congress gave Peale's daughter, Anna, the $10,000 in an act for her relief in 1873.[21] Perhaps in return, Peale's widow, Caroline, gave the Mint a fine bust of her late husband (fig. 133).[22] Bob Patterson conveyed it to the Mint.[23] However, its stay was brief as the family gave it to the Pennsylvania Academy of Fine Arts in 1876.

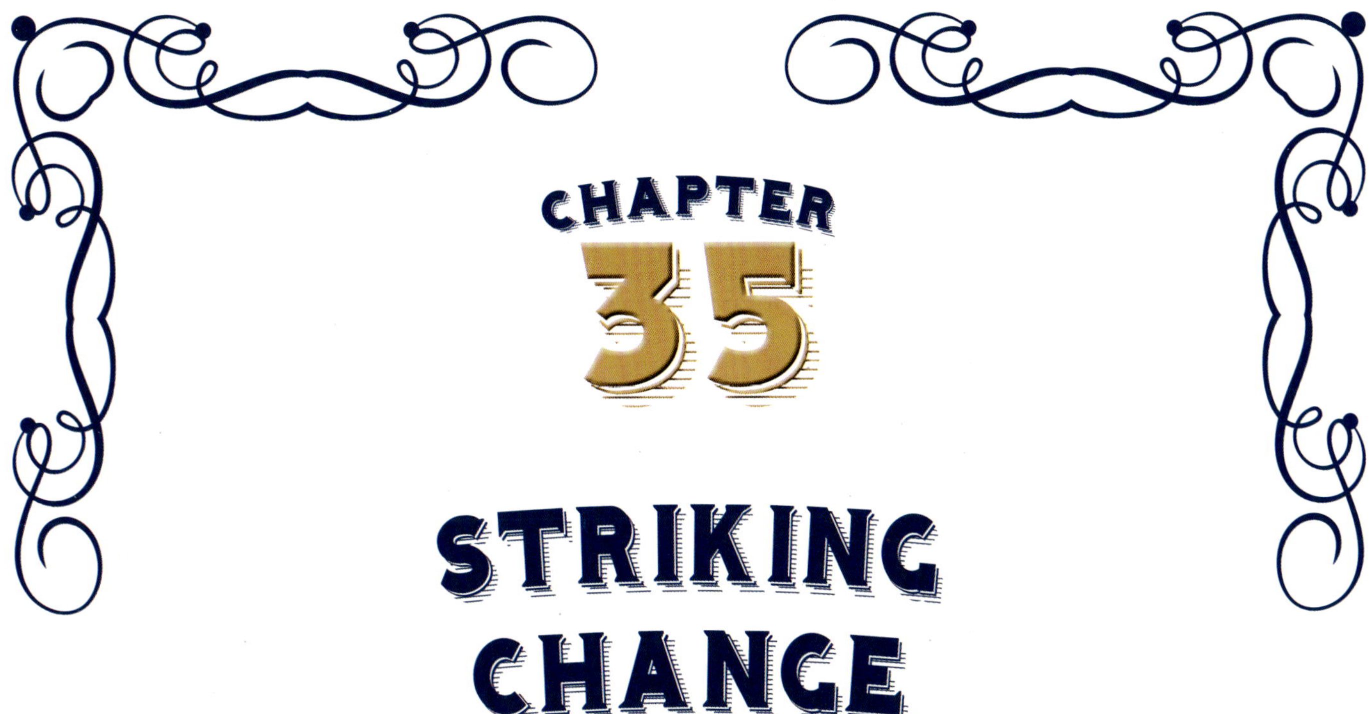

CHAPTER 35

STRIKING CHANGE

James Longacre had one character trait that had stood him in good stead during his time as engraver at the Mint: he was persistent in the face of adversity. On the other hand, Mint director James Ross Snowden needed competent talent in the engraver's department. The last session of the Thirty-Second Congress had placed two mandates on his plate. He had been authorized to seek new designs for the subsidiary silver coinage and to issue a $3 gold piece. In addition, Treasury Secretary James Guthrie brought another issue to his attention—the diameter of the gold $1 coin needed to be enlarged.

Snowden turned his focus first to seeking new designs. He sought permission from Guthrie to solicit the engravers of the country to furnish designs on paper for the obverse and reverse of the silver coins and the $3 gold piece. Once a design was chosen, the artist might be asked to prepare a die for the half dollar. In an added twist, Snowden told Guthrie that when the designs were submitted, he would be able to judge who was best qualified to hold the position of engraver at the Philadelphia Mint. Albert Stewart of Philadelphia had approached Snowden seeking Longacre's job but Snowden had judged his work to be inferior to Longacre's. However, Snowden was not ruling out a change. He intended to encourage Longacre to enter the competition.[1]

On July 26, 1853, Snowden issued a circular letter inviting the "cooperation" of artists, engravers, and persons of taste to submit such designs as they deemed appropriate for the silver coinage by October 1. The $3 gold piece design was on hold. Since the law had imposed no restrictions in relation to required devices, Snowden declined to stipulate any such requirements. An impartial examination would be made of the designs submitted and a liberal remuneration would be made for the three designs considered best suited.[2]

Here was an opportunity to radically redesign American coinage, freeing it from congressionally mandated motifs. The problem lay with the circular letter. Would it reach the right people and would they take the call seriously?

Longacre chose not to participate. His overall attitude was positive regarding outside designs. While he did not consider himself responsible for designs or devices that had not originated from him, he believed it was his job to faithfully reproduce those designs in the die. Even if he perceived flaws in a design, it was not the duty of the engraver to "improve" or modify an outside design. On the contrary, if the design was good, Longacre felt it would enhance the value and interest of his place in public service.[3] However, had he known that the winning artist would most likely be offered his job, he might have had a different attitude. It was now in Longacre's best interest for the competition to fail. Once again, his job was in play.

October came and went, without Snowden receiving anything approaching an acceptable design (fig. 134). In an about-face, Longacre reconsidered his refusal to par-

Fig. 134. Pictured are some of the surviving public submittals from the 1853 competition. Lacking the necessary attributes of a coinable design, these submittals were dead on arrival at the Mint.

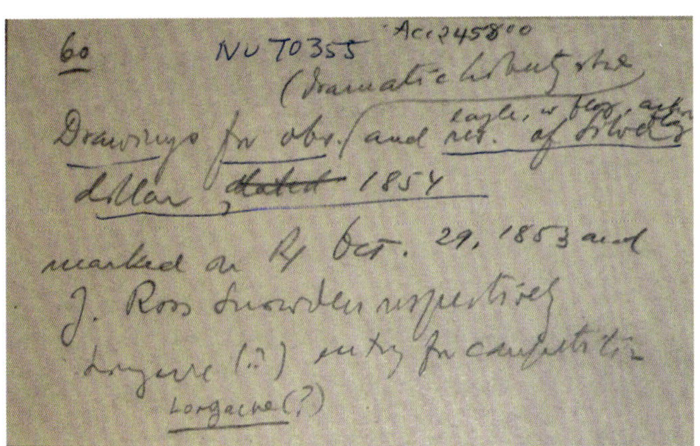

Fig. 135. The notation accompanying this sketch reads: "Drawings for obverse, dramatic Liberty seated and reverse, eagle with flag and anchor for silver dollar dated 1854. Marked on reverse October 29, 1853, and J. Ross Snowden respectively. Longacre (?) entry for competition." While the question mark implies uncertainty by the writer, the work is almost certainly that of Longacre.

ticipate and submitted a dollar coin design at the last minute. The obverse was a variation of the seated Liberty theme, with a standing eagle on the reverse. In a departure from the norm, Longacre substituted "United We Stand" for "E Pluribus Unum" and employed two ribbons wrapping a column containing the words "Liberty" and "Union." Clearly he was influenced by the troubled political times. The hurried sketch was good, although it suffered from a lack of simplicity (fig. 135).

Now Snowden turned to Longacre for advice. The engraver flatly told the director that he was not surprised by the failure. First, the space available for artistic embellishment was extremely limited. Second, and more importantly, the rigid limitations imposed by the coining process upon the relief of the design fettered the hands of the artist. Longacre was still scarred from his experience with the double eagle. While an artist might successfully address the restricted canvas presented by a coin surface, he would, in almost every instance, have no knowledge of the restrictions in relief. As a result, the drawings submitted were almost bound to have little practical application for coinage.

There was evidently some question in Snowden's mind concerning the use of a heraldic eagle on the reverse of U.S. coinage. Reinforcing this notion, Longacre added that there was nothing of a national character except the shield. The practice of using a heraldic device on the reverse of coins was common to most independent and sovereign countries. The only objection that Longacre had to this device was its central distribution on the die. In making this statement, Longacre was considering the required metal movement of both the obverse and reverse toward the center of the planchet. Again, he was recalling the pain of having to reduce the relief of the reverse of his double eagle in order for the design on the obverse to completely strike up. To get around this problem, Longacre suggested using a wreath on the reverse. In fact, all of his designs going forward would gravitate toward this motif.

Fig. 136. One of the three submittals in the competition cited by Snowden as being the best. It is really hard to understand from this sketch by Charles Nahl why Snowden did not pursue it further in spite of possible relief issues.

While commenting on the designs received for the competition, Longacre stated that they all had merit, but that they would not adapt to relief requirements. He observed that the existing legally required motifs were amenable to a more artistic development without materially changing them. This objective might be obtained by asking artists like Hiram Powers or Thomas Crawford to furnish emblematic designs at a specified relief. However, both sculptors resided in Italy, making their participation in such a process problematic.[4]

With the competition a failure, Longacre's job was safe. In addition, Snowden gave Longacre what he most wanted: control of all dies made at the Mint. The men from the coining department used in producing these dies would be working under Snowden's orders. It was a compromise very much in Longacre's favor.[5]

On December 29, 1853, Snowden formally delivered the news of the failed call for new designs to Secretary Guthrie. He had received designs and several medallions, some of which had artistic merit. However, Snowden was not prepared to recommend any as suitable for coinage. In other words, he was dismissing them because of relief considerations. There were three submittals worthy of remuneration. One was a medal by a Mr. Barber of Philadelphia. Another was a set of drawings submitted by Charles Nahl, a German-born trained sculptor living in San Francisco (fig. 136).[6] Snowden was disappointed that some of the best American artists had declined to participate. He certainly desired a submittal from Wright, but, unbeknownst to Snowden, the engraver was within a year of his death. At this point, Snowden had no choice but to restart the process if he wanted new designs.[7]

Snowden prepared another circular letter. He proposed to invite a few established diesinkers and engravers to provide a pair of original dies with the diameter of a half dollar. Again, there were no restrictions as to the devices that could be employed. The Mint would accept a drawing accompanied by a written explanation if the participant wished to avoid cutting a die. If a die was to be supplied, the contestant must name his price in advance. If the Mint agreed, he would be reimbursed for this added effort. Relief requirements would be provided in writing and were to be carefully observed. The dies were to be furnished within four months of reaching agreement on their price. Snowden wanted extra time in the hope that he would gain submittals from American artists living abroad.[8]

In conveying his draft to Guthrie for approval, Snowden candidly told the secretary that the cost of each die would be $400. He was specifically targeting four individuals from whom he wanted submittals: C.C. Wright, F.N. Mitchell of Boston, Edward Stabler of Sandy Spring, Maryland, and Albert Stewart of Philadelphia. Snowden estimated that the overall cost would be $2,700. The Mint director argued that, if the experiment resulted in an improvement to the coinage, the money would have been well spent. If, on the contrary, the dies offered were not approved, the effort would show the Mint wished to improve the coin designs, insulating them from any criticism on the subject.[9]

Guthrie rejected this second attempt. After the first failure, he judged the probability of the success of the second attempt as slender. The cost was too much. Instead, he wanted Snowden to confine his efforts to improving the dies and the mechanical execution of the coins.[10] For sure, Longacre had now weathered the storm.

After the failure of the first round, Longacre also picked up the assignment for the $3 gold piece. Since using a standard planchet thickness produced a coin very similar in size to the quarter eagle, a decision had to be made. To prevent as much confusion on the public's part as possible, there was no choice but to go with a thinner planchet, producing a coin midway in diameter between the quarter eagle and the half eagle. Little was documented about this design work. Sketches were sent to Guthrie for approval in October 1853.[11] After that, the record went blank until May 1, 1854, when the new coins were issued. The obverse exhibited an "ideal head" with a feathered headdress bearing the inscription "Liberty" on the band. Encircling the head was the inscription "United States of America." On the reverse was a wreath composed of the staple produce of the country—wheat, cotton, Indian corn, and tobacco. In the center were the denomination and the date (fig. 137).

Longacre would always consider this design his very best. In justifying the use of the headdress, Longacre stated that the feathered tiara was as characteristic of the primitive races of this hemisphere as the turban was of the Asiatic. There was nothing repulsive in its character, as opposed to the Phrygian cap, which was the emblem of a freed slave. Longacre regarded the headdress as a proper, well-defined part of the national inheritance. It was a memorial to American liberty. Why not use it?[12]

The $3 gold piece solved the problem of the size of the gold dollar coin. Longacre had experimented with annular versions prior to Snowden's arrival as Mint director. At issue were the production problems associated with punching out the annular portion. Now, with the reduced thickness of the $3 gold piece a success, Longacre applied this same principle to the $1 coin, expanding its diameter by one-tenth of an inch.[13] He slightly modified the head from the obverse of the $3 coin, copied the reverse, and produced the new issue (fig. 138). He would change the obverse in 1856 to enlarge the head of Liberty and bring the image exactly in line with the $3 gold piece.

With the issue of the coinage designs resolved in Longacre's favor, he undertook a medal project, which showed just how obtuse the engraver could be to the politics of the Mint. With chief coiner Franklin Peale barely gone from office, Longacre negotiated a contract on April 14, 1855, with the Navy department for $2,200 to execute a medal awarded to Commander Duncan Ingraham. With the help of Peter Cross, Longacre executed the dies, with one gold and ten bronze medals struck at the Mint in December (fig. 139).

The engraver took this business in spite of the fact that Snowden had formally opened a medals department on April 1, 1855. Snowden had sought permission the prior

Fig. 137. This would always be James Longacre's favorite design. Despite the thin planchet, the coin struck up well. The design devices on the obverse and reverse were not in conflict but instead complemented each other. In spite of the good composition, the coin also showed Longacre's limits as a diesinker; the letters in "Liberty" on the obverse are poorly spaced.

Fig. 138. The $1 gold piece was enlarged from previous issues by two millimeters, and Longacre slightly modified the headband of Liberty from the $3 gold piece. However, it seemed that he failed to take into account the larger tondo, as the head seems too small for the field. This particular coin also suffers from severe clash marks on the reverse.

Fig. 139. James Longacre came to grief when he took the commission from the Department of the Navy to execute this medal. With the furor over Franklin Peale taking medal commissions barely over, Longacre was forced to repay this commission to the government. Designed in large part within the Navy department, the medal has few redeeming features. The exception is the partial wreath of oak on the reverse, which would grace Longacre's famous one-cent design in 1860.

year and set forth his case in his January 30, 1855, annual report to the president.[14] The work would be consistent with the operations of the Mint, with no additional remuneration paid to either officers or employees of the Mint. It had even come before the House of Representatives for inquiry.[15] Permission was granted on March 7, 1855, before Longacre had accepted the Ingraham commission.[16]

The Treasury Department got wind of the transaction and requested justification from Longacre for his actions. Considering Peale still had friends at the Mint, the source of the leak, while never disclosed, was obvious. The engraver argued that the work was done outside of his Mint duties and in the "recess" of his official work. Artfully worded arguments were not going to work, given the uproar over Peale's activities. Longacre had to repay the government, with interest, from his salary.[17]

Fig. 140. Shown in this 1893 print, the New York Assay Office sits conspicuously next to the New York Stock Exchange.

With the ouster of Peale, Richard McCulloh had won the battle. However, his hopes for implementing his zinc-refining method were dead. McCulloh moved on, applying for a position as a professor of natural and experimental philosophy and chemistry at Columbia College in New York City. He was the dark-horse candidate. The favored candidate was an alumnus of Columbia with broad support. However, the trustees voted in favor of McCulloh on April 3, 1854. Controversy swirled around this vote. Particular criticism was leveled at one trustee, Senator Hamilton Fish, for his "polite neutrality."[18] Senator William Gwin had come to the aid of McCulloh.

At the opening of the New York assay office, Andrew Mason, a Philadelphia Mint clerk, transferred to that facility to serve as the assistant assayer. In 1865 he became the melter and refiner. In this position, he brought about the adoption of the European method of using sulfuric acid in place of nitric acid in the parting operation. This process was particularly effective in refining silver bullion containing gold in less proportion than could be economically separated using nitric acid. The savings to the government were estimated at no less than $300,000. A grateful Congress awarded Mason $10,000 in 1874.[19] He would go on to become superintendent of the assay office in 1883.

• • • •

By 1856 the Mint and its branches had settled into a pattern of operations. The push to turn out the reduced-weight silver coins was over. While there had been some movement in 1854 for Congress to authorize coinage capability at the New York assay office, the effort made no headway whatsoever. New York City would issue bars only. The total amount of gold processed at all the mints in 1856 amounted to $59 million. San Francisco led all operations with $28 million, including $23.5 million in double eagles and $3 million in unparted bars. Those numbers were to be expected. The surprise occurred when Philadelphia's output was compared to that of New York City. Philadelphia's output in gold was $11 million, including 183 refined bars at a value of $80,000. While half of production was in double eagles, there was a substantial amount of smaller gold coins struck as well. At New York City, the assay office cast 4,727 bars at a value of $19 million.[20] The production of bars at New York City eclipsed the entire gold output at Philadelphia. It wasn't even close.

The battle between New York City and the Philadelphia Mint was resolved. In the end, neither got what they wanted, yet they both got what they needed. New York would cast the bars that fueled the international financial markets (fig. 140). Philadelphia would make the coins used in the everyday domestic economy.

First and foremost of Philadelphia's production would be James Longacre's beautiful double eagle. While it did not circulate, it was an object of desire for Americans as a symbol of wealth—both treasured and tucked away for a rainy day. This $20 gold piece would become a kind of talisman for the American people.

EPILOGUE

JANUARY 25, 1861

Daniel Ullmann (fig. 141) sat at his desk in New York City, pen in hand and writing paper before him. On that desk lay a medal. It sat in a red velvet flip inside a handsome morocco case. Enclosed with the medal was a silk cloth imprinted with the events of that day, almost nine years previous, that meant so much to Ullmann.

The copper-bronzed medal with its mahogany finish projected beautifully. The work of the Mint's then–chief coiner, Franklin Peale, could not have been better. It was one of 150 pieces struck after the gold presentation piece. Charles Cushing Wright had engraved the dies; he was the best that America had—an artist in steel. Never mind that Wright's fee for the gold medal and the copper-bronzed versions was $2,630.[1]

The middle-aged attorney thought back to the genesis of the medal. By 1851, everybody knew that Henry Clay's days were numbered. On January 11, 1851, Ullmann broke the news to Clay that a project to honor the man was afoot. It was a letter of introduction for Wright to meet with Clay in Washington. A committee of New Yorkers that he chaired wished to have a gold medal struck in Clay's honor, commemorating his "exulted services to the Republic." They wanted the medal to be the most perfect specimen yet produced of American art. To that end, they had chosen Wright to execute the commission. They asked Clay to give what aid Wright required to produce

Fig. 141. Daniel Ullmann organized a final and fitting tribute to Henry Clay in the form of a commemorative medal engraved by Charles Cushing Wright.

an immortal work. They wanted the medal to enable future generations to see the lineaments of the "Great Commoner" and "Pacificator" of his age.[2]

Thomas Dow Jones had prepared a plaster relief of Clay for the medal.[3] Having just relocated to New York, Jones had been the logical choice. One of his first pieces in the early 1840s was a marble bust of Clay. He knew the statesman's profile intimately. Ullmann had given that plaster to the Maryland Historical Society in 1853.

The issue of the medal's reverse was not so easily resolved. In April Wright provided the committee with the specifications required for the reverse engraving. If modeled in wax or plaster, the design had to be at least six inches in diameter and drawn within a circle of that size. Wright wanted it in low bas-relief. No sketch would do, it had to be a finished drawing or well-modeled design. Wright needed it in three weeks. He had settled upon a three-and-one-half–inch diameter for the medal.[4]

Ullmann had to move; he had not even finalized his list of potential artists to prepare the reverse.[5] Worse, once that decision was made, Ullmann could not jump in the cars and go to Washington to meet with Clay. With the close of the Thirty-First Congress, Clay had gone home to his Ashland estate in Lexington, Kentucky. His input would have to be by correspondence.

July found the committee no farther along with the reverse.[6] It was not until fall that the reverse resolved itself. Wright had provided an outline drawing. A wreath of the six American crop staples—wheat, corn, cotton, tobacco, rice, and hemp—designed by William Walcutt, a New York City transplant from Columbus, Ohio, would encircle a list of Clay's accomplishments with associated dates. Settling upon which of the great man's accomplishments should be enumerated had been the hard part. Henry Clay had kept adding more, while telling the committee in the next breath that the list could be abridged or shortened.[7]

Clay returned to Washington with the convening of the first session of the Thirty-Second Congress in December 1851. However, everyone understood that this was the old man's last political appearance; he submitted his resignation on December 15, 1851, to take effect in September 1852. Ullmann knew he had to wrap it up.

On January 16, 1852, Wright gained permission from George Eckert to have the gold medal struck at the Mint.[8] The medal, made of pure California gold, would be about a half-inch thick. On January 22, Wright wrote to Ullmann that the dies were ready to send to the Mint. Due to family illness, he could not attend to it personally, but he assured Ullmann that they would be perfectly safe. Wright had full confidence in Peale. The case for the medal was ready, except for the engraving, and that would be finished before the medal. The case would have an image on one side of the Capitol as envisioned with both wings completed, and on the other, two images—the commemorative monument of Clay on the Cumberland Road, and below, a view of Ashland. The goal was to strike the medal during the last week of the month, for presentation in early February.[9]

Bringing Henry Clay to New York City for a proper celebration was out of the question. Wracked by a vicious cough, Clay was virtually confined to his bed at the National Hotel in Washington, D.C. As chairman, Ullmann would lead a delegation to Washington to make the presentation.

Ullmann remembered February 9, 1852, as vividly as if it were yesterday. The weather had been absolutely delightful, as mild as spring.[10] For just a moment, the dull, gloomy gray of winter had been banished. The presentation had been a formal ceremony, and Ullmann's speech had been touching. He told Clay that the committee hoped that the medal would be valuable as a specimen of an art little practiced in the United States. No medal struck in the country surpassed its beauty. It was the best likeness of Clay's features ever yet attempted in any art form. Ullmann then got carried away with the emotions of the event, declaring that he hoped Clay's likeness upon this medal would be fondly cherished, as were the likenesses of Cicero and Brutus. Ullmann noted that previously, all national medals struck in the United States commemorated the triumphs of American arms; he wished for the first American victor of peace to thus be commemorated.

Clay accepted the gift just as formally. This day would be one of the most interesting and gratifying of his life. In public life, he was never sure of the motives of his supporters. Were they driven by patriotism or were they actuated by self-interest? In this case, there could be no doubt. In contemplating the medal, he talked first of the reverse, which listed his great measures adopted by the national councils. Of the obverse, he stated that it was a remarkable and accurate likeness.

The remainder of the great man's formal acceptance had saddened Ulmann. Clay was about to retire from public life and he did not expect to live much longer. He talked of his legacy. He stood ready for the judgment of his public deeds and career by history and posterity.[11]

Clay acknowledged that this medal was the spontaneous offering of private citizens, from their private purses, for his public services. He intended to fondly and gratefully cherish and preserve it while his life endured. He would transmit it to his descendants with the hope that they would receive it and guard it carefully as the proudest and richest legacy that he could leave them.

Ullmann and the committee had been deeply touched by these words. However, the day had not been all formality. Henry Clay had joked that after he was laid low in the grave, some Goth might be tempted to break off his nose (on the medal) and use the valuable metal that it contained.[12]

Ullmann winced as he thought of what had happened next. There had been a clamor by Washingtonians to see the medal. Clay had graciously given it to a goldsmith to exhibit in his shop. However, Wright had not been happy with the lettering. He wanted the medal back in New York. Clay had confessed that he could not see the defect, but he would return it nevertheless.[13] Ullmann had wanted him to send the medal by Adams Express. If only Clay had listened.

Clay had the medal back in his hands on March 11, and he was prepared to send it as instructed. However, during that day, Anna Charlotte Lynch visited him.[14] She was a noted New York City society hostess who maintained a well-attended salon. She had a flare for sculpture and, of course, wanted to see the medal. Since she was returning to New York City the following day, she offered to carry the medal personally, saving Clay the expense and trouble

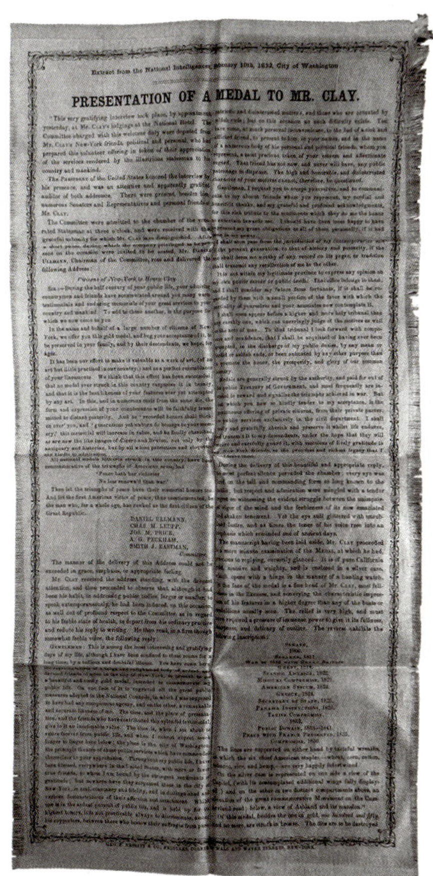
PRESENTATION OF A MEDAL TO MR. CLAY.

Fig. 142. Engraved by Charles Cushing Wright, this presentation medal to Henry Clay represented the best of American medallic art. Struck in gold for Clay, it has remained with his descendants in accordance with his wishes. The fact that it is identical to the accompanying bronze specimen argues that it is a second strike rather than the flawed first strike. Accompanying the bronze medal is an extract of the presentation from the *National Intelligencer* printed on silk.

of shipping it. Clay, always susceptible to a lady's charm, did not refuse her offer.

Miss Lynch caught the cars at nine o'clock the next morning.[15] Escorting her and her mother was noted New York lawyer and philanthropist Charles Butler. They decided to put the medal in his carpetbag for safekeeping. This bag also contained Butler's writing desk and other valuables. When they arrived in New York City at two the next afternoon, the carpetbag was placed on the hack that would take them to their residences. The baggage master set it on the seat next to the driver. When they arrived at Miss Lynch's residence on Ninth Street, the bag was gone. Everyone was mortified.[16]

There was no question of Butler not standing good for the loss of the medal, but it was a difficult letter that Ullmann had had to write to Clay, telling him of the loss. Clay was understanding; he wanted not one word of reproach to Miss Lynch.[17] Everybody believed the medal would be returned, as its unique character would have no street value. However, that was not to be. The bag was later found without the medal. It pained Daniel Ullmann to think about it. A second medal had been struck by the committee.[18] There was one fleeting moment of hope in October after Henry Clay's death. A convicted felon named Frederick Nolecke had been arrested in Hannover, Germany. In his possession was $2,000 in American coins and a large gold medal, undescribed.[19] With that single tease, the original medal vanished into thin air. At least Ullmann had had the pleasure of sending two copper-bronzed medals to Clay, which he believed had turned out even better than the original gold medal.[20]

Now, in 1861, Ullmann picked up his pen and dipped it in ink. "Dear Sir" he began.

> Some years ago a number of citizens of New York caused dies to be sunk, in which to strike a medal commemorative of the life and public services of the great Clay;—in order that they might thereby transmit to remote posterity, in the most enduring and classic form, a correct resemblance of the lineaments.
>
> A medal was accordingly struck in gold and presented to him. One hundred and fifty were also struck in bronze. After which the dies were broken.
>
> Many of the medals were presented to various States of the Union and to leading public institutions, at home and abroad.
>
> I reserved at the time, one of them with the intention, if ever such result should occur in my day, of presenting it to the citizen of the school of Henry Clay, who should first be elected to the Presidency of the United States.
>
> I rejoice that that event has at last occurred, and, recognizing in you a true disciple of our illustrious friend, I take great pleasure in carrying out my purpose, by hereby transmitting the medal to you, and begging your kind acceptance of it.

Ullmann then addressed the letter to His Excellency, Abraham Lincoln, President Elect of the United States.[21]

The medal that Ullmann enclosed represented the best of American artistry, engraving, and execution at the United States Mint for its era (fig. 142). It would stand the test of time.

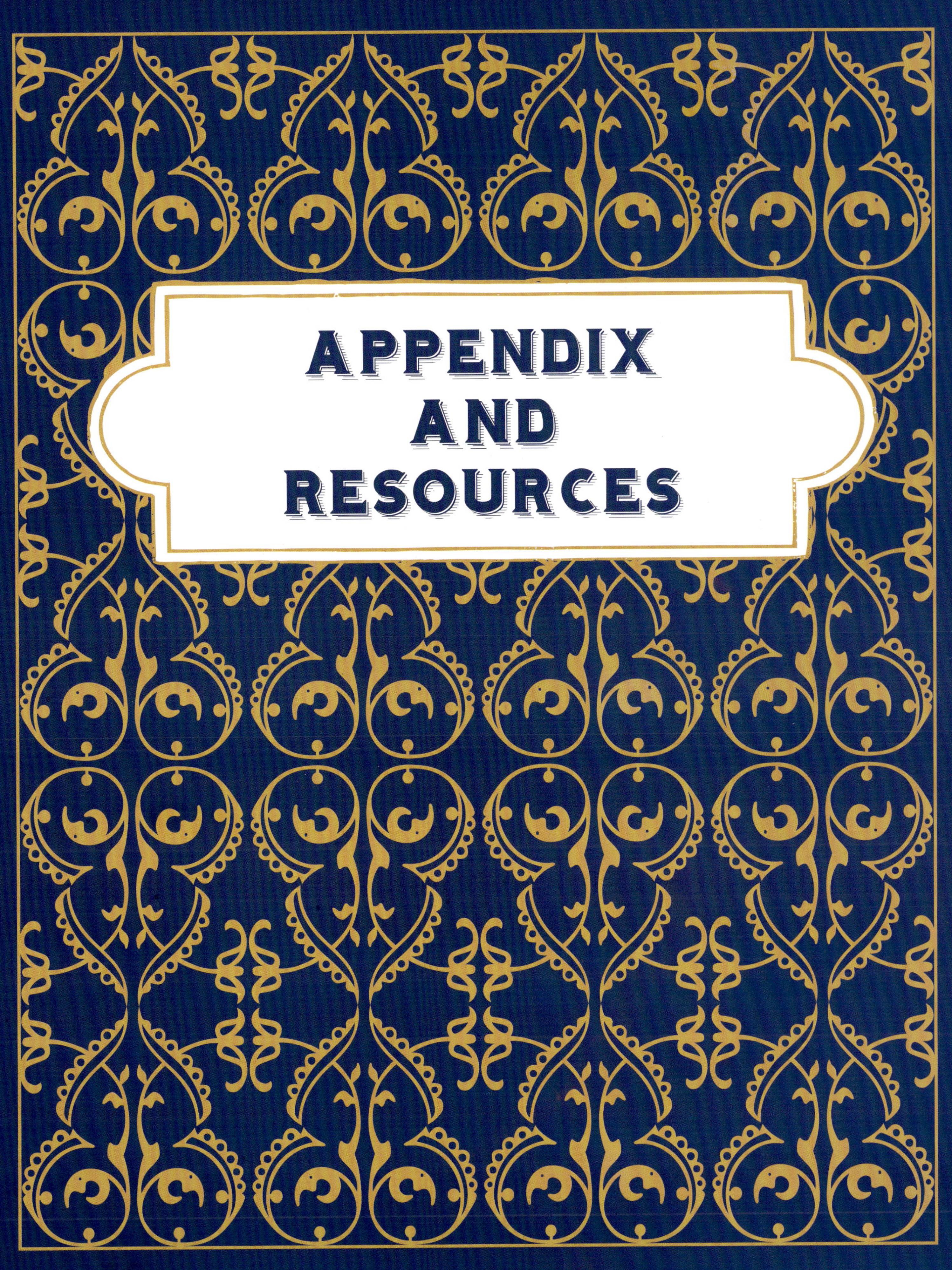

APPENDIX AND RESOURCES

1849

APPENDIX

DOUBLE EAGLES OF 1849 TO 1866 IN THE NATIONAL NUMISMATIC COLLECTION

1849, Proof

Mintage: Unknown

The Smithsonian 1849 double eagle is probably the most iconic and desirable coin in its vast collection. The coin is a direct result of the California Gold Rush, and is a tangible link to one of the most important phases of American history. Its place in the Smithsonian Museum of American History is very fitting. As is well documented in this book, the flow of bullion from the gold fields of California led to the legislation of March 3, 1849, authorizing the production gold dollars and double eagles.

Chief Engraver James B. Longacre engraved the dies for the new coinage. With great difficulty, he supervised an attempt to strike the new denomination. In a letter dated December 24, 1849, from chief coiner Franklin Peale to Mint director Robert Patterson, Peale wrote: "It is with extreme regret and after the most earnest endeavors to overcome the difficulty that I am compelled to inform you that the impression upon the new die, for the double eagle, cannot be brought up by the usual coining processes." The relief of the portrait was too high, and the coins could not be struck properly for mass production. These delays in production resulted in just a handful of coins being struck, late in 1849. (It has not been uncom-

mon in the history of U.S. coinage for the first year of issue to be problematic. Several interesting coins have been redesigned because the relief was too high. Although aesthetically attractive, actual production of high-relief coins is very difficult. The 1907 Saint-Gaudens High Relief double eagle is probably the most famous example. Others include the 1921 Peace dollar and 1849 gold dollar.)

All but two 1849 double eagles were melted. One was sent to Secretary of the Treasury W.M. Meredith and another to the Mint Cabinet in Philadelphia. The Meredith coin may have gone to the Steven Nagy collection in Philadelphia, but it is unknown to numismatists today. Researcher Dave Akers mentions that there was a photograph of one taken when the Nagy estate was sold. Neither the coin nor a photograph has surfaced.

The Mint Cabinet example has been on display in the Smithsonian Institution and is one of the most popular attractions of the numismatic collection. The Smithsonian 1849 double eagle grades PF-63, with a rather distinct series of bag marks near the first star. It is reported that in 1909 J.P. Morgan offered $35,000 for the coin, a tremendous amount for the era.

Although the only known example resides in the Smithsonian Institution, the missing Meredith coin could appear one day. Most experts agree that the 1849 double eagle is much more desirable than the 1933 double eagle. The two make incredible bookends to an extremely popular series and denomination. It can only be speculated what an example would bring if offered for sale. It is certain the eight-figure mark would be broken, and $25 million is not out of the question.

The only known example of this great coin is currently the centerpiece of the new "Value of Money" exhibit at the Smithsonian Museum of American History. The coin has often been called the "Ruby Slippers" of numismatics. Hopefully, with the publication of this book, readers will gain a better appreciation of this coin's history and the creation of a very popular denomination.

Note: This coin is included among the *100 Greatest U.S. Coins* (Garrett and Guth).

1850

Mintage: 1,170,261

The Smithsonian collection contains three examples of 1850 double eagles, the finest grading AU-58.

The 1850 double eagle is extremely popular as the first collectible year of the type and denomination. The date is moderately scarce, but more than 2,000 coins have been certified by NGC and PCGS. Most of those seen grade between Very Fine and Extremely Fine. Mint State coins are quite scarce, and only three or four coins are known in MS-64 or MS-65. The finest-known circulation strike of the date appears to the Harry W. Bass Jr. coin, which is now certified as MS-65 and last sold at auction in 2007 for $161,000. The American Numismatic Society collection also contains an MS-65 example, which is probably forever impounded in that institution. There is reportedly a Proof example of the date that has been seen in Paris, France. This double eagle could be from Longacre's estate sold at auction January 21, 1870. It was described in the Thomas & Sons catalog as "Proof from the first dies (January 1850) and might be termed a trial piece." This coin would be an incredible addition to the population of great double eagles. Perhaps the coin will someday reach the shores of the United States. The SS *Central America* hoard originally comprised 29 examples of the date, but all were circulated. Recently more examples were found at the shipwreck site, and an additional 12 or so examples will someday enter the market. These are all circulated as well.

Hoard Information: The "Baltimore Hoard" found in 1934 contained 92 examples of the date. The SS *Republic* held 55 coins and the SS *Brother Jonathan* contained a single coin. To date, 38 coins have been found on the shipwreck of the *Central America*. The Saddle Ridge hoard contained 1 example.

1850-O

Mintage: 141,000

The Smithsonian collection contains two examples, the highest grade being Extremely Fine, with traces of wax on the reverse from an old exhibit mounting.

The 1850-O is popular as the first year of issue for the regular series and the first double eagle struck at a branch mint. It is scarce, but an ample number enter the market each year. More than 500 have been certified, but most are Very Fine or Extremely Fine. Mint State coins are extremely rare, and no choice examples are known. Most coins seen are softly struck, particularly around the stars. The current auction record for the issue is a PCGS MS-61 coin that sold for $111,625 in 2014. It has been reported that a hoard of 50 to 100 coins entered the market in the 1990s. These have long since been dispersed. The recently excavated site of the SS *Central America* hoard yielded two more examples of the date, both grading About Uncirculated.

Hoard Information: The SS *Republic* contained 10 examples of the date and the SS *Central America* shipwreck site has yielded 1 example to date.

1851

Mintage: 2,087,155

The Smithsonian contains two examples, both grading About Uncirculated, although one is considerably better than the other in terms of eye appeal. With the vast quantities of gold pouring into the Philadelphia Mint from the California Gold Rush, the production of double eagles soared to levels that would not be exceeded until 1861. Most of these coins saw very heavy use and nearly all seen today are well worn. Examples, almost all of which were circulated, were found on the SS *Central America* and the SS *Republic*. The recent exploration of the *Central America* site yielded examples as well. Mint State examples for the date are quite scarce and only three or four coins are known in MS-64, one of which sold at auction in 2010 for $34,500.

Hoard Information: The "Baltimore Hoard" found in 1934 contained 79 examples of the date. The SS *Central America* hoard contained 33 coins, with another 10 or 11 found in 2014. The SS *Republic* wreck site contained 53 examples of the date.

1851-O

Mintage: 315,000

The Smithsonian collection has two examples, one that grades Extremely Fine and the other About Uncirculated.

The 1851-O was struck in ample numbers so that today the date can be found with moderate effort. More than 1,000 coins have been certified by the grading services. Most of those seen are heavily circulated and the average grade is Very Fine or Extremely Fine. Examples of the date were found on the SS *Central America* and the SS *Republic*. None were Mint State quality. There are probably only about 15 to 20 coins known that would qualify as Mint State. The finest is a single MS-63 that sold privately in April 2002 for $56,000.

Hoard Information: The "Baltimore Hoard" found in 1934 contained 10 examples of the date. The SS *Central America* hoard contained 7 coins, with another 2 coins. The SS *Republic* contained 15 examples of the date.

1852

Mintage: 2,053,026

The mintage for this issue was extremely large, nearly matching that seen in 1851. More than 2,000 coins have been certified in all grades, and the date is considered one of the most common of Type 1 double eagles (the Liberty Head type with no IN GOD WE TRUST motto on the reverse, minted from 1849 to 1866). Most examples, however, are well worn, as the bulk of the mintage entered circulation and very few were preserved for future generations. Most of the known Mint State examples are from hoards found over the years. This includes about 130 pieces found on the SS *Central America* and SS *Republic* shipwrecks. Another 17 coins surfaced in the 2014 excavation of the SS *Central America*, one of which grades MS63 or better. NGC has certified one example as MS65, but the current auction record for the date is a PCGS MS64 that sold for $82,250 in 2012. The Smithsonian examples for the date grade AU-50 and AU-58 respectively.

Hoard Information: The "Baltimore Hoard" found in 1934 contained 42 examples of the date. The SS *Central America* hoard contained 32 coins, with another 7 coins found in 2014. The SS *Republic* contained 104 examples of the date. The Saddle Ridge hoard contained 1 example.

1852-O

Mintage: 190,000

This date has a very similar survival ratio to that of the 1851-O. About 900 coins have been certified in all grades, most in the range of Very Fine or Extremely Fine. The date becomes much rarer in the higher states of preservation and only a few dozen are known in all grades of Mint State. There were 20 examples of the date on the SS *Republic*, one of which graded Mint State. The SS *Central America* yielded five coins in the 1980s and just a single piece in 2014. The finest known example by far is an NGC MS-65 that sold in 2011 for $276,000 (the Dallas Bank Collection specimen was the finest seen until the coin mentioned surfaced in 2011). Many high-grade examples for the date are seen with partially prooflike surfaces. The Smithsonian example is of relatively high grade with lustrous surfaces that would rate the coin as AU-50.

Hoard Information: The "Baltimore Hoard" contained two examples of the date. The SS *Central America* hoard contained four coins. The SS *Republic* contained twenty examples of the date. The Saddle Ridge hoard contained one example.

1853

Mintage: 1,261,326

Examples of the date in the Smithsonian collection consist of two coins, one which is MS-61 and the other a cleaned AU. Although the mintage for the 1853 double eagle is much lower than for the 1851 and 1852, the survival numbers are about the same. About this time $20 gold pieces were also being produced in California by the United States Assay Office. Nearly 2,000 1853 double eagles have been certified, most in circulated condition. Of the coins certified, only about 100 are Mint State in quality, nearly all of which are MS-61 and MS-62. A single example of the date has been certified as Gem condition. This coin sold at auction in 2014 for $152,750.

Hoard Information: More than 100 coins of the date were found on the wrecks of the SS *Central America* and the SS *Republic*, most of which graded About Uncirculated. The "Baltimore Hoard" contained 27 examples of the date. The Saddle Ridge hoard contained 1 example.

1853, 3 Over 2

Mintage: Unknown (included as part of the year's mintage of 1,261,326)

No example of this variety is represented in the Smithsonian collection. The 1853, 3 Over 2, double eagle is a rather controversial issue. Its true overdate status is questioned by some experts. The variety that is collected as the "overdate" shows the remnants of a numeral beneath the 3 of the date, which is most pronounced near the bottom. All so-called overdates seen by the author display a small die bulge below the R of LIBERTY. Numismatists have seen coins, however, with the die bulge that could not be identified as the overdate. This variety was discovered in the 1950s and is the only so-called overdate Liberty Head double eagle. Fewer than a dozen examples of this scarce issue have been certified as Mint State. The finest graded is a single MS-62 that sold at auction for $41,400 in 2004.

Hoard Information: The SS *Republic* contained nine examples of the date and the SS *Brother Jonathan* listed one example of the variety.

1853-O

Mintage: 71,000

The Smithsonian collection has two examples of this scarce issue. One coin is a lustrous AU-55, and the other grades EF-40. As can be predicted from the much lower mintage figure, the 1853-O is considerably rarer than earlier New Orleans issues. About 300 coins have been certified by the grading services combined, most of them grading Very Fine to About Uncirculated. Currently, just five coins have been deemed to be Mint State, the finest being a single MS-63. This coin has not appeared at auction in recent years.

Hoard Information: Two examples were originally found on the SS *Central America*. None were found during the 2014 excavation. The SS *Republic* contained seven examples of the date.

1854, Small Date

Mintage: Unknown (included as part of the year's mintage of 757,899)

The single Smithsonian example of this issue grades AU-55.

There are two major varieties of the 1854 double eagle. The first and more common variety is the 1854, Small Date. Most 1854 double eagles are of this variety. The Small Date is not greatly different from the Large Date and comparing photographs of both is helpful in accurate identification. More than 1,000 coins have been certified of the issue, most of which grade Extremely Fine or About Uncirculated. Mint State examples are seldom seen, and the date is extremely rare in Gem condition. Just a single example has been certified as MS-65, and it has not crossed the auction block in many years.

Hoard Information: The "Baltimore Hoard" contained 12 examples of the date. The SS *Central America* hoard contained 20 coins, with another 12 or 13 coins found in 2014. The SS *Republic* listed 42 examples of the date, but did not signify variety.

1854, Large Date

Mintage: Unknown (included as part of the year's mintage of 757,899)

The Smithsonian does not have an example of this scarce variety. The Large Date variety is much rarer than the Small Date. The grading services have certified fewer than 200 coins in all grades. This is about 15 percent of the totals seen for the Small Date. The date size difference is not hugely dramatic, but the issue has become extremely popular due to its rarity. This is a rare coin that an astute collector could possibly cherrypick, as many are unaware of its true rarity. Most examples seen fall into the Extremely Fine to About Uncirculated range. Mint State coins are rare at every level. Only about a dozen have been certified as Mint State, the finest being MS-64. One of these sold in 2008 for $96,600.

Hoard Information: The SS *Central America* hoard that was recovered in the 1980s contained seven of the Large Date variety. None were found in more recent excavations.

1854-O

Mintage: 3,250

The 1854-O is one of the great rarities of the double eagle series. There are probably 35 or fewer examples known in all grades. The Smithsonian collection contains a relatively high-grade 1854-O double eagle. The coin grades AU-50 and was once part of the famed Lilly collection. Genuine examples of this date exhibit raised die lines on the TY of LIBERTY. A few examples are also seen with minor planchet defects. The low mintage for the issue was a result of the shifting priorities at the New Orleans Mint. Most production for the year was focused in silver coinage, and other gold denominations.

Most examples seen grade Very Fine or Extremely Fine, and coins with any luster are seldom seen. No Mint State 1854-O double eagles are known to have survived. The finest example the author has seen is the coin recovered from the wreckage of the SS *Republic*. This coin was one of the highlights of the coins recovered from that shipwreck. It has been certified by NGC as AU-58 and was reportedly sold by private treaty in 2004 for $675,000. A PCGS AU-55 sold at auction in 2005 for $603,750.

Hoard Information: The SS *Republic* contained one example of the date.

Note: This coin is included among the *100 Greatest U.S. Coins* (Garrett and Guth).

1854-S

Mintage: 141,468

As discussed in this book, the San Francisco Mint was finally producing gold coins from the California Gold Rush in 1854. The 1854-S quarter eagle and 1854-S half eagle are extremely rare. Only three examples of the half eagle are known, two of which reside in the Smithsonian collection. The only coin in private hands (Pogue collection) is scheduled for sale in the near future. Most of the mint's production focused on double eagles, and they were widely distributed. The Smithsonian collection contains two examples, both with moderate wear. Most Mint State examples of the date can be traced to the wrecks of the SS *Yankee Blade*, SS *Republic*, and SS *Central America*. The auction record for the issue is a PCGS example that sold in 2008 for $115,000.

Hoard Information: The SS *Central America* hoard that was recovered in the 1980s contained 25 examples. None were found in recent excavations. The SS *Republic* contained 9 examples of the date.

1854-S, Proof

Mintage: Unknown

While doing numismatic research at the Smithsonian Institution, the author had the privilege of personally examining the trays in the cabinet of the National Numismatic Collection. This was well before the 100 or so greatest coins were housed in custom-designed museum slabs. The coins from the year 1854 are fairly routine until you come to the Proof 1854 double eagle. The coin is an 1854-S and is a deeply mirrored example, and would easily grade Specimen- or Proof-65. It was first noticed in 1951 by Walter Breen and Stuart Mosher (then curator of the collection and editor of *The Numismatist*). The coin is recorded as having been sent to the Mint Cabinet by San Francisco Mint superintendent Lewis A. Birdsall. The Mint Cabinet was transferred to the Smithsonian in 1923. The coin has always been categorized as a branch-mint Proof. The surfaces of the coin are prooflike, but without the deep, orange-peel appearance that true Proofs of the era display. It is our opinion that the coin would be more accurately described as a presentation strike. The coin is probably the first coin struck for the year, being a presentation example to recognize the opening of the San Francisco Mint. It is nonetheless an extraordinary coin, and one of the most important double eagles ever struck. The 1854-S double eagle is considered one of the legendary rarities in the National Numismatic Collection, which is housed in the Smithsonian Museum of American History. It is now prominently displayed in the new "Value of Money" exhibit that opened in the summer of 2015.

Note: This coin is included among the *100 Greatest U.S. Coins* (Garrett and Guth).

1855

Mintage: 364,666

The vast majority of 1855 double eagles seen are well worn. The issue is a solid condition rarity and Mint State examples number fewer than 25 or 30 pieces. The Smithsonian cabinet contains two pieces, one of which grades MS-61. Only two coins have been graded at the MS-64 level, one of which sold for an astounding $126,500 in 2006. It is interesting how these coins were distributed so widely, as seven examples made their way to California and then were lost of the return voyage back east when the SS *Central America* sank in 1857.

Hoard Information: The "Baltimore Hoard" contained 6 examples of the date. The SS *Central America* hoard contained 7 coins. The SS *Republic* contained 18 examples of the date.

1855-O

Mintage: 8,000

As can be guessed from the very low mintage, the 1855-O double eagle is a serious rarity. Fewer than 100 coins are known for the issue in all grades. The Smithsonian collection is blessed with two examples, one of which was part of the Lilly donation in the 1960s. Both coins grade surprisingly high, and are AU-50 with ample mint luster. The highest graded for the date is a single MS-61. That coin sold for $141,000 in 2014.

Hoard Information: The SS *Republic* hoard contained three examples, all of which were graded AU-58 at one time.

1855-S

Mintage: 879,675

The mintage for the 1855-S double eagle is quite large, reaching nearly one million coins. The coins were very widely distributed and at times most examples seen were worn or damaged. The Smithsonian collection contains three, the best being graded MS-60. The condition rarity for the issue was completely turned upside-down when more than 300 coins were discovered on the wreckage of the SS *Central America*. Nearly 100 examples graded Mint State, and one was nearly perfectly preserved and was graded MS-66 by PCGS. That coin sold at auction in 2000 for $120,750.

There are two distinctly different mintmarks found for the issue: the Medium S and the Large S.

Hoard Information: The SS *Central America* hoard contained 338 coins when they were first discovered in the 1980s. Another 50 to 60 were found in 2014. The SS *Republic* hoard listed 57 coins of the date. The SS *Brother Jonathan* listed 2 examples found. The Saddle Ridge hoard contained 1 example.

1856

Mintage: 329,878

Like most of other dates from the 1850s struck at the Philadelphia Mint, this issue is usually seen with considerable wear. Of the more than 500 coins that have been certified, fewer than 10 percent qualify as Mint State. Very few examples of the date were found on the SS *Central America* or SS *Republic*. The Smithsonian collection contains a single piece, grading About Uncirculated but with signs of an old cleaning. Examples of the date are also seen that display granular seawater surfaces. The coins are probably from an undocumented shipwreck discovery. Choice coins for the date are very rare, with only four having been certified at the MS-63 level. One of these sold at auction in 2014 for $41,125.

Hoard Information: The SS *Central America* hoard that was recovered in the 1980s contained 6 examples. None were found in recent excavations. The SS *Republic* hoard listed 17 coins of the date.

1856-O

Mintage: 2,250

The 1856-O is one of the "kings" of the Liberty Head double eagle series. Only about 25 examples are known in all grades. The Smithsonian collection features two examples of the great rarity, one coming from the Lilly donation and the other having been in the collection for many decades. The Lilly example grades AU-53 and the other piece is EF-40 with traces of an old cleaning. After the San Francisco Mint opened in 1854, the production of double eagles dropped significantly in New Orleans, creating two of the great rarities of American numismatics, the 1854-O and 1856-O double eagles. The majority of the 23 coins that have been certified to date fall into the grade range of Extremely Fine to About Uncirculated.

The three finest examples certified are AU-58, but this probably includes at least one resubmission.

Note: This coin is included among the *100 Greatest U.S. Coins* (Garrett and Guth).

1856-O, Specimen

Mintage: Unknown

As noted above, the 1856-O double eagle is unknown in Mint State. There is, however, an incredible example of this date that has been certified as Specimen-63. The coin was discovered by New England Rare Coin Galleries and was purchased directly from descendants of New Orleans Mint superintendent Charles Bienvenu in 1979. The coin is well struck, with fully mirrored surfaces, and its Specimen credentials are unquestioned. The Smithsonian lacks this great coin in its collection, but maybe someday a generous benefactor will donate the only known example to the collection. It would have plenty of great company!

The one known example last sold at auction in 2009 for $1,437,500.

Note: This coin is included among the *100 Greatest U.S. Coins* (Garrett and Guth).

1856-S

Mintage: 1,189,750

As can be seen from the mintage figure, the San Francisco Mint stayed very busy turning bullion from the gold fields of California into coinage. Years ago the 1856-S double eagle was usually seen in circulated condition. The coins saw heavy commerce. The four examples of the date in the Smithsonian collection are average at best, with the finest grading MS-61. The discovery of the SS *Central America* profoundly changed the rarity of this issue. There were more than 1,000 coins found, with the majority being Mint State. There are several Gem examples. The date was also found in quantity in other shipwrecks of the era.

When the double eagles from the *Central America* entered the market, they were closely studied for die-variety attribution. At least 18 different varieties were identified.

Hoard Information: The "Baltimore Hoard" contained 23 examples of the date. The SS *Central America* hoard contained 1,153 coins, with another 200 to 300 found in 2014. The SS *Republic* hoard listed 65 coins of the date. The SS *Brother Jonathan* listed 3 examples as found.

1857

Mintage: 439,375

As can be guessed from the relatively high mintage, this date is not very difficult to locate in circulated conditions. Most of the coins seen grade Very Fine to About Uncirculated. The Smithsonian collection has a single Extremely Fine piece, grading in the middle of the above-mentioned range. Mint State examples are scarce. While the treasure of the SS *Central America* revealed thousands of examples from the San Francisco Mint, only two 1857 Philadelphia coins were found among the hoard. One of the finest examples of this date seen by the author was in the Harry W. Bass Jr. collection.

Hoard Information: The SS *Central America* hoard contained two coins when it was first discovered in the 1980s. The SS *Republic* hoard listed 26 coins of the date. The SS *Brother Jonathan* listed 1 example as found.

1857-O

Mintage: 30,000

The mintage for double eagles rebounded sharply in 1857 after the tiny output of 1856. Most of the 30,000 coins saw heavy circulation and of the 200-plus coins that have been certified, most are Very Fine to About Uncirculated. The Smithsonian collection contains two very nice AU-55 examples, one of which displays prooflike surfaces. Prooflike surfaces can be found on many of the high-grade examples seen for the date. Interestingly, the mintmark is weakly struck on many coins seen for the date. The finest example seen was once part of the famed Harry W. Bass Jr. collection. This coin graded MS-63 and sold for the handsome sum of nearly $100,000 more than 15 years ago. The SS *Republic* shipwreck revealed just four examples. One coin was graded MS-62 Prooflike and sold for $176,250 in 2014.

Hoard Information: The SS *Republic* hoard listed four coins of the date.

1857-S

Mintage: 970,500

Prior to the discovery of the SS *Central America* the 1857-S date was normally seen in circulated condition. The Smithsonian collection has four examples, none of which are Mint State. The coins were heavily used in commerce in California and around the country. The discovery of the *Central America* changed the landscape of collecting double eagles profoundly.

On September 12, 1857, the steamship SS *Central America* sank in the Atlantic Ocean, 200 miles off the coast of North Carolina, on the way to New York with treasure fresh from the California Gold Rush. On board was an incredible quantity of gold bars, gold dust, and more than 7,000 gold coins. Unfortunately, nearly 600 people were also making the trip home from the land of opportunity. When the ship sank below the waves, 425 lives were lost. The story of the *Central America* is one the most heart-wrenching episodes of bravery and courage in American history. Because of a Herculean effort on the part of the passengers and crew, 153 passengers survived the ravages of the storm.

The ship and her golden bounty lay on the ocean floor in 7,200 feet of water for the next 130 years. In 1985 a group of explorers and investors formed the Columbus-America Discovery Group to locate the treasure. The wreck was found in September 1986. It was one the largest discoveries of treasure ever made. Over the next few years the artifacts were brought to the surface. A legal battle ensued with insurance companies over the ownership of the find. A settlement was reached, and the gold was finally brought to market. The California Gold Marketing Group, headed by Dwight Manley, was formed to market the rare coins and gold bars.

Recently the grave of the *Central America* has yielded yet more treasure. The shipwreck company Odyssey Marine has been conducting successful dives and the full extent of the lost gold is still being explored.

There were more than 7,000 examples of the 1857-S double eagle on board when the ship sank. More than 5,000 were recovered in the original excavation of the shipwreck. Many of the coins were in nearly pristine condition and looked as if they had just been struck. The fabulous condition is what makes these coins so special. These are the only Type 1 double eagles readily available in Gem condition. The original hoard was expertly marketed and most have been widely distributed among collectors. Another 1,000 to 2,000 coins were found in the most recent excavation of the *Central America* site. When these enter the market, there will probably be another round of renewed interest in collecting double eagles. At least eight different varieties of the 1857-S were identified for marketing purposes.

Hoard Information: The SS *Central America* hoard contained more than 5,000 coins, with another 1,000 to 2,000 coins found in 2014. The SS *Republic* hoard listed 86 coins of the date. The SS *Brother Jonathan* listed 5 examples as found.

Note: This coin is included among the *100 Greatest U.S. Coins* (Garrett and Guth).

1858

Mintage: 211,714

This date can be found in Extremely Fine and About Uncirculated conditions without too much difficulty. The date becomes increasingly rare in Mint State and choice examples are extremely elusive. More than 500 coins have been certified and fewer than 10 percent have attained Mint State. Surprisingly, the Smithsonian collection lacks an example of this date in the circulation-strike format. Early collectors preferred Proof examples of Philadelphia coinage. The Harry W. Bass Jr. example in MS-63 is the finest of this date seen by the author. The coin sold for $29,900 in the 2000 sale of Bass's collection. One interesting variety of the date exists with a misplaced date: the curved top of an 8 is hidden in the dentils below the 5.

Hoard Information: The SS *Republic* hoard listed nine coins of the date.

1858, Proof

Mintage: Unknown

The year 1858 is the first in which regular-issue Liberty Head double eagles are known in Proof. The exact mintage for 1858 is unknown, but today there are only three or four coins known. Two examples are in the collection of the Smithsonian; one coin is from the Mint Collection and grades PF-64, and the other from the Lilly Collection, grading PF-62. Both examples display cameo devices. Another specimen resides in the collection of the American Numismatic Society, a gift to the museum by

J.P. Morgan. A fourth example was last offered for public sale in the Memorable Collection, which was sold in 1948 by Numismatic Gallery. The Proof status of the Memorable coin has been questioned, however. John Jay Pittman stated that he did not think the coin was Proof and that if it had been, then he would have purchased it.

1858-O

Mintage: 35,250

The 1858-O double eagle is scarce in any condition and there are thought to be only about 200 coins known in all grades. Most of the coins known fall into the Very Fine to About Uncirculated grade range. The Smithsonian collection has two examples, both grading About Uncirculated. Just four or five examples of the 1858-O known would qualify as Mint State. Two of the finest 1858-O double eagles seen are the Harry W. Bass Jr. specimen, which graded MS-62, and the stunning example that was found in the wreckage of the SS *Republic*. This coin has been certified as MS-63 and last sold in January 2015 for $164,500.

Hoard Information: The SS *Republic* hoard listed eight coins of the date.

1858-S

Mintage: 846,710

As can be guessed from the large mintage, this date can be found with relative ease in grades from Extremely Fine to About Uncirculated. The issue saw extensive circulation and more than 1,000 coins have been certified in all grades. The Smithsonian collection retains three examples, all grading either Very Fine or About Uncirculated. Perhaps two dozen are known in Mint State, virtually all of which grade MS-61. The finest graded is a single MS-63 that sold at auction in 2012 for $37,375. The SS *Republic* hoard contained 68 examples of the date, most of which were About Uncirculated or MS-61.

Hoard Information: The SS *Republic* hoard listed 68 coins of the date. The SS *Brother Jonathan* contained 7 coins. The Saddle Ridge hoard contained 2 examples.

1859

Mintage: 43,597

The 1859 double eagle is one of the scarcest issues of the Type 1 double eagle struck at the Philadelphia Mint. Only about 200 coins have been certified in all grades. Nearly all are Very Fine to About Uncirculated. Also, the issue was ignored by early collectors, who preferred Proof examples of Philadelphia coinage. The Smithsonian lacks an example of this issue in the circulation-strike format. The SS *Republic* hoard contained only two examples of the date compared to much larger quantities struck at the San Francisco Mint. The finest example known for the date is a single MS-62 that was sold privately in early 2005 for $55,000.

Hoard Information: The SS *Republic* hoard listed three coins of the date.

1859, Proof

Mintage: 80

The reported mintage for the issue is 80 coins. If this many coins were actually struck, most were certainly melted, as the 1859 double eagle is exceedingly rare in Proof. There are nine coins known in all grades (based on a census prepared by Heritage Auctions), including at least one impaired example. The Smithsonian retains two examples that are of choice quality. Another resides at the American Numismatic Society. Two coins are also known in complete 1859 Proof sets. One of these was in a set formed by the late John Jay Pittman. He purchased the double eagle for his 1859 set in 1952 for $525. In 1997, the Pittman 1859 Proof set sold for $426,250. A complete gold 1859 Proof set was sold at the 2015 Central States auction for around $750,000. The double eagle in the set grades PF-66 and is considered the finest known example.

1859-O

Mintage: 9,100

The 1859-O is one of the rarest double eagles struck at the New Orleans Mint. Only about 100 coins are known in all grades, including two in the Smithsonian collection. Those pieces grade EF-45 and AU-53, which is above par for this rare issue. The 1859-O is extremely rare in high grade, with only one coin having been certified as Mint State. One of the finest examples seen in recent years, an AU-58, sold at auction in 2014 for $76,375. There were reportedly two examples of the date found in the SS *Republic* shipwreck hoard. Many examples seen for the date are heavily bagmarked and several coins are known with harsh cleaning or other impairments. The date is in very high demand with double eagle collectors.

Hoard Information: The SS *Republic* hoard listed two coins of the date.

1859-S

Mintage: 636,445

A substantial number of this issue have survived, with more than 1,000 coins having been certified to date. Like the two coins in the Smithsonian collection that grade AU-50 and AU-58, most survivors seen are circulated to some degree. Finding a lustrous example in About Uncirculated is not too difficult of a task. The shipwreck of the SS *Republic* yielded 67 examples, and most were About Uncirculated. A single example graded Mint State. Another 14 circulated examples of the date were found on the SS *Brother Jonathan*. The finest known example is a single MS-63 that sold at auction in 2012 for $54,625. There is a very interesting variety known for the date with portions of the word LIBERTY doubled. These coins are quite desirable and sought after by specialists of the series.

Hoard Information: The SS *Republic* hoard listed 67 coins of the date. The SS *Brother Jonathan* listed 14 coins as found. The Saddle Ridge hoard contained 2 examples.

1860

Mintage: 577,670

Until the recovery of the SS *Republic* this date was very difficult to locate in Mint State. The Smithsonian holdings for the date are very modest with two examples, both grading Extremely Fine. The *Republic* contained nearly 100 examples, with almost half grading Uncirculated. One coin was certified as MS-65 and last sold at auction in 2006 for $69,000. After the 1861, this date is the most available Type 1 double eagle seen from the Philadelphia Mint.

Hoard Information: The SS *Republic* hoard listed 96 coins of the date.

1860, Proof

Mintage: 59

Although the reported mintage for the 1860 double eagle is 59 coins, most were melted or lost to numismatics in subsequent years. In 1860, $20 was a hefty sum of money, and only a few well-heeled collectors could have saved an example. There are fewer than ten coins known today, including two that are in the museum collections of the Smithsonian and the American Numismatic Society. The Smithsonian specimen grades PF-63, with nice cameo contrast. Fourteen examples of the 1860 Proof double eagle are listed on the population reports. That number is not a true reflection of the coin's rarity as there are most likely several coins that have been submitted more than once. The finest Proof offered for sale in recent years was a PF-66 example that sold at auction in 2014 for $367,188.

1860, Paquet Reverse, Proof

Mintage: Unknown

The 1861 Paquet double eagle is now considered a regular-issue United States gold coin. In 1860 Anthony Paquet, an engraver at the Philadelphia Mint, modified the reverse design for the double eagle. The new design was very similar to the original but the reverse letters are much taller and more slender in appearance. There are also several technical variations with regard to the positioning and size of the lettering. Only one example of this true pattern is known. The coin is part of the Smithsonian's National Numismatic Collection. It is prominently displayed in the new "Value of Money" exhibit that opened at the Museum of American History in the summer of 2015. This interesting transitional issue is superb, and grades PF-65. Many gold patterns are very rare and they generally command astounding prices when offered. The 1860 Paquet Reverse Proof would generate even more excitement due to the rarity and high degree of collectability of the 1861 regular-issue Paquet design. The U.S. Mint also struck copper examples of this intriguing pattern, with reportedly three known.

1860-O

Mintage: 6,600

This date is rare and highly sought-after in all grades. Only about 100 or so coins are known for the issue. Most of the coins seen have heavy abrasions, and the average coin is Extremely Fine. The Smithsonian example is AU-50 with partially prooflike surfaces, which is characteristic of many the author has seen. The strike for the date can sometimes be weak on the borders. Only one example was found on the SS *Republic*, and the coin was a remarkable MS-60 Prooflike. The coin has not sold at auction, but it would surely bring a healthy six-figure price if offered. The Eliasberg coin sold in 1982 is also reportedly in Mint State; it has been in a private collection for decades. The finest example sold at auction was an NGC AU-58 for $64,625 in 2015.

Hoard Information: The SS *Republic* hoard listed one coin of the date.

1860-S

Mintage: 544,950

The 1860-S is relatively common in circulated conditions. Nearly 1,200 coins have been certified to date. In low-grade condition, the date can found in large lots of Type 1 double eagles. Mint State coins are another story and there are only about 40 to 50 known at that level. The two Smithsonian examples grade EF-40 and AU-50. This is a reflection of the scarcity of these early-date double eagles before the discovery of several shipwrecks that contained more examples. The Lilly family collection contained the best coins available at the time, and a lightly circulated example was the best to be found. There were 63 coins of the date found on the SS *Republic* and another 18 on the SS *Brother Jonathan*. A single MS-64 example has been certified, but it has not appeared at auction.

Hoard Information: The SS *Republic* hoard listed 70 coins of the date. The SS *Brother Jonathan* listed 17 coins as found.

1861, Paquet Reverse

Mintage: Unknown

In late 1860, the Paquet Reverse became the standard design that was adopted for the regular-issue coinage of 1861 double eagles. Dies were shipped to the branch mints of New Orleans and San Francisco. Actual coinage on high-speed presses began in January of 1861 in Philadelphia. It was feared that the wider fields and narrow rim would cause breakage of the dies, so the use of Paquet dies was discontinued. However, those dies that were used for coinage experienced no problems at all, proving their withdrawal was unnecessary.

Mint director James Ross Snowden recalled the new design and ordered the melting of the 1861 double eagles made at the Philadelphia Mint. The entire Philadelphia run was destroyed, with the exception of a few coins. Snowden also ordered production to cease in New Orleans and San Francisco. The order reached New Orleans in time to prevent any coinage. Because the transcontinental railroad was still several years from completion and the telegraph did not extend past St. Joseph, Missouri, word to stop coinage did not reach San Francisco until 19,250 coins had been struck. Charles H. Hempstead, superintendent of the San Francisco Mint, replied to the instructions on February 9, 1861: "I was unable to prevent the striking and issuing of a large number of double eagles, coined with the new dies." No effort was made to recall the issue.

The 1861 Paquet Reverse double eagle has been a known rarity since nearly the year it was struck. Today, just two examples of the Philadelphia mintage are known of this extremely rare coin. The Smithsonian lacks an example of this fabled rarity. Only two examples are known from the Philadelphia Mint. One coin, a PCGS-graded MS-61, was part of the Dallas Bank Collection sold by Sotheby's and Stack's in 2001. That coin was discovered in Paris in the 1970s. The coin last sold at auction in 2014 for $1,645,000. The other surviving example is Gem Uncirculated and traces its pedigree to 1865 (when it was sold by W. Elliot Woodward for $37). The coin subsequently resided in many famous collections, among them those of Ambassador and Mrs. R. Henry Norweb, King Farouk, and Colonel E.H.R. Green. The Norweb/Farouk specimen has been graded by NGC as MS-67 and is the ultimate combination of rarity and condition.

Note: This coin is included among the *100 Greatest U.S. Coins* (Garrett and Guth).

1861

Mintage: 2,976,453

The mintage figure for the 1861 double eagle is staggering for the time, and until the discovery of the SS *Central America* this date was by the far the most common Type 1 double eagle. It was not until 1904 that the mintage for double eagles exceeded that of the 1861 issue. Despite the high mintage and rather plentiful supply of available coins, the 1861 is very desirable for its Civil War date. Collectors are quite intrigued with coins from this important time period of American history. Surprisingly, the Smithsonian collection has just a single example that grades only AU-50. To date nearly 5,000 coins of this date have been certified. The finest by far is an incredible MS-67 that sold at auction in 2013 for $352,000. That coin is the finest Type 1 double eagle that was not found in a shipwreck hoard.

Hoard Information: The SS *Republic* hoard listed 459 coins of the date. The SS *Brother Jonathan* contained 4 coins of the date. The Saddle Ridge hoard contained 1 example.

1861, Proof

Mintage: 66

The circulation-strike double eagles of 1861 are among the most common for the type. Proof examples, however, are incredibly rare. Of the 66 coins reportedly struck in Proof, only a few remain. Most were probably melted as unsold. At the start of the Civil War, numismatic interest was surely diminished, especially for high-denomination issues. Besides examples in the museum collections of the Smithsonian and the American Numismatic Society, there are only three or four coins known today. The most recent example to have crossed the auction block sold in 2006 for $483,000. The Smithsonian example cited above grades PF-63 and has cameo devices.

1861-O

Mintage: 17,741

The 1861-O double eagle is very rare and one of the more historically interesting Type 1 double eagles. The issue was struck by three different governmental authorities. It has been estimated that the federal government struck 5,000 coins, the state of Louisiana 9,750 coins, and the Confederacy 2,991 coins. Unfortunately, it cannot be determined with certainty which coins were struck under which jurisdiction. There are probably fewer than 200

coins known in all grades, most of which are Very Fine or Extremely Fine. High-grade examples are very rare and desirable. Most display partially prooflike surfaces. An NGC MS-60 sold at auction for $146,875 in 2014. The finest known example, which is a prooflike NGC MS-62, is reported to have sold privately for $430,000 in early 2004. The finest 1861-O double eagle that resides in the collection of the Smithsonian is an amazing AU-53 coin with prooflike surfaces.

Hoard Information: The SS *Republic* hoard listed 2 coins of the date.

1861-S, Paquet Reverse

Mintage: 19,250

At one time the 1861-S Paquet Reverse double eagle was thought to be a pattern coin. It has been proven that the issue was intended for circulation and is now considered a rare, regular issue. Before the Mint director's order to stop production could reach California, $385,000 of the coins had been struck and released into circulation. Today there about 100 coins known in all grades, none of which have certified as Mint State. A few examples have been graded AU-58, one of which sold for $184,000 in 2012. Surprisingly, the Smithsonian collection does not contain an example of this interesting variety. A single coin of the issue was found on the SS *Republic.*

Hoard Information: The SS *Republic* hoard listed one example of the date.

1861-S

Mintage: 768,000

After a small run of the Paquet Reverse design the San Francisco Mint produced three quarters of a million coins from the regular dies. Large numbers of the date are known today, with more than 1,000 having been certified. Mint State examples are very rare, however, and fewer than two dozen are known at that level. The Smithsonian collection contains two examples, neither of which grade Uncirculated. Ample quantities of the date were found on the shipwrecks of the SS *Republic* and SS *Brother Jonathan.*

A single example has been graded at MS-63 and that coin has been in a private collection for decades.

Hoard Information: The SS *Republic* hoard listed 98 coins of the date. The SS *Brother Jonathan* listed 44 coins as found. The Saddle Ridge hoard contained 6 examples.

1862

Mintage: 92,133

With the Civil War escalating, the number of double eagles struck at the Philadelphia Mint dropped significantly. Only about 150 coins of the date have been certified. The Smithsonian collection lacks an example of the date in the circulation-strike format. Early collectors ignored the circulation-strike issues from the Philadelphia Mint. Most coins seen grade Extremely Fine or About Uncirculated. The only significant group found has been the eight coins discovered on the SS *Republic.* The finest known for the date is a single MS-64 that last sold in 2005 for $62,100. This is a Civil War issue very popular with collectors.

Hoard Information: The SS *Republic* contained nine examples for the date. The SS *Brother Jonathan* listed one coin found.

1862, Proof

Mintage: 35

The 1862 issue is probably the earliest Type 1 double eagle likely to be encountered in Proof. Although the mintage is smaller than for the previous few years, more examples have survived. There are about a dozen examples known, including two in the Smithsonian and another in the collection of the American Numismatic Society. The Smithsonian examples grade PF-63 and PF-64. Any Type 1 double eagle is a major rarity in Proof, and the demand for the issue far outstrips the supply. The auction record for the date in Proof is held by a PF-65 Cameo coin that sold in 2014 for $381,875.

1862-S

Mintage: 854,173

The large mintage for this issue has led to a plentiful supply for today's collectors. More than 1,000 coins have been certified to date. The date is available in the lower grades for the same as the most common issues of the type. The Smithsonian collection has two examples, an AU-53 and a cleaned EF. Mint Sate examples were very rare until the discovery of significant numbers on the shipwrecks of the SS *Republic* and the SS *Brother Jonathan.* About 11 or 12 examples from the *Republic* were certified as Mint State, including 4 or 5 as MS-63. An MS-63 sold in 2011 for $57,000. Small numbers of this issue are found with repunching of the 86 in the date.

Hoard Information: The SS *Republic* hoard listed 127 coins of the date. The SS *Brother Jonathan* listed 68 coins as found. The Saddle Ridge hoard contained 7 examples.

1863

Mintage: 142,790

The 1863 double eagle is another issue that is not represented in the vast Smithsonian collection. The mintage for all gold coins was very low in 1863 and as could be expected, the 1863 double eagle is a rarity in all grades. Only a few hundred have been certified. No examples of the date were found on the SS *Brother Jonathan*, and only 35 were located when the SS *Republic* was discovered. Just one coin has been certified as MS-64 and it has remained in its collection for many years. One of the finest seen by the author was a beautiful MS-63 that sold for $85,000 at the 2015 Florida United Numismatists auction.

Hoard Information: The SS *Republic* hoard listed 35 coins of the date. The Saddle Ridge hoard contained 1 example.

1863, Proof

Mintage: 30

The actual rarity of the 1863 double eagle can be difficult to determine. Although 30 coins reportedly were struck, it is nearly certain that fewer were actually sold. The population data is misleading, as the numbers include resubmissions. There are probably about a dozen examples known today, including the pieces in the museum collections of the Smithsonian and the American Numismatic Society. Of these, at least a few are impaired. The Smithsonian collection has two examples, one grading PF-63 and the other slightly finer, grading PF-64. The current auction record for the date is for a coin graded PF-66 that sold in 2014 for $381,375.

1863-S

Mintage: 966,750

Until the discovery of the SS *Republic* and the SS *Brother Jonathan* this date was nearly always seen with varying degrees of circulation. The Smithsonian examples are typical, grading Very Fine and About Uncirculated. The two shipwreck hoards yielded nearly 300 coins, many of which were in Mint State. Two examples of the date have been certified as MS-64, one of which sold for $43,125 in 2012. This issue is extremely popular with collectors of Civil War–era coinage.

Hoard Information: The SS *Republic* hoard listed 180 coins of the date. The SS *Brother Jonathan* listed 116 coins as found. The Saddle Ridge hoard contained 5 examples.

1864

Mintage: 204,235

The 1864 is another date in circulation strike that is missing from the Smithsonian's incomparable collection of Liberty double eagles. As mentioned earlier, early coin collectors were more than satisfied with a Proof example and did not consider them to be two separately collectible issues. As would be expected from the relatively low mintage, this issue is scarce in most grades. The discovery of the SS *Republic* hoard greatly increased the number of Mint State examples available to collectors. Surprisingly, the finest known example, graded PCGS MS-65, was not from the SS *Republic* hoard. The coin last sold at auction in 2014 for $282,000.

Hoard Information: The SS *Republic* hoard listed 42 coins of the date.

1864, Proof

Mintage: 50

Despite the fact that only 12 to 15 examples of the Proof 1864 double eagle are known, it is probably the most readily available year for the type in the Proof format. Two examples are in the museum collection of the Smithsonian, grading PF-63 and PF-64, and another resides at the American Numismatic Society. Most of the mintage was probably melted as unsold, not surprising considering the ravages of the Civil War at the time. The population-report numbers are misleading due to resubmissions. Examples of any Type 1 double eagle must be considered a major rarity. NGC has graded one example of the date as PF-67 Ultra Cameo and this is the finest known of the type. A PF-65 example sold in 2012 for $352,500.

1864-S

Mintage: 793,660

The Smithsonian collection example of this date was acquired before the discovery of high-grade examples on the shipwrecks of the SS *Republic* and the SS *Brother Jonathan*. The coin grades Extremely Fine with traces of an old cleaning. Before the discovery of those hoards, the average coin seen would grade Very Fine or Extremely Fine. More than 250 coins were added to the known population for this issue when the shipwrecks were found. Nearly 100 coins were of Mint State quality. Several examples of the date have been certified as MS-63, and one or two in grades above that. The single MS-65 example sold for $115,000 in 2012.

Hoard Information: The SS *Republic* hoard listed 168 coins of the date. The SS *Brother Jonathan* listed 108 coins as found. The Saddle Ridge hoard contained 5 examples.

1865

Mintage: 351,175

This is another issue that is missing from the Smithsonian double eagle collection. Early collectors were quite satisfied with a Proof example for the date.

Before the discovery of the SS *Republic* most collectors were restricted to the average circulated examples usually seen. The best Harry W. Bass Jr. could find was graded About Uncirculated. Everything changed for this date when the SS *Republic* hoard came to light. The 1865 was the most plentiful date found on the shipwreck. More than 300 coins were discovered, one of which has been graded MS-66. An MS-65 specimen sold at auction for $88,125 in 2013.

Hoard Information: The SS *Republic* hoard contained 320 examples of this date. The SS *Brother Jonathan* listed 1 coin found.

1865, Proof

Mintage: 25

With the lowest mintage figure for any Type 1 double eagle after 1858, it is not surprising that the 1865 date is much rarer than the 1862, 1863, or 1864 issues. Fewer than 10 examples are known, including the pieces in the collections of the Smithsonian and American Numismatic Society. The Smithsonian collection has two examples of this great rarity, one grading PF-63 and the other PF-64. The population numbers for this date are most certainly skewed by resubmissions. Many major collections offered in the last few decades did not have an example of the date. This includes the spectacular Harry W. Bass Jr. Collection. The auction record for the date is a PF-66 that sold for 440,625 in 2014.

Hoard Information: The SS *Republic* hoard contained 253 examples of this date.

1865-S

Mintage: 1,042,500

Prior to the discovery of the shipwrecks of the SS *Brother Jonathan* and SS *Republic*, this date was very scarce in the higher states of preservation. The Smithsonian has three examples, none of which grade better than AU-50. More than 750 coins of the date surfaced when the shipwrecks were uncovered. Nearly 100 examples of the date have been certified as MS-65 or better. Today the 1865-S double eagle is available in grades that would have seemed impossible a few decades ago. The finest certified have been MS-66, one of which sold for $46,000 in 2012.

Hoard Information: The SS *Republic* hoard contained 253 examples of this date. The SS *Brother Jonathan* listed 586 coins found. The Saddle Ridge hoard contained 11 examples.

1866-S, Without Motto

Mintage: 120,000

The 1866-S double eagle is the last of the Without Motto type (without the motto IN GOD WE TRUST on the reverse). In 1866 the San Francisco Mint issued both the Without and the With Motto varieties. The Without Motto is by far the rarer of the two. This issue is also a condition rarity, with the average coin seen being Very Fine or Extremely Fine. There are about 200 to 300 examples known in all grades. The Smithsonian collection contains a surprisingly nice example that grades AU-58. Ten or fifteen years ago the date was considered unknown in Mint State. In recent years a few coins have been graded at that level, and one example was even discovered in the Saddle Ridge hoard. That coin is graded MS-62 and is considered the finest known. It has been offered for sale at $1,200,000, but to date has not been sold.

Hoard Information: The Saddle Ridge Hoard contained one example of the date.

National Numismatic Collection Inventory of Type 1 Double Eagles (1849–1866)

Circulation-Strike Format

Date/Variety	Grade
1850	AU-58
1850	AU-58
1850	AU, Cleaned
1850-O	EF-40
1850-O	VF-35
1851	AU-58
1851	AU-50
1851-O	AU-50
1851-O	EF-45
1852	AU-58
1852	AU-50
1852-O	AU-50
1853	MS-61
1853	AU, Cleaned
1853, 3 Over 2	(none in collection)
1853-O	AU-55
1853-O	EF-40
1854, Small Date	AU-55
1854, Large Date	(none in collection)
1854-O	AU-50
1854-S	AU-50
1854-S	EF-40
1855	MS-61
1855	EF-45
1855-O	AU-50
1855-O	AU-50
1855-S	MS-60
1855-S	AU-55
1855-S	EF, Cleaned
1856	AU-50, Cleaned
1856-O	AU-53
1856-O	EF, Cleaned
1856-S	MS-61
1856-S	AU-58
1856-S	AU-50
1856-S	EF-45
1857	EF-45
1857-O	AU-55, Prooflike
1857-O	AU-55
1857-S	AU-55
1857-S	AU-50
1857-S	VF-35
1857-S	EF-45
1858	(none in collection)
1858-O	AU-53
1858-O	AU-50
1858-S	AU-55
1858-S	AU-50
1858-S	VF-35
1859	(none in collection)

Circulation-Strike Format

Date/Variety	Grade
1859-O	AU-53
1859-O	EF-45
1859-S	AU-58
1859-S	AU-50
1860	EF-40
1860	EF, Cleaned
1860-O	AU-50, Prooflike
1860-S	AU-50
1860-S	EF-40
1861	AU-50
1861, Paquet Reverse	(none in collection)
1861-O	AU-53
1861-O	EF-45
1861-S	AU-55
1861-S	EF-45
1861-S, Paquet Reverse	(none in collection)
1862	(none in collection)
1862-S	AU-53
1862-S	EF, Cleaned
1863	(none in collection)
1863-S	AU-50
1863-S	VF-35
1864	(none in collection)
1864-S	EF, Cleaned
1865	(none in collection)
1865-S	AU-50
1865-S	EF-40
1865-S	VF-20
1866-S, Without Motto	AU-58

Proof Format

Date/Variety	Grade
1849	PF-63
1854-S	PF-65
1858	PF-64 Deep Cameo
1858	PF-62 Deep Cameo
1859	PF-64 Deep Cameo
1859	PF-64 Deep Cameo
1860	PF-63 Deep Cameo
1860, Paquet Reverse	PF-65
1861	PF-63 Deep Cameo
1862	PF-64 Deep Cameo
1862	PF-63 Deep Cameo
1863	PF-64 Deep Cameo
1863	PF-63 Cameo
1864	PF-64 Deep Cameo
1864	PF-63 Deep Cameo
1865	PF-64 Deep Cameo
1865	PF-63 Deep Cameo

This book is dedicated to the memory of Dr. Richard G. Doty (1942–2013), senior curator of the National Numismatic Collection at the Smithsonian Institution, National Museum of American History.

As my wife and I were walking down the street in downtown Lexington in November 2008, a tapping noise from a restaurant window caught my attention. It was Jeff Garrett with his wife, having dinner. He motioned us in and the embryo of this book was created. I had never pictured myself writing about this period of either American or numismatic history. However, the more I researched the viability of the project, the more I was swept up by its potential. Yet the twists and turns that the story eventually took were not even in our wildest dreams that night.

Historical research has changed a lot in the decade that I have been authoring numismatic literature. What once took days of following leads—many false—to run down a single fact can now be found literally at my fingertips courtesy of Google or print-on-demand books. Unexpected information that I would not have known existed is now expected in any Google search. Acknowledgements, which once were extensive, are now just a handful.

Still, some research must be done on the ground. Many U.S. government archives are, unfortunately, not digitized. It takes a knowledgeable researcher to unlock some of those files. Pam Scott, a dear friend in Washington, did that for me in so many instances. I know the Mint records well, but this book extends far beyond the confines of those documents. It was Pam who opened these doors for me. Without her broad knowledge, this book would be incomplete.

Jeff Garrett has been my cheerleader for some time. I can't say enough about our friendship and his numismatic contributions to this book. I regret Dick Doty's passing. His guidance over the years was invaluable. His work on early American coppers gave me insight into the origin of some of the early dissatisfaction with the U.S. Mint that I would certainly have missed. His research into the issues facing the second mint's construction sent me back to the Mint correspondence to dig deeper. I also want to thank John Dannreuther for patiently walking me through his most recent work on the Gobrecht dollar. While much is known about this outstanding coin design, much is not known about the circumstances surrounding its striking. John's guidance in trying to nail down this moving target has been invaluable. Likewise Dr. Don Kagin stepped in to help with his most up-to-date information on the private mints of California.

In no particular order I would also like to acknowledge the help of others who have contributed to the completion of this book. Tom Mulvaney not only provided the coin illustrations in the book from the National Numismatic Collection, but he even worked with me for a couple days in the mid-Atlantic regional archives. With Dick Doty's passing, Karen M. Lee picked up the slack at the Smithsonian. Mark Van Winkle of Heritage Auctions was most helpful in getting me started with the Gobrecht dollars. From the Philadelphia area was Matthew Dibiase of NARA's mid-Atlantic region; David Haugaard and Dana Lamparello with the Historical Society of Pennsylvania; Valerie-Anne Lutz van Ammers with the American Philosophical Society; and Cornelia King, Sarah Weatherwax, Nicole Joniec, and Linda Wisniewski of the Library Company of Philadelphia. Elizabeth Hahn was my source at the American Numismatic Society.

Dr. Thomas Coens helped lift the veil on William McKendree Gwin from his work editing the Andrew Jackson papers. Additional help in this area came from Lee Anne Titangos of the Bancroft Library. There was Jim Witham at the Lexington Public Library when the interlibrary loan program could do what Google could not. For information on Henry Clay, I want to thank Eric Brooks at the Henry Clay Estate in Lexington. Also, Tammy Kiter at the New-York Historical Society provided the Ullman papers.

I would be remiss if I did not recognize the work of Sean Willentz, Daniel Walker Howe, and Robert E. Wright, authors of *The Rise of American Democracy: Jefferson to Lincoln*, *What Hath God Wrought: The Transformation of America, 1815–1848*, and *The First Wall Street: Chestnut Street, Philadelphia, and the Birth of American Finance*, respectively. These three books provided the wallpaper against which I set my story.

I also want to thank my readers, Q. David Bowers, Roger Burdette, Nancy Oliver, and Richard Kelley, for sharing their time and knowledge in reviewing my manuscript.

Without these people I could not have written this book.

Finally, because I serve as a special government employee on the Citizens Coinage Advisory Committee at the United States Mint, it is necessary to state that I neither sought nor received any assistance with this book from anyone associated with the Mint. Anything to the contrary would be a conflict of interest. I have nothing but the highest regard for that fine organization.

NOTES

Prologue: "California"

1. Donald H. Kagin, *Private Gold Coins and Patterns of the United States* (New York: Arco, 1981), 180.
2. This oyster can was described in newspaper reports at the time as a tea caddy.
3. General W.T. Sherman, *Personal Memoirs of Gen'l W.T. Sherman*, 37–88.
4. "California Gold, Important Official Report," *New York Tribune*, December 9, 1848: 2. In some cases facts in the official report drafted by Sherman differ somewhat from his memoirs published in 1891. In all such cases I relied upon the official report.

Chapter 1: Stepchild

1. American State Papers, 3rd Congress, 2nd Session, Finance: Volume 1, No. 71, Mint: 317.
2. Don Taxay, *The U.S. Mint and Coinage* (New York: Arco, 1966), 79–82.
3. Annals of Congress, House of Representatives, 3rd Congress, December 9, 1794.
4. The law specified a standard of 10 ounces 14 pennyweights and 19.104 parts pure silver in 1 troy pound of standard silver. Boudinot recommended changing it to 10 ounces 16 pennyweight in 1 troy pound of standard silver. There are 20 pennyweights in 1 troy ounce and 12 troy ounces in 1 troy pound. Boudinot's recommendation would essentially allow 1 part alloy for each 9 parts pure silver, a much easier fraction with which to work.
5. Annals of Congress, 3rd Congress, February 9, 1795: 1402–1410,
6. Statutes at Large, 3rd Congress, 2nd Session, March 3, 1795: 439–440,
7. Benjamin Rush, *The Autobiography of Benjamin Rush, Commonplace Book*, 1792–1813: 233–234.
8. Jacob E. Cooke, *Tench Coxe and the Early Republic* (Chapel Hill: University of North Carolina Press, 1978), 217–272.
9. American State Papers, 4th Congress, 1st Session, December 14, 1795.
10. Robert E. Wright and David J. Cowen, *Financial Founding Fathers, The Men Who Made America Rich* (Chicago and London: University of Chicago Press, 2006): 14. King's College would later change its name to Columbia College.
11. *Journal of the Executive Proceedings of the Senate* 1 (December 10, 1795): 194.
12. Timothy Pickering to George Washington, September 18, 1795. George Washington Papers, Library of Congress, Series 4, General Correspondence, 1697–1799.
13. American State Papers, House of Representatives, 5th Congress, 2nd Session, Finance: Volume 1, May 19, 1798.
14. American State Papers, Senate, 4th Congress, 2nd Session, Finance: Volume 1, December 19, 1796.
15. *Journal of the Executive Proceedings of the Senate* 1 (January 2, 1797): 219,
16. American State Papers, House of Representatives, 5th Congress, 2nd Session, Finance: Volume 1, December 11, 1797.
17. Annals of Congress, House of Representatives, 5th Congress, 2nd Session, December 13–14, 1797: 717–735.
18. Annals of Congress, House of Representatives, 5th Congress, 2nd Session, December 20, 1797: 746–757.
19. Annals of Congress, House of Representatives, 5th Congress, 2nd Session, December 13–14, 1797: 717–735.
20. Annals of Congress, House of Representatives, 5th Congress, 2nd Session, December 20, 1797: 746–757.
21. Annals of Congress, House of Representatives, 5th Congress, 2nd Session, December 13–14, 1797: 717–735.
22. Annals of Congress, House of Representatives, 5th Congress, 2nd Session, December 20, 1797: 746–757.
23. American State Papers, House of Representatives, 5th Congress, 2nd Session, Finance: Volume 1, January 11, 1798.
24. Ibid.
25. Statutes at Large, 7th Congress, 1st Session: 173.
26. Elias Boudinot to William Russell, August 16, 1799. RG 104, Records of the Bureau of the Mint, U.S. Mint at Philadelphia 1791–1936, Correspondence 1792–1904, General Correspondence 1792–1899, NC 152, Entry 1, NM 1992, Box 3.
27. Elias Boudinot to Benjamin Rush, October 12, 1799. RG 104 Records of the Bureau of the Mint, U.S. Mint at Philadelphia 1791–1936, Correspondence 1792–1904, General Correspondence 1792–1899, NC 152, Entry 1, NM 1992, Box 3.
28. Richard G. Doty, "Early United States Copper Coinage: The English Connection," *British Numismatic Journal, Proceedings of the British Numismatic Society for the Year 1987* 57 (1988): 57–61.

Chapter 2: Bare-Knuckles Brawling

1. There is uncertainty as to the location of "Mint Square" in the plan. The article "Mint Reservation," printed on September 15, 1849, in the

Baltimore Sun (page 4), stated that it was the square south of Virginian Avenue SE at about 3rd or 4th Street. A paper by Mary F. Bugbee, "The Early Planning of Sites for Federal and Local Use in Washington D.C.," presented before the Columbia Historical Society on February 13, 1951 (Records of the CHS, volumes 51–52, pages 19–31), places the square between Constitution Avenue and C Street, and 3rd Street and John Marshall Place (formerly 4 1/2 Street).

2. Annals of Congress, 6th Congress, January 8, 1800: 1255–1256.

3. American State Papers, Senate, 6th Congress, 1st Session, Finance: Volume 1, March 14, 1800: 632.

4. Statutes at Large, 6th Congress, 1st Session, May 14, 1800: 86.

5. Statutes at Large, 6th Congress, 2nd Session, March 3, 1801: 111.

6. American State Papers, House of Representatives, 7th Congress, 1st Session: 744–745.

7. *Journal of the House of Representatives* 4 (April 2, 1802): 174.

8. Elias Boudinot to Thomas Jefferson, April 17 1802. Thomas Jefferson Papers, Library of Congress, Series 1, General Correspondence, 1651–1827, Library of Congress.

9. *Journal of the House of Representatives* 4 (April 20, 1802): 211.

10. Annals of Congress, House of Representatives, 7th Congress, 1st Session, April 23, 1802: 1238–1243.

11. *Journal of the House of Representatives*, 7th Congress, April 26, 1802.

12. Annals of Congress, House of Representatives, 7th Congress, 2nd Session, December 23, 1802.

13. *Journal of the House of Representatives* 4 (January 25, 1803): 297.

14. Annals of Congress, House of Representatives, 7th Congress, 2nd Session, January 28, 1803: 445–446.

15. Bills and Resolutions, House of Representatives, 7th Congress, 2nd Session, Bill 24, February 1, 1803.

16. Annals of Congress, House of Representatives, 7th Congress, 2nd Session, March 3, 1803: 611.

17. *The Letters of Benjamin Rush*, edited by L.H. Butterfield (Princeton: Princeton University Press, 1951), 1209

18. *Journal of the Executive Proceedings of the Senate* 1 (November 24–27, 1797).

19. Benjamin Rush to John Adams, April 5, 1808. *The Letters of Benjamin Rush*.

20. Benjamin Rush to Ashton Alexander, February 20, 1798. *The Letters of Benjamin Rush*.

21. Elias Boudinot to Albert Gallatin, August 18, 1801. Thomas Jefferson Papers, Library of Congress, Series 1, General Correspondence, 1651–1827, Library of Congress.

22. Taxay, *The U.S. Mint and Coinage*, 115–118.

23. Benjamin Rush to Thomas Jefferson, April 29, 1805. *The Letters of Benjamin Rush*.

Chapter 3: The Coming of the Pattersons

1. Stephen Ambrose, *Undaunted Courage* (New York: Simon & Schuster: 1996), 81.

2. "Two Centuries on, a Cryptologist Cracks the Presidential Code," *Wall Street Journal* 253, no. 153 (July 2, 2009): 1.

3. Image 300, Thomas Jefferson to Robert Patterson, April 27, 1805. Thomas Jefferson Papers, Library of Congress, Series 1, General Correspondence, 1651–1827.

4. Image 1005, Robert Patterson to Thomas Jefferson, October 14, 1806. Thomas Jefferson Papers, Library of Congress, Series 1, General Correspondence, 1651–1827.

5. Image 1031, Thomas Jefferson to Robert Patterson, October 17, 1806. Thomas Jefferson Papers, Library of Congress, Series 1, General Correspondence, 1651–1827. For years a story has persisted that these dollar coins were hemorrhaging to the West Indies where they could be exchanged profitably at par for Spanish specie. Merchants would then bring these Spanish coins back to the United States, where they commanded a premium in the export market. This story does not ring true. International monetary markets would not have allowed such an anomaly. In addition, after dollar production was discontinued, half dollars would have worked just as well; yet this pattern never developed.

6. Oscar G. Schilke and Raphael E. Solomon, *America's Foreign Coins: An Illustrated Catalogue with Valuations of Foreign Coins With Legal Tender Status in the United States 1793–1857* (New York: The Coin and Currency Institute, 1964), 34.

7. Wright and Cowen, *Financial Founding Fathers*, 154.

8. Image 1295, Robert Patterson to Thomas Jefferson, December 14, 1805.Thomas Jefferson Papers, Library of Congress, Series 1, General Correspondence, 1651–1827.

9. Taxay, *The U.S. Mint and Coinage*, 49.

10. Image 195, Robert Patterson to Thomas Jefferson, April 3, 1807. Thomas Jefferson Papers, Library of Congress, Series 1, General Correspondence, 1651–1827.

11. Image 115, Robert Patterson to Thomas Jefferson, March 25, 1807. Thomas Jefferson Papers, Library of Congress, Series 1, General Correspondence, 1651–1827.

12. Patterson DuBois, "Our Mint Engravers," *American Journal of Numismatics* 18, no. 1 (July 1883): 12–16.

13. *Journal of the House of Representatives* 18 (December 9, 1824): 30.

14. Image 697. Thomas Jefferson to Henry Voigt, January 16, 1802. Thomas Jefferson Papers, Library of Congress, Series 1, General Correspondence, 1651–1827.

15. Image 1097, Elias Boudinot to Thomas Jefferson, June 16, 1801. Thomas Jefferson Papers, Library of Congress, Series 1, General Correspondence, 1651–1827.

16. Image 409–411, Henry Voigt to Thomas Jefferson, December 29, 1801. Thomas Jefferson Papers, Library of Congress, Series 1, General Correspondence, 1651–1827.

17. Image 697, Thomas Jefferson to Henry Voigt, January 16, 1802.

18. Image 409–411, Henry Voigt to Thomas Jefferson, December 29, 1801.

19. Image 697, Thomas Jefferson to Henry Voigt, January 16, 1802.

20. Image 1035–1037, John Lithgow to Thomas Jefferson, December 24, 1804. Thomas Jefferson Papers, Library of Congress, Series 1, General Correspondence, 1651–1827.

21. Image 298–299, Thomas Jefferson to John Reich, June 27, 1806. Thomas Jefferson Papers, Library of Congress, Series 1, General Correspondence, 1651–1827.

22. Image 115, Robert Patterson to Thomas Jefferson, March 25, 1807.

23. Samuel Moore to Levi Woodbury, October 6, 1834. RG 104, Records of the Bureau of the Mint, U.S. Mint at Philadelphia 1791–1936, Correspondence 1792–1904, General Correspondence 1792–1899, NC 152, Entry 1, NM 1992, Box 15.

24. Eric Brothers, "John Reich: The Mint's Overworked and Underappreciated Engraver," *Numismatist*, March 2011: 39–43.

25. Statutes at Large, 10th Congress, 1st Session, April 1, 1808: 481.

26. Annals of Congress, House of Representatives, 11th Congress, 3rd Session, December 13–14, 1810: 399–402.

27. Schilke and Solomon, *America's Foreign Coins*, 35.

28. Annals of Congress, House of Representatives, 11th Congress, 3rd Session, December 27, 1810: 468–473.

29. Robert V. Remini, *Henry Clay: Statesman for the Union* (New York and London: W.W. Norton, 1991), 69–71.

30. Wright and Cowen, *Financial Founding Fathers*, 173–178.

31. Albert Gallatin to Robert Patterson, December 6, 1811. RG 104 Records of the Bureau of the Mint, U.S. Mint at Philadelphia 1791–1936, Correspondence 1792–1904, General Correspondence 1792–1899, NC 152, Entry 1, NM 1992, Box 5.

32. Annals of Congress, House of Representatives, 12th Congress, 2nd Session, November 16, 1812: 150,

33. Robert Patterson to James Madison, April 20, 1813. James Madison Papers, Library of Congress.

34. *Journal of the Executive Proceedings of the Senate* 2 (May 31, 1813): 347.

35. Ibid., February 12, 1814, 473.

36. Nicholas B. Wainwright, *History of the Philadelphia National Bank: A Century and a Half of Philadelphia Banking, 1803–1953* (Philadelphia: William F. Fell, 1953), 41.

37. American State Papers, 14th Congress, 1st Session, Finance: Volume 3, January 8, 1816: 56.

Chapter 4: Like a Slumbering Phoenix

1. Image 922, Robert Patterson to James Madison, January 11, 1816. James Madison Papers, Library of Congress.

2. American State Papers, 14th Congress, 2nd Session, Finance: Volume 3, January 6, 1817: 148.

3. Bills and Resolutions, House of Representatives, 15th Congress, 1st Session, Bill 4, December 9, 1817.

4. Statutes at Large, 15th Congress, 1st Session: 403.

5. American State Papers, House of Representatives, 14th Congress, 1st Session, Finance: Volume 3, March 20, 1816: 108.

6. *Journal of the House of Representatives* 10 (April 30, 1816): 765.

7. Wright and Cowen, *Financial Founding Fathers*, 173–178.

8. American State Papers, 14th Congress, 2nd Session, Finance: Volume 3, January 6, 1817: 148.

9. *Early Engineering Reminiscences (1815–40) of George Escol Sellers* edited by Eugene S. Ferguson (Washington D.C.: Smithsonian Institution, 1965): 72.

10. William H. Crawford to John W. Eppes, December 29, 1818. American State Papers, Senate, 15th Congress, 2nd Session, Finance: Volume 3, January 25, 1819: 393–397.

11. William H. Crawford to John W. Eppes, January 6, 1819. Robert Patterson to William H. Crawford, December 28, 1818. American State Papers, Senate, 15th Congress, 2nd Session, Finance: Volume 3, January 25, 1819: 393–397.

12. Hamilton used 1/12 dilution for the alloy to arrive at 405 grains of standard silver in a dollar. Working through the same math, an eagle coin would contain 270 grains of standard gold.

13. American State Papers, House of Representatives, 15th Congress, 2nd Session, Finance: Volume 3, January 26, 1819: 398–401.

14. Bills and Resolutions, House of Representatives, 15th Congress, 2nd Session, Bill 292, January 26, 1819.

15. Statues at Large, 15th Congress, 2nd Session, March 3, 1819: 525.

16. Sean Willentz, *The Rise of American Democracy Jefferson to Lincoln* (New York and London: W.W. Norton, 2005), 204–205.

17. Wright and Cohen, *Financial Founding Fathers*, 173–178.

18. American State Papers, Senate, 16th Congress, 1st Session, March 10, 1820: 517–518.

19. American State Papers, Senate, 16th Congress, 2nd Session, January 16, 1821: 674–675.

20. American State Papers, Senate, 16th Congress, 1st Session, April 17, 1820: 30.

21. *Journal of the Senate* 10 (March 3, 1821): 272.

22. American State Papers, House of Representatives, 16th Congress, 2nd Session, Finance: Volume 3, February 2, 1821.

23. Bills and Resolutions, House of Representatives, 16th Congress, 2nd Session, Bill 243, February 2, 1821.

24. Wright and Cohen, *Financial Founding Fathers*, 173–178.

25. American State Papers, House of Representatives, 17th Congress, 2nd Session, Finance: Volume 4, February 4–5, 1823: 225–227.

26. Annals of Congress, House of Representatives, 17th Congress, 2nd Session, January 22, 1823: 663–664.

27. Annals of Congress, House of Representatives, 17th Congress, 2nd Session, February 4, 1823: 804–806.

28. Statutes at Large, 17th Congress, 2nd Session, March 3, 1823: 774.

29. Ibid., 778.

30. American State Papers, House of Representatives, 17th Congress, 2nd Session, Finance: Volume 4, February 6, 1823. William H. Crawford to W.B. Rochester, February 3, 1823.

31. American State Papers, Senate 17th Congress, 1st Session, Finance: Volume 3, January 7, 1822: 663–664.

32. William H. Crawford to W.B. Rochester, February 3, 1823. American State Papers, House of Representatives, 17th Congress, 2nd Session, Finance: Volume 4, February 6, 1823.

33. My grandfather started me collecting coins in the mid-1950s. Before long, out came the proverbial cigar box where denizens of old and curiosities of days past had been tossed. I was left to wonder how the French crown with the well-worn profile of Napoleon and the two five-franc pieces from the 1820s and 1830s found their way into that box. In addition, there was fractional Spanish silver, also well worn, from the 18th and 19th centuries. Little did I know that these were the coins used in the United States during the 18th and 19th century.

34. R.W. Julian, *Medals of the United States Mint: The First Century 1792–1892*, edited by N. Neil Harris (El Cajon, CA: Token and Medal Society, 1977), 147–148.

35. Julian, *Medals of the United States Mint*, 157.

36. Christian Gobrecht Papers, Historical Society of Pennsylvania.

37. R.M. Patterson to Levi Woodbury, December 31, 1840. RG 104, Records of the Bureau of the Mint, U.S. Mint at Philadelphia 1791–1936, Correspondence 1792–1904, General Correspondence 1792–1899, NC 152, Entry 1, NM 1992, Box 21.

38. Julian, *Medals of the United States Mint*, 112–113.

39. DuBois, *American Journal of Numismatics*, 12–16.

40. *Journal of the House of Representatives* 18 (December 9, 1824): 30.

41. Ibid., January 13, 1825, 128.

42. *Proceedings of the American Philosophical Society*, a list of its members, 1860.

43. *Journal of the House of Representatives* 13 (January 13, 1820): 31.

44. Annals of Congress, House of Representatives, 16th Congress, 1st Session, March 2, 1820: 1585–1588.

45. *Journal of the House of Representatives* 14 (February 2, 1821): 192–197.

46. Annals of Congress, House of Representatives, 16th Congress, 2nd Session, February 26, 1821: 1237–1240.

47. Patterson Family Papers 1809–1876, American Philosophical Society, P274.2, Samuel Moore Biography.

48. Image 819, Samuel Moore to Thomas Jefferson, September 21, 1824. Thomas Jefferson Papers, Library of Congress, Series 1, General Correspondence, 1651–1827.

Chapter 5: Mr. Biddle's Mint

1. Congressional Serial Set, 20th Congress, 2nd Session, House Document 51, Mint of the United States to Accompany the Bill H.R. 356, December 23, 1828.

2. Samuel Moore to John Quincy Adams, August 3, 1825. RG 104, Records of the Bureau of the Mint, U.S. Mint at Philadelphia 1791–1936, Correspondence 1792–1904, General Correspondence 1792–1899, NC 152, Entry 1, NM 1992, Box 6.

3. Image 1236, Samuel Moore to Thomas Jefferson, February 3, 1825. Thomas Jefferson Papers, Library of Congress, Series 1, General Correspondence, 1651–1827.

4. Thomas Jefferson to Samuel Moore, March 3, 1825, Image 1292. Thomas Jefferson Papers, Library of Congress, Series 1, General Correspondence, 1651–1827.

5. Samuel Moore to John Quincy Adams, August 3, 1825. RG 104, Records of the Bureau of the Mint, U.S. Mint at Philadelphia 1791–1936, Correspondence 1792–1904, General Correspondence 1792–1899, NC 152, Entry 1, NM 1992, Box 6.

6. Samuel Moore to Richard Rush, September 16, 1825. RG 104, Records of the Bureau of the Mint, U.S. Mint at Philadelphia 1791–1936, Correspondence 1792–1904, General Correspondence 1792–1899, NC 152, Entry 1, NM 1992, Box 6.

7. Richard Rush to Samuel Moore, January 12, 1826. RG 104, Records of the Bureau of the Mint, U.S. Mint at Philadelphia 1791–1936, Correspondence 1792–1904, General Correspondence 1792–1899, NC 152, Entry 1, NM 1992, Box 7.

8. Samuel Moore to Richard Rush, January 14, 1826. RG 104, Records of the Bureau of the Mint, U.S. Mint at Philadelphia 1791–1936, Correspondence 1792–1904, General Correspondence 1792–1899, NC 152, Entry 1, NM 1992, Box 7.

9. American State Papers, House of Representatives, 19th Congress, 2nd Session, Finance: Volume 5, February 24, 1827: 619.

10. *Journal of the House of Representatives* 21 (May 21, 1828): 803.

11. John Sergeant to Nicholas Biddle, January 5, 1828. Nicholas Biddle Papers, Library of Congress, Manuscript Division, General Correspondence, Reel 7.

12. Samuel Moore to John Sergeant, January 10, 1828. RG 104, Records of the Bureau of the Mint, U.S. Mint at Philadelphia 1791–1936, Correspondence 1792–1904, General Correspondence 1792–1899, NC 152, Entry 1, NM 1992, Box 7.

13. John Sergeant to Samuel Moore, January 21, 1828. RG 104, Records of the Bureau of the Mint, U.S. Mint at Philadelphia 1791–1936, Correspondence 1792–1904, General Correspondence 1792–1899, NC 152, Entry 1, NM 1992, Box 7.

14. Bills and Resolutions, H.R. 106, House of Representatives, 20th Congress, 1st Session, January 23, 1828. In addition, the bill provided that the depositor must pay the cost of assaying his deposit and, should his deposit contain gold, the cost of separation. If the gold could not be separated advantageously, the Mint would coin the bullion as ordinary silver with the depositor's permission.

15. Register of Debates, 2579–2580, May 6, 1828.

16. *Journal of the Senate* 17 (May 16, 1828): 422.

17. Nicholas Biddle to Churchill C. Cambreleng, December 5, 1828. Nicholas Biddle Papers, Library of Congress, Manuscript Division, Reel 42, Letterbooks, February 1, 1823–February 2, 1829.

18. *Journal of the House* 22 (December 16, 1828): 63.

19. U.S. Congressional Series Set, 21st Congress, 2nd Session, Senate Document 51, Report Mint of the United States to Accompany Bill H.R. 356, January 5, 1829.

20. John Sergeant to Samuel Moore, January 5, 1829. RG 104, Records of the Bureau of the Mint, U.S. Mint at Philadelphia 1791–1936, Correspondence 1792–1904, General Correspondence 1792–1899, NC 152, Entry 1, NM 1992, Box 8.

21. Samuel Moore to John Sergeant, January 17, 1829. RG 104, Records of the Bureau of the Mint, U.S. Mint at Philadelphia 1791–1936, Correspondence 1792–1904, General Correspondence 1792–1899, NC 152, Entry 1, NM 1992, Box 8.

22. Samuel Moore to S.D. Ingham, January 29, 1829. RG 104, Records of the Bureau of the Mint, U.S. Mint at Philadelphia 1791–1936, Correspondence 1792–1904, General Correspondence 1792–1899, NC 152, Entry 1, NM 1992, Box 8.

23. Samuel Moore to John Sergeant, February 9, 1829. RG 104, Records of the Bureau of the Mint, U.S. Mint at Philadelphia 1791–1936, Correspondence 1792–1904, General Correspondence 1792–1899, NC 152, Entry 1, NM 1992, Box 8.

24. John Sergeant to Samuel Moore, February 19, 1829. RG 104, Records of the Bureau of the Mint, U.S. Mint at Philadelphia 1791–1936, Correspondence 1792–1904, General Correspondence 1792–1899, NC 152, Entry 1, NM 1992, Box 8.

25. Samuel Moore to William Strickland, March 19, 1829. RG 104, Records of the Bureau of the Mint, U.S. Mint at Philadelphia 1791–1936, Correspondence 1792–1904, General Correspondence 1792–1899, NC 152, Entry 1, NM 1992, Box 8.

26. Samuel Moore to Joseph Anderson, April 27, 1829. RG 104, Records of the Bureau of the Mint, U.S. Mint at Philadelphia 1791–1936, Correspondence 1792–1904, General Correspondence 1792–1899, NC 152, Entry 1, NM 1992, Box 8.

27. John Haviland to Samuel Moore, April 1829. RG 104, Records of the Bureau of the Mint, U.S. Mint at Philadelphia 1791–1936, Correspondence 1792–1904, General Correspondence 1792–1899, NC 152, Entry 1, NM 1992, Box 8.

28. Taxay, *The U.S. Mint and Coinage*, 149. The cornerstone was discovered in May 1903 when this building was razed. It weighed 300 pounds and revealed an old-fashioned candy jar with a petrified cork. The jar held three coins, two newspapers, and a scroll giving a skeleton history of the old mint and the establishment of the new one.

29. Samuel Moore to S.D. Ingham, August 8, 1829. RG 104, Records of the Bureau of the Mint, U.S. Mint at Philadelphia 1791–1936, Correspondence 1792–1904, General Correspondence 1792–1899, NC 152, Entry 1, NM 1992, Box 8.

30. Samuel Moore to Major W.G. Buckner, November 10, 1829. RG 104, Records of the Bureau of the Mint, U.S. Mint at Philadelphia 1791–1936, Correspondence 1792–1904, General Correspondence 1792–1899, NC 152, Entry 1, NM 1992, Box 9.

31. R.G. Doty, "Early United States Copper Coinage: The English Connection," *British Numismatic Journal, Proceedings of the British Numismatic Society for the Year 1987* 57 (1988): 68–69.

Chapter 6: A Fly in the Ointment

1. *Journal of the Senate* 18 (December 29, 1828): 54.

2. Congressional Serial Set, 21st Congress, 1st Session, Senate Document 19, Report of the Select Committee to Consider the State of the Current Coins, January 11, 1830.

3. Congressional Serial Set, 21st Congress, 1st Session, House Document 117, Report from the Secretary of the Treasury Respecting the Relative Value of Gold and Silver, May 29, 1830.

4. Register of Debates, Appendix 131–136, in the Senate, December 15, 1830.

5. Bills and Resolutions, S.6, Senate, 21st Congress, 2nd Session, December 15, 1830

6. Samuel Moore to Nathan Sanford, January 4, 1830. RG 104, Records of the Bureau of the Mint, U.S. Mint at Philadelphia 1791–1936, Correspondence 1792–1904, General Correspondence 1792–1899, NC 152, Entry 1, NM 1992, Box 10.

7. Register of Debates, Appendix 142–143, in the House, January 5, 1831.

8. *Journal of the House of Representatives* 24 (January 14, 1831): 185.

9. Register of Debates, Appendix 145, in the House, January 22, 28, and February, 1831.

10. Register of Debates, Appendix 143–148, in the House, January 22, 28 and February 1831.

11. Register of Debates, Appendix 137–142, in the House, February 22, 1831.

12. Register of Debates, Appendix 147–159, in the House, February 22, 1831.

13. As Quoted from R.W. Julian, "Another Look at the 1804 Dollar," *Numismatist* 83 (January 1970): 5–13.

14. Dies used in 1834 to strike the 1804 dollar for a diplomatic mission at the request of the State department had beaded dentils and rims, a characteristic not in use when the dollar was discontinued. John Dannreuther concludes that they were made between 1831 and 1834. In his 1970 article, Bob Julian theorized they were made in 1831 because four obverse dies were prepared. That many were not necessary for the several coins required in 1834.

15. U.S. Congressional Serial Set, 1817–1980, 23rd Congress, 1st Session, House of Representatives, Report 8, December 11, 1833.

16. *Journal of the House* 23 (February 20, 1830): 316. *Journal of the Senate* 19 (May 31, 1830): 359.

Chapter 7: The Twenty-Niners

1. Bruce Roberts, *The Carolina Gold Rush: America's First* (Charlotte, NC: Heritage Printers, 1971), 5–7.

2. Ibid., 15–19.

3. David Williams, *The Georgia Gold Rush: Twenty-Niners, Cherokees and Gold Fever* (Columbia, SC: University of South Carolina Press, 1993), 24–28.

4. Ibid., 13.

5. *Cherokee Editor: The Writings of Elias Boudinot*, edited by Theda Perdue (Athens, GA: The University of Georgia Press, 1996), 3.

6. Williams, *The Georgia Gold Rush*, 18–19.

7. Ibid., 61.

8. Roberts, *The Carolina Gold Rush*, 31–33.

9. Dexter C. Seymour, "Templeton Reid: His Life and Coinage in Georgia," *Numismatist*, July 1978: 1375–1383.

10. Rodney Barfield and Keith Strawn, *The Bechtlers and Their Coinage: North Carolina Mint Masters of Pioneer Gold* (Raleigh, NC: North Carolina Museum of History, 1980), 10. Between 1831 and 1840, Becht-

ler would coin $2,250,000, as well as convert another $1,384,000 into bars and ingots. The Charlotte branch-mint superintendent reported that through December 31, 1839, the U.S. mints had coined $3,000,000 of North Carolina gold. Bechtler had coined or handled $3,625,000, and manufacturers, brokers, and others had transacted another $3,375,000.

11. Barfield and Strawn, *The Bechtlers and Their Coinage*, 1–20.

12. Williams, *The Georgia Gold Rush*, 44. Some attribute to Jackson words to the effect that John Marshall had made a decision, now let him enforce it. While this may or may not be true, Jackson's position was at odds with the one he took over the South Carolina nullification controversy.

13. Ibid., 56–57.

14. Ibid., 83.

15. Ibid., 97.

16. Samuel Moore to John C. Calhoun, December 20, 1833. *Papers of John C. Calhoun, Volume 12*, edited by Clyde N. Wilson, 194.

17. John C. Calhoun to James E. Calhoun, September 23, 1835. *Papers of John C. Calhoun, Volume 12*, edited by Clyde N. Wilson, 555.

18. Williams, *The Georgia Gold Rush*, 77.

19. Samuel Moore to Franklin Peale, May 15, 1834. RG 104, Records of the Bureau of the Mint, U.S. Mint at Philadelphia 1791–1936, Correspondence 1792–1904, General Correspondence 1792–1899, NC 152, Entry 1, NM 1992, Box 14.

Chapter 8: Gridlock

1. *Biographical Directory of the United States Congress 1774–2005* (Washington, D.C.: United States Government Printing Office, 2005), 2147.

2. *Journal of the House of Representatives* 25 (December 15, 1831): 57.

3. Register of Debates, 23rd Congress, 1st Session, March 17, 1832: 256.

4. Ibid., 250–257.

5. Bills and Resolutions, House of Representatives, 22nd Congress, 1st Session, Bill 487.

6. Bills and Resolutions, House of Representatives, 22nd Congress, 1st Session, Bill 488.

7. Register of Debates, 22nd Congress, 1st Session, March 20, 1832: 2207–2228.

8. *Journal of the House of Representatives* 25 (March 21, 1832): 523.

9. Register of Debates, 22nd Congress, 1st Session, March 22, 1832: 2234–2237.

10. Register of Debates, 22nd Congress, 1st Session, March 23, 1832: 2239–2241.

11. Campbell White to Samuel Moore, April 25, 1832. Bills and Resolutions, House of Representatives, 23rd Congress, 1st Session, February 19, 1834.

12. Register of Debates, 22nd Congress, 1st Session, April 28, 1832: 2241.

13. Samuel Moore to Campbell White, May 4, 1832. Register of Debates, 23rd Congress, 1st Session, February 19, 1834: 275–276.

14. Samuel Moore to Campbell White, May 25, 1832. Register of Debates, 23rd Congress, 1st Session, February 19, 1834: 276–282.

15. Bills and Resolutions, House of Representatives, 22nd Congress, 1st Session, Bill 603.

16. Remini, *Henry Clay*, 379–400.

17. Register of Debates, House of Representatives, 22nd Congress, 2nd Session, December 14, 1832: 864.

18. Samuel Moore to Andrew Stevenson, January 11, 1833. Register of Debates, House of Representatives, 22nd Congress, 2nd Session, January 14, 1833: 98–103.

19. *Journal of the House of Representatives* 26 (March 1, 1833): 452.

Chapter 9: Chestnut Street

1. State House Yard was renamed Independence Square in 1824.

2. "Great Meeting in Philadelphia," *Niles Weekly Register*, April 5, 1834: 92.

3. U.S. Congressional Serial Set, 1817–1980, 22nd Congress, 2nd Session, House of Representatives, Report 54, January 21, 1833.

4. Samuel Moore to S.D. Ingham, January 29, 1831. RG 104, Records of the Bureau of the Mint, U.S. Mint at Philadelphia 1791–1936, Correspondence 1792–1904, General Correspondence 1792–1899, NC 152, Entry 1, NM 1992, Box 11.

5. S.D. Ingham to Samuel Moore, February 1, 1831. RG 104, Records of the Bureau of the Mint, U.S. Mint at Philadelphia 1791–1936, Correspondence 1792–1904, General Correspondence 1792–1899, NC 152, Entry 1, NM 1992, Box 11.

6. Bills and Resolutions, H.R. 588, House of Representatives, 22nd Congress, 1st Session, May 26, 1832.

7. Samuel Moore to Louis McLane, January 29, 1833. RG 104, Records of the Bureau of the Mint, U.S. Mint at Philadelphia 1791–1936, Correspondence 1792–1904, General Correspondence 1792–1899, NC 152, Entry 1, NM 1992, Box 13.

8. Samuel Moore to Levi Woodbury, January 15, 1834. Register of Debates, 23rd Congress, 2nd Session, Appendix: 155–160.

9. Samuel Moore to Levi Woodbury, January 16, 1835. RG 104, Records of the Bureau of the Mint, U.S. Mint at Philadelphia 1791–1936, Correspondence 1792–1904, General Correspondence 1792–1899, NC 152, Entry 1, NM 1992, Box 15. There is belief that family ties also played a part. Charles Willson Peale's third wife was Hannah Moore Peale. However, the author could find no record of direct kinship with Samuel Moore. If the two of them were related, it would have been as cousins once or twice removed. Hannah Peale died in 1821 and the author believes that 11 years later this relation would not have played much, if any role, in Samuel Moore's selection of Franklin Peale.

10. Samuel Moore to R.M. Patterson, February 20, 1833. RG 104, Records of the Bureau of the Mint, U.S. Mint at Philadelphia 1791–1936, Correspondence 1792–1904, General Correspondence 1792–1899, NC 152, Entry 1, NM 1992, Box 13.

11. U.S. Congressional Serial Set, 1817–1980, 23rd Congress, 1st Session, House of Representatives, Report 48, January 16, 1834.

12. "The Philadelphia Mint—Refining Gold with Zinc—Its Troubles and Trials," *Scientific American* 7, no. 4 (October 9, 1852): 29. This article, written much later, stated that the silver required was two-thirds the weight of the gold recognizing improvements made to the process with the onslaught of California gold. Taxay stated in his book, *The U.S. Mint and Coinage*, that the silver required in 1833 was much greater. I have used the amount quoted by Taxay.

13. Samuel Moore to unknown (last page of letter missing), May 15, 1834. RG 104, Records of the Bureau of the Mint, U.S. Mint at Philadelphia 1791–1936, Correspondence 1792–1904, General Correspondence 1792–1899, NC 152, Entry 1, NM 1992, Box 14.

14. *U.S. Mint Centennial 1792–1892*, edited by George Evans (Philadelphia: George G. Evans, 1892), 118–121.

Chapter 10: A Corrupt Bargain?

1. U.S. Congressional Serial Set, 1817–1980, 23rd Congress, 1st Session, House of Representatives, Report 8, December 11, 1833.

2. U.S. Congressional Serial Set, 1817–1980, 23rd Congress, 1st Session, House of Representatives, Report 278, February 19, 1834.

3. Bills and Resolutions, House of Representatives, H.R. 255, 23rd Congress, 1st Session, January 29, 1834.

4. Bills and Resolutions, House of Representatives, H.R. 312, 23rd Congress, 1st Session, February 19, 1834.

5. Bills and Resolutions, House of Representatives, H.R. 313, 23rd Congress, 1st Session, February 19, 1834.

6. Robert V. Remini, *Daniel Webster: The Man and his Time* (New York and London: W.W. Norton, 1997), 398–423.

7. "In the Senate on Saturday," *Delaware Gazette and State Journal*, April 4, 1834: 5.

8. "Paper System vs. Gold Currency," *Eastern Argus*, April 9, 1834: 2.

9. *Journal of the Senate* 23 (April 9, 1834), 217.

10. *Journal of the House of Representatives* 27 (May 27, 1834), 662.

11. Samuel Moore to James Harper, May 5, 1834. RG 104, Records of the Bureau of the Mint, U.S. Mint at Philadelphia 1791–1936, Correspondence 1792–1904, General Correspondence 1792–1899, NC 152, Entry 1, NM 1992, Box 14.

12. Register of Debates, House of Representatives, 23rd Congress, 1st Session, June 14, 1834: 4498–4499

13. Register of Debates, House of Representatives, 23rd Congress, 1st Session, June 21, 1834: 4643–4673.

14. *Journal of the House of Representatives* 27 (June 21, 1834): 801–805.

15. Bills and Resolutions, House of Representatives, 23rd Congress, 1st Session, June 21, 1834.

16. Register of Debates, Senate, 23rd Congress, 1st Session, June 28, 1834: 2121–2122.

17. Statutes at Large, 23rd Congress, 1st Session, June 28, 1834: 699–700.

18. *Niles Weekly Register*, August 9, 1834.

19. "The Golden Humbug," *Globe*, August 18, 1834.

20. "Gold," *Farmers Gazette*, August 22, 1834.

21. "The Golden Humbug," *Globe*, August 18, 1834.

22. "The Gold Bill," *New Bedford Mercury*, July 11, 1834: 2.

23. "Questions for the Editor of the Globe," *Alexandria Gazette*, September 13, 1834.

24. Samuel Moore to Levi Woodbury, July 5, 1834. RG 104, Records of the Bureau of the Mint, U.S. Mint at Philadelphia 1791–1936, Correspondence 1792–1904, General Correspondence 1792–1899, NC 152, Entry 1, NM 1992, Box 14.

25. Levi Woodbury to Samuel Moore, July 12, 1834. RG 104, Records of the Bureau of the Mint, U.S. Mint at Philadelphia 1791–1936, Correspondence 1792–1904, General Correspondence 1792–1899, NC 152, Entry 1, NM 1992, Box 14.

26. Samuel Moore to Levi Woodbury, August 1, 1834. RG 104, Records of the Bureau of the Mint, U.S. Mint at Philadelphia 1791–1936, Correspondence 1792–1904, General Correspondence 1792–1899, NC 152, Entry 1, NM 1992, Box 14.

27. "Mint of the United States," *New Bedford Mercury*, August 29, 1834: 2.

28. Samuel Moore to Levi Woodbury, January 15, 1834. Register of Debates, 23rd Congress, 2nd Session, Appendix: 155–160.

29. Levi Woodbury to Samuel Moore, December 7, 1834. RG 104, Records of the Bureau of the Mint, U.S. Mint at Philadelphia 1791–1936, Correspondence 1792–1904, General Correspondence 1792–1899, NC 152, Entry 1, NM 1992, Box 14.

30. "Gold Eagles," *Alexandria Gazette*, October 22, 1834: 2.

Chapter 11: Branch-Mint Follies

1. U.S. Congressional Serial Set, 1817–1980, 23rd Congress, 1st Session, House of Representatives, Report 391, April 4, 1834.

2. Williams, *The Georgia Gold Rush*, 105.

3. *Journal of the House of Representatives* 24 (January 4, 1831): 141, January 4, 1831.

4. Bills and Resolutions, House of Representatives, 21st Congress, 2nd Session, Bill 630, February 15, 1831.

5. *Journal of the House of Representatives* 25 (December 15, 1831): 57.

6. Bills and Resolutions House of Representatives, 22nd Congress, 1st Session, Bill 84, December 22, 1831.

7. Samuel Moore to Henry Conner, January 21, 1834. U.S. Congressional Serial Set, 1817–1980, 23rd Congress, 1st Session, House of Representatives, Report 391, April 4, 1834.

8. Register of Debates, House of Representatives, 22nd Congress, 2nd Session, December 19, 1832: 886–890.

9. Register of Debates, House of Representatives, 22nd Congress, 2nd Session, December 20, 1832: 894–895.

10. Register of Debates, House of Representatives, 22nd Congress, 2nd Session, December 27, 1832: 918–926.

11. *Journal of the House of Representatives* 28 (December 10, 1834): 706.

12. Ibid., December 15, 1834, 90.

13. Ibid., 91.

14. Levi Woodbury to James K. Polk, January 15, 1835. Register of Debates, 23rd Congress, 2nd Session, Appendix: 155–160.

15. Bills and Resolutions, House of Representatives, 23rd Congress, 2nd Session, H.R. 731, February 12, 1835.

16. *Journal of the Senate* 24 (February 3, 1835): 133.

17. Ibid., February 5, 1835, 312.

18. Bills and Resolutions, Senate, 23rd Congress, 2nd Session, S.155, February 20, 1835.

19. Register of Debates, Senate, 23rd Congress, 2nd Session, February 20, 1835: 522.

20. Remini, *Henry Clay*, as quoted, 382–383.

21. Register of Debates, Senate, 23rd Congress, 2nd Session, February 20, 1835: 522.

22. Register of Debates, Senate, 23rd Congress, 2nd Session, February 21, 1835: 576–581.

23. Register of Debates, Senate, 23rd Congress, 2nd Session, February 24, 1835: 595–613.

24. Register of Debates, House of Representatives, 23rd Congress, 2nd Session, March 3, 1835: 1645.

25. Ibid., 1655–1656.

26. Williams, *The Georgia Gold Rush*, 108–112.

27. Samuel Moore to Levi Woodbury, January 16, 1835. RG 104, Records of the Bureau of the Mint, U.S. Mint at Philadelphia 1791–1936, Correspondence 1792–1904, General Correspondence 1792–1899, NC 152, Entry 1, NM 1992, Box 16.

28. Patterson to Samuel Moore, May 29, 1835. Patterson Family Papers 1809–1876, American Philosophical Society, P274.2, R.M.

Chapter 12: Changing of the Guard

1. "The Late Dr. Robert M. Patterson," *Pennsylvanian*, September 22, 1854: 1.

2. Joseph C. Cabell to organizing committee, September 24, 1835. Patterson Family Papers 1809–1876, American Philosophical Society, P274.2.

3. Napoleon refused to grant exequatur to Patterson. Exequatur is a patent that a head of state issues to a foreign consul which guarantees the consul's rights and privileges of office and ensures recognition in the state in which the consul is appointed to exercise such powers.

4. John K. Kane, *Autobiography of the Honorable John K. Kane 1795–1858* (Philadelphia: privately printed, 1949), 63–65.

5. Image 102, Thomas Jefferson to James Monroe, July 22, 1824. Thomas Jefferson Papers, Library of Congress, Series 1, General Correspondence, 1651–1827.

6. Image 819, Samuel Moore to Thomas Jefferson, September 21, 1824. Thomas Jefferson Papers, Library of Congress, Series 1, General Correspondence, 1651–1827.

7. Dr. Robert Maskell Patterson, *Alumni Bulletin* 3, no. 3 (November 1896): 61–65. Published quarterly by the faculty of the University of Virginia.

8. Charles Coleman Sellers, *Mr. Peale's Museum: Charles Willson Peale and the First Popular Museum of Natural Science* (New York: W.W. Norton, 1980): 245–265. This book gives the date of Patterson's appointment as 1827. However, a letter from Rubens Peale to Patterson dated March 5, 1821, in the Patterson Family Papers of the APS P274.2 notes the earlier date of Patterson's appointment.

9. Robert M. Patterson to David Baillie Warden, April 13, 1833. Peale Family Papers, Series IX-A, Correspondence of Benjamin Franklin Peale, American Philosophical Society Library, courtesy of the University of Oregon.

10. Levi Woodbury to R.M. Patterson, May 18, 1835. Patterson Family Papers 1809–1876, American Philosophical Society, P274.2.

11. R.M. Patterson to Levi Woodbury, May 21, 1835. Patterson Family Papers 1809–1876, American Philosophical Society, P274.2.

12. Samuel Moore to Levi Woodbury, January 16, 1835. RG 104, Records of the Bureau of the Mint, U.S. Mint at Philadelphia 1791–1936, Correspondence 1792–1904, General Correspondence 1792–1899, NC 152, Entry 1, NM 1992, Box 16.

13. Kane, *Autobiography*, 27–32.

14. Samuel Moore to R. M. Patterson, June 15, 1835. RG 104, Records of the Bureau of the Mint, U.S. Mint at Philadelphia 1791–1936, Correspondence 1792–1904, General Correspondence 1792–1899, NC 152, Entry 1, NM 1992, Box 16.

Chapter 13: Franklin Peale!

1. Sellers, *Mr. Peale's Museum*, 12.
2. Ibid., 56.
3. Ibid., 77–80.
4. Ibid., 88.
5. Ibid., 22.
6. Introductory Biography, Peale Family Papers, Series IX-A, Correspondence of Benjamin Franklin Peale, American Philosophical Library, courtesy of the University of Oregon.
7. Sellers, *Early Engineering Reminiscences*, 69–78.
8. A statement of Charles Willson Peale, December 30, 1824, Peale Family Papers, Series IX-A, Correspondence of Benjamin Franklin Peale, American Philosophical Library, courtesy of the University of Oregon.
9. Sellers, *Early Engineering Reminiscences*, 69–78.
10. A portrait of Franklin Peale by Thomas Sully hung in the offices of the Baldwin Locomotive Works until 1925, when it was given to the Pennsylvania Academy of Fine Arts.
11. Franklin Peale to Anna Peale, May 8, 1833. Peale Family Papers, Series IX-A, Correspondence of Benjamin Franklin Peale, American Philosophical Library, courtesy of the University of Oregon.
12. Samuel Moore to Levi Woodbury, November 25, 1835. Peale Family Papers, Series IX-A, Correspondence of Benjamin Franklin Peale, American Philosophical Library, courtesy of the University of Oregon.
13. Franklin Peale to Anna Peale, November 6, 1833. Peale Family Papers, Series IX-A, Correspondence of Benjamin Franklin Peale, American Philosophical Library, courtesy of the University of Oregon.
14. Franklin Peale to Samuel Moore, January 1, 1834. Peale Family Papers, Series IX-A, Correspondence of Benjamin Franklin Peale, American Philosophical Library, courtesy of the University of Oregon.
15. *Journal of the American Institute* 4, no. 2 (November 1838): 107.
16. Samuel Moore to Franklin Peale, January 14, 1834. Peale Family Papers, Series IX-A, Correspondence of Benjamin Franklin Peale, American Philosophical Library, courtesy of the University of Oregon.
17. R.M. Patterson to Levi Woodbury, September 26, 1835. Peale Family Papers, Series IX-A, Correspondence of Benjamin Franklin Peale, American Philosophical Library, courtesy of the University of Oregon.
18. Franklin Peale to R.M. Patterson, June 16, 1835. Peale Family Papers, Series IX-A, Correspondence of Benjamin Franklin Peale, American Philosophical Library, courtesy of the University of Oregon.
19. Franklin Peale to Professor Ducatel, March 4, 1832. Peale Family Papers, Series IX-A, Correspondence of Benjamin Franklin Peale, American Philosophical Library, courtesy of the University of Oregon.
20. Franklin Peale, February 16, 1855, *Early Proceedings of the American Philosophical Society for the Promotion of Useful Knowledge* 6, no. 55 (January–April 1855). Edited by Henry Phillips and J.P. Lesley.

Chapter 14: A Design of Great Merit

1. Samuel Moore to the auditor of the Treasury, July 16, 1835. Peale Family Papers, Series IX-A, Correspondence of Benjamin Franklin Peale, American Philosophical Library, courtesy of the University of Oregon.
2. Samuel Moore to R.M. Patterson, June 15, 1835. RG 104, Records of the Bureau of the Mint, U.S. Mint at Philadelphia 1791–1936, Correspondence 1792–1904, General Correspondence 1792–1899, NC 152, Entry 1, NM 1992, Box 16.
3. Levi Woodbury to Samuel Moore, June 20, 1835. RG 104, Records of the Bureau of the Mint, U.S. Mint at Philadelphia 1791–1936, Correspondence 1792–1904, General Correspondence 1792–1899, NC 152, Entry 1, NM 1992, Box 16.
4. Samuel Moore to R.M. Patterson, June 27, 1835. RG 104, Records of the Bureau of the Mint, U.S. Mint at Philadelphia 1791–1936, Correspondence 1792–1904, General Correspondence 1792–1899, NC 152, Entry 1, NM 1992, Box 16.
5. R.M. Patterson to Samuel Moore, June 29, 1835. RG 104, Records of the Bureau of the Mint, U.S. Mint at Philadelphia 1791–1936, Correspondence 1792–1904, General Correspondence 1792–1899, NC 152, Entry 1, NM 1992, Box 16.
6. R.M. Patterson to Samuel Moore, June 24, 1835. Patterson Family Papers 1809–1876, American Philosophical Society, P274.2.
7. Lewis Cass to Samuel Moore, May 15, 1835. Patterson Family Papers 1809–1876, American Philosophical Society, P274.2.
8. Samuel Moore to R.M. Patterson, June 29, 1835. Patterson Family Papers 1809–1876, American Philosophical Society. P274.2.
9. Franklin Peale, February 16, 1855, *Early Proceedings* 6, no. 55 (January–April 1855).
10. R.W. Julian, "Another Look at the 1804 Dollar," *Numismatist*, January 1970: 5–13.
11. Kneass sketch with date noted, James Barton Longacre Papers, Library Company of Philadelphia.
12. R.M. Patterson to Thomas Sully, August 1, 1835. RG 104, Records of the Bureau of the Mint, U.S. Mint at Philadelphia 1791–1936, Correspondence 1792–1904, General Correspondence 1792–1899, NC 152, Entry 1, NM 1992, Box 16.
13. Patterson would increase this number to 26, assuming the admission to the Union of Arkansas and Michigan prior to the completion of this design and issuance of the dollar coin.
14. R.M. Patterson to Titian Peale, August 1, 1835. RG 104, Records of the Bureau of the Mint. U.S. Mint at Philadelphia 1791 to 1936 Entry 23, Peale Correspondence 1829–1886, NC 152, HM 1992, Box 1.
15. Sully's portrait of Andrew Jackson appears on the current $20 bill.
16. Cornelius Vermeule, *Numismatic Art in America* (Atlanta: Whitman, 2007): 42.
17. Levi Woodbury to R.M. Patterson, August 31, 1835. RG 104, Records of the Bureau of the Mint, U.S. Mint at Philadelphia 1791–1936, Correspondence 1792–1904, General Correspondence 1792–1899, NC 152, Entry 1, NM 1992, Box 16.
18. Jane Kneass to Levi Woodbury, October 12, 1840. RG 104, Records of the Bureau of the Mint, U.S. Mint at Philadelphia 1791–1936, Correspondence 1792–1904, General Correspondence 1792–1899, NC 152, Entry 1, NM 1992, Box 21. In the words of Kneass's wife, it took nearly a year for Gobrecht to learn the ins and outs of Mint engraving.
19. Persico had recently departed the United States to return to his native Italy. While in the United States, he had executed a bust of Lafayette and had become a favorite of John Quincy Adams with his neoclassical style. In 1834 he had come back to America to deliver statues of War and Peace for the Capitol rotunda, commissioned while Adams was president.
20. *Wikipedia*, "Luigi Persico," last modified June 24, 2014.
21. Thomas Sully to R.M. Patterson, September 14, 1835. RG 104, Records of the Bureau of the Mint, U.S. Mint at Philadelphia 1791–1936, Correspondence 1792–1904, General Correspondence 1792–1899, NC 152, Entry 1, NM 1992, Box 16.
22. R.M. Patterson to Levi Woodbury, October 15, 1835. RG 104, Records of the Bureau of the Mint, U.S. Mint at Philadelphia 1791–1936, Correspondence 1792–1904, General Correspondence 1792–1899, NC 152, Entry 1, NM 1992, Box 16.
23. Mark Van Winkle, "Gobrecht Dollars," in *The Gobrecht Dollars 1836–1839*, by R.W. Julian: 29.
24. Mark Van Winkle, "Gobrecht Dollars," in *From the Drawingboard of a Coin-Engraver: Sketches of Christian Gobrecht for the Coinage of 1836–1839* by Elvira Clain-Stefanelli: 18.
25. R.M. Patterson to Joseph Cloud, October 28, 1835. RG 104, Records of the Bureau of the Mint, U.S. Mint at Philadelphia 1791–1936, Correspondence 1792–1904, General Correspondence 1792–1899, NC 152, Entry 1, NM 1992, Box 16.
26. R.M. Patterson to Levi Woodbury, November 27, 1835. RG 104, Records of the Bureau of the Mint, U.S. Mint at Philadelphia 1791–1936, Correspondence 1792–1904, General Correspondence 1792–1899, NC 152, Entry 1, NM 1992, Box 16.
27. Levi Woodbury to R.M. Patterson, December 21, 1835. Peale Family Papers, Series IX-A, Correspondence of Benjamin Franklin Peale, American Philosophical Library, courtesy of the University of Oregon.
28. R.M. Patterson to Thomas Hart Benton, December 30, 1835. Peale Family Papers, Series IX-A, Correspondence of Benjamin Franklin Peale, American Philosophical Library, courtesy of the University of Oregon.
29. Annual Report of the Mint, January 1, 1836. RG 104, Records of the Bureau of the Mint, U.S. Mint at Philadelphia 1791–1936, Corre-

spondence 1792–1904, General Correspondence 1792–1899, NC 152, Entry 1, NM 1992, Box 17.

30. R.M. Patterson to Thomas Ewing, January 6, 1835. Peale Family Papers, Series IX-A, Correspondence of Benjamin Franklin Peale, American Philosophical Library, courtesy of the University of Oregon.

31. R.M. Patterson to Franklin Peale, January 11, 1836. Peale Family Papers, Series IX-A, Correspondence of Benjamin Franklin Peale, American Philosophical Library, courtesy of the University of Oregon.

32. R.M. Patterson, January 11, 1836. RG 104, Records of the Bureau of the Mint, U.S. Mint at Philadelphia 1791–1936, Correspondence 1792–1904, General Correspondence 1792–1899, NC 152, Entry 1, NM 1992, Box 17.

33. R.M. Patterson to Levi Woodbury, January 7, 1836. RG 104, Records of the Bureau of the Mint, U.S. Mint at Philadelphia 1791–1936, Correspondence 1792–1904, General Correspondence 1792–1899, NC 152, Entry 1, NM 1992, Box 17.

34. R.M. Patterson to Levi Woodbury, January 8, 1836. RG 104, Records of the Bureau of the Mint, U.S. Mint at Philadelphia 1791–1936, Correspondence 1792–1904, General Correspondence 1792–1899, NC 152, Entry 1, NM 1992, Box 17.

35. R.M. Patterson to Levi Woodbury, January 14, 1836, as quoted in *The U.S. Mint and Coinage*, by Don Taxay, 171.

36. Charles Cushing Wright to Rembrandt Peale, February 11, 1836. RG 104, Records of the Bureau of the Mint, U.S. Mint at Philadelphia 1791–1936, Correspondence 1792–1904, General Correspondence 1792–1899, NC 152, Entry 1, NM 1992, Box 17.

37. Rembrandt Peale to R.M. Patterson, March 2, 1836. RG 104, Records of the Bureau of the Mint, U.S. Mint at Philadelphia 1791–1936, Correspondence 1792–1904, General Correspondence 1792–1899, NC 152, Entry 1, NM 1992, Box 17.

38. There is some disagreement among numismatic historians as to whether models were prepared at this point. Don Taxay states that the Contamin lathe was placed into service at the Mint in 1836. This is based upon a story by George Escol Sellers in 1893 concerning the preparation of a Berlin iron casting from a six-inch model for use in the lathe to cut the master die in 1836. However, the Mint correspondence does not indicate the existence of any model at this point in time and does not mention the lathe whatsoever. A more likely date for the arrival of the lathe was March or April 1837, as supported by R.W. Julian in his article in the April 5, 2011, issue of *Coins Magazine*. The Contamin lathe was most likely used when the dies were reworked in 1838.

39. Franklin Peale to R.M. Patterson, March 8, 1836. Peale Family Papers, Series IX-A, Correspondence of Benjamin Franklin Peale, American Philosophical Library, courtesy of the University of Oregon.

40. The camera lucida was in vogue by the 1830s. It provided an optical superimposition of the subject being viewed upon the surface on which the artist was drawing. The artist saw both the scene and drawing surface simultaneously, as in a photographic double exposure. This allowed the artist to duplicate key points of the scene on the drawing surface, aiding in the accurate rendering of perspective.

41. Franklin Peale to R.M. Patterson, February 28, 1836. Peale Family Papers, Series IX-A, Correspondence of Benjamin Franklin Peale, American Philosophical Library, courtesy of the University of Oregon.

42. Franklin Peale to R.M. Patterson, March 8, 1836. Peale Family Papers, Series IX-A, Correspondence of Benjamin Franklin Peale, American Philosophical Library, courtesy of the University of Oregon.

43. There were 26 stars, anticipating the admission of Michigan on January 26, 1837.

44. R.M. Patterson to Levi Woodbury, April 8, 1836. RG 104, Records of the Bureau of the Mint, U.S. Mint at Philadelphia 1791–1936, Correspondence 1792–1904, General Correspondence 1792–1899, NC 152, Entry 1, NM 1992, Box 17.

45. Levi Woodbury to R.M. Patterson, April 11, 1836 as quoted in *The U.S. Mint and Coinage*, by Don Taxay, 174,

46. R.M. Patterson to Levi Woodbury, April 14, 1836. RG 104, Records of the Bureau of the Mint, U.S. Mint at Philadelphia 1791–1936, Correspondence 1792–1904, General Correspondence 1792–1899, NC 152, Entry 1, NM 1992, Box 17.

47. R.M. Patterson to Levi Woodbury, June 18, 1836. RG 104, Records of the Bureau of the Mint, U.S. Mint at Philadelphia 1791–1936, Correspondence 1792–1904, General Correspondence 1792–1899, NC 152, Entry 1, NM 1992, Box 17.

48. R.W. Julian, "Gobrecht's Dollar: Originals Show Eagle Flying Upward," *Coins Magazine*, April 5, 2011.

49. Heretofore, no engraver's name had been displayed on a circulating United States coin. The phrase "C. Gobrecht F." was from Latin, standing for "Christian Gobrecht made it," and was in the style typically found on medals. Previously only Reich had inserted a tiny "R" at the edge of a star on his capped-bust half dollar design. There is numismatic support to the effect that Gobrecht first placed his name in the field between the plinth and the date. Only after objections to its prominence did he move it to the plinth. Surviving dollars showing Gobrecht's name in the field are restrikes made starting in the late 1850s to satisfy collector demand.

50. R.M. Patterson to Adam Eckfeldt, September 22, 1836. RG 104, Records of the Bureau of the Mint, U.S. Mint at Philadelphia 1791–1936, Correspondence 1792–1904, General Correspondence 1792–1899, NC 152, Entry 1, NM 1992, Box 17.

51. R.M. Patterson to Levi Woodbury, November 8, 1836, as quoted in *The U.S. Mint and Coinage*, by Don Taxay, 174,

52. Craig Sholley, John Dannreuther, and Saul Teichman, "New Data Supports Revisionist Theory of the Gobrecht Dollars," Numismatic Theater Presentation, 2012 ANA August Convention. Courtesy of John Dannreuther.

53. *Early Proceedings of the American Philosophical Society for the Promotion of Useful Knowledge*, edited by Henry Phillips and J.P Lesley (Philadelphia: Press of McCalla and Stavely, 1884), 679. Sadly, this coin has disappeared.

54. *Early Proceedings*, 679.

Chapter 15: Whirlwind of Change

1. *Mechanics Magazine and Journal of the Mechanics Institute* 9, no. 1 (January 1837): 43.

2. Samuel Moore to R.M. Patterson, June 26, 1835. RG 104, Records of the Bureau of the Mint, U.S. Mint at Philadelphia 1791–1936, Correspondence 1792–1904, General Correspondence 1792–1899, NC 152, Entry 1, NM 1992, Box 16.

3. Sellers, *Early Engineering Reminiscences*, 76.

4. R.M. Patterson to Levi Woodbury, September 26, 1835. Peale Family Papers, Series IX-A, Correspondence of Benjamin Franklin Peale American Philosophical Library, courtesy of the University of Oregon.

5. Joe Levine, Exonumia Auction catalogue 83, June 22, 2013.

6. Franklin Peale to R.M. Patterson, March 8, 1836. Peale Family Papers, Series IX-A, Correspondence of Benjamin Franklin Peale American Philosophical Library, courtesy of the University of Oregon.

7. Julian, *Medals of the United States Mint*, 193.

8. Sellers, *Early Engineering Reminiscences*, 76–77.

9. *Mechanics Magazine and Journal of the Mechanics Institute*, January 1837: 43. First presented at the Franklin Institute.

10. *Mechanics Magazine and Journal of the Mechanics Institute* 9, no. 2 (February 1837): 66.

11. *Journal of the House of Representatives* 29 (February 1, 1836): 270.

12. Ibid., February 13, 1836, 340.

13. R.M. Patterson to Joseph R. Ingersoll, February 16, 1836. RG 104, Records of the Bureau of the Mint, U.S. Mint at Philadelphia 1791–1936, Correspondence 1792–1904, General Correspondence 1792–1899, NC 152, Entry 1, NM 1992, Box 17.

14. R.M. Patterson to Levi Woodbury, March 23, 1836. RG 104, Records of the Bureau of the Mint, U.S. Mint at Philadelphia 1791–1936, Correspondence 1792–1904, General Correspondence 1792–1899, NC 152, Entry 1, NM 1992, Box 17.

15. U.S. Congressional Serial Set, 1817–1980, 24th Congress, 1st Session, House of Representatives, Report 513, March 26, 1836.

16. *Journal of the House of Representatives* 29 (June 23, 1836): 1082.

17. *Journal of the Senate* 25 (February 8, 1836): 149.

18. Levi Woodbury to Martin Van Buren, February 11, 1836. U.S. Congressional Serial Set, 1817–1980, 24th Congress, 1st Session, Senate, Report 162, February 15, 1836.

19. Bills and Resolutions, House of Representatives, 24th Congress, 1st Session, Bill 529, April 5, 1836.

20. R.M. Patterson to Thomas Hart Benton, March 23, 1836. RG 104, Records of the Bureau of the Mint, U.S. Mint at Philadelphia 1791–1936, Correspondence 1792–1904, General Correspondence 1792–1899, NC 152, Entry 1, NM 1992, Box 17.

21. Register of Debates, Senate, 24th Congress, 1st Session, April 5, 1836: 1090–1091.

22. R.M. Patterson to Levi Woodbury, April 14, 1836. RG 104, Records of the Bureau of the Mint, U.S. Mint at Philadelphia 1791–1936, Correspondence 1792–1904, General Correspondence 1792–1899, NC 152, Entry 1, NM 1992, Box 17.

23. Statutes at Large, 24th Congress, 1st Session, May 9, 1836: 21.

24. Sellers, *Early Engineering Reminiscences*, 76.

25. Franklin Peale to R.M. Patterson, February 28, 1836. Peale Family Papers, Series IX-A, Correspondence of Benjamin Franklin Peale American Philosophical Library, courtesy of the University of Oregon. Also, Sellers, *Early Engineering Reminiscences*, 71.

26. U.S. Congressional Serial Set, 1817–1980, 24th Congress, 2nd Session, House of Representatives, Report 96, January 23, 1837.

27. R.M. Patterson to J.W. Webster, October 10, 1844. Peale Family Papers, Series IX-A, Correspondence of Benjamin Franklin Peale American Philosophical Library, courtesy of the University of Oregon.

28. Franklin Peale to R.M. Patterson, December 16, 24, 1836. Peale Family Papers, Series IX-A, Correspondence of Benjamin Franklin Peale, Courtesy of the University of Oregon.

29. Bills and Resolutions, House of Representatives, 24th Congress, 2nd Session, December 13, 1836.

30. Levi Woodbury to R.M. Patterson, October 31, 1836. RG 104, Records of the Bureau of the Mint, U.S. Mint at Philadelphia 1791–1936, Correspondence 1792–1904, General Correspondence 1792–1899, NC 152, Entry 1, NM 1992, Box 17.

31. R.M. Patterson to George Newbold, November 11, 1836. RG 104, Records of the Bureau of the Mint, U.S. Mint at Philadelphia 1791–1936, Correspondence 1792–1904, General Correspondence 1792–1899, NC 152, Entry 1, NM 1992, Box 17.

32. Bills and Resolutions, Senate, 24th Congress, 2nd Session, S.33, December 19, 1836.

33. *Journal of the House of Representatives* 30 (December 20, 1836): 78.

34. Register of Debates, House of Representatives, 24th Congress, 2nd Session, December 22, 1836: 1144–1147.

35. Register of Debates, House of Representatives, 24th Congress, 2nd Session, December 28, 1836: 1171–1172.

36. *Journal of the Senate* 26 (January 18, 1837): 134.

37. *Journal of the House of Representatives* 30 (December 31, 1836): 156.

Chapter 16: Choppy Waters

1. A Citizen to R.M. Patterson, March 7, 1836. RG 104, Records of the Bureau of the Mint, U.S. Mint at Philadelphia 1791–1936, Correspondence 1792–1904, General Correspondence 1792–1899, NC 152, Entry 1, NM 1992, Box 17.

2. Petition to R.M. Patterson, January 20, 1837. RG 104, Records of the Bureau of the Mint, U.S. Mint at Philadelphia 1791–1936, Correspondence 1792–1904, General Correspondence 1792–1899, NC 152, Entry 1, NM 1992, Box 18.

3. R.M. Patterson to Levi Woodbury, October 17, 1840. RG 104, Records of the Bureau of the Mint, U.S. Mint at Philadelphia 1791–1936, Correspondence 1792–1904, General Correspondence 1792–1899, NC 152, Entry 1, NM 1992, Box 21.

4. Daniel Walker Howe, *What Hath God Wrought: The Transformation of America 1815–1848* (Oxford: Oxford University Press, 2007), 502–504. In the author's opinion the Gold Coin Act of 1834 had been too little too late. Had Secretary of the Treasury Crawford not been ill in 1823 before the fissures within the Democratic Republicans took hold, he might have been able to gain the necessary legislation to maximize retention of American gold coins in domestic circulation. The Panic of 1837, at the point when the land speculation bubble burst, would not have been avoided but its pain would have been manageable. However, Jackson's vengeful destruction of the Second BUS and the removal of federal deposits to state banks was economic mismanagement so gross as to be criminal negligence. The president's actions were the root cause for the length and depth of this depression.

5. R.M. Patterson to Levi Woodbury, November 8, 1836, as quoted in *The U.S. Mint and Coinage*, by Don Taxay, 174.

6. Franklin Peale to R.M. Patterson, December 24, 1836. Peale Family Papers, Series IX–A, Correspondence of Benjamin Franklin Peale, American Philosophical Society, courtesy of the University of Oregon.

7. "The New Dollar Coin," *Philadelphia Public Ledger*, December 19, 1836: 2.

8. "New Dollar," *Philadelphia Public Ledger*, December 21, 1836: 4.

9. Franklin Peale to R.M. Patterson, January 8, 1837, courtesy of John Dannreuther.

10. Sholley, Dannreuther, and Teichman, "New Data Supports Revisionist Theory of the Gobrecht Dollars." Dannreuther does not subscribe to the assumption that the steam press was used, assuming the screw press was used instead.

11. Weight courtesy of John Dannreuther.

12. "New Coin," *Niles Weekly Register*, November 21, 1840: 2.

13. R.W. Julian, "New Information on the Gobrecht Dollar," *Numismatic News*, October 6, 2009.

14. Information courtesy of Q. David Bowers.

15. Sellers, *Early Engineering Reminiscences*, 71–74. In *The United States Mint at Charlotte, North Carolina: Its History and Coinage* (Easley, SC: Southern Historical Press, 1984), 14–15, Clair Birdsall states that other records indicate that Merrick received the contract for the draw benches, cut-out press, coining press, and milling machines.

16. Birdsall, *The United States Mint at Charlotte, North Carolina: Its History and Coinage*, 11.

17. Richard G. Doty, "An Onerous and Delicate Task: Franklin Peale's Mission South, 1837," presented to the Coinage of the Americas conference at the ANS, November 4–5, 1989. Courtesy of Richard G. Doty.

18. Carl N. Lester, "A Brief History of the United States Branch Mint at Dahlonega, Georgia," 2.

19. Franklin Peale to R.M. Patterson, December 23, 1837. Peale Family Papers, Series IX–A, Correspondence of Benjamin Franklin Peale, American Philosophical Library, courtesy of the University of Oregon.

20. Birdsall, *The United States Mint at Charlotte, North Carolina: Its History and Coinage*, 15.

21. U.S. Congressional Serial Set, 1817–1980, 25th Congress, 2nd Session, House of Representatives, Report 110, January 17, 1838.

22. R.M. Patterson to Franklin Peale, October 24, 1837. Peale Family Papers, Series IX–A, Correspondence of Benjamin Franklin Peale, American Philosophical Library, courtesy of the University of Oregon.

23. Levi Woodbury to R.M. Patterson, November 6, 1837. RG 104, Records of the Bureau of the Mint, U.S. Mint at Philadelphia 1791–1936, Correspondence 1792–1904, General Correspondence 1792–1899, NC 152, Entry 1, NM 1992, Box 18.

24. *Early Proceedings of the American Philosophical Society for the Promotion of Useful Knowledge* 6, no. 55 (January–April 1855), February 16, 1855, Presentation to the APS by Franklin Peale.

25. Sellers, *Early Engineering Reminiscences*, 77.

26. J. Hewitt Judd, M.D., *United States Pattern Coins Experimental and Trial Pieces*, 8th edition, edited by Q. David Bowers (Atlanta: Whitman, 2003), 46–50.

27. Walter Breen, *Walter Breen's Complete Encyclopedia of U.S. and Colonial Coins* (New York: Doubleday, 1988), 345.

28. Breen, *Complete Encyclopedia*, 548–549. Gobrecht could only have worked from an engraving. The painting was in England and did not reach the United States until 1851.

29. Sholley, Dannreuther, and Teichman, "New Data, Supports Revisionist Theory of the Gobrecht Dollars."

30. Sellers, *Early Engineering Reminiscences*, 74–76. There is a story published by George Escol Sellers, which has only a shred of creditability,

that he and Franklin Peale prepared the iron casting of the reverse model for use in the Contamin lathe for die preparation. Sellers erroneously associated this iron casting with the first Gobrecht dollars struck in 1836. However, with the lathe not on site until March or April 1837, the next opportunity for its use with this dollar design could not have come until the 1838 patterns were struck. More likely, it was used to make the bronze model of Titian Peale's flying eagle, which was briefly considered for the reverse of the half dollar. Sellers wrote this story from memory in either 1884 or 1893.

Chapter 17: Party Politics

1. *Wealthy Citizens of Philadelphia, Memoirs and Autobiography of some of the Wealthy Citizens of Philadelphia* (Booksellers, 1846). Adam Eckfeldt was listed with a net worth of $50,000, a substantial sum for someone salaried at $1,500 per year for most of his career at the Mint. The same document listed Robert Maskell Patterson with an identical net worth of $50,000, derived from the income of a fortune and a large salary as director of the Mint.
2. W.E. DuBois to R.M. Patterson, "Saturday Evening", 1839. RG 104, Records of the Bureau of the Mint, U.S. Mint at Philadelphia 1791–1936, Correspondence 1792–1904, General Correspondence 1792–1899, NC 152, Entry 1, NM 1992, Box 20.
3. R.M. Patterson to Martin Van Buren, March 11, 1839. Peale Family Papers, Series IX-A, Correspondence of Benjamin Franklin Peale, American Philosophical Society, courtesy of the University of Oregon.
4. Adam Eckfeldt to Martin Van Buren, March 12, 1839. Peale Family Papers, Series IX-A, Correspondence of Benjamin Franklin Peale, American Philosophical Society, courtesy of the University of Oregon.
5. Henry Gilpin to R.M. Patterson, March 16, 1839. RG 104, Records of the Bureau of the Mint, U.S. Mint at Philadelphia 1791–1936, Correspondence 1792–1904, General Correspondence 1792–1899, NC 152, Entry 1, NM 1992, Box 20.
6. Henry D. Gilpin to R.M. Patterson, March 23, 1839. RG 104, Records of the Bureau of the Mint, U.S. Mint at Philadelphia 1791–1936, Correspondence 1792–1904, General Correspondence 1792–1899, NC 152, Entry 1, NM 1992, Box 20.
7. R.M. Patterson to Jonas R. McClintock, March 23, 1839. RG 104, Records of the Bureau of the Mint, U.S. Mint at Philadelphia 1791–1936, Correspondence 1792–1904, General Correspondence 1792–1899, NC 152, Entry 1, NM 1992, Box 20.
8. George Wolf to Martin Van Buren, March 26, 1839, and William Findlay to Martin Van Buren, March 24, 1839. RG 56, Records of the Department of the Treasury, Entry 288, Applications for Positions as Assistant Treasurers and Mint Officers 1836–1898 and 1902–1904, Box 24.
9. Marriage Announcement, May 1, 1839. Peale Family Papers, Series IX-A, Correspondence of Benjamin Franklin Peale, American Philosophical Society, courtesy of the University of Oregon.
10. Franklin Peale to R.M. Patterson, January 8, 1848 (probably 1849 given the document sequence). RG 104, Records of the Bureau of the Mint. U.S. Mint at Philadelphia 1791–1936, Peale Correspondence 1829–1886, NC 152, Entry 23, HM 1992, Box 1.
11. R.M. Patterson to Adam Eckfeldt, June 7, 1839.RG 104, Records of the Bureau of the Mint, U.S. Mint at Philadelphia 1791–1936, Correspondence 1792–1904, General Correspondence 1792–1899, NC 152, Entry 1, NM 1992, Box 20.
12. R.M. Patterson to Levi Woodbury, August 15, 1839. RG 104, Records of the Bureau of the Mint, U.S. Mint at Philadelphia 1791–1936, Correspondence 1792–1904, General Correspondence 1792–1899, NC 152, Entry 1, NM 1992, Box 20.
13. John Dannruether, "Robert Ball Hughes—More than a Coin Designer?" *Rare Coin Market Report*, April 2007: 17.
14. R.W. Julian, "New Information on the Gobrecht Dollars," *Numismatic News*, October 6, 2009.
15. "Report on a Coining Press at the United States Mint, Philadelphia," *Journal of the Franklin Institute*, May 14, 1840: 298.
16. R.M. Patterson to Horatio Greenough, November 25, 1842. RG 104, Records of the Bureau of the Mint. U.S. Mint at Philadelphia 1791–1936, Peale Correspondence 1829–1886, NC 152, Entry 23, HM 1992, Box 1.
17. Bills and Resolutions, Senate, 25th Congress, 2nd Session, S.357, June 7, 1838.
18. *Journal of the Senate* 28 (June 29, 1838): 508.
19. *Journal of the House of Representatives* 32 (July 4, 1838): 1230.
20. *Journal of the Senate* 29 (December 20, 1838): 64.
21. Ibid., January 25, 1839, 160.
22. Congressional Globe, 25th Congress, 3rd Session, January 29, 1839: 148.
23. U.S. Congressional Serial Set, 1817–1980, 25th Congress, 3rd Session, House of Representatives, Report 189, February 13, 1839.
24. *Journal of the Senate* 29 (February 4, 1839): 189.
25. Bills and Resolutions, Senate, 26th Congress, 1st Session, S.114, December 31, 1839.
26. *Journal of the House of Representatives* 34 (February 10, 1840): 376.
27. Congressional Globe, Senate, 26th Congress, 1st Session, April 17, 1840: 314–318.
28. *Journal of the House of Representatives* 34 (April 21, 1840): 812.
29. Peter Duponceau to William Henry Harrison, Undated. RG 56, Records of the Department of the Treasury, Applications for Positions as Assistant Treasurers and Mint Officers 1836–1898 and 1902–1904, Entry 288, Box 25.
30. R.M. Patterson to Thomas Ewing, May 10, 1841. RG 104, Records of the Bureau of the Mint, U.S. Mint at Philadelphia 1791–1936, Correspondence 1792–1904, General Correspondence 1792–1899, NC 152, Entry 1, NM 1992, Box 21.
31. Kane, *Autobiography*, 36–42.
32. R.M. Patterson to Thomas Ewing, June 16, 1841. Patterson Family Papers 1809–1876, American Philosophical Society, P274.2.
33. R.M. Patterson to Thomas Ewing, July 22, 1841. Patterson Family Papers 1809–1876, American Philosophical Society, P274.2.
34. "The Case of Governor Ritter," September 14, 1841, Patterson Family Papers 1809–1876, American Philosophical Society, P274.2, unidentified newspaper clipping.
35. *Journal of the Executive Proceedings of the Senate* 5 (June 17, 1841): 386.
36. Ibid., June 29, 1841, 396.
37. Ibid., July 15, 1841, 406.
38. Ibid., September 10, 1841, 434.
39. Ibid., September 11, 1841, 386.
40. *Wealthy Citizens of Philadelphia.*
41. U.S. Congressional Serial Set, 1817–1980, 25th Congress, 3rd Session, House of Representatives, Report 97, January 19, 1839.
42. R.M. Patterson to Thomas Hart Benton, February 17, 1840. RG 104, Records of the Bureau of the Mint, U.S. Mint at Philadelphia 1791–1936, Correspondence 1792–1904, General Correspondence 1792–1899, NC 152, Entry 1, NM 1992, Box 20.
43. R.M. Patterson to Silas Wright, Jr., December 12, 1840. RG 104, Records of the Bureau of the Mint, U.S. Mint at Philadelphia 1791–1936, Correspondence 1792–1904, General Correspondence 1792–1899, NC 152, Entry 1, NM 1992, Box 21.
44. U.S. Congressional Serial Set, 1817–1980, 26th Congress, 2nd Session, House of Representatives, Report 75, January 25, 1841.
45. Bills and Resolutions, Senate, 27th Congress, 2nd Session, S.229, April 13, 1842.
46. *Journal of the Senate* 33 (July 22, 1842): 493.
47. Bills and Resolutions, House of Representatives, 27th Congress, 2nd Session, H.R. 313, March 31, 1842.
48. U.S. Congressional Serial Set, 1817–1980, 26th Congress, 1st Session, House of Representatives, Report 91, February 12, 1840.
49. U.S. Congressional Serial Set, 1817–1980, 26th Congress, 2nd Session, House of Representatives, Report 75, January 25, 1841. The answer was simple. The government made money from the seigniorage on copper but not on silver or gold.
50. *Journal of the Senate* 34 (January 5, 1843): 75.
51. R.M. Patterson to Thomas Hart Benton, January 9, 1843. RG 104, Records of the Bureau of the Mint, U.S. Mint at Philadelphia 1791–1936,

Correspondence 1792–1904, General Correspondence 1792–1899, NC 152, Entry 1, NM 1992, Box 22.

52. Statutes at Large, 27th Congress, 3rd Session, March 3, 1843: 607.

53. R.M. Patterson to George Evans, February 27, 1843. RG 104, Records of the Bureau of the Mint, U.S. Mint at Philadelphia 1791–1936, Correspondence 1792–1904, General Correspondence 1792–1899, NC 152, Entry 1, NM 1992, Box 22.

54. Robert J. Morgan, *A Whig Embattled, The Presidency Under John Tyler* (Lincoln, NE: University of Nebraska Press, 1954), 161.

55. *Journal of the Executive Proceedings of the Senate* 6 (February 27, 1843): 173.

Chapter 18: An American Sir Isaac Newton

1. United States Mint, Philadelphia, *The American Repertory of Arts, Sciences and Manufactures*, June 1840: 342

2. R.M. Patterson to Franklin Peale, December 8, 1836. Peale Family Papers, Series IX-A, Correspondence of Benjamin Franklin Peale, American Philosophical Society, courtesy of the University of Oregon.

3. R.M. Patterson to Walter Forward, November 25, 1841. Archives, RG 104, Correspondence of the Office of the Secretary of the Treasury, Letters Received from the Director and Superintendent of the Mint, Philadelphia, 1832–1910, NC 152, Entry 169, Box 1.

4. *Early Proceedings of the American Philosophical Society for the Promotion of Useful Knowledge*, September 18, 1836: 675.

5. *Early Proceedings of the American Philosophical Society for the Promotion of Useful Knowledge*, July 18, 1836: 706.

6. *Proceedings of the American Philosophical Society* 1, no. 3 (January–March 1838).

7. *Proceedings of the American Philosophical Society* 1, no. 5 (September–October 1838).

8. Charles Coleman Sellers, *Mr. Peale's Museum: Charles Willson Peale and the First Popular Museum of Natural History and Art* (New York: W,W, Norton, 1980), 270–295. Ironically, all those specimens shipped to the Smithsonian were lost in a fire in 1865. Those going to the Philadelphia Museum were dispersed at its liquidation, with many surviving in the leading American museums today.

9. *Proceedings of the American Philosophical Society* 1, no. 7 (April–August 1839).

10. Robert Maskell Patterson Papers, APS, P274 and P274.1, *Short Biography of Robert M. Patterson, M.D., Samuel Breck, President of the Pennsylvania Institution for the Instruction of the Blind, prepared for The Managers of That Institution, Printed by order of the Board of Managers*, Philadelphia, John C. Clark & Son, Printers 68 dock Street, 1854, American Philosophical Society.

11. Christian Gobrecht to R.M. Patterson, November 10, 1843. RG 104, Records of the Bureau of the Mint, U.S. Mint at Philadelphia 1791–1936, Correspondence 1792–1904, General Correspondence 1792–1899, NC 152, Entry 1, NM 1992, Box 22.

12. R.M. Patterson to Levi Woodbury, January 15, 1840. RG 104, Records of the Bureau of the Mint. U.S. Mint at Philadelphia 1791–1936, Peale Correspondence 1829–1886, NC 152, Entry 23, HM 1992, Box 1.

13. Thomas Spencer, "On the Mode of Producing Fac-Simile Copies of Medals, etc, by the Agency of Voltaic Electricity," *The American Repertory of Arts, Sciences, and Manufactures* 1, no. 4 (May 1840): 278.

14. "The Electrotype, or Casting by Electricity", *New-Yorker* 10, no. 5 (October 17, 1840): 77.

15. Jane Kneass to Levi Woodbury, October 12, 1840. RG 104, Records of the Bureau of the Mint, U.S. Mint at Philadelphia 1791–1936, Correspondence 1792–1904, General Correspondence 1792–1899, NC 152, Entry 1, NM 1992, Box 21.

16. *Journal of the Executive Proceedings of the Senate* 5 (December 17, 1840): 316

17. R.M. Patterson to Levi Woodbury, R.M. Patterson to Martin Van Buren, August 28, 1840. RG 104, Records of the Bureau of the Mint, U.S. Mint at Philadelphia 1791–1936, Correspondence 1792–1904, General Correspondence 1792–1899, NC 152, Entry 1, NM 1992, Box 21.

18. R.M. Patterson to Walter Forward, November 25, 1841. RG 56, Correspondence of the Office of the Secretary of the Treasury, Letters Received from the Director and Superintendent of the Mint, Philadelphia, 1832–1910, NC 152, Entry 169, Box 1.

19. *Proceedings of the American Philosophical Society* 1, no.6 (January–March 1839).

20. Dannruether, "Robert Ball Hughes—More than a Coin Designer?", *Rare Coin Market Report*, April 2007: 16–18. Dannruether in 2014 backtracked on much of this article, saying that he only felt sure of Hughes having worked on one pattern piece, J-110.

21. R.M. Patterson to Horatio Greenough, November 25, 1842. RG 104, Records of the Bureau of the Mint. U.S. Mint at Philadelphia 1791–1936, Peale Correspondence 1829–1886, NC 152, Entry 23, HM 1992, Box 1.

22. Horatio Greenough to R.M. Patterson, November 27, 1842. RG 104, Records of the Bureau of the Mint, U.S. Mint at Philadelphia 1791–1936, Correspondence 1792–1904, General Correspondence 1792–1899, NC 152, Entry 1, NM 1992, Box 22.

23. R.M. Patterson to Horatio Greenough, December 2, 1842. RG 104, Records of the Bureau of the Mint, U.S. Mint at Philadelphia 1791–1936, Correspondence 1792–1904, General Correspondence 1792–1899, NC 152, Entry 1, NM 1992, Box 22.

24. R.M. Patterson to John C. Spencer, May 19, 1843. RG 104, Records of the Bureau of the Mint, U.S. Mint at Philadelphia 1791–1936, Correspondence 1792–1904, General Correspondence 1792–1899, NC 152, Entry 1, NM 1992, Box 22.

25. R.M. Patterson to James M. Porter, July 31, 1843. RG 104, Records of the Bureau of the Mint. U.S. Mint at Philadelphia 1791–1936, Peale Correspondence 1829–1886, NC 152, Entry 23, HM 1992, Box 1.

26. Joseph Hopkinson was the son of a signer of the Declaration of Independence. He was a Federalist from Philadelphia, serving in Congress from 1815 to 1819. Clearly the officers of the Mint were not the only individuals hooked into the gravy train of medal commissions given by Congress.

27. R.M. Patterson to John C. Spencer, August 11, 1843. RG 104, Records of the Bureau of the Mint, U.S. Mint at Philadelphia 1791–1936, Correspondence 1792–1904, General Correspondence 1792–1899, NC 152, Entry 1, NM 1992, Box 22.

28. John C. Spencer to R.M. Patterson, August 16, 1843. RG 104 Records of the Bureau of the Mint, U.S. Mint at Philadelphia 1791–1936, Correspondence 1792–1904, General Correspondence 1792–1899, NC 152, Entry 1, NM 1992, Box 22.

29. R.M. Patterson, July 24, 1844. RG 104, Records of the Bureau of the Mint, U.S. Mint at Philadelphia 1791–1936, Correspondence 1792–1904, General Correspondence 1792–1899, NC 152, Entry 1, NM 1992, Box 23. Gobrecht had died the previous day.

30. Franklin Peale to Charles A. Wells, August 11, 1844. Peale Family Papers, Series IX-A, Correspondence of Benjamin Franklin Peale, American Philosophical Society, courtesy of the University of Oregon.

Chapter 19: New Faces

1. Sean Wilentz, *The Rise of American Democracy: Jefferson to Lincoln* (New York and London: W.W. Norton, 2005), 568. Calhoun's so-called Packenham letter berated Great Britain for interfering in Texas affairs in the name of abolition. Calhoun went on to a spirited defense of slavery. He made sure the letter became public by including it in material sent to the Senate in support of the annexation treaty. The letter became a litmus test for national Democrats and Whigs: support Texas annexation and its pro-slavery rationale and alienate the North, or oppose it and forever lose the South.

2. Wilentz, *The Rise of American Democracy*, 563–573.

3. R.M. Patterson to John C. Spencer, January 31, 1844. RG 104, Records of the Bureau of the Mint, U.S. Mint at Philadelphia 1791–1936, Correspondence 1792–1904, General Correspondence 1792–1899, NC 152, Entry 1, NM 1992, Box 23.

4. R.M. Patterson to James J. McKay, January 23, 1844. RG 104, Records of the Bureau of the Mint, U.S. Mint at Philadelphia 1791–1936, Correspondence 1792–1904, General Correspondence 1792–1899, NC 152, Entry 1, NM 1992, Box 23.

5. Birdsall, *The United States Branch Mint at Charlotte, North Carolina*, 27–29. Feeling ill, the superintendent had not been in his quarters at the

branch mint early that morning. The man he delegated to stay the night also had not done so. The superintendent afterwards felt that the fire had been set to cover a possible robbery of his quarters. No supporting evidence was ever unearthed.

6. *Journal of the House of Representatives* 39 (January 12, 1844): 213.

7. Thomas Sully to R.M. Patterson, July 30, 1844. RG 104, Records of the Bureau of the Mint, U.S. Mint at Philadelphia 1791–1936, Correspondence 1792–1904, General Correspondence 1792–1899, NC 152, Entry 1, NM 1992, Box 23.

8. Biographical Sketch, January 11, 1918. James Barton Longacre Papers, Philadelphia Library Company.

9. J.B. Longacre to Mr. Humphreys, March 4, 1861. James Barton Longacre Papers, Philadelphia Library Company.

10. J.B. Longacre to William M. Meredith, March 2, 1850. James Barton Longacre Papers. Philadelphia Library Company.

11. *Journal of the Executive Proceedings of the Senate* 6 (December 18, 1844): 362.

12. R.M. Patterson to Robert Walker, June 22, 1844. RG 104, Records of the Bureau of the Mint, U.S. Mint at Philadelphia 1791–1936, Correspondence 1792–1904, General Correspondence 1792–1899, NC 152, Entry 1, NM 1992, Box 23.

13. Patterson Family Papers, American Philosophical Society, Robert Patterson Biography.

14. George M. Bibb to R.M. Patterson, October 7, 1844. RG 104, Records of the Bureau of the Mint, U.S. Mint at Philadelphia 1791–1936, Correspondence 1792–1904, General Correspondence 1792–1899, NC 152, Entry 1, NM 1992, Box 23.

15. Remini, *Henry Clay*, 649.

16. Henry Simpson, *Biographies The Lives of Eminent Philadelphians now Deceased* (Danvers, MA: General Books, 2009): John K. Kane.

17. Remini, *Henry Clay*, 663–665.

18. Kane, *Autobiography*, 46–48.

19. S.F. Chapman to R.M. Patterson, December 17, 1844. RG 104, Records of the Bureau of the Mint, U.S. Mint at Philadelphia 1791–1936, Correspondence 1792–1904, General Correspondence 1792–1899, NC 152, Entry 1, NM 1992, Box 23.

20. U.S. Congressional Serial Set, 1817–1980, 28th Congress, 2nd Session, House of Representatives, Report 23, December 19, 1844.

21. *Journal of the House of Representatives* 40 (January 21, 1845): 329.

22. *Journal of the Senate* 36 (February 10, 1845): 152–153.

23. U.S. Congressional Serial Set, 1817–1980, 28th Congress, 2nd Session, House of Representatives, Report 99, February 5, 1845.

24. Roy F. Nichols and G.M. Dallas, *The Mystery of the Dallas Papers*, 364.

25. Alexander D. Bache to Robert J. Walker, May 9, 1845. RG 104, Records of the Bureau of the Mint, U.S. Mint at Philadelphia 1791–1936, Correspondence 1792–1904, General Correspondence 1792–1899, NC 152, Entry 1, NM 1992, Box 24.

26. R.M. Patterson to J.B. Longacre, October 15, 1844. James Barton Longacre Papers, Philadelphia Library Company.

27. Undated manuscript. James Barton Longacre Papers, Philadelphia Library Company.

28. Undated notes. James Barton Longacre Papers, Philadelphia Library Company.

29. Franklin Peale to R.M. Patterson, December 24, 1849. James Barton Longacre Papers, Philadelphia Library Company.

30. Draft, August 1853. James Barton Longacre Papers, Philadelphia Library Company.

31. C.C. Wright to J.B. Longacre, August 7, 1848. James Barton Longacre Papers, Philadelphia Library Company.

32. J.B. Longacre to William M. Meredith, March 2, 1850. James Barton Longacre Papers, Philadelphia Library Company.

33. Allen Leonard to R.M. Patterson, June 19, 1845. RG 104, Records of the Bureau of the Mint, U.S. Mint at Philadelphia 1791–1936, Correspondence 1792–1904, General Correspondence 1792–1899, NC 152, Entry 1, NM 1992, Box 24.

34. R.M. Patterson to Robert Walker, August 20, 1845. RG 104, Records of the Bureau of the Mint, U.S. Mint at Philadelphia 1791–1936, Correspondence 1792–1904, General Correspondence 1792–1899, NC 152, Entry 1, NM 1992, Box 24.

35. Allen Leonard to R.M. Patterson, September 22, 1845. RG 104, Records of the Bureau of the Mint, U.S. Mint at Philadelphia 1791–1936, Correspondence 1792–1904, General Correspondence 1792–1899, NC 152, Entry 1, NM 1992, Box 24.

36. Allen Leonard to R.M. Patterson, November 21, 1845. RG 104, Records of the Bureau of the Mint, U.S. Mint at Philadelphia 1791–1936, Correspondence 1792–1904, General Correspondence 1792–1899, NC 152, Entry 1, NM 1992, Box 24.

37. R.M. Patterson to Robert Walker, December 19, 1845. RG 104, Records of the Bureau of the Mint, U.S. Mint at Philadelphia 1791–1936, Correspondence 1792–1904, General Correspondence 1792–1899, NC 152, Entry 1, NM 1992, Box 24.

38. J.B. Longacre to Mint director (?), August 21, 1858. James Barton Longacre Papers, Philadelphia Library Company.

39. R.M. Patterson to Isaac Roach, March 16, 1844. RG 104, Records of the Bureau of the Mint, U.S. Mint at Philadelphia 1791–1936, Correspondence 1792–1904, General Correspondence 1792–1899, NC 152, Entry 1, NM 1992, Box 23.

40. R.M. Patterson to J.W. McCulloh, March 27, 1843. RG 104, Records of the Bureau of the Mint, U.S. Mint at Philadelphia 1791–1936, Correspondence 1792–1904, General Correspondence 1792–1899, NC 152, Entry 1, NM 1992, Box 22. J.W. McCulloh's audit of Mint expenditures in the fourth quarter of 1842 disallowed $3: $1 for a washing towel overcharge and $2 for Christmas gifts to the watchmen. Patterson had to write objecting to the Christmas gift disallowance. City watchmen guarded the streets adjoining the Mint. There were no other guards for the outside premises. These men were pledged to keep a sharp eye out for anything out of the ordinary. They had in the past spotted a fire in the building. This payment was a custom and given by all citizens in Philadelphia. Adam Eckfeldt had assured Patterson that this practice had been in place for 50 years.

41. A.D. Bache to R.M. Patterson, January 20, 1846. RG 104, Records of the Bureau of the Mint, U.S. Mint at Philadelphia 1791–1936, Correspondence 1792–1904, General Correspondence 1792–1899, NC 152, Entry 1, NM 1992, Box 25.

42. *Journal of the Executive Proceedings of the Senate* 7 (April 1, 1846): 58.

43. R.M. Patterson to J.W. Webster, October 10, 1844. RG 104, Records of the Bureau of the Mint. U.S. Mint at Philadelphia 1791–1936, Peale Correspondence 1829–1886, NC 152, Entry 23, HM 1992, Box 1.

44. The American Philosophical Society, John C. Clark & Son, A Listing of its Members, #1228.

45. R.M. Patterson to Robert Walker, November 16, 1846. RG 104, Records of the Bureau of the Mint. U.S. Mint at Philadelphia 1791–1936, Peale Correspondence 1829–1886, NC 152, Entry 23, HM 1992, Box 1.

46. W. Medill to R.M. Patterson, February 21, 1846. RG 104, Records of the Bureau of the Mint, U.S. Mint at Philadelphia 1791–1936, Correspondence 1792–1904, General Correspondence 1792–1899, NC 152, Entry 1, NM 1992, Box 25.

47. *Early Proceedings of the American Philosophical Society for the Promotion of Useful Knowledge* 5, no. 36 (July–December 1846), December 18, 1846.

48. Julian, *Medals of the United States Mint*, 84.

49. R.S. McCulloh to Thomas Corwin, January 4, 1853. *The Proceedings of the Late Director of the Mint in Relation to the Official Misconduct of Franklin Peale, ESQ., Chief Coiner, and Other Abuses at the Mint*, July 11, 1853.

50. Hutchinson was recognized and apprehended on the island of St. Thomas by Jonathan Eckfeldt, captain of the brig *W.I. Watson*. Eckfeldt was the son of a half brother of Adam Eckfeldt. (Courtesy of Nancy Oliver and Richard Kelly)

51. R.M. Patterson to McClintock Young, February 12, 1848. RG 104, Records of the Bureau of the Mint, U.S. Mint at Philadelphia 1791–1936, Correspondence 1792–1904, General Correspondence 1792–1899, NC 152, Entry 1, NM 1992, Box 27.

52. RG 104, Records of the Bureau of the Mint, U.S. Mint at Philadelphia 1791–1936, Correspondence 1792–1904, General Correspondence 1792–1899, NC 152, Entry 1, NM 1992, Box 28, January 4, 1849.

53. R.M. Patterson to James Buchanan, May 10, 1845. RG 104, Records of the Bureau of the Mint, U.S. Mint at Philadelphia 1791–1936, Correspondence 1792–1904, General Correspondence 1792–1899, NC 152, Entry 1, NM 1992, Box 24.

54. R.M. Patterson to Robert Walker, March 12, 1847. RG 104, Records of the Bureau of the Mint, U.S. Mint at Philadelphia 1791–1936, Correspondence 1792–1904, General Correspondence 1792–1899, NC 152, Entry 1, NM 1992, Box 26.

55. "The Mint," *New Bedford Mercury*, June 18, 1847: 4.

56. *Journal of the Executive Proceedings of the Senate* 7 (February 16, 1848): 299.

57. Kane, *Autobiography*, 60.

Chapter 20: Philadelphia v. New York

1. Message to the joint session of Congress from President Polk as delivered by Robert Walker, secretary of the Treasury, December 5, 1848.

2. U.S. Congressional Serial Set, 1817–1980, 30th Congress, 1st Session, Senate, Report 17, January 31, 1848.

3. J.R. Ingersoll to R.M. Patterson, December 10, 1845. RG 104, Records of the Bureau of the Mint, U.S. Mint at Philadelphia 1791–1936, Correspondence 1792–1904, General Correspondence 1792–1899, NC 152, Entry 1, NM 1992, Box 24.

4. R.M. Patterson to J.R. Ingersoll RG 104, Records of the Bureau of the Mint, U.S. Mint at Philadelphia 1791–1936, Correspondence 1792–1904, General Correspondence 1792–1899, NC 152, Entry 1, NM 1992, Box 24.

5. R.M. Patterson to J.R. Ingersoll, December 26, 1845. RG 104, Records of the Bureau of the Mint, U.S. Mint at Philadelphia 1791–1936, Correspondence 1792–1904, General Correspondence 1792–1899, NC 152, Entry 1, NM 1992, Box 24.

6. R.M. Patterson to James J. McKay, January 10, 1846. RG 104, Records of the Bureau of the Mint, U.S. Mint at Philadelphia 1791–1936, Correspondence 1792–1904, General Correspondence 1792–1899, NC 152, Entry 1, NM 1992, Box 25.

7. *Journal of the House of Representatives* 41 (January 8, 1846): 206. *Journal of the Senate* 37 (January 20, 1846): 108.

8. Bills and Resolutions, Senate, 29th Congress, 1st Session, S.163, April 22, 1846

9. Bills and Resolutions, Senate, 29th Congress, 1st Session, S.160, April 22, 1846.

10. R.M. Patterson to George Evans, January 31, 1845. RG 46, Records of the U.S. Senate, Sen. 29A-D4, Committee on Finance.

11. *Journal of the House of Representatives* 42 (December 8, 1846): 39.

12. R.M. Patterson to A.D. Bache, February 4, 1847. RG 104, Records of the Bureau of the Mint, U.S. Mint at Philadelphia 1791–1936, Correspondence 1792–1904, General Correspondence 1792–1899, NC 152, Entry 1, NM 1992, Box 26.

13. Bills and Resolutions, Senate, 29th Congress, 2nd Session, Volume 7, S.19, December 17, 1846 and Bills and Resolutions, Senate, 29th Congress, 2nd Session, Volume 7, S.16, December 17, 1846.

14. Congressional Globe, House of Representatives, 29th Congress, 2nd Session, March 3, 1847: 574.

15. Congressional Globe, Senate, 29th Congress, 2nd Session, March 3, 1847: 572.

16. *Journal of the Senate* 39 (December 7, 1847): 33.

17. R.M. Patterson to J.R. Ingersoll, December 30, 1847. RG 104, Records of the Bureau of the Mint, U.S. Mint at Philadelphia 1791–1936, Correspondence 1792–1904, General Correspondence 1792–1899, NC 152, Entry 1, NM 1992, Box 26.

18. Bills and Resolutions, Senate, 30th Congress, 1st Session, S.6, December 14, 1847.

19. Bills and Resolutions, House of Representatives, 30th Congress, 1st Session, H.R. 396, April 13, 1848.

20. Congressional Globe, 30th Congress, 1st Session, July 14, 1848: 936–937.

21. J.R. Ingersoll to R.M. Patterson, July 15, 1848. RG 104, Records of the Bureau of the Mint, U.S. Mint at Philadelphia 1791–1936, Correspondence 1792–1904, General Correspondence 1792–1899, NC 152, Entry 1, NM 1992, Box 27.

Chapter 21: Sherman's Gold

1. *Annual Reunion, June 10th 1897*, United States Military Academy, Association of Graduates: 68–69.

2. W.L. Marcy to R.M. Patterson, August 28, 1847. RG 104, Records of the Bureau of the Mint, U.S. Mint at Philadelphia 1791–1936, Correspondence 1792–1904, General Correspondence 1792–1899, NC 152, Entry 1, NM 1992, Box 26.

3. W.L. Marcy to R.M. Patterson, October 2, 1847. RG 104, Records of the Bureau of the Mint, U.S. Mint at Philadelphia 1791–1936, Correspondence 1792–1904, General Correspondence 1792–1899, NC 152, Entry 1, NM 1992, Box 26.

4. R.M. Patterson to W.L. Marcy, October 5, 1847. RG 104, Records of the Bureau of the Mint, U.S. Mint at Philadelphia 1791–1936, Correspondence 1792–1904, General Correspondence 1792–1899, NC 152, Entry 1, NM 1992, Box 26.

5. W.L. Marcy to R.M. Patterson, October 7, 1847. RG 104, Records of the Bureau of the Mint, U.S. Mint at Philadelphia 1791–1936, Correspondence 1792–1904, General Correspondence 1792–1899, NC 152, Entry 1, NM 1992, Box 26.

6. Julian, *Medals of the United States Mint*, 134–135.

7. "The Gold Region of California", *National Intelligencer*, December 4, 1848, 2. Reprint from the New Orleans *Picayune*, November 24, 1848.

8. "The President's Message", *Philadelphia Public Ledger*, December 2, 1848, 2.

9. *Journal of the Senate* 40 (December 5, 1848): 14–15.

10. W.L. Marcy to R.M. Patterson, December 8, 1848. RG 104, Records of the Bureau of the Mint, U.S. Mint at Philadelphia 1791–1936, Correspondence 1792–1904, General Correspondence 1792–1899, NC 152, Entry 1, NM 1992, Box 27.

11. R.M. Patterson to Robert Walker, December 8, 1848. RG 104, Records of the Bureau of the Mint, U.S. Mint at Philadelphia 1791–1936, Correspondence 1792–1904, General Correspondence 1792–1899, NC 152, Entry 1, NM 1992, Box 27.

12. R.M. Patterson to Robert Walker, December 11, 1848. RG 104, Records of the Bureau of the Mint, U.S. Mint at Philadelphia 1791–1936, Correspondence 1792–1904, General Correspondence 1792–1899, NC 152, Entry 1, NM 1992, Box 27.

13. R.M. Patterson to W.L. Marcy, December 12, 1848. RG 104, Records of the Bureau of the Mint, U.S. Mint at Philadelphia 1791–1936, Correspondence 1792–1904, General Correspondence 1792–1899, NC 152, Entry 1, NM 1992, Box 27.

14. R.S. Yeoman, "The 1848 Quarter Eagle With CAL", *Numismatist*, July 1953: 674–686, R.M Patterson to W.L. Marcy, January 5, 1849.

15. Catalogue of a Valuable Collection of Coins and Medals, January 21, 1870. James Barton Longacre Papers, Philadelphia Library Company: 8.

Chapter 22: William McKendree Gwin

1. Lately Thomas, *Between Two Empires: The Life Story of California's First Senator William McKendree Gwin* (Boston: Houghton Mifflin, 1969), 3–5.

2. Ibid., 27–30.

3. James Gwin to Andrew Jackson, December 18, 1830. *The Papers of Andrew Jackson, Volume VIII*, (University of Tennessee): 696–697.

4. "The Jackson Feast," *National Journal*, July 15, 1830: 3.

5. "Celebration of American Independence at Washington City," *New Hampshire Gazette*, July 19, 1831: 2.

6. Edwin A. Miles, "Andrew Jackson and Senator George Poindexter," *Journal of Southern History* 24, no. 1 (February 1958): 51–66.

7. Samuel Gwin to George Poindexter, October 14, 1831. J.F.H. Claiborne, *Mississippi as a Province, Territory, and State with Biographical Sketches of Eminent Citizens* (Jackson, MS: Power and Barksdale, 1880).

8. "Gwin's Case," *Hartford Times*, August 2, 1832: 2.

9. "Mr. Gwin," *New Hampshire Gazette*, August 7, 1832: 2.

10. Senate, 24th Congress, 1st Session, Public Lands: Volume 8, June 1, 1836: 724–726.
11. Untitled, *Daily National Intelligencer*, March 12, 1833: 4.
12. *Journal of the Senate*, Volume 23, Appendix: 447–455.
13. William Gwin to Andrew Jackson, August 9, 1834. Library of Congress, ALS.
14. Senate, 24th Congress, 1st Session, Public Lands: Volume 8: 746.
15. *The Papers of Jefferson Davis, Volume II, 1841–1846*, edited by James T. McIntosh (Baton Rouge: Louisiana State University Press, 1974): 104–106.
16. James P. Shenton, *Robert John Walker: A Politician from Jackson to Lincoln* (New York and London: Columbia University Press, 1961), 16.
17. Senate, 24th Congress, 1st Session, Public Lands: Volume 8: 746 and 753.
18. *Journal of Executive Proceedings of the Senate* 4 (January 21, 1834): 345.
19. U.S. Congressional Serial Set, 1817–1980, 23rd Congress, 2nd Session, Senate, Report 22, December 15, 1834.
20. *Journal of the Executive Proceedings of the Senate* 4 (May 29, 1834): 412.
21. Ibid., June 17, 1834, 423.
22. Ibid., June 28, 1834, 436.
23. Ibid., June 30, 1834, 441.
24. Andrew Jackson to William Gwin, July 3, 1834. Jackson Papers, Bancroft Library, ALS, University of California at Berkeley.
25. Andrew Jackson to William Gwin, July 3, 1834. Jackson Papers, Bancroft Library, ALS, University of California at Berkeley.
26. William Gwin to Andrew Jackson, August 9, 1834. Library of Congress, ALS.
27. Edwin A. Miles, "Andrew Jackson and Senator George Poindexter," *Journal of Southern History* 24, no. 1 (February 1958): 51–66.
28. Samuel Gwin to Andrew Jackson, June 27, 1835. Andrew Jackson Papers, AJC Library of Congress–46.
29. Samuel Gwin to Andrew Jackson, September 23, 1835. Library of Congress, Andrew Jackson Papers.
30. Andrew Jackson to A. Campbell, July 29, 1835, and R.J. Walker to John Black, March 1, 1834. "Political Incidents," *Niles Weekly Register* 49, no.1, 255: 92–93.
31. Shenton, *Robert John Walker*, 21.
32. "Fatal Duel," *Richmond Enquirer*, February 4, 1836: 3.
33. Henry Stuart Foote, *Casket of Reminiscences* (Washington, D.C.: Chronicle, 1874), 442–443.
34. Untitled, *Rhode Island Republican*. Reprint of a dispatch from Clinton, Mississippi, February 2, 1836: 2.
35. Untitled, *Richmond Enquirer*, June 24, 1836: 4.
36. Andrew Jackson to R.E.W. Earl, September 23, 1836. Per Thomas Coens, associate editor, Papers of Andrew Jackson, University of Tennessee.
37. "Mississippi," *New Hampshire Gazette*, December 19, 1837: 3.
38. Thomas, *Between Two Empires*, 20. Also, *The Papers of Jefferson Davis, Volume II, 1841–1846*, 712.
39. Jefferson Davis to John Jenkins, January 30, 1846. *The Papers of Jefferson Davis, Volume II, 1841–1846*, 424–429.
40. Nichols and Dallas, *The Mystery of the Dallas Papers*, 363.
41. Thomas, *Between Two Empires*, 21.
42. *The Papers of Jefferson Davis, Volume II, 1841–1846*, 261–262.
43. , William Gwin to Andrew Jackson, April 28, 1845. Jackson Papers, Library of Congress.
44. , Andrew Jackson to William Gwin, May 9, 1845. Unpublished Letters of Andrew Jackson, *Overland Monthly* 19, no. 110 (February 1892).
45. Notice of the Proceedings of the Warren County Democratic Convention, June 23, 1845. *The Papers of Jefferson Davis, Volume II, 1841–1846*, 256–263.
46. Notice of the Proceedings of the State Democratic Convention–First Day, July 7, 1845. *The Papers of Jefferson Davis, Volume II, 1841–1846*, 289–294.
47. Notice of the Proceedings of the State Democratic Convention–Second Day, July 8, 1845. *The Papers of Jefferson Davis, Volume II, 1841–1846*, 295–304.
48. *The Papers of Jefferson Davis, Volume II, 1841–1846*, 84.
49. Thomas, *Between Two Empires*, 22.
50. "Affairs in California," *National Intelligencer*, June 28, 1849: 2.
51. "Further on the Gold Mines," *National Intelligencer*, December 11, 1848: 2. Extract of a letter written from Monterrey, CA, on August 29, 1848.
52. Edgar H. Adams, *Private Gold Coinage of California 1849–55: Its History and Its Issues* (Brooklyn: Edgar H. Adams, 1913), xiii.
53. "The State of California," *Georgia Telegraph*, December 1, 1849: 1.
54. Adams, *Private Gold Coinage of California 1849–55:*, vi.
55. "California Convention," *Massachusetts Spy*, December 4, 1849.
56. Charles T. Botts, *Richmond Whig*, December 11, 1849.
57. Francis J. Lippitt, *Reminiscences of Francis J. Lippitt: Written for His Family, His Near Relatives and Intimate Friends*, 79–82.
58. "California Convention," *Massachusetts Spy*, December 4, 1849.
59. "Bayard Taylor's Letter," *New Jersey State Gazette*, December 10, 1849: 1.
60. "Highly Interesting from California," *Weekly Herald* 15, no. 52 (December 29, 1849): 414.
61. "Doings of the Legislature," *Daily Alta California* 1, no. 5 (December 19, 1849).
62. "Interesting from California," *Daily Picayune*, February 4, 1850: 1.
63. "Local Matters," *Daily Alta California* 1, no. 10, December 31, 1849.
64. General W.T. Sherman, *Personal Memoirs of Gen'l W.T. Sherman*, 109–110.
65. "Further from California," *Daily National Intelligencer*, February 8, 1850: 3.

Chapter 23: Lame Ducks

1. William L. Marcy to R.M. Patterson, January 8, 1848[9]. RG 104, Records of the Bureau of the Mint, U.S. Mint at Philadelphia 1791–1936, Peale Correspondence 1829–1886, NC 152, Entry 23, HM 1992, Box 1.
2. Mitchell was a map engraver.
3. C.C Wright to R.M. Patterson, January 24, 1849. RG 104, Records of the Bureau of the Mint, U.S. Mint at Philadelphia 1791–1936, Peale Correspondence 1829–1886, NC 152, Entry 23, HM 1992, Box 1.
4. R.S. McCulloh to R.M. Patterson, January 4, 1849. RG 104, Records of the Bureau of the Mint, U.S. Mint at Philadelphia 1791–1936, Correspondence 1792–1904, General Correspondence 1792–1899, NC 152, Entry 1, NM 1992, Box 28. This was a bound report. It sat in the archives without a crease on it until the author copied it, indicating that this particular document has never been read.
5. *Journal of the House of Representatives* 39 (January 1, 1844): 167. Also, *Journal of the House of Representatives* 41 (January 13, 1846): 252.
6. James I. McKay, January 20, 1844. RG 104, Records of the Bureau of the Mint, U.S. Mint at Philadelphia 1791–1936, Correspondence 1792–1904, General Correspondence 1792–1899, NC 152, Entry 1, NM 1992, Box 23.
7. Bills and Resolutions, House of Representatives, 28th Congress, 1st Session, March 15, 1844.
8. R.M. Patterson to James I. McKay, February 3, 1846. RG 104, Records of the Bureau of the Mint, U.S. Mint at Philadelphia 1791–1936, Correspondence 1792–1904, General Correspondence 1792–1899, NC 152, Entry 1, NM 1992, Box 25.
9. *Journal of the Senate* 40 (January 2, 1849): 94.
10. *Journal of the House of Representatives* 44 (January 15, 1849): 253. Pollock would become director of the Mint under Lincoln in 1861.
11. "Gold Dollar," *Daily Globe*, January 20, 1849: 3.
12. "Gold Dollar," *Washington Union*, January 27, 1849: 3. The article does not identify McKay as its source but only McKay and the other Ways and Means Committee members had access to these coins.
13. R.M. Patterson to James I. McKay, January 30, 1849, in *The U.S. Mint and Coinage*, by Don Taxay, 202.
14. Congressional Globe, 30th Congress, February 20, 1849: 566–568.
15. Bills and Resolutions, Senate, 30th Congress, 2nd Session, February 22, 1849.

16. Statutes at Large and Treaties of the United States of America, December 1, 1845–March 3, 1851: 397–398.

17. Richard Lewis Ashhurst, "William Morris Meredith 1797–1873," *American Law Register* 55, no. 4 (April 1907): 201–243.

18. Miscellany, *Literary Union* 1, no. 8 (May 26, 1849): 120.

19. James B. Longacre, undated manuscript, not before 1854. James Barton Longacre Papers, Philadelphia Library Company, Box 2.

20. James B. Longacre to W.M. Meredith, February 18, 1850. James Barton Longacre Papers, Philadelphia Library Company, Box 2.

21. James B. Longacre to W.M. Meredith, March 1, 1850. James Barton Longacre Papers, Philadelphia Library Company, Box 2. Also, James B. Longacre to James Ross Snowden (?), August 21, 1858. James Barton Longacre Papers, Philadelphia Library Company, Box 2. Longacre states in this letter that the $3 gold piece design of 1854 was the first opportunity of any practical expression of his own. It would have been out of character for Patterson to give Longacre complete artistic license to develop the head of Liberty design independently. Patterson must be given at least some, if not all, of the credit for the selection of *Venus Accroupie* as the basis for this design.

22. R.M. Patterson to W.M. Meredith, March 19, 1849. RG 104, Records of the Bureau of the Mint, U.S. Mint at Philadelphia 1791–1936, Correspondence 1792–1904, General Correspondence 1792–1899, NC 152, Entry 1, NM 1992, Box 28.

23. James B. Longacre to R.M Patterson, undated draft, late January 1850. James Barton Longacre Papers, Philadelphia Library Company, Box 2.

24. James B. Longacre to W.M. Meredith, February 18, 1850. James Barton Longacre Papers, Philadelphia Library Company, Box 2.

25. Diary entries, April 30–May 8, 1849. James Barton Longacre Papers, Philadelphia Library Company, Box 4.

26. James B. Longacre to John C. Calhoun, May 8, 1849. James Barton Longacre Papers, Philadelphia Library Company, Box 2.

27. Anonymous to R.M. Patterson, May 3, 1849. RG 104, Records of the Bureau of the Mint, U.S. Mint at Philadelphia 1791–1936, Correspondence 1792–1904, General Correspondence 1792–1899, NC 152, Entry 1, NM 1992, Box 28.

28. "The Gold Dollar," *Washington Union*, May 6, 1849: 2.

29. Untitled, *Washington Union*, May 19, 1849: 3.

30. "Letter to the Editor," *Turf, Agriculture, Field Sports, Etc.*, July 21, 1849.

31. Miscellany, *Literary Union* 1, no. 8 (May 26, 1849): 120.

32. R.M. Patterson to W.M. Meredith, March 12, 1850. RG 104, Records of the Bureau of the Mint, U.S. Mint at Philadelphia 1791–1936, Correspondence 1792–1904, General Correspondence 1792–1899, NC 152, Entry 1, NM 1992, Box 29.

33. "The Gold Dollar," *Washington Union*, May 31, 1849: 3.

34. Untitled, *Scientific American* 4, no. 43 (July 14, 1849): 339.

35. R.S. McCulloh, *Memorial to the Congress of the United States, An Investigation and Legislation in Relation to the New Method for Refining Gold*, February 24, 1851.

36. James C. Booth Rebuttal, Letter to Millard Fillmore, University of Michigan Library, February 17, 1853.

37. R.M. Patterson to George Crawford, July 5, 1849. RG 104, Records of the Bureau of the Mint. U.S. Mint at Philadelphia 1791–1936, Peale Correspondence 1829–1886, NC 152, Entry 23, HM 1992, Box 1.

38. R.S. McCulloh to Thomas Corwin, January 4, 1853. *The Proceedings of the Late Director of the Mint in Relation to the Official Misconduct of Franklin Peale, Esq., Chief Coiner, and Other Abuses in the Mint, Reviewed by R.S. McCulloh, Formerly the Melter and Refiner of the Mint*, Princeton, New Jersey, July 11, 1853.

39. James C. Booth Rebuttal, Letter to Millard Fillmore, University of Michigan Library, February 17, 1853.

40. *The Proceedings of the Late Director of the Mint in Relation to the Official Misconduct of Franklin Peale, Esq.*

41. C.C. Wright to R.M. Patterson, August 11, 1849. RG 104, Records of the Bureau of the Mint, U.S. Mint at Philadelphia 1791–1936, Peale Correspondence 1829–1886, NC 152, Entry 23, HM 1992, Box 1.

42. R.S. McCulloh to R.M. Patterson, August 23, 1849. RG 104, Records of the Bureau of the Mint, U.S. Mint at Philadelphia 1791–1936, Peale Correspondence 1829–1886, NC 152, Entry 23, HM 1992, Box 1.

43. R.M. Patterson to George Crawford, August 25, 1849. RG 104, Records of the Bureau of the Mint. U.S. Mint at Philadelphia 1791–1936, Peale Correspondence 1829–1886, NC 152, Entry 23, HM 1992, Box 1.

44. *The Proceedings of the Late Director of the Mint in Relation to the Official Misconduct of Franklin Peale, Esq.*

45. McCulloh, *Memorial to the Congress of the United States.*

46. R.M. Patterson to W.M. Meredith, October 26, 1849. RG 104, Records of the Bureau of the Mint, U.S. Mint at Philadelphia 1791–1936, Correspondence 1792–1904, General Correspondence 1792–1899, NC 152, Entry 1, NM 1992, Box 28.

47. R.M. Patterson to W.M. Meredith, September 17, 1849. RG 104, Records of the Bureau of the Mint, U.S. Mint at Philadelphia 1791–1936, Correspondence 1792–1904, General Correspondence 1792–1899, NC 152, Entry 1, NM 1992, Box 28.

48. R.M. Patterson to W.M. Meredith, October 8, 1849. RG 104, Records of the Bureau of the Mint, U.S. Mint at Philadelphia 1791–1936, Correspondence 1792–1904, General Correspondence 1792–1899, NC 152, Entry 1, NM 1992, Box 28.

49. McCulloh, *Memorial to the Congress of the United States.*

50. James C. Booth Rebuttal, Letter to Millard Fillmore, University of Michigan Library, February 17, 1853.

51. James C. Booth Rebuttal.

52. *Proceedings of the American Philosophical Society* 27, no. 131 (November 1889): 161.

53. "The Explosion at Philadelphia," *Times Picayune*, May 23, 1851: 2. Also, *Proceedings of the American Philosophical Society* 5, no. 46 (June 20, 1851): 206.

54. U.S. Congressional Series Set, 1817–1980, 31st Congress, 1st Session, House of Representatives, Report 31, Table C, January 28, 1850.

Chapter 24: Something of Value

1. J.B. Longacre to W.M. Meredith, February 18, 1850. James Barton Longacre Papers, Philadelphia Library Company.

2. J.B. Longacre to W.M. Meredith, March 1, 1850. James Barton Longacre Papers, Philadelphia Library Company.

3. Early draft of J.B. Longacre to R.M. Patterson, January 30, 1850. James Barton Longacre Papers, Philadelphia Library Company.

4. The Eckfeldt lineage is courtesy of Nancy Oliver and Richard Kelly.

5. J.B. Longacre to G.N. Eckert, November 11, 1851. James Barton Longacre Papers, Philadelphia Library Company.

6. J.B. Longacre to R.M. Patterson, January 30, 1850. James Barton Longacre Papers, Library Company of Philadelphia.

7. Undated statement (1851) from Franklin Peale to G.N. Eckert. James Barton Longacre Papers, Philadelphia Library Company.

8. Longacre diary, November 6, 1849. James Barton Longacre Papers, Philadelphia Library Company.

9. J.B. Longacre to W.M. Meredith, February 18, 1850. James Barton Longacre Papers, Philadelphia Library Company.

10. R.S. McCulloh to J.B. Longacre, September 30, 1856. James Barton Longacre Papers, Philadelphia Library Company.

11. Longacre diary, December 20, 1849. James Barton Longacre Papers, Philadelphia Library Company. Cross collected pay for six weeks and two days.

12. J.B. Longacre to R.M. Patterson, January 30, 1850. James Barton Longacre Papers, Library Company of Philadelphia.

13. Longacre diary, December 22, 1849. James Barton Longacre Papers, Philadelphia Library Company.

14. As quoted from United States Gold Coins An Illustrated History, Q. David Bowers, Page 299, R. M. Patterson to William Meredith, December 22, 1849.

15. Undated statement (1851) from Franklin Peale to G.N. Eckert. James Barton Longacre Papers, Philadelphia Library Company. The letter from Patterson to Peale on December 24, 1849, is transcribed in the text of Peale's statement to Eckert.

16. As quoted from United States Gold Coins An Illustrated History, Q. David Bowers, Page 299, R. M. Patterson to William Meredith, December 25, 1849.

17. J.B. Longacre to R.M. Patterson, January 30, 1850. James Barton Longacre Papers, Library Company of Philadelphia.

18. Roger W. Burdette notes the following: "In addition to improper annealing, the gold might have been contaminated with small amounts of antimony, lead, or iron, which would make the metal hard and brittle." (From correspondence with the publisher.)

19. RG 104, Records of the Bureau of the Mint, Records of the U.S. Mint a Philadelphia, Operating Records, Records Relating to Bars, Coins, and Coinage, Chief Coiner's Accounts Concerning the Working of Gold 1847–1872, NC 152, Entry 51, Box 1, Double Eagles, December 1849: 82.

20. J.B. Longacre's Rebuttal of Franklin Peale's Charges, draft of August 1853. James Barton Longacre Papers, Library Company of Philadelphia.

21. Undated statement (1851) from
Franklin Peale to G.N. Eckert. James Barton Longacre Papers, Philadelphia Library Company.

22. R.M. Patterson to C.C. Wright, December 29, 1849. RG 104, Records of the Bureau of the Mint, U.S. Mint at Philadelphia 1791–1936, Correspondence 1792–1904, General Correspondence 1792–1899, NC 152, Entry 1, NM 1992, Box 28.

23. C.C. Wright to R.M. Patterson, February 12, 1850. RG 104, Records of the Bureau of the Mint, U.S. Mint at Philadelphia 1791–1936, Correspondence 1792–1904, General Correspondence 1792–1899, NC 152, Entry 1, NM 1992, Box 29.

24. Longacre diary, January 9–11, 1850. James Barton Longacre Papers, Philadelphia Library Company.

25. J.B. Longacre to W.M. Meredith, February 18, 1850. James Barton Longacre Papers, Philadelphia Library Company.

26. J.B. Longacre to G.N. Eckert, November 13, 1851. James Barton Longacre Papers, Philadelphia Library Company.

27. J.B. Longacre to R.M. Patterson, January 30, 1850. James Barton Longacre Papers, Philadelphia Library Company.

28. Undated statement (1851) from Franklin Peale to G.N. Eckert. James Barton Longacre Papers, Philadelphia Library Company.

29. J.B. Longacre to R.M. Patterson, January 30, 1850. James Barton Longacre Papers, Philadelphia Library Company.

30. J.B. Longacre to R.S. McCulloh, September 2, 1851. James Barton Longacre Papers, Philadelphia Library Company.

31. J.B. Longacre to W.M. Meredith, February 12, 1850. James Barton Longacre Papers, Philadelphia Library Company.

32. Longacre diary, February 12, 1850. James Barton Longacre Papers, Philadelphia Library Company.

33. J.B. Longacre to Thomas Corwin, October 3, 1850. James Barton Longacre Papers, Philadelphia Library Company.

34. J.B. Longacre to R.S. McCulloh, September 2, 1851. James Barton Longacre Papers, Philadelphia Library Company.

35. J.B. Longacre to Thomas Corwin, October 3, 1850. James Barton Longacre Papers, Philadelphia Library Company.

36. J.B. Longacre to W.M. Meredith, February 18, 1850. James Barton Longacre Papers, Philadelphia Library Company.

37. J.B. Longacre to Mr. Humphreys, March 4, 1861. James Barton Longacre Papers, Philadelphia Library Company. R.S. McCulloh related this conversation second hand to Longacre.

38. C.C. Wright to R.M. Patterson. RG 104, Records of the Bureau of the Mint, U.S. Mint at Philadelphia 1791–1936, Correspondence 1792–1904, General Correspondence 1792–1899, NC 152, Entry 1, NM 1992, Box 29.

39. J.B. Longacre to W.M. Meredith, March 1, 1850. James Barton Longacre Papers, Philadelphia Library Company.

40. R.M. Patterson to W.M. Meredith, March 12, 1850. RG 104, Records of the Bureau of the Mint, U.S. Mint at Philadelphia 1791–1936, Correspondence 1792–1904, General Correspondence 1792–1899, NC 152, Entry 1, NM 1992, Box 29.

41. Administrator's sale, January 21, 1870 James Barton Longacre Papers, Philadelphia Library Company: 8. The whereabouts of this piece today is unknown.

42. Untitled, *The Farmer's Cabinet*, March 28, 1850: 2.

43. "Commercial and Money Matters," *New York Tribune*, March 14, 1850: 3.

44. "Twenty-Dollar Gold Pieces," *Pittsfield Sun*, March 21, 1850: 2.

45. Untitled, *Gloucester Telegraph*, March 20, 1850: 2.

46. R.M. Patterson to W.M. Meredith, April 1, 1850. RG 104, Records of the Bureau of the Mint, U.S. Mint at Philadelphia 1791–1936, Correspondence 1792–1904, General Correspondence 1792–1899, NC 152, Entry 1, NM 1992, Box 29.

47. Longacre diary, April 6–June 2, 1850. James Barton Longacre Papers, Philadelphia Library Company.

48. Franklin Peale to R.M. Patterson, September 10, 1850. RG 104, Records of the Bureau of the Mint, U.S. Mint at Philadelphia 1791–1936, Peale Correspondence 1829–1886, NC 152, Entry 23, HM 1992, Box 1. Also, Franklin Peale to R.M. Patterson, January 16, 1850. *The Proceedings of the Late Director of the Mint in Relation to the Official Misconduct of Franklin Peale, Esq.*.

49. Statutes at Large, 31st Congress, 1st Session, May 15, 1850: 426.

50. Bills and Resolutions, House of Representatives, 31st Congress, 1st Session, H.R. 118, February 25, 1850.

51. Senate Documents, RG 46, Sen. 31A-F5, W.M. Meredith to Hannibal Hamlin, March 22, 1850.

Chapter 25: Bad Chemistry

1. James C. Booth to R.M. Patterson, September 10, 1850. RG 104, Records of the Bureau of the Mint, U.S. Mint at Philadelphia 1791–1936, Correspondence 1792–1904, General Correspondence 1792–1899, NC 152, Entry 1, NM 1992, Box 30.

2. "Commercial Chronicle and Review," *Merchants' Magazine and Commercial Review*, March 1, 1850: 319.

3. James C. Booth Rebuttal, Letter; Millard Fillmore, February 17, 1853.

4. James C. Booth Rebuttal.

5. R.S. McCulloh, *Memorial to the Congress of the United States, An Investigation and Legislation in Relation to the New Method for Refining Gold*, February 24, 1851.

6. George M. Dallas to Sophia Dallas, January 24, 1849. Diary and Letters of George M. Dallas, December 4, 1848–March 6, 1849, Historical Society of Pennsylvania.

7. *Journal of the Senate* 41 (December 24, 1849): 25.

8. Lately Thomas, *Between Two Empires, The Life Story of California's First Senator William McKendree Gwin*, 63–64.

9. *Journal of the Senate* 41 (January 4, 1850): 54.

10. Ibid., January 7, 1850, 58.

11. *Journal of the House of Representatives* 45 (January 3, 1850): 212.

12. Bills and Resolutions, H.R. 24, 31st Congress, 1st Session, February 4, 1850.

13. *Journal of the Senate* 41 (May 9, 1850): 328.

14. Congressional Globe, House of Representatives, 31st Congress, 1st Session, May 22, 1850: 1034.

15. Bills and Resolutions, House of Representatives, 31st Congress, 1st Session, H.R. 294, May 22, 1850.

16. Congressional Globe, Senate, 31st Congress, 1st Session, May 24, 1850: 1302.

17. New York Branch Mint to Accompany H.R. 294, September 14, 1850. RG 233, House of Representatives, 31st Congress, 1st Session, Report 490.

18. Congressional Globe, Senate, 31st Congress, 1st Session, May 27, 1850: 1072–1074.

19. Congressional Globe, Senate, 31st Congress, 1st Session, May 29, 1850: 1098–1105.

20. Congressional Globe, Senate, 31st Congress, 1st Session, May 31, 1850: 1108–1109.

21. Bills and Resolutions, S.24, 31st Congress, 1st Session, July 22, 1850.
22. *Journal of the Senate* 41 (July 17, 1850): 453.
23. Congressional Globe, Senate, 32nd Congress, 2nd Session, December 29, 1852: 43–47.
24. Bills and Resolutions, S. 355, 31st Congress, 1st Session, September 19, 1850.
25. Bills and Resolutions, S. 356, 31st Congress, 1st Session, September 19, 1850.
26. Over the years the silver requirement had been reduced from three pounds per one pound of gold to two pounds.
27. *Journal of the Senate* 41 (July 6, 1850): 438.
28. Franklin Peale to Titian Peale, July 9, 1850. Peale Family Papers, Series IX-A, Correspondence of Benjamin Franklin Peale, American Philosophical Library, courtesy of the University of Oregon.
29. James C. Booth, *Letter to the Honorable Millard Fillmore, President of the United States, In Reply to the Charges of Professor R.S. McCulloh*, January 17, 1853.
30. RG 46, Records of the U.S. Senate, SEN 31 A-H 5.1, January 22, 1850–February 15, 1850.
31. James C. Booth and Henry M. Morfit to W.M. Meredith, September 9, 1850. RG 104, Records of the Bureau of the Mint, U.S. Mint at Philadelphia 1791–1936, Correspondence 1792–1904, General Correspondence 1792–1899, NC 152, Entry 1, NM 1992, Box 30.
32. McCulloh, *Memorial to the Congress of the United States.*
33. James C. Booth to R.M. Patterson, September 11, 1850. RG 104, Records of the Bureau of the Mint, U.S. Mint at Philadelphia 1791–1936, Correspondence 1792–1904, General Correspondence 1792–1899, NC 152, Entry 1, NM 1992, Box 30.
34. Booth, *Letter to the Honorable Millard Fillmore.*
35. Joseph R. Chandler to R.M. Patterson, September 7, 1850. RG 104, Records of the Bureau of the Mint, U.S. Mint at Philadelphia 1791–1936, Correspondence 1792–1904, General Correspondence 1792–1899, NC 152, Entry 1, NM 1992, Box 30.
36. Jacob Eckfeldt and William E. Dubois to R.M. Patterson, September 9, 1850. RG 104, Records of the Bureau of the Mint, U.S. Mint at Philadelphia 1791–1936, Correspondence 1792–1904, General Correspondence 1792–1899, NC 152, Entry 1, NM 1992, Box 30.
37. *Journal of the Senate* 41 (September 11, 1850): 622.
38. James C. Booth to R.M. Patterson, September 11, 1850. RG 104, Records of the Bureau of the Mint, U.S. Mint at Philadelphia 1791–1936, Correspondence 1792–1904, General Correspondence 1792–1899, NC 152, Entry 1, NM 1992, Box 30.
39. U.S. Congressional Series Set, 1817–1980, 31st Congress, 1st Session, House of Representatives, Report 490, September 14, 1850.
40. *Journal of the House of Representatives* 45 (September 28, 1850): 1582.
41. *Journal of the Senate* 41 (September 28, 1850): 698–699.
42. Booth, *Letter to the Honorable Millard Fillmore.*
43. Statutes at Large, 31st Congress, 1st Session, September 30, 1850: 531.
44. Kagin, *Private Gold Coinage and Patterns of the United States*, 98.
45. Edgar H. Adams, *Private Gold Coinage of California 1849–55, Its History and its Issues*, 58–62.
46. Ibid., 73–74, as quoted from the April 17, 1851, issue of the *Pacific News.*
47. Diary entry for April 17, 1850. James Barton Longacre Papers, Philadelphia Library Company, Box 4.
48. Adams, *Private Gold Coinage of California 1849–55*, 71–73.
49. Kagin, *Private Gold Coinage and Patterns of the United States*, 87.
50. Adams, *Private Gold Coinage of California 1849–55*, 13–17.
51. Ibid,, 3–12.
52. Ibid., 18–19.
53. Ibid., 18.
54. Ibid., 19.
55. Ibid., 21. Taken from the editorial page of the January 30, 1851, *Alta California.*
56. Statues at Large, 31st Congress, 1st Session, September 30, 1850: 531.

Chapter 26: Besieged

1. Wainwright, *History of the Philadelphia National Bank*, 70.
2. J.B. Trevor to J.R. Chandler, September 23, 1850. RG 56, Records of the Department of the Treasury, Entry 288, Applications for Positions as Assistant Treasurers and Mint Officers 1836–1898 and 1902–1904, James Ross Snowden, Box 26.
3. Wainwright, *History Philadelphia National Bank*, 241.
4. J.B. Longacre to Thomas Corwin, October 3, 1850. James Barton Longacre Papers, Philadelphia Library Company, Box 2.
5. R.S. McCulloh to J.B. Longacre, October 12, 1850. James Barton Longacre Papers, Philadelphia Library Company, Box 2.
6. Thomas Corwin to J.B. Longacre, October 15, 1850. Peale Family Papers, Series IX–A, Correspondence of Benjamin Franklin Peale, American Philosophical Library, courtesy of the University of Oregon.
7. J.B. Longacre to Thomas Corwin, October 17, 1850. James Barton Longacre Papers, Philadelphia Library Company, Box 2.
8. R.S. McCulloh to J.B. Longacre, October 19, 1850. James Barton Longacre Papers, Philadelphia Library Company, Box 2.
9. Petition to Thomas Corwin, October 19, 1850. RG 56, Records of the Department of the Treasury, Applications for Positions as Assistant Treasurers and Mint Officers 1836–1898 and 1902–1904, Robert Maskell Patterson, Entry 288, Box 25.
10. W.M. Gwin to R.M. Patterson, October, 1850. Congressional Globe, Senate, 32nd Congress, 2nd Session, December 29, 1852: 43–47.
11. McCulloh, *Memorial to the Congress of the United States.*
12. R.S. McCulloh to J.B. Longacre, October 12, 1850. James Barton Longacre Papers, Philadelphia Library Company, Box 2.
13. C.C. Wright to R.M. Patterson, November 5, 1850. RG 104, Records of the Bureau of the Mint, U.S. Mint at Philadelphia 1791–1936, Correspondence 1792–1904, General Correspondence 1792–1899, NC 152, Entry 1, NM 1992, Box 30.
14. Thomas Corwin to R.M. Patterson, November 18, 1850. Peale Family Papers, Series IX–A, Correspondence of Benjamin Franklin Peale, American Philosophical Library, courtesy of the University of Oregon.
15. *Journal of the Senate* 44 (January 6, 1853): 77.
16. This computation assumes that the raw bullion had a silver content of 11 percent. The refined bullion prior to the change was assumed to be 3 percent, up from the more traditional level of 2 percent. Booth had stated in a testimonial that the silver content had increased a modest amount over the summer of 1850 without giving specifics.
17. R.M. Patterson to Thomas Corwin, November 18, 1850. Peale Family Papers, Series IX–A, Correspondence of Benjamin Franklin Peale, American Philosophical Library, courtesy of the University of Oregon.
18. R.S. McCulloh to J.B. Longacre, November 18, 1850. James Barton Longacre Papers, Philadelphia Library Company, Box 2.
19. Congressional Globe, 31st Congress, 2nd Session, Report of the Secretary of the Treasury, December 31. 1850: 25. Corwin erroneously refers to the process as a new method of assaying.
20. George N. Eckert to Thomas Corwin, October 14, 1851. RG 104, Records of the Bureau of the Mint, U.S. Mint at Philadelphia 1791–1936, Correspondence 1792–1904, General Correspondence 1792–1899, NC 152, Entry 1, NM 1992, Box 31. Eckert quotes the letter from Patterson to Corwin of March 18, 1851.
21. *Report Made to the Hon. Thomas Corwin Secretary of the Treasury by Prof. R.S. McCulloh on his Operations at the U.S. Mint in Refining California Gold by his Zinc Method* (Washington: Gideon, 1852).
22. Booth, *Letter to the Honorable Millard Fillmore*: 2.
23. McCulloh, Exhibits 1–70, *Memorial to the Congress of the United States.*
24. U.S. Congressional Series Set, 1817–1980, 31st Congress, 2nd Session, House of Representatives, Report 50, March 3, 1851. Annual Report of the Mint and its branches, January 27, 1851.

Chapter 27: Barbarians at the Gates

1. *Journal of the Senate* 42 (December 2, 1850): 13, December 2, 1850.
2. *Journal of the House of Representatives* 46 (December 16, 1850): 59.
3. Congressional Globe, House of Representatives, 31st Congress, 2nd Session, January 13, 1851: 226.
4. "Silver Coins," *Philadelphia Inquirer*, January 11, 1851: 2.
5. Congressional Globe, House of Representatives, 31st Congress, 2nd Session, January 29, 1851: 367.
6. Congressional Globe, House of Representatives, 31st Congress, 2nd Session, January 30–31, 1851: 380–400.
7. Congressional Globe, House of Representatives, 31st Congress, 2nd Session, February 4, 1851: 412–423.
8. Bills and Resolutions, Senate, 31st Congress, 2nd Session, S.455, February 19, 1851.
9. Congressional Globe, Senate, 31st Congress, 2nd Session, February 19, 1851: 611.
10. R.M. Patterson, March 1851. RG 104, Records of the Bureau of the Mint, U.S. Mint at Philadelphia 1791–1936, General Correspondence 1792–1899, NC 152, Entry 1, NM 1992, Box 31.
11. Bills and Resolutions, Senate, 31st Congress, 1st Session, S.230, May 13, 1850.
12. Bills and Resolutions, Senate, 31st Congress, 2nd Session, H.R. 351, January 20, 1851.
13. Statues at Large, 31st Congress, 2nd Session, March 3, 1851: 591.
14. R.M. Patterson, March 1851. RG 104, Records of the Bureau of the Mint, U.S. Mint at Philadelphia 1791–1936, General Correspondence 1792–1899, NC 152, Entry 1, NM 1992, Box 31.
15. R.M. Patterson to Thomas Corwin, March 8, 1851. RG 104, Records of the Bureau of the Mint, U.S. Mint at Philadelphia 1791–1936, General Correspondence 1792–1899, NC 152, Entry 1, NM 1992, Box 31.
16. W.L. Hodge to R.M. Patterson, March 11, 1851. RG 104, Records of the Bureau of the Mint, U.S. Mint at Philadelphia 1791–1936, General Correspondence 1792–1899, NC 152, Entry 1, NM 1992, Box 31.
17. R.M. Patterson to W.L. Hodge, March 27, 1851. RG 104, Records of the Bureau of the Mint, U.S. Mint at Philadelphia 1791–1936, General Correspondence 1792–1899, NC 152, Entry 1, NM 1992, Box 31.

Chapter 28: Sacked!

1. R.S. McCulloh to Thomas Corwin, January 4, 1851. *Memorial to the Congress of the United States.*
2. Bancroft Library, University of California, William M. Gwin Papers 1833–1897, Box 2, William M. Gwin, March, April 1851, extracted from the Corwin collection, Library of Congress, Volume 4: 123 and 294.
3. J.B. Trevor to Thomas Corwin, February 11, 1851. Thomas Corwin Papers, Library of Congress, Manuscript Division, book 6, leaf 23.
4. "Manufacture of Iron," *American Quarterly Register and Magazine*, May 1848: 101. Written by Stephen Colwell.
5. J.B. Trevor to Thomas Corwin, March 5, 1851. RG 56, Records of the Department of the Treasury, Applications for Positions as Assistant Treasurers and Mint Officers 1836–1898 and 1902–1904, Entry 288, Box 21.
6. RG 56, Records of the Department of the Treasury, Applications for Positions as Assistant Treasurers and Mint Officers 1836–1898 and 1902–1904, Entry 288, Box 21, J.B. Trevor to Thomas Corwin, March 11, 1851.
7. J.B. Trevor to Jonathan Biddle, March 12, 1851. RG 56, Records of the Department of the Treasury, Applications for Positions as Assistant Treasurers and Mint Officers 1836–1898 and 1902–1904, Entry 288, Box 21.
8. R.M. Patterson to Millard Fillmore, March 15, 1851. Patterson Family Papers 1809–1876, American Philosophical Society, P274.2.
9. R.M. Patterson to Millard Fillmore, April 7, 1851. Patterson Family Papers 1809–1876, American Philosophical Society, P274.2.
10. William A. Kein to Ferdinand Hayes, May 6, 1851. RG 56, Records of the Department of the Treasury, Applications for Positions as Assistant Treasurers and Mint Officers 1836–1898 and 1902–1904, Entry 288, Box 21.
11. Franklin Peale to the Hutchinsons, December 29, 1846. Patterson Family Papers 1809–1876, American Philosophical Society, P274.2.
12. Col. Jno. Swift to Francis Smith, January 7, 1847. Patterson Family Papers 1809–1876, American Philosophical Society, P274.2.
13. J.B. Trevor to John McLean, forwarded to Millard Fillmore, April 12, 1851. RG 56, Records of the Department of the Treasury, Applications for Positions as Assistant Treasurers and Mint Officers 1836–1898 and 1902–1904, Entry 288, Box 21.
14. Stephen Colwell to Thomas Corwin, April 15, 1851. RG 56, Records of the Department of the Treasury, Applications for Positions as Assistant Treasurers and Mint Officers 1836–1898 and 1902–1904, Entry 288, Box 21.
15. Samuel Moore to Millard Fillmore, April 16, 1851. RG 56, Records of the Department of the Treasury, Applications for Positions as Assistant Treasurers and Mint Officers 1836–1898 and 1902–1904, Entry 288, Box 21.
16. George N. Eckert to Millard Fillmore, April 25, 1851. RG 56, Records of the Department of the Treasury, Applications for Positions as Assistant Treasurers and Mint Officers 1836–1898 and 1902–1904, Entry 288, Box 21.
17. Stephen Colwell to Thomas Corwin, May 9, 1851. RG 56, Records of the Department of the Treasury, Applications for Positions as Assistant Treasurers and Mint Officers 1836–1898 and 1902–1904, Entry 288, Box 21.
18. Stephen Colwell to Thomas Corwin, May 9, 1851. Library of Congress, Manuscripts Division, Thomas Corwin Papers, Volume 8, Leaf 28.
19. J.B. Trevor to Millard Fillmore, May 23, 1851. RG 56, Records of the Department of the Treasury, Applications for Positions as Assistant Treasurers and Mint Officers 1836–1898 and 1902–1904, Entry 288, Box 21.
20. "Interesting from Washington," *Cleveland Plain Dealer*, June 10, 1851.
21. James C. Booth to R.M. Patterson, May 2, 1851. RG 104, Records of the Bureau of the Mint, U.S. Mint at Philadelphia 1791–1936, Correspondence 1792–1904, General Correspondence 1792–1899, NC 152, Entry 1, NM 1992, Box 31.

Chapter 29: J'accuse

1. *The Proceedings of the Late Director of the Mint in Relation to the Official Misconduct of Franklin Peale, Esq.*
2. Wainwright, *History of the Philadelphia National Bank*, 99–100.
3. W.H.D. to James Thompson, September 24, 1850. RG 56, Records of the Department of the Treasury, Applications for Positions as Assistant Treasurers and Mint Officers 1836–1898 and 1902–1904, Entry 288, Box 26.
4. *Journal of the House of Representatives* 46 (February 25, 1851): 343.
5. R.S. McCulloh to Millard Fillmore, August 1, 1851. *The Proceedings of the Late Director of the Mint in Relation to the Official Misconduct of Franklin Peale, Esq.*
6. George Eckert to Thomas Corwin, October 14, 1851. RG 104, Records of the Bureau of the Mint, U.S. Mint at Philadelphia 1791–1936, Correspondence 1792–1904, General Correspondence 1792–1899, NC 152, Entry 1, NM 1992, Box 31.
7. Taxay, *The U.S. Mint and Coinage*, 178–179.
8. *The Proceedings of the Late Director of the Mint in Relation to the Official Misconduct of Franklin Peale, Esq.*
9. "The Assay Office," *Alta California*, April 14, 1851: 3.
10. "California Gold," *Alta California*, August 1, 1851: 4.
11. Kagin, *Private Gold Coinage and Patterns of the United States*, 146–150.
12. Miscellaneous, *Bankers' Magazine and Statistical Register*, June 1852: 1008. The magazine gives the date of the letter as April 23, 1851. However, it identifies the director as George Eckert. Given the publishing date, it can be assumed that the date of this letter is stated incorrectly in the magazine and should be April 23, 1852.

13. Kagin, *Private Gold Coinage and Patterns of the United States*, 146.

Chapter 30: Mr. Wizard

1. United States Mint, Philadelphia. *Gleason's Pictorial Drawing-Room Companion*, July 17, 1852, 40.
2. *The Proceedings of the Late Director of the Mint in Relation to the Official Misconduct of Franklin Peale, Esq.*
3. "The Philadelphia Mint—Refining Gold with Zinc—its Troubles and Trials," *Scientific American*, 29.
4. Actually, gold melts at 1,948 °F and zinc at 787 °F. However, Booth's basic point remains correct.
5. Booth, *Letter to the Honorable Millard Fillmore.*
6. Ibid.
7. George Eckert to U.S. Patent Office, March 4, 1852. RG 104, Records of the Bureau of the Mint, U.S. Mint at Philadelphia 1791–1936, Correspondence 1792–1904, General Correspondence 1792–1899, NC 152, Entry 1, NM 1992, Box 32.
8. U.S. Congressional Series Set, 1817–1980, 32nd Congress, 1st Session, House of Representatives, Report 59, February 12, 1852.
9. *Report Made to the Hon. Thomas Corwin Secretary of the Treasury, Prof. R.S. McCulloh of His Operations at the U.S. Mint in Refining California Gold by His Zinc Method*, August 3, 1852.
10. George Eckert to Thomas Corwin, June 21, 1852. RG 104, Records of the Bureau of the Mint, U.S. Mint at Philadelphia 1791–1936, Correspondence 1792–1904, General Correspondence 1792–1899, NC 152, Entry 1, NM 1992, Box 32.
11. McCulloh, *Report Made to the Hon. Thomas Corwin.*
12. Taxay, *The U.S. Mint and Coinage*, 186.
13. Franklin Peale to George Eckert, September 2, 1852. Peale Family Papers, Series IX–A, Correspondence of Benjamin Franklin Peale, American Philosophical Library, courtesy of the University of Oregon.
14. R.S. McCulloh to George Eckert, November 16, 1852. RG 104, Records of the Bureau of the Mint, U.S. Mint at Philadelphia 1791–1936, Correspondence 1792–1904, General Correspondence 1792–1899, NC 152, Entry 1, NM 1992, Box 33.
15. R.S. McCulloh to George Eckert, November 26, 1852. RG 104, Records of the Bureau of the Mint, U.S. Mint at Philadelphia 1791–1936, Correspondence 1792–1904, General Correspondence 1792–1899, NC 152, Entry 1, NM 1992, Box 33.
16. The Philadelphia Mint—Refining Gold with Zinc—its Troubles and Trials, *Scientific American*, 29.
17. The Philadelphia Mint—Refining Gold, Its Troubles and Trials, *Scientific American*, April 25, 1853: 250.
18. J.B. Longacre to George Eckert, November 10, 1851. J.B. Longacre Papers, Philadelphia Library Company.
19. W.L. Hodge to George Eckert, December 13, 1851. RG 104, Records of the Bureau of the Mint, U.S. Mint at Philadelphia 1791–1936, Correspondence 1792–1904, General Correspondence 1792–1899, NC 152, Entry 1, NM 1992, Box 32.
20. Franklin Peale to George Eckert, January 7, 1852. RG 104, Records of the Bureau of the Mint, U.S. Mint at Philadelphia 1791–1936, Correspondence 1792–1904, General Correspondence 1792–1899, NC 152, Entry 1, NM 1992, Box 32.
21. Franklin Peale to George Eckert, April 15, 1852. *The Proceedings of the Late Director of the Mint in Relation to the Official Misconduct of Franklin Peale, Esq.*
22. Patterson Family Papers 1809–1876, American Philosophical Society, P274.2,
Robert Patterson to Robley Dunglison, May 4, 1852.
23. *The Proceedings of the Late Director of the Mint in Relation to the Official Misconduct of Franklin Peale, Esq.*
24. R.S. McCulloh to J.B. Longacre, September 25, 1852. Philadelphia Library Company, J.B. Longacre Papers.

Chapter 31: Hardball Politics

1. *Journal of the Senate* 43 (December 4, 1851): 32.
2. Ibid., December 8, 1851, 40.
3. Ibid., December 15, 1851, 62.
4. Ibid., December 9, 1851, 45.
5. Bills and Resolutions, Senate, 32nd Congress, 1st Session, S.21, December 11, 1851.
6. *Journal of the House of Representatives* 47 (December 18, 1851): 118.
7. Ibid., January 5, 1852, 165,.
8. *Journal of the Senate* 43 (February 3, 1852): 171.
9. Ibid., February 9, 1852, 185.
10. Ibid., February 23, 1852, 224.
11. Congressional Globe, House of Representatives, 32nd Congress, 1st Session, April 12, 1852: 1051.
12. Theodore Adams to Thomas Corwin, March 9, 1852. Library of Congress, Manuscript Division, Thomas Corwin Papers, Volume 15, Number 201.
13. Congressional Globe, House of Representatives, 32nd Congress, 1st Session, June 14, 1852: 1564–1565; June 15, 1852: 1581–1586.
14. Congressional Globe, House of Representatives, 32nd Congress, 1st Session, June 22, 1852: 1596–1599.
15. Statutes at Large, 32nd Congress, 1st Session, July 3, 1852: 11–12.
16. *Journal of the Executive Proceedings of the Senate* 8 (August 30, 1852): 442.
17. Statutes at Large, 32nd Congress, 1st Session, August 30, 1852: 96.
18. Congressional Globe, Senate, 32nd Congress, 2nd Session, December 29, 1852: 43.
19. Statutes at Large, 32nd Congress, 1st Session, August 30, 1852: 97–98.
20. Untitled, *Daily National Intelligencer*, August 11, 1852, 3.
21. Curtis Perry and Ward to Thomas Corwin, September 3, 1852. Library of Congress, Manuscript Division, Thomas Corwin Papers, Volume 18, Number 9.
22. Clay Mudd to Thomas Corwin, October 31, 1852. Library of Congress, Manuscript Division, Thomas Corwin Papers, Volume 19, Number 175.
23. *Journal of the Senate* 44 (January 10, 1853): 82–83.
24. Congressional Globe, Senate, 32nd Congress, 2nd Session, December 29, 1852: 43–47.
25. *Journal of the Senate* 44 (January 6, 1853): 77.
26. Eckert noted that of the $12 million of gold coins minted before the change in the standard fineness, only $1.5 million were returned to the mint for recoinage. Of these, about $1 million came in during the last half of 1834.
27. U.S. Congressional Series Set, 1817–1980, 32nd Congress, 2nd Session, Senate, Report 21, January 19, 1853. Report of the Acting Secretary of the Treasury. George Eckert to William L. Hodge, January 17, 1853.
28. Bills and Resolutions, Senate, 32nd Congress, 2nd Session, S.596, January 26, 1853.
29. Congressional Globe, House of Representatives, 32nd Congress, 2nd Session, January 18, 1853: 332–333.
30. Congressional Globe, House of Representatives, 32nd Congress, 2nd Session, January 19, 1853: 343–349.
31. Congressional Globe, 32nd Congress, 2nd Session, January 20, 1853: 357–360.
32. Congressional Globe, House of Representatives, 32nd Congress, 2nd Session, January 26, 1853: 406–408.
33. Congressional Globe, Senate, 32nd Congress, 2nd Session, February 14, 1853: 605.
34. Congressional Globe, House of Representatives, 32nd Congress, 2nd Session, February 28, 1853: 917–922.
35. Congressional Globe, Senate, 32nd Congress, 2nd Session, March 1, 1853: 944–945.
36. J.R. Chandler to George Eckert, March 1, 1853. RG 104, Records of the Bureau of the Mint, U.S. Mint at Philadelphia 1791–1936, Correspondence 1792–1904, General Correspondence 1792–1899, NC 152, Entry 1, NM 1992, Box 32.
37. George Eckert to J.R. Chandler, March 3, 1853. RG 104, Records of the Bureau of the Mint, U.S. Mint at Philadelphia 1791–1936, Corre-

spondence 1792–1904, General Correspondence 1792–1899, NC 152, Entry 1, NM 1992, Box 32.

38. Statutes at Large, 32nd Congress, 2nd Session, March 3, 1853: 209.

39. *Journal of the Senate* 44 (March 3, 1853): 282.

40. "Hon. George Briggs—Tender of a Public Dinner," *New York Times*, April 19, 1853. Letters from Joseph N. Barnes, F.A. Tallmadge, and William S. Wood to George Briggs, April 10, 1853, and from George Briggs to Joseph N. Barnes, et. al., April 18, 1853.

41. "The San Francisco Mint," *Bankers Magazine and Statistical Register*, September 1854, 220.

Chapter 32: Backwoods Legislatin'

1. "The Currency—Gold and Silver," *Merchants' Magazine and Commercial Review* 26, no. 3 (March 1, 1852): 326.

2. Report on Finances, *Congressional Globe*, Treasury Department, December 8, 1853.

3. George Eckert to Thomas Corwin, November 29, 1851. RG 104, Records of the Bureau of the Mint, U.S. Mint at Philadelphia 1791–1936, Correspondence 1792–1904, General Correspondence 1792–1899, NC 152, Entry 1, NM 1992, Box 31.

4. Bills and Resolutions, Senate, 32nd Congress, 1st Session, S.271, March 8, 1852.

5. Bills and Resolutions, Senate, 32nd Congress, 1st Session, S.271, March 8, 1852. In the Senate, Report 104, March 8, 1852.

6. Congressional Globe, Senate, 32nd Congress, 1st Session, March 29, 1852: 907.

7. *Journal of the House of Representatives* 47 (March 30, 1852): 529.

8. Congressional Globe, House of Representatives, 32nd Congress, 2nd Session, February 1, 1853: 190–194.

9. Congressional Globe, House of Representatives, 32nd Congress, 2nd Session, February 1, 1853: 458–459.

10. Congressional Globe, House of Representatives, 32nd Congress, 2nd Session, February 2, 1853: 475–477.

11. Congressional Globe, 32nd Congress, 2nd Session, February 3, 1853: 490–494.

12. Congressional Globe, House of Representatives, 32nd Congress, 2nd Session, February 15, 1853: 629–630.

13. Statutes at Large, 32nd Congress, 2nd Session, February 21, 1853: 160–161.

14. *Journal of the Senate* 44 (March 3, 1853): 282.

15. Congressional Globe, House of Representatives, 32nd Congress, 2nd Session, February 28, 1853.

16. Congressional Globe, Senate 32nd Congress, 2nd Session, February 28, 1853: 896.

17. Statutes at Large, 32nd Congress, 2nd Session, March 3, 1853: 212.

18. U.S. Congressional Series Set, 1817–1980, 32nd Congress, 2nd Session, House of Representatives, Report 42, February 12, 1853. Annual Mint Report, George Eckert to Millard Fillmore, January 29, 1853.

19. J.B. Longacre to unknown, February 5, 1853. J.B. Longacre Papers, Library Company of Philadelphia.

20. George Eckert to J.B. Longacre, February 23, 1853. RG 104, Records of the Bureau of the Mint, U.S. Mint at Philadelphia 1791–1936, Correspondence 1792–1904, General Correspondence 1792–1899, NC 152, Entry 1, NM 1992, Box 33.

21. J.B. Longacre to George Eckert, February 28, 1853. RG 104, Records of the Bureau of the Mint, U.S. Mint at Philadelphia 1791–1936, Correspondence 1792–1904, General Correspondence 1792–1899, NC 152, Entry 1, NM 1992, Box 33.

22. George Eckert to J.B. Longacre, February 28, 1853. RG 104, Records of the Bureau of the Mint, U.S. Mint at Philadelphia 1791–1936, Correspondence 1792–1904, General Correspondence 1792–1899, NC 152, Entry 1, NM 1992, Box 33.

23. George Eckert to J.B. Longacre, March 3, 1853. RG 104, Records of the Bureau of the Mint, U.S. Mint at Philadelphia 1791–1936, Correspondence 1792–1904, General Correspondence 1792–1899, NC 152, Entry 1, NM 1992, Box 33.

24. J.B. Longacre to George Eckert, March 4, 1853. RG 104, Records of the Bureau of the Mint, U.S. Mint at Philadelphia 1791–1936, Correspondence 1792–1904, General Correspondence 1792–1899, NC 152, Entry 1, NM 1992, Box 33.

25. Richard McCulloh to J.B. Longacre, March 9, 1853. J.B. Longacre Papers, Philadelphia Library Company.

26. George Eckert to J.B. Longacre, March 7, 1853. RG 104, Records of the Bureau of the Mint, U.S. Mint at Philadelphia 1791–1936, Correspondence 1792–1904, General Correspondence 1792–1899, NC 152, Entry 1, NM 1992, Box 33.

27. J.B. Longacre to George Eckert, March 7, 1853. RG 104, Records of the Bureau of the Mint, U.S. Mint at Philadelphia 1791–1936, Correspondence 1792–1904, General Correspondence 1792–1899, NC 152, Entry 1, NM 1992, Box 33.

28. Taxay, *The U.S. Mint and Coinage*, 224–225.

29. "Our Silver Coinage," *Bankers Magazine and Statistical Register*, September 1855, 234.

30. George Eckert to Thomas Corwin, March 1. 1853. RG 104, Records of the Bureau of the Mint, U.S. Mint at Philadelphia 1791–1936, Correspondence 1792–1904, General Correspondence 1792–1899, NC 152, Entry 1, NM 1992, Box 33.

Chapter 33: End of the Line

1. Robert Patterson, Helen Patterson to Jane Pierce, December 1852. RG 56, Records of the Department of the Treasury, Applications for Positions as Assistant Treasurers and Mint Officers 1836–1898 and 1902–1904, Entry 288, Box 25.

2. Wing of the Democratic Party noted for political and economic caution.

3. Richard McCulloh to J. Ross Snowden, November 29, 1852. James Ross Snowden Papers, Society Collection, Historical Society of Pennsylvania.

4. Robert Patterson, Helen Patterson to Franklin Pierce, February 10, 1853. RG 56, Records of the Department of the Treasury, Applications for Positions as Assistant Treasurers and Mint Officers 1836–1898 and 1902–1904, Entry 288, Box 25.

5. Various recommendations, March 1853. Robert Maskell Patterson Papers, American Philosophical Society, P274 and P274.1.

6. J. Ross Snowden to James Buchanan, February 20, 1845, and March 25, 1847. James Ross Snowden Papers, Society Collection, Historical Society of Pennsylvania.

7. J. Ross Snowden to James Buchanan, March 2, 1853. James Ross Snowden Papers, Society Collection, Historical Society of Pennsylvania.

8. Robert Patterson to Jefferson Davis, March 21, 1853. RG 56, Records of the Department of the Treasury, Applications for Positions as Assistant Treasurers and Mint Officers 1836–1898 and 1902–1904, Entry 288, Box 26.

9. Robert Patterson to William Marcy, March 25, 1853. RG 56, Records of the Department of the Treasury, Applications for Positions as Assistant Treasurers and Mint Officers 1836–1898 and 1902–1904, Entry 288, Box 26.

10. Robert Patterson to Franklin Pierce, March 3, 1853. RG 56, Records of the Department of the Treasury, Applications for Positions as Assistant Treasurers and Mint Officers 1836–1898 and 1902–1904, Entry 288, Box RG 26.

11. Thomas Pettit to Franklin Pierce, March 1, 1853. RG 56, Records of the Department of the Treasury, Applications for Positions as Assistant Treasurers and Mint Officers 1836–1898 and 1902–1904, Entry 288, Box 25.

12. Robert Patterson to Franklin Peirce, undated. RG 56, Records of the Department of the Treasury, Applications for Positions as Assistant Treasurers and Mint Officers 1836–1898 and 1902–1904, Entry 288, Box 25.

13. James Guthrie to Thomas Pettit, April 21, 1853. RG 104, Records of the Bureau of the Mint, U.S. Mint at Philadelphia 1791–1936, Correspondence 1792–1904, General Correspondence 1792–1899, NC 152, Entry 1, NM 1992, Box 33.

14. Helen Patterson to William Bigler, letter fragment, February 27, 1861. RG 56, Records of the Department of the Treasury, Applications for Positions as Assistant Treasurers and Mint Officers 1836–1898 and 1902–1904, Entry 288, Box 25.

15. George Ticknor Curtis, *The Life of James Buchanan, Fifteenth President of the United States, Volume II* (New York: Harper & Brothers, Franklin Square, 1883), 76–83. Undated notes in Buchanan's handwriting.

16. Helen Patterson to William Bigler, January 25, 1861. RG 56, Records of the Department of the Treasury, Applications for Positions as Assistant Treasurers and Mint Officers 1836–1898 and 1902–1904, Entry 288, Box 25.

17. Helen Patterson to William Bigler, undated letter fragment (1861). RG 56, Records of the Department of the Treasury, Applications for Positions as Assistant Treasurers and Mint Officers 1836–1898 and 1902–1904, Entry 288, Box 25.

18. James Buchanan to Helen Patterson, June 7, 1853. Robert Maskell Patterson Papers, American Philosophical Society, P274 and P274.1.

19. Curtis, *The Life of James Buchanan, Volume II*, 91.

20. James Guthrie to Thomas Pettit, May 20, 1853. RG 104, Records of the Bureau of the Mint. U.S. Mint at Philadelphia 1791–1936, Peale Correspondence 1829–1886, NC 152, Entry 23, HM 1992, Box 1.

21. Robert Patterson to James Guthrie, May 28, 1853. Peale Family Papers, Series IX-A, Correspondence of Benjamin Franklin Peale, American Philosophical Library, courtesy of the University of Oregon.

22. "U.S. Assay Office, New York," *Bankers Magazine and Statistical Register* 4, no. 4 (October 1854): 290.

23. "Assay Office in New York," *Bankers Magazine and Statistical Register*, August 1853, 112, and reprint from *U.S. Gazette*, June 28, 1853.

24. "From Washington—More Appointments," *Portsmouth Journal of Literature and Politics*, 3.

25. Helen Patterson to William Bigler, January 25, 1861. RG 56, Records of the Department of the Treasury, Applications for Positions as Assistant Treasurers and Mint Officers 1836–1898 and 1902–1904, Entry 288, Box 25.

26. Miscellaneous, *The Bankers Magazine and Statistical Register*, September 1853, 260.

27. James Guthrie to J. Ross Snowden, February 8, 1854. RG 104, Records of the Bureau of the Mint, U.S. Mint at Philadelphia 1791–1936, Correspondence 1792–1904, General Correspondence 1792–1899, NC 152, Entry 1, NM 1992, Box 35.

28. James Guthrie to Thomas Pettit, May 21, 1853. RG 104, Records of the Bureau of the Mint, U.S. Mint at Philadelphia 1791–1936, Correspondence 1792–1904, General Correspondence 1792–1899, NC 152, Entry 1, NM 1992, Box 33.

29. J. Ross Snowden to James Guthrie, July 29, 1856. RG 104, Records of the Bureau of the Mint. U.S. Mint at Philadelphia 1791–1936, Peale Correspondence 1829–1886, NC 152, Entry 23, HM 1992, Box 1.

30. *Journal of the Executive Proceedings of the Senate* 9 (March 29, 1853): 120.

31. "Affairs of Honor—Fatal Termination of One of Them," *Weekly Herald*, July 16, 1853, 230.

32. *Cleveland Plain Dealer*, May 17, 1854, 3.

33. U.S. Congressional Series Set, 1817–1980, 33rd Congress, 1st Session, House of Representatives, Report 40, Annual Report of the Director of the Mint, February 2, 1854.

34. "A Branch Mint and Assay Office," *Placer Times*, October 3, 1854, 2.

35." Letter to the Hon. Wm. M. Gwin," *Alta California*, October 24, 1854, 2.

36. Bills and Resolutions, Senate, 33rd Congress, 1st Session, S.380, May 23, 1854.

37. *Journal of the House of Representatives* 49 (August 3, 1854): 1290.

Chapter 34: Smith and Pickett

1. Franklin Peale to J. Ross Snowden, July 22, 1853. Correspondence of Benjamin Franklin Peale, Series IX-A, American Philosophical Library, courtesy of the University of Oregon.

2. J. Ross Snowden to Franklin Peale, July 22, 1853. Correspondence of Benjamin Franklin Peale, Series IX-A, American Philosophical Library, courtesy of the University of Oregon.

3. Franklin Peale to J. Ross Snowden, December 15, 1853. Correspondence of Benjamin Franklin Peale, Series IX-A, American Philosophical Library, courtesy of the University of Oregon.

4. J. Ross Snowden to James Guthrie, July 29, 1856. RG 104, Records of the Bureau of the Mint, U.S. Mint at Philadelphia 1791–1936, Peale Correspondence 1829–1886, NC 152, Entry 23, HM 1992, Box 1.

5. Franklin Peale to J. Ross Snowden, May 17, 1854. RG 104, Records of the Bureau of the Mint, U.S. Mint at Philadelphia 1791–1936, Peale Correspondence 1829–1886, NC 152, Entry 23, HM 1992, Box 1.

6. R.S. McCulloh to J. Ross Snowden, June 6, 1854. James Ross Snowden Papers, Society Collection, Historical Society of Pennsylvania.

7. Executive Documents, House of Representatives, 2nd Session, 33rd Congress, Volume 2, Document 3: 366–389.

8. J. Ross Snowden to the Officers of the Mint, June 1, 1854. RG 104, Records of the Bureau of the Mint, U.S. Mint at Philadelphia 1791–1936, Correspondence 1792–1904, General Correspondence 1792–1899, NC 152, Entry 1, NM 1992, Box 36.

9. J. Ross Snowden to Franklin Peale, July 5, 1854. Peale Family Papers, Series IX-A, Correspondence of Benjamin Franklin Peale, American Philosophical Society Library, courtesy of the University of Oregon.

10. J.M. Ramsey to J. Ross Snowden, August 12, 1854. RG 104, Records of the Bureau of the Mint, U.S. Mint at Philadelphia 1791–1936, Correspondence 1792–1904, General Correspondence 1792–1899, NC 152, Entry 1, NM 1992, Box 37.

11. James Guthrie to J. Ross Snowden, October 4, 1854. RG 104, Records of the Bureau of the Mint, U.S. Mint at Philadelphia 1791–1936, Correspondence 1792–1904, General Correspondence 1792–1899, NC 152, Entry 1, NM 1992, Box 38.

12. J. Ross Snowden to James Guthrie September 4, 1854. RG 104, Records of the Bureau of the Mint, U.S. Mint at Philadelphia 1791–1936, Correspondence 1792–1904, General Correspondence 1792–1899, NC 152, Entry 1, NM 1992, Box 37.

13. Proposed Regulations of the Mint, September 4, 1854. RG 104, Records of the Bureau of the Mint, U.S. Mint at Philadelphia 1791–1936, Correspondence 1792–1904, General Correspondence 1792–1899, NC 152, Entry 1, NM 1992, Box 37.

14. Regulations for the Chief Coiner's Department, September 13, 1854. RG 104, Records of the Bureau of the Mint, U.S. Mint at Philadelphia 1791–1936, Correspondence 1792–1904, General Correspondence 1792–1899, NC 152, Entry 1, NM 1992, Box 37.

15. Franklin Peale to J. Ross Snowden, September 19, 1854. RG 104, Records of the Bureau of the Mint, U.S. Mint at Philadelphia 1791–1936, Correspondence 1792–1904, General Correspondence 1792–1899, NC 152, Entry 1, NM 1992, Box 37.

16. J.B. Longacre to J. Ross Snowden, September 25, 1854. RG 104, Records of the Bureau of the Mint, U.S. Mint at Philadelphia 1791–1936, Correspondence 1792–1904, General Correspondence 1792–1899, NC 152, Entry 1, NM 1992, Box 37.

17. Julian, *Medals of the United States Mint*, xxiv.

18. U.S. Congressional Series Set, 1817–1980, 34th Congress, 1st Session, Senate, Report 185, Report of the Committee of Claims to Whom was Referred the Memorial of Franklin Peale, May 23, 1856.

19. James Guthrie to J. Ross Snowden, July 21, 1856. RG 104, Records of the Bureau of the Mint, U.S. Mint at Philadelphia 1791–1936, Correspondence 1792–1904, General Correspondence 1792–1899, NC 152, Entry 1, NM 1992, Box 33.

20. J. Ross Snowden to James Guthrie, July 29, 1856. RG 104, Records of the Bureau of the Mint, U.S. Mint at Philadelphia 1791–1936, Peale Correspondence 1829–1886, NC 152, Entry 23, HM 1992, Box 1.

21. H.R. 3877 of the 42nd Congress. Correspondence of Benjamin Franklin Peale, Series IX-A, American Philosophical Society Library, courtesy of the University of Oregon.

22. Caroline E.G. Peale to James Pollock, April 30, 1873. RG 104, Records of the Bureau of the Mint, U.S. Mint at Philadelphia 1791–1936, Peale Correspondence 1829–1886, NC 152, Entry 23, HM 1992, Box 1.

23. Robert Patterson to James Pollock, May 3, 1873. RG 104, Records of the Bureau of the Mint, U.S. Mint at Philadelphia 1791–1936, Peale Correspondence 1829–1886, NC 152, Entry 23, HM 1992, Box 1.

Chapter 35: Striking Change

1. J. Ross Snowden to James Guthrie, July 19, 1853. RG 104, Records of the Bureau of the Mint, U.S. Mint at Philadelphia 1791–1936, Correspondence 1792–1904, General Correspondence 1792–1899, NC 152, Entry 1, NM 1992, Box 34.

2. Taxay, *The U.S. Mint and Coinage*, 223.

3. J.B. Longacre to J. Ross Snowden, August 21, 1858. James Barton Longacre Papers, Philadelphia Library Company.

4. J.B. Longacre to J. Ross Snowden, November 26, 1853. James Barton Longacre Papers, Philadelphia Library Company.

5. J.B. Longacre to J. Ross Snowden, November 14, 1853. RG 104, Records of the Bureau of the Mint, U.S. Mint at Philadelphia 1791–1936, Correspondence 1792–1904, General Correspondence 1792–1899, NC 152, Entry 1, NM 1992, Box 35.

6. This was most likely William Barber, who later become Longacre's assistant and succeeded to the chief engraver's position upon Longacre's death on January 1, 1869.

7. J. Ross Snowden to James Guthrie, December 29, 1853. RG 104, Records of the Bureau of the Mint, U.S. Mint at Philadelphia 1791–1936, Correspondence 1792–1904, General Correspondence 1792–1899, NC 152, Entry 1, NM 1992, Box 35.

8. J. Ross Snowden, Draft Circular, January 7, 1854. RG 104, Records of the Bureau of the Mint, U.S. Mint at Philadelphia 1791–1936, Correspondence 1792–1904, General Correspondence 1792–1899, NC 152, Entry 1, NM 1992, Box 35.

9. J. Ross Snowden to James Guthrie, January 7, 1854. RG 104, Records of the Bureau of the Mint, U.S. Mint at Philadelphia 1791–1936, Correspondence 1792–1904, General Correspondence 1792–1899, NC 152, Entry 1, NM 1992, Box 35.

10. James Guthrie to J. Ross Snowden, January 12, 1854. RG 104, Records of the Bureau of the Mint, U.S. Mint at Philadelphia 1791–1936, Correspondence 1792–1904, General Correspondence 1792–1899, NC 152, Entry 1, NM 1992, Box 35.

11. J. Ross Snowden to James Guthrie, November 2, 1853. RG 104, Records of the Bureau of the Mint, U.S. Mint at Philadelphia 1791–1936, Correspondence 1792–1904, General Correspondence 1792–1899, NC 152, Entry 1, NM 1992, Box 35.

12. J.B. Longacre to J. Ross Snowden, August 21, 1858. James Barton Longacre Papers, Philadelphia Library Company.

13. J.B. Longacre to J. Ross Snowden, August 17, 1854. RG 104, Records of the Bureau of the Mint, U.S. Mint at Philadelphia 1791–1936, Correspondence 1792–1904, General Correspondence 1792–1899, NC 152, Entry 1, NM 1992, Box 37.

14. U.S. Congressional Series Set, 1817–1980, 33rd Congress, 2nd Session, Report 62, Annual Report of the Director of the Mint, February 8, 1855.

15. *Journal of the House of Representatives* 49 (May 19, 1854): 869.

16. Julian, *Medals of the United States Mint*, xxv.

17. Julian, *Medals of the United States Mint*, 172.

18. Milton Haley Thomas, "Professor McCulloh of Princeton, Columbia and Points South," *The Princeton University Library Chronicle*, 9, no. 1 (November 1947): 17–29. The controversy of his election dogged McCulloh for his full time at Columbia. A week after the New York City draft riots of July 1863, McCulloh resigned to fight for the Confederacy. Depending upon the source, he was commissioned either a lieutenant colonel or a brigadier general assigned to the Bureau of Nitre and Mining. Here blogs state that he developed a lethal chemical for use on the battlefield that the Confederacy declined to use. He was involved in an incendiary plot to attack northern shipping, arrested after the war and imprisoned for a year. Afterwards Robert E. Lee called him to be a professor at Washington College. In 1877 he left to teach at Louisiana State University for 11 stormy years. He died on September 15, 1894.

19. Congressional Record, House of Representatives, 43rd Congress, 1st Session, May 22, 1874: 4189–4190.

20. U.S. Congressional Series Set, 1817–1980, 34th Congress, 3rd Session, Report 63, Annual Report of the Director of the Mint, February 4, 1857

Epilogue: January 25, 1861

1. C.C. Wright to Daniel Ullmann, January 4, 1851. Daniel Ullmann Papers, New-York Historical Society.

2. Daniel Ullmann to Henry Clay, January 11, 1851. Daniel Ullmann Papers, New-York Historical Society.

3. According to Georgia Chamberlain in her article in *The Numismatist*, January 1961, Jones used Lexington stone-cutter Mahlon Pruden's 1847 marble bust of Clay, created when he was 73.

4. C.C. Wright to Daniel Ullmann, April 21, 1851. Daniel Ullmann Papers, New-York Historical Society. Ultimately the medal had a diameter of 90 millimeters.

5. Charles M. Leap to Daniel Ullmann, April 20, 1851. Daniel Ullmann Papers, New-York Historical Society.

6. C.C. Wright to Daniel Ullmann, July 2, 1851. Daniel Ullmann Papers, New-York Historical Society.

7. Henry Clay, "Henry Clay to Daniel Ullmann, September 26, 1851," *The Private Correspondence of Henry Clay*, edited by Calvin Colton (Boston: Frederick Parker, 1856), 620–622.

8. George Eckert to C.C. Wright, January 16, 1852. Daniel Ullmann Papers, New-York Historical Society.

9. C.C. Wright to Daniel Ullmann, January 22, 1852. Daniel Ullmann Papers, New-York Historical Society.

10. Editor's Correspondence, *Daily National Intelligencer*, February 10, 1852, 3.

11. Transcript from the *Daily National Intelligencer*, February 10, 1852. Engrossed on silk to accompany the copper-bronzed medals.

12. Henry Clay to Daniel Ullmann, March 18, 1852. Daniel Ullmann Papers, New-York Historical Society.

13. Henry Clay to Daniel Ullmann, March 6, 1852. Daniel Ullmann Papers, New-York Historical Society.

14. She married Vincenzo Botta in 1855.

15. Henry Clay to Daniel Ullmann, March 12, 1852. Daniel Ullmann Papers, New-York Historical Society.

16. Charles Butler to Daniel Ullmann, March 15, 1852. Daniel Ullmann Papers, New-York Historical Society.

17. Henry Clay to Daniel Ullmann, March 18, 1852. Daniel Ullmann Papers, New-York Historical Society.

18. C.C. Wright to Daniel Ullmann, et al., July 31, 1852. Daniel Ullmann Papers, New-York Historical Society.

19. "Arrest in Hanover for Robberies Committed in this Country," *The New York Times*, October 7, 1852.

20. Papers of Henry Clay, University of Kentucky, May 3, 1852.

21. Daniel Ullmann to Abraham Lincoln, January 25, 1861. Library of Congress, Abraham Lincoln Papers.

Archival Materials

Biddle, Nicholas, Papers. Library of Congress.

A Century of Lawmaking for a New Nation: U.S. Congressional Documents and Debates, 1774–1875. American State Papers, Annals of Congress, Bills and Resolutions of the House of Representatives and the Senate, *Congressional Globe*, *Congressional Record*, Executive Documents of the House of Representatives, *Journal of the House of Representatives*, *Journal of the Senate*, *Journal of the Executive Proceedings of the Senate*, Register of Debates, Statutes at Large. Law Library of Congress.

Clay, Henry, Papers. University of Kentucky.

Corwin, Thomas, Papers. Manuscript Division, Library of Congress.

Department of the Treasury: Record Group 56, Philadelphia Mint Employment. Entry 169, Letters Received from the Director of the Mint, Philadelphia, 1832–1910.

Department of the Treasury: Record Group 56, Records of the Department of the Treasury. Entry 288, Applications for Positions as Assistant Treasurers and Mint Officers, 1836–1898 and 1902–1904.

Executive Documents, Report on Finances, Examination of the Mint at Philadelphia, House of Representatives, June 1, 1854.

Gobrecht, Christian, Papers. Historical Society of Pennsylvania.

Gwin, William McKendree, Papers. The Bancroft Library. University of California, Berkeley.

Jackson, Andrew, Letters. Library of Congress.

———, Papers. The Bancroft Library. University of California, Berkeley.

———, Papers. University of Tennessee.

Jefferson, Thomas, Papers. Series 1, General Correspondence. Library of Congress.

Lincoln, Abraham, Papers. Library of Congress.

Longacre, James Barton, Papers. The Library Company of Philadelphia.

Madison, James, Papers. Library of Congress.

Message to the Joint Session of Congress From President Polk as Delivered by Robert Walker, Secretary of the Treasury, December 5, 1848.

Patterson Family Papers, American Philosophical Society, Philadelphia.

Patterson, Robert Maskell, Papers. American Philosophical Society, Philadelphia.

Peale Family Papers. Correspondence of Franklin Peale. American Philosophical Society, courtesy of the University of Oregon.

Snowden, James Ross, Papers. Society Collection, Historical Society of Pennsylvania.

Ullmann, Daniel, Papers. New-York Historical Society.

U.S. Mint Documents: Record Group 104, Records of the Bureau of the Mint, U.S. Mint at Philadelphia, 1791–1936. Entry 1, General Correspondence, 1792–1899.

U.S. Congressional Serial Set, 1817–1994. The official collection of reports and documents of the United States Congress.

U.S. Mint Documents: Record Group 104, Records of the Bureau of the Mint, U.S. Mint at Philadelphia, 1791–1936. Entry 23, Peale Correspondence, 1829–1882.

Vermeule, Cornelius. *Numismatic Art in America*. Atlanta: Whitman Publishing, 2007.

Washington, George, Papers. Series 4, General Correspondence. Library of Congress.

Articles

"Affairs in California." *National Intelligencer*, June 28, 1849.

"Affairs of Honor–Fatal Termination of One of Them." *Weekly Herald*, July 16, 1853.

"Annual Reunion, June 10th, 1897." United States Military Academy, Association of Graduates.

"Arrest in Hannover for Robberies Committed in this Country." *New York Times*, October 7, 1852.

Ashhurst, Richard Lewis. "William Morris Meredith 1797–1873." *American Law Register*, April 1907.

"The Assay Office." *Daily Alta California*, April 14, 1851.

"Assay Office in New York." *Bankers' Magazine and Statistical Register*, September 1853.

"Bayard Taylor's Letter." *New Jersey State Gazette*, December 10, 1849.

"A Branch Mint and Assay Office." *Placer Times*, October 3, 1854.

"California Convention." *Massachusetts Spy*, December 4, 1849.

"California Gold." *Daily Alta California*, August 1, 1851.

"California Gold, Important Official Report." *New York Tribune*, December 9, 1848.

"Celebration of American Independence at Washington City." *New Hampshire Gazette*, July 19, 1831.

Colwell, Steven. "Manufacture of Iron." *American Quarterly Register and Magazine*, May 1848.

"Commercial and Money Matters." *New York Tribune*, March 14, 1850.

"The Currency–Gold and Silver." *Merchants' Magazine and Commercial Review*, March 1, 1852.

Dannreuther, John. "Robert Ball Hughes–More than a Coin Designer?" *Rare Coin Market Report*, April 2007.

"Doings of the Legislature." *Daily Alta California*, December 19, 1849.

Doty, R.G. "Early United States Copper Coinage: The English Connection." *British Numismatic Journal* 58 (1988).

———. "'An Onerous and Delicate Task:' Franklin Peale's Mission South, 1837." Coinage of Americas Conference Presentation, November 4, 1989.

"Dr. Robert Maskell Patterson." *Alumni Bulletin* 3, no. 3 (November 1896).

Dubois, Patterson. "Our Mint Engravers." *American Journal of Numismatics* 18, no. 1 (July 1883).

"Editor's Correspondence." *Daily National Intelligencer*, February 10, 1852.
"The Electrotype, or Casting by Electricity." *New-Yorker*, October 17, 1840.
"The Explosion at Philadelphia." *Times Picayune*, May 23, 1851.
"Fatal Duel." *Richmond Enquirer*, February 4, 1836.
"From Washington–More Appointments." *Portsmouth Journal of Literature and Politics* (1853).
"Further from California." *Daily National Intelligencer*, February 8, 1850.
"Further on the Gold Mines." *National Intelligencer*, December 11, 1849.
"Gold." *Farmers Gazette*, August 22, 1834.
"The Gold Bill." *New Bedford Mercury*, July 11, 1834.
"Gold Dollar." *Daily Globe*, January 20, 1849.
"Gold Dollar." *Washington Union*, January 27, 1849.
"The Gold Dollar." *Washington Union*, May 6, 1849.
"The Gold Dollar." *Washington Union*, May 31, 1849.
"The Golden Humbug." *Globe*, August 18, 1834.
"The Gold Region of California." Reprint from the New Orleans *Picayune. National Intelligencer*, December 4, 1848.
"Great Meeting in Philadelphia." *Niles Weekly Register*, April 5, 1834.
"Highly Interesting from California." *Weekly Herald*, December 29, 1849.
"Hon. George Briggs–Tender of a Public Dinner." *New York Times*, April 19, 1853.
"Interesting from California." *Daily Picayune*, February 4, 1850.
"Interesting from Washington." *Cleveland Plain Dealer*, June 10, 1851.
"The Jackson Feast." *National Journal*, July 15, 1830.
Julian, R.W. "Another Look at the 1804 Dollar." *Numismatist*, January 1970.
———. "Gobrecht's Dollar: Originals Show Eagle Flying Upward." *Coins Magazine*, April 5, 2011.
———. "New Information on the Gobrecht Dollar." *Numismatic News*, October 6, 2009.
"The Late Dr. Robert M. Patterson." *Pennsylvanian*, September 22, 1854.
Lester, Carl N. "A Brief History of the United States Branch Mint at Dahlonega, Georgia." Undated.
Letter to the Editor, *Turf, Agriculture, Field Sports, Etc.*, July 21, 1849.
"Letter to the Hon. Wm. M. Gwin." *Daily Alta California*, October 24, 1854.
"A Listing of its Members." The American Philosophical Society.
"Local Matters." *Daily Alta California*, December 31, 1849.
Miles, Edwin A. "Andrew Jackson and Senator George Poindexter." *Journal of Southern History*, February 1958.
"Mint of the United States." *New Bedford Mercury*, August 29, 1834.
"Miscellaneous." *Bankers' Magazine and Statistical Register*, June 1852.
"Miscellaneous." *Bankers' Magazine and Statistical Register*, September 1853.
"Miscellany." *Literary Union*, May 26, 1849.
Mr. Charles T. Botts." *Richmond Whig*, December 11, 1849.
"New Coin." *Niles Weekly Register*, November 21, 1840.
"New Dollar." *Philadelphia Public Ledger*, December 21, 1836.
"The New Dollar Coin." *Philadelphia Public Ledger*, December 19, 1836.
Nichols, Roy F. and G.M. Dallas. *Mystery of the Dallas Papers*.
"Our Silver Coinage." *Bankers' Magazine and Statistical Register*, September 1855.
"The Philadelphia Mint–Refining Gold with Zinc–Its Troubles and Trials." *Scientific American* 7, no. 4 (October 9, 1852).
"The Philadelphia Mint–Refining Gold, Its Troubles and Trials." *Scientific American*, April 25, 1853.
"Political Incidents." *Niles Weekly Register*, March 1, 1834.
"The President's Message." *Philadelphia Public Ledger*, December 2, 1848.
Proceedings of the American Philosophical Society.
"Questions for the Editor of the Globe." *Alexandria Gazette*, September 13, 1834.
"Report on a Coining Press at the United States Mint, Philadelphia." *Journal of the Franklin Institute*, May 14, 1840.
"The San Francisco Mint." *Bankers' Magazine and Statistical Register*, September 1854.
Seymour, Dexter C. "Templeton Reid: His Life and Coinage in Georgia." *Numismatist*, July 1978.
"Silver Coins." *Philadelphia Inquirer*, January 11, 1851.
Solly, Craig, John Dannreuther, and Saul Teichman. "New Data Supports Revisionist Theory of the Gobrecht Dollars." Numismatic Theater Presentation, August 2012.
Spencer, Thomas. "On the Mode of Producing Fac-Simile Copies of Medals, etc. by the Agency of Voltaic Electricity." *American Repertory of Arts, Sciences and Manufactures*, May 1840.
"The State of California." *Georgia Telegraph*, December 1, 1849.
Thomas, Milton Haley. "Professor McCulloh of Princeton, Columbia and Points South." *Princeton University Library Chronicle*, November 1947.
"Twenty-Dollar Gold Pieces." *Pittsfield Sun*, March 21, 1850.
"Two Centuries on, a Cryptologist Cracks the Presidential Code." *Wall Street Journal* 253, no. 153 (July 2, 2009).
"The United States Mint, Philadelphia." *American Repertory of Arts, Sciences and Manufactures*, June 1840.
"Unpublished Letters of Andrew Jackson." *Overland Monthly*, February 1892.
Untitled. *Cleveland Plain Dealer*, May 17, 1854.
Untitled. *Daily National Intelligencer*, March 12, 1833.
Untitled. *Daily National Intelligencer*, August 11, 1852.
Untitled. *Farmer's Cabinet*, March 28, 1850.
Untitled. *Gloucester Telegraph*, March 20, 1850.
Untitled. *Mechanics Magazine and Journal of the Mechanics Institute*, January 1837 and February 1837.
Untitled. *Rhode Island Republican*, February 2, 1836.
Untitled. *Richmond Enquirer*, June 24, 1836.
Untitled. *Scientific American*, July 14, 1849.
Untitled. *Washington Union*, May 19, 1849.
Yeoman, R.S. "The 1848 Quarter Eagle With CAL." *Numismatist*, July 1953.

Books

Adams, Edgar H. *Private Gold Coinage of California, 1849–55: Its History and its Issues*. Brooklyn: Edgar H. Adams, 1913.
Ambrose, Stephen. *Undaunted Courage: Meriwether Lewis, Thomas Jefferson, and the Opening of the American West*. New York: Simon & Schuster, 1996.
Barfield, Rodney and Keith Strawn. *The Bechtlers and Their Coinage: North Carolina Mint Masters of Pioneer Gold*. Raleigh, NC: North Carolina Museum of History, 1980.
Benton, Thomas H. *Thirty Years' View: A History of the Working of the American Government for Thirty Years*. New York: D. Appleton, 1854.
Birdsall, Clair M. *The United States Branch Mint at Charlotte, North Carolina: Its History and Coinage*. Easley, SC: Southern Historical Press, 1988.
———. *The United States Branch Mint at Dahlonega, Georgia: Its History and Coinage*. Easley, SC: Southern Historical Press, 1984.
Boudinot, Elias. *Cherokee Editor: The Writings of Elias Boudinot*. Edited by Theda Perdue. Athens, GA: University of Georgia Press, 1996.
Breen, Walter. *Walter Breen's Complete Encyclopedia of U.S. and Colonial Coins*. New York, London, Toronto, Sydney, Auckland: Doubleday, 1988.
Calhoun, John C. *The Papers of John C. Calhoun: Volume XII*. Edited by Clyde Wilson. Columbia, SC: University of South Carolina Press, 1979.
Chambers, William Nisbet. *Old Bullion Benton: Senator from the New West*. Boston and Toronto: Little, Brown, 1956.
Claiborne, J.F.H. *Mississippi as a Province, Territory, and State with Biographical Sketches of Eminent Citizens*. Jackson, MS: Power and Barksdale, 1880.
Clain-Stefanelli, Vladimir. *History of the National Numismatic Collections*. Washington, D.C.: United States Government Printing Office, 1968.
Clay, Henry. *The Private Correspondence of Henry Clay*. Edited by Calvin Colton. Boston: Frederick Parker, 1856.
Cole, Donald B. *Amos Kendall and the Rise of American Democracy*. Baton Rouge: Louisiana State University Press, 2004.
Congress of the United States. *Biographical Directory of the United States Congress 1774–2005*. Washington, D.C.: United States Government Printing Office, 2005.
Cooke, Jacob E. *Tench Coxe and the Early Republic*. Chapel Hill: University of North Carolina Press, 1978.

Curtis, George Ticknor. *The Life of James Buchanan, Fifteenth President of the United States.* New York: Harper & Brothers, Franklin Square, 1883.

Davis, Jefferson. *The Papers of Jefferson Davis.* Edited by James T. McIntosh. Baton Rouge: Louisiana State University Press, 1974.

Evans, George, ed. *U.S. Mint Centennial 1792–1892.* Philadelphia: George G. Evans, 1892.

Foote, Henry Stuart. *Casket of Reminiscences.* Washington, D.C.: Chronicle, 1874.

Howe, Daniel Walker. *What Hath God Wrought: The Transformation of America, 1815–1848.* Oxford: Oxford University Press, 2007.

Hoyt, Edwin P. *James Buchanan.* Chicago: Reilly & Lee, 1966.

Hutchinson Family. *Excelsior: Journals of the Hutchinson Family Singers, 1842–1846.* Edited and annotated by Dale Cockrell. Stuyvesant, NY: Pendragon Press, 1989.

Judd, J. Hewitt. *United States Pattern Coins Experimental and Trial Pieces.* Edited by Q. David Bowers. 8th ed. Atlanta: Whitman, 2003.

Julian, R.W. *Medals of the United States Mint: The First Century 1792–1892.* Edited by N. Neil Harris. El Cajon, CA: Token and Medal Society, 1977.

Kagin, Donald H. *Private Gold Coins and Patterns of the United States.* New York: Arco, 1981.

Kane, John K. *Autobiography of the Honorable John K. Kane 1795–1858.* Philadelphia: privately printed, 1949.

Kendall, Amos. *Autobiography of Amos Kendall.* Edited by William Stickney. Boston: Lee and Shepard; New York: Lee, Shepard and Dillingham, 1872.

Lippitt, Francis J. *Reminiscences of Francis J. Lippet: Written for His Family, His Near Relatives and Intimate Friends.* Providence, RI: Preston & Rounds, 1902.

Morgan, Robert J. *A Whig Embattled: The Presidency Under John Tyler.* Lincoln, NE: University of Nebraska Press, 1954.

O'Meara, James. *Broderick and Gwin: The Most Extraordinary Contest for a Seat in the Senate of the United States Ever Known.* San Francisco: Bacon & Company, 1881.

Phillips, Henry and J.P. Lesley, eds. *Early Proceedings of the American Philosophical Society for the Promotion of Useful Knowledge.* Philadelphia: Press of McCalla and Stavely, 1884.

Quinn, Arthur. *The Rivals: William Gwin, David Broderick, and the Birth of California.* New York: Crown Publishers, 1994.

Remini, Robert V. *Daniel Webster: The Man and his Time.* New York and London: W.W. Norton, 1997.

———. *Henry Clay: Statesman for the Union.* New York and London: W.W. Norton, 1991.

Roberts, Bruce. *The Carolina Gold Rush: America's First.* Charlotte, NC: Heritage Printers, 1971.

Rush, Benjamin. *The Autobiography of Benjamin Rush; His "Travels Through Life" Together with His Commonplace Book for 1789–1813.* Princeton: Princeton University Press, 1948.

———. *The Letters of Benjamin Rush.* Edited by L.H. Butterfield. Princeton: Princeton University Press, 1951.

Schilke, Oscar G. and Raphael E. Solomon. *America's Foreign Coins: An Illustrated Standard Catalogue with Valuations of Foreign Coins with Legal Tender Status in the United States, 1793–1857.* New York: The Coin and Currency Institute, 1964.

Sellers, Charles Coleman. *Mr. Peale's Museum: Charles Willson Peale and the First Popular Museum of Natural Science and Art.* New York: W.W. Norton, 1980.

Sellers, George Escol. *Early Engineering Reminiscences (1815–40) of George Escol Sellers.* Edited by Eugene S. Ferguson. Washington, D.C.: Smithsonian Institution, 1965.

Shenton, James P. *Robert John Walker: A Politician from Jackson to Lincoln.* New York and London: Columbia University Press, 1961.

Sherman, General W.T. *Personal Memoirs of Gen'l W. T. Sherman.* New York: Charles L. Webster, 1891.

———. *Personal Memoirs of Gen'l W.T. Sherman.* New York: Harcourt, Brace, 1932.

Simpson, Henry. *The Lives of Eminent Philadelphians, Now Deceased.* Danvers, MA: General Books, 2009.

Snowden, James Ross. *A Description of Ancient and Modern Coins in the Cabinet Collection of the Mint of the United States.* Philadelphia: J.B. Lippincott, 1860.

Taxay, Don. *The U.S. Mint and Coinage.* New York: Arco, 1966.

Thomas, Lately. *Between Two Empires: The Life Story of California's First Senator William McKendree Gwin.* Boston: Houghton Mifflin, 1969.

Wainwright, Nicholas B. *History of the Philadelphia National Bank: A Century and a Half of Philadelphia Banking, 1803–1953.* Philadelphia: William F. Fell, 1953.

Wealthy Citizens of Philadelphia, Memoirs and Autobiography of some of the Wealthy Citizens of Philadelphia. Philadelphia: Booksellers, 1846.

Wilentz, Sean. *The Rise of American Democracy: Jefferson to Lincoln.* New York and London: W.W. Norton, 2005.

Williams, David. *The Georgia Gold Rush: Twenty-Niners, Cherokees, and Gold Fever.* Columbia, SC: University of South Carolina Press, 1993.

Wright, Robert E. *The First Wall Street: Chestnut Street, Philadelphia, and the Birth of American Finance.* Chicago and London: University of Chicago Press, 2005.

Wright, Robert E. and David J. Cowen. *Financial Founding Fathers: The Men Who Made America Rich.* Chicago and London: University of Chicago Press, 2006.

Pamphlets

Booth, James C. *Letter to Millard Fillmore.* February 17, 1853.

McCulloh, Richard Sears. *Memorial to the Congress of the United States of Prof. Richard S. McCulloh, An Investigation and Legislation in Relation to the New Method for Refining Gold.* February 24, 1851.

McCulloh, Richard Sears. *The Proceedings of the Late Director of the Mint in Relation to the Official Misconduct of Franklin Peale, Esq., Chief Coiner, and Other Abuses in the Mint, as Reviewed by R.S. McCulloh, Formerly the Melter and Refiner of the Mint.* July 11, 1853.

McCulloh, Richard Sears. *Report Made to the Hon. Thomas Corwin Secretary of the Treasury by Prof. R. S. McCulloh on his Operations at the U. S. Mint in Refining California Gold by his Zinc Method.* Washington, D.C.: Gideon, 1852.

ABOUT THE AUTHORS

Michael F. Moran has been a numismatist since childhood, when his grandfather got him started collecting Indian Head cents. He fell in love with the art of Augustus Saint-Gaudens in 1960, and spent his summer lawn-mowing money on one of the artist's $20 gold pieces.

Moran holds a bachelor's degree in civil engineering and a master's in industrial administration from Purdue University. He has spent a business career in corporate mergers and acquisitions in the energy fields and now serves as a managing partner in several diverse businesses. He says only half jokingly that he learned to write by the seat of his pants, while providing economic justifications for major capital projects and acquisitions that he then presented for approval to his board of directors.

Since leaving his corporate career, Moran has turned to numismatic writing. He has written cover articles for *Numismatist* and received the American Numismatic Association's Heath Literary Award for his 2006 article about the survival of the San Francisco Mint during the earthquake of 1906. In 2007 he completed his first book, *Striking Change, the Great Artistic Collaboration of Theodore Roosevelt and Augustus Saint-Gaudens*. For this work he received the Robert Friedberg Award of the Professional Numismatists Guild in 2008. This book was a labor of love combining his enthusiasm for the art of Saint-Gaudens with his admiration of Theodore Roosevelt.

Opportunities subsequently opened. In 2011 Senator Mitch McConnell appointed Mr. Moran to a four-year term on the Citizens Coinage Advisory Committee at the United States Mint. In this capacity Moran with ten other individuals reviews the designs proposed for all coins and medals issued by the Mint. His activities on the committee have included chairing of a subcommittee recommending the initiation of an art-medals program at the Mint. He has also played a lead role in the introduction of legislation to restore the image of Liberty to a portion of the circulating coinage issued by the United States.

In addition to his numismatic activities Moran serves on the Advisory Board of the Theodore Roosevelt Association. He also is the past chairman of the Advisory Board of the Art Museum at the University of Kentucky.

Moran lives in Lexington, Kentucky.

Jeff Garrett began his coin collecting in 1969, when a family friend gave him a Lincoln cent board. Since then, coins have been the focus of his life. Growing up in the Tampa Bay area, Garrett became very active in several local clubs. He was mentored at an early age by many of the area's dealers, and attended his first American Numismatic Association convention in 1974. He has not missed one since. In 2015, after serving on the ANA's board of governors for six years, he was elected to lead the congressionally chartered association as its 59th president.

At the age of 17 Garrett was offered a position with Florida Coin Exchange; two years later he became a partner in the firm. In 1984 he founded Mid-American Rare Coin Galleries, which continues to operate today. He is also co-owner of the Sarasota Rare Coin Gallery. He organized the Bluegrass Coin Club in Lexington, Kentucky, to foster the atmosphere of enthusiasm that encouraged him as a youth.

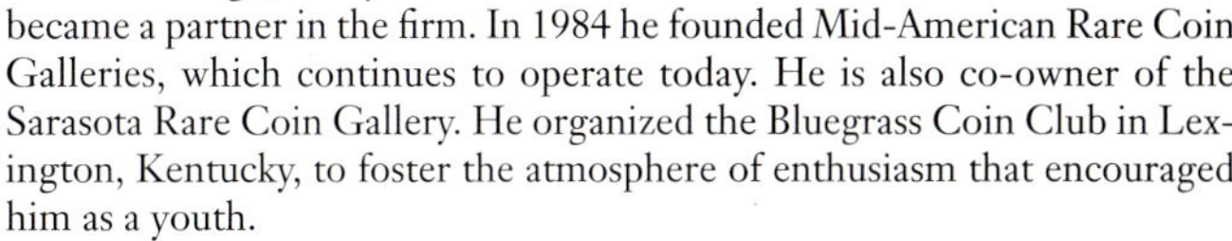

Over the course of his career, Garrett has handled nearly every United States numismatic rarity. During the ANA convention in 2003 he was one of the experts called upon to authenticate the long-lost 1913 Liberty Head nickel. In 2004, he handled one of the greatest gold coin collections ever assembled, the famed Dukes Creek set of Georgia gold.

Garrett has belonged to the Professional Numismatists Guild since 1982 and has served as its president. In 2003 the PNG awarded him the Abe Kosoff Founder's Award, its highest honor, for work promoting the hobby and the organization.

While Garrett spends most of his time buying and selling coins, he also enjoys research and the study of rare coins, and is a published author in the field. In 2003 the first edition of *100 Greatest U.S. Coins* was awarded by both the Numismatic Literary Guild and the Professional Numismatists Guild. Garrett is coauthor of *the Official Red Book of Auction Records;* the award-winning *Encyclopedia of U.S. Gold Coins 1795–1933*, a project done in cooperation with the Smithsonian Institution; *United States Coinage: A Study by Type*; and *100 Greatest U.S. Modern Coins*. He serves as valuation editor for the annually issued *Guide Book of United States Coins* (the hobby's best-selling "Red Book").

ILLUSTRATIONS

The images of coins and medals used in this book have been taken wherever possible from the National Numismatic Collection at the Smithsonian Institution. The purpose for this action was twofold. First, it shows the great breadth of this collection of American numismatics. Second, some of the coins covered in this narrative are one of a kind, such as the great 1849 double eagle. These coins simply exist nowhere else. This collection is truly a national treasure.

The full story of the National Numismatic Collection deserves its own book. In short, credit for its genesis belongs to chief coiner Adam Eckfeldt. Having been at the Mint from its inception in one capacity or another, he was in a unique position with the foresight to set aside certain "master coins" of the different annual Mint strikings. Thus the collection contains some spectacular Proof quarter and half eagles from the 1820s, when it seemed every gold coin struck at the Mint ended up in the melting pots of Europe. Eckfeldt did not stop with coins of the United States; he also pulled out the finest foreign specimens submitted for recoinage. Still, Eckfeldt's actions were personal in nature; they lacked the institutional endorsement to ensure the collection's continuance and continuity. Indeed, there were holes throughout Eckfeldt's collecting activities.

It was Eckfeldt's son, Jacob (a Mint assayer), and Eckfeldt's son-in-law, William DuBois (the assistant assayer), who picked up the activity in 1838. Within a year of officially relinquishing the chief coiner's position, the elder Eckfeldt turned over the coins he had accumulated. Aided that same year by a special congressional appropriation specifically to fund this activity's continuation, the collection became an entity unto itself.

Ironically, that same year, the Mint received 104,960 gold sovereigns for recoinage into U.S. specie. This comprised the bequest of James Smithson, a British citizen, to the United States for the diffusion of knowledge. Eventually, in fulfillment of this obligation, an act of Congress on May 10, 1846, established the Smithsonian Institution. Two sovereigns were retained to commemorate the bequest. Early numismatic activity at this national museum did not compete with the Mint's collection. Collecting instead focused upon medals and decorations. Foreign coins and currency also found their way into the Smithsonian collection.

Meanwhile, the annual retention of Proof specimens struck at the Philadelphia Mint for its collection progressed. Even private gold issues were retained. However, regular circulation coins, particularly the smaller denominations, and coins from the new branch mints were hit or miss. No particular value was placed upon branch-mint issues, leaving gaping holes in the collection. An exception was the first double eagle struck at San Francisco in 1854.

The growing numismatic collection was featured prominently at the Philadelphia Mint and gained its own curator, Lewis Comparette, in the early years of the 20th century. He at once began to acquire pieces previously not considered for the collection.

In the early 1920s Secretary of the Treasury Andrew Mellon began to contemplate the combination of the Mint collection and the numismatic accumulation at the Smithsonian. The opportunity for this action took place with the sudden death of Comparette in July 1922. At the same time, public access to the mints—and hence the Mint collection—had been terminated as the result of a robbery at the Denver branch that year. Secretary Mellon then effected the removal of the Mint collection to the Smithsonian in 1923. Specimens totaling 18,291 pieces were removed from Philadelphia and combined with the Smithsonian's collection of 21,523 items to form what would become the National Numismatic Collection.

For many years the collection remained largely out of the public eye, and it was only after the Second World War that it received the attention it deserved. The Paul Straub gift added both silver and gold coins and had been designed in part to fill the gaps in the Smithsonian collection. Theodore Roosevelt's family gifted an ultra high-relief double eagle once owned by the president. Finally, the National Numismatic Collection gained a much-deserved reputation for its richness when it went on display in March 1964 at the Hall of Monetary History and Medallic Art in the newly completed Museum of History and Technology.

In 1968 the collection received its most important gift since that of Adam Eckfeldt: it gained the Josiah K. Lilly holdings of 6,150 gold coins, including an almost complete U.S. gold-coin collection. Now the holes in the collection were virtually filled, making it truly unique.

While the collection's exhibition space at the Smithsonian was downsized in the first decade of the 21st century, its many treasures remain in the public eye through an aggressive targeted exhibition program. It is in this vein that the illustrations from this book pull from the National Numismatic Collection to give its rare and beautiful pieces the added exposure that they so assuredly deserve.

For a complete history of this great collection please see Vladimir Clain-Stefanelli's *History of the National Numismatic Collections* (U. S. Government Printing Office, Washington, D. C., 1968).

Part 1: Laying the Foundations

Prologue: California

1. Lieutenant W.T. Sherman. Image courtesy of *The Generals of the American Civil War*, November 1907.

Chapter 1: Stepchild

2. First U.S. Mint.
3. Elias Boudinot.
4. Albert Gallatin. Image courtesy of the Metropolitan Museum of Art.

Chapter 2: Bare-Knuckles Brawling

5. John Randolph. Image courtesy of the National Portrait Gallery, Smithsonian Institution.

Chapter 17: Party Politics

71. Adam Eckfeldt, MT-18. Images courtesy of Stack's Bowers Galleries.
72. 1839 pattern half dollar, J-93. Images courtesy of the National Numismatic Collection, Smithsonian Institution.
73. 1840 eagle. Images courtesy of the National Numismatic Collection, Smithsonian Institution.
74. 1839 Gobrecht pattern dollar, J-104. Images courtesy of the National Numismatic Collection, Smithsonian Institution.
75. Gobrecht sketch for the dollar-coin reverse. Image courtesy of the National Numismatic Collection, Smithsonian Institution.
76. Joseph Ritner.

Chapter 18: An American Sir Isaac Newton

77. Robert Ball Hughes.
78. Ball Hughes modifications. Images courtesy of the National Numismatic Collection, Smithsonian Institution.
79. Horatio Greenough. Image courtesy of the National Portrait Gallery of the Smithsonian Institution.
80. Franklin Institute, Julian AM-17. Images courtesy of Stack's Bowers Galleries.

Chapter 19: New Faces

81. James B. Longacre.
82. Polk Inaugural Medal, PR-9. Images courtesy of Stack's Bowers Galleries.

Chapter 20: Philadelphia v. New York City

83. Robert Walker.
84. Alexander Dallas Bache.

Chapter 21: Sherman's Gold

85. Major General Zachary Taylor, Julian MI-22 and MI-23. Images courtesy of Stack's Bowers Galleries.
86. 1848 "CAL" quarter eagle. Images courtesy of the National Numismatic Collection, Smithsonian Institution.

Part 3: The Great Meltdown

Chapter 22: William McKendree Gwin

87. William McKendree Gwin. Image courtesy of the Library of Congress, Prints and Photographs Division.
88. George Poindexter.
89. San Francisco Harbor.
90. Mormon double eagle. Images courtesy of Jeff Garrett.

Chapter 23: Lame Ducks

91. Major General Zachary Taylor, Julian MI-24. Images courtesy of Stack's Bowers Galleries.
92. James Iver McKay.
93. Stephen A. Douglas.
94. *Venus Accroupie*.
95. Longacre Liberty Head sketches. Images courtesy of the Library Company of Philadelphia.
96. 1849 Liberty Head gold dollar, open- and closed-wreath reverses. Images courtesy of the National Numismatic Collection, Smithsonian Institution.
97. Franklin Peale. Image courtesy of the Pennsylvania Academy of the Fine Arts.
98. Major General Winfield Scott, Julian MI-26. Image courtesy of the author.
99. James C. Booth.

Chapter 24: Something of Value

100. Early study for double eagle reverse. Image courtesy of the Library Company of Philadelphia.
101. Late study for double eagle reverse. Image courtesy of the Library Company of Philadelphia.
102. 1849 double eagle. Images courtesy of the National Numismatic Collection, Smithsonian Institution.
103. Weak obverse second-die splasher. Image courtesy of the Library Company of Philadelphia.
104. William Meredith. Image courtesy of the author.
105. Probable second-obverse die splashers. Images courtesy of the Library Company of Philadelphia.

Chapter 25: Bad Chemistry

106. Richard Sears McCulloh. Image courtesy of University Archives, Rare Book & Manuscript Library, Columbia University in the City of New York.
107. J.R. Chandler.
108. Jefferson Davis.
109. Henry Clay.
110. 1851 Augustus Humbert $50 gold piece. Image courtesy of the National Numismatic Collection, Smithsonian Institution.

Chapter 26: Besieged

111. Thomas Corwin.

Chapter 27: Barbarians at the Gates

112. George Briggs. Image courtesy of the Library of Congress, Prints and Photographs Division.
113. Californians at the Mint.
114. Thaddeus Stevens. Image courtesy of the Library of Congress, Prints and Photographs Division.
115. 1850 pattern three-cent piece. Image courtesy of the National Numismatic Collection, Smithsonian Institution.
116. 1851 three-cent piece. Image courtesy of the National Numismatic Collection, Smithsonian Institution.

Chapter 28: Sacked!

117. George Eckert.
118. Stephen Colwell.
119. Robert Maskell Patterson, Julian MT-2. Images courtesy of Stack's Bowers Galleries.

Chapter 30: Mr. Wizard

120. The U.S. Mint in 1852.

Part 4: To the Brink and Back

Chapter 31: Hardball Politics

121. Edward C. Marshall. Image courtesy of the University of Kentucky Special Collections, Wilson Family Photographic Collection.
122. James Brooks. Image courtesy of the Library of Congress, Prints and Photographs Division.
123. Hamilton Fish. Image courtesy of the Library of Congress, Prints and Photographs Division.
124. First San Francisco Mint.

Chapter 32: Backwoods Legislatin'

125. R.M.T. Hunter. Image courtesy of the Library of Congress Division of Prints and Photographs.
126. 1853, Arrows at Date, Rays Around Eagle, half dollar. Images courtesy of the National Numismatic Collections, Smithsonian Institution.

Chapter 33: End of the Line

127. James Buchanan. Image courtesy of the Library of Congress, Prints and Photographs Division.
128. James Ross Snowden. Image courtesy of the author.
129. Franklin Pierce. Image courtesy of the Library of Congress, Prints and Photographs Division.
130. David Broderick. Image courtesy of the Library of Congress, Prints and Photographs Division.

Chapter 34: Smith and Pickett

131. James Guthrie.
132. 1854-S double eagle. Images courtesy of the National Numismatic Collection, Smithsonian Institution.

133. Bust of Franklin Peale. Image courtesy of the Pennsylvania Academy of the Fine Arts.

Chapter 35: Striking Change

134. 1853 public competition submittals. Images courtesy of the National Numismatic Collection, Smithsonian Institution.
135. 1853 competition submittal of Longacre. Images courtesy of the National Numismatic Collection, Smithsonian Institution.
136. 1853 competition submittal of Charles Nahl. Image courtesy of the National Numismatic Collection, Smithsonian Institution.
137. 1854 $3 gold piece. Images courtesy of the National Numismatic Collection, Smithsonian Institution.
138. 1854, Type 2, $1 gold piece. Images courtesy of the National Numismatic Collection, Smithsonian Institution.
139. The Rescue of Martin Koszta, Julian NA-26. Image courtesy of Stack's Bowers Galleries.
140. New York Assay Office.

Epilogue: January 25, 1861

141. Daniel Ullmann.
142. Henry Clay, Julian PE-7. Gold images courtesy of the Clay descendents. Copper images courtesy of the author.

INDEX